Data Analytics, Bioinformatics
and
Machine Learning

ISBN 978-0-578-22302-5

Data Analytics, Bioinformatics
and
Machine Learning

Stephen Winters-Hilt

Meta Logos Systems
Denver, Colorado

ISBN 978-0-578-22302-5

Golden Tao Publishing
USA

Preface

In this book I describe how to use computational/algorithmic, statistical, and informatics methods to analyze any data that is captured in digital form, whether it be text, sequential data in general (such as experimental observations over time, or stock market and econometric histories), symbolic data (genomes), or image data. Active learning will be emphasized with frequent reference to small exercises (many Chapters end with an Exercise Section). In Ch. 2, for example, we implement a program to identify statistical anomalies or 'signatures', so have exercises accordingly.

This book is an accumulation of lecture notes and interesting research tidbits from over a decade of teaching courses in: Bioinformatics, Machine Learning, Data Analytics, Signal Processing, and Pattern Recognition. The material draws from my undergraduate and graduate education at Caltech, and further graduate studies at Oxford, U. Wisconsin, and UCSC. The material then draws from my teaching experience and research efforts at the University of New Orleans, where I was tenured in the CS Department, and the Research Institute for Children, Children's Hospital New Orleans, where I was a tenured 'Fellow' and a Principal Investigator/Director of a protein channel biochemistry lab. The material also draws from teaching experience at Connecticut College where I created an undergraduate-level curriculum in bioinformatics and machine learning (from the graduate-level curriculum previously established at UNO).

The Chapters in this book can be traversed in different ways for different course offerings, that range from First Year Undergraduate level to Doctoral Graduate Level. The first four Chapters are shared by many of the courses, and form the basis of much of the First Year Undergraduate course (and with material included in the Appendix, there are no prerequisites). The First Year course is 'rounded out' with small parts of Ch.s 7 and 11-13 to get a high level survey of top Machine Learning methods. Here's a more complete breakdown on the suggested Chapters for the some of the other course offerings that could be made with this material:

Courses where this text has been used:
(i) Data Analytics and Informatics (UG level, First Year, no prerequisites)
(ii) Machine Learning (UG level)
(iii) Bioinformatics and Molecular Biology (UG level)
(iv) Cheminformatics, Proteomics, and Biotechnology (Grad level)
(v) Graduate Machine Learning with focus on HMMs and generative methods (Grad)
(vi) Graduate Machine Learning with focus on SVMs and discriminative methods (Grad)
(vii) Genomics, Transcriptomics, and Proteomics

Here are the recommended course traversals:

Chapter	Courses using:
Ch 1. Introduction	(i) – (vii)
Ch 2. Probabilistic Reasoning	(i) – (iii)
Ch 3. Information Entropy	(i) – (iii)
Ch 4. Ad hoc Signal Acquisition	(i) – (vi)
Ch 5. Information Encoding Molecules	(iii), (iv), (vii)
Ch 6. Sequential Alignment	(iii), (iv), (vii)
Ch 7. Hidden Markov Models (HMMs)	(i) – (vi)
Ch 8. Cell & Virus	(iii),(vii)
Ch 9. Transcriptomics	(iii), (iv), (vii)
Ch 10. Proteomics	(iii), (iv), (vii)
Ch 11. Classification, Clustering, and SVMs	(i) – (vi)
Ch 12. Search Metaheuristics	(i) – (iii), (vi)
Ch 13. Stochastic Sequential Analysis	(i) – (vi)
Ch 14. The Nanoscope – A Case Study	(iii) – (vi), (vii)

This textbook is one of three texts that are closely related and being published at the same time. Ch. 14 on the Nanoscope is self-contained, but substantially more material exists, and this has led to a parallel text "The Nanoscope" where more many details are elaborated further. Likewise, the Machine Learning intensive chapters (Ch. 7 and 11 especially) have more material as well, and this has led to a third textbook: "Informatics and Machine Learning, from Martingales to Metaheuristics". The latter textbook also has many application outside of biology, such as text analytics and stock (financial) analysis.

Acknowledgement

This book wouldn't have been possible without support of family and friends. So I'd like to thank my wife and sons foremost: Cindy, Nathaniel, and Zachary. I'd also like to thank my mother, sister, and brothers: Sybil, Teresa, Eric and Joshua. Josh also helped with some of the experiments and software. I'd also like to thank my grandparents and my aunts and uncles: Wilbur, Beulah, Bruce, Richard, Diana, Mark, Susan, and John. I'd also like to thank Rob and family.

This book wouldn't have been possible without having several 'genuises' as advisors or instructors over the years (including Nobel Prize winners), whose insights I was inspired to try to capture in some instructional form. During my time at Caltech I was fortunate to have as advisor or instructor: Kip Thorne (graduate advisor), Richard Feynman, Murry Gell-Mann, David Middlebrook, Amnon Yariv, Ron Drever, and Barry Barish (undergraduate advisor). During my time at Oxford I was fortunate to have as advisor or instructor: Roger Penrose and Nick Woodhouse. During my time at UWM I was fortunate to have as advisor or instructor: Nick Papastamatiou, Leonard Parker, John Friedman, and Jourma Louko. During my time at UCSC: David Haussler, David Deamer, and Mark Akeson.

I'd also like to thank the student researchers, postdocs, and lab technicians that I've advised and worked with: Eric Morales, Andrew Duda, Iftelhar Amin, Amanda Alba, Amanda Davis, Evenie Horton, Joshua Morrison, Anand Prabhakaran, Alex Ortiz, Raja Iqbal, Srikanth Sendamangalam, Charlie McChesney, Matthew Landry, Molly Oehmichem, Kenneth Armond Jr., Sepehr Merat, Daming Lu, Hang Zhang, Carl Baribault, Zuliang Jiang, Alexander Churbanov, and Alexander Stoyanov.

Contents

Chapter 1

Introduction

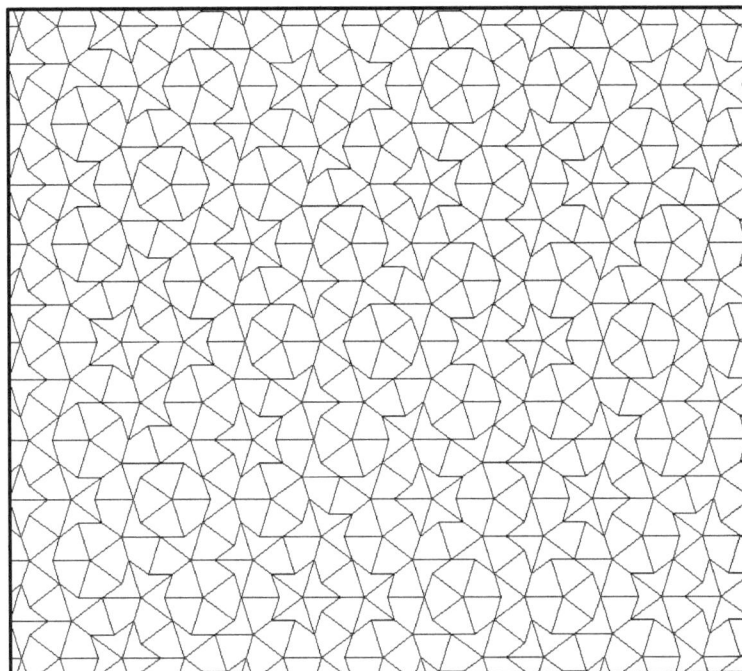

Fig. 1.1. A Penrose Tiling*.

Informatics provides new avenues of understanding and inquiry in any medium that can be captured in digital form. Areas as diverse as text analysis, signal analysis, and genome analysis, to name a few, can be studied with informatics tools. Computationally-powered informatics tools are having a phenomenal impact in many fileds, including engineering, nanotechnology, and the biological sciences.

In this text I provide a background on various methods from Informatics and Machine Learning that together comprise a 'complete toolset' for doing data analytics work at all levels -- from a first year undergraduate introductory level to advanced topics in subsections suitable for graduate students seeking a deeper understanfing (or a more detailed example). Prior book and journal publications by the author, in topics such as Machine Learning, Nanopore Detection, and Physics [1-55], are drawn upon extensively throughout the text. The application domain is practically everything, as mentioned above, but in this text the focus will be on core methodologies with specific application in either bioinformatics or cheminformatics (nanopore detection, in particular). Other disciplines can also be analyzed with informatics tools. Basic questions about human origins (anthrogenomics) and behavior (econometrics) can also be explored with informatics based pattern recognition methods, with a huge impact on new research directions in anthropology, sociology, political science, economics, and psychology. The complete toolset of statistical learning tools can be used in any of these domains.

---

* A non-repeating tiling with two shapes of tiles, with 5-point local symmetry and both local and global (emergent) Golden Ratio.

In the chapter that follows an overview is given of the various information processing stages to be discussed in the text, with some highlights to help explain the order and connectivity of topics, as well as motivate their presentation in further detail in what is to come. The Biology overview, however, is not included in this 'informatics' overview, but done separately with the introduction to the Ch. 5 material on the information encoding molecules of life.

Data Science: statistics, probability, calculus … perl, or python, and Linux

Knowledge construction using statistical and computational methods is at the heart of data science and informatics. Counts on data features (or events) are typically gathered as a starting point in many analyses [56,57]. Computer hardware is very well-suited to such counting tasks. Basic operating system commands and a popular scripting language (Perl) will be taught to enable doing these tasks easily. Computer software methods will also be shown that allow easy implementation and understanding of basic statistical methods, whereby the counts, for example, can be used to determine event frequencies, from which statistical anomalies can be subsequently identified. The computational implementation of basic statistics methods then provides the framework to perform more sophisticated knowledge construction and discovery by use of information theory and basic machine learning methods. Machine learning can be thought of as a specialized branch of statistics where there is minimal assumption of a statistical 'model' based on prior human learning. This book shows how to use computational, statistical, and informatics/algorithmic methods to analyze any data that is captured in digital form, whether it be text, sequential data in general (such as experimental observations over time, or stock market/econometric histories), symbolic data (genomes), or image data. Along the way there will be a brief introduction to probability and statistics concepts (Ch 2) and basic Perl/Linux system programming methods (Ch 2 and App. A).

Informatics and data analytics

It is commonplace to need to acquire a signal where the signal properties are not known, or the signal is only suspected and not discovered yet, or the signal properties are known but they may be too much trouble to fully enumerate. There is no common solution, however, to the acquisition task. For this reason the initial phases of acquisition methods unavoidably tend to be *ad hoc*. As with data dependency in non-evolutionary search metaheuristics (where there is no optimal search method that is guaranteed to always work well), here there is no optimal signal acquisition method known in advance. In what follows methods are described for bootstrap optimization in signal acquisition to enable the most general-use, almost 'common', solution possible. The bootstrap algorithmic method involves repeated passes over the data sequence, with improved priors, and trained filters, among other things, to have improved signal acquisition on subsequent passes. The signal acquisition is guided by statistical measures to recognize anomalies. Informatics methods and information theory measures are central to the design of a good finite state automata acquisition method, and will be reviewed in signal acquisition context in Chapters 2-4. Code examples are given in Perl and C (with introductory Perl described in Ch. 2 and App. A). Bootstrap acquisition methods may not automatically provide a common solution, but appear to offer a process whereby a solution can be improved to some desirable level of general-data applicability.

The signal analysis and pattern recognition methods described in this book are mainly applied to problems involving stochastic sequential data: power signals and genomic sequences in particular. The information modeling, feature selection/extraction, and feature-vector discrimination, however, were each developed separately in a general-use context. Details on the theoretical underpinnings are given in Ch. 3, including a collection of *ab initio* information theory tools to help "find your way around in the dark". One of the main *ab initio* approaches is to search for statistical anomalies using information measures, so various information measures will be described in detail [58-70].

The background on information theory and variational/statistical modeling has significant roots in variational calculus. Chapter 3 describes information theory ideas and the information "calculus" description (and related anomalous detection methods). The involvement of variational calculus methods and the possible parallels with the nascent development of a new (modern) 'calculus of information' motivates the detailed overview of the highly successful physics development/applications of the calculus of variations (App. B). Using variational calculus, for example, it is possible to establish a link between a choice of information measure and statistical formalism (maximum entropy, Sec. 3.1). Taking the maximum entropy on a distribution with moment constraints leads to the classic distributions seen in mathematics and nature (the Gaussian for fixed mean and variance, etc.). Not surprisingly, variational methods also help to establish and refine one of the main Machine Learning methods that will be described, the Support Vector Machine (to be described in Ch. 11). Support Vector Machines (SVMs) are the main tool presented for both classification (supervised learning) and clustering (unsupervised learning), and everything in between (such as bag learning).

FSA-based signal acquisition and bioinformatics
Many signal features of interest are time limited and not band limited in the observational context of interest, such as noise 'clicks', 'spikes', or impulses. To acquire these signal features a time-domain FSA (tFSA) is often most appropriate [71-79]. Human hearing, for example, is a non-linear system that thereby circumvents the restrictions of the Gabor limit (to allow for musical geniuses, for example, who have 'perfect pitch'), where time-frequency acuity surpasses what would be possible by linear signal processing alone [71], such as with Nyquist sampled linear response recording devices that are bound by the limits imposed by the Fourier uncertainty principle (or Benedick's theorem) [72]. Thus, even when the powerful Fourier Transform or HMM feature extraction methods are utilized to full advantage, there is often a sector of the signal analysis that is only conveniently accessible to analysis by way of FSA's (without significant oversampling), such that a parallel processing with both HMM and FSA methods is often needed (results demonstrating this in the context of channel current analysis [1] will be described in Ch. 14). Not all of the methods employed at the FSA processing stage derive from standard signal processing approaches, either, some are purely statistical such as with oversampling [73] (used in radar range oversampling [74,75]) and dithering [76] (used in device stabilization and to reduce quantization error [77,78]).

All of the tFSA signal acquisition methods described in Chapters 2-4 are O(L), i.e., they scan the data with a computational complexity no greater than that of simply seeing the data (via a 'read' or 'touch' command, O(L) is known as 'order of', or 'big-oh', notation). Because the signal acquisition is only O(L) it is not significantly costly, computationally, to simply repeat the acquisition analysis multiple times with a more informed process with each iteration, to have arrive at a 'bootstrap' signal acquisition process. In such a setting, signal acquisition is often done with bias to very high specificity initially (and sensitivity very poor), to get a 'gold standard' set of highly likely true signals that can be data mined for their attributes. With a filter stage thereby trained, later scan passes can pass suspected signals with very weak specificity (very high sensitivity now) with high specificity then recovered by use of the filter. This then allows a bootstrap process to a very high specificity (SP) and sensitivity (SN) at the tFSA acquisition stage on the signals of interest (see [1], Ch. 2, and Ch. 13 for more details).

An example of a bootstrap FSA from genomic analysis is to first scan through a genome base-by-base and obtain counts on nucleotide pairs with different gap sizes between the nucleotides observed [1]. This then allows a mutual information analysis on the nucleotide pairs taken at the different gap sizes (shown in Ch. 3 & 4). What is found for prokaryotic genomes, with their highly dense gene placement, that is mostly protein coding (i.e., where there is little 'junk' DNA and no introns), is a clear signal indicating anomalous statistical linkages on bases three apart [1,39]. What is discovered thereby is codon structure, where the coding information comes in groups of three bases. Knowing this, a repeated pass (bootstrap) with frequency analysis of the 64 possible 3-base groupings can then be done, at which point the anomalously low counts on 'stop' codons is then observed. Upon identification of the stop codons their placement (topology) in the genome can then be examined and it is found that their counts are anomalously low because there are large stretches of regions with no stop codon (e.g., there are stop codon 'voids', known as open reading frames, or 'ORF's). The codon void topologies are examined in a comparative genomic analysis in [39] (and shown in Ch. 3). The stop codons, which should occur every 21 codons on average if DNA sequence data was random, are sometimes not seen for stretches of several hundred codons. For the genomic data what is found are the regions that contain the longer genes (whose anomalous, clearly non-random DNA sequence, is being maintained as such, and not randomized by mutation, as this would be selected against in the survival of the organism that is dependent on the gene discovered). This basic analysis can provide a gene-finder on prokaryotic genomes that comprises a one-page Perl script that can perform with 90 to 99% accuracy depending on the prokaryotic genome (shown in Ch. 3). A second page of Perl coding to introduce a 'filter', along the lines of the bootstrap learning process mentioned above, leads to an *ab initio* prokaryotic gene-predictor with 98.0 to 99.9% accuracy. Perl code to accomplish this is shown in Ch. 4. In this bootstrap acquisition process all that is used is the raw genomic data (with its highly structured intrinsic statistics) and methods for identifying statistical anomalies and informatics structural anomalies: (i) anomalously high mutual information is identified (revealing codon structure); (ii) anomalously high (or low) statistics on an attribute or event is then identified (low stop codon counts, lengthy stop codon voids); then anomalously high sub-sequences (binding site motifs) are found in the neighborhood of the identified ORFs (used in the filter).

Ad hoc signal acquisition refers to finding the solution for 'this' situation (whatever 'this' is) without consideration of wider application. The solution is strongly *data dependent* in other words. Data dependent methodologies are, by definition, not defined at the outset, but must be invented as the data begins to be understood. As with data dependency in non-evolutionary search metaheuristics, where there is no optimal search method that is guaranteed to always work well, here there is no optimal signal acquisition method known in advance. This is simply restating a fundamental limit from non-evolutionary search metaheuristics in another form [193]. What can be done, however, is assemble the core tools and techniques from which a solution can be constructed and to perform a bootstrap algorithmic learning process with those tools (examples in what follows) to arrive at a functional signal acquisition on the data being analyzed. A universal, automated, bootstrap learning

4

process may eventually be possible using evolutionary learning algorithms (related to the co-evolutionary Free Lunch Theorem [194]), and this is discussed in Ch. 13.

"Bootstrap" refers to a method of problem solving when the problem is solved by seemingly paradoxical measures (the name references Baron von Munchausen who freed the horse he was riding from a bog by pulling himself, and the horse with him, up by his bootstraps [195]). Such algorithmic methods often involve repeated passes over the data sequence, with improved priors, or a trained filter, among other things, to have improved performance. The bootstrap amplifier from electrical engineering is an amplifier circuit where part of the output is used as input, particularly at start-up (known as bootstrapping), allowing proper self-initialization to a functional state (by amplifying ambient circuit noise in some cases) [196]. The bootstrap FSA proposed here is a meta-algorithmic method in that performance 'feedback' with learning is used in algorithmic refinements with iterated meta-algorithmic learning to arrive at a functional signal acquisition status.

Acquisition is often all that needed in a signal analysis problem, where a basic means to acquire the signals is sought, to be followed by a basic statistical analysis on those signals and their occurrences. Various methods for signal acquisition using Finite State Automaton (FSA) constructs are described in what follows that focus on statistical anomalies to identify the presence of signal and 'lock on' [1,197]. The signal acquisition is initially only guided by use of statistical measures to recognize anomalies. Informatics methods and information theory measures are central to the design of a good FSA acquisition method, however, and will be reviewed in the signal acquisition context [1], along with hidden Markov Models (HMMs).

Thus, FSA processes allow signal regions to be identified, or 'acquired', in O(L) time. Furthermore, in that same order of time complexity, an entire panoply of statistical moments can also be computed on the signals (and used in a bootstrap learning process). The O(L) feature extraction of statistical moments on the signal region acquired may suffice for *localized* events and structures. For sequential information or events, however, there is often a *non-local*, or extended structural, aspect to the signal sought. In these situations we need a general, powerful, way to analyze sequential signal data that is stochastic (random, but with statistics, such as average, that may be unchanging over time if 'stationary', for example). The general method for performing stochastic sequential analysis is via Hidden Markov Models (HMMs), as will be extensively described in Ch. 7, and briefly summarized in what follows.

Feature extraction and gene structure identification
HMMs offer a more sophisticated signal recognition process than FSAs, but with greater computational space and time complexity [80,81]. Like electrical engineering signal processing, HMMs usually involve pre-processing that assumes linear system properties or assumes observation is frequency band limited and not time limited, and thereby inherit the time-frequency uncertainty relations, Gabor limit, and Nyquist sampling relations. FSA methods can be used to recover (or extract) signal features missed by HMM or classical electrical engineering signal processing. Even if the signal sought is well understood, and a purely HMM-based approach is possible, this is often needlessly computationally intensive (and slow), especially in areas where there is no signal. To address this there are numerous hybrid FSA/HMM approaches (such as BLAST [82]) that benefit from the O(L) complexity

on length L signal with FSA processing, with more targeted processing at $O(LN^2)$ complexity with HMM processing (where there are N states in the HMM model).

Hidden Markov models, unlike tFSAs, have a straightforward mathematical and computational foundation at the nexus where Bayesian probability and Markov models meet dynamic programming. To properly define or choose the HMM model in a machine learning context, however, further generalization is usually required. This is because the 'bare-bones' HMM description has critical weaknesses in most applications, which are described in Ch. 7, *along with their 'fixes'*. Fortunately, each of the standard HMM weaknesses can be addressed in computationally efficient ways. The generalized HMMs described in Ch. 7 allow for a generalized Viterbi Algorithm (see Fig. 1.2) and a generalized Baum-Welch Algorithm. The generalized algorithms retain path probabilities in terms of a sequence of likelihood ratios, which satisfy Martingale statistics under appropriate circumstances [57], thereby having Martingale convergence properties (where here convergence is associated with 'learning' in this context). Thus, HMM learning proceeds via convergence to a limit state that provably exists in a similar sense to that shown with the Hoeffding inequality [59], via its proven extension to Martingales [63]. The Hoeffding inequality is a key part of the VC Theorem in Machine Learning, whereby convergence for the Perceptron learning process to a solution in an infitie solution space is proven to exist in a finite number of learning steps [64]. Further details on the Fundamental Theorems [57,59,63,64] are summarized in Ch. 7 and App. C.

Hidden Markov model (HMM) tools have recently been developed with a number of computationally efficient improvements (described in detail in Ch. 7), where application of the HMM methods will be described for gene-finding, alt-splice gene-finding, and nanopore-detector signal analysis.

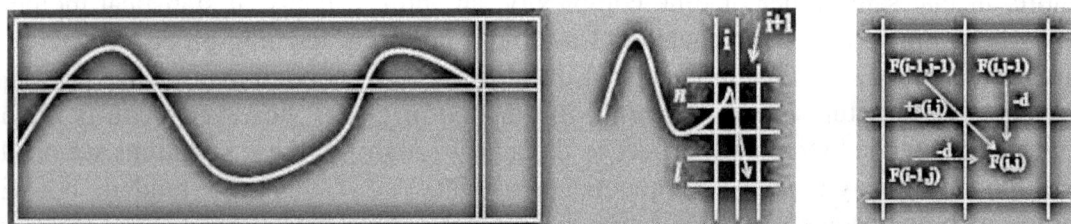

Fig. 1.2. The Viterbi Path. Left. The Viterbi path is recusively defined, thus tabulatable, with one column only, recursively, dependent on the prior column. **Right.** A related recursive algrithm used to perform sequence alignment extensions with gaps (the Smith-Waterman algorithm, Ch. 6) is provided by the neighbor-cell recursively-defined relation shown.

HMM methods are powerful, especially with the enhancements described in Ch. 7, but this would all be for naught in a real-time, $O(L)$, processing on L size data if the core $O(LN^2)$ algorithm (N states in the HMM) couldn't be distributed, onto $O(N^2)$ nodes, say, to get back to an overall distributed process involving HMM feature extraction with $O(L)$ processing (to be part of our real-time signal processing pipeline). So need a way to distribute the core algorithms for HMM learning: Viterbi and Baum-Welch. It turns out distributed processing, or 'chunking', method is possible for the single sweep Viterbi algorithm (ignoring the trivial traceback optimal path recovery that does not cause table alteration). The key to having this chunking capability on the other core learning algorithm, Baum-Welch, is to have a similar single-pass table production. The standard Baum-Welch requires a forward and a backward sweep across the table during production of the result (with algorithms named accordingly for this purpose in Ch 3). This would disallow the chunking solution, so what is needed is a single sweep Baum Welch algorithm, and such has been discovered and is described in Ch 3, where it is known as the Linear Memory HMM (at the time of its discovery it was most notable to reviewers due to another oddity, that it required only linear space memory during computation – but memory is cheap, while being able to do distributed processing with massive speed-up operationally is much more important). With distributability (asynchronous), computational time is directly reduced by ~ N on a cluster with N nodes (see Fig. 1.2). The HMM with single-sweep Linear Memory (distributable) for EM also allows distribution (massive parallel asynchronous processing) for the generalized Viterbi and Baum-Welch algorithms on the Meta-HMM and HMMD variants described in Ch 3 as well.

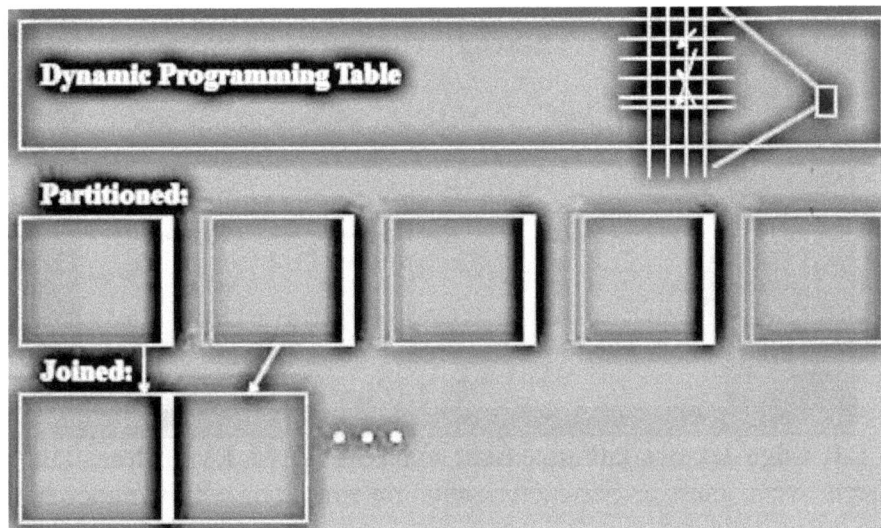

Fig. 1.3. Chunking on a Dynamic Table. Works for an HMM using a simple join recovery.

HMMs for analysis of Information Encoding Molecules

The main application areas for HMMs covered in this book are Bioinformatics and Cheminformatics (the main reviews and applications discussed are from [83-89]).. For Bioinformatics, we have information encoding molecules that are polymers, giving rise to sequential data format, thus HMMs well suited to analysis. To start to understand Bioinformatics, however, we need to know not only the biological encoding rules, largely rediscoverd on the basis of their statistical anomalies in Ch.s 1-4. But also need to know the idiosyncratic stuctures seen (genomes and transcriptomes) that are full of evolutionary artifacts and similarities to evolutionary cousins. To know the nature of the statistical imprinting on the polymeric encodings also requires an understanding of the biochemical constraints that give rise to the statistical biases seen. Once taken altogether, bioinformatics offers a lot of clarity on why Nature has settled on the particular 'mess', with optimizations, that it has selected. For this reason, the molecular biology is reviewed from introductory concepts, to advanced biochemical effects, in Ch.s 5 and 8-10.

HMMs for Cheminformatics and Generic Signal Analsyis

The prospect of having an HMM feature extraction in the streaming signal processing pipeline (and O(L), for size L data process) offers powerful real-time feature extraction capabilities and specialized filtering (all of which is implemented in the Nanoscope, Ch. 14). One such processing method, decribed in Ch. 7, is HMM/EM EVA (Emission Variance Am-

7

plification) Projection which has application in providing simplified automated tFSA Kinetic Feature Extraction from channel current signal. What is needed is the equivalent of low-pass filtering on blockade levels while retaining sharpness on the timing of the level changes. This is not possible with the standard low-pass filter because the edges get blurred out in the local filtering process, but notice how this does not happen with the HMM-based filter, for the data shown in Fig. 1.4.

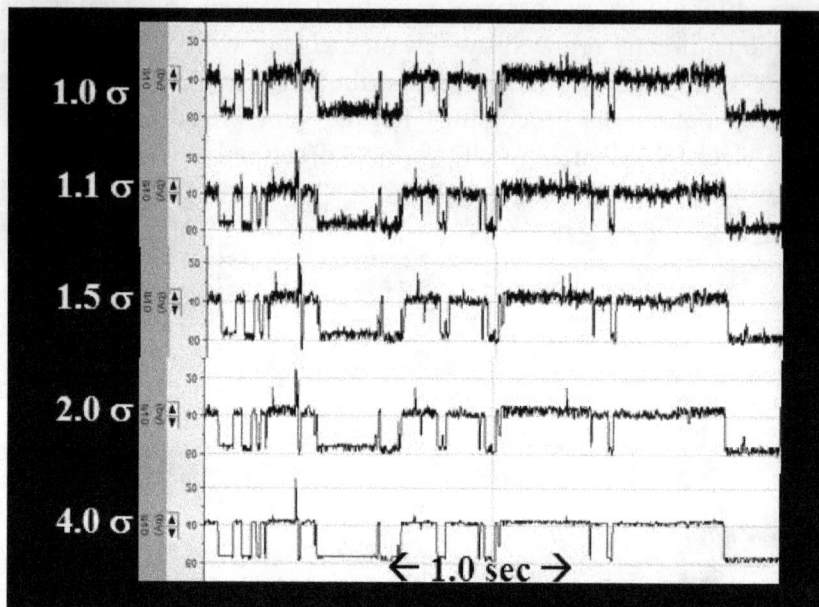

Fig. 1.4. Edge feature enhancement via HMM/EM EVA filter. The filter "projects" via a gaussian parameterization on emissions with variance boosted by the factor indicated.

HMMs are a common *intrinsic* statistical sequence modeling method (implementations and applications are mainly drawn from [90-113] in what follows), so the question naturally arises -- how to optimally incorporate *extrinsic* "side-information" into an HMM? This can be done by treating duration distribution information *itself* as side-information and a process is shown for incorporating side-information into an HMM. It is thereby demonstrated how to bootstrap from an HMM to a HMM-with-duration (more generally, a hidden semi-Markov model or HSMM, as it will be described in Ch. 7).

In many applications, the ability to incorporate the state duration into the HMM is very important because conventional HMM-based, Viterbi and Baum-Welch algorithms are otherwise critically constrained in their modeling ability to distributions on state intervals that are geometric (this is shown in Ch. 7). This can lead to a significant decoding failure in noisy environments when the state-interval distributions are not geometric (or approximately geometric). The starkest contrast occurs for multimodal distributions and *heavy-tailed* distributions, the latter occurring for exon and intron length distributions (thus critical in gene finders). The hidden Markov model with binned duration (HMMBD) algorithm eliminates the HMM geometric distribution modeling constraint, as well as the HMMD maximum duration constraint, and offers a significant reduction in computational time for all HMMBD-based methods *to approximately the computational time of the HMM-process alone.*

In adopting any model with 'more parameters', such as an HMMBD over an HMM, there is potentially a problem with having sufficient data to support the additional modeling. This is generally not a problem in any HMM model that requires thousands of samples of non-self transitions for sensor modeling, such as for the gene-finding that is described in what follows, since knowing the boundary positions allows the regions of self-transitions (the durations) to be extracted with similar sample number as well, which is typically sufficient for effective modeling of the duration distributions in a HMMD.

Improvement to overall HMM application rests not only with the aforementioned improvements to the HMM/HMMBD, but also with improvements to the hidden state model and emission model. This is because standard HMMs are at low Markov order in transitions (first) and in emissions (zeroth), and transitions are decoupled from emissions (which can miss critical structure in the model, such as state transition probabilities that are sequence dependent). This weakness is eliminated if we generalize to the largest state-emission clique possible, fully interpolated on the data set, as is done with the generalized-clique hidden Markov model (HMM), where gene finding is performed on the *C. elegans* genome (Computational genomics results shown in Ch 8). The clique generalization improves the modeling of the critical signal information at the transitions between exon regions and non-coding regions, e.g., intron and junk regions. In doing this we arrive at a HMM structure identification platform that is novel, and robustly-performing, in a number of ways.

Prior HMM-based systems for stochastic sequential analysis (SSA) had undesirable limitations and disadvantages. For example, the speed of operation made such systems difficult, if not impossible, to use for real-time analysis of information. The the SSA Ptotocol described here, distributed generalized HMM processing together with the use of the SVM-based Classification and Clustering Methods (described next) permit the general use of the SSA Protocol free of the usual limitations. After the HMM and SSA methods are described, their synergistic union is used to convey a new approach to signal analysis with HMM methods, including a new form of stochastic-carrier wave (SCW) communication.

Classification and clustering
Support Vector Machines (SVMs) can be used for classification and clustering (to be described in detail in Ch. 11), as well as aiding with signal analysis and pattern recognition on stochastic sequential data. The signal processing material described next, and in detail later, mainly draw from prior journal publications [114-144]. Analysis tools for stochastic sequential data have broad-ranging application in that any device producing a sequence of measurements can be made more sensitive, or "smarter," by efficient learning of measured signal/pattern characteristics. The SVM and HMM/SVM application areas described in this book include cheminformatics, biophysics, and bioinformatics. The cheminformatics application examples pertain to channel current analysis on the alpha-hemolysin nanopore detector (Ch. 14).

The biophysics and 'information flows' associated with the nanopore transduction detector in Ch. 14 are analyzed using a generalized set of hidden Markov model (HMM) and Support Vector Machine (SVM) based tools, as well as *ad hoc* finite state automata (FSA) based methods, and a collection of distributed genetic algorithm methods for tuning and selection. Used with a nanopore detector, the channel current cheminformatics for the stationary signal channel blockades (with 'stationary statistics') enables a method for a highly sensitive nanopore detector for single molecule biophysical analysis.

The SVM implementations described involve SVM algorithmic variants, kernel variants, and chunking variants; as well as SVM classification tuning metaheuristics; and SVM clustering metaheuristics. The SVM tuning metaheuristics typically enable use of the SVM's confidence parameter to bootstrap from a strong classification engine to a strong clustering engine via use of label changes, and repeated SVM training processes with the new label information obtained.

SVM Methods and Systems are given in Ch. 11 for classification, clustering, and stochastic sequential analysis in general, with a broad range of applications:

- sequential-structure identification
- pattern recognition
- knowledge discovery
- bioinformatics
- nanopore detector cheminformatics
- computational engineering with information flows

SVM binary discrimination outperforms other classification methods with or without dropping weak data (while many other methods can't even identify weak data).

Stochastic sequential analysis (SSA) protocol (Deep Learning without NNs)
The SSA protocol is shown in Fig. 1.5 is a general signal-processing flow topology and database schema (Left Panel), with specialized variants for channel current cheminformatics (Center) and kinetic feature extraction based on blockade-level duration observations (Right). The SSA Protocol allows for the discovery, characterization, and classification of localizable, approximately-stationary, statistical signal structures in channel current data, or genomic data, or sequential data in general. The core signal processing stage in Fig. 1.5 is usually the feature extraction stage, where central to the signal processing protocol is a generalized Hidden Markov model. The SSA Protocol also has a built-in recovery protocol for weak signal handling, outlined next, where the HMM methods are complemented by the strengths of other Machine Learning methods.

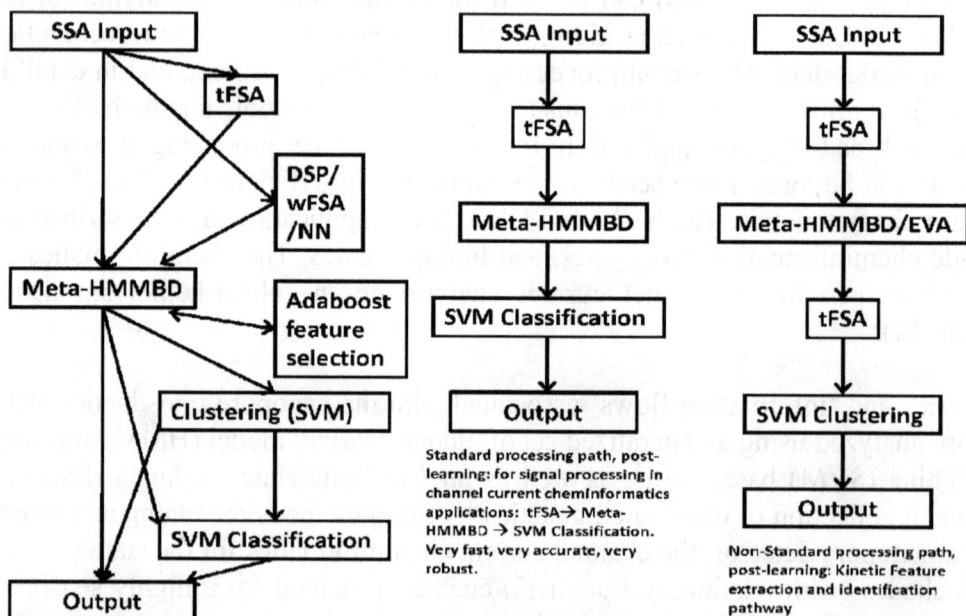

Figure 1.5. Left. The general stochastic sequential analysis flow topology. **Center.** The general signal processing flow in performing channel current analysis is typically Input →

tFSA→ Meta-HMMBD → SVM → Output. **Right.** Notable differences occur in channel current cheminformatics during state discovery when EVA-projection (emission variance amplification projection), or a similar method, is used to achieve a quantization on states, then have Input → tFSA → HMMBD/EVA (state discovery) → meta-HMMBD-side → SVM → Output. While, in gene-finding just have: Input → meta-HMMBD-side → Output. In gene-finding, however, the HMM internal 'sensors' are sometimes replaced, locally, with profile-HMMs [1] (equivalent to position-dependent Markov Models, or pMM's, see Ch. 7), or SVM-based profiling [1], so the topology can differ not only in the connections between the boxes shown, but in their ability to embed in other boxes as part of an internal refinement.

The sequence of algorithmic methods used in the SSA Protocol, for the information-processing flow topology shown in Fig. 1.5, comprise a weak signal handling protocol as follows: (i) the weakness in the (fast) Finite State Automaton (FSA) methods will be shown to be their difficulty in non-local structure identification, for which HMM methods (and tuning metaheuristics) are the solution; (ii) for the HMM, in turn, the main weakness is in local sensing 'classification' due to conditional independence assumptions. Once in the setting of a classification problem, however, the problem can be solved via incorporation of generalized SVM methods [26]. If facing only classification task (data already preprocessed), the SVM will also be the method of choice in what follows. (iii) The weakness of the SVM, whether used for classification or clustering, but especially for the latter, is the need to optimize over algorithmic, model (kernel), chunking, and other process parameters during learning. This is solved via use of metaheuristics for optimization such as simulated annealing, and genetic algorithm optimization in (iv). The main weaknesses in the metaheuristic tuning effort is partly resolved via use of the "front-end" methods, like the FSA, and partly resolved by a knowledge discovery process using the SVM clustering methods. The SSA Protocol weak signal acquisition and analysis method thereby establishes a robust signal processing platform.

The HMM methods are the central methodology or stage in the SSA Protocol, particularly in the gene finders, and sometimes with the channel current cheminformatics (CCC) protocol or implementation, in that the other stages can be dropped or merged with the HMM stage in many incarnations. For example, in some CCC analysis situations the time-domain Finite State Automaton (tFSA) methods could be totally eliminated in favor of the more accurate (but time consuming) HMM-based approach to the problem, with signal states defined or explored in much the same setting, but with the optimized Viterbi path solution taken as the basis for the signal acquisition.

The HMM features, and other features (from neural net, wavelet, or spike profiling, etc.) can be fused and selected via use of various data fusion methods, such as a modified Adaboost selection (from [1], and Ch. 11). The HMM-based feature extraction provides a well-focused set of 'eyes' on the data, no matter what its nature, according to the underpinnings of its Bayesian statistical representation. The key is that the HMM not be too limiting in its state definition, while there is the typical engineering trade-off on the choice of number of states, N, which impacts the order of computation via a quadratic factor of N in the various dynamic programming calculations (comprising the Viterbi and Baum-Welch algorithms among others).

The HMM 'sensor' capabilities can be significantly improved via switching from profile-MM (pMM) sensors to pMM/SVM-based sensors, as indicated in [1,26] and Ch. 7, where the improved performance and generalization capability of this approach is demonstrated.

In standard band-limited (and not time-limited) signal analysis with periodic waveforms, sampling is done at the Nyquist rate to have a fully reproducible signal. If the sample information is needed elsewhere, it is then compressed (possibly lossy) and transmitted (a 'smart encoder'). The received data is then decompressed and reconstructed (by simply summing wave components, e.g., a 'simple' decoder). If the signal is sparse or compressible, then compressive sensing [145] can be used, where sampling and compression are combined into one efficient step to obtain compressive measurements (the simple encoding in [145] since a set of random projections are employed), which are then transmitted (general details on noise in this context are described in [146] and [147]). On the receiving end, the decompression and reconstruction steps are, likewise, combined using an asymmetric 'smart' decoding step. This progression towards asymmetric compressive signal processing can be taken a step further if we consider signal sequences to be equivalent if they have the same stationary statistics. What is obtained is a method similar to compressive sensing, but involving stationary-statistics generative-projection sensing, where the signal processing is non-lossy at the level of stationary statistics equivalence. In the SCW signal analysis the signal source is generative in that it is describable via use of a hidden Markov model, and the HMM's Viterbi-derived generative projections are used to describe the sparse components contributing to the signal source. In SCW encoding the modulation of stationary statistics can be man-made or natural, with the latter in many experimental situations involving a flow phenomenology that has stationary statistics. If the signal is man-made, usually the underlying stochastic process is still a natural source, where it is the changes in the stationary statistics that is under the control of the man-made encoding scheme. Transmission and reception are then followed by generative projection via Viterbi-HMM template matching or via Viterbi-HMM feature extraction followed by separate classification (using SVM). So in the SCW approach the encoding is even simpler (possibly non-existent, other than directly passing quantized signal) and is applicable to any noise source with stationary statistics (e.g., a stationary signal with reproducible statistics, the case for many experimental observations). The decoding must be even 'smarter', on the other hand, in that generalized Viterbi algorithms are used, and possibly other machine learning methods as well, SVMs in particular. An example of the stationary statistics sensing with a machine learning based decoder is described in application to channel current cheminformatics studies in Ch 14.

Stochastic carrier wave (SCW) analysis – Nanoscope signal analysis
The Nanoscope described in Ch. 14 builds from nanopore detection with introduction of reporter molecules to arrive at a nanopore transduction detection paradigm. By engineering reporter molecules that produce stationary statistics (a stochastic carrier wave, or SCW) together with machine learning signal analysis methods designed for rapid analysis of such signals, we arrive at a functioning 'nanoscope'.

Nanopore detection is made possible by the following well-established capabilities: (i) classic electrochemistry; (ii) pore-forming protein toxin in a bilayer; and (iii) patch clamp amplifier. Nanopore *transduction* detection leverages the above detection platform with (iv) an event-transducer pore-blockader that has stationary statistics and (v) machine learning tools for real-time SCW signal analysis. The meaning of 'real-time' is dependent on the application. In the Nanoscope implementation discussed in Ch. 14, each signal is usually identified in less than100 ms, where calling accuracy is 99.9% if rejection is employed, and improved even further if signal sample duration, when a call is forced, is used with duration greater than 100 ms.

Nanopore transduction detection offers prospects for highly sensitive and discriminative biosensing. The NTD 'Nanoscope' functionalizes a single nanopore with a channel current modulator that is designed to transduce events, such as binding to a specific target. Nanopore event transduction involves single-molecule biophysics, engineered information flows, and nanopore cheminformatics. In the NTD functionalization the transducer molecule is drawn into the channel by an applied potential but is too big to translocate, instead becoming stuck in a bistable capture such that it modulates the channel's ion-flow with stationary statistics in a distinctive way. If the channel modulator is bifunctional in that one end is meant to be captured and modulate while the other end is linked to an aptamer or antibody for specific binding, then we have the basis for a remarkably sensitive and specific biosensing capability.

The NTD approach has significant improvement in versatility via use of non-covalently 'captured' modulators that can be electrophoretically swapped out on a given channel by voltage reversal. The improvements in sensitivity derive from the measurable, non-trivial, stationary statistics of the channel blockades (and how this can be used to classify state with very high accuracy). The overall improvement in versatility is because all that needs to be redesigned for a different NTD experiment (or binding assay) is the linkage-interaction moiety portion of the bifunctional molecules involved. There is also the versatility that *mixtures* of different types of transducers can be used, a method that can't be employed in single-channel devices that use covalently bound binding moieties (or that discriminate by dwell-time in the channel).

At the nanopore channel one can observe a sampling of bound/unbound states, each sample only held for the length of time necessary for a high accuracy classification. Or, one could hold and observe a single bound/unbound system and track its history of bound/unbound states or conformational states. The *single* molecule detection, thus, allows measurement of molecular characteristics that are obscured in ensemble-based measurements. Ensemble averages, for example, lose information about the true diversity of behavior of individual molecules. For complex *bio*molecules there is likely to be a tremendous diversity in behavior, and in many cases this diversity may be the basis for their function. The NTD 'Nanoscope' may provide the means to 'see' individual biomolecular kinetics and dynamic behavior. There can also be a great deal of diversity via post-translational modifications, as well, such as with heterogeneous mixtures of protein glycoforms, such as thyroid stimulating hormone (TSH), that typically occur in living organisms (e.g., for TSH and hemoglobin proteins in blood serum and red blood cells, respectively). The hemoglobin 'A1c' glycoprotein, for example, is a disease diagnostic (diabetes), and for TSH, glycation is critical component in the TSH-based regulation of the endocrine axis. Multi-component regulatory systems and their variations (often sources of disease) could also be studied much more directly using the NTD approach, as could multi-component (or multi-cofactor) enzyme systems. Glycoform assays, characterization of single-molecule conformational variants, and multi-component assays are significant capabilities to be developed further with the NTD approach, further details on NTD analysis and assaying are in Ch. 14.

In the Nanopore Transduction Detector (NTD) Nanoscope experiments [27], the molecular dynamics of a (single) captured non-translocating transducer molecule provide a unique stochastic reference signal with stable statistics on the observed, single-molecule blockaded channel current, somewhat analogous to a carrier signal in standard electrical engineering signal analysis. Discernible changes in blockade statistics, coupled to SSA signal processing protocols, enable the means for a highly detailed characterization of the interactions of the transducer molecule with binding targets (cognates) in the surrounding (extra-channel) environment.

The transducer molecule is engineered to generate distinct channel blockade signals depending on its interaction with target molecules [27]. Statistical models are trained for each binding mode, bound and unbound, for example, by exposing the transducer molecule to zero or high (excess) concentrations of the target molecule. The transducer molecule is engineered so that these different binding states generate distinct signals with high resolution. Once the signals are characterized, the information can be used in a real-time setting to determine if trace amounts of the target are present in a sample through a serial, high-frequency sampling, and pattern recognition, process.

Thus, in Nanoscope applications of the SSA Protocol, due to the molecular dynamics of the captured transducer molecule, a unique reference signal with strongly stationary (or weakly, or approximately stationary) signal statistics is engineered to be generated during transducer blockade, analogous to a carrier signal in standard electrical engineering signal analysis. In these applications a signal is deemed 'strongly' stationary if the EM/EVA projection (HMM method from Ch. 7) on the entire dataset of interest produces a discrete set of separable (non-fuzzy domain) states. A signal is deemed 'weakly' stationary if the EM/EVA projection can only produce a discrete set of states on subsegments (windowed sections) of the data sequence, but where state-tracking is possible across windows (i.e., the non-stationarity is sufficiently slow to track states – similar to the adiabatic criterion in statistical mechanics). A signal is approximately stationary, in a general sense, if it is sufficiently stationary to still benefit, to some extent, from the HMM-based signal processing tools (that assume stationarity).

The adaptive SSA machine learning algorithms, for real-time analysis of the stochastic signal generated by the transducer molecule can easily offer a "lock and key" level of signal discrimination. The heart of the signal processing algorithm is a generalized Hidden Markov Model (gHMM) based feature extraction method, implemented on a distributed processing platform for real-time operation. For real-time processing, the gHMM is used for feature extraction on stochastic sequential data, while classification and clustering analysis are implemented using a Support Vector Machine. In addition, the design of the machine learning based algorithms allow for scaling to large datasets, via real-time distributed processing, and are adaptable to analysis on any stochastic sequential dataset. The machine learning software has also been integrated into the NTD Nanoscope [27] for "real-time" pattern-recognition informed (PRI) feedback [20] (see Ch. 14 for results). The methods used to implement the PRI feedback include *distributed* HMM and SVM implementations, which enable the processing speedup that is needed.

Nanoscope Cheminformatics – A Case Study for device 'smartening'
The Nanoscope example can also be considered a case study for device 'smartening', whereby device state is tracked in terms of easily measured device characteristics, such as

the ambient device "noise". A familiar example of this would be the sound of your car engine. In essence, you could eventually have an AI listening to the sound of your engine to similarly track state and issue warnings like an expert mechanic with that car, without the need for sensors, or to supplement sensors (reducing expense, providing secondary fail-safe). Such an AI might even offer predictive fault detection.

Bioinformatics Overview

As mentioned at the start of this chapter, the overview of the biology specific details, such as about the polymeric information encoding molecules of life and their development [148-192] are provided separately, for those interested, at the start of Ch. 5.

Chapter 2

Probabilistic Reasoning and Bioinformatics

In this chapter a review is given of statistics and probability concepts, with implementation of many of the concepts in Perl. Perl scripts are then used to do a preliminary examination of the randomness of genomic (virus) sequence data. A short review of Linux OS setup (with Perl automatically installed) and Perl syntax is given in App. A.

2.1 Perl shell scripting

A 'fair' die has equal probability of rolling a 1, 2, 3, 4, 5 or 6, i.e., a probability of 1/6 for each of the outcomes. Notice how the sum all of the discrete probabilities for the different outcomes all add up to 1, this is always the case for probabilities describing a complete set of outcomes.

A 'loaded' die has a non-uniform distribution, for prob=0.5 to roll a '6' and uniform on the other die rolls you have loaded die_roll_probability = (1/10,1/10,1/10,1/10,1/10,1/2).

The first program to be discussed is named prog1.pl and will introduce the notion of discrete probability distributions in the context of rolling the familiar six-sided die. Comments in Perl are the portion of a line to the right of any '#' symbol (except for the first line of code with "#!.....", that's explained later)..

The Shannon entropy of a discrete probability distribution is the measure of its amount of randomness, with the uniform probability distribution having the greatest randomness (e.g., it is most lacking in any statistical 'structure' or 'information'). Shannon entropy is the sum of each outcome probability times its log probability, with an overall negative placed in front to arrive at a definition involving a positive value. Further details on the mathematical formalism will be given in Ch. 3, but for now we can implement this in our first Perl program:

```
----------------------------------------------- prog1.pl -----------------------------------------------
#!/usr/bin/perl
use strict; # this helps prevent scope errors on variables
my @die_roll_probability = (1/6,1/6,1/6,1/6,1/6,1/6);
#my @die_roll_probability = (1/10,1/10,1/10,1/10,1/10,1/2);
# let's print the probability to roll a '1'
print "$die_roll_probability[0]\n";

my $shannon_entropy=0;
my $numterms = scalar(@die_roll_probability);
my $index;
for $index (0..$numterms-1) {
    $shannon_entropy += $die_roll_probability[$index]
                          *log($die_roll_probability[$index]);
}
$shannon_entropy = -$shannon_entropy;
my $test = log(6);
print "test=$test\n";
print "shannon_entropy=$shannon_entropy\n";

----------------------------------------------- end prog1.pl -----------------------------------------------
```

The maximum Shannon entropy on a system with six outcomes is log(6). In the prog1.pl program above we evaluate that number, print it, and compare it to the calculation for the Shannon entropy (they should be equal). Further tests are left to the Exercises (Sec. 2.7).

Let's now move on to some basic statistical concepts. How do we know the probabilities for the outcomes of the die roll? In practice you would observe numerous die rolls and get counts of how many times the various outcomes were observed. Once you have counts, you can divide by the total counts to have the frequency of occurrence of the different outcomes. If you have enough observational data, the frequencies then become better and better estimates of the true underlying probabilities for those outcomes for the system observed (a result due to the law of large numbers, which is rederived in Sec. 2.6.1). Let's proceed with adding more code in prog1.pl that begins with counts on the different die rolls:

```
----------------------------------------------- prog1.pl addendum 1-----------------------------------------------
my @rolls = (3435,3566,3245,3600,3544,3427);
my $numterms = scalar(@rolls);
my @probs;
my $total_count=0;
for $index (0..$numterms-1) {
    $total_count+=$rolls[$index];
}
print "total=$total_count\n";

for $index (0..$numterms-1) {
    $probs[$index] = $rolls[$index]/$total_count;
}
print "@probs\n";

----------------------------------------------- end prog1.pl addendum 1-----------------------------------------------
```

Some notes on syntax: 'scalar' is a Perl function that returns a scalar (single) value no matter what it operates on. In the case of an array, it returns the number of terms in the array. 'my' is seen in front of the FIRST introduction of a variable, this is done to clarify the scope of a variable and to help avoid misspelling syntax errors, one of the most typical "bugs," from occurring. More discussion of its role in establishing 'scope' will be done later.

At this point we can estimate a new probability distribution based on the rolls observed, for which we are interested in evaluating the Shannon entropy. To avoid repeatedly copying and pasting the above code for evaluating the Shannon entropy, let's create a subroutine, called 'shannon' that will do this standard computation. This is a core software engineering process, whereby tasks that are done repeatedly become recognized as such, and become rewritten as subroutines, and then need no longer be rewritten. Subroutines also avoid clashes in variable usage, compartmentalizing their variables (whose scope is only in their subroutine), and more clearly delineate what information is 'fed in' and what information is returned (e.g., the application programming interface, or API).

```
-------------------------------------- prog1.pl addendum 2---------------------------------------
sub shannon {
    my ($ref)=@_; # @_ is the special array that holds
                  # the arguments passed to the subroutine
    my @probs = @{$ref};
    my $shannon_entropy=0;
    my $numterms = scalar(@probs);
    my $index;
    for $index (0..$numterms-1) {
        $shannon_entropy += $probs[$index]*log($probs[$index]);
    }
    $shannon_entropy = -$shannon_entropy;
    return $shannon_entropy;
}

my @fair_die = (1/6,1/6,1/6,1/6,1/6,1/6);
my @loaded_die = (1/10,1/10,1/10,1/10,1/10,1/2);
my $fairnum = shannon(\@fair_die);
my $loadednum = shannon(\@loaded_die);
print "fair shannon entropy = $fairnum\n";
print "loaded shannon entropy = $loadednum\n";

my $testnum = shannon(\@probs);
print "test_approx_fair shannon entropy = $testnum\n";

------------------------------------- end prog1.pl addendum 2-------------------------------------
```

Some notes on syntax: subroutines typically return a scalar variable, as shown here with the 'return' command. Subroutines are often called with arguments (variables) that are scalars. So, how to pass an array to a subroutine? This is typically done by creating a 'reference' to the array that is a scalar-valued entity that indicates where the start of the array is in memory. The array can then be reconstituted from this reference inside the subroutine by 'de-referencing'. The reference for an array '@array' is obtained by preceding the array name with a '\': \@array in this example. De-referencing can then be done with @{...}, where the reference scalar is placed inside the brackets.

If we do another set of observations, getting counts on the different rolls, we then need to repeat the process of converting those counts to frequencies... so it is time to elevate the count-to-frequency computation to subroutine status as well, as is done next. The standard syntactical structure for defining a subroutine in Perl is hopefully starting to become apparent (more detailed Perl notes are in App. A).

```
-------------------------------------------- prog1.pl addendum 3--------------------------------------------
my @loaded_rolls = (3435,3566,3245,3600,3544,14427);
sub count_to_freq {
    my ($ref)=@_;
    my @counts = @{$ref};

    my $numterms = scalar(@counts);
    my @probs;
    my $total_count=0;
    for $index (0..$numterms-1). {
        $total_count+=$counts[$index];
    }

    for $index (0..$numterms-1) {
        $probs[$index] = $counts[$index]/$total_count;
    }
    return @probs;
}
my @loaded_probs = count_to_freq(\@loaded_rolls);
my $testnum = shannon(\@loaded_probs);
print "test_approx_loaded shannon entropy = $testnum\n";
-------------------------------------------- end prog1.pl addendum 3--------------------------------------------
```

Is genomic dna random? Let's read thru a dna file, consisting of a sequence of a,c,g, and t's, and get their counts.... then compute the shannon entropy vs random (uniform distribution, e.g., p=1/4 for each of the four possibilities). In order to do this we must learn file input/output (i/o) to 'read' the data file:

```
-------------------------------------------- prog1.pl addendum 4--------------------------------------------
use FileHandle;
my $data_input_fh = new FileHandle "Norwalk_Virus.txt";
my $sequence;
while (<$data_input_fh>) {
    chomp;
    s/\s//g;
    s/\d//g;
    $sequence .= $_;
}
print "$sequence\n";
-------------------------------------------- end prog1.pl addendum 4--------------------------------------------
```

Notes on syntax: the example above shows the standard template for reading a data file, where the datafile's name is Norwalk_Virus.txt. FileHandle is a Perl module that handles file i/o. As its name suggests, it provides a 'handle' on a datafile. A module is a block of code that is already written and that provides specialized subroutines and functionalities. The while loop is a type of loop that runs as long as its argument is 'true', where its argument is the odd looking syntax '<$data_input_fh>' in this example. The <...> expression is known as the 'angle operator' in Perl and is a deceptively simple looking bit of code that does all the heavy lifting of accessing a file, line-by-line, and keeping track of where it's at, in doing that line-by-line access, until it reaches the end of the datafile being accessed. In the example shown, the while loop will repeatedly access the angle operator on the datafile, getting the next line in the file on each pass through the while block of code, until the last line of the file is 'read', at which point the angle operator will return with a 'false' evaluation and the while loop will be exited by moving to the first line of code after the while block.

The Norwalk virus file has non-standard format and is shown in its entirety in Fig. 2.1 below. The *e. coli* genome (Fig. 2.2) has standard FASTA format.

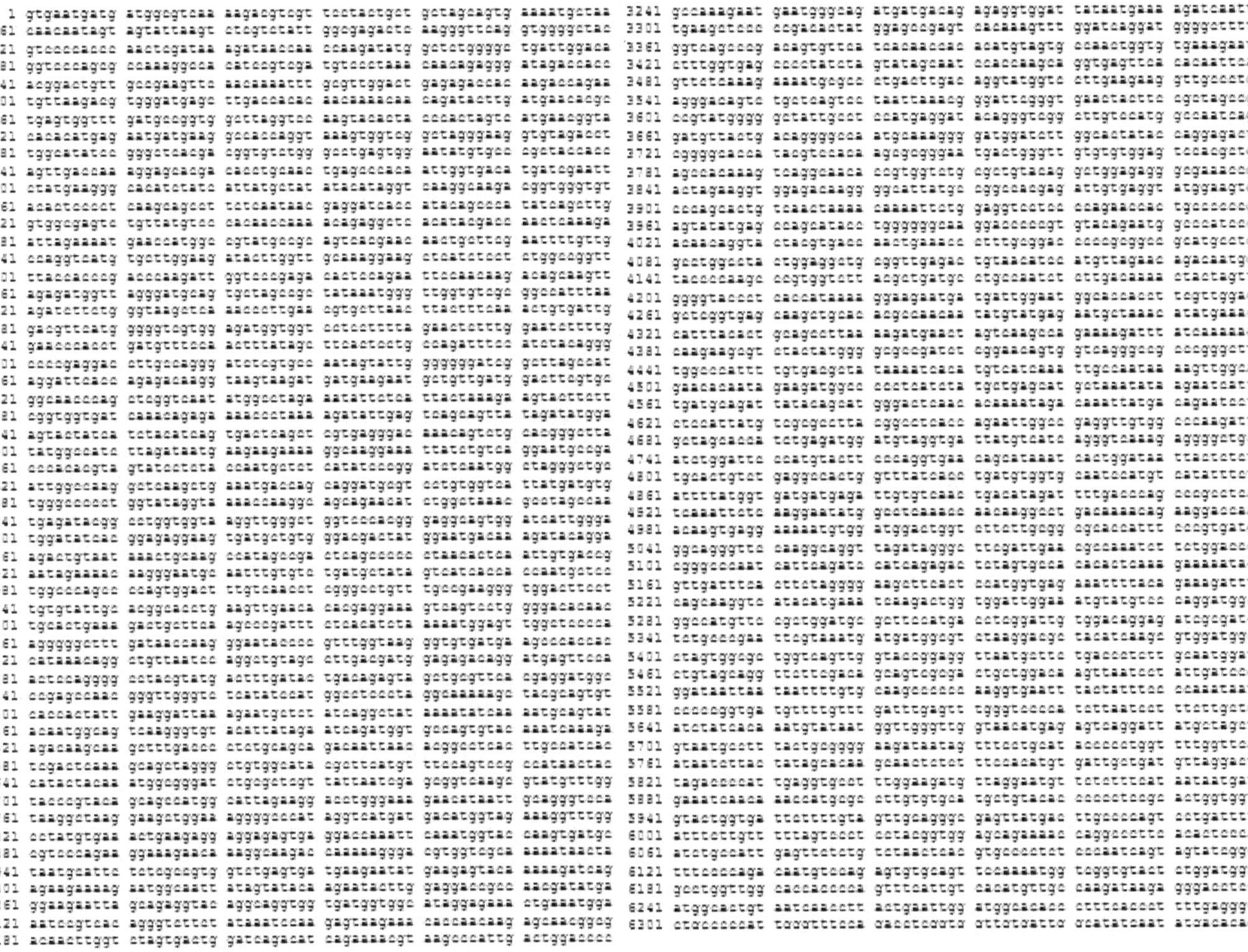

Fig. 2.1. The Norwalk virus genome (the "cruise ship virus").

The e. coli genome file is shown only for the first part (it's 4.6Mb) in Fig. 2.2, where the key feature of the FASTA file is apparent on line #1, where a ">" symbol should be present indicating a label (or comment -- information that will almost always be present).

```
>gi|556503834|ref|NC_000913.3| Escherichia coli str. K-12 substr. MG1655,
complete genome
AGCTTTTCATTCTGACTGCAACGGGCAATATGTCTCTGTGTGGATTAAAAAAAGAGTGTCTGATAGCAGC
TTCTGAACTGGTTACCTGCCGTGAGTAAATTAAAATTTTATTGACTTAGGTCACTAAATACTTTAACCAA
TATAGGCATAGCGCACAGACAGATAAAAATTACAGAGTACACAACATCCATGAAACGCATTAGCACCACC
ATTACCACCACCATCACCATTACCACAGGTAACGGTGCGGGCTGACGCGTACAGGAAACACAGAAAAAAG
CCCGCACCTGACAGTGCGGGCTTTTTTTTTCGACCAAAGGTAACGAGGTAACAACCATGCGAGTGTTGAA
GTTCGGCGGTACATCAGTGGCAAATGCAGAACGTTTTCTGCGTGTTGCCGATATTCTGGAAAGCAATGCC
AGGCAGGGGCAGGTGGCCACCGTCCTCTCTGCCCCCGCCAAAATCACCAACCACCTGGTGGCGATGATTG
AAAAAACCATTAGCGGCCAGGATGCTTTACCCAATATCAGCGATGCCGAACGTATTTTTGCCGAACTTTT
GACGGGACTCGCCGCCGCCCAGCCGGGGTTCCCGCTGGCGCAATTGAAAACTTTCGTCGATCAGGAATTT
GCCCAAATAAAACATGTCCTGCATGGCATTAGTTTGTTGGGGCAGTGCCCGGATAGCATCAACGCTGCGC
TGATTTGCCGTGGCGAGAAAATGTCGATCGCCATTATGGCCGGCGTATTAGAAGCGCGCGGTCACAACGT
TACTGTTATCGATCCGGTCGAAAAACTGCTGGCAGTGGGGCATTACCTCGAATCTACCGTCGATATTGCT
GAGTCCACCCGCCGTATTGCGGCAAGCCGCATTCCGGCTGATCACATGGTGCTGATGGCAGGTTTCACCG
CCGGTAATGAAAAAGGCGAACTGGTGGTGCTTGGACGCAACGGTTCCGACTACTCTGCTGCGGTGCTGGC
TGCCTGTTTACGCGCCGATTGTTGCGAGATTTGGACGGACGTTGACGGGGTCTATACCTGCGACCCGCGT
CAGGTGCCCGATGCGAGGTTGTTGAAGTCGATGTCCTACCAGGAAGCGATGGAGCTTTCCTACTTCGGCG
```

Fig. 2.2 The start of the _e.coli_ genome file, FASTA format.

Code blocks in Perl, and most languages (except Python) are delineated by curly braces '{ … }'.Inside the while block we start with the colorful command 'chomp;'. When you read in a line from a file you have the visible text followed by a newline control character that is not displayed (the \n control character). The command chomp is designed to chomp off the newline control character at the end of a line (if present). A more general command, called 'chop', will simply chop off the last character whether it be a normal text character or the newline control character. The 's/\s//g;' command accesses a regular expression (regex) matching mini-language inside perl that is a very powerful tool for doing text search and re-placement. In this instance, the starting 's' stands for substitute and the regex machine operates by s/match/replace/g, where the matched string is given between the first two slashes ('/') and the substitution is given between the second and third slashes. In this example the first match is done on something that starts with a backslash, which means that something is a control character of some sort or a special sub-class of characters. In this in-stance, '\s', is the special control character for whitespace, and '\d' is the special control character for matching on a number (d for decimal). In both substitutions nothing is speci-fied for what is being substituted, so the matching is substituted with nothing, i.e., the whitespace and numbers will be stripped from each line of data read from the datafile. The 'g' at the end of each of these regex commands stands for 'global' which means the substitu-tion will be done globally throughout the line of data being processed and not halt after the first substitution as it will do by default otherwise. Normally a string variable is indicated for what the regex engine operates on, but if not provided it will operate on the special string '$_'.

In Perl, when the angle operator reads in a line from a datafile, that line of data, a string of the characters from that line in the file, is placed in the default scalar variable '$_'. So this is how the regex operations know to operate on the latest line of data read in. After the substi-tutions of whitespace and numbers with 'nothing', the cleaned line of data, still held in $_, is now concatenated to the growing scalar variable named $sequence. In the end, the entire ge-nome file will be read in and the genomic sequence, consisting only of the {a,c,g,t} symbols, will reside in the variable $sequence. One last note on this example. See how the $sequence variable is declared on first use with 'my' OUTSIDE the while loop. In this context it is ref-ered to as a global variable as it 'lives' outside the while loop, with the while loop updating the $sequence variable as it grows it line by line, via concatenation, to hold the entire ge-nomic sequence indicated in the file accessed in the while loop. This is an example of how proper declaration of the scope of a variable is critical. If $sequence was declared with 'my' inside the while loop it would have re-initialized the variable (to be nothing, the empty string) on each pass thru the while loop and would have been undefined outside the block it was declared in. Lets now get counts on the occurrences of the {a,c,g,t} DNA bases:

-- prog1.pl addendum 5---

```
my @dna = split //, $sequence;
my $seq_length = scalar(@dna);
print "sequence length of Norwalk virus Genome is $seq_length.\n";

my $index;
my $a_count;
my $c_count;
my $g_count;
my $t_count;
for $index (0..$seq_length-1) {
    if ($dna[$index] eq 'a') { $a_count++; }
    elsif ($dna[$index] eq 'c') { $c_count++; }
    elsif ($dna[$index] eq 'g') { $g_count++; }
    elsif ($dna[$index] eq 't') { $t_count++; }
}
my @norwalk_counts = ($a_count,$c_count,$g_count,$t_count);


my @norwalk_probs = count_to_freq(\@norwalk_counts);

my $testnum = shannon(\@norwalk_probs);
print "Norwalk Genome has base-level shannon entropy = $testnum\n";
my @uniform_probs = (1/4,1/4,1/4,1/4);
my $testnum = shannon(\@uniform_probs);
print "Uniform Prob dist has base-level shannon entropy = $testnum\n";
```

-- end prog1.pl addendum 5---

Note on syntax: notice how the comparison test uses 'eq'. When comparing characters or strings in Perl, 'eq' must be used, while when comparing numbers in Perl '==' must be used.

Note on informatics result: notice how the Shannon entropy for the frequencies of {a,c,g,t} in the genomic data differs only slightly from the Shannon entropy that would be found for a perfectly random, uniform, probability distribution. This shows that the genomic data is not random, i.e., the genomic data holds 'information' of some sort, but we are only weakly seeing it at the level of single base usage.

In order to see clearer signs of non-randomness, let's try evaluating frequencies at the base-pair, or dinucleotide, level. There are 16 (4x4) dinucleotides that we must now get counts on:

-- prog1.pl addendum 6---
```
my $types = 16; #types of dinucleoties
my @di_uniform;
my $index;
for $index (0..$types-1) {
    $di_uniform[$index] = 1/16;
}
```

23

```
my %count;
for $index (0..$seq_length-1-1) {
    my $dinucleotide = "$dna[$index]$dna[$index+1]";
    $count{$dinucleotide}++;
}
my @dinucleotides = keys %count;
my $dinucleotide_types = scalar(@dinucleotides);
my @dinucleotide_counts;
my $index;
for $index (0..$dinucleotide_types-1) {
    $dinucleotide_counts[$index] = $count{$dinucleotides[$index]};
}

my @di_norwalk_probs = count_to_freq(\@dinucleotide_counts);
my $testnum = shannon(\@di_norwalk_probs);
print "Norwalk Genome has dibase-level shannon entropy = $testnum\n";
my $testnum = shannon(\@di_uniform);
print "Uniform Prob dist has dibase-level shannon entropy =$testnum\n";
```
-- end prog1.pl addendum 6--

In the above example we see our first use of hash variables in keeping tabs on counts of occurrences of various outcomes. This is a fundamental way to perform such counts without enumerating all of the outomes beforehand (which results in what's known as the 'enumeration problem', which isn't really a problem, just a poor algorithmic approach). Further discussion of the enumeration 'problem' and how it can be circumvented with use of hash variables will be described in Sec. 2.2.

The sequence information is traversed in a manner such that each of the dinucleotides is counted in the order seen, where the dinucleotide is extracted as a 'window' of width two bases is *slid* across the genomic sequence. Each dinucleotide is entered into the count hash variable as a 'key' entry, with the associated 'value' being an increment on the count already seen and held as the old 'value'. These counts are then transferred to an array to make use of our prior subroutines count_to_freq and Shannon.

In the results for Shannon entropy on dinucleotides, we still don't see clear signs of nonrandomness. Similarly, let's try trinucleotide level. There are 64 (4x4x4) trinucleotides that we must now get counts on:

-- prog1.pl addendum 7--
```
my $types = 64; #types of trinucleoties
my @tri_uniform;
my $index;
for $index (0..$types-1) {
    $tri_uniform[$index] = 1/64;
}
my %count;
for $index (0..$seq_length-1-2) {
    my $trinucleotide = "$dna[$index]$dna[$index+1]$dna[$index+2]";
    $count{$trinucleotide}++;
}
my @trinucleotides = keys %count;
```

```
my $trinucleotide_types = scalar(@trinucleotides);
my @trinucleotide_counts;
my $index;
for $index (0..$trinucleotide_types-1) {
    $trinucleotide_counts[$index] = $count{$trinucleotides[$index]};
}
my @tri_norwalk_probs = count_to_freq(\@trinucleotide_counts);
my $testnum = shannon(\@tri_norwalk_probs);
print "Norwalk Genome has tribase-level shannon entropy = $testnum\n";
my $testnum = shannon(\@tri_uniform);
print "Uniform Prob dist has tribase-level shannon entropy = $testnum\n";
```
-- end prog1.pl addendum 7--

Still don't see real clear signs of non-random at tribase-level! So let's try 6-nucleotide level.
There are 4096 6-nucleotides that we must now get counts on:

-- prog1.pl addendum 8--
```
my $types = 4096; #types of 6nucleoties
my @six_uniform;
my $index;
for $index (0..$types-1) {
    $six_uniform[$index] = 1/$types;
}
my %count;
for $index (0..$seq_length-1-5) {
    my $sixnucleotide = "$dna[$index]$dna[$index+1]$dna[$index+2]"
                        . "$dna[$index+3]$dna[$index+4]$dna[$index+5]";
    $count{$sixnucleotide}++;
}
my @sixnucleotides = keys %count;
my $sixnucleotide_types = scalar(@sixnucleotides);
if ($trinucleotide_types != $types) {
    print "numtypes=$sixnucleotide_types!\n";
}
my @sixnucleotide_counts;
my $index;
for $index (0..$types-1) {
    $sixnucleotide_counts[$index] = $count{$sixnucleotides[$index]};
    if ($sixnucleotide_counts[$index]==0) {
        $sixnucleotide_counts[$index]=0.0000000001;
    }
}
my @six_norwalk_probs = count_to_freq(\@sixnucleotide_counts);
my $testnum = shannon(\@six_norwalk_probs);
print "Norwalk Genome has sixbase-level shannon entropy = $testnum\n";
my $testnum = shannon(\@six_uniform);
print "Uniform Prob dist has sixbase-level shannon entropy = $testnum\n";
```

-- end prog1.pl addendum 8--

Sample Size Complications
The sixnucleotide statistics analyzed in prog1.pl in the preceding is typically called a hexamer statistical analysis. Where the window-size for extracting the substrings has "-mer"
appended, thus six-mer or hexamer. The term '-mer' comes from oligomer, a polymer containing a small number of monomers in its specification. In the case of the hexamers we saw
that there were 4,096 possible hexamers, or length six substrings, when the 'alphabet' of

```
```

monomer types consists of four elements: a, c, g, and t. In other words, there are $4^6 = 4{,}096$ such substrings. In this case of the Norwalk virus analysis this large number of different types of things that we are counting raises sampling questions. The Norwalk virus has a genome that is only 7,654 nucleotides long. As we sweep the six-base window over that string to extract all of the hexamer counts we then obtain only 7,654–5=7,649 hexamer samples! Even with uniform distribution we will be getting barely two counts for most of the different hexamer types! Limitations due to sample size play a critical role in these types of analysis.

The Norwalk virus genome is actually smaller than the typical viral genome, which ranges between 10,000 and 100,000 bases in length. Prokaryotic genomes typically range between 1 and 10 million bases in length. While the human genome is approximately 3 Billion bases in length (3.23Gb per haploid genome, 6.46Gb total diploid). Significantly more detail will be given on genome sizes and structures in later chapters. To go forward with a 'strong' statistical analysis in the current discussion, the key as with any statistical analysis, is sample size, which is obviously dictated in this analysis by genome size. So to have 'good statistics' meaning to have sufficient samples that frequencies of outcomes provide a good estimation of the underlying probabilities for those outcomes, we will apply the methods developed thus far to a bacterial genome in Ch. 3 (the classic model organism, *E. coli.*). In this instance the genome size will be approximately four and a half million bases in length, so much better counts should result than with the 7,654 base Norwalk virus genome.

2.2 Counting, the enumeration problem, and statistics

In the example in the previous section we left off with doing counts on all 4096 hexamers seen in a given genome. If we go from counts on substrings of length 6 to substrings of length 30 we run into a problem – there are now a million million million (10^{18}) substrings to get counts on. No genome is even remotely this large, so when getting counts on substrings in this situation most will necessarily be zero. Due to the large number of substrings, this is often referred to as 'the enumeration problem', but since most of those substring counts are zero, by proper programming techniques, counts need only be maintained that are non-zero, bounded by genome size, for which there is no enumeration problem. The main mechanism for capturing count information on substrings without dedicated (array) memory, is by use of associative memory constructs, such as the hash variable, and this technique will be employed in the code in later sections.

2.3 From counts to frequencies to probabilities

The conventional relations on probabilities say nothing as to their interpretation. According to the Frequentist (frequency-based) interpretation, probabilities are defined in terms of fractions of a set of observations, as the number of observations tends to infinity (where the law of large numbers works to advantage). In practice, infinite observations aren't done, and often only one observation is done (predicting the winner of a marathon, for example). In the case of one race, however, it seems intuitive that prior information would still be beneficial to predicting winners. With the formal introduction of prior probabilities we then arrive at the Bayesian interpretation. From the Bayesian perspective, prior probabilities can be encoded as "pseudocounts" in the frequentist framework (i.e., observation counts don't necessarily initialize from zero). In the computer implementations used here there are typically tuned/selected psuedocounts and minimum/maximum probability cutoffs, thus the implementations can be formally described on a Bayesian footing [1].

Whenever you can list all the outcomes for some situation (like rolls on a six-sided die), it is natural to think of the 'probabilities' of those outcomes, where it is also natural for the outcome probabilities sum to one. So, with probability we assume there are 'rules' (the probability assignments), and using those rules we make predictions on future outcomes. The rules are a mathematical framework, thus probability is a mathematical encapsulation of outcomes.

How did we get the 'rules', the probability assignments on outcomes? This is the realm of statistics, where we have a bunch of data and we want to distill any rules that we can, such as a complete set of outomes (observed) and their assigned (estimated) probabilities. If the analysis to go from raw data to a probability model was somehow done in one step, then it could be said that statistics is whatever takes you from raw data to a probability model, and hopefully do so without dependency on a probability model. In practice, however, the statistical determination of a probability model suitable for a collection of data is like the identification of a physical law in mathematical form given raw data – it's math and a lot more, including an iterative creative/inventive process where models are attempted and discarded, and built from existing models.

2.4 Identifying emergent/convergent statistics & anomalous statistics

Expectation, E(X), of random variable X:

$$E(X) \equiv \sum_{i=1}^{L} x_i\, p(x_i) \text{ if } x_i \in \Re.$$

X = total of rolling two six sided dice: X =2 can occur in one way, rolling 'snake eyes", while rolling X = 7 can be done in six ways, etc. E(X) = 7. Now consider the expectation for rolling a single die, now E(X) = 3.5. Notice that the value of the expectation need not be one of your possible outcomes (it's really hard to roll a 3.5).

The expectation, E(g(X)), of a function g of random variable X:

$$E(X) \equiv \sum_{i=1}^{L} x_i\, p(x_i) \text{ if } x_i \in \Re.$$

$$E(g(X)) \equiv \sum_{i=1}^{L} g(x_i)\, p(x_i) \text{ if } x_i \in \Re.$$

Consider special case g(X) where $g(x_i) = -\log(\,p(x_i)\,)$:

$H(X) \equiv E[g(X)] = -\sum_{i=1}^{L} p(x_i)\, \log(p(x_i))$ if $p(x_i) \in \Re^{+}$, which is Shannon Entropy for the discrete distribution $p(x_i)$.

For Mutual Information, similarly, use $g(X,Y) = \log(p(x_i,y_i)/p(x_i)p(y_i))$:

$I(X;Y) \equiv E[g(X,Y)] \equiv \sum_{i=1}^{L} p(x_i,y_i)\, \log(p(x_i,y_i)/p(x_i)p(y_i))$ if $p(x_i)$, $p(y_i)$, $p(x_i,y_i)$ are all

$\in \Re^{+}$, which is the Relative Entropy between a joint distribution and the same distribution if r.v.'s independent: $D(\,p(x_i,y_i) \,||\, p(x_i)p(y_i)\,)$.

Jensen's Inequality:

Let $\varphi(\cdot)$ be a convex function on a convex subset of the real line: $\varphi: \chi \to \Re$. Convexity by definition: $\varphi(\lambda_1 x_1 + \dots y_n x_n) \leq \lambda_1 \varphi(x_1) + \dots + \lambda_n \varphi(x_n)$, where $\lambda_i \geq 0$ and $\Sigma\, \lambda_i = 1$. Thus, if $\lambda_1 =$

$p(x_1)$, we satisfy the relations for line interpolation as well as discrete probability distributions, so can rewrite in terms of the Expectation definition:

$$\varphi(\,E(X)\,) \leq E(\,\varphi(X)\,)$$

Since $\varphi(x) = -\log(x)$ is a convex function:

$$\log(\,E(X)\,) \geq E(\,\log(X)\,) = -H(X)$$

Variance:

$$\mathrm{Var}(X) \equiv E(\,[X - E(X)]^2\,) = \sum_{i=1}^{L}\big(x_i - E(X)\big)^2 p(x_i) = E(X^2) - (E(X))^2$$

Chebyshev's Inequality:

For $k>0$, $P(|X - E(X)|>k) \leq \mathrm{Var}(X)/k^2$

Proof: $\mathrm{Var}(X) = \sum_{i=1}^{L}\big(x_i - E(X)\big)^2 p(x_i)$

$$= \sum_{\{x_i\,||x_i - E(X)|>k\}}\big(x_i - E(X)\big)^2 p(x_i)$$

$$+ \sum_{\{x_i\,||x_i - E(X)|\leq k\}}\big(x_i - E(X)\big)^2 p(x_i)$$

$$\geq k^2\, P(|X - E(X)|>k)$$

2.5 Statistics, Conditional Probability, and Bayes' Rule

So far we have counts and probabilities, but what of the probability of X when you know Y has occurred (where X is dependent on Y)? How to account for a greater state of knowledge? It turns out the answer to this was not put on a formal mathematical footing until half way thru the 20th century, with the Cox derivation [56].

The Calculus of Conditional Probabilities: The Cox derivation

The rules of probability, including those describing conditional probabilities, can be obtained using an elegant derivation by Cox [56]. The Cox derivation uses the rules of logic (Boolean algebra) and two simple assumptions. The first assumption is in terms of "**b|a**," where **b|a** $\equiv$ "likelihood" of proposition **b** when proposition **a** is known to be true. (The interpretation of "likelihood" as "probability" will fall out of the derivation.) The first assumption is that likelihood **c-and-b|a** is determined by a function of the likelihoods **b|a** and **c|b-and-a**:

(Assumption 1)   c-and-b|a = F(c|b-and-a, b|a),

for some function **F**. Consistency with the Boolean algebra then restricts F such that (**Assumption 1**) reduces to:

$$Cf(\text{c-and-b|a}) = f(\text{c|b-and-a})f(\text{b|a}),$$

where **f** is a function of one variable and **C** is a constant. For the trivial choice of function and constant there is:

$$p(c,b|a) = p(c|b,a)\,p(b|a),$$

which is the conventional rule for conditional probabilities (and **c-and-b|a** is rewritten as **p(c,b|a)**, etc.). The second assumption relates the likelihoods of propositions **b** and ~**b** when the proposition **a** is known to be true:

(Assumption 2) $\qquad\qquad\qquad$ ~b|a = S(b|a),

for some function **S**. Consistency with the Boolean algebra of propositions then forces two relations on **S**:

$$S[S(x)]=x \text{ and } xS[S(y)/x]=yS[S(x)/y],$$

which together can be solved to give:

$$S(p)=(1-p^m)^{1/m},$$

where **m** is an arbitrary constant. For **m=1** we obtain the relation **p(b|a) + p(~b|a) = 1**, the ordinary rule for probabilities. In general, the conventions for **Assumption 1** can be matched to those on **Assumption 2**, such that the likelihood relations reduce to the conventional relations on probabilities. Note: conditional probability relationships can be grouped:

$$p(b|a) = p(a|b)\ p(b)/p(a),$$

to obtain the classic Bayes Theorem.

Bayes' Rule

The derivation of Bayes' rule is obtained from the property of conditional probability:

$$p(x_i, y_j) = p(x_i|y_j)\ p(y_j) = p(y_j|x_i)\ p(x_i)$$

$$p(x_i|y_j) = p(y_j|x_i)\ p(x_i)/\ p(y_j) = \frac{p(y_j|x_i)\ p(x_i)}{\sum_{i=1}^{L} p(y_j|x_i)\ p(x_i)}$$

$$p(x_i|y_j) = \frac{p(y_j|x_i)\ p(x_i)}{\sum_{i=1}^{L} p(y_j|x_i)\ p(x_i)}$$

Bayes' Rule provides an update rule for probability distributions in response to observed information. Terminology:

$p(x_i)$ is referred to as the "prior distribution on X" in this context.

$p(x_i|y_j)$ is referred to as the "posterior distribution on X given Y".

Estimation based on maximal conditional probabilities

There are two ways to do an estimation given a conditional problem. The first is to seek a maximal probability based on the optimal choice of outcome (MAP), versus a maximal probability (referred to as a 'likelihood' in this context) given choice of conditioning (ML).

Maximum A Posteriori (MAP) Estimate:

Provides an estimate of random variable (r.v.) X given that Y=y_j in terms of the posterior probability:

$$\hat{X}_{MAP} = \text{argmax}_{x \in X}\ p(x\ |y_j).$$

Maximum Likelihood (ML) Estimate:

Provides an estimate of r.v. X given that $Y=y_j$ in terms of the maximum likelihood:

$$\hat{X}_{MAP} = \text{argmax}_{x \in X} \, p(y_j|x)$$

2.6 Emergent Distributions and Series

In this section we consider a random variable, X, with specific examples where those outcomes are fully enumerated (such as 0 or 1 outcomes corresponding to a coin flip). We review a series of observations of the random variable, X, to arrive at the Law of Large Numbers (LLN). The emergent structure to describe a random variable is often described in terms of probability distributions, the most famous being the Gaussian Distribution (a.k.a., the Normal, or Bell curve).

2.6.1 The Law of Large Numbers (LLN)

The LLN will now be derived in the classic "weak" form. The "strong" form is derived in the modern mathematical context of Martingales in App. C.1.

Let X_k be independent identically distributed (iid) copies of X, and let X be the real number 'alphabet'. Let $\mu = E(X)$, $\sigma^2 = Var(X)$, and denote

$$\bar{x}_N = \frac{1}{N} \sum_{k=1}^{N} X_k$$

$$E(\bar{x}_N) = \mu$$

$$Var(\bar{x}_N) = \frac{1}{N^2} \sum_{k=1}^{N} Var(X_k) = \frac{1}{N} \sigma^2$$

From Chebyshev: $\qquad P(|\bar{x}_N - \mu| > k) \leq Var(\bar{x}_N)/k^2 = \frac{1}{Nk^2} \sigma^2$

As N→∞ get the <u>Law of Large Numbers (weak):</u>

If X_k are iid copies of X, for k=1,2,..., and X is a real and finite alphabet, and $\mu = E(X)$, $\sigma^2 = Var(X)$, then: $P(|\bar{x}_N - \mu| > k)$ → 0, for any k>0. The arithmetic mean of a sequence of iid r.v.s converges to their common expectation. The weak form has convergence "in probability", while the strong form has convergence "with probability one", and that derivation is done later.

2.6.2 Distributions

The Geometric distribution(emergent via maxent)

Here we talk of the probability of seeing something after k tries when the probability of seeing that event at each try is 'p'. Suppose we see an event for the first time after k tries, that means the first (k-1) tries were non-events (with probability (1-p)), and the final observation then occurs with probability p, giving rise to the classic formula for the geometric distribution:

$$P(X=k) = (1-p)^{(k-1)}p$$

As far as normalization, i.e., do all outcomes sum to one, we have:

Total Probability = $\sum_{k=1} (1-p)^{(k-1)}p = p[1+(1-p)+(1-p)^2+(1-p)^3+\ldots] = p[1/(1-(1-p))]=1$.

So total probability already sums to one with no further notmailzation needed. In Fig. 2.3 is a geoemetric distribution for the case where p=0.8:

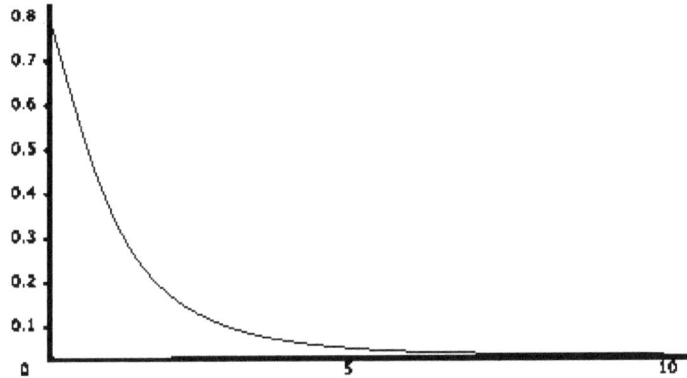

Fig. 2.4 The Geometric distribution, $P(X=k) = (1-p)^{(k-1)}p$, with p=0.8.

The Gaussian (aka Normal) distribution (emergent via LLN relation and maxent)

$$N_x(\mu,\sigma^2) = \exp(-(x-\mu)^2/(2\sigma^2))/(2\pi\sigma^2)^{(1/2)}$$

For the Normal distribution the normalization is easiest to get via comlex integration (so we'll skip that). With mean zero and variance equal one (Fig. 2.4) we get:

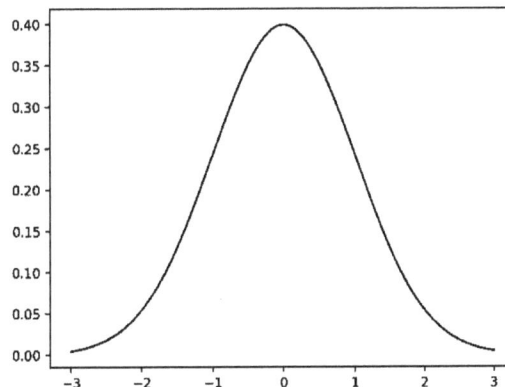

Fig. 2.4 The Gaussian distribution, aka Normal, shown with mean zero and virance equal to one: $N_x(\mu,\sigma^2) = N_x(0,1)$.

Significant distributions that are not Gaussian or Geometric
Non-geometric duration distributions occur in many familiar areas, such as the length of spoken words in phone conversation, as well as other areas in voice recognition. Although the Gaussian distribution occurs in many scientific fields (an observed embodiment of the law of large numbers, among other things), there are a huge number of significant (observed) skewed distributions, such as heavy-tailed (or long-tailed) distributions, multimodal distributions, etc.

31

Heavy-tailed distributions are widespread in describing phenomena across the sciences. The log-normal and Pareto distributions are heavy-tailed distributions that are almost as common as the normal and geometric distributions in descriptions of physical phenomena or man-made phenomena and many other phenomena. Pareto distribution was originally used to describe the allocation of wealth of the society, known as the famous 80-20 rule, namely, about 80% of the wealth was owned by a small amount of people, while 'the tail', the large part of people only have the rest 20% wealth. Pareto distribution has been extended to many other areas. For example, internet file-size traffic is a long-tailed distribution, that is, there are a few large sized files and many small sized files to be transferred. This distribution assumption is an important factor that must be considered to design a robust and reliable network and Pareto distribution could be a suitable choice to model such traffic. (Internet applications have found more and more heavy-tailed distribution phenomena.) Pareto distribution's can also be found in a lot of other fields, such as economics.

Log-normal distributions are used in geology & mining, medicine, environment, atmospheric science, and so on, where skewed distribution occurrences are very common. In Geology, the concentration of elements and their radioactivity in the Earth's crust are often shown to be log-normal distributed. The infection latent period, the time from being infected to disease symptoms occurs, is often modeled as a log-normal distribution. In the environment, the distribution of particles, chemicals, and organisms is often log-normal distributed. Many atmospheric physical and chemical properties obey the log-normal distribution. The density of bacteria population often follows the log-normal distribution law. In linguistics, the number of letters per words and the number of words per sentence fit the log-normal distribution. The length distribution for introns, in particular, has very strong support in an extended heavy-tail region, likewise for the length distribution on exons or open reading frames (ORFs) in genomic DNA. The anomalously long-tailed aspect of the ORF-length distribution is the key distinguishing feature of this distribution, and has been the key attribute used by biologists using ORF finders to identify likely protein-coding regions in genomic DNA since the early days of (manual) gene structure identification.

2.6.3 Series

A series is a mathematical object consisting of a series of numbers, variables, or observation values. When observations describe equilibrium or 'steady state', emergent phenomenon familiar from physical reality, we often see series phenomena that are martingale. The martingale sequence property can be seen in systems reaching equilibrium in both the physical setting and algorithmic learning setting.

A discrete-time martingale is a stochastic process where a sequence of random variables $\{X_1, \ldots, X_n\}$ has conditional expected value of the next observation equal to the last observation: $E(X_{n+1} \mid X_1, \ldots X_n) = X_n$, where $E(|X_n|) < \infty$. Similarly, one sequence, say $\{Y_1, \ldots, Y_n\}$, is said to be martingale with respect to another, say $\{X_1, \ldots, X_n\}$, if for all n: $E(Y_{n+1} \mid X_1, \ldots X_n) = Y_n$, where $E(|Y_n|) < \infty$. Examples of martingales are rife in gambling. For our purposes, the most critical example is the likelihood-ratio testing in statistics, with test-statistic, the "likelihood ratio" given as: $Y_n = \Pi^n_{i=1} g(X_i)/f(X_i)$, where the population densities considered for the data are f and g. If the better (actual) distribution is f, then Y_n is martingale with respect to X_n. This scenario arises throughout the HMM Viterbi derivation if local 'sensors' are used, such as with profile-HMM's or position-dependent Markov models in the vicinity of transition between states. This scenario also arises in the HMM Viterbi recognition of regions (versus transition out of those regions), where length-martingale side information will be explicitly shown in what follows, providing a pathway for incorporation of any martingale-series side information (this fits naturally with the clique-HMM generalizations described in what follows). Given that the core ratio of cumulant probabilities that is employed is itself a martingale, this then provides a means for incorporation of side-information in general (further details in App. C).

2.7 Exercises

(Ex. 2.1) Evaluate the Shannon Entropy, by hand, for the fair die probability distribution: (1/6,1/6,1/6,1/6,1/6,1/6), for the probability of rolling a 1 thru a 6 (all are the same, 1/6, for uniform prob. Dist). Also evaluate for loaded die: (1/10,1/10,1/10,1/10,1/10,1/2).

(Ex. 2.2) Evaluate the Shannon Entropy for the fair and loaded probability distribution in (2.1) computationally, by running the program described in Sec. 2.1.

(Ex. 2.3) Now consider you have two dice, where each separately rolls 'fair', but together they don't roll 'fair', i.e., each specific pair of die rolls doesn't have probability 1/36, but instead has probability:

Die 1 roll	Die 2 roll	Probability
1	1	(1/6)*(0.001)
1	2	(1/6)*(0.125)
1	3	(1/6)*(0.125)
1	4	(1/6)*(0.125)
1	5	(1/6)*(0.124)
1	6	(1/6)*(0.5)
2	any	(1/6)*(1/6)
3	any	(1/6)*(1/6)
4	any	(1/6)*(1/6)
5	any	(1/6)*(1/6)
6	1	(1/6)*(0.5)
6	2	(1/6)*(0.125)
6	3	(1/6)*(0.125)
6	4	(1/6)*(0.125)
6	5	(1/6)*(0.124)
6	6	(1/6)*(0.001)

What is Shannon Entropy for the Die 1 outcomes? (call H(1)) What is the Shannon entropy of the Die 2 outcomes (refer to as H(2))? What is the Shannon entropy on the two-dice outcomes with probabilities shown in the table above (denote (H(1,2))?

Compute the function MI(Die 1,Die 2) = H(1) + H(2) – H(1,2). Is it positive?

(Ex. 2.4) Go to genbank (https://www.ncbi.nlm.nih.gov/genbank/) and select the genome of a small virus (~10Kb). Using the perl code shown in Sec. 2.1, determine the base frequencies for {a,c,g,t}. What is the shannon entropy (if those frequencies are taken to be the probabilities on the associated outcomes)?

(Ex. 2.5) Go to genbank (https://www.ncbi.nlm.nih.gov/genbank/) and select the genome of three medius-sized viruses (~100Kb). Using the perl code shown in Sec. 2.1, determine the trinucleotide frequencies. What is the Shannon entropy of the trinucleotide frequencies for each of the three virus genomes? Using this as a distance measure phylogenetically speaking, which two viruses are most closely related?

(Ex. 2.6) Repeat (2.5) but now use symmetrized relative entropy between the trinucleotide probability distributions as a distance measure instead (re-evaluate pairwise between the three viruses). Using this as a distance measure phylogenetically speaking, which two viruses are most closely related?

(Ex. 2.7) Prove that relative entropy is always positive (hint: use Jensen's Inequality from Sec. 2.4).

(Ex. 2.8) What is the Expectation for the two-dice roll with pair outcome probabilities listed in (2.3)?

(Ex. 2.9) What is the Expectation for the two-dice roll with fair dice? Is this expectation an actual outcome possibility? What does it mean if it isn't?

(Ex. 2.10) Survey the literature and write a report on common occurences of distributions of the type: uniform, geometric, exponential, Gaussian, log-normal, heavy-tail.

(Ex. 2.11) Survey the literature and write a report on common occurences of series of the type: Martingale

(Ex. 2.12) Consider the loaded die example, where the probability of rolling a 1,2,3,4, or 5, is 0.1, and the probability of rolling a 6 is 0.5.
   (i) What is the expectation for the loaded die?
   (ii) What is its variance?
   (iii) What is its mode?
   (iv) What is its median?
   (v) The law of large numbers for the loaded die above indicates that a sequence of rolls could be done and if its average tends towards 4.5, you know it's loaded, and if it goes towards 3.5, you know it's fair. So it comes down to how soon you can resolve that its converging on these two possible expectations differing by 1.0. Suppose someone is rolling a die that is either fair or loaded as described above, how many rolls do you think you will need to see before it will be obvious how the average is trending? Is the better way to spot the anomaly? Like frequency of seeing three sixes in a row is notably skewed?

(Ex. 2.13) You have a genomic sequence of length L. (For DNA genomes you have approximately 10**4 for viruses, 10**6 for bacteria, and 10**9 for mammals.) A typical analysis is to get counts on subsequences of length N within the full sequence L, where there are L-N+1 subsequences of length N (by sliding a window of width N across the length L sequence and taking the window samples accordingly). The number of possible subsequences of length N grows exponentially with increase in that length. For DNA subsequences of length 6 bases, the 6mers, with 4 base possibilities, {a,c,g,t}, there are thus 4**6=4096 possible 6mers. If the 6mers are equally probable, then in the approximate 10,000 length of a virus each 6mer might be seen a couple times (10,000/4,096 to be precise), while a particular 6mer can be seen millions of times in mammalian genomes. Sounds fine so far, but now consider an analysis of 25mers.... The possible 25mers number 4**25=2**50=(2**10)**5 =1024**5=10**15. So, a million billion possibilities..... It turns out that DNA information doesn't have subsequences with approximately equal statistical counts (equal probabilities), but, instead, is highly structured with a variety of overlapping encoding schemes, so has subsequences with very unequal statistics. The vast majority of the 25mer subsequences, in fact, will have zero counts such that enumeration of the possibilities ahead of time in an array data-structure is not useful or even possible in some cases, which then leads to associative arrays in this context as shown in the sample code. Do a 25mer analysis on bacterial genome (get from genbank, like E. coli). What is the highest count 25mer subsequence?

Chapter 3

Information Entropy and Statistical Measures

In this chapter we start with a description of the core information entropy and statistical measures (Sec. 3.1). Using these measures we then examine genomic data and almost trivially discover a three-element encoding scheme. A few (simple) statistical queries from there, and the codon encoding scheme is revealed (Sec. 3.2). Once the coding scheme is known to exist, further structure is revealed via the anomalous placement of 'stop' codons, e.g., anomalously large open reading frames (ORFs) are discovered. A few more (simple) statistical queries from there, and ORFs and gene structure is revealed (Sec. 3.3). Once you have a clear structure in the sequential data that can be referenced positionally, it is then possible to gather statistical information for a Markov model. One example of this is to look at the positional base statistics at various positions "upstream" from the start codon (and thereby identify binding sites for critical molecular interaction in both transcription and translation). Since the Markov model is needed in analysis of sequential processes in general for what is discussed in later chapters (Ch 6 & 7 in particular), a review of Markov models, and some of their specializations, are given in Sec. 3.4 (Ch. 7 covers *Hidden* Markov models, or HMMs).

3.1 Shannon entropy, relative entropy, maxent, mutual information

If you have a discrete probability distribution P, with individual components p_k, then the rules for probabilities requires that the sum of the probabilities of the individual outcomes must be 1 (as mentioned in Ch. 2). This is written in math shorthand as:

$$\Sigma_k \, p_k = 1.$$

Furthermore, the individual outcome probabilities must always be positive, and by some conventions, nonzero. In the case of hexamers, there are 4,096 types, thus the index variable 'k' ranges from 1 to 4,096. If we introduce a second discrete probability distribution Q, with individual components q_k, those components sum to 1 as well:

$$\Sigma_k \, q_k = 1$$

The definition of Shannon Entropy in this math notation, for the P distribution, is:

$$\text{Shannon entropy of } P = - \Sigma_k \, p_k \, \log(p_k)$$

The degree of randomness in a discrete probability distribution P can be measured in terms of Shannon entropy [61].

The Khinchin derivation

In his now famous 1948 paper [61], Claude Shannon provided a qualitative measure for entropy in connection with communication theory. The Shannon entropy measure was later put on a more formal footing by A. I. Khinchin in an article where he proves that with certain assumptions the Shannon entropy is unique [62]. (Dozens of similar axiomatic proofs have since been made.) A statement of the theorem is as follows:

Khinchine Uniqueness Theorem: Let $H(p_1, p_2, \ldots, p_n)$ be a function defined for any integer **n** and for all values $p_1, p_2, \ldots, p_n$ such that $p_k \geq 0$ (**k** = 1,2,...,**n**), and $\Sigma_k p_k = 1$. If for any function **n** this function is continuous with respect to its arguments, and if the function obeys the three properties listed below, then $H(p_1, p_2, \ldots, p_n) = -\lambda \Sigma_k p_k \log(p_k)$, where λ is a positive constant (with Shannon entropy recovered for convention λ=1). The three properties are:

> (1) For given **n** and for $\Sigma_k p_k = 1$, the function takes its largest value for $p_k = 1/n$ (**k** = 1,2,...,**n**). This is equivalent to Laplace's principle of insufficient reason, which says if you don't know anything assume the uniform distribution (also agrees with Occam's Razor assumption of minimum structure).

> (2) $H(ab) = H(a) + H_a(b)$, where $H_a(b) = -\Sigma_a p(a) \log(p(b|a))$, is the conditional entropy. This is consistent with $H(ab) = H(a) + H(b)$, for probabilities of **a** and **b** independent, with modifications involving conditional probability being used when not independent.

> (3) $H(p_1, p_2, \ldots, p_n, 0) = H(p_1, p_2, \ldots, p_n)$. This reductive relationship, or something like it, is implicitly assumed when describing any system in "isolation."

Note that the above axiomatic derivation is still 'weak' in that it assumes the existence of the conditional entropy in property (2). Interestingly enough, there is a deep connection providing for uniqueness of Shannon entropy, but it would take until 1999 for the mathematics of differential geometry (used in Einstein's General Relativity) to make its way into information theory for this to become apparent (see [68-70] and [53]). This is described in the relative entropy uniqueness description to follow (from which Shannon entropy uniqueness then follows as a special case).

Maximum Entropy Principle

The law of large numbers (Sec. 2.6.1), and related central limit theorem, explain the ubiquitous appearance of the Gaussian (a.k.a., Normal) distribution in Nature and statistical analysis. Even when speaking of a probability distribution purely in the abstract, the Gaussian distribution (amongst a collection) still stands out in a singular way. This is revealed when seeking the discrete probability distribution that maximizes the Shannon entropy subject to constraints. The Lagrangian optimization method is a mathematical formalism to solve problems of this type, where you want to optimize something, but must do so subject to constraints. Lagrangians are described in detail in Ch. 7. For our purposes here, once you know how to group the terms to create the Lagrangian expression appropriate to your problem, the problem is then reduced to simple differential calculus and algebra (you take a derivative of the Lagrangian and solve for it being zero -- the classic way to find an extremum from calculus). I'll skip most of the math here, and just state the Lagrangians and their solutions in the small examples that follow.

If no constraint on probabilities, other than that they sum to 1, the Lagrangian form for the optimization is as follows:

$$L(\{p_k\}) = -\Sigma(p_k \log(p_k)) - \lambda\,(1 - \Sigma(p_k)\,),$$

where $\partial L/\partial p_k = 0 \rightarrow p_k = e^{-(1+\lambda)}$ for all k, thus $p_k = 1/n$ for system with n outcomes. Thus, the maximum entropy hypothesis in this circumstance results in Laplace's Principle of Insufficient Reasoning, a.k.a., principle of indifference, where if you don't know any better, use the uniform distribution.

If you have as prior information the existence of the mean, μ, of some quantity x, then you have the Lagrangian:

$$L(\{p_k\}) = -\Sigma(p_k \log(p_k)) - \lambda\,(1 - \Sigma(p_k)\,) - \delta\,(\mu - \Sigma(p_k x_k)\,),$$

where $\partial L/\partial p_k = 0 \rightarrow p_k = A\exp(-\delta x_k)$, leading to the exponential distribution. If for the latter we had the mean of the function, $f(x_k)$, of some random variable X, then a similar derivation would again yield the exponential distribution $p_k = A\exp(-\delta f(x_k)\,)$, where now A is not simply a normalization factor, but is known as the partition function and it has a variety of generative properties vis-à-vis statistical mechanics and thermal physics.

If you have as prior information the existence of the mean and variance of some quantity (the first and second statistical moments), then you have the Lagrangian:

$$L(\{p_k\}) = -\Sigma(p_k \log(p_k)) - \lambda\,(1 - \Sigma(p_k)\,) - \delta\,(\mu - \Sigma(p_k x_k)\,) - \gamma\,(\nu - \Sigma(p_k(x_k)^2)\,)\,,$$

where $\partial L/\partial p_k = 0 \rightarrow$ the Gaussian distribution.

With the introduction of Shannon entropy above, ca. 1948, a reformulation of statistical mechanics was indicated (Jaynes [67]) whereby entropy could be made the starting point for the entire theory by way of maximum entropy with whatever system constraints -- immediately giving rise to the classic distributions seen in nature for various systems (itself an alternate derivation starting point for statistical mechanics already noted by Maxwell over 100 years ago). So instead of introducing other statistical mechanics concepts (ergodicity, equal *a priori* probabilities, etc.) and matching the resulting derivations to phenomenological thermodynamics equations to get entropy, with the Jaynes derivation we start with entropy and maximize it directly to obtain the rest of the theory.

Relative Entropy and its Uniqueness

Relative entropy ($\rho = \Sigma_x \, p(x) \, \log(p(x)/q(x)) = D(P\|Q)$) uniquely results from a geometric (differentiable manifold) formalism on families of distributions -- the Information Geometry formalism was described by S. Amari [68-70] (a synopsis is given in [53]). Together with Laplace's principle of insufficient reason on the choice of "reference" distribution in the relative entropy expression, this will reduce to Shannon entropy, and thus uniqueness on Shannon entropy from a geometric context. The parallel with geometry is the Euclidean distance for "flat" geometry (simplest assumption of structure), vs. the "distance" between distributions as described by the Kullback-Leibler divergence.

Thus, when comparing discrete probability distributions P and Q, both referring to the same N outcomes, the proper measure of their difference is measured in terms of their symmetrized relative entropy [60] (a.k.a. Kullback-Leibler Divergence), D(P,Q):

$$D(P,Q) = [D(P\|Q) + D(Q\|P) \,]/2,$$

where

$$D(P\|Q) = \Sigma_k \, p_k \, \log(p_k/q_k),$$

where P and Q have outcome probabilities $\{p_k\}$ and $\{q_k\}$.

Relative entropy has some oddities that should be explained right away. First, it doesn't have the negative sign in front to make it a positive number (recall this was done for the Shannon entropy definition since all of the $\log(p_k)$ factors are always negative, since log of a number less than 1 is always negative, thus giving rise to an overall negative sum if not for the sign flip with the overall negation placed out front). The reason relative entropy doesn't need the negative sign is that it is provably always positive as is! (The proof uses Jensen's Inequality from 2.6.1.) For relative entropy there is also the constraint to the convention mentioned above where all the outcome probabilities are *nonzero* (otherwise have a divide by zero or a log(0) evaluation, either of which is undefined). Relative entropy is also asymmetric in that $D(P\|Q)$ is not equal to $D(Q\|P)$

One of the most powerful uses of Relative entropy is in the context of evaluating the statistical linkage between two sets of outcomes, e.g., in determining if two random variables are independent are not. In probability we can talk about the probability of two events happening, such as the probabilities for the outcomes of rolling two dice P(X,Y), where X is the first die, with outcomes $x_1 = 1, \ldots, x_6 = 6$, and similarly for the second die Y. If they are both fair dice, they act independently of each other, then their joint probability reduces to: P(X,Y) = P(X)P(Y), if {X,Y} are independent of eachother.

If using loaded dice, but with dice that have no interaction, then they are still independent of eachother, and their probabilities are thus still independent, reducing to the product of two simpler probability distributions (with one argument each) as shown above. In games of dice where two dice are rolled (craps) it is possible to have dice that individually roll as fair, however, having uniform distribution on outcomes, but that when rolled together interact such that their combined rolls are biased. This can be accomplished with use of small bar magnets oriented from the '1' to '6' faces, such that the dice tend to come up with their magnets anti-aligned (one showing its '1' face, the other showing its '6' face, for a total roll count of '7', where the roll of a '7' has special significance in the game of craps). In the instance of the dice with magnets, the outcomes of the individual die rolls are not independent, and the simplification of P(X,Y) to P(X)P(Y) cannot be made.

In evaluating if there is a statistical linkage between two events we are essentially asking if the probability of those events are independent, e.g., does P(X,Y) = P(X)P(Y) ? In this situation we are again in the position of comparing two probability distributions, P(X,Y) and P(X)P(Y), so if relative entropy is best for such comparisons, then why not evaluate D(P(X,Y) || P(X)P(Y))? This is precisely what should be done and in doing so we've arrived at the definition of what's known as 'mutual information' (finally a name for an information measure that is perfectly self-explanatory!).

MI(X,Y) = mutual information between X an Y = D(P(X,Y) || P(X)P(Y))

The use of mutual information is very powerful in bioinformatics, and informatics in general, as it allows statistical linkages to be discovered that are not otherwise apparent. In the following program example we will start with evaluating the mutual information between genomic nucleotides at various degrees of separation. If we see nonzero mutual information in the genome for bases separated by certain, specified, gap distances, we will have uncovered that there is 'structure' of some sort.

Information measures recap
The fundamental information measures are, thus, Shannon entropy, mutual information, and relative entropy (also known as the Kullback-Leibler divergence). Shannon entropy, $\sigma = -\Sigma_x p(x) \log(p(x))$, is a measure of the information in distribution $p(x)$. Relative Entropy (Kullback-Leibler divergence): $\rho = \Sigma_x p(x) \log(p(x)/q(x))$, is a measure of distance between two probability distributions. MI(X,Y) , $\mu = \Sigma_x \Sigma_y p(xy) \log(p(xy)/p(x)p(y))$, is a measure of information one random variable has about another random variable. As shown above, Mutual Information is a special case of relative entropy. Let's now write code to implement these measures, and then apply them to analysis of genomic data.

The next program, cleverly named prog2.pl, will build off the code devised previously, with the file i/o operation now 'lifted' into a subroutine for safer encapsulation (to avoid scope errors, etc.) and to avoid the confusing clutter of copying and pasting such a large block of code repeatedly that would be required otherwise. By now, this has hopefully made a convincing case for why subroutines are a big deal in the evolution of software engineering constructs (and the computer languages that implement them). Similarly, a subroutine is also introduced for handling the oligomer counting with the 'order' or length of the substring that is to be sampled being a specifiable parameter. In the case of the oligo counter subroutine, we see how simple it is to increase from passing in one variable to two in this case. The code is then used to compute the probability distributions on a particular order of oligomer for both the Norwalk and *E. coli*, or 'EC', genomes.

```
-------------------------------------------- prog2.pl -------------------------------------------------
#!/usr/bin/perl
use strict;
use FileHandle;
sub shannon {
    my ($ref)=@_;                    # @_ is the special array that holds
```

```perl
    my @probs = @{$ref};        # the arguments passed to the subroutine
    my $shannon_entropy=0;
    my $numterms = scalar(@probs);
    my $index;
    for $index (0..$numterms-1) {
        $shannon_entropy += $probs[$index]*log($probs[$index]);
    }
    $shannon_entropy = -$shannon_entropy;
    return $shannon_entropy;
}
sub count_to_freq {
    my ($ref)=@_;
    my @counts = @{$ref};
    my $numterms = scalar(@counts);
    my @probs;
    my $total_count=0;
    my $index;
    for $index (0..$numterms-1) {
        $total_count+=$counts[$index];
    }
    for $index (0..$numterms-1) {
        $probs[$index] = $counts[$index]/$total_count;
    }
    return @probs;
}
sub slurp_fasta_file {
    my ($filename) = @_;
    my $data_input_fh = new FileHandle "$filename";
    my $sequence;
    my $label;
    while (<$data_input_fh>) {
        chomp;
        s/\s//g;
        s/\d//g;
        if (s/^>//) { $label = $_; }
        else {
            tr/ACGT/acgt/;
            $sequence .= $_;
        }
    }
    if ($label eq "") { $label = "nolabel"; }
    print "file slurp complete on fasta file with label:$label\n";
    #print "$sequence\n";
    return $sequence;
}
```

-- prog2.pl end--

Note: the use of 'use strict' forces first-use of any variable to be declared with 'my'. This then forces proper coding style, where proper attention must be paid to the scope of the variables. Some of the worst, and yet most trivial, code bugs result from a variable being accessed outside of its intended scope.

Regarding "s/^>//", if a match occurs with the first character of the line being '>' this is standard notation in 'fasta' files for a label/comment specification. By doing the recognition by way of a substitution attempt the line that remains in the $_ default is stripped of the '>'.

Regarding "tr/ACGT/acgt", the tr/.../.../ command is for 'transliteration' and the syntax is such that the first element in the first is transliterated to the first element of the second list, and so on, the effect in this case being to shift the base specification from uppercase to lower case.

As mentioned previously, when comparing two probability distributions on the same set of outcomes, it's natural to ask if they can be compared in terms of the difference in their scalar-valued Shannon entropies. Similarly, there is the standard manner of comparing multicomponent features by treating them as points in a manifold and performing the usual Euclidean distance calculation generalized to whatever dimensionality of the feature data. Both of these approaches are wrong, especially the latter, when comparing discrete probability distributions (of the same dimensionality). The reason being, when comparing two discrete probability distributions there are the additional constraint on the probabilities (sum to 1, etc.), and the provably optimal difference measure under these circumstances, as described previously, is relative entropy. This will be explored in the problems, so some related subroutines are included in the first addendum to prog2.pl:

```
---------------------------------------- prog2.pl addendum 1----------------------------------------

sub eucl_dist_sq {
    my ($refP,$refQ)=@_;
    my @Pprobs = @{$refP};
    my @Qprobs = @{$refQ};
    my $num_P_terms = scalar(@Pprobs);
    my $num_Q_terms = scalar(@Qprobs);
    if ($num_P_terms != $num_Q_terms) {
        print "Pprobs an Qprobs have diff numbers of prob terms\n";
        die;
    }
    my $euclidean_dist_sq=0;
    my $index;
    for $index (0..$num_P_terms-1) {
        my $p = $Pprobs[$index];
        my $q = $Qprobs[$index];
        $euclidean_dist_sq += ($p-$q)**2;
    }
    return $euclidean_dist_sq;
}
my $eucl_dist_sq = eucl_dist_sq(\@EC_xmer_probs,\@Norwalk_xmer_probs);
print "Euclidean Dist Squared between EC an Norwalk prob arrays is:";
print " $eucl_dist_sq\n";

sub relative_entropy {
    my ($refP,$refQ)=@_;
    my @Pprobs = @{$refP};
    my @Qprobs = @{$refQ};
    my $num_P_terms = scalar(@Pprobs);
    my $num_Q_terms = scalar(@Qprobs);
    if ($num_P_terms != $num_Q_terms) {
        print "Pprobs an Qprobs have diff number of prob terms\n";
        die;
    }
    my $relative_entropy=0;
    my $index;
    for $index (0..$num_P_terms-1) {
        my $p = $Pprobs[$index];
```

```
        my $q = $Qprobs[$index];
        $relative_entropy += $p*log($p/$q);
    }
    return $relative_entropy;
}
my $re = relative_entropy(\@EC_xmer_probs,\@Norwalk_xmer_probs);
print "Relative entropy divergence between EC and Norwalk Prob ";
print "Distributions is: $re\n";
my $re = relative_entropy(\@Norwalk_xmer_probs,\@EC_xmer_probs);
print "Relative entropy divergence between norwalk and EC Prob ";
print "Distributions is: $re\n";
```

-- prog2.pl addendum 1 end--

Recall that the definiton of mutual information between two random variables, {X,Y} is simply the relative entropy between P(X,Y) 'P' and P(X)P(Y) 'p', and this is implemented in addendum #2 to prog2.pl:

-- prog2.pl addendum 2 --
```
sub mutual_information {
    my ($refP,$refp)=@_;
    my @Pprobs = @{$refP};
    my @pprobs = @{$refp};
    my $num_P_terms = scalar(@Pprobs);
    my $num_p_terms = scalar(@pprobs);
    if ($num_P_terms != $num_p_terms*$num_p_terms) {
        print "Pprobs and pprobs**2 have diff number of prob terms\n";
        die;
    }
    my $mi=0;
    my $index;
    for $index (0..$num_p_terms-1) {
        my $i;
        for $i (0..$num_p_terms-1) {
            my $joint_index = $index*4+$i;
            my $ab = $Pprobs[$joint_index];
            my $a = $pprobs[$index];
            my $b = $pprobs[$i];
            $mi += $ab*log($ab/($a*$b));
        }
    }
    return $mi;
}
my $order=1;
#### get info on EC genome
my $filename = "EC_Chr1.fasta.txt";
my $sequence = slurp_fasta_file($filename);
my @dna = split //, $sequence;
my $seq_length = scalar(@dna);
print "Sequence length of $filename Genome is $seq_length.\n";
my @xmer_counts = oligo_counter(\@dna,$order);
my @xmer_probs = count_to_freq(\@xmer_counts);
my @EC_1mer_probs = @xmer_probs; # order is 1, have base (1mer) probs
```
-- prog2.pl addendum 2 end --

3.2 Codon discovery from mutual information anomaly

As mentioned previously, mutual information allows statistical linkages to be discovered that are not otherwise apparent. Consider the mutual information between nucleotides in genomic data when different gap sizes are considered between the nucleotides as shown in Fig. 3.1 Left. When the MI for different gap sizes is evaluated (see Fig. 3.1 Right), a highly anomalous long-range statistical linkage is seen, consistent with a three-element encoding scheme (the codon structure is thereby revealed) [39].

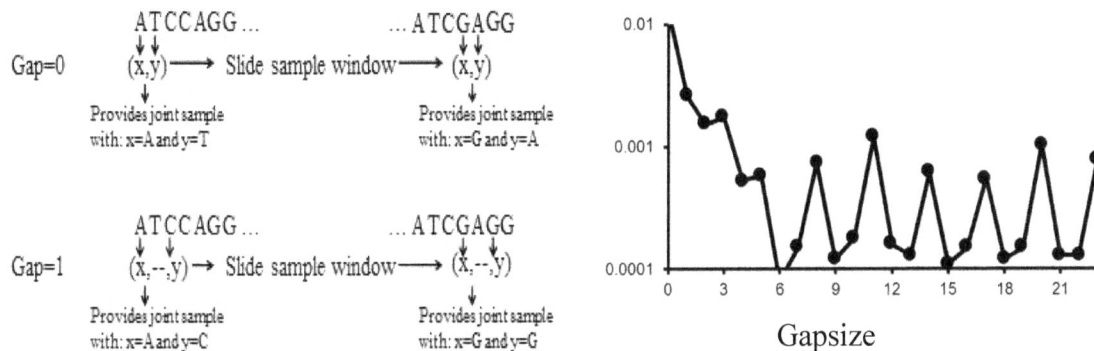

Fig. 3.1. Codon structure is revealed in the *V. cholera* genome by mutual information between nucleotides in the genomic sequence when evaluated for different gap sizes.

The next subroutine (prog2.pl addendum 3) is a recycled version of the code for the dinucleotide counter described previously, except that now the two bases in the sample window have a fixed gap size between them of the indicated size. Before, with no gap, the gapsize was zero.

```
----------------------------------------- prog2.pl addendum 3 -----------------------------------------
sub gap_dinucleotide_counter {
    my ($ref,$gap,$last_index) = @_;
    my @dna = @{$ref};
    my $seq_length = scalar(@dna);
    my $types = 16;
    my %count;
    my $index;
    for $index (0..$seq_length-1-1) { #special char cleaner
        if ($dna[$index] ne 'a' && $dna[$index] ne 'c' &&
            $dna[$index] ne 'g' && $dna[$index] ne 't') {
            print "dna[$index]=$dna[$index] replacing with 'a'\n";
            $dna[$index]='a';
        }
    }
    my $last;
    if ($last_index) { $last = $last_index; }
    else { $last = $seq_length-1-1-$gap; }
    for $index (0..$last) { # note the use of the $gap variable
        my $gapmer = "$dna[$index]$dna[$index+1+$gap]";
```

45

```
            $count{$gapmer}++;
        }
        my @seen_xmer_types = keys %count;
        @seen_xmer_types = sort(@seen_xmer_types);
        my $number_seen_xmer_types = scalar(@seen_xmer_types);
        if ($number_seen_xmer_types != $types) {
            my $zero_counts = $types-$number_seen_xmer_types;
            print "There are $zero_counts zero counts in $types xmers.\n";
            die;
        }
        my @xmer_counts;
        my $index;
        for $index (0..$number_seen_xmer_types-1) {
            $xmer_counts[$index] = $count{$seen_xmer_types[$index]};
        }
        return @xmer_counts;
}
#### get info on EC genome
my $filename = "EC_Chr1.fasta.txt";
my $sequence = slurp_fasta_file($filename);
my @dna = split //, $sequence;
my $seq_length = scalar(@dna);
print "Sequence length of $filename Genome is $seq_length.\n";

my $gap=$ARGV[0];
my @xmer_counts = gap_dinucleotide_counter(\@dna,$gap);
my @xmer_probs = count_to_freq(\@xmer_counts);
my @EC_gap2mer_probs = @xmer_probs;

my $mi = mutual_information(\@EC_gap2mer_probs,\@EC_1mer_probs);
print "mi=$mi with gap=$gap\n";
```
-- prog2.pl addendum 3 end --

Note on syntax: the special array @ARGV, accessed in the above code, is the array that holds the arguments fed to the program when invoked at the command line. By use of this we can specify different gap sizes at the command line instead of 'hard-coding' any particular choice of gap and constantly editing it for different dataruns. Working at command prompt is exactly what we want for system level programming style. This leads to perl that is C-optimized for speed at system level, but still leaves a fully functional perl environment. In Ch 4 a description of such a C-optimized setup is given where the perl solution makes use of a full-fledged Object-Oriented formulation.

At first the mutual information falls off as we look at statistical linkages at greater and greater distance, which makes sense for any information construct that is 'local', e.g, it should have less linkage with structure further away. After a certain point, however, the mutual information no longer falls off, instead cycling back to a certain level of mutual information with a cycle period of three bases. This suggests that a long-range three-element encoding scheme might exist (among other things), which can easily be tested. In doing so we ask Nature 'the right question' and the answer is the rediscovery of the codon encoding scheme, as will be shown in prog.3.pl that follows.

So, to clarify before proceeding, suppose we want to get information on a three-element encoding scheme for the *E. coli* genome (Chromosome 1), say, in file EC_Chr1.fasta.txt. We, therefore, want an order=3 oligo counting, but on 3-element windows seen 'stepping' across the genome, e.g. a 'stepping' window, not a sliding window, resulting in three choices on stepping, or framing, according to how you take your first step:

case 0: agttagcgcgt --> (agt)(tag)(cgc)gt
case 1: agttagcgcgt --> a(gtt)(agc)(gcg)t
case 2: agttagcgcgt --> ag(tta)(gcg)(cgt)

In the code that follows the case '0' above is passed as an argument for the $frame variable. Again, the code is handled via reuse of a modified count subroutine to get the 3-frame ('codon') counts:

```
----------------------------------------- prog3.pl -----------------------------------------
# include usual header and subroutines called in following
my $filename = "EC_Chr1.fasta.txt";
my $sequence = slurp_fasta_file($filename);
my @dna = split //, $sequence;
my $seq_length = scalar(@dna);
sub codon_counter {
    my ($ref,$frame) = @_;
    my @dna = @{$ref};
    my $seq_length = scalar(@dna);
    my $types = 64;
    my %count;
    my $index;
    for $index (0..$seq_length-1-2) { #special char cleaner
        if ($dna[$index] ne 'a' && $dna[$index] ne 'c' &&
            $dna[$index] ne 'g' && $dna[$index] ne 't') {
            print "dna[$index]=$dna[$index] replacing with 'a'\n";
            $dna[$index]='a';
        }
    }

    for $index (0..$seq_length-1-2) {
        if ($index%3 != $frame) { next; } # trick to perform 'stepping'
        # the operator '%' evaluates the modulus: 0%3 is 0, 0%1 is 1,
        # 2%3 is 2, 3%3 is 0 again!.... 1000%3 is 1, e.g., the
        # remainder from integer division
        my $codon = "$dna[$index]$dna[$index+1]$dna[$index+2]";
        $count{$codon}++;
    }

    my @seen_codon_types = keys %count;
    # the 'keys' operator on a hash returns the keys as a list, where
    # their order in that list is determined by their order of
    # first use in the hash
    @seen_codon_types = sort(@seen_codon_types);
    # the 'sort' operator acting on an array will reorder
    # alphabetically, for lists of strings, or in ascending order
    # numerically if lists of numbers.
    my $number_seen_codon_types = scalar(@seen_codon_types);
    if ($number_seen_codon_types != $types) {
        print "Have $number_seen_codon_types codons.\n";
        die;
    }

    my $codon;
    foreach $codon (@seen_codon_types) {
```

```
        print "$codon count is $count{$codon}\n";
    }

    my @codon_counts;
    my $index;
    for $index (0..$number_seen_codon_types-1) {
        $codon_counts[$index] = $count{$seen_codon_types[$index]};
    }
    return @codon_counts;
}
my @codon_counts = codon_counter(\@dna,0);
```

-- prog3.pl end ---

Note on syntax: the 'keys' operator on a hash returns the keys as a list, where their order in that list is determined by their order of first use in the hash @seen_codon_types = sort(@seen_codon_types). The 'sort' operator acting on an array will reorder alphabetically, for lists of strings, or in ascending order numerically if lists of numbers.

In running prog3.pl we find that the codon 'tag' has much lower counts, and similarly for the codon 'cta':

> frame 0 have tag with 8970 and cta with 8916
> frame 1 have tag with 9407 and cta with 8821
> frame 2 have tag with 8877 and cta with 9033

The tag and cta trinucleotides happen to be related – they are reverse compliments of each other. There are two other notably rare codons: taa and tga (and their reverse compliment in this all-frame genome-wide study as well).

Now that we've identified an interesting feature, such as 'tag', it is reasonable to ask about this feature's placement across the genome. Having done that, the follow-up is to identify any anomalously recurring feature proximate to the feature of interest. Such an analysis would need a generic subroutine for getting counts on sub-strings of indicated order on an indicated reference, to genome sequence data, and that is provided next as an addendum to prog3.pl.

-- prog3.pl addendum 1 ---------------------------------------
```
sub oligo_counter {
    my ($ref,$order) = @_;
    my @dna = @{$ref};
    my $seq_length = scalar(@dna);
    my $types = 4**$order; #types of $order 'mers'
    my %count;
    my $index;
    for $index (0..$seq_length-1-$order+1) { #special char cleaner
        if ($dna[$index] ne 'a' && $dna[$index] ne 'c' &&
            $dna[$index] ne 'g' && $dna[$index] ne 't') {
            print "dna[$index]=$dna[$index] replacing with 'a'\n";
            $dna[$index]='a';
        }
    }
    for $index (0..$seq_length-1-$order+1) {
        my $xmer;
        my $i;
        for $i (0..$order-1) {
```

```
        $xmer .= $dna[$index+$i];
    }
    $count{$xmer}++;
}
my @seen_xmer_types = keys %count;
@seen_xmer_types = sort(@seen_xmer_types);
my $number_seen_xmer_types = scalar(@seen_xmer_types);
if ($number_seen_xmer_types != $types) {
    my $zero_counts = $types-$number_seen_xmer_types;
    print "There are $zero_counts zero counts in $types xmers.\n";
    print "The relative entropy calculation is not guaranteed.\n";
}
my @xmer_counts;
my $index;
for $index (0..$number_seen_xmer_types-1) {
    $xmer_counts[$index] = $count{$seen_xmer_types[$index]};
}
return @xmer_counts;
}
------------------------------------------ prog3.pl addendum 1 end -----------------------------------------
```

3.3 ORF discovery from long-tail distribution anomaly

Once codon grouping is revealed, a frequency analysis on codons can be done, and the stop codons are found to be rare. Focusing on the stop codons it is easily found that the gaps between stop codons can be quite anomalous compared to the gaps between other codons (see Fig. 3.2). ORFs are "open reading frames", where the reference to what is open is lack of encounter with a stop codon when traversing the genome with a particular codon framing , e.g., ORFs are regions devoid of stop codons when traversed with the codon framing choice of the ORF. When referring to ORFs in most of the analysis we refer to ORFs of length 300 bases or greater. The restriction to larger ORFs is due to their highly anomalous occurrences and likely biological encoding origin (see Fig. 3.2), e.g., the long ORFs give a strong indication of containing the coding region of a gene. By restricting to transcripts with ORFs >= 300 in length we have a resulting pool of transcripts that are mostly *true* coding transcripts.

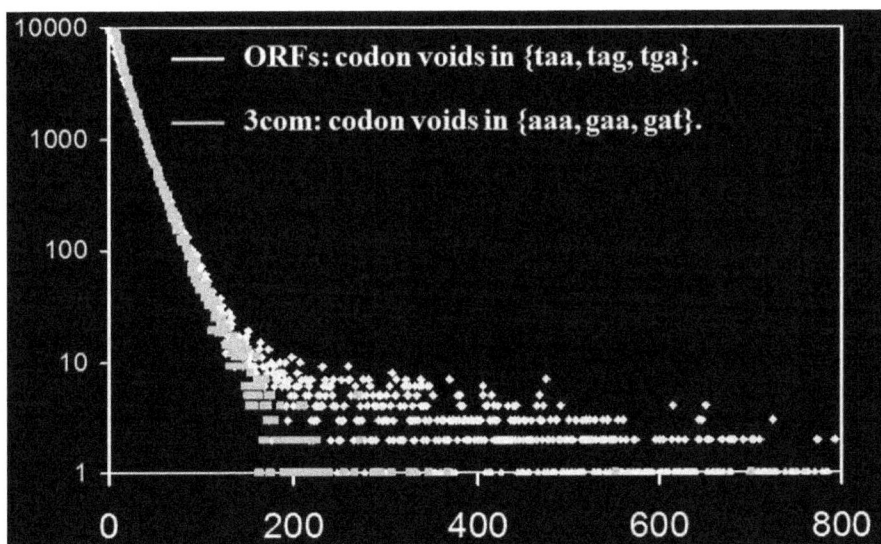

Fig. 3.2. ORF encoding structure is revealed in the *V. cholera* genome by gaps between stop codons in the genomic sequence. X-axis shows the size

of the gap in codon count between reference codons (stops for conventional ORFs, or 3com set for comparisons in table), Y-axis show the counts.

The above example shows a bootstrap FSA process on genomic data: first scan through the genomic data base-by-base and obtain counts on nucleotide pairs with different gap sizes between the nucleotides observed [1]. This then allows a mutual information analysis on the nucleotide pairs taken at the different gap sizes. What is found for prokaryotic genomes (with their highly dense gene placement), is a clear signal indicating anomalous statistical linkages on bases three apart [39]. What is discovered thereby is codon structure, where the coding information comes in groups of three bases. Knowing this, a bootstrap analysis of the 64 possible 3-base groupings can then be done, at which point the anomalously low counts on 'stop' codons is then observed. Upon identification of the stop codons their placement (topology) in the genome can then be examined and it is found that their counts are anomalously low because there are large stretches of regions with no stop codon (e.g., there are stop codon 'voids', known as open reading frames, or 'ORF's). The codon void topologies are examined in a comparative genomic analysis in [39]. As noted previously, the stop codons, which should occur every 21 codons on average if DNA sequence data was random, are sometimes not seen for stretches of several hundred codons (see Fig. 3.2). For the genomic data what is being found is the regions that contain the longer genes whose anomalous, clearly non-random DNA sequence, is being maintained as such, and not randomized by mutation, (as this would be selected against in the survival of the organism that is dependent on the gene revealed).

The preceding basic analysis can provide a gene-finder on prokaryotic genomes that comprises a one-page Perl script that can perform with 90 to 99% accuracy depending on the prokaryotic genome. A second page of Perl coding to introduce a 'filter', along the lines of the bootstrap learning process mentioned above, leads to an *ab initio* prokaryotic gene-predictor with 98.0 to 99.9% accuracy. Perl code to accomplish this is shown in what follows. In this process all that is used is the raw genomic data (with its highly structured intrinsic statistics) and methods for identifying statistical anomalies and informatics structural anomalies: (i) anomalously high mutual information is identified (revealing codon structure); (ii) anomalously high (or low) statistics on an attribute or event is then identified (low stop codon counts, lengthy stop codon voids); then anomalously high sub-sequences (binding site motifs) are found in the neighborhood of the identified ORFs (used in the filter).

Since 'tag' codons are comparatively rare, let's examine their relative placement with respect to eachother (in the frame 0 case, for example) to do this, we need to modify the codon counter to be a tag-codon gap 'counter', which in this case is a count on different length gaps between tag-codons, and is a histogram on those gap lengths. Note the code reuse in prog3.pl addendum 2, to arrive at a counting process on gaps with the indicated codon boundaries.

```
------------------------------------- prog3.pl addendum 2 -------------------------------------
sub codon_gap_counter {
    my ($ref,$frame,$codon_delimiter) = @_;
    my @dna = @{$ref};
    if (!$frame) { $frame = 0; }
    if (!$codon_delimiter) { $codon_delimiter = "tag"; }
    my $seq_length = scalar(@dna);
```

```perl
    my %count;
    my $index;
    for $index (0..$seq_length-1-2) { #special char cleaner
        if ($dna[$index] ne 'a' && $dna[$index] ne 'c' &&
            $dna[$index] ne 'g' && $dna[$index] ne 't') {
            print "dna[$index]=$dna[$index] replacing with 'a'\n";
            $dna[$index]='a';
        }
    }
    my $oldindex=0;
    for $index (0..$seq_length-1-2) {
        if ($index%3 != $frame) { next; }
        my $codon = "$dna[$index]$dna[$index+1]$dna[$index+2]";
        if ($codon eq $codon_delimiter) {
            my $gap = $index - $oldindex;
            my $quant = 100;
            my $bin = int($gap/$quant);
            if ($oldindex != 0) { $count{$bin}++; }
            $oldindex=$index;
        }
    }
    my @seen_gap_types = keys %count;
    @seen_gap_types = sort {$a<=>$b} (@seen_gap_types); #numerical sort
    my $number_seen_gap_types = scalar(@seen_gap_types);
    my $gap;
    foreach $gap (@seen_gap_types) {
        print "$gap gap count is $count{$gap}\n";
    }
    return %count;
}
my %gapcounts = codon_gap_counter(\@dna,0);
```

-- prog3.pl addendum 2 end --

Upon running the above code with codon delimiter set to 'tag', we arrive at Table 3.1, which shows the distribution on (tag) gap sizes. Bin size is 100. So gap bin 0 has the count on all gaps seen sized anywhere from 1 to 99. Bin 1 has counts on occurrences of gaps in the domain 100 to 199, etc.

Gap bin	Count
0	2115
1	1428
2	1066
3	829
4	696
5	484
6	399
7	293
8	241
9	222

Table 3.1. (tag) gap sizes, with bin size 100.

In order to see how strongly the (tag) distribution is skewed, consider some other codon to evaluate, such as for the 'aaa' gap, where aaa is most common. So, need to run the codon gap counter with the alternative delimiter:

```
my %gapcounts = codon_gap_counter(\@dna,0,"aaa");
```

The aaa gaps, shown in Table 3.2, tend to be much smaller, with a standard exponential distribution fall-off indicative of no long-range encoding linkages:

Gap bin	Count
0	21256
1	7843
2	3375
3	1665
4	827
5	480
6	287
7	163
8	86
9	70

Table 2. (aaa) gap sizes, with bin size 100.

Thus the codon tag is clearly very different from aaa, it's as if tag roughly marks the boundaries of regions, and aaa is just scattered throughout. Are any other codons similar to tag? The frequency analysis blurs counts so more subtle differences not as obvious.... have to run gap counter for each to directly see, and how to easily 'see'? Notice how the tag distribution has a long tail. The gap bins only go to 9 in the figures, but for the full dataset the last nonzero gap bin for 'tag' is at a remarkable bin 70. For 'aaa' the last nonzero bin is much earlier, at bin number 23 (even though there are ten times as many (aaa) codons as (tag) codons anyway). For 'taa' the last nonzero bin is at 60, while for tga it's at 53. The codons taa, tga, and tag are known as the stop codons and the gaps between them are known as open reading frames, or ORFs. A subtlety in the statistical analysis is that the stop codons do not have to match to define such anomalously large regions (according to observation). Thus a biochemical encoding schem must exist that works with any of the three stop codons seen as equivalent, thus the naming for this group as 'stop' codons (and their grouping as such in Fig. 3.2.). We see more the nuances of the naming convention 'stop' codon when delving into the encoding biochemistry in Ch 5.

Ab initio learning with smORF's, holistic modeling, and bootstrap learning
In work on prokaryotic gene prediction (*V. cholera* in what follows), a program (smORF) was developed for an extended ORF (open reading frame) characterization (to characterize "some more ORFs" … with different trinucleotide delimiters than stops). Using that software with a simple start-of-coding heuristic it was possible to establish good gene prediction for ORFs of length greater than 500 nucleotides. The smORF gene identification was used in a bootstrap gene-annotation process (where no initial training data was provided). The strength of the gene identification was then improved by use of a gap-interpolating-Markov-model (gIMM). When applied to the identified coding regions (most of the >500 length ORFs), six gIMMs were used (one for each frame of the codons, with forward and backward read senses). If poorly gIMM-scoring coding regions were rejected, performance improved,

with results slightly better than those of the early Glimmer gene-prediction software [80], where an interpolating Markov model was used (but not generalized to permit gaps). More recent versions of Glimmer incorporate start-codon modeling in order to strengthen predictions. One of the benefits of the gap-interpolating generalization is that it permits regulatory motifs to be identified, particularly those sharing a common positional alignment with the start-of-coding region. Using the bootstrap-identified genes from the smORF-based gene-prediction (including mis-calls) as a training set permitted an unsupervised search for upstream regulatory structure. The classic Shine-Dalgarno sequence (the ribosome binding site) was found to be the strongest signal in the 30-base window upstream from the start codon.

smORF offers information about open reading frames (ORFs), and tallies information about other such codon void regions (an ORF is a void in three codons: TAA, TAG, TGA). This allows for a more informed selection process when sampling from a genome, such that non-overlapping gene starts can be cleanly and unambiguously sampled. The goal is, initially, to identify key gene structures (e.g., stop codons, etc.) and use only the highest confidence examples to train profilers. Once this is done, Markov models (MMs) can be (bootstrap) constructed on the suspected start/stop regions and coding/noncoding regions. The algorithm then iterates again, informed with the MM information, and partly relaxes the high fidelity sampling restrictions (essentially, the minimum allowed ORF length is made smaller). A crude gene-finder can be constructed on the high fidelity ORFs by use of a very simple heuristic: scan from the start of an ORF and stop at the first in-frame "atg". This analysis was applied to the *V. cholerae* genome (Chr. I). 1253 high fidelity ORFs were identified out of 2775 known genes. This first-"atg" heuristic provided a gene prediction accuracy of 1154/1253 (92.1% of predictions of gene regions were exactly correct). If small shifts are allowed in the predicted position of the start-codon relative to the first-"atg" (within 25 bases on either side), then prediction accuracy improves to 1250/1253 (99.8%). This actually elucidates a key piece of information needed to improve such a prokaryotic gene-finder: information is needed to help identify the correct start codon in a 50 base window from the first ATG. Such information exists in the form of DNA motifs corresponding to the binding footprint of regulatory biomolecules (that play a role in transcriptional or translational control). Further bootstrap refinements along these lines are done in Ch 4 to produce a prokaryotic gene finder.

Comparative topological structure analysis via smORFs
Ab initio gene-finding can identify the stop codons and, thus, (standard) ORFs. A generalization to codon void regions, with all six frame passes, then leads to recognition of different, overlapping, potential gene regions (with two orientations). A genome-topology scoring as shown in Fig. 3.3 clearly shows differences between bacteria (Fig. 3.4) – and is thus a possible "fingerprinting" tool.

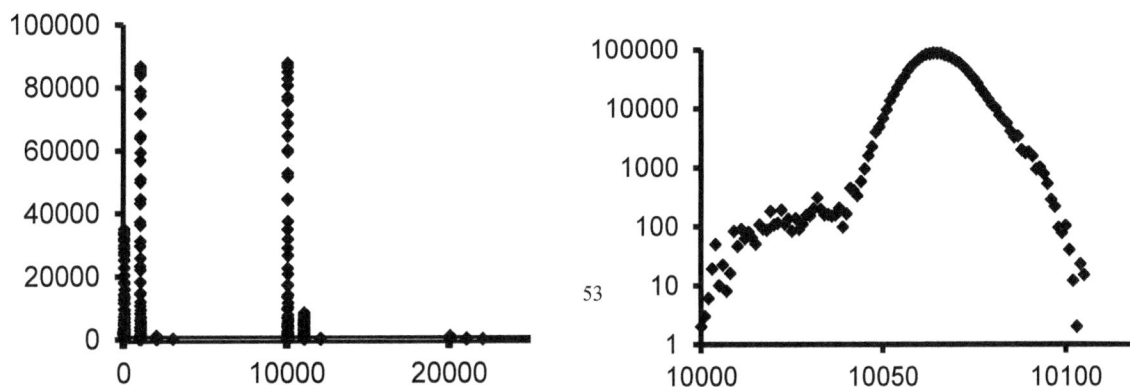

53

Fig. 3.3. Left. Topology Index Histograms shown for the _V. cholerae_ CHR. I genome, where the x-axes are the topology index, and the y-axes show the event counts (i.e., occurance of that particular topolgy index in the genome). The topology indeex is computed by the following scheme: (i) initialize index for all bases in sequesnce to zero. (ii) Each base in a forward sense ORF, with length greater than a specified cut-off, is incremented by +10,000 for each such ORF overlap. Similarly, bases in reverse sense ORFs are incremented by +1,000 for each such overlap. Voids larger than the cut-off length in the non-standard smORFs each give rise to an increment of +1. The Top panel above shows that _V. cholerae_ only has a small portion of its genome involved in multiple gene encodings.The Right panel shows a "blow-up" of the 10000 peak.

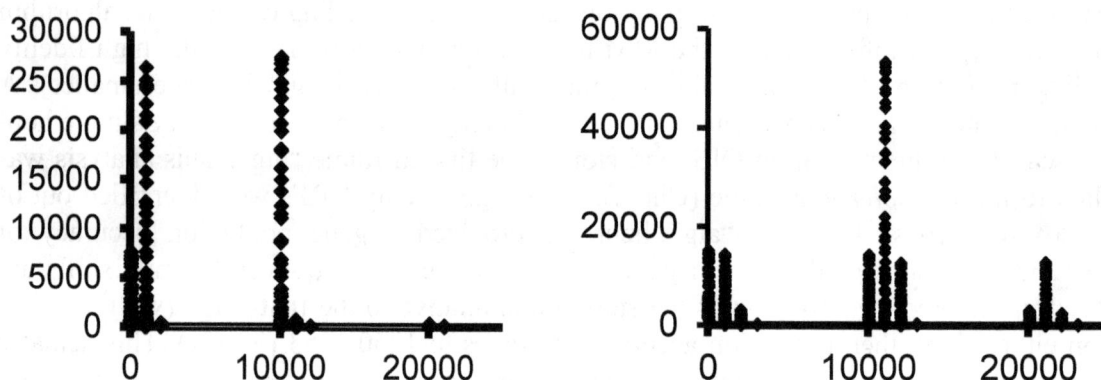

Fig. 3.4. Topology-Index histograms are shown for the _Chlamydia trachomatis_ genome, Left panel, and _Deinococcus radiodurans_ genome, Right panel. _C. trachomatis_, like _V. cholerae_, shows very little overlapping gene structure. _D. radiodurans_, on the other hand, is dominated by genes that overlap other genes (note the strong 11000 peak).

The prokaryotic genome analysis is similar to both the prokaryotic _and eukaryot_ic transciptome analysis (the latter is explored in Ch. 9), where eukaryotic _transcriptome_ analysis is similar since the introns have been removed. The analysis tools for prokaryotic genomes, described thus far, are primarily what are needed for either prokaryotic or eukaryotic transcriptome analysis (since the introns are removed).Surprisingly, the same overlapping void topologies, with reverse overlap orientation ("duals"), are seen at transcriptome level in eukaryotes as in prokaryotes. For eukaryotic transcripts with overlaps that are 'dual', however, this has special significance (see Ch. 9 for full description). Recall that a transcript that encodes overlapping read direction 'duality' (with regulatory regions intact and lengthy ORF size, so highly likely functional), is only from a _single_ genome-level pre-mRNA due to intron splicing in eukaryotes. This is a very odd arrangement (artifact) for eukaryotes unless they evolved from an ancient prokaryote as hypothesized in a number of theories where such an overalp topology would already be in place to 'imprint thru'. The specific nature of this transcriptome artifact, however, is best explained in the viral eukaryogenesis hypothesis (see Ch 8).

3.4 Sequential Processes and Markov Models

Just as Ch 2 finished with a Math review, we do the same again here in the context of sequential processes. The core mathematical tool for describing a sequential process (where limited memory suffices) is the Markov chain, so that will be defined first. In the context of genome analysis, however, the standard Markov chain based feature extraction is no longer optimal (especially given the nature of the computational resources). Thus, novel mathematical generalization of the Markov chain description, interpolatedMarkov models, will be given as well.The gap/hash interpolated Markov model, in particular, can be used to 'vacuum-up' all motif information in specified regions. This could be used and directly integrated into an HMM-based gene finder (Ch. 7 & 8), or, alternatively, identification of a typical motif set for some circumstance, such as occurrence immediately upsteam from start of coding could be used (as will be done in Ch 4).

Markov Chains

A Markov chain is a sequence of random variables S_1; S_2; S_3; ... with the Markov property of limited memory, where a first-order Markov assumption on the probability for observing a sequence '$s_1s_2s_3s_4$ ... s_n' is:

$$P(S_1=s_1, ..., S_n=s_n) = P(S_1=s_1) \, P(S_2=s_2 \, |S_1=s_1) ... P(S_n=s_n \, |S_{n-1}=s_{n-1})$$

In the Markov chain model, the states are also the observables. For a hidden Markov model (HMM) we generalize to where the states are no longer directly observable (but still 1st-order Markov), and for each state, say S_1, we have a statistical linkage to a random variable, O_1, that has an observable base emission, with the standard (0th-order) Markov assumption on prior emissions.

The key "short-term memory" property of a Markov chain is: $P(x_i|x_{i-1}, ..., x_1) = P(x_i|x_{i-1}) = a_{i-1,i}$, where $a_{i-1,i}$ are sometimes referred to as "transition probabilities", and we have: $P(x) = P(x_L, x_{L-1} ..., x_1) = P(x_1) \prod_{i=2..L} a_{i-1,i}$. If we denote C_y for the count of events y, C_{xy} for the count of simultaneous events x and y, T_y for the count of strings of length one, and T_{xy} for the count of strings of length two: $a_{i-1,i} = P(x \mid y) = P(x,y)/P(y) = [C_{xy}/T_{xy}] / [C_y/T_y]$. Note: since $T_{xy}+1 = T_y \rightarrow T_{xy} \cong T_y$ (sequential data sample property if one long training block), $a_{i-1,i} \cong C_{xy}/C_y = C_{xy}/\sum_x C_{xy}$, so counts C_{xy} is complete information for determining transition probabilities.

For prokaryotic gene prediction much of the problem with obtaining high-confidence training data can be circumvented by using a bootstrap gene-prediction approach. This is possible in prokaryotes because of their simpler and more compact genomic structure: simpler in that long ORFs (open reading frames) are usually long genes, and compact in that motif searches upstream usually range over hundreds of bases rather than thousands (as in human).

Interpolated Markov Model (IMM): the order of the MM can be interpolated according to a *globally* imposed cut-off criterion (se Fig. 3.5), such as a minimum sub-sequence count: 4th-order passes if Counts(x_0; x_{-1}; x_{-2}; x_{-3}; x_{-4})>cutoff for all $x_{-4}...x_0$ sub-sequences (100, for example), the utility of this becomes apparent with the following re-expression:

$$P(x_0| x_{-1}; x_{-2}; x_{-3}; x_{-4}) = P(x_0; x_{-1}; x_{-2}; x_{-3}; x_{-4})/P(x_{-1}; x_{-2}; x_{-3}; x_{-4})$$
$$= Counts(x_0; x_{-1}; x_{-2}; x_{-3}; x_{-4})/Counts(x_{-1}; x_{-2}; x_{-3}; x_{-4})$$

TotalCounts(length5)/TotalCounts(length4)

$$= \text{Counts}(x_0; x_{-1}; x_{-2}; x_{-3}; x_{-4})/\text{Counts}(x_{-1}; x_{-2}; x_{-3}; x_{-4}) \, [(L-4)/(L-3)]$$

$$\cong \text{Counts}(x_0; x_{-1}; x_{-2}; x_{-3}; x_{-4})/\text{Counts}(x_{-1}; x_{-2}; x_{-3}; x_{-4})$$

Suppose $\text{Counts}(x_0; x_{-1}; x_{-2}; x_{-3}; x_{-4}; x_{-5}) < \text{cutoff}$ for some $x_{-5} \ldots x_0$ sub-sequence, then the interpolation would halt (globally), and the order of MM used would be 4th order.

Gap Interpolated Markov Model (gIMM): like IMM with its count cutoff, but when going to higher order in the interpolation there is no constraint to contiguous sequence elements -- i.e., 'gaps' are allowed. The resolution of what gap-size to choose when going to the next higher order is resolved by evaluating the Mutual Information. I.e., when going to 3rd order in the Markov context, $P(x_0| x_{-5}; x_{-2}; x_{-1})$ is chosen over $P(x_0| x_{-3}; x_{-2}; x_{-1})$ if

$$MI(\{x_0; x_{-1}; x_{-2}\}, \{x_{-5}\}) > MI(\{x_0; x_{-1}; x_{-2}\}, \{x_{-3}\}).$$

Or, in terms of Kullback-Leibler divergences, if

$$D[P(x_0; x_{-1}; x_{-2}; x_{-5})\|P(x_0; x_{-1}; x_{-2})P(x_{-5})] > D[P(x_0; x_{-1}; x_{-2}; x_{-3})\|P(x_0; x_{-1}; x_{-2})P(x_{-3})].$$

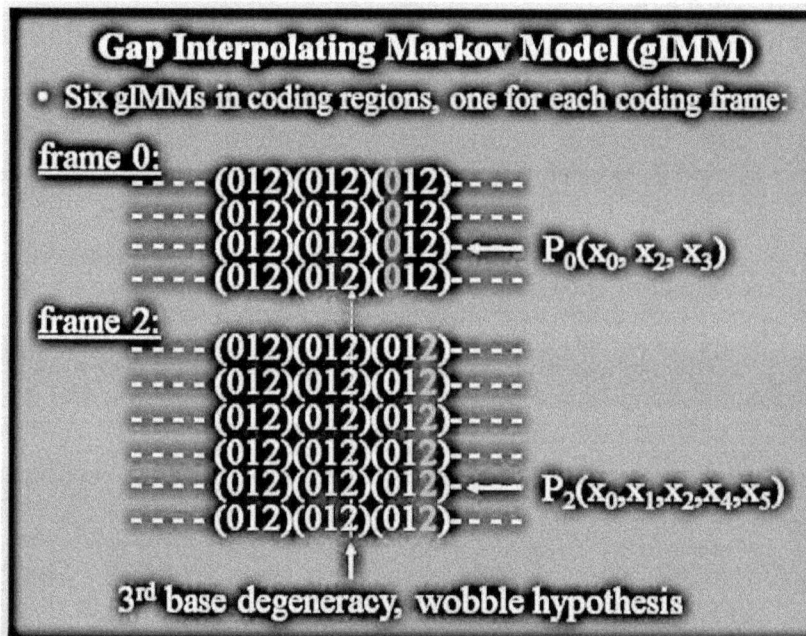

Fig. 3.5. Hash Interpolated Markov Model (hIMM) and gap/hash interpolated Markov model (ghIMM): now no longer employ a global cutoff criterion --- count cutoff criterion applied at the sub-sequence level. Given the current state and the emitted sequence as x1,...., xL; compute: $P(xL \mid x1,...., xL-1) \approx \text{Count}(x1,...., xL)/\text{Count}(x1,...., xL-1)$. Iff $\text{Count}(x1,...., xL-1) \geq 400$ i.e. only if the parental sequence shows statistical significance (consider 400=4*100, or requiring >100 counts on observations assuming uniform distribution for count cut-off determination), store $P(xL \mid x1,...., xL-1)$ in the hash. (If gene finding, have at least five states, e.g., need to maintain a separate hash for each of the following states – Junk, Intron and Exon0, 1, 2.)

3.5 Exercises

(Ex. 3.1) In Sec. 3.1 the Maximum Entropy Principle is introduced. Using the Lagrangian formalism, find a solution that maximizes on Shannon entropy subject to the constraint of the 'probabilities' sum to one.

(Ex. 3.2) Repeat the Lagrangian optimization of (Ex. 3.1) subject to the added constraint that there is a mean value, $E(X)=\mu$.

(Ex. 3.3) Repeat the Lagrangian optimization of (Ex. 3.2) subject to the added constraint that there is a variance value, $Var(X) = E(X^2)-(E(X))^2=\sigma^2$.

(Ex. 3.4) Using the 2-die roll probabilities from (Ex. 2.3) compute the mutual information between the two die using the relative entropy form of the definition. Compare to the pure Shannon definition: $MI(X,Y) = H(X) + H(Y) - H(X,Y)$.

(Ex. 3.5) Go to genbank (https://www.ncbi.nlm.nih.gov/genbank/) and select the genomes of three medius-sized bacteria (~1Mb), where two bacteria are closely related. Using the perl code shown in Sec. 2.1, determine their hexamer frequencies (as in Ex. 2.5 with virus genomes). What is the Shannon entropy of the hexamer frequencies for each of the three bacterial genomes? Consider the following three ways to evaluate distances between the genome hexamer-frequency profiles (denoted Freq(genome1), etc.), try each, and evaluate their performance at revealing the 'known' (that two of the bacteria are closely related):
(i) distance = Shannon difference = | H(Freq(genome1))-H(Freq(genome2))|.
(ii) distance = Euclidean distance = d(Freq(genome1),Freq(genome2)).
(iii) distance = Symmetrized Relative Entropy
$\qquad$ = [D(Freq(genome1)||Freq(genome2))+D(Freq(genome2)||Freq(genome1))]/2

Which distance measure provides the clearest identification of phylogenetic relationship? Typically it should be (iii).

(Ex. 3.6) Exercise 3.5, if done repeatedly, will eventually reveal that the best distance measure (between distributions) is the symmetrized relative entropy (case (iii)). Notice that this means that when comparing two distributions we quantify their difference not by a difference on shannon entropies, case (i). In other words, we choose:
Difference(X,Y) = MI(X,Y)=H(X)+H(Y)–H(X,Y),
Not Difference = |H(X)–H(Y)|.
The latter case satisfies the metric properties, including triangle inequality, in order to be a 'distance' measure, is this true for the mutual information difference as well?

(Ex. 3.7) Go to genbank (https://www.ncbi.nlm.nih.gov/genbank/) and select the genome of the K-12 strain of *E.coli*. (The K-12 strain was obtained from the stool sample of a diphtheria patient in Palo Alto, CA, in 1922, so that seems like a good one.) Reproduce the MI codon discovery described in Fig. 3.1.

(Ex. 3.8) Using the *E.coli* genome (the one described above) and using the codon counter code, get the frequency of occurence of the 64 different codons genome-wide (without even restricting to coding regions or to a particular'framing', these are still unknowns, initially, in an *ab initio* analysis). This should reveal oddly low counts for what will turn out to be the 'stop' codons.

(Ex. 3.9) Using the code examples with stops used to mark boundaries, identify long ORF regions in the *E.coli* genome (the one described in (Ex. 3.7)). Produce an ORF length histogram like that shown in Fig. 3.2.

(Ex. 3.10) Create an overlap-encoding topology scoring method (like that described for Fig. 3.3), and use it to obtain topology histograms like those shown in Fig. 3.3 Left and Fig. 3.4. Do this for the following genomes: *E.coli* (K-12 strain); *V. cholera*; and *Deinococcus Radiodurans*.

(Ex. 3.11) In a highly trusted coding region, such as the top 10% of the longest ORFs in the E.coli genome analysis, perform a gap IMM analysis, which should approximately reproduce the result shown in Fig. 3.5.

Text Analytics

(Ex. 3.12) Do text analysis on a text of your choice. Generally this will include word frequency and sentiment analysis (get sentiment table off of internet). Sometimes punctuation usage, such as the exclamation point can be very distinctive (Tolkien). So include a punctuation frequency analysis as well. The default text, if you can't decide on one, is to use Machiavelli's IlPrincipe in the original italian.

(Ex. 3.13) Find the most common 3-word grouping in the works of Shakespeare. Submit your code with your answer. Why did Shakepeare do this, was it to "stay true to the meter"?

(Ex. 3.15) Have a way to map words to syllables, get histogram of syllable counts per line of Shakespeare. There should be a peak at 10 syllabes for iambic pentameter.

(Ex. 3.16) Get an 'iambic pentameter profile' on Part I and Part II of Shakespeare's Henry VI. Is there a notable shift in the iambic signature of the two Part's ? (the second is known to have actually been written by Marlowe). By profile, get a histogram of counts on syllables in the lines of Shakespeare -- it should peak at 10, with a side-peak at 11.

Chapter 4

Ad Hoc, Ab Initio, and Bootstrap Signal Acquisition Methods

In this chapter concepts introduced in chapters 2 and 3 are combined with efficient implementation details and objective measures of performance, as well as signal analysis tools from electrical engineering and statistics. This permits *ad hoc*, *ab initio*, signal acquisition.

4.1 Signal acquisition, or scanning, at linear order time-complexity

All of the tFSA signal acquisition methods described in this chapter are O(L), i.e., they scan the data with a computational complexity no greater than that of simply seeing the data (via a 'read' or 'touch' command). Because the signal acquisition is only O(L) it is not significantly costly, computationally, to simply repeat the acquisition analysis multiple times with a more informed process with each iteration, to have arrive at a 'bootstrap' signal acquisition process. In such a setting, signal acquisition is often done with bias to very high specificity initially (and sensitivity very poor), to get a 'gold standard' set of highly likely true signals that can be data mined for their attributes. With a filter stage thereby trained, later scan passes can pass suspected signals with very weak specificity (very high sensitivity now) with high specificity then recovered by use of the filter. This then allows a bootstrap process to a very high specificity (SP) and sensitivity (SN) at the tFSA acquisition stage on the signals of interest.

The same procedure outlined for the above signal discovery and acquisition on genomic data can be applied to analysis of any set of stochastic sequential data. If the data is numerical, e.g., observational data on an electrical current, or stock price, or time series in general, then even more tools from statistics can be brought to bear (e.g., the expectation of a real number observational sequence can be calculated, while the same can't be done, directly, with the symbol-based {a,c,g,t} genomic data). In what follows a description of a time-domain FSA on real-number observational data (channel current readings) will be given. Details include practical implementation considerations such as working with raw integer encoded data, not floating point representation until absolutely needed. Working with integer representation, in some settings, allows a significant speedup for every processing loop working with integer multiplications instead of floating point multiplications.

In [198], a time-domain finite state automaton with eight states is used for signal identification and acquisition (based on the first 100 ms of channel current blockade signal in Fig. 4.1). Two states, sequentially connected, were used for reset and initialization on the FSA. Transition between the two states, from reset-start to reset-ready, was accomplished upon measuring a short section of acceptable baseline current (200 μs). An abrupt drop in current to 70% residual current (determined by the holistic tuning that is described in what follows), or less, then triggered transition from the reset-ready state to the signal-active state. From the signal-active state, processing advanced to one of two states (good- and bad-end-level states) according to an end-of-signal profile. The profile rule simply required that the last end-level-range observations had to have current above minimum-end-level-value. Satisfying the rule led to the good-end-level state, otherwise the bad-end-level state was reached. If there was a normal return to baseline (good-end-level state), or a signal-blockade scan exited due to truncation (bad-end-level state), the signal complete state was reached, otherwise further scanning was performed. Further scanning involved transition through the internal active state, where local signal properties, observation less than maximum-cutoff and observation greater than minimum-cutoff, were used to decide whether to exit (to the reset-end state) or continue the blockade scan (return to the signal-active state). Similar to the local blockade signal properties that determined how to transition from the internal-active state, transition to the acquire-signal state from the signal-complete state was based on several global properties of the signal trace: maximum blockade sample less than maximum-cutoff and greater than min-max-internal, minimum blockade sample greater than minimum-cutoff and less than max-min-internal, and signal duration greater than or equal to minimum-duration.

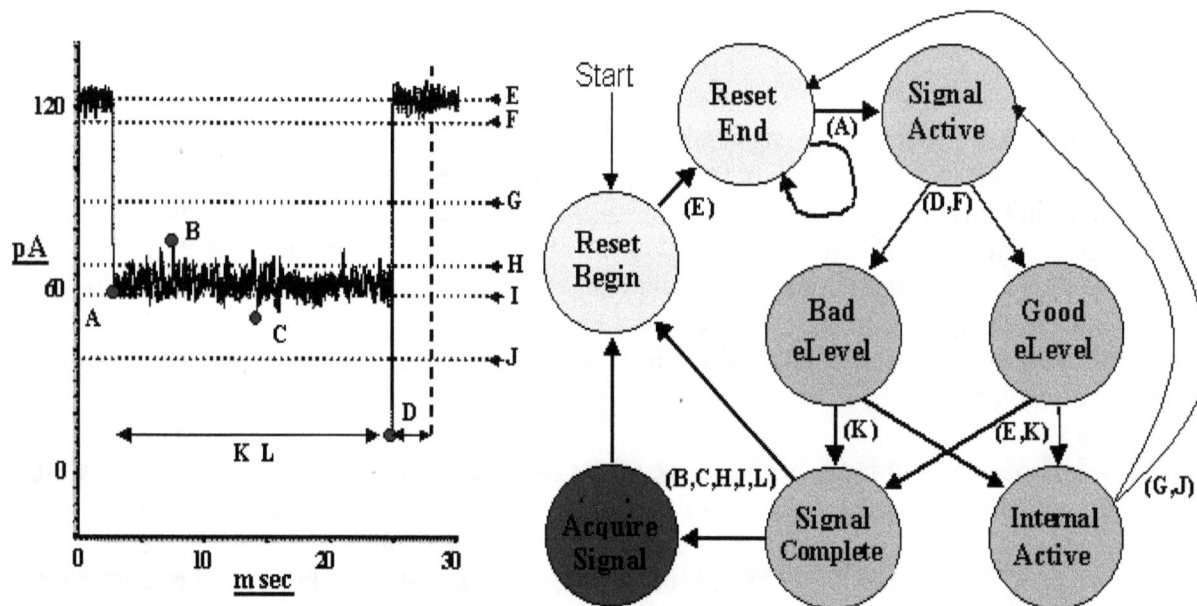

Fig. 4.1. Schematic for the finite state automaton used for acquisition of 6 base-pair DNA hairpin blockade signals observed in [198], where a sample signal is shown to the left. The letters label various types of feature extraction parameters and their placement in the FSA diagram indicate where the decision-making or thresholding is dependent on those parameters.

4.2 Genome analytics: the Gene-finder

Let's now return, briefly, to the gene-finder developments begun in Ch. 3. We now continue the 'bootstrap' evolution of the FSA-based prokaryotic gene-finder code is given in Ch. 3. Variations on the FSA-based ORF-finder code for prokaryotic genomes can be applied to both prokaryotic and eukaryotic transcriptomes, but these are described and used elsewhere [4] and, [5], and in Ch 9. In Sec. 4.4.2 tFSA methods are given for channel current cheminformatics (CCC) when there is stable channel baseline reference signal. In Sec. 4.4.3 are tFSA methods for CCC with unstable baseline. In Sec. 4.5 are efficient implementations of the FSA and core statistical tools.

The code that follows is an example of a bootstrap learning process, beginning with a sub-routine that finds ORFs longer than a specified cutoff, and moves in-frame from the left to the first 'atg' codon, for which a tentative coding region is identified, as well as the up-stream '*cis*' region and downstream '*trans*' regions. Extracts of the coding, *cis*, and *trans* regions are taken. The crude `longORFfirstATG_geneFinder` indicated will catch many true gene regions, but the 'first atg' heuristic for the start of the coding region will fail 1-10% of the time depending on the genome. This is where a filter is obtained by looking for anomalous high count motif structures in the cis region. Even if 10% of the genes so indicated are incorrect, the strongly recurring motifs tallied from the 90% correctly delineated genes will provide a clear indication of the *cis* regulatory motifs found in valid *cis* regions. This then provides a filter test for a second-pass (bootstrap) genefinder that has a validation test on the *cis* region. This boosts the genefinder accuracy to 99% for many prokaryotes genomes (if not sufficiently accurate for a genome of interest, similar refinements could be made for validation on *trans* motifs and on codon usage).

Let's proceed under the assumption that the gene starts with the first 'atg' in the ORF and try to find associated structures that will offer a means to validate the first 'atg' as the start, so begin effort by capturing the 'first atg genes' in the long-ORFs, along with their pre (*cis*) and post (*trans*) regions as in the Perl subroutine shown Fig. 4.2 below:

```
sub longORFfirstATG_geneFinder {
    my ($ref,$frame,$start,$length,$ciswindow) = @_;
    my @dna = @{$ref};
    if (!$frame) { $frame = 0; }
    if (!$start) { $start= "atg"; }
    if (!$length) { $length= 500; }
    if (!$ciswindow) { $ciswindow= 30; }
    my $seq_length = scalar(@dna);
    my %count;
    my $index;
    my $gene_file = "genefile";
    my $cisgene_file = "cisfile";
    my $transgene_file = "transfile";
    my $gene_output_fh = new FileHandle ">$gene_file";
    my $cisgene_output_fh = new FileHandle ">$cisgene_file";
    my $transgene_output_fh = new FileHandle ">$transgene_file";
    my $oldindex=0;
    for $index (0..$seq_length-1-2) {
        if ($index%3 != $frame) { next; }
        my $codon = "$dna[$index]$dna[$index+1]$dna[$index+2]";
        if ($codon eq 'taa' ||
            $codon eq 'tag' ||
            $codon eq 'tga') {
            my $gap = $index - $oldindex;
            if ($gap>$length) {
                my $i;
FOR2:                for $i ($oldindex+3..$index-3) {
```

```
            if ($i%3 != $frame) { next FOR2; }
            my $cdn = "$dna[$i]$dna[$i+1]$dna[$i+2]";
            if ($cdn eq $start) {
                my @gene = @dna[$i..$index+2];
                my $geneseq = join('',@gene);
                my @cisgene = @dna[$i-$ciswindow..$i-1];
                my $cisgeneseq = join('',@cisgene);
                my @transgene = @dna[$index+3..$index+$ciswindow];
                my $transgeneseq = join('',@transgene);
                $gene_output_fh->print("$geneseq\n");
                $cisgene_output_fh->print("$cisgeneseq\n");
                $transgene_output_fh->print("$transgeneseq\n");
                last FOR2;  # taking only first start
            }
        }
    }
    $oldindex=$index;
    }
  }
}
```

Fig. 4.2. The `longORFfirstATG_geneFinder` **perl method.**

By running longORFfirstATG_geneFinder we generate output files for the hypothesized gene region and the preceding (*cis*) region and the following (*trans*) region. We now want to look through the collection of *cis* regions to see if there are any anomalously occurring DNA substrings (motifs) that may associate with the hypothesized start of gene region, as shown in Fig. 4.3 next:

```
longORFfirstATG_geneFinder(\@dna,0,'atg',500,30);
sub line_oligo_counter {
    my ($filename,$order,$anom_mult) = @_;
    if (!$anom_mult) { $anom_mult = 5; }
    my $data_input_fh = new FileHandle "$filename";
    my $types = 4**$order; #types of $order 'mers'
    my $samples=0;
    my $lines=0;
    my $label;
    my %count;
    while (<$data_input_fh>) {
        chomp;
        s/\s//g;
        s/\d//g;
        if (s/^>//) {
            $label = $_;
        }
        else {
            tr/ACGT/acgt/;
            my @dna = split //, $_;
            my $seq_length = scalar(@dna);
            $lines++;
            $samples += $seq_length-$order+1;
            my $index;
            for $index (0..$seq_length-1-$order+1) {
                my $xmer;
                my $i;
                for $i (0..$order-1) {
                    $xmer .= $dna[$index+$i];
                }
                $count{$xmer}++;
            }
        }
    }

    my @seen_xmer_types = keys %count;
    my $expected_average_count = $samples/$types;
    my $anomalous_count_cutoff = $expected_average_count*$anom_mult;
    print "acc=$anomalous_count_cutoff\n";
    print "number of dna segments = $lines\n";
    print "anom_mult=$anom_mult\n";

    my $above_acc_count=0;
```

```
    my %motifs;
    my $xmer;
    foreach $xmer (@seen_xmer_types) {
        if ($count{$xmer}>$anomalous_count_cutoff) {
            $above_acc_count++;
            print "count{$xmer}=$count{$xmer}\n";
            $motifs{$xmer}=$count{$xmer};
        }
    }
    print "above_acc_count=$above_acc_count\n";
    return %motifs;
}
```

Fig. 4.3. The `line_oligo_counter` (motif finder) perl method.

In the above while loop, we are getting counts on the xmers (oligomers, or subsequences) of the specified order (length). In what follows we then estimate the number of occurences of a particular type of xmer when the data is random (uniform probability distribution) – this is referred to as the expected_average_count. A cutoff is then introduced for when the number of occurrences of a particular motif is anomalous by use of a multiplier, anom_mult. All motifs with counts above the indicated cutoff are deemed anomalous and thus potentially of interest as a signaling motif that is paired with the 'atg' start of coding.

There is found to be a lengthy list of anomalous 6mers occurring in the window 15 bases prior to the start codon – going forward, we can simply look for an occurrence of one of these 6mers to validate any hypothesized start codon. Failure to validate on the first 'atg' would then lead to looking for the next, in-frame, 'atg' as a possible start. It turns out that 'atg' is used for start only 90 to 99% of the time, the other main start codon being 'gtg'. The percentage of genes starting with 'atg' is genome (thus organism) specific. For some strains of *E. Coli*, about 99% of the genes start with 'atg', for the most common strain of *Vibrio Cholerae*, only about 93% of the genes start with 'atg', 6.9% starting with 'gtg'. 0.1% starting with 'ttg', and very rarely, some genes starting with 'ctg'. To handle this, if we don't have validation via an occurrence of the Shine-Dalgarno or other *cis* motifs in the window 15 based prior to the hypothesized start, then we want to continue to step codon-by-codon (in-frame) into the ORF (from left to right) until the next 'atg' or 'gtg' is encounted, where the validation is attempted again. This is then repeated until either validation achieved, or the remaining length of the ORF becomes drops below our cutoff. In the code thus far we have focused on ORFs>500 in length, to ensure the very likely collection of true gene regions. Now that we have a validation test, we can relax the length-anomaly filter to not be quite so stringent, to 300 initially, and repeat the datarun (see Fig. 4.4 next).

```
longORFfirstATG_geneFinder(\@dna,0,'atg',300,15);
my $file = "cisfile";
my %motifs=line_oligo_counter($file,6,3);
my $motifref = \%motifs;


sub geneFinder {
    my ($ref,$frame,$start,$length,$motifref,$ciswindow) = @_;
    my @dna = @{$ref};
    my %motifs = %{$motifref};
    if (!$frame) { $frame = 0; }
    if (!$start) { $start= "atg"; }
    if (!$length) { $length= 500; }
    if (!$ciswindow) { $ciswindow= 15; }
    my $seq_length = scalar(@dna);
    my %count;
    my $index;
    my $gene_file = "newgenefile";
    my $cisgene_file = "newcisfile";
    my $transgene_file = "newtransfile";
```

```perl
        my $gene_output_fh = new FileHandle ">$gene_file";
        my $cisgene_output_fh = new FileHandle ">$cisgene_file";
        my $transgene_output_fh = new FileHandle ">$transgene_file";
        my $oldindex=0;
        for $index (0..$seq_length-1-2) {
            if ($index%3 != $frame) { next; }
            my $codon = "$dna[$index]$dna[$index+1]$dna[$index+2]";
            if ($codon eq 'taa' ||
                $codon eq 'tag' ||
                $codon eq 'tga') {
                my $gap = $index - $oldindex;

                my $alt_start = 'atg';
                if ($gap>$length) {
                    my $i;
FOR2:               for $i ($oldindex+3..$index-3) {
                        if ($i%3 != $frame) { next FOR2; }
                        my $cdn = "$dna[$i]$dna[$i+1]$dna[$i+2]";
                        if ($cdn eq $start || $cdn eq $alt_start) {
                            my @motifs_list = keys %motifs;
                            my $motif;
                            my @cisgene = @dna[$i-$ciswindow..$i-1];
                            my $cisgeneseq = join('',@cisgene);
                            my @transgene = @dna[$index+3..$index+$ciswindow];
                            my $transgeneseq = join('',@transgene);
                            foreach $motif (@motifs_list) {
                                if ($cisgeneseq =~ m/$motif/) {
                                    my @gene = @dna[$i..$index+2];
                                    my $gene_length = scalar(@gene);
                                    if ($gene_length<90) {
                                        print "exiting ORF search at $i\n";
                                        last FOR2;
                                    } #length cutoff
                                    my $end = $index+2;
                                    print "gene: start=$i, end=$end\n";
                                    my $geneseq = join('',@gene);
                                    $gene_output_fh->print("$geneseq\n");
                                    $cisgene_output_fh->print("$cisgeneseq\n");
                                    $transgene_output_fh->print("$transgeneseq\n");
                                    last FOR2;  # ORF extraction complete
                                }
                            }
                            # if here then no motif match, so next 'atg' OR 'gtg'
                            $alt_start = 'gtg';
                            print "doing repeat start pass at index=$i\n";
                            next FOR2;  # taking next possible start
                        }
                    }
                }
                $oldindex=$index;
            }
        }
    }
    geneFinder(\@dna,0,'atg',240,$motifref);
```

Fig. 4.4. The geneFinder perl method.

At this point we have a complete genefinder, with cis motif discovery code and code for use of those motifs for start-of-gene validation. What is missing however are the repeated passes over the genomic data for the different frames (referred to as frame 0, 1, and 2 in what follows). As noted in the Ch. 3 discussions on this matter, there are actually three possible framings that can occur on the genomic data when you have a three-element encoding scheme. As indicated there, the other framings can be obtained by repeating the analysis just done with the first base removed (for the frame '1' case), or the first two bases removed (for the frame '2' case). Having obtained the gene predictions for the three possible framings there is a further subtlety that must be dealt with having to do with the fact that the genomic sequence information provided is for only 'half' of the genome. This is because the sequence information is actually obtained from double stranded DNA genomes, such that we need to repeat the entire analysis for the other strand. The other strand is fully specified by the first, however, since the second strand pairs with the first strand according to the Watson-Crick base-pairing scheme, where you have A pairing with T (and vice-versa) and C pairing with G. The read direction of the other strand is also in the opposite direction to the read direction of the first (an explanation of the biochemistry is in Ch 5 and [1]). This means that the gene count is actually approximately six times that indicated from the frame 0 'positive' strand analysis done thus far. If we use the motif results from just the frame 0 positive strand above, to keep thing simple we can repeat the analysis directly for the other strands with some simple alterations on the DNA data for the repeated passes with different framing.

4.3 Objective performance evaluation: Sensitivity and Specificity

Now that we have a gene-finder, a predictive algorithm as to whether a gene has streamed into view, we want to know how well it works. A similar need for performance measure for classifiers in general will be needed (in Ch. 11 especially), so will be covered with sufficient detail to cover the three conventions (shown in Fig. 4.5 & 4.6) and why the one chosen is optimal for prediction (or classification), when not wanting to use, or concerned about, counts on true negatives (TNs).

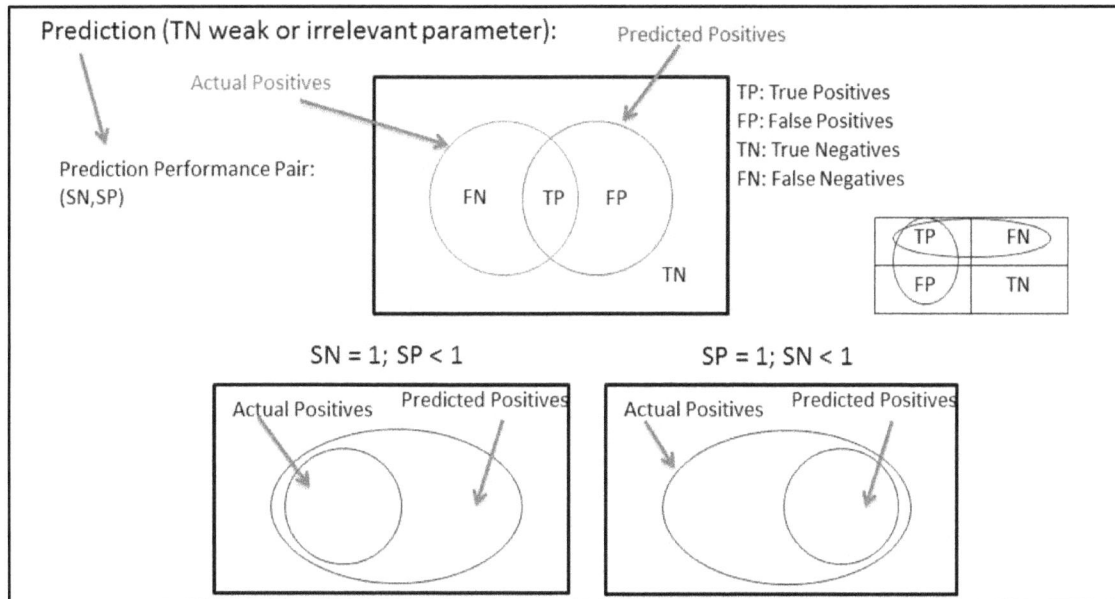

Fig. 4.5. Sensitivity (SN) and Specificity (SP). For the predictor evaluator convention(with Venn diagram set correspondence) we have SN = TP/(TP+FN) and SP = TP/(TP+FP). The Venn diagram correspondence is shown with the above {SN,SP} conventions. To report a score, both {SN,SP} values must be given (according to any of the three conventions), as indicated by the extreme cases whereby either SN=1 or SP =1 is possible, as indicated in the lower Venn diagrams, but where the other score parameter was very poor. Often, Score = (SN+SP)/2 is used.

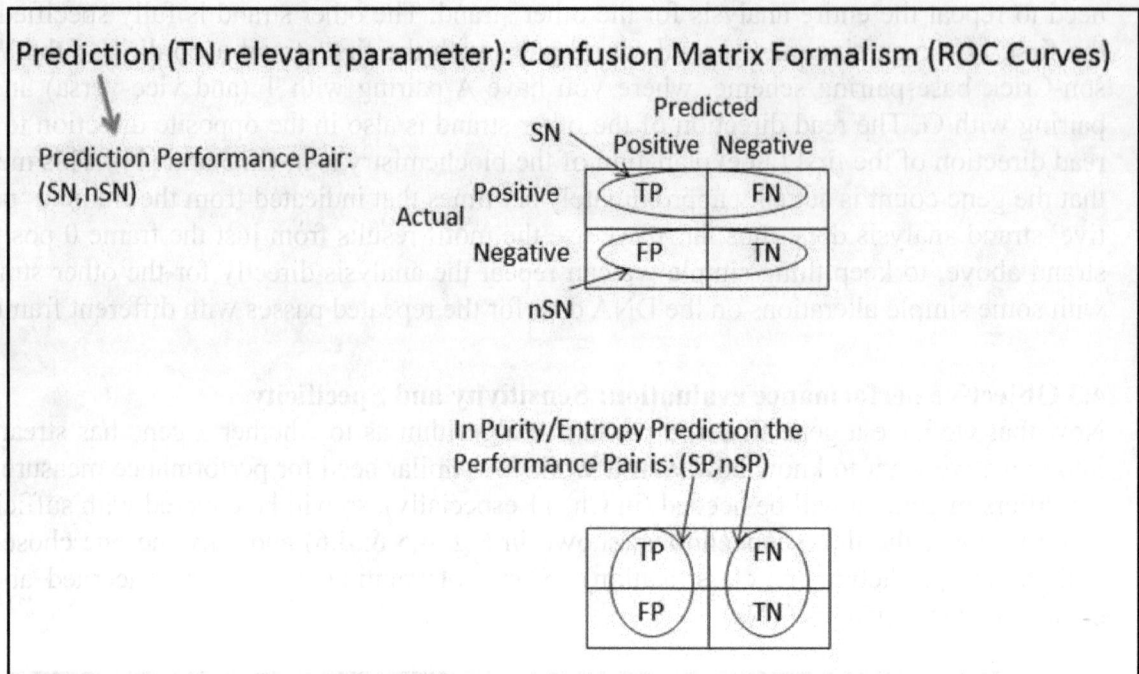

Fig. 4.5. Sensitivity (SN) and Specificity (SP) for other two conventions (used in EE with ROC curves, and purity/entropy in clustering analysis), we have nSN = TN/(TN+FP) and nSP = TN/(TN+FN). The alternative predictive performance pairs, {SN,nSN} and {SP,nSP} are shown diagrammatically in terms of the EE 'confusion matrix'.

4.4 Signal analytics: the time-domain Finite State Automaton (tFSA)

The FSA shown in Fig. 4.1 [1] was eventually tuned to operate such that it would rarely miss signal acquisitions (low false negatives) by allowing for large numbers of mistaken signal acquisitions (to be initiated), followed by filtering to achieve high specificity (see Fig. 4.6). The acquisition bias was accomplished by imposing constraints on valid starts that were weak while maintaining constraints on valid interior and ends that were strong. The bias towards high sensitivity for *initiating* acquisition permitted tuning on FSA parameters with a simplified objective (part of the benefit of a multi-pass bootstrap tuning process). For the blockade signatures studied, the FSA parameters for maximal signal acquisition shared a broad, common range, allowing one set of FSA parameters (a single generic FSA) to acquire all signals.

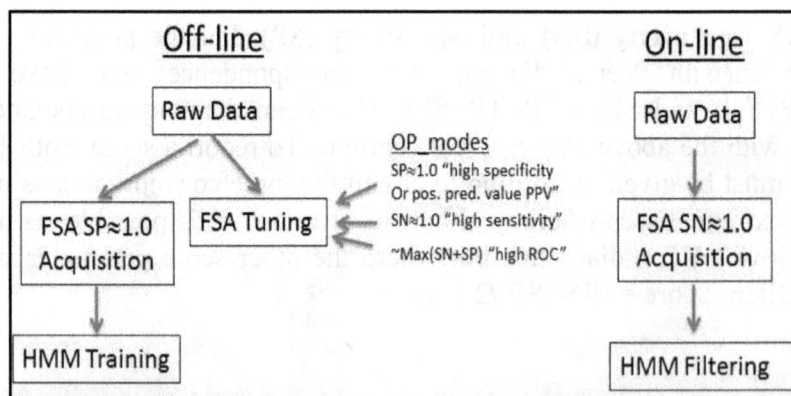

Fig. 4.6. FSA with alternating SP:SN optimized tuning. Step 1: Acquire signals with high specifity (SP=1, SN = whatever), obtain a 'gold standard'

66

reference set (if you have an expert, have them provide as much of this as they can manually). Step 2: Extract feature information from the gold standard set, to know what "it" looks like. (HMMs will often be used for this in what follows.) Step 3: Do acquisition with high sensitivity, followed by a specificity filter learned at Step 2. In other words, have (SN=1, SP= whatever) → (filter boosts to SP=1 with minimal drop in SN).

The FSA described in Fig. 4.1 enables acquisition of localizable channel current signals using 'holistic' tuning and 'emergent grammar' tuning. (Emergent grammar tuning, and use of wavelets, is described in [198] and won't be discussed further here.) When attempting to tune the FSA it can be viewed as a "holistic engine" of a multiply connected set of variables and states. For acquisition we seek minimal feature identification comprising identification of signal beginnings and ends (and thus durations as well). *Holistic tuning is mainly done by testing global features for anomalous changes, or 'phase transitions'.* One of the main global features of the acquisition process is the number of acquisitions itself, made under a particular set of tuning parameters. In Fig. 4.7 is shown the result of a holistic tuning process on the signal acquisition count for different start_drop_value parameter. A critical requirement for holistic tuning is having a viable initial tuning state to initialize the process, e.g., multiple parameters must be within their live 'lock range' on tuning parameters analogous to the phase-locked loop (PLL) lock-range constraint [1]. The code description with the core tuning parameters highlighted is in Sec. 4.4.2.

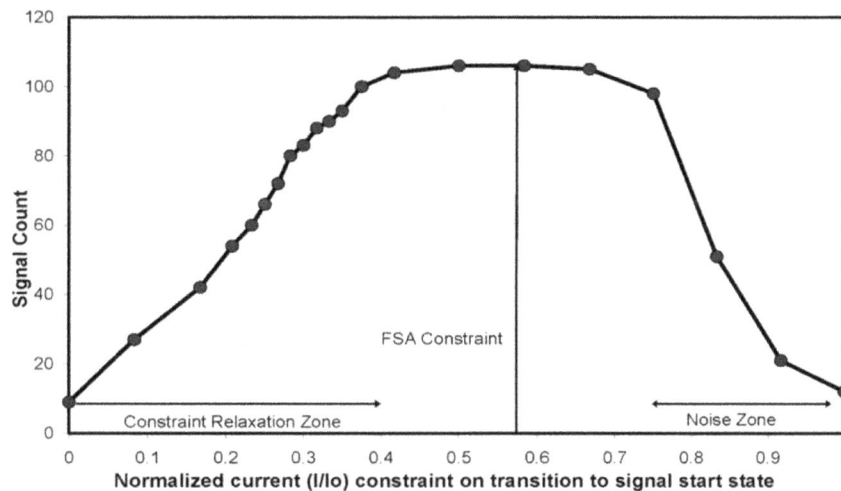

Fig. 4.7. Tuning on 'start_drop_value for a collection of blockade signals resulting from channel captures of DNA hairpins with 6 base-pair stem length. For baseline-normalized current constrained to drop to 0 channel current to trigger possible acquisition we see that very few acquisitions succeed (approximately 10 signal acquisitions shown). As we relax this start of acquisition constraint on possible signal acquisitions, we steadily see more signal counts until it plateaus starting at a baseline-normalized current of 0.4 to a baseline-normalized current of 0.7. The paradoxical seeming drop in signal acquisitions for the more hair-trigger acquisitions for baseline-normalized current drop, to only 0.8 or greater, is due to the FSA often triggering on noise, and eventually rejecting the indicated signal as invalid, but in doing so sometimes missing a valid signal start, resulting in fewer overall signal acquisitions. The holistic tuning process seeks the plateau region (that is not

directly responsive to change in cutoff over a broad range) as an indication of a robust acquisition setting, with the 0.57 value chosen in the example shown.

The O(L) time-complexity feature identification "scan" process can be employed for simultaneous feature extraction on various statistical moments, as mentioned previously. Identification of sharply localizable 'spike' behavior can also be done in the scan process (still with only O(L) time complexity) based on a nonparametric method that is described next.

4.4.1 tFSA spike detector

A channel current spike detector algorithm can be used to characterize the brief, very strong, blockade "spike" behavior observed for duplex DNA molecular termini that occasionally fray in the region exposed to the limiting aperture's strong electrophoretic force region. (See [54] for details, where nine base-pair hairpins were studied, the spike events were attributed to a fray/extension event on the terminal base-pair.) A complication with the spike feature extraction is the blockade level from which the spike event occurs is not known, or too variable to use to identify the spike blockade event. To have a robust feature extraction a test-level-crossing heuristic was used, where for a fixed blockade level the number of signal crossings at that level are counted (such as from spikes). The test level used in the crossing analysis is then shifted to higher levels, with increasing crossing counts as the level passes thru the signal region. What results is linear increase in crossing count for actual spike features as the test level used in the crossing analysis is increased, until the main signal region is reached. In the case of the channel current analysis the various levels of blockade seen for a particular molecular blockade typically have Gaussian noise about the average of each level. Thus, as the line-crossing sweeps thru the signal blockade level and probes the tail of the Gaussian noise distribution about that signal blockade level an exponential increase in level crossings is seen (see Fig. 4.8). Focusing on the linearly increasing count region, and extrapolating to the counts up to the average of the signal blockade level from which the spike deflections are seen, a count on spike events (or a frequency on spike events) can then be robustly ascertained.

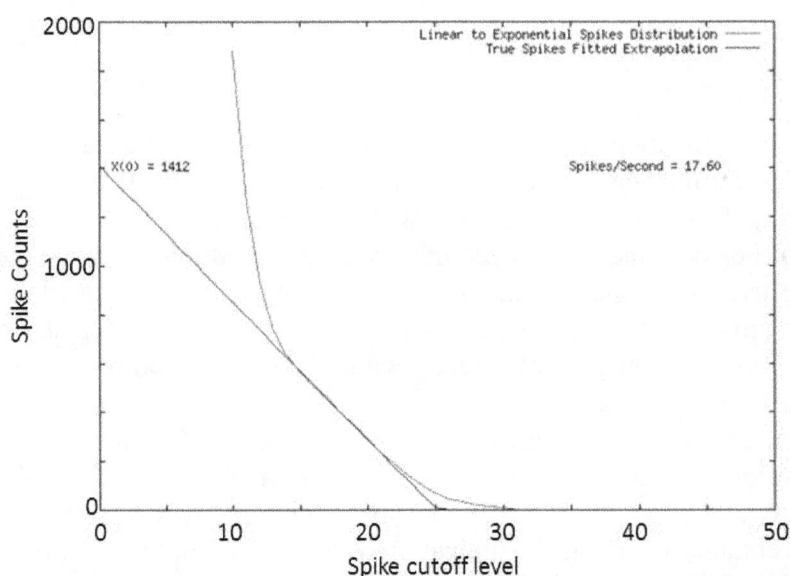

Fig. 4.8. Robust Spike feature extraction: radiated DNA. A time-domain FSA is used to extract fast time-domain features, such as "spike" blockade

events. Automatically generated "spike" profiles are created in this process. One such plot is shown here for a radiated 9 base-pair hairpin, with a fraying rate indicated by the spike events per second (from the lower level sub-blockade). Results: the radiated molecule has more "spikes" which are associated with more frequent "fraying" of the hairpin terminus--the radiated molecules were observed with 17.6 spike events per second resident in the lower sub-level blockade.

The spike detector software is designed to count "anomalous" spikes, i.e., spike noise not attributable to the Gaussian fluctuations about the mean of the dominant blockade-level. The extrapolations provide an estimate of "true" anomalous spike counts. Together, the formulation of HMM-EM, FSAs and Spike Detector provide a robust method for analysis of channel current data [1,54]. In Fig. 4.8 the plot is automatically generated for spike characteristics for blockade data for DNA hairpins examined: one with cross-linking radiation damage and one without damage. The plots are also automatically fit with extrapolations of their linear phases. By this method, the non-radiated DNA exhibited a full-blockade "spike" from its lower-level blockade with a frequency of 3.58 spikes per second (indicating a fraying of the blunt ended terminus of the molecule at that rate). For the radiated molecule the frequency of spikes was 17.6 spikes per second, indicating a much greater fraying rate (and associated dissociation of the terminal base-pair), consistent with that molecule being weakened by radiation such that its terminal base-pair frays more frequently.

The additional "spike" frequency feature is found to improve classification accuracy between two species of DNA hairpins by approximately 5% in the hairpin discrimination SVM tuning that is scored for various kernel parameters in Fig. 4.9. This is an example of how non band limited signal features can be extracted without the limitations of a HMM state quantization pre-processing (or Fourier transform method feature extraction from electrical engineering signal processing) to arrive at a more informed process than seems possible given the usual constraint of the Gabor limit, as mentioned previously.

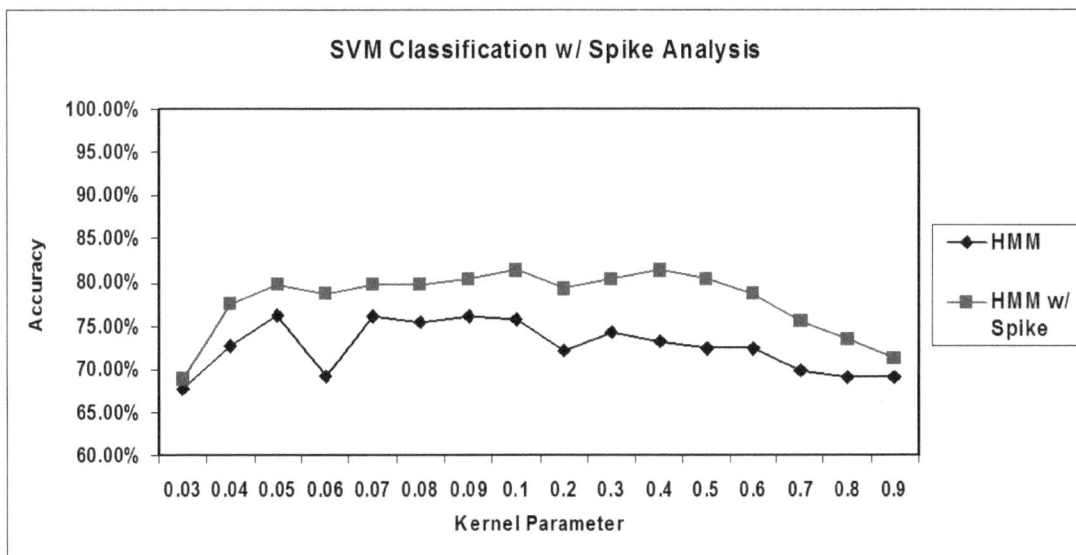

Figure 4.9. SVM classification results with and without spike analysis. Adding a spike feature significantly improves classification accuracy, by approximately 5%, over a wide range of kernel parameters.

Once the lifetimes of the various levels are obtained, information about a variety of other kinetic properties is accessible. If the experiment is repeated over a range of temperatures, a full set of kinetic data is obtained (including the aforementioned "spike" feature frequency analysis). This data may be used to calculate k_{on} and k_{off} rates for binding events, as well as indirectly calculate forces by means of the van't Hoff Arrhenius equation.

4.4.2 tFSA-based channel signal acquisition methods with stable baseline

The tFSA program (shown in C code version) begins with State="Reset Begin" (see Fig. 4.10 and comments in code below) with a loop to self a minimum of 10 times on the sample data being scanned, where the data in [1,54,198] was sampled at 20us, thus minimum time to advance from the "Reset Begin" state is 0.2 ms in the code shown (via baseline_to_reset=10). In order to only do a reset loop 10 times, the observed blockade value must exceed the open_channel_avg value on each sample of the 10 observations. Until 10 such observations exceeding the open_channel_avg value are tallied, whether consecutively or not, the loop will not advance from "Reset Begin" to "Reset End". The baseline_to_reset parameter is reset to 10 after each possible signal acquisition is resolved (with acquisition or rejection). The value of 10 is itself chosen by a 'holistic' tuning process.

```
while (index<length) {
    // data is read from (binary) datafile, or taken from streaming (buffered)
    // data from a live experiment, and placed in the variable 'rescale'
    /* Now at State="Reset Begin" */
    if (baseline_to_reset>0) {
        if (rescale>open_channel_avg) { baseline_to_reset--; }
        index++; continue;
    }
    /* Now at State="Reset End".*/
    if (start_active<1 && rescale<start_drop_value && rescale>start_drop_limit) {
        signal_start[j] = index;
        signal_max[j] = rescale;
        signal_min[j] = rescale;
        sigindex=0;
        sigdata[sigindex] = rescale;
        start_active = 1;
        get_base_lead = 0;
        index++; continue;
    }
    if (start_active<1) { index++; continue; }
    else {
        /* Now at State="Signal Active". */
        sigindex++;
        sigdata[sigindex] = rescale;
        bad_end_level=0;
        for (i=0;i<end_level_range;i++) {
            if (data[i]<end_level_value) { bad_end_level=1; i=end_level_range; }
        }
        signal_end[j] = index-1-end_level_range;
        signal_length = signal_end[j] - signal_start[j] + 1;
        if (signal_length>max_length) {
            signal_end[j] += 1+end_level_range;
            signal_length += 1+end_level_range;
        }
        if ((bad_end_level<1&&rescale>open_channel_avg)||(signal_length>max_length)){
            /* Exit condition is obtained. */
            if (signal_length>min_length && signal_min[j]<max_min_internal) {
                /* Now at State="Acquire Signal". */
                t = sigindex-end_level_range;
                do_simple_profile(sigfile,signal_start,signal_end,signal_max,signal_min,t,sigdata,j);
                printf("signal %d processing complete\n",j);
                sigindex=0; //resets signal info
                j++;
            }
            baseline_to_reset=10;
            start_active=0; //resets
            /* Now Reset to State="Reset Begin". */
            get_base_lead = 1;
            index++; continue;
        }
        /* Now at State="Bad eLevel". */
        else if (((index-signal_start[j]>end_level_range) &&
                (data[end_level_range-1]>max_internal)) || rescale<min_internal) {
            start_active=0; //resets
            // Now at State="Reset End". Note, not a full reset to
            // State="Reset Start" since baseline_to_reset not reset to 10.
            get_base_lead = 1;
            index++; continue;
        }
        // Now fall-through to State="Signal Active", for another blockade
        // sample iteration, after some min and max evaluations and sweep
        // boundary avoidance.
        else if (mod_index>0 && ((index%mod_index<mod_index_range) ||
                          (index%mod_index>mod_index-mod_index_range))) {
            start_active=0; //resets
            get_base_lead = 1;
            index++; continue;
        }
        else {
            if ((index-signal_start[j]>end_level_range) && (data[end_level_range-1]>signal_max[j])) {
                signal_max[j]=data[end_level_range-1];
            }
            if (rescale<signal_min[j]) { signal_min[j]=rescale; }
            index++; continue;
        }
    }
    index++;
}
```

Fig. 4.10. The main while loop for signal scanning for the FSA diagram shown in Fig. 4.1.

Once at the State "Reset End", the blockade sample values are checked (shown as self-loop in Fig. 4.1) to see if they've dropped significantly from the reset condition (e.g., dropped below baseline). This will be the first of a series of instances where weak conditions are used on initiating signal acquisitions, while much stricter conditions must be satisfied later (when better informed about the signal) in order to complete, and fully acquire, the signal. A blockade sample observation is deemed to have "dropped significantly" from its reset condition if it drops below a cutoff named the "start_drop_value" in Fig. 4.1, to arrive at the next state, "signal active", for initiating signal acquisition. Sometimes a blockade sample drops right through the floor, however, to large negative values, etc., due to noise or a shock, etc. These falsely triggered signals are excluded by excluding start drops that go below the "start_drop_limit" value. (Again, all parameters are tuned.) Once at the State "Signal Active", each subsequent blockade sample is read into an array, for possible signal acquisition and recording, and for use by O(1) data analysis algorithms (keeping the overall FSA operation O(L) on L observation samples). Such algorithms are used to calculate simple statistical properties of the blockade region (in an O(1) process), such as the maximum, minimum, duration, and (running) average of the blockade signal, and the (running) standard deviation of the blockade signal. The notion of a 'running' statistical evaluation is that the initialization of the statistical parameter may be O(N), for N length observation in the signal scan window, but that as the windowing on data used in the scan operation is slid along the data observation sequence, further updates on that sliding-window statistical parameter is only O(1). This sliding-window, or 'running', evaluation, then allows higher order statistical moments to be computed at O(L) on the full observation sequence under study (code implementations for this will be shown in detail for the first few statistical moments in what follows).

As a preliminary step for each new sample acquisition, to minimize bad-acquisition blocking on good signal that might immediately follow, exit conditions are tested for channel blockade completion (i.e., a return to the baseline, open channel, current readings). In Fig. 4.1, the exit condition is obtained either by a return to baseline (bad_end_level=0, or State="Good eLevel"), or due to acquisition truncation (case with State="Bad eLevel", due to truncation, even though good for acquisition). Once an exit condition is reached without rejection, a proper signal acquisition has occurred (with data already loaded into the acquisition array), and we now arrive at the State "Signal Complete". A collection of signal conditions are then tested on the total signal data for the final acceptance or rejection decision.

Recall from Fig 4.1 that we had onset of possible signal acquisition triggered by a significant drop in the blockade level average (evaluated O(windowsize) on data, so 'real-time' with minimal memory buffering needs). We could also trigger on change of blockade level standard deviation in that same window evaluation (still just O(windowsize) evaluation). A diagram showing the latter, and related methods, for acquisition of unstable signals, is given in Fig. 4.11.

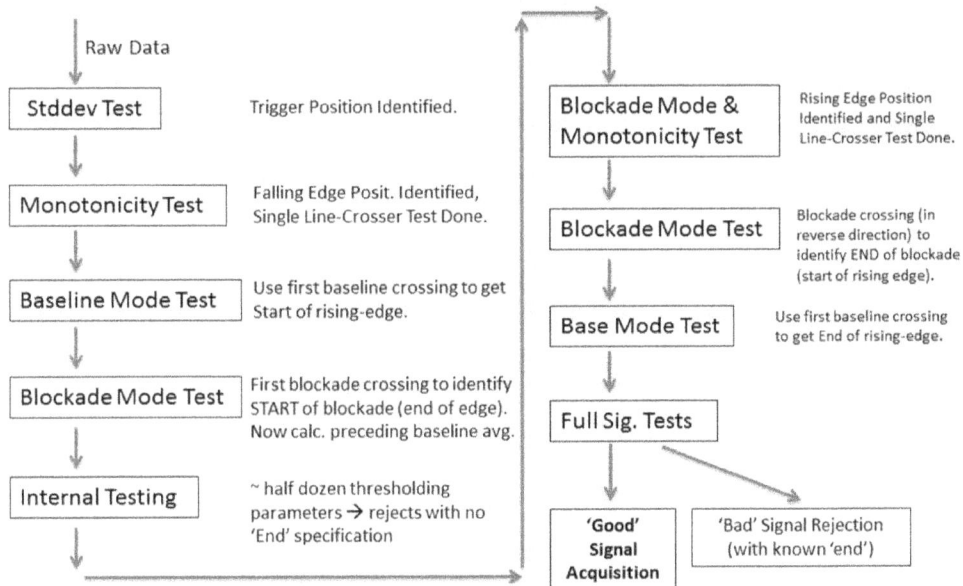

Fig. 4.11. FSA acquisition flowchart.

4.4.3 tFSA-based channel signal acquisition methods without stable baseline

In channel current blockade analysis, and electrical signal analysis in general, the tFSA signal acquisition is much more difficult if the reference baseline is not stable. For electrical signals one type of unstable baseline that typically results is from capacitive discharge/charge giving rise to an exponential rise (or fall) in the baseline current when event sampling is necessary before system relaxation can occur (to steady baseline). If the exponential rise/fall in the channel current signal was the same this could simply be factored out, but typically the charge/discharge reset is incomplete, and the capacitive properties themselves variable under load, giving rise to (effectively) different exponential rise/fall baseline references with every device reset. Even this extreme case can be handled with a properly designed tFSA (one making use of filters analogous to boxcar filters from electrical engineering, for example). A tFSA signal acquisition for stable baseline scenarios, but still with very challenging noisy data, is described first, followed by the enhancements needed for handling unstable baseline.

Using the start_drop_value parameter introduced already one seeks to identify onset of blockade events by their deviation, typically expressed by some multiple of standard deviations, from the baseline mean (see Fig. 4.11 above). A 'three-sigma' rule is often used, i.e., event acquisition onset is triggered when a channel current reduction by more than three standard deviations of baseline noise, from the baseline mean, is observed. The falling edge of the blockade onset can then be precisely fixed (down to a specific sample observation in many cases) by performing a monotonicity test on the falling edge, which can be done with an O(L) line-crosser analysis like that used in the spike analysis [1,54]. Fixing the start of blockade then depends on the data processing conventions adopted (often one chooses whatever convention yields the best classification/clustering at later SVM processing stages, if in use). Whatever the convention, the core, 'stable', information that guides the blockade level identification is a modal analysis on the different blockade levels seen. What is revealed by this is a mode identifying the baseline level (at least in the region just prior to the triggered signal acquisition) and the blockade level. If there is stable baseline, or even stable capaci-

73

tive discharge baseline (i.e., a single exponential profile occurring with each sampling reset), then the modal analysis will directly reveal that baseline, or identification of the asymptotic, 'relaxed', exponential baseline level. Once a suspected blockade signal onset has occurred, passing the standard deviation, monotonicity, and mode tests, signal acquisition commences on further streaming signal, with ongoing 'running' O(L) measurement of statistical moments and max, min sample values, with rejection if the 'internal' signal statistics does not fall within the desired range of possibilities. Identification of end-of-blockade, i.e., identification of the rising edge back to baseline current with no blockade, is then much the same as the falling edge identification, with use of standard deviation, monotonicity and modal tests. Typically identification of return to baseline requires additional measurement of a minimum number of baseline samples after return to baseline to avoid truncation on signal acquisitions that are sufficiently noisy that their internal blockade fluctuations occasionally 'spike' back to baseline level.

Sample code for a modal scan is given in Fig. 4.12 (Code Sample 1), where use is also made of integer-based variables for speedup on multiplications with integer variables instead of floating point variables. Working with integer-valued data is not as lossy as it might seem at first since the data encoding schemes used by third-party DAQs and amplifier developers, and by their efficient binary datafile encodings (if saved to file), are themselves integer-based with shift and float multiplication operations to bring the data back to the floating value and precision originally observed, with the resolution (number of significant figures) used in the recording or quantization process. Note: the hardest part of this process is often 'cracking' the binary file to learn the data encoding scheme and the shift and float-multiplication conversion values needed to recover the original data values direct from the binary data (using a 'known ciphertext' attack is often the quickest way to proceed).

Code Sample 1:

```
sub Scan_Data_Modes { # used to do binary data read and identify stat
modes
    my ($self,$input_file,$type,$mode) = @_;
    if (!$input_file) { $input_file = "data_file"; }
    $self->{input_file} = $input_file;
    # generate conversion lookup array for speedup over float mult
    my $maxrawint; # must be set, depends on file-formatting
    my $rawint;
    my @conversion_array;
    my $factor; # must be set, depends on file-formatting
    $self->{factor}=$factor;
    for $rawint (-$maxrawint..$maxrawint) {
        $conversion_array[$maxrawint+$rawint]=$rawint*$factor;
    }
    # begin binary read and mode count
    # details and some initializations deleted
    my $Data_fh = new FileHandle "$input_file";
    binmode($Data_fh);
    while (read($Data_fh,$buffer,4)) {
        $index++;
        my ($value,$vvalue) = unpack 'ss', $buffer;
        $data_index = $index-$header_skip;
        $data[$data_index]=$value;
        my $binned_sample_value = $data[$data_index];
        $mode_count($binned_sample_value)++;
    }
    close($Data_fh);
    # 'housekeeping' code that is omitted
}
```

Fig. 4.12. Code to scan channel current data and do a modal analysis.

If the channel current blockade signals have an unstable baseline, then the window-based FSA shown in Fig. 4.13, and elaborations on it, can be critical to locking onto the signal, but may not be optimal at calling the edges, thus multiple passes may be needed (bootstrap acquisition again), with early passes involving the window-based tFSA to get a preliminary lock so that the unstable base-line moving average can be subtracted, shifting to a simpler acquisition where a sample-based tFSA can then take over for the final signal acquisition with the most precise edge recognition possible.

```perl
while ($sample_index<$total_sample_count) {
    $sample_index++;
    my $sample_value = $data[$sample_index];
    if (!$reset_start) {
        if ($sample_value>$reset_value) { next; }
        else { $reset_start=1; next; }
    }
    elsif (!$reset_end) {
        if ($sample_value<$reset_value) { next; }
        else {
            $reset_end=1;
            $active{start}[$sweep_count]=$sample_index;
            print "active signal region starting at $sample_index... ";
            next;
        }
    }
    # do look-ahead for end of active signal region
    my $lookahead_sample_index = $sample_index+10;
    my $lookahead_sample_value = $data[$lookahead_sample_index];
    if ($lookahead_sample_index>$total_sample_count-1) {
        $lookahead_sample_value = $signal_end_cutoff+1;
    }
    if ($lookahead_sample_value>$signal_end_cutoff) {
        $active{end}[$sweep_count]=$sample_index;
        print "and ending at $sample_index\n";
        $reset_start=0;
        $reset_end=0;
        $sweep_count++;
        $lowpass_initialized=0;
        next;
    }
    # only here if ready to process active signal region
    ###
    # identify rising edge from baseline
    if ($lowpassdiff_value>$rising_diff_cutoff) {
        if ($sample_index-$prior_cutoff_index>20) {
            $prior_cutoff_index=$sample_index;
            my $dref = $self->{data_ref};
            my $std_dev = $Get_Std_Dev->($dref,$sample_index,-30,$window_size,$factor);
            if ($std_dev>$std_dev_cutoff) { $fail_count++; }
            else {
                my $edge_start=$sample_index;
                $signal{start}[$j]=$sample_index-5;
                $signal{start_baseline}[$j]=$lowpass_baseref;
                $start_flag=1;
                $running_signal_length=0;
                $running_signal_max=100;
                $running_signal_min=400;
                $running_signal_sum=0;
            }
        }
        else { $prior_cutoff_index=$sample_index; }
    }
    # identify falling edge to baseline
    if ($lowpassdiff_value<-$falling_diff_cutoff) {
        my $lowpass_baseref =
        $Get_Lowpass->($self->{data_ref},$sample_index,$pref,$window_size,$factor);
        if ($lowpass_baseref<($factor*$self->{highest_count_asympt_mode}+100) ) {
            my $dref = $self->{data_ref};
            my $std_dev2 = $Get_Std_Dev->($dref,$sample_index,50,$window_size,$factor);
        }
    }
    # perform running signal evaluation
    if ($start_flag==1) {
        $running_signal_length = $sample_index-$signal{start}[$j]-5;
        if ($running_signal_length>0) {
            my $rescaled_data = $sample_value*$factor-$signal{start_baseline}[$j];
            if ($rescaled_data<$running_signal_min) { $running_signal_min=$rescaled_data; }
            if ($rescaled_data>$running_signal_max) { $running_signal_max=$rescaled_data; }
            $running_signal_sum+=$rescaled_data;
            $running_signal_avg=$running_signal_sum/$running_signal_length;
        }
    }
}
```

Fig. 4.13. While loop for window-based tFSA signal acquisition.

4.5 Signal statistics (Fast): Mean, Variance, and Boxcar filter

Sometimes the more sophisticated window-based tFSA methods can be avoided entirely by use of a boxcar filter (a form of lowpass notch filter) as a preprocessing stage, which is shown in Fig. 4.14. In the worst case scenario, all of these methods need to be used, with the boxcar filter used in a post-processing validation method (as well as throwing the kitchen sink at the problem) in order to get the signal acquisition to work. The process that might be undertaken on a challenging signal acquisition, thus, might go as follows:

(1) scan for asymptotic baseline statistics
(2) do a preliminary window-based FSA scan to get a handle on the baseline
(3) estimate the baseline signal
(4) perform a sample-based tFSA scan on the baseline-subtracted signal
(5) perform repeated tFSA scans (since fast) with different biases to lock onto all signal regions
(6) perform boxcar filter on raw signal in indicated signal regions with identified baseline attributes used to determine the optimal boxcar filter.
(7) perform merge on signal acquisitions indicated at steps (5) and (6)

```
sub Boxcar_Filter {
    my ($self,$notch_window,$buffer_window) = @_;
    my @data = @{$self->{data_ref}};
    my $total_sample_count=$self->{total_sample_count};
    if (!$notch_window) { $notch_window=1000; }
    if (!$buffer_window) { $buffer_window=100; }
    # running calc to obtain window array for notch_filter_data calc
    # not valid if sample_index<notch_window_size+1
    # this is a running stat calc
    my @notch_filter_data;
    my @lowpass_filter_data;
    my @notch_window_array;
    my $sample_index;
    my $notch_window_sum;
    my $notch_window_avg;
    for $sample_index (0..$total_sample_count-1) {
        my $sample_value = $data[$sample_index];
        if ($sample_index < $notch_window) {
            my $pop = $notch_window_array[0];
            my $i;
            for $i (0..$notch_window-2) {
                $notch_window_array[$i] = $notch_window_array[$i+1];
            }
            $notch_window_array[$notch_window-1] = $sample_value;
            $notch_window_sum += ($sample_value-$pop);
            $notch_window_avg = $notch_window_sum/($sample_index+1);
            $lowpass_filter_data[$sample_index]=$notch_window_avg;
        }
        else {
            my $pop = $data[$sample_index-$notch_window];
            my $push = $data[$sample_index];
            $lowpass_filter_data[$sample_index]=
            $lowpass_filter_data[$sample_index-1]+($push-$pop)/$notch_window;
        }
    }
    for $sample_index (0..$total_sample_count-1) {
        my $sample_value = $data[$sample_index];
        if ($sample_index < $notch_window+$buffer_window) {
            $notch_filter_data[$sample_index]=$data[$sample_index]-
            $lowpass_filter_data[$sample_index+2*$notch_window+$buffer_window];
        }
        else {
            $notch_filter_data[$sample_index]=$data[$sample_index]-
            0.5*($lowpass_filter_data[$sample_index-$notch_window-$buffer_window]
            +$lowpass_filter_data[$sample_index+2*$notch_window+$buffer_window]);
        }
    }
    $self->{notch_filter_data}=\@notch_filter_data;
}
```

Fig. 4.14. Subroutine example for Boxcar filter.

Efficient implementations for statistical tools (O(L))

Working with the native integer encoded binary representation of the data is faster on multiple levels. This would not be of much benefit, however, if the subroutines for the statistical moments (mean, standard deviation, etc.) could not operate at the integer variable level for most of their evaluation. An implementation of statistical methods for evaluating the mean and standard deviation at integer-variable level is shown in Fig. 4.15. A *window-based* tFSA implementation using these methods (instead of single-sample based tFSA implementation like that shown in Fig. 4.10) is then shown in Fig. 4.13 (the main acquisition while loop is shown). The window-based implementation is more robust with variable, unstable, baseline, but is less precise at identifying falling edges and other sharp transitions. Since the window based method often involves sums over the window, it is sometimes called an integration (or calculus-based) tFSA.

```perl
my $Get_Lowpass = sub {
    my ($ref,$sample_index,$offset,$window_size,$factor) = @_;
    my @data;
    if ($ref) {
        @data = @{$ref}[$sample_index+$offset-$window_size+1..$sample_index+$offset];
    }
    else {
        print "error in passing raw data array\n";
    }
    my $i;
    my $window_sum=0;
    for $i (0..$window_size-1) {
        $window_sum += $data[$i];
    }
    my $mean = $factor*$window_sum/$window_size;
    return $mean;
};
my $Get_Std_Dev = sub {
    my ($ref,$sample_index,$offset,$window_size,$factor) = @_;
    my @data;
    if ($ref) {
        @data = @{$ref}[$sample_index+$offset-$window_size+1..$sample_index+$offset];
    }
    my $mean = $Get_Lowpass->($ref,$sample_index,$offset,$window_size,$factor);
    my $i;
    my $sum_squared_central_moment=0;
    my $factorlessmean = int($mean/$factor+0.5);
    for $i (0..$window_size-1) {
        my $diff = $data[$i]-$factorlessmean;
        $sum_squared_central_moment += $diff*$diff;
    }
    my $variance=$sum_squared_central_moment/$window_size;
    my $std_dev = $factor*sqrt($variance);
    return $std_dev;
};
```

Fig. 4.15. Code examples for non-lossy statistical moment evaluations that are integer-based.

4.6 Signal spectrum: Nyquist Criterion, Gabor Limit, Power Spectrum

In discussions of noise properties spectral analysis plays a large role. The fundamental tool in spectral analysis is the Fourier transform (FT), which gives the frequency decomposition of the transformed signal [199]. For noise fluctuations in an electrical signal, attention is usually focused on the FT of the signal squared. This is because the square of a voltage or current signal is proportional to the power. Depending on the incorporation of that proportionality constant (i.e., impedance value) the spectral densities obtained are known as voltage, current, or power spectral density [146]. Due to properties of FTs, convolution, such as in the definition of the autocorrelation function, transforms to multiplication. This provides a FT relationship between a signal's power spectral density and its autocorrelation function (the Weiner-Khinchine theorem).

Nyquist Sampling Theorem
Let x(t) be a band limited signal with $X(\omega) = 0$ for $|\omega| > \omega_M$. Then x(t) is uniquely determined by its samples $x(nT)$, $n=0, \pm1, \pm2, \ldots$ if $\omega_S > 2\omega_M$, where $\omega_S = 2\pi/T$. The frequency $2\omega_M$

is known as the Nyquist rate and must be exceeded by the sampling frequency to satisfy the sampling theorem [199].

Fourier Transforms, and other classic Transforms

The response of a linear (i.e., superposition property) time-invariant system (time-shift in input leads to same output but with that time-shift) to a complex exponential input (a phasor) is the same phasor with a change in amplitude: $e^{i\omega t} \rightarrow H(\omega)e^{i\omega t}$. This motivates phasor recon-struction of a periodic signal x(t), with fundamental period $T=2\pi/\omega$, using $x(t) = \Sigma_k a_k e^{ik\omega t}$, where k summation is over both positive and negative integers. Evaluation of the Fourier series components a_k is via: $a_k = 1/T \int x(t)e^{-ik\omega t}dt$ [199]. (Similar form for continuous time transform.) Other classic transforms include the Laplace, Mellin, Hankel, and Z-transform. There are also a variety of (non-lossy) data-compression methods that can be used as trans-forms insofar as feature extraction purposes.

Power Spectral Density

The power spectral density, S(f), of a signal, x(t), is a real, even, nonnegative function of frequency. Integration over S(f) gives total average power per ohm: $P=\int S(f)df=<x^2(t)>$ (fre-quency integration $-\infty$ to ∞ unless specified otherwise). The autocorrelation function, $R(\tau) = <x(t)x(t+\tau)>$, of a power signal, x(t), is defined as the time average $<x(t)x(t+\tau)> = \lim_{T\rightarrow\infty} (1/2T) \int x(t)x(t+\tau)dt$. For an ergodic process, S(f) and $R(\tau)$ are a Fourier Transform pair (Weiner-Khinchine theorem): $R(\tau) = \int S(f) e^{i2\pi ft} df$ and $S(f) = \int R(\tau) e^{-i2\pi ft} df$ [147].

Power-spectrum based feature extraction

Typical power spectra for captured nine-base-pair DNA hairpins are shown in Ch. 14, along with a spectrum for the open channel. Below 10 kHz, the current fluctuation caused by the captured DNA molecule (i.e. the blockade noise) is greater than all other noise sources. Such blockade noise typically arises from changes in transient bonds with the protein channel, DNA conformational changes in molecular structure or overall orientation vis-a-via the channel, changes in DNA conplexation/solvation (involving waters of hydration and salt ions), and changes in internal chemical bonds (terminus fraying, for example). The power spectra for all the signals examined in [45] had approximately Lorentzian profiles, indicative of a predominately two-state switching process (seen as random telegraph noise). Discrimi-nating between the DNA hairpins on the basis of their power spectral (or other Fourier transform properties, or wavelet properties) is possible for small sets of hairpins. For larger sets of hairpins, or for very similar hairpins like here, the HMM-based feature extraction proved critical, due to their strengths at extracting features from aperiodic (stochastic) se-quential data. HMMs can be used for classification as well as feature extraction. In Ch. 14 HMMs are mainly used for feature extraction in conjunction with a Support Vector Machine (SVM). The resulting signal processing and pattern recognition architecture enabled real-time single molecule classification on blockade samplings of only 100 milliseconds [45].

Cross-Power Spectral Density

For ergodic processes, time and ensemble averages are interchangeable, in particular, $R(\tau) = <x(t)x(t+\tau)> = E\{x(t)x(t+\tau)\}$. If the ergodic processes for two power signals are present the net power signal (noise voltage, for example) is z(t) = x(t) + y(t) and $P_z = E\{z^2(t)\} = P_x+P_y+2P_{xy}$, where $P_{xy} = E\{x(t)y(t)\}$. The latter quantity is the $\tau=0$ case of the cross-correlation function: $R_{xy}(\tau) = E\{x(t)y(t+\tau)\}$. Similarly, cross-power spectral density, $S_{xy}(f)$, is the Fourier transform of $R_{xy}(\tau)$ [147].

AM/FM/PM Communications Protocol

Amplitude modulation involves addition of a DC bias to a message signal and using this as an amplitude modulation factor on some carrier frequency [147]: $x(t) = [A+m(t)] \cos(\omega t)$, this is often rewritten as:

$x(t) = A[1 + am_N(t)] \cos(\omega t)$, where $m_N(t) = m(t)/|\min m(t),|$ and $a = |\min m(t)|/A$.

The parameter 'a' is the modulation index and envelope detection can only be used if $a < 1$. The total power in the AM modulated signal is proportional to: $< x^2(t) > = <[A+m(t)]^2 \cos^2(\omega t)>$. If $m(t)$ is more slowly varying than $\cos(\omega t)$, then the latter time integration can be performed to yield a factor of ½: $< x^2(t) > = [A^2+2A<m(t)> + <m^2(t)>]/2$, which typically reduces with $<m(t)>=0$ to: $< x^2(t) > = [A^2+<m^2(t)>]/2$. Note: the AM signal power with maximum information content is for square-wave signal max $m(t) =1$ and min $m(t) = -1$, efficiency is 50%. For sinusoidal, efficiency is 33%.

AM does not require a coherent reference for demodulation, this leads to AM radios that are simple and inexpensive. Similarly, this is one point for a branching in the communications theory to other instances where there is not necessarily a coherent reference, such as with the stochastic carrier wave methods.

4.7 Exercises

(Ex. 4.1) Objective is to identify gene regions via the long open reading frame (long ORF) anomaly. It is found that there is an anomalous spike in ATG codon frequency just inside the left ORF boundary – we use the first (in-frame) ATG seen from the left as our purported gene 'start'. The gene 'end' is the stop codon at the right boundary of the ORF. The first-ATG heuristic, thereby defined, turns out to be true 90% or more of the time! (for prokaryotes). We now want to boost the performance by looking for motifs to the left ("upstream") of the purported 'start', at the first ATG of the ORF (from the left). The idea from biology is that there are regulatory molecules that would bind upstream, thereby having a binding-site 'footprint' in the statistics that we could possibly pick up. So we look for anomalous hexamer motifs upstream from the ATG for the region extending 30 bases upstream (to the left). We then use the presence of these anomalous motifs to validate a purported start...... So consider what happens if initially we're 90% accurate, that means that we are 10% wrong, thus 10% of the count data on hexamers (there are 4,096) would be mostly random nonsense. By the nature of the counting on indivuda hexamer frequencies, however, the anomolous counts coming from the other 90% of the data clearly wins out for still identifying anything anomalous. In fact, the 'noise' could be the significantly greater and this method still work. As is, those anomolous motifs (counts significantly higher than would occur if random) can be used to validate. So, here's the assignment:

Run `longORFfirstATG_geneFinder` , to identify 'cis' region 30 bases upstream of ATG start

Run `line_oligo_counter` , to identify anomalous hexamer motifs in cis regions

List the top 20 anomolous motifs. Does 'aaggaa' show among them?

(Ex. 4.2) Building on (Ex. 4.1), now that you've identified motifs to use to validate a start, then proceed with modification to boost to genefinder performance that is approximately 99% correct. The modified heuristic: start = first ATG unless doesn't have motif validation, if validation fails, take try next ATG or GTG (moving in-frame), repeat until validation. This is what is done in genefinder, so here's the next assignment:

Run `geneFinder` (Fig. 4.4), to get gene predictions (for frame 0). Repeat for other two forward frames and three reverse frames to get full gene prediction. How do the counts of genes observed (above length cut-off of 300 bases) compare on the different frame passes?

(Ex. 4.3-4.6)
The non-HMM bootstrap approach is now carried over to analysis of eukaryotic genomes (C. elegans), where we will be able to 'discover' introns (and their rules), but not much more will be easy (this will motivate moving to an HMM representation in Ch. 7 to fully solve this):

Here is the prokaryotic gene-structure we have 'discovered' thus far, where the coding region maps to a complete protein product and usually starts with the codon (ATG):

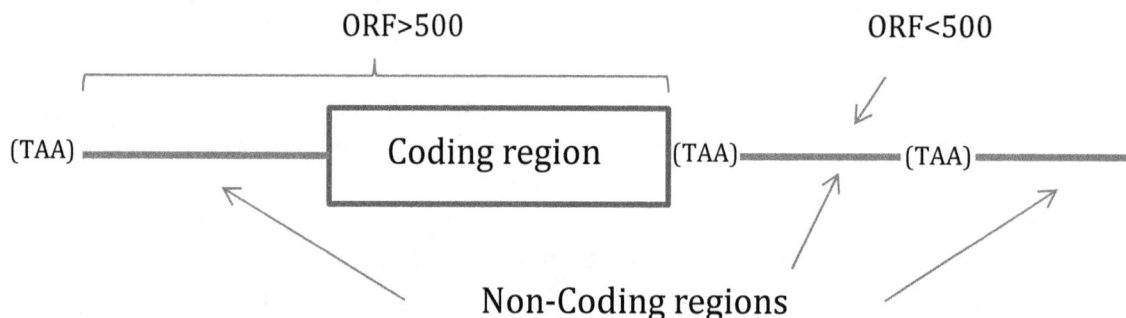

Notice how we distinguish between two types of 'stop codon' delimiters in the ORF-finder approach: (i) those that delimit regions of coding (upstream) from non-coding (Center 'TAA' and downstream); and (ii) those that delimit regions of non-coding from other non-coding:

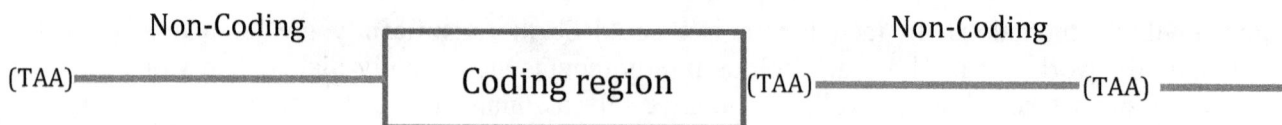

In what follows we will want to leverage this ability to identify 'true' stop codons in a eukaryotic setting, and will thereby attempt to rediscover eukaryotic gene structure by starting from recognized stop-codon structures.

(Ex. 4.3) Scan the eukaryotic genome of C. elegans to identify the 'true' stop codons on ORF's>500. This requires a means to differentiate non-codong from coding (to know a 'true' stop' has coding on left and non-coding on right.

(Ex. 4.4) Suppose the splice signal just upstream of the true stop codon was unknown and we wanted to discover it. A reasonable guess would be that it would border the coding region at its upstream end and further upstream from there would be the ORF's leftmost (TAA) boundary. Note that such a picture (shown below) would indicate the mystery 5' splice signal motif (shown as 'AG') would necessarily be separated by a *non-coding* region from its upstream stop.

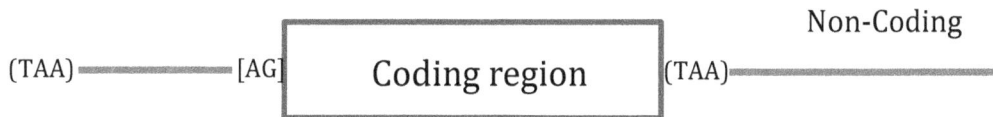

Given 3 stops and 64 codons, and random sequence in the non-coding (non true, but certainly random when compared to coding), we'd expect to 'see' a stop every 21 codons or so. Thus, if we take a window of 60 bases downstream from the stop codon that is itself just upstream from a 'true' stop, then we'd probably capture much of the anomalous statistics from the signal we are seeking in the window (shown overlaid on picture below):

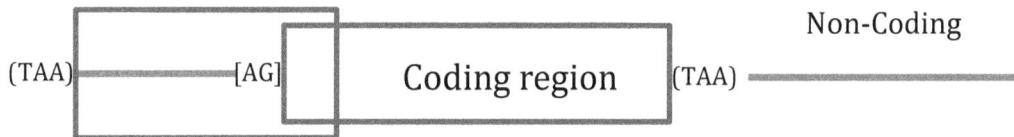

Collect all of the 60-base windows, relative to the 'true' stops as indicated. Then obtain a histogram of the 2-base elements ('AG' should be a significant peak) and 3-base elements ('ATG' will be a significant peak if there are a lot of 'singleton' genes that have only one exon).

(Ex. 4.5) Suppose 'AG' is the most common 2-base element in your 60-base window. There might be too many 'AG's in a 60-base window, however, in which case the question becomes which one is associated with a splice site ….in other words, you will need to validate that you have a splice-signal AG by performing a test to confirm that the region downstream is coding and upstream is non-coding.

(Ex. 4.6) Once the 'AG' consensus is identified for the intron boundary, we can examine the bulk intron statistics (and find that it is similar to junk away from the splice-boundaries). Also, upstream from the 'AG' signaling area we expect to see a series of stop codons (every 21 codons or so). Eventually, with possibly a different absolute framing, we encounter a ORF>500 bases (we crossed the intron moving upstream and now have encountered the >500 ORF because it is enclosing a coding region). We now face the reverse of the argument that motivated our AG search – now the >500 ORF is bordered on its rightmost side by a stop codon that is, on average, 21 codons from whatever coding boundary resides further upstream. So, again, we try a 60 base window (you may need to adjust, a window of 30, or a window of 120, etc) on the region upstream from the >500 ORF's rightmost boundary. **Again, need histograms on 2-base and 3-base elements, and here we aim to rediscover the 'GT' consensus signaling.**

In doing Ex.s 4.3-4.6 you get to re-discover the core gene-structure elements at the eukaryotic level. If you then wanted to cobble it all together to make a gene-finder you would have an optimization task on how to bring the various components together for best performance. If this optimization was pushed to the highest level of refinement (base-level coding/noncoding identification) you would effectively arrive at an HMM, to be described in Ch. 7.

(Ex. 4.7-4.10)

The exercizes that follow involve generating signal data ("Throw" section) using the tfsa_generate.pl Perl script below (Ex. 4.7), acquiring signal data (Ex. 4.8, using "Catch" script -- a toy version of the tFSA shown in Fig. 4.1 called tfsa_acquire.pl below), tuning for improved acquisition (Ex. 4.9). Also, a brief analysis of stock market data (CSCO) is done using the FSA to capture events and outcome information (good or bad, used to label as positive or negative), which can then be used to train a classifier (whose classification in the moment can be used to determine buy orders).

(Ex. 4.7) Throw: Run tfsa_generate.pl and generate the datafile (in 'gendata2') and annot via redirection of printed output (so run as "./tfsa4.pl > annot" to get annotation file).

(Ex. 4.8) Catch: Run tfsa_catch.pl to catch the signals in the gendata2 file and place predicted signal regions in 'predict' file (start with argument start_drop_percentage = 0.8). Run scoring.pl to score predict against annot. Indicate the accuracy score (SN+SP)/2 for the given start_drop_percentage chosen. Indicate the signal counts for the given start_drop_percentage chosen.

(Ex. 4.9) Repeat (Ex. 4.8) to get plots of accuracy and sig counts for different choice of start_drop_percentage – produce these tuning plots using whatever plotting method you want.

(Ex. 4.10) Repeat 4.7-4.9 (e.g. generate data again) for the more challenging case of overlapping noise bands – perhaps modify tfsa_generate.pl to where you hard code changes to the gaussians to have the same mean but wider noise bands (greater sigmas), so the new {mean,sigma} is {70,15} for the baseline level and {40,15} for the blockade level. (If this doesn't work well, try less noise, 10 instead of 15).

Throw:
tfsa generate.pl

```
use strict;
use FileHandle;
my $data_range=100;
my $output_fh2 = new FileHandle ">gendata2";
my $pi = 3.1415;

my $event_number = 100;
my $event_index=0;
for $event_index (0..$event_number) {

# no indent>>>>>>>>>>>>
```

```perl
my $mean = 70;
my $sigma = 3;
my $data_length = 500*rand();
for $index (0..$data_length-1) {
    # use Box-Muller transform
    my $gen_value1 = rand()+0.00000001;
    my $gen_value2 = rand()+0.00000001;
    my $Z1 = sqrt(-2*log($gen_value1)) * sin(2*$pi*$gen_value2);
    my $Z2 = sqrt(-2*log($gen_value1)) * cos(2*$pi*$gen_value2);
    my $X1 = $mean + $Z1 * $sigma;
    my $X2 = $mean + $Z2 * $sigma;

    my $int_gen_val = int($X1);
    print "$int_gen_val\n";
    $output_fh2->print("$int_gen_val\n");

    my $int_gen_val = int($X2);
    print "$int_gen_val\n";
    $output_fh2->print("$int_gen_val\n");
}

my $mean = 40;
my $sigma = 6;
my $data_length = 200*rand();
for $index (0..$data_length-1) {
    # use Box-Muller transform
    my $gen_value1 = rand()+0.00000001;
    my $gen_value2 = rand()+0.00000001;
    my $Z1 = sqrt(-2*log($gen_value1)) * sin(2*$pi*$gen_value2);
    my $Z2 = sqrt(-2*log($gen_value1)) * cos(2*$pi*$gen_value2);
    my $X1 = $mean + $Z1 * $sigma;
    my $X2 = $mean + $Z2 * $sigma;

    my $int_gen_val = int($X1);
    print "$int_gen_val\n";
    $output_fh2->print("$int_gen_val\n");

    my $int_gen_val = int($X2);
    print "$int_gen_val\n";
    $output_fh2->print("$int_gen_val\n");
}
# end no indent <<<<<<<<<<<<<<<<<<

}
```

Catch:
tfsa_acquire.pl

```perl
#!/usr/bin/perl

use strict;
use FileHandle;
my $input_fh = new FileHandle "gendata2";
my $output_fh = new FileHandle ">predict";

my $start_drop_percentage=$ARGV[0];


my @data;
my $data_index=-1;
while (<$input_fh>) {
    $data_index++;
    chop;
    $data[$data_index]=$_;
}

my $data_length = scalar(@data);
```

```perl
my $sig_count;
my $sig_avg;
my $start_drop_seen=0;
my $baseline;
my $index;
my $last_index=0;
for $index (0..$data_length-1) {
    my $value = $data[$index];
    my $past_avg=0;
    if ($index>4) {
        $past_avg += $data[$index-5];
        $past_avg += $data[$index-4];
        $past_avg += $data[$index-3];
        $past_avg += $data[$index-2];
        $past_avg += $data[$index-1];
    }
    $past_avg=$past_avg/5;
    if ($value<$start_drop_percentage*$past_avg && !$start_drop_seen) {
        if ($index>$last_index+20) {
            print "possible start region at index=$index\n";

            my $start = $index+1;
            $output_fh->print("$start\t");


            $start_drop_seen=1;
            $baseline = $past_avg;
        }
        $last_index=$index;
    }

    if ($start_drop_seen) {
        $sig_avg+=$value;
    }

    my $fut_avg=0;
    if ($index<$data_index-6) {
        $fut_avg += $data[$index+5];
        $fut_avg += $data[$index+4];
        $fut_avg += $data[$index+3];
        $fut_avg += $data[$index+2];
        $fut_avg += $data[$index+1];
    }
    $fut_avg=$fut_avg/5;

    my $end_drop_percentage=$start_drop_percentage;
    if ($value>$end_drop_percentage*$baseline && $start_drop_seen
        && $fut_avg<1.1*$baseline && $fut_avg>0.9*$baseline) {
        print "possible end region at index=$index\n";
        my $end = $index;
        $output_fh->print("$end\t");

        my $signal_duration = $index-$last_index;

print "baseline=$baseline\n";
print "index=$index\n";
print "last_index=$last_index\n";

        print "signal_duration = $signal_duration\n";
        if ($signal_duration> 10 ) {
            $sig_avg = $sig_avg/$signal_duration;
            if ($sig_avg>30 && $sig_avg<50 && $baseline>65) {
                $sig_count++;
                $output_fh->print("good\n");
            }
        }
```

```perl
        else {
            $output_fh->print("bad\n");
        }

print "sig_avg=$sig_avg\n";
        $sig_avg=0;
        $start_drop_seen=0;
    }
}
print "signal count = $sig_count\n";
```

Stock Scanner:

```perl
#!/usr/bin/perl

use strict;
use FileHandle;

my $input_fh = new FileHandle "CSCO.txt";
my $output_fh = new FileHandle ">CSCO_events";


my @closes;
my @opens;
my $index=-2;

while (<$input_fh>) {
    my ($date,$open,$high,$low,$close,$adjclose,$volume) = split;
    $index++;
    if ($index<0) { next; }
    $closes[$index]=$close;
    $opens[$index]=$open;
}

my $length = scalar(@closes);
my $i = 0;

my $window=7;
my @past_opens;
my $start_drop_percentage = 0.90;
my $past_open_sum=0;
for ($i=0; $i<$length; $i++) {
    unshift @past_opens, $opens[$i];
    if (scalar(@past_opens)>$window) {
        my $pop_val = pop @past_opens;
        $past_open_sum += $opens[$i];
        $past_open_sum -= $pop_val;
    }
    else {
        $past_open_sum += $opens[$i];
    }
    my $past_open_avg = $past_open_sum/$window;

#    print @past_opens;
#    print "\t $past_open_avg";
#    print "\n";

    my $j = $i +1;
    if ($j<$length) {
        my $new_open = $opens[$j];
        if ($new_open < $start_drop_percentage*$past_open_avg) {
            print "triggered at index $j\n";
            my $label;
            if ($closes[$j]>$opens[$j]) { $label = 1; }
            else {$label = -1; }
```

```perl
            my @data_instance = ($label,$new_open,@past_opens);
            my $inst_length = scalar(@data_instance);
            my $k;
            for ($k=0; $k<$inst_length; $k++) {
                $output_fh->print("$data_instance[$k]");
                if ($k<$inst_length-1) {
                    $output_fh->print("\t");
                }
                else {
                    $output_fh->print("\n");
                }
            }
        }
    }
}
```

Scoring:
scoring.pl

```perl
#!/usr/bin/perl

use strict;
use FileHandle;

my $annot_fh = new FileHandle "annot";
my $predict_fh = new FileHandle "predict";

my %annot;
my %pred;

my $TP;
my $FP;
my $FN;

while (<$annot_fh>) {
    my ($start,$end) = split;
    $annot{$start}{$end} = 1;
}
close($annot_fh);

while (<$predict_fh>) {
    my ($start,$end) = split;
    $pred{$start}{$end} = 1;
    if ($annot{$start}{$end} == 1) { $TP++; }
    else { $FP++; }
}

my $annot_fh = new FileHandle "annot";
while (<$annot_fh>) {
    my ($start,$end) = split;
    if ($pred{$start}{$end} != 1) { $FN++; }
}

print "TP=$TP\t FP=$FP\t FN=$FN\n";

my $SN = $TP/($TP+$FN);
my $SP = $TP/($TP+$FP);
print "SN=$SN\t SP=$SP\n";
```

Chapter 5

Information Encoding Molecules of Life

Like a classic Shakespearean play, let's describe the story of the information encodng molecules of Life in five Acts. The first Act is to set the geophysical stage. The second act will focus on the entry of polymeric nucleic acids in arrangments and concentrations such that we begin to have nucleic information, auto-catalytic self-replication, and RNA World. RNA World may have existed in a pre-cellular phase, with partial compartmentalization or containment (undersea clay beds near volcanic vents, for example), and then been present in the initial proto-cellular expansions into the oceans. In the third Act, clear cell-lines became established according to the two membrane types currently known to exist, and the viral co-evolutionary partners are similarly stabilized into specialization according to these cell lines. Initially, without significant protein-based cytosol processing, a key distinction between between cellular life and viral life hasn't evolved yet, thus this phase is sometimes just referred to as Virus World. In the fourth Act, Darwinian selection on cell lines has led to an amino acid (AA) polymer (protein) encoding and production scheme. (AA's available from primitive metabolic and membrane peptide stabilizers.) In the new language of protein sequences 20 common amino acids are coded, plus two rarer amino acids, for a total of 22 amino acids in the protein alphabet. From a maximal information propagation context, it may be that encodings with 22 element alphabets are optimal [3], so this would demonstrate the remarkable power of Darwinian selsection to recover this upon optimizing/selecting on protein 'words'. The fifth Act is still happening. It starts with a description of the standard dogma and then describes modifications indicated by recent results (some presented in Ch 8 & 9) that give rise to much more complex system description. The fifth Act closes with a description of what we must now contend with in terms of systems-complexity karma (such as autonomous, reproducing, AI).

We start in Sec. 5.1 with a brief description and history of the physical environment to understand the timescales involved. Similarly, a brief description and history is then provided as regards the formation, and 'pre-processing', of the chemical environment. How this might have established the initial conditions for life, and initiated the ensuing phase of Darwinian evolution that brings us to where we are today, is unclear. The sedimentation-ordering emphasis is partly chosen so as to exhibit the pre-processing orderings that may have enabled the proto-biotic possibilities in a broad ranging description of information preserving and propagating contexts. The period of Darwinian evolution eventually settled on the "DNA/RNA→mRNA→Protein & DNA/RNA→ncRNA" models that we see in all living things currently known, as will be discussed. Viruses aren't usually described with this picture, but the genomic data doesn't make sense until viral co-evolution is considered, so the role of viruses will be mentioned throughout. Bioinformatics methods relevant to examining the evolutionary information flows will be discussed, and include PCR, BLAST (Sec. 5.6 & Ch. 6), and HMM-based gene-structure identification (Ch. 7). SVM applications for classification and clustering problems are covered separately in Ch. 11.

Beyond gene structure identification, there is the issue of motif identification and reconstructing gene regulatory networks, and that is just the information processing at the DNA level. There is still the mRNA and ncRNA (such as miRNAs) transcriptome, where expression varies according to cell type, cell environment, and cell cycle. For the mRNA's, we can find the proteins that are encoded, for which the bioinformatics task is to then use that information to identify protein, their similarities to other proteins, and their conformation states and function, and with that metabolic pathway identification and function. One of the main sequence analysis tools in RNA and Protein analysis is the same as in DNA analysis, HMMs, although with different emphasis on different issues (alignment instead of internal structure identitification, in some cases, for example).

5.1 Act 1: Setting the Geophysical Stage
5.1.1 Formation of the Pre-Life Physical Environment

The age of the universe is currently estimated to be: 13.75 ± 0.11 Ga (where 'Ga' is the standard geological term for 'a billion yers ago') [148]. Solar Nebula collapse begins around 4.6 Ga, and the Earth accretes from solar nebula around 4.54 Ga. Earth's initial geological formation is mostly done in 10 Million years, with core differentiation and crust formation. Sometime in the 150 Million years after 4.53 Ga the proto-Earth is hit by a large Moon-sized object. Possibly an L5 accretion object ('Theia' hypothesis) that finally oscillates into a collision. Impact thought to be low velocity, grazing, allowing for core exchange (loss) by the smaller body. The result a moon made of crust material and minimal core, and an Earth with a large core (eventually provides a large magnetic 'shield'), a 23.5 axial tilt, and sped-up rotation. (The Moon is the only known object of its size in the solar system that lacks a significant core.) Most theories consider there to be both crust and ocean formation prior to Theia impact. After Theia impact, around 4.4 Ga, the earth's geological ordering processes hit the 'reset' button, with a reset on crust formation, with initial water recovery vaporized by molten surface, e.g., with sterilization of the waters. Eventually, during 4.4 Ga – 4.2 Ga the oceans reform (for the second time). Tectonic plate motion eventually forces up emergent landmasses (the cratons) around 4.0 Ga.(The oldest rocks date to 4.0 Ga, and are found in the cratons, the ocean bottoms are subduction plates, on the other hand, leading to 'memory' being erased every 200 Million years or so). Sedimentation processes and atmospheric erosion begin on the exposed land; have clay formation with water of various levels of salinity, including very little salinity (e.g., fresh-water); and heating of water and clays may be present due to volcanic vent activity. As new land is pushed up by tectonic action, have large collection of water/clay pools and vents, an environment conducive to establishing the Stage 1 of the Chemical environment (described in the next section).

The amount of water found on Earth currently cannot be explained by volcanism and outgassing alone, so must be accounted for partly via cometary impact [149]. Comets are, basically, dirty snowballs. Comets have been found to contain nucleic acids, PAH's, even amino acids (glycine, found on survey by NASA Stardust probe [150]). While not possible to explain the oceans solely from volcanism, it is possible to do so via a reasonable number of cometary impacts (a million over a billion years). Thus, much of our oceans come from comets. The hypothesis of life originating from a sedimentation-ordering is the main thread of this discussion, so life doesn't start with the oceans, but with land formation rising from the oceans, in this hypothesis. Land offers obvious compartmentalization into separate pools, and clay beds, and still has potentially adjacent hydrothermal heating and volcanic venting. Anther leading possibility is of life originating in solvation-ordering in water, possibly originating in underwater hydrothermal vents. If life can directly originate in the primordial oceans, in hydrothermal vents for example, then this opens the possibility for life starting as early as 4.4 Ga on planet Earth. The ocean-vent and clay-bed life origination theories, and other theories, tend to converge on a RNA World hypothesis, regardless, as will be described in what follows.

If life on Earth is dated to 4.0 Ga, with land emergence, and the earliest archaen fossils date to 3.5 Ga (stromatalites [151] still extant today), that leaves a 500 million year window for RNA World & Virus World dominance. In another 500 million years after the emergence of Archaens, at 3.0 Ga, we have the emergence of oxygenic photosynthesis and the resulting oxygen revolution/catastrophe in the Earth's biome. The critical formation of the chemical environment for life begins with the sedimentation derived clay/organic mixture, possibly heated, with low salinity water, and the chemical environment co-evolves with the virus/cell world from 4.0 Ga to 3.0 Ga, with a shift to a higher oxygen concentration in the atmosphere, among other things.

If life on Earth is dated to the end of the heavy meteorite bombardment phase, at 3.9 Ga, the window for RNA World & Virus World correspondingly shrinks. In recent results the date of earliest archaen fossils has moved from 3.5 Ga up to 3.7 Ga [200]. This would leave a period of only 200 million years for all of the developments indicated for RNA World to occur. Given the latest preliminary results, and the ratchet-like nature of new discoveries closing this 200 million year window even further, it may be that RNA World either 'began in a flash' or happened over a prior 500 Million year period on Mars (with impact-transfer event to get to Earth, see Sec. 5.1.4.

5.1.2 Pre-Life Chemical Environment and the RNA Splice-World Hypothesis
Stage 1. Establishing Initial Chemical Environment – physical ordering. To recap the physical ordering above, we have: (i) sedimentation – microporous clay depositions rich in organic compounds and phosphate [152,153]; (ii) complex solvation – microporous eutectic freezing rich in organic compounds and phosphate; (iii) pooling; and (iv) heating.

Clays, or a surface covering with water in a freeze/thaw cycle, are both ubiquitous upon land formation (tectonic plate action leads to dry land formation, the cratons). Clay minerals are typically formed by erosion of rocks via weathering and small particulate transport to form large beds away from original rock-bound location. Have fresh water (rain) on land, possibly heated by volcanism, with organic components partly from comets (entirely so in case of space "panspermia" [154]). The ubiquitous aspect of the oceans alone at this stage does not appear sufficient to manage the chemical reactions leading to life without a containment mechanism.

Stage 2. Pre-processing with Chemical Environment: have initial formation of a replicator in the physical-ordering partial containment established in Stage 1. This is 'PAH World', where we have metabolism without genes or full containment. PAHs have been found in a nebula [155], and appear common, giving rise to suggestions of a "PAH World" phase of proto-life [156]. In some origin of life theories it is early metabolism that is the origin of life processes. These theories are often, effectually dual origin theories, or explicitly so, as with Dyson [201], where a nucleic acid information-carrying processes originates separately. In the works of Margulis [202-204] the role of nucleic acid in an infectious role are emphasized throughout (and Dyson references this in his theory for the dual origins, where nucleic-acid enters as a toxic accumulation that turns into an infectious process).

Stage 3. Establishing Initial Replicator: a replicator forms that is partly contained via loose encapsulation inside membrane-forming biomolecules that self-assemble in water due to hydrophobicity properties, or in microporous clays. This is 'Lipid/pre-RNA World' (precursor to Intron World in Sec. 5.2.2), where we have biopolymer pre-genes with minimal metabolism (autocatalytic and self-splicing). Any replicator initiation in a resource-rich semi-contained environment will then propagate to that entire environment: the clay-beds or a eutectic freeze/thaw zone, for example. The dual origin hypothesis mentioned above has a new twist in Sec. 5.1.4, where there's not enough time on early Earth, given the chronology, for the initial nucleic acid information-handling development, so it's possible that this may have been done separately on Mars [1], and then successfully transferred to Earth via impact and meteorite bombardment.

5.1.3 Encapsulation of chemical interactions and information structures
The physical/chemical emergence of proto-biological ordering, from universe formation, to planetary coalescence, up to formation of sediments, with related formation of clay beds (possibly hot with volcanic vent proximity), occurs over a period of around 9.75 billion years (from 13.75 Ga to 4.0 Ga). Earth and Mars [190,191] are examples of sediment-forming planets in our solar system.

Once initiated ca. 4.0 Ga, the biological emergence of fantastically complex information structures occurred over 500 million years via selection. This is due to the rapid emergence of complexity under conditions of selection acting on units of encapsulated, replicative, information structures, in the vast primordial oceans.

Life is known to have occurred at least as early as (3.5 Ga) from the fossil record. Viral and primitive single-celled life forms are not viewable in the fossil record, however, so the fossil records don't provide information about precisely the era thought to have occurred when going before 3.5 Ga. So, to be specific about timelines, suppose the 500 million years from 4.0 Ga to fossil record life at 3.5 Ga could be spent in establishing a replicator on Earth (the Mars case to be covered in the next section), and then rapidly disseminating that replicator in the oceans (in a geological-time 'blink') once a self-contained replicator/container system is found -- a fast-start to the fossil record at 3.5 Ga, in other words. For example, consider that from 4.0 Ga to 3.8 Ga Earth establishes a nucleic acid replicator (initiates RNA World, or its PAH +RNA 'artifact-precursor' World); then from 3.8 Ga to 3.7 Ga Earth finds replicator/container (initiates RNA World with cell). From 3.7 Ga to 3.5 Ga Earth has selection and evolution up to the point of life-forms that can be observed in the fossil record (at 3.5 Ga).

So, have biological informatics, or bioinformatics, of encapsulated chemical interactions involving information structures, where those informations structures could be RNA-based, or, as will be seen, eventually protein-based, so not just information encoding (the transcriptome), but the information inherent in the protein construct and the related metabolic pathways (the proteome and metabalome).

In the dual origin theories metabolism and nucleic-acid information processing have separate origins, with protein production resulting later (post RNA-World). If asking why Earth would be special to this process it might actually relate to the later phases, particularly the era of protein production and, thus, the standard dogma DNA→mRNA→protein. This is because Earth has a 22-year orbital cycle within one cycle of the Sun's magnetosphere, giving rise to 22 yearly Earth states, sequentially visited, repeatedly, with minor variation. Systems with 22 states, and propagation of information via alphabets with 22 letters (or 22 amino acids), is found to be optimal in some circumstances (discussed in Sec. 5.4, and extensively in [3]), thus special attention to their emergence in a variety of circumstances, here a a 22-cycle driver and the production of a 22-element protein language, seems warranted.

5.1.4 Possible Role for Mars [1]

Mars may have had a meteor impact generated transfer of a nucleic acid based replicator system to Earth, providing at least a 500 million year headstart on such development on the geologically 'reset' Earth/Moon system.

Mars cooled approximately 200 million years before Earth. Mars had oceans/sedimentation around 4.5 Ga (while Earth doesn't have oceans until around 4.3Ga).This is partly because Mars is smaller, and thus cooled faster and lower gravity, and partly because Proto-Earth had a developmental reset during this time with its hypothesized L5 'theia' collision that resulted in Earth/Moon system (ca. 4.54 GA): Mars, thus, reached the sedimentation production phase before Earth. Mars had plate tectonics, as revealed by the tell-tale pole-flipping imprint of the magnetic field in the cooling magma of its rift-zone magma fields [190]. Land formation would have been easier on Mars, given its lower gravity. And, the distinctive seasonal layering of sedimentation beds have been conclusively observed on Mars in recent years [191]. (Earth has five beats to the bar, while Mars has the expected ten due to its more complex axial wobble.)

At time of land emergence on Earth (4.0Ga), Mars is hit by a Pluto-sized object (this may be Mars finally crossing paths with one of its own L5 condensates). Mars does not recover much of its oceans and atmosphere.....so where does it go? A small fraction could have made it to earth... and given the inherent replication ability of a nucleic acid replicator that is all that would be needed. If a functional replicator is delivered to Earth, then Earth has a head start by at least 500 million years on replicator development. Since most water-soluble containers (lipid vesicles, etc.) would be easily disrupted or stripped away by such an interplanetary transfer, its more likely that a DNA based replicator in a clay-matrix (possibly pyrite-based) might make such a transfer, to alter earth sedimentation clay beds (or eutectic zones) that have appropriate replicator substrate (such as in the pyrite-based clays of the Rio Tinto Valley [205]).

It is thus conceivable that replicator transfer from Mars Noachian meteor impacts, up to and including the big one (at ~4.0 Ga), would have seeded the Earth's oceans, clay beds, and eutectic zones, etc., upon meteoric transfer to Earth. This would provide up to a 500 million year head start on replicator development. As mentioned in [1], Earth may have cheated on the cradle-of-life exam, and borrowed some answers from Mars, notably a nucleic acid replicator system.

5.2 Act 2: Enter Nucleic Acids: Nucleic Information and RNA World
5.2.1 Nucleic Acids
DNA bases are made up of a phosphate group, nitrogenous base (A, G, T, or C), and a (deoxy) ribose sugar (replace T with U for RNA). Single-strand DNA (ssDNA) can anneal with a 'complementary' DNA strand to form a highly stable DNA helix. Annealing is made possible by base-paring between the strands via hydrogen bonds (G-C pair has 3 hydrogen bonds, A-T has 2, G-T has 1). The helix is further stabilized by 'stacking energy' due to the overlapping pi bonds from one planar base-pair in the helix to the next (where the planar-base-paired molecules 'stack' with the next base-pair planar molecule). In RNA or DNA, alternatively, ssDNA can coil onto itself in places where it is G rich, allowing for guanine tetraplexes (G4s) to form (using Hoogsteen hydrogen bonding, not Watson-Crick hydrogen bonding). The G4 motif is $G_{\geq3}N_xG_{\geq3}N_xG_{\geq3}N_xG_{\geq3}$. A single, planar, G4 (G-qurtet) is shown in Fig. 5.1, along with a diagram showing how sacks of G4s give rise to structure (the basis of aptamers both natural and synthetic).

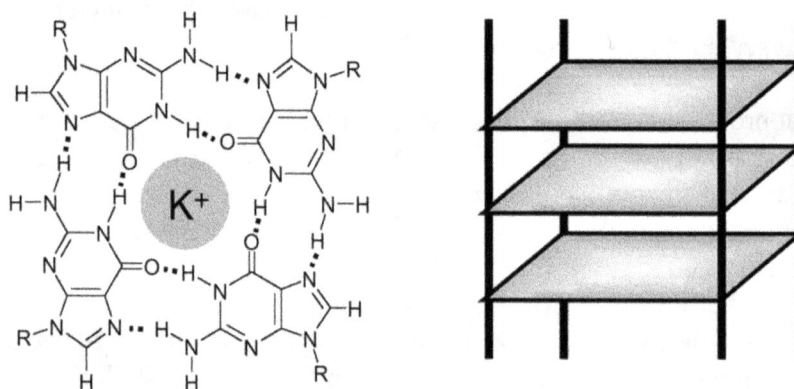

Fig. 5.1. The G4 motif is $G_{\geq3}N_xG_{\geq3}N_xG_{\geq3}N_xG_{\geq3}$.

Naturally occurring riboswitches (some ribozymes that are still in use), found by Breaker and Nudler in 2002, are nucleic acid based polymers that take on a 3-D conformation with function. This is similar to what is obtained with the aptamers found via SELEX in biotechnology applications (Sec. 5.6).

In order to have ssDNA polymerization, minimally need formation of phosphodiester bonds, where nucleotides are added only at the 3' end. To go from DNA to RNA we need a DNA-dependent RNA polymerase (DdRp) ribozyme. Eventually we arrive at the protein-based DdRp enzyme in use in living organisms today.

RNA Polymerase synthesizes mRNA strands based on DNA template. It was discovered in 1960. Because transcriptional regulation is critical to cells, RNA polymerase is highly regulated. RNA polymerase will bind to promoter region and begin transcription and then release its transcript at specific sites along the DNA sequence. DdRp produces: mRNA; Non-coding RNA (tRNA & rRNA); microRNAs; and Ribozymes. After binding to DNA, RNA polymerase transitions to open conformation and is also able to unwind the DNA about 13 bases upstream. At first RNA polymerase is strongly bound to the promoter. Once longer transcripts begin to be produced, the enzyme clears the promoter. Mg^{2+} ions are used by the enzyme to coordinate phosphate groups during the elongation. In prokaryotes, transcript termination can be Rho dependent/independent. Independent termination involves formation of a hairpin loop in the RNA at the site of termination which helps it to dissociate from the DNA. In eukaryotes RNA polymerase II is responsible for most mRNA production

The transcriptome is the set of all RNAs produced in one or a population of cells. The genome is, roughly, fixed (not strictly fixed due to virus horizontal gene transfer), while the transcriptome can vary with environmental conditions.

Transcriptomics, or Expression Profiling, is the study of mRNA's in a given cell population: for high-throughput studies generally lacking in high accuracy at the single nucleotide level, DNA microarray technology is available (Ch 9 for details). If single-nucleotide level examination of the transcriptome is needed, sequencing technology with cDNAs can be done to obtain a high accuracy result. Nanopore detector based methods (Ch. 14) may be central, economically, to having both high throughput and high accuracy. (Note the subtlety that the relative amounts of mRNA in a cell are not indicative of the relative amounts of the associated proteins, as will be described in Ch 10.)

5.2.2 Intron World -- a precursor to RNA World
In 'Intron world' we begin with a means for ssRNA extension via a crude RNA-based polymerase, where the polymerase would help to generate, and regenerate, the random pools of ssRNA variants needed. A nucleotide polymerase in the form of an RNA World (precellular) aptazyme is not a strech of the imagination since special cases of such an aptazyme capability still exist in nature, where 1 to 3 bases are polymerized, and some of these cases have been modified to allow almost 100 bases of polymerization [157]. Thus, remnants of an aptazyme polymerization capability are already evident.

RNA/DNA polymers can grow by polymerase extension, aptazyme-based polymer joining, and polymer splicing (via inserts). Notice that in the latter case, splicing can be done without a separate aptazyme or ribozyme, as the splicing replicating element can itself be a ribozyme -- these are known to exist and are known to be ancient (self-splicing intron II and transposons). In this setting, call it the "Intron Earliest" hypothesis (pre-cellular RNA-World), where the first truly replicating element is the intron II / retrotransposon. This allows for an explosion in polymeric complexity at an early stage.
In the Intron World Hypothesis, introns are selected as selfish mobile elements, with self-splicing capability. A more sophisticated Intron spliceosome eventually forms. Introns are eventually demoted to artifacts (or eliminated entirely – in most prokaryotes and viruses), or co-opted as a transcript pause method, or as a spacer for selective modularity (where modularity may not be so much 'functional' as it is a language tokenization with an optimal sequence size according to the specific sequence -- with likely strong dependency on the cumulative hydrophobicity of the amino acids, e.g., a hydrophobicity gematria, for example).

There may have been, thus, intron splicing before RNA→RNA transcriptase capability in Intron World, since it would have more quickly arrived at intron ribozyme (RNA enzyme) self-splicing behavior (Group I + II introns), since selection based on existing RNA self-splicing would have existed first, then would have adopted an artifact to optimize this process and co-evolved on that artifact (a ribozyme before the protein revolution, then a protein-based enzyme afterwards) to achieve improved, faster splicing. The full fledged spliceosome eventually results, variants of which then provide basis for RNA→longer RNA polymerase and eventually RNA→DNA transcriptase (perhaps related to the splice-onto parts of the spliceosome process).

Introns are weird

Some introns are self splicing, and mainly fall into two groups: Group I and II. Group I introns are found in rRNA of lower eukaryotes. The Group I introns have a common secondary structure, and often have catalytic activity for something other than their own self-splicing. Some Group I intron code for endonucleases that promote their own mobility.

In an intron dominated early RNA World (or "Intron World") intron functionalization, and mirtron constructs, could have been the basis for early biochemical information processing.

The adoption of DNA firmly into the RNA World might be marked by the invention of the Group II intron, which allows self-splicing on introns from DNA parent sequence. As with Group I, Group II introns are self-splicing will all sorts extra (beyond self-splicing) catalytic activities. Group II introns, however, use an RNA intermediary during transport to another DNA molecule, at which point they need reverse transcriptase to allow insertion of the RNA back into the new DNA 'host' (if it sounds like a transposon, that's because it does, with different extraction via self-splicing than the standard transposon, otherwise they are very similar and undoubtedly related). Although much more complex (DNA length encodings can be longer than RNA based), Group II introns allowed much more rapid and functionalized developments (via RNA intermediate), that a transition to full "RNA World" could finally be made (with role of DNA as primary information encoding also critically established).

5.2.3 RNA World – (pre-Cellular, initially)

Once you have a lot of random RNA (and DNA) polymers, with self-splicing replicators you've established the framework for autocatalytic RNA polymer complexes with one polymer acting as an information template --- *so the precursor to the modern "gene circuit" could have been in place as far back as the pre-cellular RNA World.*

Suppose RNA World constructs helped launch the first successful 'cell' that could replicate and travel the oceans in their self-replicating cellular compartmentalization. It is likely that proteins would have been beneficial to these early cells if only to help stabilize the cell membrane. Cell-based selection for more and better protein helpers eventually led to the protein-dominated enzymatic systems we see in prokaryotic cells. Given the preceding, the RNA World Hypothesis is as follows.

RNA World Hypothesis (no indivualized 'container' yet)

(i) ribozyme replicators: polymerization of nucleotides leads to constructs with self-replicating capabilities (self-replicating, purely RNA-based, ribozymes) [157].

(ii) simple reversible transcriptase between RNA-DNA type ribozyme: introduction of DNA as storage template, and as synthesis template.

(iii) ribosome synthesizer: oligopeptides complex with RNA to form better catalysts, eventually have capability to catalyse peptidyl transfer for primitive protein polymer-

ization. Simple proteins found to be useful, perhaps as bilayer stabilizing and virus interference elements -- eventually arrive at ribosome used in modern protein synthesis.
(iv) protein-based enzymes replace ribozymes (the protein revolution): protein synthesis produces enzymes with more specificity and control and they replace most ribozymes in their various uses.
(v) in Stage 4 to follow, with proto-cell, protein becomes dominant biopolymer, and RNA/DNA take on a predominantly information centric role.

Liposomal 'space program'
What really launched the cell? Some reliable easily reproducible and extendible (for budding) lipid-based membrane material that, basically, self-orders into the desired cell wall purely on the basis of hydrophobicity? Some uniformity would seem to be needed, and indeed, two types of membranes (with very different thicknesses) predominate. Once a reliable cellular unit existed, it could launch from what was probably a 2D chemical environment of a clay-water interface (or even a mostly 1D chemical environment in a channel in a microporous clay). Once a reproducible unit could launch into the 3D ocean habitat, then vastly greater complexity of biomolecular computation could be accessed.

The origin of the prokaryotic cell may be hopelessly obscured by billions of years of time, but the origin of the eukaryotic cell may have some tantalizing clues via the evolution of the spliceosome and RNAi (as will be discussed further in Ch. 8).

5.3 Act 3: Enter Cell/Virus: Virus World
At the start of the third Act we have compartmentalization, thus cell+virus simultaneously born, giving rise to two forms of transmission of selfish information. Although, the virus seeking compartments, or approximately such, may have existed pre-cellular, according to how things are defined. At this early phase there would be rapid selection and optimization over cell 'compartment' features. The role/benefits of proteins as bilayer constituents may have played a critical role. A tipping point for protein functionality may have been at an early phase in cell membrane evolution to be compatible with protein-based ion-selective channels. It is already hard enough to arrive at an ion-selective channel, bridging the cell membrane, using protein, with its clearly delinated hydrophobic segments. Doing the same with nucleic acid, on the other hand, seems very difficult and likely 'leaky', with likely non-optimal function even if discovered. (It turns out it is possible to engineer nuclei acid based channels that are ion selective [206], known as nucleic acid origami, but the constructs are unlikey to arise in Nature, or if they did, would be very leaky.)

Stage 4. Replicator/container emerges that conquers (populates) the oceans of the world. This is the ancient Virus/ Cell World. Lipids and amphiphilic peptide compounds have both hydrophobic and hydrophilic portions. Coupled with mild agitations, such as a wave-zone that is crashing and foaming in a replicator-infested region (if bordering on an infested clay bed or eutectic freze/thaw zone), then we have what is likely to have been a frequently occurring scenario with conditions that allow replicator containment in lipid vesicles, etc., where primitive budding of the vesicle may have been the basis for reproduction on this first replicator/container arrangement. Eventually some stable replicator/container arrangement will be selected by its successful spread into the oceans.

The dominant replicator/container system may have been a primitive RNA-based system. This may have been the initialization of the primitive cellular RNA World hinted at by the various RNA-based artefacts in all known living organisms. This is 'RNA World with proto-cell', where we have metabolism with primitive genes and individualized containment. In the case of RNA World with container (individualized, cellular) – the containment is itself an important artifact.

Stage 5. Natural selection acts on the stable set of simple RNA World cellular/viral entities. Eventually select on RNA World entity that has better fitness due to co-evolution with artifact, in this case a primitive protein, or protein pre-cursor, and the ability to produce/acquire and manipulate that 'artifact' to added benefit in evolutionary selection. As mentioned, we see no RNA World artifacts involving ion-selective channels (that are very small), indicating the early introduction of such was accomplished via a stable set of complex RNA World entities together with protein synthesis forms providing selection advantage in early cellular life. Protein synthesis may have initially been an artifact that simply provided a membrane strengthening result (with selection), or spliceosomal strengthening artifact or added critical compartment stabilization and functionalization with proten-based channels. Darwinian evolution then acts with Natural selectio with DNA/RNA → mRNA → Protein and DNA/RNA → ncRNA systems.

In the Modern Synthesis [158], the transmitted unit of heredity is the gene; the unit of selection is the individual; and the evolving unit is the population. Darwin describes the evolutionary mechanism of natural selection in [159], but not the intial formation of first replicating organism. In neo-Darwinism – evolution is driven by natural selection acting on variation produced by simple mutation and cross-over mutation. In more recent versions of evolutionar theory, Richard Dawkins suggests the gene is the unit of selection [160], as well as non-biological evolutionary systems, such as memes in culture [161], in agreement with prior meme'like ideas described in [162]. More generally, any 'selfish' biomolecule will comprise a unit of selection (see next Sec. for details), and all evolution is co-evolution with such entities.What results is co-evolution with other species (or with virus and other selfish constructs – see next Sec.), or co-evolution with artifact (the Sec. after next).

RNA World type chemical processing also occurs in biotechnology applications: Selection on soups of RNA/DNA molecules is now done in biotechnology in the aptamer selection procedure known as SELEX, where selection isn't for self-replication etc. (as in Nature), but for local binding to some target, with amplification on those found to bind target best.

Role of Viruses and other 'selfish', co-evolving, or parasitic, genomic elements
In the Intron World Hypothesis we have full intron spliceosome before RNA transcriptase replication ability. The premise that the nucleus might be virus-derived (the viral eukaryo-genesis hypothesis [163]) is now strengthened in that viral endosymbiogenesis can be accompanied by nucleus formation with a spliceosome at the outset, since it's possible for a virus to have sliceosome machinery given its antiquity. To understand why a virus might contribute its own spliceosome consider the miRNA and RNAi viral defenses of the cell. RNA/DNA silencing methods may date to pre-cellular antiquity. The RNAi defense, on the other hand, may have been largely developed after cell formation, to attack the dsRNA intermediary that is a common molecular complex of most viruses upon introduction to their cellular host (whether originating as ssRNA, or DNA). Thus, there are two mechanisms that might have provided selection pressure for a nuclear membrane: (1) Protection from the RNAi defenses; and (2), separation of translation molecular machinery from pre-processing (splicing) molecular machinery. Splicing by spliceosomes (faster than self-splicing) can be

at a rate of one intron every 100-200 seconds (this is organism dependent and highly variable, so just an example). Thus, one role of a nuclear membrane is clear, it must let the slower spliceosome finish its splicing before the translation process can begin.

Thus, the response of some viruses to RNAi may have been to introduce an outer membrane so as to fully construct their single stranded mRNA's and pre-miRNAs (the latter released to cytosol to alter the RNAi-based regulation of gene expression for the cell). The 'nuclear' membrane provided by the virus then allows splicing and dsRNA intermediates to not be exposed to the cell's RNAi defense upon entering the cytosol, and to not have wasteful translation on unspliced pre-mRNA, such that fully constructed ssRNA can be released outside the viral outer membrane (such as with the pox viruses). Even though the spliceosome is thrown in as fortuitous event at this point, such a selection possibility was available, and its amazing success is now apparent, eukaryogenesis -- a virus, with membrane-defense against RNAi, forms the proto-eukaryotic nucleus in an endosymbiotic fusion. It may not be possible to conclusively identify a particular parent in this early genomic sharing, or a direct fusion mechanism of their parent genes, as reshuffling of genes via mobile genetic elements, and immense amounts of time, blurs many of the distinctions provided by a particular initialization.) We shall see in Ch 8, however, that distinctive transcriptome artifacts of this fusion event may still be present, a statistical footprint that is frozen in the eukaryotic genomes since earliest formation.

So viruses may have seeded the formation of the eukaryotic cell itself (further results shown in Ch. 9 appear to strengthen this hypothesis). What is only beginning to be appreciated, however, is the extent to which viral co-evolution has both benefited and cursed cell-based lifeforms. Benefit: accelerated evolution on population, horizontal gene transfer enrichment, greater fitness/competitiveness; and the future tools of medicine and nanotechnology machinery in general.

Bacteriophages are the most abundant life form. There are more viral genes than genes in cellular compartments. It was thought that viruses might be precursors to cells as far back as 1922 [164]. Haldane poses an early viral stage in evolution in 1928 [165]. An intesting and critical detail of viruses is that they have host specificity. For bacteriophages the host cell is usually a single species of bacterium (a detail used in 'phage typing', see Sec. 5.7).

In the mammalian genome [157], approximately 60% of the genome consists of intergenic regions consisting of mobile elements in various stages of decay. Another 30% of the mammalian genome is introns. Introns are thought to allow greater (more modular, safer) modulation via mobile elements (among other things), such as transposons and virus HGT.

In the RNA World, introns may have provided an early mechanism for rate control. In protein world introns provide a means to tokenize into what are called 'exons', that translate to groupings of 50-100 amino acids, whose protein hydrophobicity gematria score represents mostly neutral charge, etc. We could see similar optimized parameters occurring, with the exon-based protein gematria strings, resulting in the observed exon size range (tokenization size). If timing is nuanced for some reason, this can also be managed via use of intron size. Another odd aspect of introns is that they appear to have a "grammar" of their own, but what it encodes is unknown. One possibility is that the intron "grammar" is meant to perform a reset on the transcriptase/polymer uncoiling so that it has no excessive coiling strain when it reaches exonic regions where high fidelity transcription is most important. Although introns are found in everything, including prokaryotes and viruses, they appear to be selected against in these organisms, however, where there is no nucleus to mature the spliced mRNA, and where timing is streamlined for the fastest replication possible.

The origin of viruses has traditionally been placed into three variant theories: (i) viruses were there from the beginning (see RNA World); (ii) the viruses resulted from plasmids or some other selfish mobile genetic element that became parasitic; (iii) the viruses derived from specialized parasitic bacteria (regressive hypothesis). Although all reasonable ideas in their time, and to some extent all describing phenomena that are found to occur in nature. The main thread of evolutionary genomic data appears to support the RNA World case (i). The new understanding of the extensive role of viruses derives from the amazing complexity discerned in just 5000 of the viral genomes sequenced. There are estimated to be hundreds of millions of viral genomes, so more surprises are probably in store.

Transposons are sequences of DNA that can move or transpose themselves (also known as 'jumping genes' [166]). The transposition can either be 'copy and paste' (Class I) or 'cut and paste' (Class II). Class I retrotransposons copy themselves from DNA to RNA by transcription, then from RNA back to DNA by reverse transcription. The reverse transcriptase is often encoded in the transposon itself (similar to retroviruses, such as HIV). Class II DNAtransposons do not involve an RNA intermediate. Transposase makes a staggered cut at target site, cuts out transposon and ligates to target, with DNA polymerase to fill sticky ends and DNA ligase reconnects the backbone. Insertion sites of DNA transposons may be identified by short direct repeats followed by inverted repeats. Some transposons have lost their ability to synthesize reverse transcriptase or transposase, yet continue to be viable because other transposons are still present in the community that do synthesize reverse transcriptase and/or transposase.

The 'P element' transposon family appears to have entered the fruit fly genome in only the past 50 years, having become *globally* disseminated in that time – this provides a hint at the strong HGT pressures from virus (and other mobile element) co-evolution.

In bacteria, transposons can jump from chromosomal DNA to plasmid DNA and back, allowing for the transfer of genes by this manner. This was alluded to in the description of the proto-eubacterial cell, as a means for genome consolidation. This has been observed in the transfer of antibiotic resistance, for example. When the transposable elements lack genes (entirely selfish construct), they are known as insertion sequences.The most common transposon in humans is the ALU insertion sequence. It is approximately 300 bases long and is found copied between 300,000 and 1,000,000 times in the human genome. The Mariner transposon is found in numerous species (found in everything with habitat near the ocean), including human, suggesting distant horizontal transfers might occur as well.

As with viruses, their more independent counterpart, transposons are mutagens. Many transposons (and viruses) contain promoters which drive transcription of their own transposase. More recently, viruses have been found to contain miRNAs, evidently in an attempt to modulate the cells miRNA regulatory system and the antiviral response of the cells innate immunity defenses. The transposons or proviral mutagens with promoters and/or miRNAs can cause altered expression in host genes, a source of disease and evolution. In addition to what is thought to be a primitive form of RNAi (CRISPRi), Bacteria also protect themselves from viruses, and related selfish genomic elements, by producing enzymes, restriction endonucleases, that cut targeted viral DNA/RNA sequences (see Sec. 5.6 for biotechnology applications for restriction endonucleases)..

5.4 Act 4: Enter Amino Acids: Protein Gematria optimal with 22 letters
5.4.1 Mutual Information reveals Codons

In Ch. 3 we saw codon structure revealed in terms of a three-cycle in mutual information (MI) linkages between nucleotides in prokaryotic genome-wide studies (e.g., dinucleotide MI linkages with different base separations). The three-element codon (with a four-element alphabet) has 64 possibilities. Their mapping to amino acid, or 'stop', is shown in Table 5.1.

	U (middle)	C(middle)	A(middle)	G(middle)	
U (5' base)	phe	ser	tyr	cys	U (3' base)
U (5' base)	phe	ser	tyr	cys	C (3' base)
U (5' base)	leu	ser	stop	stop	A (3' base)
U (5' base)	leu	ser	stop	trp	G (3' base)
C (5' base)	leu	pro	his	arg	U (3' base)
C (5' base)	leu	pro	his	arg	C (3' base)
C (5' base)	leu	pro	gln	arg	A (3' base)
C (5' base)	leu	pro	gln	arg	G (3' base)
A (5' base)	ile	thr	asn	ser	U (3' base)
A (5' base)	ile	thr	asn	ser	C (3' base)
A (5' base)	ile	thr	lys	arg	A (3' base)
A (5' base)	met (start)	thr	lys	arg	G (3' base)
G (5' base)	val	ala	asp	gly	U (3' base)
G (5' base)	val	ala	asp	gly	C (3' base)
G (5' base)	val	ala	glu	gly	A (3' base)
G (5' base)	val	ala	glu	gly	G (3' base)

Table 5.1. The codon assignment for the 64 codons. Standard amino acid (AA) abreviations shown for the 20 (main) AA's. The stop codon (UGA) sometimes codes for selenocysteine, a 21st AA. The stop codon (UGA) codes for a 22nd AA, pyrolysine. Thus, the alphabet on AA's appears to encompass 22 letters, but no more. This is a significant number of letters to have in a sequential transmission (propagation) of information, as outlined in mathematical physics analysis of maximal information propagation [3].

5.4.2 The Ribosome: Nature's fantastic nanomachine

The ribosome is a nucleoprotein consisting of two ribosomal RNA (rRNA) subunits: the small subunit reads mRNA and the large subunit catalyzes the linkage of amino acids. After reading the mRNA, the two subunits split apart. Each ribosome contains the A, P, and E sites: A binds aminoacyl- tRNA; P binds peptidyl-tRNA (growing peptide strand); and E binds free tRNA before it exits the ribosome. Since the core catalytic activity is in the large RNA subunit, ribosomes are classified as ribozymes. Their origin is thus likely ancient, going back to the ribozyme dominated RNA World and the earliest introduction of protein production processes.

Ribosomes can be free or membrane-bound. Free ribosomes are present in the cytosol and because it is a reducing environment, proteins with disulfide bonds cannot be made there. Membrane-bound ribosomes are found in the "rough" endoplasmic reticulum, where proteins are usually part of a secretory pathway.

5.4.3 Peptide bond and 22-letter alphabet

So why is stringing together 'words' with an alphabet of 22 letters better than 4 letters? Perhaps even optimal? To explore and capture information in the larger structural space available (the eventual protein structure-function paradigm), it is found that information propagation is optimal with 22 propagation parameters [3], where in the symbolic sequence context described here, this corresponds to an alphabet of 22 letters, or 22 AAs. Why not simply 22 nucleic acids, in that case, and avoid the big shift to an amino acid based formulation? As has long been noted, this comes down to the adoption of the peptide bond as the polymer linker instead of a phosphodiester bond used in nucleic acids, imparting thereby more rigidity, but still retaining critical degrees of freedom in two rotation angles along the backbone at each C-alpha (see Fig. 5.2).

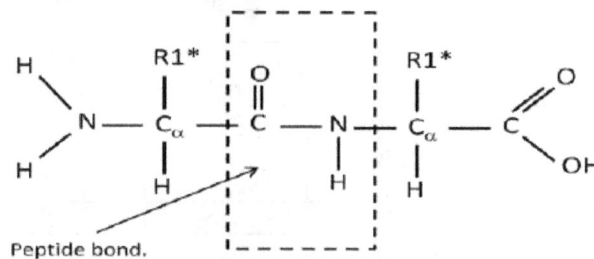

Fig. 5.2. The peptide bond. Shown for the beginning of a homopolymer with R1 residue linking to another R1 residue. The side-chain residue can be non-polar hydrophobic; polar hydrophilic; or charged (acidic, basic). The peptide bond imparts critical rigidity and leads to alpha helix and other stable conformational structures. A critical bond hybridization leads to planar peptide bond, leaving the polymer's conformational degrees of freedom largely simplified to the two orientation angles along the backbone at each C-alpha.

A protein is a polypeptide biomolecule in stable 3-D conformation. A polypepetide is any length, but implies lacking in complex 3-D conformation. A peptide is a short amino acid oligomer often lacking defined 3-D conformation. After translation, the residues of a protein are often modified by posttranslational modifications (glycosylations, etc.). After release of synthesized polypeptide, the molecule is selected for its ability to form a 3-D conformation with sufficient rigidity and surface attributes to have function.

Protein sequence cannot be modified as easily as nucleic acid sequence. Even a basic splicing operation, which may trace to antiquity in nucleic acids (Intron Earliest Hypothesis) is almost unheard of in amino acid polmers, where proteins with post translational modification by internal sequence splicing are almost unheard of (but do occur, and are known as inteins). This is not to say post-translational modifications are far easier and more significant with proteins in other ways, where elaborate glycosylation structures exist, among other things.

5.5 Act 5: Enter dogma, Exit karma

Once a DNA → RNA → Protein in a membrane encapsulation was reproducing, a rapid evolutionary exploration began for all sorts of protein function (see Ch. 9 for details).

5.5.1 Cellular nucleic acid information

DNA is replicated by DNA polymerase (DdDp). DNA Polymerase I was discovered by Arthur Kornberg in 1956 from *E. coli.* DdDp's generally require an existing nucleotide (3' OH) on which to add the new nucleotide . Exonuclease (proofreading) activity is found in some but not all DNA polymerases (DdDp's). DdDp polymerases have processivity along their guide strands, and can add multiple nucleotides per second

RNA is *transcribed* from DNA through RNA polymerase activity (DdRp). The ribosome *translates* the information encoded in the mRNA into protein. As mentioned, DNA in coding regions codes for one of the standard 20 amino acids, and a 21st and 22nd that are coded for in archaic organisms. Genes are transcribed from 5' to 3' ends. The region preceding the 5' end is the *cis* regulatory region, and the region following the 3' end is the *trans* regulatory region.

For viruses, there is RNA → protein (initially, to get viral RdRp, etc.) , then RNA → mRNA → protein (capsid), but now using the virus RdRp. In all, viral genomes can be constructed using a variety of number of nucleic acids (standard DNA or RNA bases, and variants) in any number of forms (ss/ds; circular/linear).

In prokaryotes, genes are often linked under joint regulatory control (i.e., operon structure), as described in Ch. 8. Eukaryotes also have various DNA motifs that encode information about translation start sites and modulation of transcription. Methylation of Cs in GC rich sites can turn off gene transcription (known as CpG Islands, shown as GC blocks in Fig. 5.3). CpG islands- regions where cytosine is surrounded by guanine, where the cytosine can be methylated at these locations as a way to turn off gene expression.

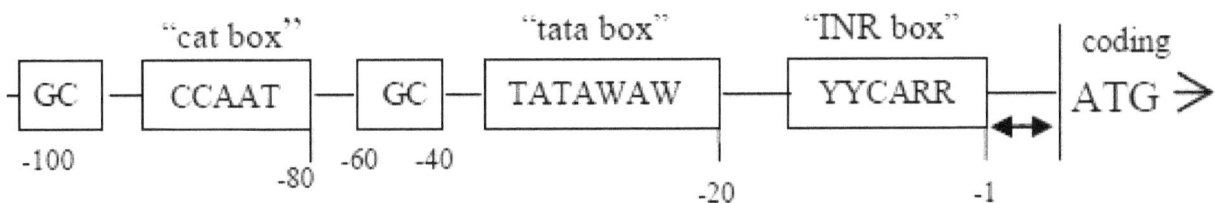

Fig. 5.3. Cis-regulatory control.

C. elegans is odd in that it has some genome structure in prokaryotic style, with operons, and some in eukaryotic style, with introns. Furthermore, *C. elegans* has an 'outron' (Fig. 5.4), essentially an intron on the outside (has a 3' consensus splice site).

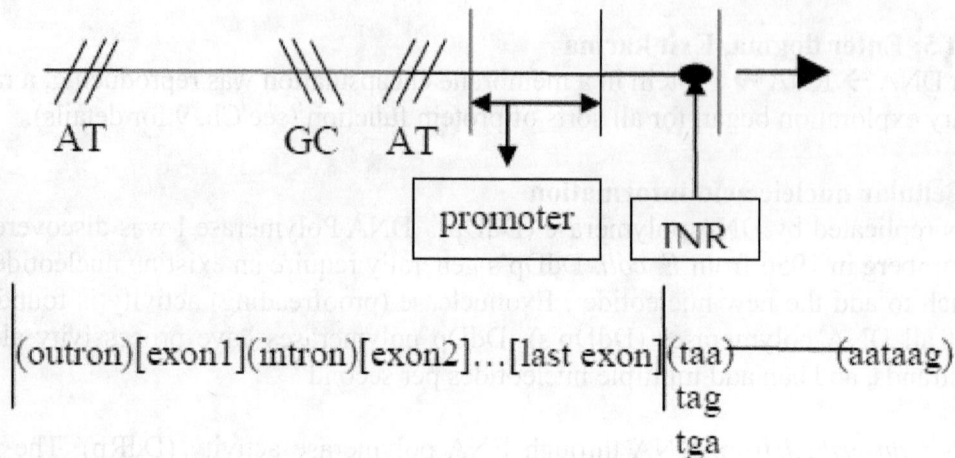

AT   GC AT

promoter INR

(outron)[exon1](intron)[exon2]…[last exon](taa)————(aataag)
               tag
               tga

Fig. 5.4. *C. elegens* genome structures.

When introns are cut out, the cut does not necessarily respect the codon boundaries, roughly 50% of the time we get a 'cut' like: (…)(…)(.)-----------(..)(…)(…). Synteny, on the other hand, does describe the strict preservation on the *order* of exons, i.e., the specific order of exons that are spliced together to make a mature mRNA is maintained in different species. Introns are significantly more free to change relative to exons, due to more constaint on the latter. The end of gene coding structure helps to produce the poly-A tail found on mature mRNAs (see Ch. 9, one of many 'tricks' stolen from viruses.)

More detail on the genomes seen is given in Ch 8, here we focus on the nucleic acids in a general, information encoding, context with overall system level optimization (5.5.2); in the presence of viral co-evolution (5.5.3); and the original role of peptide artifact before extensive use of protein (5.5.4).

5.5.2 Cellular system information and co-evolutionary optimization

Transposons are pervasive, just like viruses, making their relation all the more apparent. If looking for a middle-ground between the two, consider the family of endogenous retroviruses (ERVs). As with transposons, the ERVs are thought to endow the host with another mode of competitive viral inhibition against related activities by exogenous retroviruses [167].Transposable elements can be defended by use of siRNAs (small interfering RNAs that trigger the RNAi against the intended target), that perform silencing on the transcribed (mobile) transposon product. In eukaryotes, RNAi is used to inhibit transposon activity in this way (review of RNAi in next section).

Transposition can be classified as either "autonomous" or "non-autonomous" in both Class I and Class II TEs. Autonomous TEs can move by themselves, whereas non-autonomous TEs require the presence of another TE to move. This is often because dependent TEs lack transposase (for Class II) or reverse transcriptase (for Class I).

Co-evolution of virus-human has greatly shaped human molecular evolution and the human genome [168]. Common patterns of nucleotide motif usage are found between virus and host, sometimes moreso than common patterns found in the hosts' nearby species relatives [169].Viruses are hypothesized to play developmental and expression-modification roles. Maternal immune activation (MIA) is found to give rise to pro-viral activation in both mother and fetus. This can lead to a process where the mother gets a viral infection, with the usual inflammatory response, including interleukin-6 (IL-6), in particular. IL-6 alone is found to alter fetal brain development in mice [170], and IL-6, and other stress indicators, also appear to play a critical role in awakening pro-viruses from dormancy [171-173]. The retrovirus XMRV is one such pro-viruses that may be activated during fetal development and is found to have a high correlation to children with autism and adults with schizophrenia. Not all viruses are detrimental to humans, since some viruses target tumor cells (perhaps some ERVs have such benefit). The use of viruses in cancer therapy dates back to the 1940's. In recent advances in this area, in 2007, a virus has been identified that is very efficacious at eliminating neuroendicrine cancers [174].

The evolutionary notion of saltation is evidenced in the viral genomic record via its evident antiquity in some portions, and not in others: evidently selection pressure on the components of an organism can greatly shift, causing the sensitive components of yesteryear to "freeze" in their configurations due to their evolutionary response to the selection pressures becoming minor in comparison to the selection pressures acting on some new component (a specific gene, or antibiotic protein, etc.). Any 'artifact revolution' is hypothesized to be accompanied by a major saltation event in the genomic record. Remarkably, this may allow ancient genomic lineages to still be traceable [157], given the immense geologic time that should have erased these lineages if some portions not 'frozen' [175].

The role of artifact is given in the next section. A new exploration area/method in Bioinformatics, and one that complements efforts in metaheuristics (Ch. 12) will be described. The new tool involves assessing hypothesized evolutionary mechanism (and linkages) according to metaheuristic optimization performance. The demonstration of the advantages of GA+Viral evolution (both vertical and horizontal gene transfer in host) over standard GA (vertical only), are beginning to be explored [176,177]. For example, if the evolutionary hypothesis to test was regarding artifact revolutions; one could examine introduction of an artifact into a GA-artifact metaheuristic. This is discussed in Ch. 12, where GA, GA-artifact, and GA-virus metaheuristics are described and their comparison discussed in the context of testing various evolutionary dynamics (e.g., artifact saltation).

The Cell's RNAi and miRNA/RNAi defenses, and hyper-mutational defenses

In ssRNA gene silencing experiments in 1998 [178] it was found that the ssRNA was not as effective as dsRNA at silencing. In fact, the dsRNA form of silencing resulted in far more silencing than small concentrations could justify, such that a protein catalytic cascade was thought to have been initiated. This was clarified in 2001 [179] with the description of the enzyme Dicer, which cleaves dsRNA into 22bp segments, referred to as small interfering RNAs (siRNAs), that are subsequently inducted into the RNA-induced silencing complex (RISC), which is then able to suppress target sequences similar to the template, here the dsRNA swept up by Dicer. RNA intereference (RNAi) is thus a gene-silencing process, it appears widespread, and thus likely ancient. Even so, RNAi probably only become established after cell formation, after development of the transmembrane TLR3 receptor ('Toll Receptor'), that recognize dsRNA and initiates the interferon response. Once developed, the RNAi machinery provides a highly effected means for viral defense and gene regulation in general.

Depending on the length of dsRNA molecules introduced into the cytosol of a eukaryotic cell there are two responses. For dsRNA longer than 30 base-pairs in length the Toll Receptors are activated, with production of proinflammatory cytokines known as interferons. The interferons, in turn, initate tha adaptive immune response in mammals. For introduction of dsRNA less than 30 base-pairs ('small RNAs') in length a gene-specific response is triggered via the RNAi machinery. There are three types of small RNAs: (1) small interfereing RNAs (siRNAs), between 20-25 bps, typically 21-22 bps, found to be generated by Dicer, an element of the RNAi defense; (2) micro RNAs (miRNAs), generated from genome-encoded hairpin precursors; and (3) repeat-associated small interfering (rasiRNAs), a distinct class of 28 nt siRNAs that are found to silence transposons. Longer dsRNA (29 nt) silencing is found to be stronger at gene silencing than 21 nt templates [180], indicating the significance of the transposon suppression to the fitness of the organism. The small RNAs introduced, or produced by Dicer, are then picked up by the cells RNA-induced silencing complex (RISC).

By introducing dsRNA homologous to target mRNAs those mRNAs can be regulated or silenced (this is done by the genome itself via the miRNAs). Evidently the length of the dsRNA (up to about 29 nts) is a strong indicator of suppression strength by the RISC, as is the degree of match between the miRNA and its intended target. If the intended target is an exact match, or very close, such as occurs with introduction of viral dsRNA, the target is cleaved, and this is enzymatically driven to nearly full gene-silencing. If the intended target is a good match, but with a few mismatches, the RNAi mechanism binds and disables, but does not cut (or very slow cut, so does not go on cutting others as fast), thus partial suppression of expression. The miRNAs operate more in this latter capacity in animals, possibly with a good match to multiple targets, for an overall suppression on a number of genes (and more than one type of miRNA may lead to very controlled gene suppression, allowing further adjustment in extent of suppression and correlation with other, homologous, genes).

The discovery of miRNAs in the encoding of the HIV virus, and other viruses, has led to a new understanding of how viruses have highly evolved strategies for highjacking the cell's RNAi machinery to its own ends [181], including the ability to mediate latent infection ("hide") [182] and modify miRNA expression overall [183]. This has also brought attention to the role of miRNAs in epigentics and human cancer as it is found that the epigenetic machinery of the cell is partly regulated by a subgroup of miRNAs (denoted "epi-miRNAs" in [184]). The role of RNAi and miRNA is only beginning to be understood.

One of the innate defense mechanisms of the cell involves hypermutational biomolecules. HIV researchers have known since 1992 [185] that HIV viruses without the viral infectivity factor (e.g., without the Vif gene), could not infect most human cells. It wasn't until 2002 [186] that this was understood: Vif blocks the DNA-editing enzyme known as APOBEC3G, a cytadine deaminase [187],[188]. If unblocked, the APOBEC3G protein hypermutates the viral DNA to non-functionality. Several other members of the APOBEC family have antiviral activity as well, and the highly radiated structure of the family is highly indicative of strong selection pressure [168]. The APOBEC family are part of a large gene family that includes AID (activation-induced deaminase), the protein responsible for the hypermutation that takes place in the Ig genes during antibody production [189]. Further description of antibody protein is given in Ch 10.

5.5.3 RdRp & Viral Eukaryogensis (karma – we are virus)
Pre-eukaryotes may have co-evolved an early form of RNAi with a megavirus, where the battle for RNAi control of host, eventually gave rise to the eukaryotic cell via modulation of RNAi. If nothing else, RdRp's have a pervasive role in eukaryotes in defense against foreign nucleic acids, developmental regulation, genome maintenance, and transcriptome modula-

tion (to be discussed further in Ch. 8). Viral eukaryogenesis has been proposed in a variety of forms, all consistent with the lack of RdRp in prokaryotes/archaea (as with RNAi), while RdRp is found in eukaryotes and viruses (as is RNAi). So the important role of RdRp for RNAi purposes clearly explains why RdRp would have singular importance to eukaryotes, but is there a non-RNAi role for RdRp as well? In some RdRp RNA productions lengthy antisense strands are produced, and this suggests a possible non-RNAi role, as will be discussed later.

The viral endosymbiosis could have been a very slow transitional process given the likely mutualism 'melting pot' of endosymbionts, including both proteobacteria (eventually leading to mitochondria, etc.) and viruses (including megaviruses) that could have existed at the LECA. This could have existed then since it still exists now, in present day *Acanthamoeba*, which is the host to the megaviruses Mimivirus, Marseillesvirus, and other nucleocytoplasmic large DNA viruses (the NCLDVs), as well as a variety of bacteria, often hosting multiple virus and bacterial visitors at the same time. Furthermore, phylogenetic analysis shows that the NCLDV viruses have an ancient relation to eukaryotes, thus the LECA, placing them in the mutualism context at the time of the hypothesized viral eukaryogenesis. The NCLDV viruses possess their own mRNA capping protein (eIF4E), mRNA capping enzyme, and DdRp, to ensure preferential production of their mRNAs by the host, and eIF4E, at least, is thought to be unique to the virus (not obtained from the host *Acanthamoeba*). The mutualism 'melting pot' environment of the early eukaryote formation is further supported by viral mutualism in the form of favorable RdRp exchange from T7 to the mitochondrial host genome, which is thought to have occurred at the time of the LECA (or earlier) since it is present in all known eukaryotic mitochondria (with only one known exception).

The viral eukaryogenesis theory leaves little opportunity for testing since it relates to a hypothesized ancient historical event, and for this reason testing the viral eukaryogenesis theory has been grouped with other hypothesized endosymbiosis events, such as those endosymbiosis events leading to the mitochondria and chloroplasts. The viral eukaryogenesis hypothesis, however, involves a shift of non-eukaryotic cytosol based genomic data into the newly formed nucleus of the organism, so may leave more evolutionary artifacts in the genomic sequence information than could be obtained in the case of the organelles (see Sec. 8.7).

5.5.4 Role of Artifact (karma – we are the tools we use)
We continue to borrow extensively from virus, including the methylated cap and polyA maturation on eukaryotic mRNA (not done by the original prokaryotic mRNA, see Table 5.2 below):

Property	Prokaryotic mRNA	Eukaryotic mRNA
Cis regulation	polycistronic	monocistronic
5' termination	triphosphate	methylated cap (a virus trick)
3' processing	termination to release mRNA	cleavage to release mRNA
3' termination	last base of mRNA	polyA
Transport	n/a (no nuclear membrane)	necessary
Translation	~54 nt/sec	~20nt/sec
Half-life	< 5 min.	> 4 hours
Ribosomes/mRNA	>20	>10

Table. 5.2. Comparison of gene structure and transcript properties for bacterial (single cellular prokaryotic) mRNA and animal (multicellular eukaryotic) mRNA.

The role of artifact in co-evolutionary schemes appears throughout the history of life, and this is only beginning to be understood (see ACO and related methods in Ch. 9 for analysis and comparison of such systems in a metaheuristic optimization setting). Some important artifacts: (i) the artifact of containment; (ii) RNA may have been an artifact in PAH World evolutionary selection; (iii) Protein & DNA may have been an artifacts in RNA World evolutionary selection (eventually to become tools outright for more efficient enzymatic activity or more reliable information storage); (iv) Organelles in eukaryotes are thought to be symbiotic co-evolutionary artefacts. The nucleus may be viral in origin (see poxvirus description in viral eukaryogenesis hypothesis), and may have directly led to introduction of sliceosomal introns in the protected nucleus region. The mitochondria still have their own DNA. (v) for human evolution artifacts take on special meaning, as they cover everything from tool use to concept use, such as use of fire; non-verbal concepts; and language. The co-evolution of humans and cultural artifact shows that, not just genes drive evolution, which has long been suspected, but only recently begun to be tested by direct analysis of individual genomic information, such as in recent studies of the serotonin transporter gene [161].

5.6 Biotechnology Methods
5.6.1 Restriction endonucleases
Restriction endonucleases (originally from prokaryotes) cleave certain palindromic DNA sequences and sometimes produce sticky ends (unpaired DNA overhangs). Restriction endonuclease works by making cuts through the sugar-phosphate backbone of each strand. Found in bacteria and archaea and thought to be an early defense against viruses. Native DNA that bears those sequences is methylated to prevent it being cleaved.

Restriction endonuclease was first identified in λ phage. It recognizes palindromic sites. Some cuts produce blunt ends while others leave sticky ends with bases overhanging on either side. Typically used to digest DNA before performing a Southern Blot (see next section). Also useful for inserting DNA sequences into plasmid vectors and identifying SNPs in target sequences

5.6.2 Blots
Southern Blot (named after Edwin Southern) – used for detection of specific DNA sequences in a DNA sample. Uses annealing, in modern applications typically on ~23 unique length of DNA, arranged in (immobilized onto) an array (a DNA microarray) allowing parallel processing (often with an optical read-out by having a fluorophore activatable ending on the 23 base immobilized strands that activates upon annealing). In Southern's original 'blot' method blotting was used to transfer DNA (separated) onto a membrane where it would become immobilized. A sample would then be presented to the membrane under conditions conducive to DNA annealing. By reading out where binding occurs, the sample can be probed for DNA in common with the immobilized DNA probes.

Northern Blot – like Southern, but instead of DNA use RNA instead.

Western Blot – used to detect specific proteins, where the proteins are separated and blotted/immobilized prior to exposure to antibodies with specific targeting (that carry label info for easy optical read-out).

5.6.3 Electrophoresis and GELs

Electrophoresis and other electrochemistry methods have a long, multi-century, history in Chemistry. Gel-based methods are electrophoretic approaches where the different mobilities of molecules (thus how they separate) are exaggerated by use of agarose gels and other multicellular matrices (a short description of various types of gels to follw). Molecules can be separated by molecular weight, charge, isoelectric point, and in numerous other ways. Fig. 5.5 shows how digested DNA samples can be pipetted at the top (the two dark bands) and then have its constituent parts drawn electrophoretically to the other side of the gel, creating the separated bands shown. For DNA one can easily perform forensics -- the digested DNA profiles would separate differently for different people, for example). If the molecules examined in the gel were protein, then the bands could correspond to different molecular weight glycoproteins (in some gels). A limitation of the gel approach, however, is that isoforms and glycoform variants will all be grouped into one band – this is where the nanopore detector described in Ch. 14 may offer a solution when operated in GEL mode, where similar information is sought as with Gels, except with the nanopore we can potentially resolve the isoforms and glycoform variants.

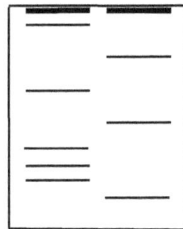

Fig. 5.5. A schematic for a Gel, with material drawn from top to bottom, and faster molecules separating into separate bands at the bottom.

Gel electrophoresis: Charged molecules are drawn through a "gel" by an applied potential. The gel obstructs flow such that larger objects (or longer polymers, or higher molecular weight molecules) move more slowly.

For porous gels the opposite can be arranged, by doing what is known as size exclusion chromatography, where the smaller molecules have to traverse a larger volume in a porous matrix.

Gels, porous or not, appear to promote self-ordering behavior, thus provide an interesting framework for gel-like clays involved in RNA World hypotheses.

Can have column separation based on:
(1) hydrophobicity;
(2) ion exchange (magnitude of charge slows traversal)
(3) affinity (glycoproteins can be separated by lectin affinity chromatography)
(4) divalent metal ion binding to polyhistidine tags
(5) immunoaffinity
(6) immunoprecipitation using proteins 'tagged' (engineered) with an antigen peptide tag

HPLC: High Performance Liquid Chromatography
Seek to have a high pressure solute driven against hydrophobic column material ("reversed phase"), where higher pressure means less diffusion times, and better resolution.

Have different types of gels:
(1) Denaturing: protein unfolds to linear form, and can have separation based on polymer length;
(2) Native: natural (folded) structure retained during separation
(3) Isoelectric Focusing (IEF): using ampholyte solutions with immobilized pH gradient (IPG) gels obtained by the continuous change in the ratio of immobilites (weak acids or bases defined by pK).

Understanding the isoelectric point for a protein can be very significant. By modification of the isoelectric point (pI) of an enzyme by phosphorylation (or by production of an isozyme variant with altered pI), the cell can transfer molecules of the enzyme between different parts of the cell interior. Cells appear to use isoelectric focusing of proteins to overcome a limitation on the rate of metabolic reaction by limiting diffusion of enzymes and their reactants.

For 2D Gel Electrophoresis, proteins are separated in a 2D gel based on isoelectric points (first dimension) and molecular weights (second dimension). A typical problem with 2D Gels is spot quantification under conditions of 'smearing' and "warping", this often leads to mostly qualitative results, where further quantification on a particular "spot" requires cutting out the spot part of the gel and running it through a mass spectrometer (MS).

5.6.4 PCR
Polymerase Chain Reaction (PCR) is a biochemistry method that is used in DNA sequencing, SELEX, and DNA profiling forensics, and provides sensitivity boosting via PCR amplification on tags for a variety of other methods (specificity, e.g., error rate, however, can be limiting in some situations). PCR has an error rate of approximately one in a thousand. PCR can amplify a single or a few copies of DNA across several orders of magnitude. The method uses thermocycling to repeatedly heat (to melt the DNA) and cool (to activate enzymatic replication). Primers containing sequences complimentary to the target region (a known, nearby, genomic sub-sequence 'landmark' for example, along with a DNA polymerase (Taq polymerase from *Thermus aquaticus*) to proceed with processive replication, with themocycling to reset (and grow exponentially). PCR methods can processively amplify 10-40 kb sequences [192]. The three phases of the PCR amplification are as follows:

(1) Denaturation phase: 94-98 degrees, 20-30 seconds
(2) Annealing phase: 50-65 degrees, 20-40 seconds (3-5 degrees below melting Tm of the primers used)
(3) Extension phase: Taq polymerase has optimum activity at 75-80, and commonly use 72.

The tools to capture the information include polymer sequencing capability, where we have this for DNA via DNA polymerase, and have for mRNA via cDNA from reverse transcriptase. Once genomic, expression profile, and proteomic sequences identified from raw data, have task of identifying their properties via relation to other sequences (either directly or via identification of functional structures).

5.6.5 DNA Sequencing

DNA Sequencing involves determining the order of nucleotide bases {a.c.g.t} in a molecule of DNA. Sequencing began in the early 1970's, but an economical method wasn't obtained until Sanger et al. developed the chain-termination method in 1975 [207,208], where a kit-deployment was possible due to the use of fewer toxic chemicals and greater efficiency.

The chain-termination method involves a DNA polymerase that is used to replicate a DNA molecule in the presence of not only standard deoxynucleotides (dATP, dCTP, dGTP; dTTP; e.g., 'dNTP'), but also in the presence, separately, of each of the dideoxynucleotide triphosphates (ddNTPs) as DNA chain terminators (where the polymerase can no longer make a phosphodiester bond, is halted, and eventually disengages). If appropriate concentration of one of the ddNTPsis used in relation to the dNTP's in the polymerization of DNA template, then DNA fragments of varying length are obtained that terminate with the 'N' nucleotide of the ddNTP used. The DNA fragments can be separated by gels with one nucleotide resolution. For the four possible ddNTP terminators, can lay four parallel tracks of gel bands, thereby reading the sequence from the sequence of bands indicated (when viewing all four gels together). Later developments, in 1985 by Leroy Hood et al. [209,210], with fluorescently labeled ddNTPs allowed multiplexing (where length separation was done using capillary electrophoresis, not gel-based electrophoresis). Since then, starting around 2005, and later in 2010, combination amplication and sequencing kits have been developed (Ampliseq and SeqSharp) that avoid cloning and other amplification methods [211,212].

The price of the standard, enzyme-based, DNA sequencing effort is dropping precipitously. Even if this price drop is slowed or halted by limitations of the current methods, it is likely that the price of the standard DNA sequencing information won't be significant going forward. The catch is that the sequence data produced has an error rate of approximately one in a thousand (with re-sequencing, etc. accounted for), and for many SNP-based medical diagnostics this is too high since many disease conditions occur with frequency less than approximately one in a thousand (see problems in Ch. 2 for further elaboration). The NTD Nanoscope in Ch. 14 may offer a means to obtain cheap, sensitive, and specific SNP detection.

5.6.6 Expression analysis: DNA microarrays & RNA-seq

Expression analysis involves examination of the RNA population present in a cell or tissue sample, at a particular time. The two main methods that have arisen for these studies are DNA microarray methods and RNA-seq methods.

DNA microarrays are a multiplex technology that grew out DNA probe immobilization [213] ca. 1984 and out of Southern blotting ca. 1992 [214], where a fixed substrate is 'blotted' with DNA. The blotted, immobilized, DNA probes can then have a sample solution washed over them, with hybridization-based detection. An earlier form of transcript immobilization, ca. 1982, involved immobilization of lysed bacterial communities with oligonucleotide detection at the overall transcriptome level [215]. The error rate on DNA microarrays is approximately 1/100, although less economical approaches may allow this to be reduced to 1/1000.

RNA-seq is used in expression analysis methods to reverse transcribe the messenger RNA active at a particular instant into DNA and sequence the resulting cDNA to get information about RNA expression. Due to the low cost of 1/1000 base-level resolution, RNA-seq is rapidly replacing DNA microarray based methods [216]. Higher fidelity data results and the ability to capture unkown data (not using a known template as in DNA microarrays) is also an advantage. The multiplexing strengths of the DNA microarrays will still have a niche, going forward, but one favoring a stronger pre-processing role, with hybridization selection on a collection of related molecules for example (specificity not required as being used as a 'notch filter' capture system).

An important diagnostic in disease recognition involves discovery and identification of single nucleotide polymorphisms (SNPs) in genomic DNA data and RNA expression data. SNP arrays have been devised for this purpose, among other things. More recently, DNA enzyme methods have been able to push the limits of SNP discovery via use of pooled genomic DNA data [217] to the 1/1000 error rate. What is still needed, in many cases, is much greater specificity, however, for SNP information to provide a useful diagnostic. The Archon X Prize [218] awards $10,000,000 to the fist method that provides sequence information at an error rate below 1/100,000 (along with other constraints effectively restricting to economical solutions), which further elucidates the critical role of economical re-sequencing in gene coding regions with much greater specificity in order to have further progress in SNP-based medical diagnostics. The 1/1000 error rate might be reduced in a single-enzyme interaction observation approach, and this was described ca. 2003 in [219]. Any polymerase-based approach may be fundamentally weakened by the error rate of the enzyme. The use of polymerases is avoided in a SNP array approach ca. 2004 [220], where a hybridization-based approach is used involving sandwich probe hybridization with gold nanoparticle tagged sandwich probes in a second washing step. A method that leverages the the hybridization-based approach (no enzyme error rate introduced), with the single-molecule observation/validation (lower hybridization error rate), is the nanopore transduction method described in Ch. 14.

5.6.7 Phage Typing & Metagenomic Environmental Testing

Given the pervasive nature of the viral presence, often in many-to-one correspondence (ten bactiophage might have the same, sole, host – a detail used in phage typing), we have the means for viral monitoring of environmental conditions. In other words, with DNA profiling based on a probe set of organisms, such as with an environmental sample, we can profile based on examining phage DNA (e.g., a metagenomic profile).

The main use for microarrays in the future may be as targeted concentrators for sequences of interest. The resolution of SNP variants, or other state, could then be resolved by passing the DNA-array filter/concentrates onto a nanopore detector. The NTD approach may offer improved resolution of DNA or protein variants involving isoform, a single monomer, or a single surface nanopore-epitope alteration (or related glycation-profile, in case of focus on glycoproteins).

5.7 Exercizes

(Ex. 5.1) Heavy meteorite bombardment phase on Earth ends 3.9 Ga (Ga = billion years ago) and earliest archaeon fossils potentially dated at 3.7 Ga (as of 2019), leaving only a 200 million year window for life to start and settle on cellular life governed by the standard model (DNA→mRNA→protein). Do a literature update on earliest archaeon dates (in particular), has the window for RNA World been reduced further?

(Ex. 5.2) What are the two types of cell membranes? Give their description in detail (lipid length, overall membrane width, extent ot channel and sensor usage).

(Ex. 5.3) Do any of the iron-processing extremophiles have the less common, thicker, membrane type? Is the lipid of the thicker membrane type associated with pyrite?

(Ex. 5.4) Indirect test of Mars Impact transfer hypothesis (of a DNA transposon and a bunch of DNA, perhaps). (i) How long can life live inside a rock? And How long can DNA be recoverable from inside a rock (for genome sequencing purposes)? (ii) How long to transfer a rock from Mars to Earth (assume blast sends crust in all directions, so select the direction satisfying the most optimal trajectory for Earth crossing)?

(Ex. 5.5) RNA World evolved the best aptamers. Current aptamer design libraries 'seed' off of well known ribozyme structures. Write a current assessment of what aptamer designs are leveraged off of what ancient ribozymes?

(Ex. 5.6) Once you have an established RNA World encapsulation (or two) then you have two strategies going forward: cell and virus. Early in this process there would have been little or no protein production (the ribosome might not exist yet), so cell and virus wouldn't have had as much to differentiate on. Once protein becomes prevalent, and the cell with modern dogma is operational, the cell/virus differentiation would have become significant. Suppose they shared Intron II pre-protein, but had stronger separation and divergent Intron II afterward? Look at the latest Intron I & II data and report on it's sequence information and possible divergence.

(Ex. 5.7) Analyze the megaviridae of Amoeba for introns, by use of annotation files (see genbank). Repeat for Amoeba itself. Compare intron structures. Do the megaviridae appear to have their own distinct intron structure? (They are known to have their own distinctive spliceosomes.)

(Ex. 5.8) The protein-fold (functionalization) repertoire, like the immune repertoire, number from 10^6 to 10^7 as of 2019. Do a report to provide updated numbers, but they are probably fairly stable at roughly a million. This means, in other words, that AA polymer 'words' are roughly one million in number without being a synonym (functional equivalent). Thus an AA polymer with its peptide bond constraints and 22-letter alphabet allows for roughly one million functionalized variants. How can we discriminate between those variants? Some separation is easy, such as into one of the four protein families, then by more specific gene families, but in the end there is probably still a 'hard' discrimination task between 1,000 proteins (repeatedly, but reduced to this level of difficulty). How would you perform this task, with scalable technology?

(Ex. 5.9) What Eukaryotes are currently known to produce their own RdRp?

(Ex. 5.10) Co-evolution with virus is more significant than people realize, especially during development. Virus is able to affect in obvious ways when crippling, but less obvious when causing heart damage that doesn't manifest until 30 years later, say, or cause neural developmental damage that manifests as a form of autism or propensity for schizophrenia. Do a survey of viruses and HERV's active or common among developing fetuses and infants. Search literature for recent word associations between survey viruses and keyword autism or schizophrenia.

(Ex. 5.11) One possibility is that a particular, common, viral infection (possibly common, minor, un-noticed), or a particular HERV (human endogenous retrovirus), MUST be present (and active) to avoid a disease condition (not the other way around). I.e., there may be some symbiosis that we are unaware of… such could lead to accidental antiviral knockout of a virus/HERV that is critically needed, symbiotically, to avoid non-optimal development (autism spectrum). Search literature for recent HERV, autism, antiviral articles, or for other complex traits (swap out keyword autism for other).

(Ex. 5.12) Draft your own eukaryogenesis theory accounting for RNAi, etc., as discussed in the chapter.

(Ex. 5.13) "Virus 9". What if a virus wasn't host specific…. then maybe it could spread more quickly and dangerously via every cellular life form (virus-9 like ice-9)? How is this not a transposon, such as a Mariner variant? RNAi can stop transposons. Do a report on small viruses with more universal cellular attack, that are currently known.

(Ex. 5.14) Obtain a histogram of Gematria scores on words – is there a peak at 137?

(Ex. 5.15) Adapt AA weighting scheme on protein 'words' until it scores 137 in a similar distributional peak structure to that seen in (Ex. 5.14). Is this weighting scheme predominantly a hydrophobicity measure?

(Ex. 5.16) "Mars is your Daddy". In the Mars DNA Transfer Hypothesis, Intron World at Mars transfers to Metabolic World at Earth. Dual origin of reproducing nucleic acid based information processing at Mars and reproducing metabolic autocycle at Earth [201]. Like an unfertilized egg (Earth) getting sperm (Mars), a new type of life-process can begin (dual origin, Dyson). [202-204] refers to similar paradigm but DNA as infective agent, but that would imply that at initiation the unfertilized egg could ever be more (which it can't be by assumptions of hypothesis). How long for transfer? How long to have reconstructable genome? How long to have revivable amoeba from frozen Siberian lake ice? Etc…..

(Ex. 5.17) MirTrons are microRNAs that result from intron splicing. This offers a new mechanism for miRNA production that is DROSHA independent, and that sometimes bypasses Dicer entirely as well. Since some intron-splicing is self-splicing, this allows for a purely RNA/DNA route to miRNA production. To quote a former Vice Pres., "this is a

[BFD]".... If mirtrons are ancient, they might be really ancient. Delve into this possibility, that mirtrons might be ancient, and how to test for it.

(Ex. 5.18) (Halloween Scary!) Suppose a 'virus' happens to get loose that happens to alter human miRNA expression profile to cause zombie-like behavior and contagion (shedding a particular miRNA? Or the viruses pick it up and 'shed' virus....). And I'm talking fast 'rage' zombies, not your slow walkers. In detail, with references, describe how you would use miRNA expression arrays to determine what miRNA to target in zombie-infected patients, by way of appropriately designed lncRNA injections.

(Ex. 5.19) If Mars only had RNA World, what would remain after the smash? If no compartmentalization, can't go deep like a methanogen, so pre-cellular 'life' only in thin clay-like layer. Once desiccated, it's over, all that's left is the detritus of RNA-World's oceans (or clay-layer between ocean and non-coastal or sedimentary deposition). Mars does have the odd surface red-dust trait due to pyrite. Could remnants of a Mars RNA World still be around? Paradoxically, to find proof of life on Mars you would have to look to the Moon and the Earth's L5 attractors. Alternatively, L5 and the Moon may hold remnants of any nearby Earth-blasted nucleic acid, so an interesting graveyard for astropaleontological purposes as well as test Mars Transfer. Write a mission proposal to NASE to sweep thru the L5 zone and scoop up samples. What are you seeking, what form migt it be in, how would you focus on getting it and not a bunch of space rock?

Chapter 6

Analysis of sequential data using alignment

Genomic data consists of a sequence of nucleic acid residues. Proteomic data largely consists of a sequence of amino acid residues (the primary structure of a protein), although significant post-translational modifications can be made (such as glycosylation). We can arrive at a sequence function relationship for many protein sequences due to alignment to known sequence (with similar function by inference). We can thereby sidestep the classic structure-function paradigm. Getting structure is the gold-standard, however, for training information, for reference, and for model refinement, but involves methods that do not scale well, thus the significant benefit of sequence-function association without knowing the structure explicitly. For this reason there is little discussion of the protein structure-function paradigm in Ch 10, where proteins are discussed in more detail. When function is solely defined in terms of binding interactions, or where sequence-function association fails, structure determination can be avoided by using binding state function characterization using a nanopore detector (Ch 14), exploration of dynamic binding states is also possible. Clearly a lot can be accomplished with sequence alignments to the sequence information we already have, however, and that is the focus of the chapter.

6.1 Properties of notably similar sequences – no gaps
When comparing genomic sequence data notably similar sequences are found to be common, consistent with the evolutionary hypothesis of a common ancestor (if you just look back far enough). Also consistent is that the more distantly separated genomic sequence information corresponds to more distantly back in time to reach a common ancestor.

As sequencing of nucleic acids gets easier and cheaper the extent of databases containing genomic and transcriptomic information continues to grow. When you have new sequence data it's natural to ask if there is any notable similar sequence in the vast databases of sequences that are available. If you have a sequence that is 'notably similar', where it can't even remotely occur by chance, then there has to be an evolutionary or horizontal gene transfer connection. Suppose there is such a match, then the organism for which the match is made may be much better understood (it could be one of the 'model organisms'), and the function of the matching genomic element may be directly inferred.

About 50% of the genes can be found by identifying sections of un-annotated genomic sequence that are notably similar to known (function annotated) genomic sequence. Gene-finders can probably get 99% of the genes, but are significantly more complicated. So the powerful tool of being able to recognize when one sequence is notably similar to another sequence is paramount in bioinformatics, and to this end we now focus on the pairwise alignment comparison method described in what follows.

6.1.1 Pairwise Alignment Scoring

If two sequences are notably similar, then somewhere within these two sequences there must be a long stretch of matching residues. A long matching stretch is suggestive of a pairwise alignment scoring process, so we just need to mathematically formalize this to proceed:

Suppose our two sequences to compare are $X = $ "$x_1...x_n$" and $Y = $ "$y_1 ... y_m$", where $x_i \in \{a,c,g,t\}$ and $y_j \in \{a,c,g,t\}$. If the two sequences are unrelated, then the independent random model is best:

$$P(X,Y|\text{random}) = P(X|\text{random}) \, P(Y|\text{random})$$
$$= \prod_{i=1}^{n} P(x_i = x_i) \prod_{j=1}^{m} P(y_j = y_j)$$

If the two sequences are related, then the shorter sequence, X say, must have a maximal scoring 'alignment', with the Y overhangs considered independent factors (that divide out) in what follows:

$$P(X,Y|\text{match}) = \prod_{i=1}^{n} P(x_i = x_i; \, y_i = y_i)$$

The odds ratio, $P(X,Y|\text{match})/ P(X,Y|\text{random})$ is then used to identify the strength of the alignment.

6.1.2 The log odds ratio

The odds ratio is usually computed as the *log* odds ratio to avoid underflow, and to arrive at an additive scoring system:

$$\text{Log Odds Ratio} = \log\big(P(X, Y|\text{match})/ P(X, Y|\text{random})\big)$$
$$= \sum_{i=1}^{n} \log[P(x_i = x_i; \, y_i = y_i)/ P(x_i = x_i)P(y_i = y_i)]$$
$$= \sum_{i=1}^{n} s(x_i; y_i)$$

In this form we have the alignment score reduced to the sum of the pairwise residue alignment scores, or 'substitution' matrix in the evolutionary context.

Recall from Ch. 3 and App. C that this sum is a Martingale series, thus a stable convergence, and a limit exists given sufficient duration.

6.2 Nucleotide substitution rates

Consider the number of substitutions two sequences have had since they last referred to a common ancestor (and were the same sequence). Note: the estimation in this approach requires two sequences (typically from two different species) and the time since their divergence.

K = number of substitutions
T = divergence time

Since have T substitution time on two sequences, treat as 2T substitution time on one sequence (where the 'other' sequence is taken as unchanged, i.e., effectively referencing the ancestral sequence). The rate of substitution is then $r=K/(2T)$. The substitution analysis that follows assumes the number of substitutions is few enough that overlapping (repeated) substitutions are sufficiently rare to be left out of the analysis. (When this is not the case will be discussed in Sec. 6.2.5.)

Recall with ORFs we had lengthy anomalous stretches with no in-frame stop codons. Thus, substitutions must be strongly suppressed in these regions to avoid randomly generating an in-frame stop (which would eliminate the 'read out' of the remainder of the protein coding, creating a likely non-functional mutant protein). Thus, we expect the substitution rate on coding sequence to be notably less than the substitution rate on non-coding sequence.

In the analysis comparing two sequences it is convenient if they have the same length and are mostly similar. This level of conservation holds for certain protein families, such as the globins. In an instructional example presented in [221] beta-like globin genes are compared between a collection of mammals (human, mouse, rabbit, and cow sequence information from Genbank accession numbers V00497 and V00879, see Table 6.1):

Gene Region	Substitution Rate*
5' Flanking	3.39
5' UTR	1.86
Coding (all exons)	1.58
Intron1	3.48
3' UTR	3.00
3' Flanking	3.60

Table 6.1. Substitution rates according to gene region. *Substitution rate is in substitutions per site per billion years.

Clearly substitutions are suppressed in coding, but would have expected a greater difference. Consider, however, that the encoding has a degeneracy. Perhaps when there is truly only one encoding substitution is more significantly suppressed? Thus, looking into the different codon bases themselves, insofar as their substitution rates (given the degenerate mapping) results are shown in the next table (Table 6.2):

Coding Region	Substitution Rate*
Nondegenerate	0.56
Two-fold Degenerate	1.67
Four-fold Degenerate	2.35

Table 6.2. Positional substitution rates inside codon consistent with synonymous 'wobble' substitutions. The codon MI imprint and gIMM results (Ch. 2) similarly reveal the statistical footprint of weak third-base, 'wobble', linkage, indicating consistency between biochemical and statistical couplings. *Substitution rate is in substitutions per site per billion years.

Thus, substitutions that change coding information (in mammals) are suppressed sixfold over non-coding or non-regulatory regions for the globin family of proteins.

6.2.1 Types of substitution (single-point mutation)

The type of substitution involving a locus of a single nucleotide is the focus of this subsection. The types of such substitutions when made on nucleotide sequence with as protein coding role can be decomposed into synonymous vs. non-synonymous substitutions, where-synonymous changes at nucleotide level, but not at amino acid level, and non-synonymous change at nucleotide level effects change at amino acid level.

So far no mention has been made of substitution of something for nothing (a deletion) or the reverse (an addition). In transcriptionally active regionsd there is a very strong bias against insertions or deletions (indels) in the sequence due to the resulting frame shift – indels are approximately ten times less likely than substitutions. Although substitution in non-synonymous coding is almost a magnitude less frequent than in nearby non-coding "junk", substitutions in some parts of the coding region are even more reduced, sometimes greatly in areas of functionalization. Functional parts of a coding region (catalytic or structural) tend to allow significantly fewer substitutions (or none).

6.2.2 Gene duplication (multi-point mutations, the primary driver of evolution)

Gene duplication occurs primarily by:

(1) Homologous recombination
(2) Retrotransposons
(3) Chromosome duplication
(4) Genome duplication

In each of the above cases, the primary driver of the duplication process is due to transposons and viruses directly, or indiectrly. Viruses, in turn, are traceable to the early cell-virus world, even in its earliest RNA World form. Transposons (and Type I and II introns) may even go further, to the hypothesized 'Intron World' (Introns Earliest Hypothesis, Ch 5), to a distinct nucleic acid 'cook' made possible on Earth (the Rio Tinto Valley), or perhaps on a larger scale, via a slow 'cook' (500 million years) that simmered in pockets over the entire surface of the planet Mars and then had meteoric transfer (the Mars Transfer Hypothesis, see [1] and Ch. 5 for details).

Regarding whole multi-genome duplication, this is common in plants, not animals, beyond diploid form. At diploid form (duplicated) the genome is common with sexually reproducing organisms. Sexually reproducible species must have an even number of chromosomes for the division/recombination process to proceed. The familiar banana is not sexually reproducing, for example, having 33 copies of its ancestral genome, while the sexually reproducing banana species (plantain) has 22 copies of its ancestral genome. Wheat is hexaploidal, having six copies of its ancestral genome. Plants tend to evolve by gene duplication at the level of the chromosome or genome (cases 3 and 4), while animals tends to evolve by duplication at the single-gene level (cases 1 and 2). Trisomy 21 in humans is where three copies of chromosome 21 are retained instead of 2 (Down's Syndrome).

6.2.3 Retrogenes and Pseudogenes

If viral or transposon proteins mistakenly attach to cellular mRNA they can reverse transcribe copies of genes into the host organism's DNA, called 'retrogenes', that have no introns and a poly-A tail.

Transposons can be understood as a domesticated retrovirus insofar as function (and possibly in their derivation, for some). Transposons and viral co-evolution are the primary drivers of gene duplication (thus evolution) in animals. Gene duplication basically builds from what already 'works'.

Suppose you have a gene duplication and the gene copy has a mutation that disables it, such as an indel, or possibly a mutation in its critical promoter region. You then have what is known as a 'pseudogene'. Mutation rates in pseudogenes match that of the 'junk' DNA in the 3' flanking regions of genes.

We only see the 'winners'. We can easily compute the substitution rates on organisms that have passed the filter of natural selection. We can't easily compute the true mutation rate. Knowing the difference is knowing how functionally constrained a sequence is. Synonymous and pseudogene substitution rates are considered to provide good estimates to the true mutation rate (where natural selection is neutral).

6.2.4 Fixation of Alleles
Different versions of any gene within a species of organism are known as alleles. This includes not only differences in promoter and other regulatory regions, but differences seen in digestion products due to restriction endonuclease mapping.

Humans differ in about 1 base in every 200 bases. Suppose you have N reproductively active diploid organisms. A new allele appears with a frequency of $q=1/(2N)$, where we are assuming only a single copy of the gene (i.e., gene-copy complications are not considered in this analysis). The new allele frequency will either go back to zero, or grow towards 1 (the latter is referred to as 'fixation', where all members of the species would have the new allele). The mean time for fixation of a neutral allele is the time for *4N generations*. The probability for loss of a neutral allele is *1-q*.

6.2.5 Estimating Substitution Rates
If optimal alignment shows a low density of substitutions, then simple counts and a naïve model are okay. But if the density of substitutions indicates it's probable to have *overlapping* substitutions at any particular base, then we need a more sophisticated model. Note: multiple substitutions at a single base will only be seen as one substitution... if even that, e.g., the last in a multiple substitution could return the base to its original base, appearing as no substitution occurring at all.

Jules-Cantor (J-C) Substitution Model:
The assumption of the J-C model: all nucleotides change amongst themselves at the same rate (α). Suppose you have a 'C' at a particular base position at time '0':

At time '1' still have a C with probability: $P_C(1) = 1-3\alpha$; and $P_G(1) = \alpha = P_T(1) = P_A(1)$.

At time '2' still have a C with probability: $P_C(2) = (1-3\alpha)P_C(1) + \alpha(1- P_C(1))$.

Therefore, in general:

$$P_C(t) = \frac{1}{4} + \frac{3}{4} e^{-4\alpha t}.$$

If 'p' is the substitution fraction, '(1-p)' is the probability to stay the same, and the 'actual' number of substitutions, k, at a site is k=3αt, thus:

$$(1-p) = \tfrac{1}{4} + \tfrac{3}{4}\, e^{-4/3\,(3\alpha t)}$$

which can be rewritten as: $k = -3/4 \ln(1 - 4/3\, p)$.

Kimura Substitution Model:

Recall that purines, guanine and adenine, have two rings while pyrimidines, cytosine and thymine, have one ring. It is found, not surprisingly, that substituting one purine for another is easier than a purine for a pyrimidine. So introducing two substitution parameters to differentiate these two types of substitution we have the transition substitution rate (α) *within* purine or pyrimidine groups; and the transversion substitution (β) *between* purine and pyrimidine groups, where transitions are roughly three times more frequent than transversions. If we solve similarly as before, and eventually express in terms of k, the actual substitution fraction: $k = \tfrac{1}{2} \ln(1/[1-2P-Q]) + \tfrac{1}{4} \ln(1/[1-2Q])$, where, P = transition fraction; and Q = transversion fraction.

Histones have lots of specific binding, and have very slow evolutionary substitution rate, so can be used as basis for molecular clock. Apolipoproteins have a high rate of substitutions – any hydrophobic substitution will do. Human mitochondrial DNA (mtDNA) mutates 10-times faster than nuclear DNA (due to oxygen free radicals in the cell's 'powerhouse'), so mtDNA can be used as a clock when studying closely related populations (less than 10M years since divergence).

BLOSUM Matrix:

A widely used substitution scoring is the BLOSUM substitution matrix [223] that is based on the BLOCKS database [222]. The BLOCKS database is a set of aligned, ungapped, regions of proteins. Sequences within the database were grouped according to percentage, L%, of exact matching, to arrive at blocks or clusters of the sequences. The frequency of seeing residue a in one cluster and b in another is then calculated as A_{ab}. Do this for all elements of each cluster against the other, and weight by $1/(n_1 n_2)$, where n_1 and n_2 are the cluster sizes. Then estimate $p_{ab} = A_{ab}/\sum_{cd} A_{cd}$ (the MLE), and it then follows that $p_a = \sum_b A_{ab}/\sum_{cd} A_{cd}$ as well, from which $s(a,b) = \log(p_{ab}/(p_a p_b))$.

BLOSUM62 and BLOSUM50:

For L=62 (62% matching to be in same group), the 'BLOSUM62' substitution table generated from the BLOCKS database has values are scaled to be in half-bits, i.e., multiplied by 2/log2 (see Table 6.3), while the BLOSUM50 matrix is scaled to be in third-bits (shown in Problems).

Blosum62 Matrix

	A	C	D	E	F	G	H	I	K	L	M	N	P	Q	R	S	T	V	W	Y
A	4																			
C	0	9																		
D	-2	-3	6																	
E	-1	-4	2	5																
F	-2	-2	-3	-3	6															
G	0	-3	-1	-2	-3	6														
H	-2	-3	1	0	-1	-2	8													
I	-1	-1	-3	-3	0	-4	-3	4												
K	-1	-3	-1	1	-3	-2	-1	-3	5											
L	-1	-1	-4	-3	0	-4	-3	2	-2	4										
M	-1	-1	-3	-2	0	-3	-2	1	-1	2	5									
N	-2	-3	1	0	-3	0	-1	-3	0	-3	-2	6								
P	-1	-3	-1	-1	-4	-2	-2	-3	-1	-3	-2	-1	7							
Q	-1	-3	0	2	-3	-2	0	-3	1	-2	0	0	-1	5						
R	-1	-3	-2	0	-3	-2	0	-3	2	-2	-1	0	-2	1	5					
S	1	-1	0	0	-2	0	-1	-2	0	-2	-1	1	-1	0	-1	4				
T	-1	-1	1	0	-2	1	0	-2	0	-2	-1	0	1	0	-1	1	4			
V	0	-1	-3	-2	-1	-3	-3	3	-2	1	1	-3	-2	-2	-3	-2	-2	4		
W	-3	-2	-4	-3	1	-2	-2	-3	-3	-2	-1	-4	-4	-2	-3	-3	-3	-3	11	
Y	-2	-2	-3	-2	3	-3	2	-1	-2	-1	-1	-2	-3	-1	-2	-2	-2	-1	2	7

Table 6.3. The Blosum62 substitution matrix.

6.3 Properties of notably similar sequences – with gaps

If gaps are allowed, then significantly better alignments can be obtained, but gaps must be associated with a penalty factor (or the alignment will simply be 100% gap). There are two main types of gap scoring, the linear penalty gap, with score $\gamma(g)=-gd$; or the affine penalty gap, with score $\gamma(g) = -d-(g-1)e$, where d is the gap-open penalty and e is the gap-extension penalty. Akin to static friction and rolling friction, the gap-extension penalty is typically less than the gap-open penalty.

In the probabilistic model, a gap of length g has probability f(g), and a gap aligns to a sub-sequence that is assumed to be independent and random in the gap region, such that its odds ratio contribution with the random alignment is cancelled and all that remains is the log of f(g) to add in when working in the log odds computation, where $\gamma(g)=\log(f(g))$, where the gap penalty scoring methods above both correspond to an assumption of a geometric distribution on gap lengths.

Once gaps are allowed, even if both sequences have the same length n, we must contend with a combinatorial explosion in the possible global alignments of the two sequences:

$$\binom{2n}{n} = \frac{(2n)!}{(n!)^2} \cong \frac{2^{2n}}{\sqrt{\pi n}},$$

which is a lot to handle, so we need a better plan, such as 'dynamic programming', which involves recording prior calculations in a table for reuse (note: there's no 'dynamic' or 'programming' in 'dynamic programming').

The exponential combinatorial explosion in the possible global alignments of two sequences of length n when allowing for gaps is simplified to a quadratic growth in calculations in the dynamic programming context, and thus made solvable. The idea is simply that sub-alignments are often shared and need only be computed once if a tabular bookkeeping is maintained on calculations already performed.

6.3.1 Needleman-Wunsch (global alignment)

In the Needleman-Wunsch alignment algorithm the idea is to construct an optimal alignment between sequences recursively by using optimal alignments between subsequences of those sequences. Let $F(i,j)$ be the score of the best alignment between initial segment $x_1, ..., x_i$ and initial segment $y_1, ..., y_j$. Then given $s(i,j) \equiv s(x_i, y_j)$ and a gap penalty $-d$, we can express the value for $F(i,j)$ recursively (see Fig. 6.1 below):

$$F(i,j) = max \begin{cases} F(i-1, j-1) + s(i,j) \\ F(i-1, j) - d \\ F(i, j-1) - d \end{cases}$$

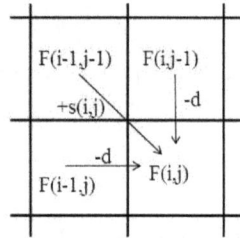

Fig. 6.1. Recursive relation for global alignment, where $F(0.0)=0$ to properly initialize. Starting from $(0,0)$ filling the table this is shown for our test alignment.

Let's align ACDEFGHYWVTSRQ and EGHGWGGRQ, with gap penalty -4 using the recursive rule shown in Table 6.4. First, let's create a Blosum62 look-up intermediate table (for convenient reference):

-	-	A	C	D	E	F	G	H	Y	W	V	T	S	R	Q
-															
E		-1	-4	2	5	-3	-2	0	-2	-3	-2	0	0	0	2
G		0	-3	-1	-2	-3	6	-2	-3	-2	-3	1	0	-2	-2
H		-2	-3	1	0	-1	-2	8	2	-2	-3	0	-1	0	0
G															
W		-3	-2	-4	-3	1	-2	-2	2	11	-3	-3	-3	-3	-2
G															
G															
R		-1	-3	-2	0	-3	-2	0	-2	-3	-3	-1	-1	5	1
Q		-1	-3	0	2	-3	-2	0	-1	-2	-2	0	0	1	5

Table 6.4. Blosum62 look-up intermediate table.

If doing global alignment (Needleman Wunsch), the idea is to construct an optimal alignment between sequences recursively by using optimal alignments between subsequences of those sequences. Let $F(i,j)$ be the score of the best alignment between initial segment x_1, ..., x_i and initial segment y_1, ..., y_j. Then given $s(i,j) \equiv s(x_i, y_j)$ and a gap penalty $-d$, we can express the value for $F(i,j)$ recursively, as shown in Fig. 6.2, where $F(0.0)=0$ is used to properly initialize. Starting from $(0,0)$ and filling the table recursively this is shown in Table 6.5.

The alignment solution is obtained from completing a table construction, recursively, as indicated, but also recording "where" each max "came from", so not just the recursively computed value is needed, but a traceback for an optimal alignment is needed at the end). The optimal global alignment is then given by tracing back from the lower right cell in the table (d: diagonal; v: vertical; h: horizontal; x=d/v; y=d/h):

-	-	A	C	D	E	F	G	H	Y	W	V	T	S	R	Q
-	0	-4,h	-8,h	-12,h	-16,h	-20,h	-24,h	-28,h	-32,h	-36,h	-40,h	-44,h	-48,h	-52,h	-56,h
E	-4,v	-1,d	-5,h	-6,d	-7,d	-11,h	-15,h	-19,h	-23,h	-27,h	-31,h	-35,h	-39,h	-43,h	-47,h
G	-8,v	-4,d	-4,d	-6,d	-8,d	-10,d	-5,d	-9,h	-13,h	-17,h	-21,h	-25,h	-29,h	-33,h	-37,h
H	-12,v	-8,v	-7,d	-3,d	-6,d	-9,d	-9,v	3,d	-1,h	-5,h	-9,h	-13,h	-17,h	-21,h	-25,h
G	-16,v	-12,x	-11,x	-7,v	-5,d	-9,v	-3,d	-1,v	0,d	-3,d	-7,h	-8,d	-12,h	-16,h	-20,h
W	-20,v	-12,v	-14,d	-11,v	-9,v	-4,d	-7,v	-5,x	1,d	11,d	7,h	3,h	-1,h	-5,h	-9,h
G	-24,v	-16,v	-15,d	-15,x	-13,x	-8,v	2,d	-2,h	-3,v	7,v	8,d	8,d	4,h	0,h	-4,h
G	-28,v	-20,v	-19,x	-16,d	-17,x	-12,v	-2,x	0,d	-4,h	3,v	4,x	9,d	8,d	4,h	0,h
R	-32,v	-24,v	-23,x	-20,v	-16,d	-16,v	-6,v	-2,d	-2,d	-1,v	0,x	5,v	8,d	13,d	9,h
Q	-36,v	-28,v	-27,x	-23,d	-18,d	-19,d	-10,v	-6,x	-3,d	-4,d	-3,d	1,v	5,d	9,x	18,d

Table 6.5. Needleman Wunsch global alignment table. The alignment solution is obtained from tracing back from the lower right cell in the table: d,d,d,d,h,d,d,d,d,h,d,h,h,h; which leads to the alignment of
`ACDEFGHYWVTSRQ` to `---E-GHGW-GGRQ`.

Starting from lower right cell, the reverse trace is: d,d,d,d,h,d,d,d,d,h,d,h,h,h:
```
ACDEFGHYWVTSRQ
---E-GHGW-GGRQ
```

6.3.2 Smith-Waterman (local alignment)

If doing local alignment (Smith Waterman): (d: diagonal; v: vertical; h: horizontal; x=d/v; y=d/h), the idea is to construct an optimal alignment between *sub*-sequences of X and Y (see Fig. 6.2 below):

$$F(i,j) = max \begin{cases} 0 \\ F(i-1, j-1) + s(i,j) \\ F(i-1, j) - d \\ F(i, j-1) - d \end{cases}$$

Fig. 6.2. Smith Waterman recursive local alignment rule, where $F(0.0)=0$ to initialize, and due to the negative gap-penalty, often take zero value in recursive computations.

Going from a nonzero score to zero in Table 6.6 corresponds to starting a new alignment. Now view table differently, want to start at highest value and end wherever it traces back:

-	-	A	C	D	E	F	G	H	Y	W	V	T	S	R	Q
-	0	0	0	0	0	0	0	0	0	0	0	0	0	0	0
E	0	0	0	2,d	5,d	1,h	0	0	0	0	0	0	0	0	2,d
G	0	0	0	0	1,v	2,d	7,d	3,h	0	0	0	1,d	0	0	0
H	0	0	0	1,d	0	0	3,v	15,d	11,h	7,h	3,h	0	0	0	0
G	0	0	0	0	0	0	6,d	11,v	12,d	9,d	5,h	4,d	0	0	0
W	0	0	0	0	0	1,d	2,v	7,v	13,d	23,d	19,h	15,h	11,h	7,h	3,h
G	0	0	0	0	0	0	7,d	3,v	9,v	19,v	20,d	20,d	16,h	12,h	8,h
G	0	0	0	0	0	0	6,d	5,d	5,v	15,v	16,x	21,d	20,d	16,h	12,h
R	0	0	0	0	0	0	2,v	6,d	3,d	11,v	12,x	17,v	20,d	25,d	21,h
Q	0	0	0	0	2,d	0	0	2,x	5,d	7,v	9,d	13,v	17,d	21,x	30,d

Table 6.6. Smith Waterman recursive local alignment table for the sequences shown.

Starting from the max value=30, which happens to be in the lower right cell, the reverse trace to 0 is: d,d,d,d,h,d,d,d,d,h,d:

```
ACDEFGHYWVTSRQ
  E-GHGW-GGRQ
```

If 'RQ' is removed from the ends of both sequences, the local alignment is indicated by the max value=23, with traceback beginning with the W alignment:

```
ACDEFGHYWVTS
  E-GHGW
```

Let's switch now to doing alignments on nucleic acid sequences, where a simpler set of substitution rules can be used. Let's do a a nucleic acid alignment where match has score 2, mismatch score 1, and gap penalty = -2, and try aligning 'gattaca' with 'gatcatttatacaa' (see Table 6.7 below):

-	-	g	a	t	c	a	t	t	t	a	t	a	c	a	a
-	0	-2	-4	-6	-8	-10	-12	-14	-16	-18	-20	-22	-24	-26	-28
g	-2	2,d	0,h	-2,h	-4,h	-6,h	-8,h	-10,h	-12,h	-14,h	-16,h	-18,h	-20,h	-22,h	-24,h
a	-4	-1,d	4,d	2,h	0,h	-2,y	-4,h	-6,h	-8,h	-10,y	-12,h	-14,y	-16,h	-18,y	-20,y
t	-6	-3,x	2,v	6,d	4,h	2,h	0,y	-2,y	-4,y	-6,h	-8,h	-10,h	-12,h	-14,h	-16,h
t	-8	-5,x	0,v	4,x	7,d	5,y	4,d	2,y	0,y	-2,h	-4,y	-6,h	-8,h	-10,h	-12,h
a	-10	-7,x	-2,v	2,v	5,v	9,d	7,h	6,d	4,h	2,y	0,h	-2,y	-4,h	-6,y	-8,y
c	-12	-9,x	-4,v	0,v	4,d	7,v	10,d	8,d	7,d	5,y	3,y	1,y	0,d	-2,h	-4,h
a	-14	-11,x	-6,v	-2,v	2,v	5,x	8,x	11,d	9,y	9,d	7,h	5,y	3,h	2,d	0,y

Table 6.7. Alignments on nucleic acid sequences *globally*. A match has score 2, mismatch score 1, and gap penalty = -2; 'h' denotes 'max' came horizontally, 'v' for vertically, 'd' from diagonally, and y = h or d.

Align #1, choose all y=d:
Traceback = d,h,d,d,d,h,d,h,h,d,h,h,h,d:

124

```
gatcatttatacaa
g---a--t-tac-a
```

Align #2, choose all y=h:
Traceback = hddhhhhddhhddd:
```
gatcatttatacaa
gat--ta----ca-
```

Note: Sometimes ties can occur and it isn't revealed by 'y' or 'x' in the traceback.

Now redo for local alignment (see Table 6.8 that follows):

-	-	g	a	t	c	a	t	t	t	a	t	a	c	a	a
-	0	0	0	0	0	0	0	0	0	0	0	0	0	0	0
g	0	2,d	1,d	1,d	1,d	1,d	1,d	1,d	1,d	1,d	1,d	1,d	1,d	1,d	1,d
a	0	1,d	4,d	2,y	2,d	3,d	2,d	2,d	2,d	3,d	2,d	3,d	2,d	3,d	3,d
t	0	1,d	2,x	6,d	4,h	3,d	5,d	4,d	4,d	3,d	5,d	3,y	4,d	3,d	4,d
t	0	1,d	2,d	4,d	7,d	5,y	5,d	7,d	6,d	5,d	5,d	6,d	4,y	5,d	4,d
a	0	1,d	3,d	3,d	5,x	9,d	7,h	6,d	8,d	8,d	6,y	7,d	7,d	6,d	7,d
c	0	1,d	2,d	4,d	5,d	7,v	10,d	8,y	7,d	9,d	9,d	7,y	9,d	8,d	7,d
a	0	1,d	3,d	3,d	5,d	7,d	8,x	11,d	9,y	9,d	10,d	11,d	9,h	11,d	10,d

Table 6.8. Alignments on nucleic acid sequences *locally*. A match has score 2, mismatch score 1, and gap penalty = -2; 'h' denotes 'max' came horizontally, 'v' for vertically, 'd' from diagonally, and y = h or d.

High value is 11 with three cases (and no x/y bifurcating subcases):
Case #1:
```
gatcatttatacaa
gattaca
```

Case #2:
```
gatcatttatacaa
    gattaca
```

Case #3:
```
gatcatttatacaa
      gattaca
```
For further elaboration, see problems in Exercises Section 6.5.

6.3.3 BLAST

The Smith-Waterman algorithm is an algorithm for finding optimal local alignments, precisely what is needed if comparing a sequence to a known set of sequences to try to find out what it is: $F(i,j)=\max\{0; F(i-1,j-1)+s(i,j); F(i-1,j)-d; F(I,j-1)-d\}$ → solve over matrix, then start at cell with highest $F(i,j)$ and start traceback from there, ends when a value of zero obtained. For $s(i,j)$ use blossum62 or other substitution tables.

BLAST (Basic Local Alignment Search Tool) [82] makes a list of k-mers, k-length subsequences (3 for protein sequences; 11 for nucleic acids sequences) in its search database, along with their index positions, and begins alignments searches with this information at hand. Once a hit occurs, it is used to seed a Smith-Waterman 'hit extension' process. BLOSUM62 is a commonly used scoring-matrix. BLAT (Basic Like Alignment Tool) relies on k-mer database indexing to generate seeds, for a fasterer version of BLAST. The Smith-Waterman algorithm can be re-expressed as a form of HMM Viterbi algorithm on a pair-HMM [81]. Thus the HMM implementations, and speed-up capabilities, described in Ch. 3 are applicable here as a form of Smith-Waterman. The BLAST algorithm is less accurate than the pure Smith-Waterman, but is approximately 50 times faster. Smith-Waterman still necessary for remote homology. Have FPGA and SMID speedup. May have fast Smith-Waterman via dual HMM formulation with O(TN) speed-up optimization [224]. In Ch 13 we shall see that BLAST is signal processing chain of the form:

[Raw data] → FSA → HMM → [identified alignments],

where an initial FSA stage is first used to identify signal regions of interest (or alignment prospects of interest in case of BLAST). Then have a process to provide the optimal alignment, or parsing of the signal in general setting, by use of Hidden Markov Models (HMMs). (The Smith-Waterman algorithm can be re-expressed in terms of the Viterbi algorithm in the HMM setting.) This signal analysis paradigm is used for both alignments (BLAST) and gene structure identification (the meta-HMM gene finder). In Ch 14 we shall make use of a similar signal analysis paradigm in the initial parts:

[Raw data] → FSA → HMM → SVM [streaming signal classification],

where an initial FSA stage is first used to identify signal regions of interest, the HMM is now for (optimal) feature extraction only. Now have SVM stage to classify the signals acquired by the FSA according to the HMM features. This paradigm occurs for power signal analysis, such as for channel currents.

6.4 Exercises

(Ex. 6.1) Amino Acids (AAs) fall into groups according to hydrophobic or charged, etc.Taking three representatives from each grou, rget the substitution within group and without and determine their average substitution score. Note: The alignments within the charged or hydrophobic groups are positive, indicating such substitutions are commonly allowed. The alignments between these groups are, on average, significantly negative, indicating such substitutions are very rare, probably due to the altered biochemical functionality that is indicated by such changes (and how this might be highly selected against for survival if a critical protein).

(Ex. 6.2) Do a global alignment of HEAGAWGHEE and PAWHEAE using the Blosum62 table.

(Ex. 6.3) Do a local alignment of HEAGAWGHEE and PAWHEAE using the Blosum62 table.

(Ex. 6.4) Do a global alignment of ACAGTCGTTCG and ACCGTCCG, where match score is +1, mismatch score = 0; and gap penalty = -1.

(Ex. 6.5) Do a local alignment of ACAGTCGTTCG and ACAGTCCG, where match score is +1, mismatch score = 0; and gap penalty = -1.

Chapter 7
Analysis of sequential data using HMMs

Generalized Hidden Markov model (HMM) methods are described for both signal feature extraction and structure identification. The generalized HMMs described also enable a new form of carrier-based communication, where the carrier is stationary but not periodic (further details in Ch. 13). HMM-with-binned-duration, and meta-HMM generalizations, shown in what follows, enable practical stochastic carrier wave encoding/decoding, where the generalized HMM methods have generalized Viterbi algorithms with all of the inherent benefits of an efficient dynamic programming implementation, as well as Martingale convergence properties when used for filtering and robust feature extraction.

7.1 Hidden Markov Models (HMMs)
7.1.1 Background and Role in Stochastic Sequential Analysis (SSA)
Hidden Markov models have been used in speech recognition since the 1970s [83], and in bioinformatics since the 1990's [89], and have an extensive, and growing, breadth of applications in other areas (especially as more computational resources become available). Other areas of HMM application include gesture recognition [101-103], handwriting and text recognition [104-106], image processing [106-108], computer vision [109], communication [110], climatology [111], and acoustics [112,113]. An HMM is the central method in all of these approaches because it is the simplest, most efficient, modeling approach that is obtained when you combine a Bayesian statistical foundation for Markovian stochastic sequential analysis [58] with the efficient dynamic programming table constructions possible on a computer.

In automated gene finding there are two types of approaches, based on data intrinsic to the genome under study [84], or extrinsic to the genome (e.g., homology, and EST data). Since c.a. 2000 the best gene finders have been based on combined intrinsic/extrinsic statistical modeling [85], [86-88]. The most common intrinsic statistical model is an HMM, so the question naturally arises -- how to optimally incorporate extrinsic side-information into an

HMM? We resolve that question in Sec 7.4 by treating duration distribution information *itself* as side-information and demonstrate a process for incorporating that side-information into an HMM. We thereby bootstrap from an HMM formalism to a HMM-with-duration formulation (more generally, a hidden semi-Markov model or HSMM).

In many applications, the ability to incorporate the state duration into the HMM is very important because the standard, HMM-based, Viterbi and Baum-Welch algorithms are otherwise critically constrained in their modeling ability to distributions on state intervals that are geometric (see Sec. 7.4 for derivation of this restrictive property). This can lead to a significant decoding failure in noisy environments when the state-interval distributions are not geometric (or approximately geometric). The starkest contrast occurs for multimodal distributions and heavy-tailed distributions. The hidden Markov model with binned duration (HMMBD) algorithm, presented in Sec. 7.4 and [21], eliminates the HMM geometric distribution constraint, as well as the HMMD maximum duration constraint, and offers a significant reduction in computational time for all HMMD-based methods to approximately the computational time of the HMM-process alone. In adopting any model with 'more parameters', such as an HMMD over an HMM, there is potentially a problem with having sufficient data to support the additional modeling. This is generally not a problem in any HMM model that requires thousands of samples of non-self transitions for sensor modeling, such as for the gene-finding that is described in what follows, since knowing the boundary positions allows the regions of self-transitions (the durations) to be extracted with similar sample number as well, which is typically sufficient for effective modeling of the duration distributions in a HMMD.

Critical improvement to overall HMM application rests not only with the aforementioned generalizations to the HMM/HMMD, but also with generalizations to the hidden state model and emission model. This is because standard HMMs are at low Markov order in transitions (first) and in emissions (zeroth), and transitions are decoupled from emissions (which can miss critical structure in the model, such as state transition probabilities that are sequence dependent). This weakness is eliminated if we generalize to the largest state-emission clique possible, fully interpolated on the data set, as is done with the generalized-clique hidden Markov model (HMM) described in Sec. 7.4 and in [18], where gene finding is performed on the *C. elegans* genome. The objective with the clique generalization is to improve the modeling of the critical signal information at the transitions between exon regions and noncoding regions, e.g., intron and junk regions. In doing this we arrive at a HMM structure identification platform that is novel, and robustly-performing, in a number of ways.

The generalized clique HMM ("meta-HMM") application to gene-finding begins by enlarging the primitive hidden states associated with the individual base labels (as exon, intron, or junk) to substrings of primitive hidden states or *footprint* states. The emissions are likewise expanded to higher order in the fundamental joint probability that is the basis of the generalized-clique, or 'meta-State', HMM. In [18] we show how a meta-state HMM significantly improves the strength of coding/noncoding-transition contributions to gene-structure identification when compared to similar, intrinsic-statistics-only, geometric models (some results shown in Ch. 8). We describe situations where the coding/noncoding -transition modeling can effectively 'recapture' the exon and intron heavy tail distribution modeling capability as well as manage the exon-start 'needle-in-the-haystack' problem. In analysis of the *C. elegans* genome, the sensitivity and specificity (SN,SP) results for both the individual-state and full-exon predictions are greatly enhanced over the standard HMM when using the generalized-clique HMM [18]. These meta-HMMBD developments provide a foundation from which to explore a core new paradigm, the holographic HMM, where generalization to multiple labels are possible at each emission. Holographic HMMs are explored theoretically and in implementations, such as alternative-splice gene finding (as described in what follows).

The improved signal resolution possible via a meta-HMMBD signal processing method will allow for reduced signal processing overhead, thereby reducing power usage. This directly impacts satellite communications where a minimal power footprint is critical, and cell phone construction, where a low-power footprint allows for smaller cell phones, or cell phones with smaller battery requirements, or cell phones with less expensive power system methodologies. For real-time signal processing, meta-HMMBD signal processing permits much more accurate signal resolution and signal de-noising than current, HMM-based, methods. This impacts real-time operational systems such as voice recognition hardware implementations, over-the-horizon radar detection systems, sonar detection systems, and receiver systems for streaming low-power digitial signal broadcasts (such an enhancement could improve receiver capabilities on various high-definition radio and TV broadcasts). For batch (off-line) signal resolution, the meta-HMMBD signal processing allows for significantly improved gene-structure resolution in genomic data, and extraction of binding/conformational kinetic feature data from nanopore detector channel current data. For scientific and engineering endeavors in general, where there is any data analysis that can be related to a sequence of measurements or observations, the meta-HMMBD signal processing systems that can be implemented permit improved signal resolution and speed of signal processing.

In a 'holographic' HMM we extend to a multi-track label-sequence (e.g., a multi-state labeling framework at each observation instance). The simplest example of this is to have two label sequnces for one observation sequence, and this is the implementation used in the alternative-splice gene-finding in the *C. elegans* genome effort described in Ch. 9 and [12], where it is shown that there is sufficient statistical support for a two-track label model.

In instances of 2-D and higher order dimensional data, such as 2-D images, the data can be reduced to a single-track sequence of measurements via a rastering process, as has been done with HMM methods in the past, *or* the reduction from the rastering could be to a multi-track hidden-label state to better track the local 2-D information, e.g., a 3x3 window with hidden states corresponding to the different 3x3 windows that can be seen, etc., in a self-consistent tiling (the center of the 3x3 grid could be the the former, single sample, datum used in the 1-D reduced rasterization, for example). This can be extended for larger 2-D 'windows', or n-D neighborhoods (the latter reducible to a 2-D representation in an extension of the holographic hypothesis [225,226]). (Another area impacted by the multi-track HMM method is protein folding and conformational analysis. This is because now contemporanious information can be absorbed into the multi-track HMM. This is an extensive application area in its own right.)

All of the HMM generalizations and feature extraction methods discussed in what follows can be optimized for speed with binned durations and through dynamic ("null") binning, distributed table-chunking, and GPU-usage. This allows the limiting speed constraint on the core HMMBD component in the Stochastic Sequential Analysis (SSA) protocol (Fig. 7.1) to be controlled as much as possible. The SSA protocol outlined in what follows is for the discovery, characterization, and classification of localizable, approximately-stationary, statistical signal structures in channel current data, or genomic data, or stochastic sequential data in general, and changes between such structures.

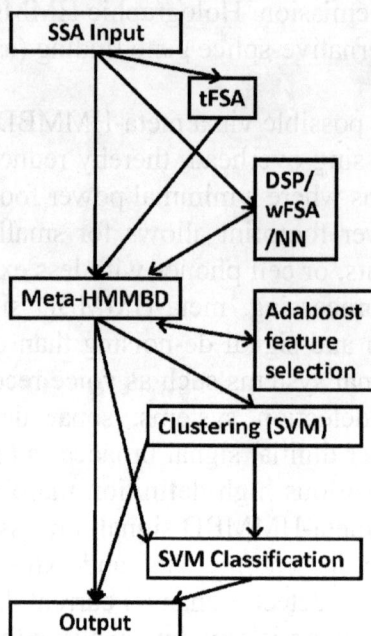

Fig. 7.1. The most common stochastic sequential analysis flow topology. The main signal processing flow is typically Input → tFSA→ Meta-HMMBD → SVM → Output. Notable differences occur in channel current cheminformatics (CCC) where there is use of EVA-projection, or similar method, to achieve a quantization on states, then have Input → tFSA → HMM/EVA → meta-HMMBD-side → SVM → Output. While, in gene-finding just have: Input → meta-HMMBD-side → Output. In gene-finding, however, the HMM internal 'sensors' are sometimes replaced, locally, with profile-HMMs [1] or SVM-based profiling [26], so topology can differ not only in the connections between the boxes shown, but in their ability to embed in other boxes as part of an internal refinement.

The core signal processing stage in Fig. 7.1 is usually the feature extraction and feature selection stage, where central to the signal processing protocol is the Hidden Markov model (HMM). The HMM methods are the central methodology/stage in the CCC protocol in that the other stages can be dropped or merged with the HMM stage in many incarnations. For example, in some data analysis situations the tFSA methods could be totally eliminated in favor of the more accurate HMM-based approach to the problem, with signal states defined/explored in much the same setting, but with the optimized Viterbi path solution taken as the basis for the signal acquisition structure identification. The reason this is not typically done is that the FSA methods are usually only $O(T)$ computational expense, where 'T' is the length of the stochastic sequential data that is to be examined, and '$O(T)$' denotes an order of computation that scales as 'T' (linearly in the length of the sequence). The typical HMM Viterbi algorithm, on the other hand, is $O(TN^2)$, where 'N' is the number of states in the HMM. So, use of the tFSA provides a faster, and often more flexible, means to acquire signal, but it is more hands-on. If the core HMM/Viterbi method can be approximated such that it can run at $O(TN)$ or even $O(T)$ in certain data regimes, for example, then the non-HMM methods can be phased out.

The HMM emission probabilities, transition probabilities, and Viterbi path sampled features, among other things, provide a rich set of data to draw from for feature extraction (to create 'feature vectors'). The choice of features in the SSA Protocol is optimized along with the classification or clustering method that will make use of that feature information. In typical operation of the protocol in Ch. 13, the feature vector information is classified using a Support Vector Machine (SVM) [224,227-230]. Once again, however, the separate classification step could be totally eliminated in favor of the HMM's log likelihood ratio classification capability, for example, when a number of template HMMs are employed (one for each signal class). This classification approach is weaker and slower than the (off-line trained) SVM methodology in many respects, but, depending on the data, there are circumstances where it may provide the best performing implementation of the protocol.

The HMM features, and other features (from neural net, wavelet, or spike profiling, etc.) can be fused and selected via use of various data fusion methods, such as a modified Adaboost selection (from [1,38,131], and described in what follows). The HMM-based feature extraction provides a well-focused set of 'eyes' on the data, no matter what its nature, according to the underpinnings of its Bayesian statistical representation. The key is that the HMM not be too limiting in its state definition, while there is the typical engineering trade-off on the choice of number of states, N, which impacts the order of computation via a quadratic factor of N in the various dynamic programming calculations used (comprising the Viterbi and Baum-Welch algorithms among others).

The HMM 'sensor' capabilities can be significantly improved via switching from profile-HMM sensors to pMM/SVM-based sensors, as indicated in [26], where the superior performance and generalization capability of this approach was demonstrated. A martingale feature vector is described in this context in [224,227-230].

Preliminary work with HMMD binning [21], clique-generalized HMMs [18], and HMMs with side information [19], lays the foundation for an intrinsic-statistics optimized HMM and shows how to optimally incorporate extrinsic side-information (if available). This is described in what follows and may provide a transformative platform for gene-structure identification. The methods described will also show how to collect data for the statistics to validate the strength of a multi-track state labeling statistical model. An analysis of the *C. elegans* genome's alternative-splice state-space complexity shows that a two-track alt.-splice modeling is possible. If successful with high accuracy, alternatively-spliced regions could be analyzed with much greater automation, possibly leading to further breakthroughs as new tracts of genomic data are then understood. The HMM speed optimizations could have a profound effect on HMM real-time applications, as well, although such optimizations may have data-dependent complexity, and this is one of the matters that will be explored. In what follows we describe how to 'upgrade' from a pMM sensor to a pMM/SVM sensor. This could significantly boost standard HMM performance, especially when used to lift the general log-liklihood ratio (LLR) terms that arise in the meta-HMM Viterbi-type algorithm into an SVM classifier.

7.1.1 When to use a Hidden Markov Model (HMM)?

Suppose you have a sequence of observations (or measurements, or samplings, etc.) and take '$b_1 b_2 \ldots b_L$' to denote an observation sequence of length L. Introduce as Bayesian parameter a hidden label associated with each observation, denote the label sequence as '$\lambda_1 \lambda_2 \ldots \lambda_L$'. The joint probability of the observations and a particular label-sequence is given via:

$$P(B;\Lambda) = P(b_1 \, b_2 \, \dots \, b_L; \lambda_1\lambda_2 \dots \lambda_L) = P(b_1 \, b_2 \, \dots \, b_L | \, \lambda_1\lambda_2 \dots \lambda_L) \, P(\lambda_1\lambda_2 \dots \lambda_L).$$

Markov assumptions for a standard 1st-order hidden Markov model then allow reduction to:

$$P(B;\Lambda;1^{st}\text{-order HMM}) = [P(b_1| \, \lambda_1) \, \dots \, P(b_L| \, \lambda_L)] \, [P(\lambda_1) \, P(\lambda_2| \, \lambda_1) \, \dots P(\lambda_L| \, \lambda_{L-1})]$$

If there are 50 labels and 50 observations (as in the quantized power signal analysis considered in that follows), then the full joint probability has $(50)^{2L}$ possibilities for labeled observation sequence of length L, which is unmanagable for typical sequences of interest, while, after reduction to the 1st-order HMM Markov assumptions on the conditional probabilities we have a set of $2 \times (50)^2$ possibilities (independent of sequence length). If n^{th}-order Markov models are employed, the set of possibilities grows as $(50)^{n+1}$, which can be easily enumerated for n up to 3 or 4, and still be accessed via hash-indexing for n>4 (as in the hIMM approach described in [39]).

In the Viterbi algorithm we seek the λ-sequence that maximizes the joint probability above for given observation sequence. In order to consider all of the possible λ-sequences in some direct enumeration for the above N-label case, we would have $(N)^L$ possible L length λ-sequences. Here we employ the classic dynamic programming solution employed by Viterbi instead, to perform a HMM Viterbi table calculation that retains information such that $O(LN^2)$ computations are needed to consider all paths.

Hidden Markov models (HMMs) are, thus, an amazing tool at the nexus where Bayesian probability and Markov models meet dynamic programming. To properly define/choose the HMM model in a machine learning context, however, further generalization is usually required. This is because the 'bare-bones' HMM description has critical weaknesses in most applications, which are summarized below. Fortunately, these weaknesses can be addressed, and in computationally efficient ways, as will be described in what follows.

7.1.2 Hidden Markov Models (HMMs) – standard formulation and terms

We define the 1st order HMM as consisting of the following:

- A hidden state alphabet, Λ, with "Prior" Probabilities $P(\lambda)$ for all $\lambda \in \Lambda$, and "Transition" Probabilities $P(\lambda_2|\lambda_1)$ for all $\lambda_1 \, \lambda_2 \in \Lambda$ -- where the standard transition probability is denoted $a_{kl} = P(\lambda_n=l|\lambda_{n-1}=k)$ for a 1st order Markov model on states with homogenous stationary statistics (i.e., no dependence on position 'n').

- An observable alphabet, B, with "Emission" Probabilities $P(b|\lambda)$ for all $\lambda \in \Lambda$ $b \in B$ – where the standard emission probability is $e_k(b) = P(b_n=b|\lambda_n=k)$, i.e., a 0th order Markov model on bases with homogenous stationary statistics.

There are three classes of problems that the HMM can be used to solve [81,83]:

(1) Evaluation - Determine the probability of occurrence of the observed sequence.

132

(2) Learning (Baum-Welch) - Determine the most likely emission and transition probabilities for a given set of observational data.

(3) Decoding (Viterbi) - Determine the most probable sequence of states emitting the observed sequence.

Most of the examples focus on the 3rd problem, the Viterbi decoding problem, but full gHMM solutions for both Viterbi and Baum-Welch have been derived and implemented, and are shown in the sections that follow.

The probability of a sequence of observables $B = b_0 \, b_1 \ldots b_{n-1}$ being emitted by the sequence of hidden states $\Lambda = \lambda_0 \, \lambda_1 \ldots \lambda_{n-1}$ is solved by using $P(B, \Lambda) = P(B|\Lambda) \, P(\Lambda)$ in the standard factorization, where the two terms in the factorization are described as the *observation model* and the *state model*, respectively. In the 1st order HMM, the state model has the 1st order Markov property and the observation model is such that the current observation, b_n, depends only on the current state, λ_n:

$$P(B|\Lambda) \, P(\Lambda) = P(b_0|\lambda_0) \, P(b_1|\lambda_1) \ldots P(b_{n-1}|\lambda_{n-1}) \text{ x}$$
$$P(\lambda_0)P(\lambda_1|\lambda_0)P(\lambda_2|\lambda_0, \lambda_1) \ldots P(\lambda_{n-1}|\lambda_0 \ldots \lambda_{n-2})$$

With first order Markov assumption in the state-model this becomes:

$$P(B|\Lambda) \, P(\Lambda) = P(b_0|\lambda_0) \, P(b_1|\lambda_1) \ldots P(b_{n-1}|\lambda_{n-1}) \text{ x } P(\lambda_0)P(\lambda_1|\lambda_0)P(\lambda_2|\lambda_1) \ldots P(\lambda_{n-1}|\lambda_{n-2})$$

7.2 Graphical Models for Markov Models and Hidden Markov Models

In this section we re-express Markov Models (MMs) and Hidden Markov Models (HMMs) in terms of graphical models (Fig.s 7.2 and 7.3, respectively). This will then be extended to a "full-clique" graphical model in Fig. 7.6 and Fig. 7.12.

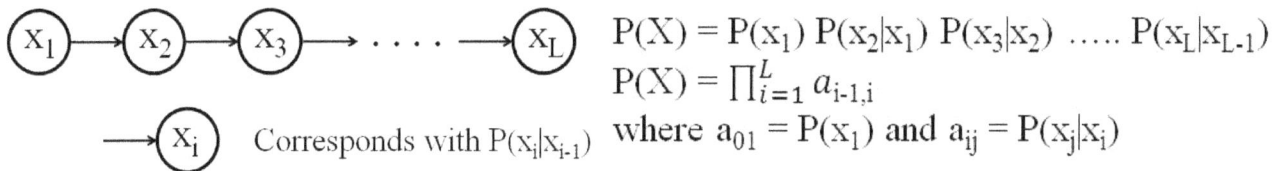

$P(X) = P(x_1) \, P(x_2|x_1) \, P(x_3|x_2) \ldots P(x_L|x_{L-1})$

$P(X) = \prod_{i=1}^{L} a_{i-1,i}$

Corresponds with $P(x_i|x_{i-1})$ where $a_{01} = P(x_1)$ and $a_{ij} = P(x_j|x_i)$

Fig. 7.2. Graphical Model for a 1st-order Markov Model

Hidden Markov Models

For (hidden) Markov state sequence $\Pi = "\pi_1 \pi_2 \pi_3 \ldots \pi_L"$, where the states take on values (e.g., $\pi_n = k$) in a finite alphabet, with transition probability $a_{kl} = P(\pi_i = l | \pi_{i-1} = k)$, and with an associated observation sequence $X = "x_1 x_2 x_3 \ldots x_L"$, and 'emission' probability $e_k(b) = P(x_i = b | \pi_i = k)$: (now viewed as an 'emission' outcome of the hidden state, not a transition process in itself, see Fig. 7.3):

133

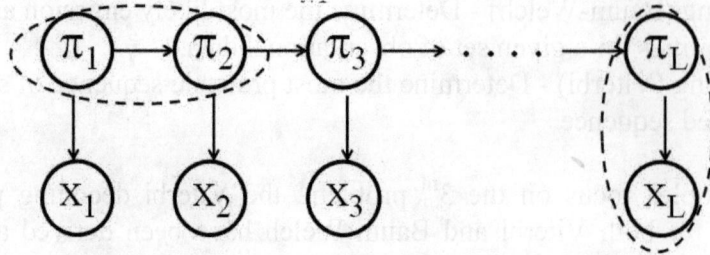

$$P(X; \Pi) = P(X|\Pi) \cdot P(\Pi) = P(X|\Pi) \cdot P(\pi_1) P(\pi_2|\pi_1) P(\pi_3|\pi_2) \ldots P(\pi_L|\pi_{L-1})$$

$$P(X; \Pi) = \prod_{i=1}^{L} P(x_i{=}x_i|\pi_i{=}\pi_i) \cdot \prod_{i=1}^{L} P(\pi_i{=}\pi_i|\pi_{i-1}{=}\pi_{i-1})$$

$$P(X; \Pi) = a_{0\pi_1} \prod_{i=1}^{L} e_{\pi_i}(xi) a_{\pi_i \pi_{i+1}}$$

where $a_{0\pi_1} = P(\pi_1)$ and $a_{\pi_i \pi_{i+1}} = P(\pi_i{=}\pi_i|\pi_{i-1}{=}\pi_{i-1})$.

Fig. 7.3. Graphical Model for a Standard Hidden Markov Model

7.2.1 Viterbi Path

In the Viterbi algorithm, a recursive variable is defined: $v_{kn} = v_k(n) = v_k(b_n) =$ *"the most probable path ending in state $\lambda_n{=}k$ with observation b_n"*. The recursive definition of $v_k(n)$ is then: $v_l(n{+}1) = e_l(b_{n+1}) \max_k [v_k(n) a_{kl}]$, where $e_l(b_{n+1})$ is the 'emission' probability for the observed b_{n+1} when in state $\lambda_{n+1}{=}l$, and a_{kl} is the transition probability from state $\lambda_n{=}k$ to state $\lambda_{n+1}{=}l$. The optimal path information is recovered according to the (recursive) trace-back:

(1) $\Lambda^* = \text{argmax}_\Lambda P(B, \Lambda) = (\lambda^*_0, \ldots, \lambda^*_{L-1}); \lambda^*_n|_{\lambda^*_{n+1}=l} = \text{argmax}_k [v_k(n) a_{kl}]$,

and where

(2) $\lambda^*_{L-1} = \text{argmax}_k [v_k(L-1)]$, for length L sequence.

The recursive algorithm for the most likely state path given an observed sequence (the Viterbi algorithm) is expressed in terms of v_{ki} (the probability of the most probable path that ends with observation $b_n = i$, and state $\lambda_n{=}k$). The recursive relation is lifted directly from the underlying probability definition: $v_{ki} = \max_n\{e_{ki}a_{nk}v_{n(i-1)}\}$, where the $\max_n\{\ldots\}$ operation returns the maximum value of the argument over different values of index n, and the boundary condition on the recursion is $v_{k0} = e_{k0}p_k$. The emission probabilities are the main place where the data is brought into the HMM-EM algorithm. An inversion on the emission probability is possible in this setting because the states and emissions share the same alphabet of states/quantized-emissions. The Viterbi path labelings are, thus, recursively defined by $p(\lambda_i|\lambda_{(i+1)}{=}n) = \text{argmax}_k\{v_{ki}a_{kn}\}$. The evaluation of sequence probability (and its Viterbi labeling) take the emission and transition probabilities as a given. Estimates on those emission and transition probabilities themselves can be obtained by an Expectation/Maximization (EM) algorithm that is known as the Baum-Welch algorithm in this context. The 50-state generic HMM described above is used extensively in [1,198], and will be described further in the EVA and other methods that follow in Sec. 2.3.4.

134

The Most Probable State Sequence

Given an observation sequence $X = "x_1 x_2 x_3 \ldots x_L"$, we often want to know the most probable hidden state sequence that might be associated with it (shown in Fig. 7.4):

$$\Pi* = \underset{\Pi}{\operatorname{argmax}} \ P(X; P)$$

aacgcgtagctagttgactctcgaaacgcgtagctagttgactctcgaacgcgtagctagttgactctcgaacgcgtagctagttgactctt

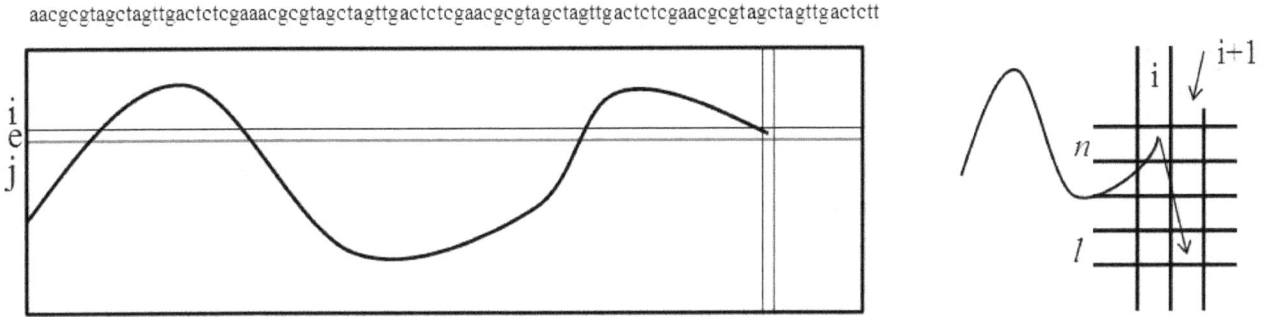

Fig. 7.4. The Most Probable State Sequence

This can be solved recursively using a dynamic programming algorithm known as the Viterbi algorithm. Let $v_k(i)$ be the probability of the most probable path ending in state "k" with i'th observation ($x_i = c$ and k=e, for exon, shown in Fig. 7.5):

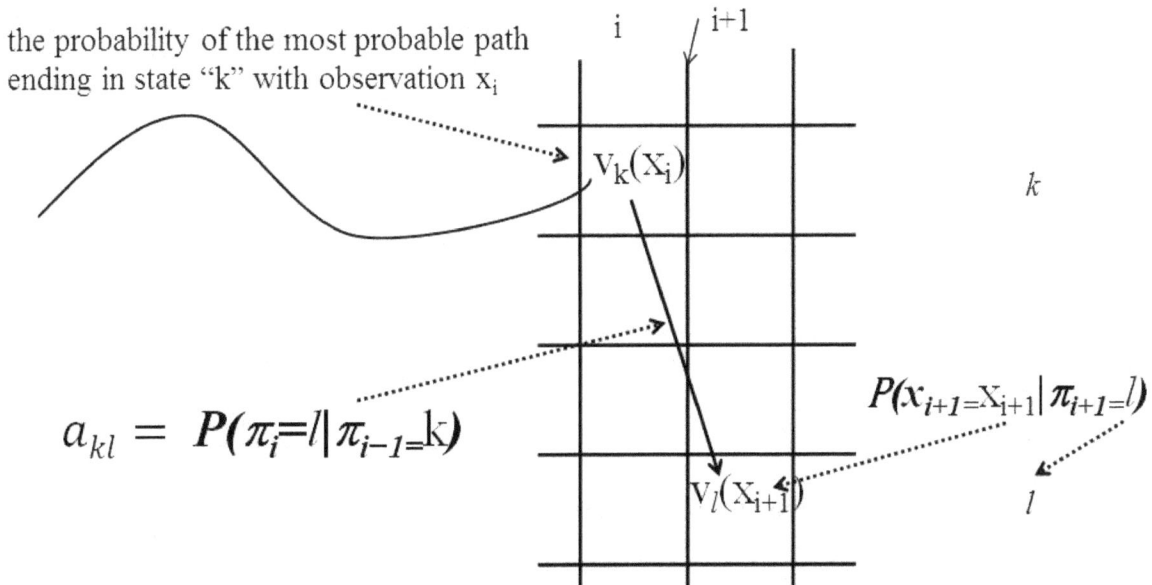

the probability of the most probable path ending in state "k" with observation x_i

$V_k(X_i)$

$a_{kl} = P(\pi_i=l|\pi_{i-1}=k)$

$P(x_{i+1}=X_{i+1}|\pi_{i+1}=l)$

$V_l(X_{i+1})$

$$v_l(i+1) = \underset{k}{\max}[P(x_{i+1}=X_{i+1}|\pi_{i+1}=l)a_{kl} \ v_k(i)] = el(xi_{+1})\underset{k}{\max}[a_{kl}v_k(i)]; \ P(X; \Pi*) = \underset{k}{\max}[v_k(L-1)]$$

$$\pi_i*|(\pi_{i+1}* = l) = \underset{k}{\operatorname{argmax}}[a_{kl}v_k(i)]; \ v_k(0) = P(x_0|\pi_0=k); \ \pi_{L-1}* = \underset{k}{\operatorname{argmax}}[v_k(L-1)]$$

Fig. 7.5. Viterbi Path. Optimal Path Identification

7.2.2 Forward and Backward Probabilities

The Forward & Backward probabilities occur when evaluating $p(b_0...b_{L-1})$ by breaking the sequence probability $p(b_0...b_{L-1})$ into two pieces via use of a single hidden variable treated as a Bayesian parameter: $p(b_0...b_{L-1}) = \Sigma_k\, p(b_0...b_i, \lambda_i=k)p(b_{i+1}...b_{L-1}, \lambda_i=k) = \Sigma_k\, f_{ki}b_{ki}$, where $f_{ki} = p(b_0...b_i, \lambda_i=k)$ and $b_{ki} = p(b_{i+1}...b_{L-1}, \lambda_i=k)$. Given stationarity, the state transition probabilities and the state probabilities at the ith observation satisfy the trivial relation $p_{qi} = \Sigma_k a_{kq}p_{k(i-1)}$, where $p_{qi} = p(\lambda_i=q)$, and $p_{q0} = p(\lambda_0=q)$, and the latter probabilities are the state priors. The trivial recursion relation that is implied can be thought of as an operator equation, with operation the product by a_{kq} followed by summation (contraction) on the k index. The operator equation can be rewritten using an implied summation convention on repeated Greek-font indices (Einstein summation convention): $p_q = a_{\beta q}p_\beta$. Transition-probabilities in a similar operator role, but now taking into consideration local sequence information via the emission probabilities, are found in recursively defined expressions for the forward variables, $f_{ki} = e_{ki}(a_{\beta k}f_{\beta(i-1)})$, and backward variables, $b_{ki} = a_{k\beta}e_{\beta(i+1)}b_{\beta(i+1)}$. The recursive definitions on forward and backward variables permit efficient computation of observed sequence probabilities using dynamic programming tables. It is at this critical juncture that side information must mesh well with the states (column components in the table), i.e., in a manner like the emission or transition probabilities. Length information, for example, can be incorporated via length-distribution-biased transition probabilities.

7.2.3 HMM: Maximum Likelihood discrimination

The maximum likelihood criterion is used to infer parameters, θ, for a model $\mathbf{M}$ from a data set $\mathbf{D}$ by simply taking the parameters that maximize $\mathbf{P(D|\theta,M)}$. Following the notation of [81] this is written:

$$\theta^{ML} = \text{argmax}_\theta\, \mathbf{P(D|\theta,M)},$$

(The terminology "likelihood" is taken to refer to the function of $\mathbf{y}$ described by $\mathbf{P(x|y)}$, while the function of $\mathbf{x}$ described by $\mathbf{P(x|y)}$ is interpreted as a probability.) Along theses same lines, the model itself could be the parameter by which to maximize. This was an actual implementation possibility: multiple HMM processes, separately trained to each individual class of current blockade signal, could be used to extend the HMMs feature extraction role to discrimination. After a few rounds of the EM filtering process, blockade probabilities could be obtained and ranked according to highest probability "template" match. The blockade signal could then be classified accordingly. As with maximum likelihood discrimination, however, there is a serious weakness with this approach given sparse data, and rejection is not as controlled as in full discriminatory frameworks like SVMs.

7.2.4 Expectation/Maximization (Baum-Welch)

Expectation/Maximization, EM, is a general method to estimate the maximum likelihood when there is hidden or missing data. The method is guaranteed to find a maximum, but it may only be a local maximum, as is shown here (along the lines of [81]). For a statistical model with parameters θ, observed quantities $\mathbf{B}$, and hidden labels Λ, the EM goal is to maximize the log likelihood of the observed quantities with respect to θ: $\log P(\mathbf{B}|\theta)=\log[\Sigma_\Lambda P(\mathbf{B},\Lambda|\theta)]$. At each iteration of the estimation process we would like the new log likelihood, $P(\mathbf{B}|\theta)$, to be greater than the old, $P(\mathbf{B}|\theta^*)$. The difference in log likelihoods can be written such that one part is a relative entropy, the positivity of which makes the EM algorithm work:

$$\log P(\mathbf{B}|\theta) - \log P(\mathbf{B}|\theta^*) = Q(\theta|\theta^*) - Q(\theta^*|\theta^*) + D[P(\Lambda|\mathbf{B},\theta^*)\|P(\Lambda|\mathbf{B},\theta)],$$

where $D[\ldots\|\ldots]$ is the Kullback-Leibler divergence, or relative entropy, and $Q(\theta|\theta^*) = \Sigma_\Lambda P(\mathbf{B},\Lambda|\theta)$. Now a greater log likelihood results simply by maximizing $Q(\theta|\theta^*)$ with respect to parameters θ. The EM iteration is comprised of two steps: (1) Estimation – calculate $Q(\theta|\theta^*)$, and (2) Maximization – maximize $Q(\theta|\theta^*)$ w.r.t. parameters θ.

For an HMM the hidden labels Λ correspond to a path of states. Along path Λ the emission and transition parameters will be used to varying degrees. Along path Λ, denote usage counts on transition probability a_{kl} by $A_{kl}(\Lambda)$ and those on emission probabilities e_{kb} by $E_k(b,\Lambda)$ (following [81] conventions), $P(\mathbf{B},\Lambda|\theta)$ can then be written:

$$P(\mathbf{B},\Lambda|\theta) = \Pi_{k=0}\Pi_b[e_{kb}]^\wedge E_k(b,\Lambda)\ \Pi_{k=0}\Pi_{l=1}[a_{kl}]^\wedge A_{kl}(\Lambda).$$

Using the above form for $P(\mathbf{B},\Lambda|\theta)$, A_{kl} for the expected value of $A_{kl}(\Lambda)$ on path Λ, and $E_k(b)$ for the expected value of $E_k(b,\Lambda)$ on path Λ, it is then possible to write $Q(\theta|\theta^*)$ as:

$$Q(\theta|\theta^*) = \Sigma_{k=1}\Sigma_b E_k(b) \log[e_{kb}] + \Sigma_{k=0}\Sigma_{l=1} A_{kl} \log[a_{kl}].$$

It then follows (relative entropy positivity argument again) that the maximum likelihood estimators (MLEs) for a_{kl} and e_{kb} are:

$$a_{kl} = A_{kl} / (\Sigma_l A_{kl}) \quad \text{and} \quad e_{kb} = E_k(b) / (\Sigma_b E_k(b)).$$

The latter estimation is for when the state sequence is known. For an HMM (with Baum-Welch algorithm) it completes the Q maximization step (M-step), which is obtained with the MLEs for a_{kl} and e_{kb}. The E-step requires that Q be calculated, for the HMM this requires that A_{kl} and $E_k(b)$ be calculated. This calculation is done using the forward/backward formalism with rescaling in the next section.

Emission and Transition Expectations with Rescaling
For an HMM, the probability that transition a_{kl} is used at position i in sequence $\mathbf{B}$ is:

$$p(\lambda_i=k, \lambda_{(i+1)}=l \mid X) = p(\lambda_i=k, \lambda_{(i+1)}=l, \mathbf{B})/p(\mathbf{B}), \text{ where}$$

$$p(\lambda_i=k,\lambda_{(i+1)}=l,\mathbf{B})=p(\mathbf{b}_0,\ldots,\mathbf{b}_i,\lambda_i=k)p(\lambda_{(i+1)}=l \mid \lambda_i=k)p(\mathbf{b}_{i+1} \mid \lambda_{(i+1)}=l)p(\mathbf{b}_{i+2},\ldots,\mathbf{b}_{L-1} \mid \lambda_{(i+1)}=l).$$

In terms of the previous notation with forward/backward variables:

$$p(\lambda_i=k, \lambda_{(i+1)}=l \mid X) = f_{ki}\, a_{kl}\, e_{l(i+1)}\, b_{l(i+1)}\, /p(\mathbf{B}),$$

So the expected number of times a_{kl} is used, A_{kl}, simply sums over all positions i (except last with indexing):

$$A_{kl} = \Sigma_i f_{ki} a_{kl} e_{l(i+1)} b_{l(i+1)} /p(\mathbf{B}),$$

Similarly, the probability that b is emitted by state k at position i in sequence $\mathbf{B}$:

$$p(\mathbf{b}_i=b, \lambda_i=k \mid X)=[p(\mathbf{b}_0,\ldots,\mathbf{b}_i,\lambda_i=k) p(\mathbf{b}_{i+1},\ldots,\mathbf{b}_{L-1} \mid \lambda_i=k) / p(\mathbf{B})]\delta(\mathbf{b}_i-b),$$

where a Kronecker delta function is used to enforce emission of b at position i. The expected number of times b is emitted by state k for sequence $\mathbf{B}$:

$$E_k(b) = \Sigma_i f_{ki} b_{ki}/ p(\mathbf{B}) \delta(\mathbf{b}_i-b),$$

In practice, direct computation of the forward and backward variables can run into underflow errors. Rescaling variables at each step can control this problem. One rescaling approach is to rescale the forward variables such that $\Sigma_i F_{ki}=1$, where F_{ki} is the rescaled forward variable, and B_{ki} is the rescaled backward variable: $F_{ki} = a_{\beta k}e_{ki}F_{\beta(i-1)}/s_i$, and $B_{ki} = a_{k\beta}e_{\beta(i+1)} B_{\beta(i+1)}/t_{i+1}$, where s_i and t_{i+1}, are the rescaling constants. The expectation on counts for the various emissions and transitions then reduce to:

$$A_{kl} = \Sigma_i F_{ki} a_{kl} e_{l(i+1)} B_{l(i+1)} /[\Sigma_k\Sigma_l F_{ki} a_{kl} e_{l(i+1)}] \text{ and } E_k(b) = \Sigma_i F_{ki} B_{ki} \delta(\mathbf{b}_i-b).$$

7.3 Standard HMM weaknesses and their GHMM fixes

A brief list of the typical weaknesses encountered with the standard HMM follows, with a description of the appropriate HMM generalization that eliminates those weaknesses (to be described in detail in later sub-sections):

(1) Standard HMMs are at low Markov order in transitions (first) and in emissions (zeroth), and transitions are decoupled from emissions, which can miss critical structure in the model (e.g., state transition probabilities that are strongly sequence dependent). This weakness is eliminated if we generalize to the largest state-emission clique possible, fully interpolated on the data set, with use of a minimal state-length constraint to obtain an efficient implementation (see Fig. 7.6).

The generalized clique HMM (Fig. 7.6) begins by enlarging the primitive hidden states associated with the individual base labels (such as with exon, intron, or junk in gene-structure identification) to substrings of primitive hidden states or footprint states. There is a key constraint, however, to keep the scaling of footprint states linear with footprint size: the footprint states are constrained to have self-transitions with a minimal length such that a footprint, and the overlapping 'next' footprint, together can only have one primitive transition between states of different type (equivalent to constraining same-state transitions to have a minimal duration). The emissions are likewise expanded to higher order in the fundamental joint probability that is the basis of the generalized-clique, or 'meta-State', HMM.

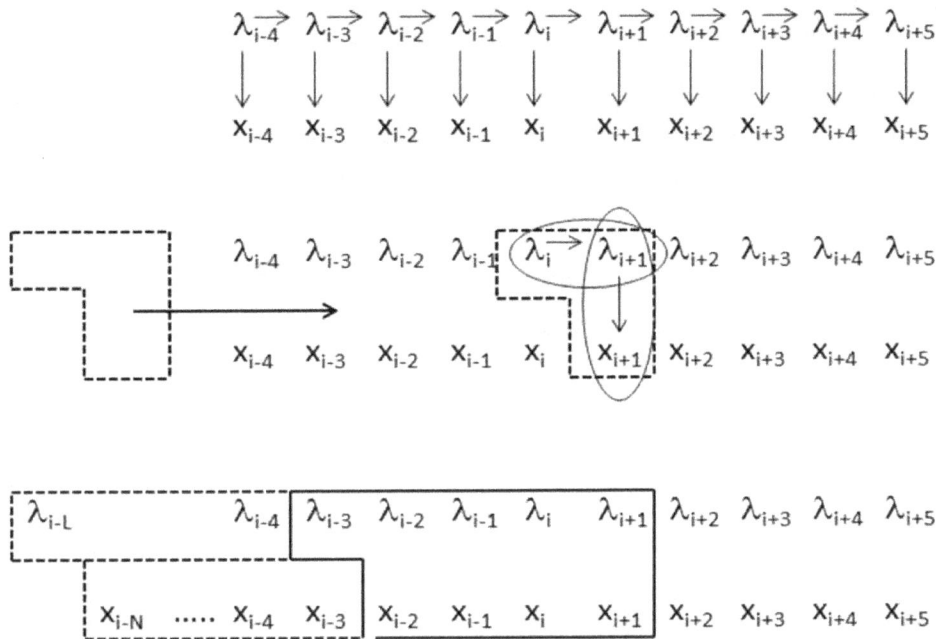

Figure 7.6. Comparison of standard HMM and the clique-generalized HMM. The upper graphical model is for the standard HMM and shows the 'emission' observation sequence x_i, and the associated hidden label sequence λ_i, and the arrows denote the conditional probability approximations used in the model (for the transition and emission probabilities). Focusing at the level of the core joint-probability construct at instant 'i' in the middle graph, the standard HMM is a subset of the joint probability construct $P(\lambda_i, \lambda_{i+1}, x_{i+1})$. The generalized-clique HMM is shown in the graphical model at the bottom for one particular clique generalization. The model can be exact on emission positionally, then extend via zone dependence and use of gIMM interpolation [1]. The model can be exact to higher order in state (referred to as footprint states', see [18]), and also extends modeling to have HMM with duration modeling. When doing the latter, zone-dependent and position dependent modeling can be incorporated via reference to the duration in the model, and can be directly incorporated into a generalized Viterbi algorithm (and other generalized HMM algorithms), as well as any other side-information of interest [1,19].

(2) Standard HMMs don't properly model self-transition durations, imposing a 'best-fit' geometric distribution on self-transition duration distributions instead. This weakness is eliminated if we generalize to a HMM-with-duration (HMMD) formalism, where direct modeling on self-transition duration distributions is incorporated. Standard HMMD methods are computationally expensive, however, when compared to Standard HMM. This weakness can be addressed, without loss of generality, via use of HMM with binned duration (HMMBD) representations [21].

(3) The standard HMM approach lacks the means for directly incorporating side-information into the dynamic programming table based optimizations (used in the Viterbi and Baum-Welch algorithms, etc.). This is solved in [21], where HMM side-information is incorpo-

rated along with state duration information in a generalized HMM-with-duration implementation.

(4) Standard HMM and HMMD methods suffer from a severe bottleneck if full table computation is used on a lengthy data sequence, where there is a need for a method for distributed processing, or 'chunking', with overlaps sufficient for recovery. A method for distributed Viterbi and Baum-Welch will be described in what follows.

(5) There is typically a need for a method for HMM Feature Extraction Selection, Compression, and Fusion. A modified form of Adaboost [65,131] is used for this purpose in [33,38].

(6) The standard HMM has one 'track' of hidden label information. There is a need for multi-track hidden Markov modeling in many applications but this is not typically addressed in this direct way due to the significantly greater number of multi-track states indicated, and associated processing overhead. Multi-track hidden state constraints (and allowed transitions) are often present that can significantly limit model complexity, however, as already seen in the meta-HMM clique generalization with application in gene-finding in [18], and mentioned in item (1). If properly handled via a preliminary allowed state/transition analysis, significant multiple hidden-track model complexity can be accommodated. Ch. 9 and [1,12] preliminary statistical results are described that indicate that a two-track HMM alternative-splice gene-finder model is statistically well-supported for bootstrap learning with a wide range of eukaryotic genomes (*C. elegans* to *H. sapiens* genomes [12]).

(7) There is a need for a standardized HMM method for handling power signal data, and this is accomplished by use of the Emission Variance Amplification (EVA) state projection pre-processing as described in Sec. 7.2, other uses for EVA are also indicated there as well, including identification of strong or weak signal stationarity.

(8) There is a need for a standardized HMM usage in signal processing systems that draw upon the strengths of other Machine Learning methods. HMMs are very strong at extracting signal features from sequential data, for example, and at performing long-range structure identification along that sequential data. HMMs don't offer a scalable means to do classification when working with many classes, however, and HMMs are often a waste of computational resource)when an $O(L)$ complexity simple finite state automaton (FSA) 'scan', for length L sequence, will often suffice for 95% of the data analysis (the popular BLAST [82] algorithm from Bioinformatics is an FSA/HMM hybrid algorithm for this same reason). The SSA Protocol is designed to handle this and other arrangements of signal processing methods.

In the SSA Protocol and the SCW Communications method (Ch. 13) the HMMD recognition of a signal's stationary statistics has benefits analogous to 'time integration' heterodyning of a radio signal with a periodic carrier in classic electrical engineering, where longer observation time is leveraged into higher signal resolution. In order to enhance the 'time integration', or longer observation, benefit in the signal recognition, one can introduce modulations (periodic, burst, or stationary stochastic) into the signal generator environment [1].

In channel current state identification in a high noise background [1], for example, modulations may be introduced such that some of the channel current state lifetimes have heavy-tailed, or multimodal, distributions. With these modifications, a state's signal could be recognizable in the presence of very high noise. The boost in sensitivity is mostly obtained by leveraging the SCW signal processing capabilities without further refinements to the channel monitoring device other than to, possibly, allow modulation. The SSA Protocol and SCW methods offer similar enhancement to signal processing capabilities in other devices as well. Any device generating a sequence of observations can be enhanced with use of SCW methods in a similar manner. Background on the SSA Protocol and its general-use is given in Ch. 13.

All of the HMM generalizations and feature extraction methods discussed in what follows can be optimized for speed with binned durations and through distributed table-chunking (and GPU-usage). This allows the limiting speed constraint on the core HMMBD component in the SSA protocol to be greatly reduced.

7.4 Generalized HMMs (GHMMs – "gems"): Minor Viterbi Variants
7.4.1. The Generic HMM
An HMM that is designed to generate a specific signal type need only have a few states and transitions. In reverse, this HMM 'template' can be used to detect signal with matching statistics. An HMM that is meant to generate a large family of signals, on the other hand, needs to have more states and associated transitions. The 'Generic' HMM or 'grayscale' HMM is an example of this in the case of the channel current analysis applications in [1] and in many of the examples in this paper.

The generic or grayscale HMM used in [1] is implemented with fifty states, corresponding to current blockades in 1% increments ranging from 20% residual current to 69% residual current. The HMM states, numbered 0 to 49, corresponded to the 50 different current blockade levels in the sequences that are processed. The state emission parameters of the HMM are initially set so that the state j, $0 <= j <= 49$ corresponding to level $L = j+20$, can emit all possible levels, with the probability distribution over emitted levels set to a discretized Gaussian with mean L and unit variance. All transitions between states are possible, and initially are equally likely.

7.4.2. pMM/SVM
For start-of-coding recognition one can create a profile Markov model (pMM) based log-likelihood ratio (LLR) classifier given by $\log[P_{start}/P_{non-start}] = \Sigma_i \log[P_{start}(x_i=b_i)/P_{non-start}(x_i=b_i)]$. Rather than a classification built on the sum of the independent log odds ratios, however, the sum of components could be replaced with a vectorization of components:

(3) $\Sigma_i \log[P_{start}(x_i=b_i)/P_{non-start}(x_i=b_i)]$ --> $\{...., \log[P_{start}(x_i=b_i)/P_{non-start}(x_i=b_i)], ...\}$
These can be viewed as feature vectors (f.v.'s), and can be classified by use of an SVM. The SVM partially recovers linkages lost with the HMM's conditional independence approximations. For the 0th order MM, for example, the positional probabilities are approximated as entirely independent -- which is typically far from accurate. The SVM approach can recover statistical linkages between components in the f.v.'s in the SVM training process. Results along these lines are shown in [26].

There are generalizations for the MM sensor and its SVM f.v. implementation, and all are compatible with the SVM f.v. classification profiling. Markov Profiling with component-sum to component feature-vector mapping for SVM/MM profiling, thus, enhances the use of

MMs, IMMs, gIMMs, hIMMs, and ghIMMs [1,39], with SVM usage via "vectorization" to SVM/MM, SVM/IMM, SVM/gIMM classification profiling.

7.4.3. EM and Feature Extraction via EVA projection

Emission variance amplification (EVA) projection is used in the SSA Protocol to go from a power signal (or anything sampled from a continuum domain of possibilities) to a discrete, projected 'EVA state', representation of the data. Once all states are discrete, higher order structure (or encoding) can be extracted by use of the meta-HMM generalization.

Using a standard implementation of a HMM with emissions probabilities parameterized by Gaussian distributions: emission_probabilities[i][k] = exp(-(k-i)*(k-i)/(2*variance)), where "i" and "k" are each a state where 0 <= i,k <= 49 in a 50 state system. To perform EVA, the variance is simply multiplied by a factor that essentially widens the gaussian distribution parameterized to best fit the emissions, and the equation simply becomes exp(-(k-i)*(k-i)/(2*variance*eva_factor)). For a sizable range of this parameter, HMM with EVA will remove the noise from the power signal while *strictly* maintaining the timing of the state transitions.

After EVA-projection, a simple FSA can easily extract level duration information (see Fig. 7.7). Each level is identified by a simple threshold of blockade readings, typically one or two percent of baseline. When EVA boosts the variance of the distribution, for states near a dominant level in the blockade signal, the transitions are highly favored to points nearer that dominant level. This is a simple statistical effect having to do with the fact that far more points of departure are seen in the direction of the nearby dominant level than in the opposite direction. When in the local gaussian tail of sample distribution around the dominant level, the effect of transitions towards the dominant level over those away from the dominant level can be very strong. In short, a given point is much more likely to transition towards the dominant level than away from it, thereby arriving at a "focusing" on the levels, while preserving level transitions.

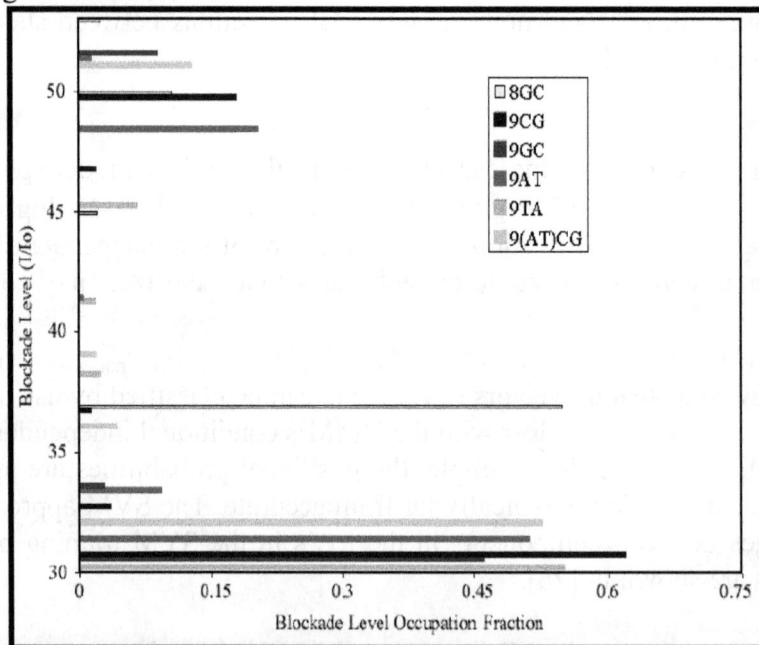

Fig. 7.7. HMM/EM Viterbi-path level occupation feature extraction. Strong EVA projection is employed to project the data onto dominant levels, a

Viterbi path Histogram then shows the barcode "fingerprints" of the different molecular species (the labels are for the DNA hairpins examined in [198], and since then used as controls).

Emission variance amplification (EVA) projection is used in the SSA Protocol to go from a power signal (or anything sampled from a continuum domain of possibilities) to a sparser, projected 'EVA state', representation of the data. Quantization on the sparser representation can then provide a discrete representation. Once all states are discrete, higher order structure (or encoding) can be extracted by use of the meta-HMM generalization described in Sec. 7.3, and other methods. EVA makes use of Expectation/Maximization, so that will be reviewed next before proceeding.

When EVA boosts the variance of the distribution, the states near a dominant level in the blockade signal are highly favored to transition to points nearer that dominant level. This is a simple statistical effect having to do with the fact that far more points of departure are seen in the direction of the nearby dominant level than in the opposite direction. When in the local Gaussian tail of sample distribution around the dominant level, the effect of transitions towards the dominant level over those away from the dominant level can be very strong. In short, a filtered datum is much more likely to transition towards the dominant level than away from it, thereby arriving at a "focusing" on the levels, while preserving level transitions.

When paired with HMMD modeling, EVA projection has additional synergy. EVA projects onto the dominant sub-levels, of which there can be many, all clearly separable after the projection. To the extent that they aren't cleanly separable HMMD can greatly enhance performance (consider two sub-levels that are close together, as a challenging case synthetic data is generated with such sub-levels where their noise level standard deviance greatly exceed their sub-level separation (by a factor ranging from 4 to 50). In the 'tight' two-level signal resolution studies in [1], the performance difference is stark: the exact and adaptive HMMD decodings are 97.1% correct, while the HMM decoding is only correct 61% of the time (where random guessing would accomplish 50%, on average, in such a two-state system). Three parameterized distributions were examined in that study: geometric, Gaussian, and Poisson. Distributions that were segmented and "messy" were also examined. In all cases the HMMD performed robustly, similar to the above, and in all cases the adaptive binning HMMD optimization performed comparably to the more computationally expensive exact HMMD.

The EVA-projected/HMMD processing offers a hands-off (minimal tuning) method for extracting the mean dwell times for various blockade states (the core kinetic information on the blockading molecule's channel interactions). The results in [1] clearly demonstrated the superior performance of the HMMD over the simpler standard HMM formulation on data with non-geometrically distributed same-state interval durations. In the stochastic carrier wave context, this describes a means to discern a stochastic stationary carrier with HMMD (while with HMM alone we are much weaker in this regard and cannot robustly discern carrier). With use of the EVA-projection method, this also affords a robust means to obtain kinetic-type (state duration) feature extraction. The HMM with duration enables accurate kinetic feature extraction when using EVA, thus the results in [1] suggest that this problem can be elegantly solved with a pairing of the HMM-with-Duration stabilization with EVA-projection.

7.4.4. Feature Extraction via Data Absorption (a.k.a. Emission Inversion)

A new form of "inverted" data injection is possible during HMM training when the states and quantized emission values share the same alphabet. This is typically the case in power signal analysis, such as the chanel current cheminformatics problem described in what follows. Results from channel current signal classification consistently show approximately 5% improvement in accuracy (sensitivity + specificity) with the aforementioned data inversion upon SVM classification (and this holds true over wide ranges of SVM kernel parameters and collections of feature sets, see Fig. 7.8). Transition & "absorption" statistical profiles are thought to work better than standard transition & emission profiles, in generalized classification performance, due to regularization with an effective SRM (structural risk minimization [120]) constraint, via optimization with an added term that depends on the relative entropy between state prior probabilities and emission posterior probabilites.

By swapping $e_b(k)$ for $e_k(b)$ we introduce a multiplicative factor, the ratio of the priors on states to the frequencies on emissions: $e_k(b) = e_b(k) [P(b)/P(k)]$. This factor weights the computations in a manner that seems to track, and minimize, on the Kullback-Leibler divergence between the state prior distribution and the emission frequency distribution. This approximate notion follows from the evaluation of the extra terms that will occur on the maximum log-prob calculation for the Viterbi path. On the Viterbi solution, using the swapped emission probabilities, the sum (on log probabilities) at the end will differ by a sum of log ratios: $\log [P(k_i)/P(b_i)] = -\log[P(b_i) / P(k_i)]$ Normalized by length 'L' over different k and b, this term is approximated by Diff Term $= - D(P(\mathbf{B})\|P(S))$, maximizing on this term is, thus, minimizing on the divergence, $D(P(\mathbf{B})\|P(S))$, between the priors and the emissions.

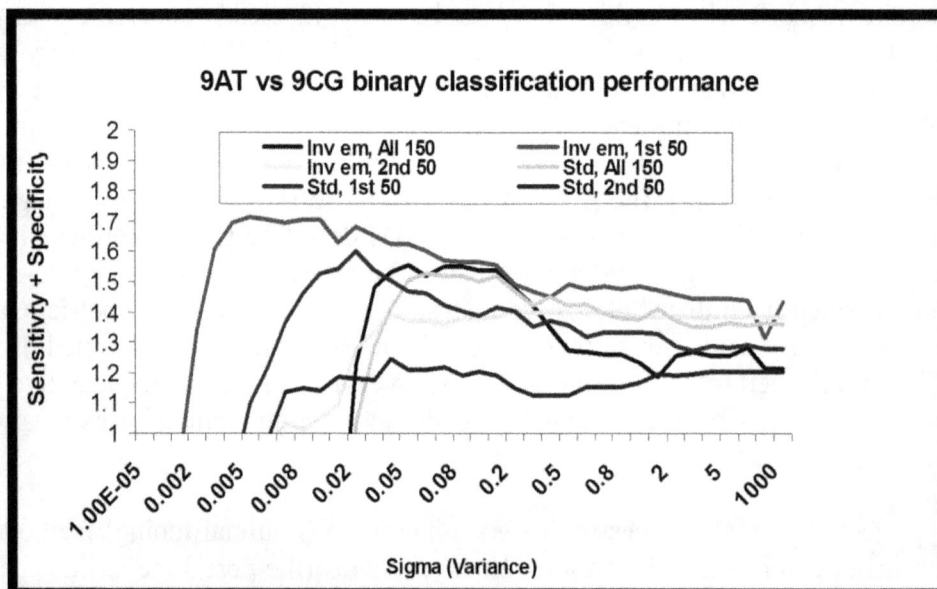

Fig. 7.8. The binary classification performance using features extracted with HMM data inversion vs. HMM standard. Blockade data was extracted from channel measurements of 9AT and 9CG hairpins (both hairpins with nine base-pair stems), the data extraction involved either standard (std) emission data representations or inverted (inv) emission data, and was based on feature sets of the full 150 features, or the first 50, with the Viterbi-path level dwell-time percentages or the second 50, the emissions variances (much weaker features as expected). The inverted data offers consistently better discriminatory performance by the SVM classifier.

7.4.5. Modified AdaBoost for Feature selection and Data fusion

AdaBoost [65,131] can take a collection of weak classifiers and boost them by forming a linear combination to have a single strong classifier. As a classification method, one of the main disadvantages of AdaBoost is that it is prone to overtraining. However, AdaBoost is a natural fit for feature selection. Here, overtraining is not a problem, as AdaBoost is only used to find diagnostic features, and those features are then passed on to a classifier that does not suffer from overtraining (such as an SVM). HMM features, and other features (from neural net, wavelet, or spike profiling, etc.), can be fused and selected via use of the Modified Adaboost selection algorithm [1].

More specifically, AdaBoost learns from a collection of weak classifiers and then boosts them by a linear combination into a single strong classifier. The input to the algorithm is a training set $\{(x_1, y_1), ..., (x_N, y_N)\}$ where $y_i \in Y = \{-1, +1\}$ is the correct label of instance $x_i \in X$ and N is the number of training examples in the data set. A weak learning algorithm is repeatedly called in a series of rounds $t = 1, ..., T$ with different weight distributions D_t on the training data. This set of weights associated with the training data at each round t is denoted by $D_t(i)$. In general, sampling weights associated with each example are initially set equal, i.e. a uniform sampling distribution is assumed. For the tth iteration, a classifier is learned from the training examples and the classifier with error $\varepsilon_t \leq 0.5$ is selected. In each iteration, the weights of misclassified examples are increased which results in these examples getting more attention in subsequent iterations. AdaBoost is outlined below. It is interesting to note that α_t measures the importance assigned to the hypothesis h_t and it gets larger as the training error ε_t gets smaller. The final classification decision H of a test point x is a weighted majority vote of the weak hypotheses.

The AdaBoost algorithm

Input: $S = \langle (x_1, y_1), ..., (x_N, y_N) \rangle$ where $x_i \in X$ and $y_i \in Y = \{-1, +1\}$

Initialization: $D_1(i) = 1/N$, for all $i = 1, ..., N$

For $t = 1$ *to* T **do**

1. Train weak learners with respect to the weighted sample set $\{S, D_t\}$ and obtain hypothesis $h_t : X \rightarrow Y$.

2. Obtain the error rates ε_t of h_t over the distribution D_t such that $\varepsilon_t = P_{i \sim D_t} [h_t(x_i) \neq y_i]$.

3. Set $\alpha_t = \frac{1}{2} ln(1 - \varepsilon_t / \varepsilon_t)$

4. Update the weights: $D_{t+1}(i) = (D_t(i)/Z_t) \, e^{-y_i h_t(x_i) \alpha_t}$, where Z_t is the normalizing factor such that $D_{t+1}(i)$ is a distribution.

5. Break if $\varepsilon_t = 0$ or $\varepsilon_t \geq \frac{1}{2}$.

end

Output: $H(x) = sign(\Sigma_{t=1}^{T} \alpha_t h_t(x_i))$

As has been shown in the tFSA spike analysis [33], careful selection of features plays a significant role in classification performance. However, adding non-characteristic or noisy features will hurt classification performance. The last set of 50 components from the standard HMM-based 150-component feature vector were chosen from compressed transition probabilities (where 50*50 transitions are compressed to 50 features). A means of compression is necessary because many of these transitions are very unlikely and contribute noise to the feature vector (e.g., they offer weak generalization performance when passed to a classifier). Without compression, classification performance suffers, yet it is possible for diagnostic information to be discarded in such a feature compression. An automated approach is possible to solve the issue of feature selection.

The modified Adaboost algorithm for feature selection

In Modified AdaBoost [33] weights are given to the weak learners as well as the training data. The key modifications here are to give each column of features in a training set a weak learner and to update each weak learner every iteration, not just updates the weights on the data. In an example where there is a set of 150-component feature vectors, 150 weak learners would be created. As previously mentioned, each weak learner corresponds to a single component and classifies a given feature vector based solely on that one component. Then, weights for these weak learners are introduced. In each iteration of this modified AdaBoost process, weights for both the input data and the weak learners are updated. The weights for the input data are updated as in the standard AdaBoost implementation, while weights on the individual weak learners are updated as if each were a complete hypothesis in the standard AdaBoost implementation. At the end of the iterative process, the weak learners with the highest weights, that is, the weak learners that represent the most diagnostic features, are selected and those features are passed to an SVM for classification (see [33] for more details). Thus, the benefits of both AdaBoost and SVMs are obtained.

Modified Adaboost in SSA Protocol

It is found that boosting from the set of 150 manuually designed features worked better than from the 2600 naive Bayes, and boosting from the 50 features in the first group worked best (see Fig. 7.9 & 7.10). This result is also consistent with the PCA filtering in [38] mostly reducing the 150 feature set to the first 50 features.

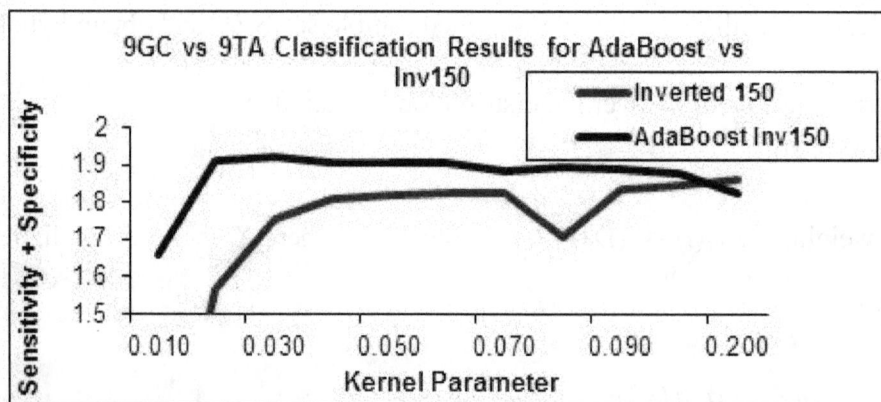

Fig. 7.9. Adaboost feature selection strengthens the SVM performance of the Inverted HMM feature extraction set. Classification improvement with Adaboost taking the best 50 from the Inverted-emission 150 feature set. 95% accuracy is possible for discriminating 9GC from 9TA hairpins with no data dropped with use of Adaboost, without Adaboosting, the accuracy is approx. 91%.

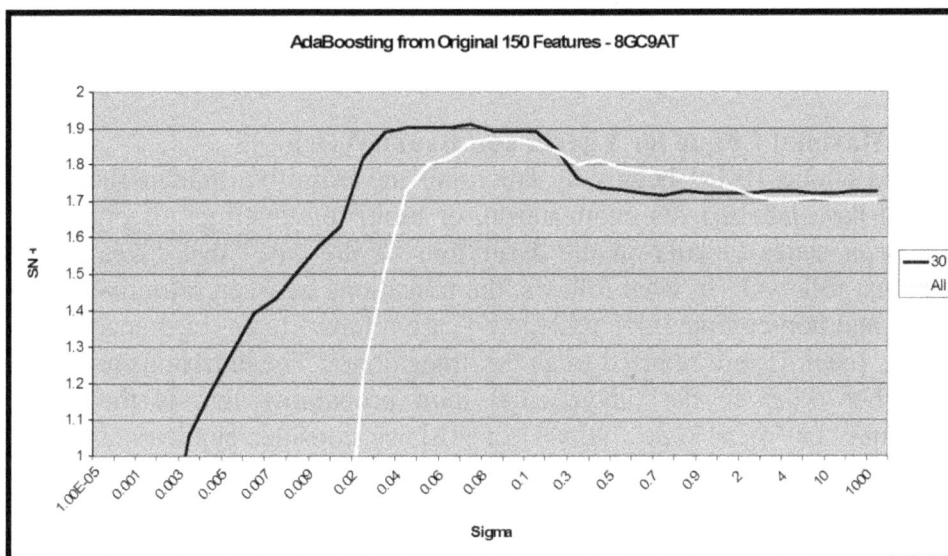

Fig. 7.10. If Adaboost operates from the 150 component manual set, a reduced feature set of 30 is found to work best, and with notable improvement in kernel parameter stability in the region of interest.

Classification improvement with Adaboost taking the best 50 from the Inverted-emission 150 feature set is shown in Fig. 7.11. An accuracy of 95% is possible for discriminating 9GC from 9TA hairpins with no data dropped with use of Adaboost. This demonstrates a significant robustness to what the SVM can "learn" in the presence of noise (some of the 2600 components have richer information, but even more are noise contributors). This also validates the effectiveness with which the 150 parameter compression was able to describe' the two-state dominant blockade data found for the nine base-pair hairpin and other types of "toggler" blockades, as well as the utility of the inverted features.

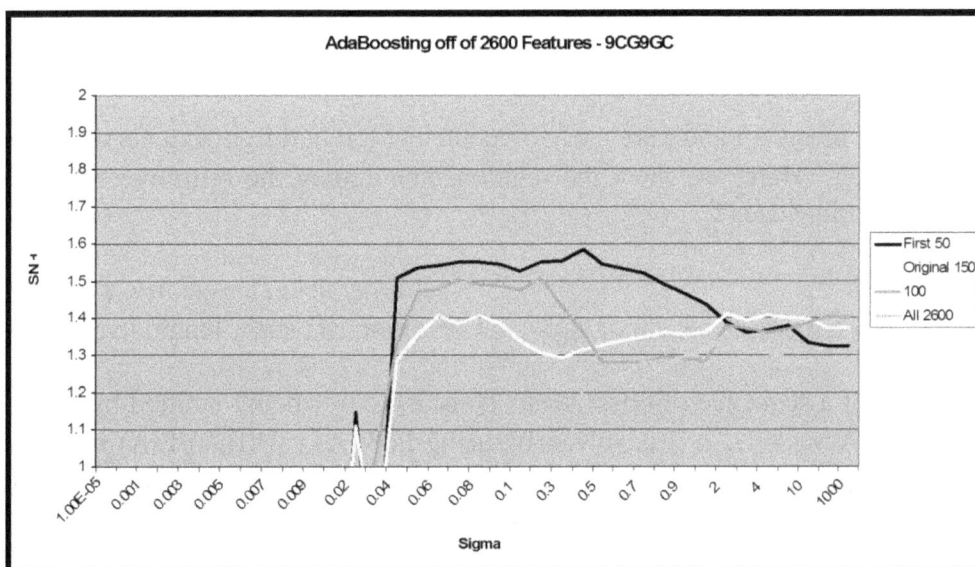

Fig. 7.11. AdaBoosting to select 100 of the full set of 2600 features improves classification over just passing all 2600 components to the SVM. The best performance is still obtained when working with the Adaboosting from the

147

manual set. (A principal component analysis (PCA) is done on the HMM projection data. 90% of the PCA information is contained in the first 50 principal components. The first 50 principal components are also listed as a feature set.)

7.5 GHMMs: Maximal Clique for Viterbi and Baum-Welch

The generalized clique HMM begins by enlarging the primitive hidden states associated with individual base labeling (as exon, intron, or junk) to substrings of primitive hidden states or *footprint* states (details on the definitions of the base-label states and footprint states are in what follows). In what follows, the transitions between primitive hidden states for coding {e} and non-coding {i,j}, {ei,ie,je,ej}, are referred to as 'eij-transitions', and the self transitions, {ee,ii,jj}, are referred to as 'xx-transitions'. The emissions are likewise expanded to higher order in the fundamental joint probability that is the basis of the generalized-clique, or 'meta-State', HMM. In [18] we consider application to eukaryotic gene finding and show how a meta-state HMM improves the strength of eij-transition contributions to gene-structure identification. It is found that the meta-state eij-transition modeling can effectively 'recapture' the exon and intron heavy tail distribution modeling capability as well as manage the exon-start 'needle-in-the-haystack' problem [18].

The meta-state, clique-generalized, HMM entails a clique-level factorization rather than the standard HMM factorization (that describes the state transitions with no dependence on local sequence information). This is described in the general formalism to follow, where specific implementations are given for application to eukaryotic gene structure identification.

Observation and state dependencies in the generalized-clique HMM (see Fig. 7.12) are parameterized according to the following:

1) Non-negative integers L and R denoting left and right maximum extents of a substring, w_n, (with suitable truncation at the data boundaries, b_0 and b_{N-1}) are associated with the primitive observation, b_n, in the following way:

$$w_n = b_{n-L+1}, \ldots, b_n, \ldots, b_{n+R}$$
$$\widetilde{w}_n = b_{n-L+1}, \ldots, b_n, \ldots, b_{n+R-1}$$

2) Non-negative integers l and r are used to denote the left and right extents of the extended (footprint) states, f. Here, we show the relationships among the primitive states λ, dimer states s, and footprint states f:

$\delta_n = \lambda_n \lambda_{n+1}$ (dimer state, length in λ's =2)

$f_n = \delta_{n-l+1}, \ldots, \delta_{n+r} \cong \lambda_{n-l+1}, \ldots, \lambda_n, \ldots, \lambda_{n+r+1}$ (footprint state, length in δ's= l+r)

The probability of a sequence of observables $B=b_0 b_1 \ldots b_{L-1}$ being emitted by the sequence of hidden states $\Lambda=\lambda_0 \lambda_1 \ldots \lambda_{L-1}$ is solved by using $P(B, \Lambda) = P(B|\Lambda) P(\Lambda)$ in the standard factorization mentioned above, where the two terms in the factorization are described as the *observation model* and the *state model*, respectively. In the 1st order HMM, the state model has the 1st order Markov property and the observation model is such that the current observation, b_n, depends only on the current state, λ_n. Given (i) sequence of observations b_n, (ii) hidden labels λ_n, and (iii) stationary Markov statistics, one can calculate: (i) p(B), or (ii) the most likely hidden labeling (path with largest contribution to p(B;Λ)), or (iii) the re-estimation of emission and transmission probabilities such that p(B;Λ) is maximized (using Expectation/Maximization).

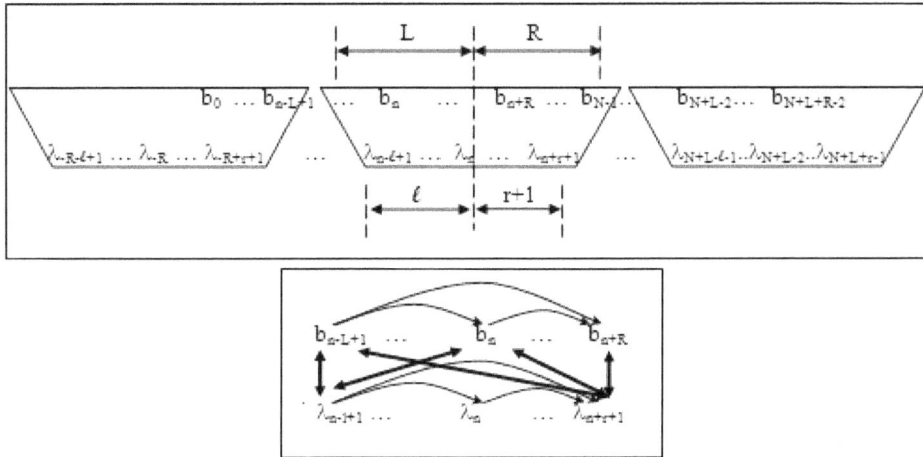

Fig. 7.12. Top Panel. Sliding-window association (clique) of observations and hidden states in the meta-state hidden Markov model, where the clique-generalized HMM algorithm describes a left-to-right traversal (as is typical) of the HMM graphical model with the specified clique window. The first observation, b_0, is included at the leading edge of the clique overlap at the HMM's left boundary. For the last clique's window overlap we choose the trailing edge to include the last observation b_{N-1}. Bottom Panel. Graphical model of the clique-generalized HMM, where the interconnectedness on full joint dependencies is only partly drawn. The graphical model is significantly constrained, as well, in a manner not represented in the graphical model, in that state sequences are only allowed with at most one non-self transition.

As in the 1st order HMM, the nth base observation b_n is aligned with the nth hidden state λ_n. Given the above, the clique-factorized HMM is as follows [18]:

$$P(B, \Lambda) = P(w_{-R}, f_{-R}) \{ \mathbf{\Pi}_{n=-R+1}^{N+L-2} [P(w_n, f_{n-1}, f_n) / P(\widetilde{w}_n, f_{n-1})] \}$$

The critical ratio of probabilities in the [...] term above retains the Martingale sequence properties on the generalized Viterbi path, as with the standard HMM/Viterbi implementation, and all of the elegant convergence and limit properties of Martingales are thereby inherited via the backward martingale convergence theorem (as discussed in [224]). The sliding-window clique overlap (see Fig. 7.12) is much more significant than with the standard HMM, giving rise to many more table look-ups on eij-transition tables.

A generalization to the Viterbi algorithm can now be directly implemented, using the above form, to establish an efficient dynamic programming table construction. Generalized expressions for the Baum-Welch algorithm are also possible. For further details on the generalized Viterbi and Baum-Welch algorithms for the meta-state HMM see [18].

The gap and hash interpolating Markov Models (gIMM and hIMM) [19,39] can be directly incorporated into meta-HMMBD gene-finding models as a further enhancement to the underlying Markov models, since they are already known to extract additional information that may prove useful, particularly in the zone-dependent emission regions (denoted 'zde's as in

[19,39]) where promoters and other gapped motifs might exist. Promoters and transcription factor binding sites often have lengthy overall gapped motif structure, and with the hash-interpolated Markov models it is also possible to capture the conserved higher order sequence information in the zde sample space. The hIMM and gIMM methods, thus, will not only strengthen the gene structure recognition, they can also provide the initial indications of anomalous motif structure in the regions identified by a gene-finder (in a post-genomic phase of the analysis) [19,39].

By viewing state transitions, such as $e_0 e_1$ or $e_0 i_0$, as transition "dimer states", or as two-element "footprint" states, we begin to shift ot a meta-HMM footing where we can model emissions more accurately. For the footprint states introduced in what follows a critical assumption is made – *at most one non-self transition is allowed per footprint transition*. This assumption is a equivalent to a minimum length constraint on regions of self-transitions to be footprint size or greater. For genomic applications this is not a problematic constraint, and when a concern, different 'gene-scans' can always be performed with different footprint sizes.

When encountered sequentially in the Viterbi algorithm, the sequence of (single) non-self state transition 'dominated' *footprint* states would conceivably score highly when computed for the footprint-width number of footprint-states that overlap the non-self transition. In other words we can expect a *natural boosting* effect for the correct prediction at such non-self transitions (compared to the standard HMM). To describe bases in the irreducible joint probability we have: $w_n = b_{n-L+1}, ..., b_n, ..., b_{n+R}$, and $\widetilde{w}_n = b_{n-L+1}, ..., b_n, ..., b_{n+R-1}$ describes the base observations, while $s_n = \lambda_n \lambda_{n+1}$ (dimer states, length in λ's =2), and $f_n = s_{n-l+1}, ..., s_{n+r} \cong \lambda_{n-l+1}, ..., \lambda_n, ..., \lambda_{n+r+1}$ (footprint state, length in s's= l+r), describes the associated labels. Given the above, the clique-factorized HMM is as shown in the previous equation.

The core term in the clique-factorization can also be written by introducing a Bayesian parameter, one that happens to provide a matching joint probability construct (to the extent possible) with the term in the numerator:

$$\rho = \frac{P(w_n, f_{n-1}, f_n)}{P(\widetilde{w}_n, f_{n-1})} = \frac{P(w_n, f_{n-1}, f_n)}{\sum_{f'_{n(allowed)}} P(\widetilde{w}_n, f_{n-1}, f'_n)}$$

$$= \frac{P(w_n | f_{n-1}, f_n) \, P(f_n | f_{n-1}) \, P(f_{n-1})}{\sum_{f'_n} P(\widetilde{w}_n | f_{n-1}, f'_n) \, P(f'_n | f_{n-1}) \, P(f_{n-1})}$$

In the standard Markov model R = 0, L = 1, r = -1, l = 0: $f_n = \lambda_n$, $w_n = b_n$, $P(\widetilde{w}_n, f_{n-1}) = P(\lambda_n)$:

$$\left. \frac{P(w_n, f_{n-1}, f_n)}{P(\widetilde{w}_n, f_{n-1})} \right|_{\substack{Standard\ Hidden \\ Markov\ Model}} = P(b_n | \lambda_n) \, P(\lambda_n | \lambda_{n-1})$$

In the above we introduce the constraint notation with the vertical bar notation, where the expression on the left is the clique factorization term with the constraint that it approximate according to the standard HMM conditional probabilities.

We now examine specific cases of this equation to clarify the novel improvements that result. *In what follows we constrain our model to have a minimum length on regions (thus self-transitions) such that footprint states, and their transitions, can only have one transition between different states.*

Consider the case with the first footprint state being of eij-transition type, and the second footprint thereby constrained to be of the appropriate xx-type:

$$\left.\frac{P(w_n, f_{n-1}, f_n)}{P(\widetilde{w}_n, f_{n-1})}\right|_{f_{n-1} \in eij} = \left.\frac{P(w_n, f_{n-1}, f_n)}{\sum_{f'_{n(allowed)}} P(\widetilde{w}_n, f_{n-1}, f'_n)}\right|_{\substack{f_{n-1} \in eij \\ [f'_n \text{ unique} \in xx]}}$$

$$= P(b_{n+R}|\widetilde{w}_n, f_{n-1}, f_n)\big|_{f_{n-1} \in eij} \; P(f_n|f_{n-1})\big|_{f_{n-1} \in eij}$$
$$= P(b_{n+R}|\widetilde{w}_n, f_{n-1})$$

Where use is made of the relation $P(f_n|f_{n-1})\big|_{f_{n-1} \in eij} = 1$ for the unique xx-footprint that follow the eij-transition given our minimum length constraint.

Consider, next, the case with the first footprint state being xx-type:

$$\left.\frac{P(w_n, f_{n-1}, f_n)}{P(\widetilde{w}_n, f_{n-1})}\right|_{f_{n-1} \in xx} = \left.\frac{P(w_n|f_{n-1}, f_n)\big|_{f_{n-1} \in xx} P(f_n|f_{n-1})}{\sum_{f'_n} P(\widetilde{w}_n|f_{n-1}, f'_n)\big|_{f_{n-1} \in xx} P(f'_n|f_{n-1})}\right|_{f_{n-1} \in xx}$$

$$= \left.\frac{P(w_n|f_n) \, P(f_n|f_{n-1})}{\sum_{f'_n} P(\widetilde{w}_n|f'_n) P(f'_n|f_{n-1})}\right|_{f_{n-1} \in xx}$$

If the second footprint is eij-transition type, then the equation has two sum terms in the denominator if the first transition is ii or jj transition, and a third sum contribution if the first transition is an ee-transition:

In what follows, dimer notation is used on footprints, since we are interested in the footprint-to-footprint transitions. Given their large overlap dependence, this notation and formalism directly generalizes to the same cases no matter the size of the footprint (due to the single major-transition in or between footprints constraint that is provided by a minimum length constraint).

If $f_{n-1} \in xx$ we have three cases: $xx \in \{ii, ee, jj\}$. For $f_{n-1} = ii$, we have two possible $f_n \in \{ii, ie\}$; for $f_{n-1} = jj$, we have two possible $f_n \in \{jj, je\}$; for $f_{n-1} = ee$, we have three possible $f_n \in \{ee, ej, ei\}$.

$$\left.\frac{P(w_n, f_{n-1}, f_n)}{P(\widetilde{w}_n, f_{n-1})}\right|_{\substack{f_{n-1} = ii, \\ f_n = ie}} = \frac{P(w_n|ie) \, P(ie|ii)}{P(\widetilde{w}_n|ie)P(ie|ii) + P(\widetilde{w}_n|ii)P(ii|ii)}$$

$$= \frac{P(b_{n+R}|\widetilde{w}_n, ie)}{1 + \left(\frac{P(\widetilde{w}_n|ii)}{P(\widetilde{w}_n|ie)}\right)\left(\frac{P(ii|ii)}{P(ie|ii)}\right)}$$

Where we have introduced the notation 'ii' to denote the dimer state or the footprint state 'ii…iii', and the notation 'ie' to denote the dimer state or the footprint state 'ii…iie'.

151

Similarly, consider $f_{n-1} = jj$ and $f_n = je$:

$$\left.\frac{P(w_n, f_{n-1}, f_n)}{P(\tilde{w}_n, f_{n-1})}\right|_{\substack{f_{n-1} = jj \\ f_n = je}} = \frac{P(w_n|je)\,P(je|jj)}{P(\tilde{w}_n|je)P(je|jj) + P(\tilde{w}_n|jj)P(jj|jj)}$$

$$= \frac{P(b_{n+R}|\tilde{w}_n, je)}{1 + \left(\frac{P(\tilde{w}_n|jj)}{P(\tilde{w}_n|je)}\right)\left(\frac{P(jj|jj)}{P(je|jj)}\right)}$$

For the $f_{n-1} = ee$ and $f_n = ej$ we get a similar expression, but a third term in the sum due to the three possibilities allowed for f_n:

$$\left.\frac{P(w_n, f_{n-1}, f_n)}{P(\tilde{w}_n, f_{n-1})}\right|_{\substack{f_{n-1} = ee, \\ f_n = ej}} = \frac{P(w_n|ej)\,P(ej|ee)}{P(\tilde{w}_n|ej)P(ej|ee) + P(\tilde{w}_n|ei)P(ei|ee) + P(\tilde{w}_n|ee)P(ee|ee)}$$

$$= \frac{P(b_{n+R}|\tilde{w}_n, ej)}{1 + \left(\frac{P(\tilde{w}_n|ei)}{P(\tilde{w}_n|ej)}\right)\left(\frac{P(ei|ee)}{P(ej|ee)}\right) + \left(\frac{P(\tilde{w}_n|ee)}{P(\tilde{w}_n|ej)}\right)\left(\frac{P(ee|ee)}{P(ej|ee)}\right)}$$

Likewise for the $f_{n-1} = ee$ and $f_n = ei$ we get a similar expression, but a third term in the sum:

$$\left.\frac{P(w_n, f_{n-1}, f_n)}{P(\tilde{w}_n, f_{n-1})}\right|_{\substack{f_{n-1} = ee, \\ f_n = ei}} = \frac{P(w_n|ei)\,P(ei|ee)}{P(\tilde{w}_n|ei)P(ei|ee) + P(\tilde{w}_n|ej)P(ej|ee) + P(\tilde{w}_n|ee)P(ee|ee)}$$

$$= \frac{P(b_{n+R}|\tilde{w}_n, ei)}{1 + \left(\frac{P(\tilde{w}_n|ej)}{P(\tilde{w}_n|ei)}\right)\left(\frac{P(ej|ee)}{P(ei|ee)}\right) + \left(\frac{P(\tilde{w}_n|ee)}{P(\tilde{w}_n|ei)}\right)\left(\frac{P(ee|ee)}{P(ei|ee)}\right)}$$

Consider now the cases involving self-transitions: $f_{n-1} = xx$ and $f_n = xx$. The derivation parallels that above for $f_{n-1} = ii$ and $f_n = ii$:

$$\left.\frac{P(w_n, f_{n-1}, f_n)}{P(\tilde{w}_n, f_{n-1})}\right|_{\substack{f_{n-1} = ii, \\ f_n = ii}} = \frac{P(w_n|ii)\,P(ii|ii)}{P(\tilde{w}_n|ie)P(ie|ii) + P(\tilde{w}_n|ii)P(ii|ii)}$$

$$= \frac{P(b_{n+R}|\tilde{w}_n, ii)}{1 + \left(\frac{P(\tilde{w}_n|ie)}{P(\tilde{w}_n|ii)}\right)\left(\frac{P(ie|ii)}{P(ii|ii)}\right)}$$

Similarly, consider $f_{n-1} = jj$ and $f_n = jj$:

$$\left.\frac{P(w_n, f_{n-1}, f_n)}{P(\tilde{w}_n, f_{n-1})}\right|_{\substack{f_{n-1} = jj \\ f_n = jj}} = \frac{P(w_n|jj)\,P(jj|jj)}{P(\tilde{w}_n|je)P(je|jj) + P(\tilde{w}_n|jj)P(jj|jj)}$$

$$= \frac{P(b_{n+R}|\tilde{w}_n, jj)}{1 + \left(\frac{P(\tilde{w}_n|je)}{P(\tilde{w}_n|jj)}\right)\left(\frac{P(je|jj)}{P(jj|jj)}\right)}$$

For the $f_{n-1} = ee$ and $f_n = ej$ we get the third term in the sum due to the three possibilities allowed for f_n:

$$\frac{P(w_n, f_{n-1}, f_n)}{P(\tilde{w}_n, f_{n-1})}\Bigg|_{\substack{f_{n-1}=ee \\ f_n=ee}} = \frac{P(w_n|ee)\,P(ee|ee)}{P(\tilde{w}_n|ej)P(ej|ee)+P(\tilde{w}_n|ei)P(ei|ee)+P(\tilde{w}_n|ee)P(ee|ee)}$$

$$= \frac{P(b_{n+R}|\tilde{w}_n, ee)}{1+\left(\frac{P(\tilde{w}_n|ei)}{P(\tilde{w}_n|ee)}\right)\left(\frac{P(ei|ee)}{P(ee|ee)}\right)+\left(\frac{P(\tilde{w}_n|ej)}{P(\tilde{w}_n|ee)}\right)\left(\frac{P(ej|ee)}{P(ee|ee)}\right)}$$

In the above expressions we clearly have sequence dependent transitions. For $f_{n-1} = ii$, and $f_n = ie$ for example, we have:

$$\rho|_{GCHMM} = \frac{P(w_n, f_{n-1}, f_n)}{P(\tilde{w}_n, f_{n-1})}\Bigg|_{\substack{f_{n-1}=ii, \\ f_n=ie}}$$

$$= \frac{P(w_n|ie)\,P(ie|ii)}{P(\tilde{w}_n|ie)P(ie|ii)+P(\tilde{w}_n|ii)P(ii|ii)} = \frac{P(b_{n+R}|\tilde{w}_n, ie)P(ie|ii)}{P(ie|ii)+P(ii|ii)\left(\frac{P(\tilde{w}_n|ii)}{P(\tilde{w}_n|ie)}\right)}$$

While the standard HMM has this ratio with w_n a single element emission sequence, and $P(w_n, f_{n-1}, f_n) = P(w_n|f_n)\,P(f_n|f_{n-1})$, thus, for the standard HMM:

$$\rho|_{Std.HMM} = \frac{P(w_n, f_{n-1}, f_n)}{P(\tilde{w}_n, f_{n-1})}\Bigg|_{\substack{f_{n-1}=ii, \\ f_n=ie, \\ Std.HMM}} = P(b_{n+R}|ie)\,P(ie|ii)$$

If we generalized the Std. HMM to higher order Markov models on emissions, to the same order as in the generalized clique, there is still the difference in the transition probability contributions:

$$\rho|_{\substack{Std.HMM \\ HO\ EMs}} = P(b_{n+R}|\tilde{w}_n, ie)\,P(ie|ii),$$

as can be seen in the ratio of their contributions, and how it is sequence dependent (i.e., dependent on '$\tilde{w}_i$'):

$$\frac{\rho|_{\substack{Std.HMM \\ HO\ EMs}}}{\rho|_{GCHMM}} = P(ie|ii) + P(ii|ii)\left(\frac{P(\tilde{w}_i|ii)}{P(\tilde{w}_i|ie)}\right).$$

Note that the sequence dependencies (in this and the other footprint transition choices) enter via likelihood ratio terms. These are precisely the type of terms examined in [26] in an effort to improve the HMM-based discriminatory ability via use of SVMs. The 'discriminatory' aspect of the key new (sequence-dependent) contribution is most evident in forms like that above, where we have a likelihood ratio for the observed sequences given the different label 'classifications' chosen. In the cases that follow we will examine the extreme cases of the likelihood-ratio discriminator strongly classifying one way or the other, or not strongly classifying either way with the given sequence information (making the contribution of knowing that sequence information negligible, which should then reduce to the std. HMM situation, as will be shown). Specifically, we will now examine the above equations in situations where the sequence-dependent likelihood-ratios strongly favor one state model over another, with particular attention as to whether there are sequence dependent scenarios offering recovery of the heavy-tail distribution in example one and recovery of contrast resolution in example two:

Example One:

For $f_{n-1} = ii$ and $f_n = ii$ we showed:

$$\rho = \left. \frac{P(w_n, f_{n-1}, f_n)}{P(\tilde{w}_n, f_{n-1})} \right|_{\substack{f_{n-1}= ii, \\ f_n= ii}} = \frac{P(b_{n+R}|\tilde{w}_n, ii)}{1 + \left(\frac{P(\tilde{w}_n|ie)}{P(\tilde{w}_n|ii)} \right) \left(\frac{P(ie|ii)}{P(ii|ii)} \right)}$$

Example One; Case 1: $P(\tilde{w}_n|ie) \cong P(\tilde{w}_n|ii)$ (likelihood ratio of probabilities is approximately one, leading to a weak (small) classification confidence if a confidence parameterized classifier, like an SVM, is referred to in place of the simple ratio)

$$\rho|_{ie\cong ii} \cong P(b_{n+R}|\tilde{w}_n, ii) \, P(ii|ii)/[P(ii|ii) + P(ie|ii)]$$
$$= P(b_{n+R}|\tilde{w}_n, ii) \, P(ii|ii)$$

Thus, in the 'uninformed' case we recover regular 1st order HMM theory, with geometric distribution on 'ii'. In this notation, $\rho|_{ie\cong ii}$ refers to the value of ρ when the observed sequence $\tilde{w}_n$ has approximately the same probability regardless of the state being 'ii' or 'ie'.

Example One; Case 2: $P(\tilde{w}_n|ie) \gg P(\tilde{w}_n|ii)$ (likelihood ratio of probabilities is very large, leading to a strong (large) classification confidence if a confidence parameterized classifier, like an SVM, is referred to in place of the simple ratio)

$$\rho|_{ie\gg ii} \cong P(b_{n+R}|\tilde{w}_n, ii) \left[\frac{P(\tilde{w}_n|ii)P(ii|ii)}{P(\tilde{w}_n|ie)P(ie|ii)} \right]$$

In this case we obtain contributions less than the regular 1st order HMM counterpart, effectively shortening the geometric distribution on 'ii' → e.g., it adaptively switches to a shorter, sharper, fall-off on the distribution in a sequence dependent manner.

Example One; Case 3: $P(\tilde{w}_n|ie) \ll P(\tilde{w}_n|ii)$ (likelihood ratio of probabilities is very small, leading to a strong (large) classification confidence if a confidence parameterized classifier, like an SVM, is referred to in place of the simple ratio)

$$\rho|_{ie\ll ii} \cong P(b_{n+R}|\tilde{w}_n, ii) \, \underline{1}$$

In this case we obtain contributions greater than the regular 1st order HMM theory. In particular, ***we recover the heavy tail distribution in a sequence dependent manner***:

$$\frac{P(w_n, f_{n-1}, f_n)}{P(\widetilde{w}_n, f_{n-1})}\bigg|_{\substack{f_{i-1} \in ie, \\ f_i \in ee}} = P(b_{n+R}|\widetilde{w}_n, f_{n-1})$$

Example Two:

One more example-case will be considered, that involving acceptor splice-site recognition. For $f_{n-1} = ii$, $f_n = ie$ we have:

$$\rho = \frac{P(w_n, f_{n-1}, f_n)}{P(\widetilde{w}_n, f_{n-1})}\bigg|_{\substack{f_{n-1} = ii, \\ f_n = ie}} = \frac{P(b_{n+R}|\widetilde{w}_n, ie)}{1 + \left(\frac{P(\widetilde{w}_n|ii)}{P(\widetilde{w}_n|ie)}\right)\left(\frac{P(ii|ii)}{P(ie|ii)}\right)}$$

Example Two; Case 1: $P(\widetilde{w}_n|ie) \cong P(\widetilde{w}_n|ii)$

$$\rho|_{ie \cong ii} \cong P(b_{n+R}|\widetilde{w}_n, ie)\, P(ie|ii)$$

We recover regular HMM theory in the uninformed situation.

Example Two; Case 2: $P(\widetilde{w}_n|ie) \gg P(\widetilde{w}_n|ii)$

$$\rho|_{ie \gg ii} \cong P(b_{n+R}|\widetilde{w}_n, ie)$$

Greater than regular 1st order HMM theory. Removes key penalty of *P(ie|ii)* factor when sequence match overrides. ***Resolves weak contrast resolution at 1st order.***

Example Two; Case 3: $P(\widetilde{w}_n|ie) \ll P(\widetilde{w}_n|ii)$

$$\rho|_{ie \ll ii} \cong P(b_{n+R}|\widetilde{w}_n, ie)\left[\frac{P(ie|ii)P(\widetilde{w}_n|ie)}{P(ii|ii)P(\widetilde{w}_n|ii)}\right]$$

Less than regular 1st Order HMM, effectively weakens ie transition strength (the classic major-transition bias factor).

Use of the meta-HMM formalism resolves complications due to heavy-tail duration distributions and weak contrast. This is a new HMM modeling capability. The form of the clique factorization in [1] also has LLR terms such as $P(\widetilde{w}_n|ie)/P(\widetilde{w}_n|ii)$ that allow for a simple switch from internal scalar-based state discriminant to a vector-based feature, allowing for a similar substitution of a discriminant based on a Support Vector Machine (SVM) as demonstrated for splice sites in [26], and described in the pMM/SVM sub-section. These alternate representations do not introduce any significant increase in computational time complexity.

7.6 GHMMs: Full Duration Model
7.6.1 HMM with Duration (HMMD)

In the standard HMM, when a state i is entered, that state is occupied for a period of time, via self-transitions, until transiting to another state j. If the state interval is given as d, the standard HMM description of the probability distribution on state intervals is implicitly given by:

$$(7.1) \qquad p_i(d) = a_{ii}^{d-1}(1 - a_{ii})$$

where a_{ii} is self-transition probability of state i. As mentioned previously, this geometric distribution is inappropriate in many cases. The standard HHMM-with-Duration (HMMD) replaces the equation above with a $p_i(d)$ that models the real duration distribution of state i. In this way explicit knowledge about the duration of states is incorporated into the HMM. When entered, state i will have a duration of d according to its duration density $p_i(d)$; it then transits to another state j according to the state transition probability a_{ij} (self-transitions, a_{ii}, are not permitted in this formalism). It is easy to see that the HMMD will turn into a HMM if $p_i(d)$ is set to the geometric distribution shown above. The first HMMD formulation was studied by Ferguson [93]. A detailed HMMD description was later given by [18]. There have been many efforts to improve the computational efficiency of the HMMD formulation given its fundamental utility in many endeavors in science and engineering. Notable amongst these are the variable transition HMM methods for implementing the Viterbi algorithm introduced in [94], and the hidden semi-Markov model (HSMM) implementations of the forward-backward algorithm [95].

In [1,19,34] it is shown how to 'lift' side information that is associated with a region, or transition between regions, by 'piggybacking' that side information with the duration side information. We use, as example, HMM incorporation of duration itself as the guide in what follows. In doing so, we arrive at a hidden semi-Markov model formalism for a HMMD. An equivalent formulation of the HSMM was introduced in [94] for the Viterbi algorithm and in [95] for Baum-Welch. In these derivations, however, the maximum-interval constraint is still present (comparisons of these methods were subsequently detailed in [96]). Other HMM generalizations include Factorial HMMs [97] and hierarchical HMMs [98]. For the latter, inference computations scaled as $O(T^3)$ in the original description, and have since been improved to $O(T)$ by [99].

The HSMM formalism introduced here, however, is directly amenable to incorporation of side-information and to adaptive speedup (as described in [1,19,34,21]). For the state duration density $p_i(x = d)$, $1 \leq x \leq D$, we have:

$$(7.2) \qquad p_i(x = d) = p_i(x \geq 1) \cdot \frac{p_i(x \geq 2)}{p_i(x \geq 1)} \cdot \frac{p_i(x \geq 3)}{p_i(x \geq 2)} \dots \frac{p_i(x \geq d)}{p_i(x \geq d-1)} \cdot \frac{p_i(x = d)}{p_i(x \geq d)}$$

where $p_i(x = d)$ is abbreviated as $p_i(d)$ if no ambiguity. Define "self-transition" variable $s_i(d)$ = probability that next state is still $\lambda_t = i$, given that i has consecutively occurred d times up to now.

(7.3)

$$p_i(x = d) = \left[\prod_{j=1}^{d-1} s_i(j)\right](1 - s_i(d)), where \; s_i(d) = \begin{cases} \frac{p_i(x \geq d+1)}{p_i(x \geq d)} & if \; 1 \leq d \leq D - 1 \\ 0 \; if \; d = D \end{cases}$$

We see with comparison of the equation for $p_i(d)$ above and $p_i(d) = (a_{ii})^{d-1}(1 - a_{ii})$, that we now have similar form, there are 'd-1' factors of 's' instead of 'a', with a 'cap term' '(1-s)' instead of '(1-a)', where the 's' terms are not constant, but only depend on the state's duration probability distribution. In this way, each 's' can mesh with the HMM's dynamic programming table construction for the Viterbi algorithm at the column-level in the same manner that 'a' does. Side-information about the local strength of EST matches or homology matches, etc., that can be put in similar form, can now be 'lifted' into the HMM model on a proper, locally optimized Viterbi-path. The derivations of the Baum-Welch and Viterbi HSMM algorithms are in [1,19,43,21].

The memory complexity of this method is O(TN). No forward table needs to be saved. The computation complexity is $O(TN^2+TND)$. In an actual implementation, a scaling procedure may be needed to keep the forward-backward variables within a manageable numerical interval. One common method is to rescale the forward-backward variables at every time index t using the scaling factor $c_t = \Sigma_i f_t(i)$. Here we use a dynamic scaling approach. For this we need two versions of $\theta(k, i, d)$. Then at every time index, we test if the numerical values is too small, if so, we use the scaled version to push the numerical values up; if not, we keep using the unscaled version. In this way, no additional computation complexity is introduced by scaling.

As with Baum-Welch, the Viterbi algorithm for the HMMD is $O(TN^2+TND)$. Because logarithm scaling can be performed for Viterbi in advance, however, the Viterbi procedure consists only of additions to yield a very fast computation. For both the Baum-Welch and Viterbi algorithms, use of the HMMBD algorithm [21] can be employed (as in this work) to further reduce computational time complexity to $O(TN^2)$, thus obtaining the speed benefits of a simple HMM, with the improved modeling capabilities of the HMMD.

The standard HMMD replaces Eq. (7.1) with a $p_i(d)$ that models the real duration distribution of state i. In this way explicit knowledge about the duration of states is incorporated into the HMM. A general HMMD can be illustrated as shown in Fig. 7.13.

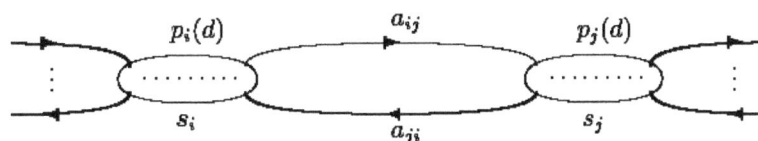

Fig. 7.13. The transition schematic for the HMM with duration (HMMD).

When entered, state i will have a duration of d according to its duration density $p_i(d)$, it then transits to another state j according to the state transition probability a_{ij} (self-transitions, a_{ii}, are not permitted in this formalism). It is easy to see that the HMMD will turn into a HMM if $p_i(d)$ is set to the geometric distribution shown in Eq. (7.1). The first HMMD formulation was studied by Ferguson [93]. A detailed HMMD description was later given by [21] (shown below). There have been many efforts to improve the computational efficiency of the HMMD formulation given its fundamental utility in many endeavors in science and engineering. Notable amongst these are the variable transition HMM methods for implementing the Viterbi algorithm introduced in [94], and the hidden semi-Markov model implementations of the forward-backward algorithm [95].

For an exact-HMMD formalism denote the following: N, the number of states; M, the number of distinct observations (where an observation sequence is denoted as: $B = b_1 b_2 \ldots b_T$); D, the maximum duration length; a_{ij}, the state transition probability; $e_i(k)$, the emission probability: probability of observing k in state i; π_i, the initial state probability: the probability of state i given the observation sequence B; $p_i(d)$, the state duration density: the probability of having exactly d consecutive state i observations after state i is entered. With these definitions the HMMD generalizations to the standard HMM resestimation formulae are as follows:

First define the forward-backward variables:
$$f_t(i) = P(b_1 \ldots b_t, \lambda_i \; end \; at \; t)$$
$$b_t(i) = P(b_{t+1} \ldots b_T | \lambda_i \; end \; at \; t)$$
$$f_t^*(i) = P(b_1 \ldots b_t, \lambda_i \; begins \; at \; t+1)$$
$$b_t^*(i) = P(b_{t+1} \ldots b_T | \lambda_i \; begins \; at \; t+1)$$
where $f_t(i)$ can be calculated by:

$$(7.4) \quad f_t(i) = \sum_{j=1}^{N} \sum_{d=1}^{D} f_{t-d}(j) \, a_{ji} p_i(d) \prod_{s=t-d+1}^{t} e_i(b_s)$$

Others can be calculated similarly. The relationships among f, f^*, b and b^* are:

$$f_t^*(i) = \sum_{j=1}^{N} f_t(j) \, a_{ji} \qquad f_t(j) = \sum_{d=1}^{D} f_{t-d}^*(i) \, p_i(d) \prod_{s=t-d+1}^{t} e_i(b_s)$$
$$b_t(i) = \sum_{j=1}^{N} b_t^*(j) \, a_{ij} \qquad b_t^*(i) = \sum_{d=1}^{D} b_{t+d}(i) \, p_i(d) \prod_{s=t+1}^{t+d} e_i(b_s)$$

Based on the above definitions and equations, we have the following maximum likelihood re-estimation formulas (the Baum-Welch algorithm) for HMMD [21]:

$$(7.5) \quad \pi_i^{new} = \frac{\pi_i b_0^*(i)}{P(B)}$$

$$(7.6) \quad a_{ij}^{new} = \frac{\sum_{t=1}^{T} f_t(i) a_{ij} b_t^*(j)}{\sum_{j=1}^{N} \sum_{t=1}^{T} f_t(i) a_{ij} b_t^*(j)}$$

$$(7.7) \quad e_i^{new}(k) = \frac{\sum_{\substack{t=1 \\ s.t. b_t = k}}^{T} \left\{ \sum_{r<t} f_r^*(i) b_r^*(i) - \sum_{r>t} f_r(i) b_r(i) \right\}}{\sum_{k=1}^{M} \sum_{\substack{t=1 \\ s.t. b_t = k}}^{T} \left\{ \sum_{r<t} f_r^*(i) b_r^*(i) - \sum_{r>t} f_r(i) b_r(i) \right\}}$$

$$(7.8) \quad p_i^{new}(k) = \frac{\sum_{t=1}^{T} f_t^*(i) p_i(d) b_{t+d}(i) \prod_{s=t+1}^{t+d} e_i(b_s)}{\sum_{d=1}^{D} \sum_{t=1}^{T} f_t^*(i) p_i(d) b_{t+d}(i) \prod_{s=t+1}^{t+d} e_i(b_s)}$$

In the above equations we can see that $D^2/2$ times more computational cost is required than the standard HMM. We now introduce a more efficient implementation of the explicit duration HMM that uses hidden semi-Markov models.

7.6.2 Hidden Semi-Markov Models (HSMM) with sid-information

It is shown in [19,21,34] how to 'lift' side information that is associated with a region, or transition between regions, by 'piggybacking' that side information along with the duration side information. We use, as example, HMM incorporation of duration itself as the guide. In doing so we arrive at a hidden semi-Markov model (HSMM) formalism. An equivalent formulation of the HSMM was introduced in [94] for the Viterbi algorithm and in [95] for Baum-Welch. In these derivations, however, the maximum-interval constraint is still present (comparisons of these methods were subsequently detailed in [96]). Other HMM generalizations include Factorial HMMs [97] and hierarchical HMMs [98]. For the latter, inference computations scaled as $O(T^3)$ in the original description, and has since been improved to $O(T)$ by [99].

The Baum-Welch algorithm in the martingale side-information HMMD formalism

We define the following three variables to simplify what follows:

$$(7.9) \quad \bar{s}_i(d) = \begin{cases} 1 - s_i(d+1) & \text{if } d = 0 \\ \frac{1 - s_i(d+1)}{1 - s_i(d)} \cdot s_i(d) & \text{if } 1 \le d \le D - 1 \end{cases}$$

$$(7.10) \quad \theta(k, i, d) = e_i(k)\bar{s}_i(d) \qquad 0 \le d \le D - 1$$

$$(7.11) \quad \varepsilon(k, i, d) = e_i(k)s_i(d) \qquad 1 \le d \le D - 1$$

Define: $f'_t(i, d) = P(b_1 b_2 \dots b_t, \lambda_t = i, \text{and } i \text{ has cons. occ. } d \text{ times up to } t)$

(7.12)

$$f'_t(i, d) = \begin{cases} e_i(b_t) \sum_{j=1, j \ne i}^{N} F_{t-1}(j)a_{ji} & \text{if } d = 1 \\ f'_{t-1}(i, d - 1)s_i(d - 1)e_i(b_t) & \text{if } 2 \le d \le D \end{cases}$$

Define:
$$\bar{f}_t(i, d) = P(b_1 b_2 \cdots b_t, \lambda_t = i \text{ ends at } t \text{ with duration } d)$$
$$= f'_t(i, d)(1 - s_i(d)) \qquad 1 \le d \le D$$

$$(7.13) \, \bar{f}_t(i, d) = \begin{cases} \theta(b_t, i, d - 1)F'_{t-1}(i) & \text{if } d = 1 \\ \theta(b_t, i, d - 1)\bar{f}_{t-1}(i, d - 1) & \text{if } 2 \le d \le D \end{cases}$$

where

$$(7.14) \quad F'_t(i) = \sum_{j=1, j \ne i}^{N} F_t(j) * a_{ji} \qquad F_t(i) = \sum_{d=1}^{D} f'_t(i, d)(1 - s_i(d))$$

Define: $b'_t(i, d) = P(b_t b_{t+1} \cdots b_T, \lambda_t = i \text{ will have a duration of } d \text{ from } t)$

$$(7.15) \, b'_t(i, d) = \begin{cases} \theta(b_t, i, d - 1)B'_{t+1}(i) & \text{if } d = 1 \\ \theta(b_t, i, d - 1)b'_{t+1}(i, d - 1) & \text{if } 1 < d \le D \end{cases}$$

Where

(7.16) $B'_t(i) = \sum_{j=1, j \neq i}^{N} a_{ij} B_t(j)$ $B_t(i) = \sum_{d=1}^{D} b'_t(i,d)$

Now *f, f*, b* and *b** can be expressed as:

$$f_t^*(i) = \frac{f'_{t+1}(i,1)}{e_i(b_{t+1})}; \quad b_t^*(i) = B_{t+1}(i); \quad b_t(i) = B'_{t+1}(i); \quad f_t(i) = F_t(i)$$

Now define

(7.17) $\omega(t,i,d) = \bar{f}_t(i,d) B'_{t+1}(i)$

(7.18) $\mu_t(i,j) = P(b_1 \cdots b_T, \lambda_t = i, \lambda_{t+1} = j) = F_t(i) a_{ij} B_{t+1}(j)$

(7.19) $\varphi(i,j) = \sum_{t=1}^{T-1} \mu_t(i,j)$

(7.20) $v_t(i) = P(b_1 \cdots b_T, \lambda_t = i) =$

$$\begin{cases} \pi(i) B_1(i) & if\ t = 1 \\ v_{t-1} + \sum_{j=1, j \neq i}^{N} (\mu_{t-1}(j,i) - \mu_{t-1}(i,j)) & if\ 2 \leq t \leq T \end{cases}$$

Using the above equations:

(7.21) $\pi_i^{new} = \frac{\pi_i b'_1(i,1)}{P(B)}$

(7.22) $a_{ij}^{new} = \frac{\varphi(i,j)}{\sum_{j=1}^{N} \varphi(i,j)}$

(7.23) $e_i^{new}(k) = \frac{\sum_{t=1\ s.t.\ O_t = k}^{T} v_t(i)}{\sum_{t=1}^{T} v_t(i)}$

(7.24) $p_i(d) = \frac{\sum_{t=1}^{T} \omega(t,i,d)}{\sum_{d=1}^{D} \sum_{t=1}^{T} \omega(t,i,d)}$

The Viterbi algorithm in the martingale side-information HMMD formalism

Define *$v_t(i, d)$* = the most probable path that consecutively occurred d times at state i at time t:

(7.25) $v_t(i,d) = \begin{cases} e_i(b_t) \max\limits_{j=1, j \neq i}^{N} V_{t-1}(j) a_{ji} & if\ d = 1 \\ v_{t-1}(i, d-1) s_i(d-1) e_i(b_t) & if\ 2 \leq d \leq D \end{cases}$

where

(7.26) $V_t(i) = max_{d=1}^{D} v_t(i,d)(1 - s_i(d))$

The goal is to find: $argmax_{[i,d]} \{ \max\limits_{i,d}^{N,D} v_t(i,d)(1 - s_i(d) \}$

Define:
$$\bar{s}_i(d) = \begin{cases} 1 - s_i(d+1) & if\ d = 0 \\ \dfrac{1-s_i(d+1)}{1-s_i(d)} \cdot s_i(d) & if\ 1 \le d \le D-1 \end{cases}$$

(7.27) $\theta(k,i,d) = \bar{s}_i(d-1)e_i(k) \quad 1 \le d \le D$

(7.28) $v_t'(i,d) = v_t(i,d)\big(1 - s_i(d)\big) \quad 1 \le d \le D$

$$= \begin{cases} \theta(b_t,i,d) \displaystyle\max_{j=1, j \ne i}^{N} V_{t-1}(j)a_{ji} & if\ d = 1 \\ v_{t-1}'(i,d-1)\theta(b_t,i,d) & if\ 2 \le d \le D \end{cases}$$

where

(7.29) $V_t(i) = \max_{d=1}^{D} v_t'(i,d).$

The goal is now:

(7.30) $argmax_{[i,d]}\{\max_{i,d}^{N,D} v_T'(i,d)\}$

If we do a logarithm scaling on $\bar{s}$, a and e in advance, the final Viterbi path can be calculated by:

(7.31) $\theta'(k,i,d) = \log\theta(k,i,d) = \log\bar{s}_i(d-1) + \log e_i(k) \quad 1 \le d \le D$

(7.32) $v_t'(i,d) = \begin{cases} \theta'(b_t,i,d) + \displaystyle\max_{j=1, j \ne i}^{N} (V_{t-1}(j) + \log a_{ji}) & if\ d = 1 \\ v_{t-1}'(i,d-1) + \theta'(b_t,i,d) & if\ 2 \le d \le D \end{cases}$

where the argmax goal above stays the same.

A summary of the Baum-Welch training algorithm is as follows:

1. initialize elements(λ) of HMMD.
2. calculate $b_t'(i,d)$ using Eq.s (7.15) and (7.16) (save the two tables: $B_t(i)$ and $B_t'(i)$).
3. calculate $\bar{f}_t(i,d)$ using Eq. (7.13) and (7.14).
4. re-estimate elements(λ) of HMMD using Eq. (7.17)-(7.24).
5. terminate if stop condition is satisfied, else goto step 2.

The memory complexity of this method is O(TN). As shown above, the algorithm first does backward computing (step (2)), and saves two tables: one is $B_t(i)$, the other is $B_t'(i)$. Then at very time index t, the algorithm can group the computation of step (3) and (4) together. So no forward table needs to be saved. We can do a rough estimation of HMMD's computation cost by counting multiplications inside the loops of $\Sigma^T \Sigma^N$ (which corresponds to the standard HMM computational cost) and $\Sigma^T \Sigma^D$ (the additional computational cost incurred by the

HMMD). The computation complexity is $O(TN^2+TND)$. In an actual implementation a scaling procedure may be needed to keep the forward-backward variables within a manageable numerical interval. One common method is to rescale the forward-backward variables at every time index t using the scaling factor $c_t = \Sigma_i f_t(i)$. Here we use a dynamic scaling approach. For this we need two versions of $\theta(k, i, d)$. Then at every time index, we test if the numerical values is too small, if so, we use the scaled version to push the numerical values up; if not, we keep using the unscaled version. In this way no additional computation complexity is introduced by scaling.

As with Baum-Welch, the Viterbi algorithm for the HMMD is $O(TN^2+TND)$. Because logarithm scaling can be performed for Viterbi in advance, however, the Viterbi procedure consists only of additions to yield a very fast computation. For both the Baum-Welch and Viterbi algorithms, use of the HMMBD algorithm [21] can be employed (as in this work) to further reduce computational time complexity to $O(TN^2)$, thus obtaining the speed benefits of a simple HMM, with the improved modeling capabilities of the HMMD.

7.6.3 HMM with Binned Duration (HMMBD)

The intuition guiding the HMMBD approach is that the standard HMM already does the desired duration modeling when the distribution modeled is geometric, suggesting that, with sufficient effort, a self-tuning explicit HMMD might be possible to achieve HMMD modeling capabilities at HMM computational complexity in an adaptive context.

The duration distribution of state i consists of rapidly changing probability regions (with small change in duration) and slowly changing probability regions. In the standard HMMD all regions share an equal computation resource (represented as D substates of a given state) -- this can be very inefficient in practice. In this section, we describe a way to recover computational resources, during the training process, from the slowly changing probability regions. As a result, the computation complexity can be reduced to $O(TN^2+TND^*)$, where D* is the number of "bins" used to represent the final, coarse-grained, probability distribution. A "bin" of a state is a group of substates with consecutive duration. For example, *f(i, d)*, *f(i, d+1)*, ...*f (i, d+δd)* can be grouped into one bin. The bin size is a measure of the granularity of the evolving length distribution approximation. A fine-granularity is retained in the active regions, perhaps with only one length state per bin, while a coarse-granularity is adopted in weakly changing regions, with possibly hundreds of length states per bin. An important generalization to the exact, standard, length-truncated, HMMD is suggested for handling long duration state intervals – a "tail bin". Such a bin is strongly indicated for good modeling on certain important distributions, such as the long-tailed distributions often found in nature, the exon and intron interval distributions found in gene-structure modeling in particular. In practice, the idea is to run the exact HMMD on a small portion, δT, of the training data, at $O(\delta TNN + \delta TND)$ cost, to get an initial estimate of the state interval distributions. Some preliminary course-graining is then performed, where strongly indicated, and the number of bins representing the length distribution is reduced from D to D′. The exact HMMD is then performed on the D′ substate model for another small portion of the training data, at computational expense $O(\delta TNN + \delta TND')$. This is repeated until the number of bin states, D*, reduces no further, and the bulk of the training then commences with the D* bin-states length distribution model at expense $O(TN^2+TND^*)$. The key to this process is the retention of training information during the 'freezing out' of length distribution states, and such that the D* bin state training process can be done at expense $O(TN^2+TND^*) \approx O(TN^2)$, which is the same complexity class as the standard HMM itself.

Starting from the above binning idea, for substates in the same bin, a reasonable approximation is applied:

$$(7.33) \quad \sum_{d'=d}^{d+\delta_d} f_t(i, d')\theta(b_t, i, d') = \theta(b_t, i, \bar{d}) \sum_{d'=d}^{d+\delta_d} f_t(i, d')$$

where $\bar{d}$ is the duration representative for all substates in this bin.

We begin in the first sub-section below with a description of the Baum-Welch algorithm in the adaptive hidden semi-Markov model (HSMM) formalism. This is followed by a sub-section with a description of the Viterbi algorithm in the adaptive HSMM formalism.

The Baum-Welch algorithm in the adaptive HMMD formalism
Define:

$$(7.34) \quad fprod_t(i, n) = \prod_{t-\delta_d(i,n)}^{t} \theta(b_t, i, \bar{d})$$

Based on the above approximation and equation, formulas (7.13) and (7.14) used by forward algorithm can be replaced by:

$(7.35) \quad fbin_t(i, n) = P(b_1 \dots b_t, \lambda_t = i \text{ ends at } t \text{ with duration between } d \text{ and } d + \delta_d(i, n))$

$$= \begin{cases} fbin_{t-1}(i, n)\theta(b_t, i, \bar{d}) - pop_t(i, n) + F'_{t-1}(i) & \text{if } n = 1 \\ fbin_{t-1}(i, n)\theta(b_t, i, \bar{d}) - pop_t(i, n) + pop_t(i, n - 1) & \text{if } 1 < n < D^* \end{cases}$$

Where

$$(7.36) \quad F_t(i) = \sum_{n=1}^{D^*} fbin_t(i, n) \quad F'_{t-1}(i) = \sum_{j=1; j\neq i}^{N} F_t(i)a_{ji}$$

$$(7.37) \quad pop_t(i, n) = queue(i, n) * fprod_t(i, n)$$

After the above calculations two updates are needed:

$$(7.38) \quad queue(i, n).push(pop_t(i, n - 1)$$

$$(7.39) \quad fprod_t(i, n) = fprod_t(i, n)/\theta(b_{t-\delta_d(i,n)}, i, \bar{d})$$

The explanation for push and pop operations, etc., begins with associating every bin with a queue $queue(i, n)$. The queue's size is equal to the number of substates grouped by this bin. At every time index, the oldest substate: $f(i, d+\delta_d(i, n))$ will be shifted out of its current bin and pushed into its next bin ('queue.push'), where $queue(i, n)$ stores the original probability of each substates in that bin when they were pushed in. So when one substate becomes old enough to move to next bin, its current probability can be recovered by first popping out its original probability, then multiplied by its "gain". Then an update is applied. Similarly, define:

$$(7.40) \quad bprod_t(i, n) = \prod_{t}^{t+\delta_d(i,n)} \theta(b_t, i, \bar{d})$$

Formulas (7.15) and (7.16) used by the backward algorithm can be replaced by

(7.41) $bbin_t(i,n) = P(b_1 \dots b_t, \lambda_t = i \text{ has remaining a duration between } d \text{ and } d + \delta_d(i,n) \text{ at } t)$

$$= \begin{cases} bbin_{t+1}(i,n)\theta(b_t, i, \bar{d}) - pop_t(i,n) + B'_{t+1}(i) & \text{if } n = 1 \\ bbin_{t+1}(i,n)\theta(b_t, i, \bar{d}) - pop_t(i,n) + pop_t(i, n+1) & \text{if } 1 < n < D^* \end{cases}$$

where

(7.42) $\quad B_t(i) = \sum_{n=1}^{D^*} bbin_t(i,n) \quad B'_t(i) = \sum_{j=1; j \neq i}^{N} B_t(j) a_{ij}$

(7.43) $\quad pop_t(i,n) = queue(i,n).pop * bprod_t(i,n)$

After the above calculation two updates are needed:

(7.44) $\quad queue(i,n).push(pop_t(i, n+1))$

(7.45) $\quad bprod_t(i,n) = bprod_t(i,n)/\theta(b_{t+\delta_d(i,n)}, i, \bar{d})$

The re-estimation formulas stay unchanged.

The Viterbi algorithm in the adaptive HMMD formalism

The idea is similar to the one for adaptive Baum-Welch training (with computation complexity also O(TN²+TND*)), where the following formulas are used:

(7.46)

$$New_t(i,n) = \begin{cases} max_{j=1, j \neq i}^{N}(m_{t-1}(j) + \log a_{ji}) & \text{if } n = 1 \\ Sum_{t-1}(i,n) - Queue(i, n-1).pop & \text{if } 1 < n \leq D^* \end{cases}$$

(7.47) $\quad Sum_t(i,n) = \begin{cases} 0 & \text{if } t = 1 \\ Sum_{t-1}(i,n) + \theta'(b_t, i, \bar{d}) & \text{if } 1 < t \leq T \end{cases}$

(7.48) $\quad D_t(i,n) = Sum_t(i,n) - New_t(i,n)$

(7.49) $\quad Queue(i,n).push(D_t(n,i))$

(7.50) $\quad Sort(i,n).insert(D_t(n,i))$

(7.51) $\quad m_t(i,n) = \max\{m_t(i,n), D_t(n,i)\}$

(7.52) $\quad m_t(i) = max_n^{D^*} m_t(i,n)$

The usage of the above relations is described in [1,21]. Note: there is non-trivial handling of many stack operations in order to attain the theoretically indicated O(TND) to O(TND*) improvement in actual implementation, as described in detail in [231].

Adaptive null-state binning for O(TN) computation

During the HMM Viterbi table construction for each of T sequence data values there is a column entry, and for each of N states there is a row. At each column the HMM Viterbi algorithm must look to the past column entries as it populates the table from left to right, thus leading to an O(TN²) computation. If we establish an adaptive binning capability, reminescent of what was done with the HMMBD method, then we can keep track of lists with respect to each state that correspond to prior column transitions to that state. If we, in particular, track those Viterbi most-probable-paths that arrive at our state cell with probability below some cutoff (with respect to the other probabilities arriving at that cell), we can ignore transitions from such cells in later column computations. What results is an initial $O(tN^2)$ $(t<<T)$ computation to learn the state lists for above cut-off transitions (suppose K on average), followed by the main body of the O(TNK) computation (with K<<N).

A method is also possible comprising use of a "fastViterbi" process where $O(TN^2)$ → O(TmN) via learned, local, max-path ordering in a given column of the Viterbi computation for the highest 'm' values. Subsequent columns first only examine the top 'm' max-paths and if their ordering is retained, and their total probability advanced sufficiently, then the other states remain 'frozen-out' with a large grouping (binning) on the probabilities on those states used to maintain their probability information (and correct normalization summing) when going forward column-by column, with reset to full column evaluation on the individual state level when the m values fall out of their initially identified ordering.

A method is possbile comprising use of a fastViterbi with null-binning process where $O(TN^2)$ → O(Tmn) → O(T) via learned global and local aspects of the data as indicated above. This approach offers significant utility as a purely HMM-based alignment algorithm that may outperform BLAST with comparable time complexity.

7.7 GHMMs: Linear Memory Baum-Welch Algorithm

Table chunking methods for the dynamic programming algorithms have been developed that involve only a single-pass computation analogous to the Viterbi algorithm (ignoring the O(L) traceback) [1]. The Viterbi algorithm efficiently calculates the most probable state path. The Baum-Welch algorithm calculates the probability of having a state at a particular index, summing over all path probabilities that arrive at that state-instance, and is usually implemented as two passes, for the forward and backward parameters. In the Linear Memory HMM introduced in [24], however, the Baum-Welch implementation has a distinctive trait other than a linear memory implementation, it's also a 'single-pass' implementation for the algorithm, which is needed for the Viterbi single-pass referenced, overlap-stitched, reconstituted signal in a distributed processing setting (described in Sec. 7.8 that follows). This can be used for brute force, and massively scalable, computational speed-up on all the HMM-based algorithms used in the SSA Protocol.

Following the notation used in [24], $t_{i,j}(t,m)$ is the weighted sum of probabilities of all possible state paths that emit subsequence $b_1,...,b_t$ and finish in state $\lambda_t = m$, taking an $\lambda_t = i$ → $\lambda_{t+1} = j$ (i→j) transition at least once (for some t) where the weight of each state path is the number of i→j transitions that it takes. Processing of the entire $t_{i,j}(t,m)$ recurrence takes memory proportional to $O(NQ)$ and processor time $O(TNQQ_{max})$.

Initially, since no transitions have been made, we have $t_{i,j}(1,m)=0$. After initialization we have the following recurrence steps

$$(7.53) \quad t_{i,j}(t,m) = f_{i(t-1)} \, a_{im} \, e_m(b_t) \, \delta(m=j) + \sum_{n=1}^{N} t_{i,j}\left(t-1,n\right) a_{nm} \, e_m(b_t)$$

The computation is in-step with the forward variable as a single-pass computation, where the delta function is defined as: $\delta(m=j) = \begin{cases} 1, & if \ m = j \\ 0, otherwise \end{cases}$. At a certain time moment t we need to score the evidence supporting transition between nodes i and j, which is the sum of probabilities of all possible state paths that emit subsequence $b_1,...,b_{t-1}$, and finish in state i (forward probability $f_{i(t-1)}$), multiplied by transition a_{ij} and emission $e_j(b_t)$ probabilities upon arrival to b_t. We extend the weighted paths containing evidence of i→j transitions made at previous time moments $1,...,t-1$ further down the trellis in the second part of the equation above. Finally, by the end of the recurrence, we marginalize the final state m out of probability $t_{i,j}(T,m)$ to get a weighted sum of state paths taking transition i→j at various time moments. Thus, we estimate transition utilization using

$$(7.54) \qquad a_{ij} = \frac{\sum_{m=1}^{N} t_{i,j}(T,m)}{\sum_{j \in out(state\ i)} \sum_{m=1}^{N} t_{i,j}(T,m)}$$

where *out(state i)* of nodes connected by edges from state *i*.

The following algorithm updates the 'emission' parameters for the set of discrete symbol probability distributions $E=\{e_1(b),..., e_N(b)\}$ in $O(NED)$ memory and $O(TNEDQ_{max})$ time. According to [24], $e_i(b,t,m)$ is the weighted sum of probabilities of all possible state paths that emit subsequence $b_1,...,b_t$ and finish in state m, for which state i emits observation b at least once where the weight of each state path is the number of b emissions that it makes from state i. Initialization step: $e_i(b,1,m)=f_{m1}\delta(i=m)\delta(b=b_1)$. After initialization we make the recurrence steps, where we correct emission recurrence presented in [100]:

$$(7.55) \quad e_i(b,t,m)= f_{mt}\delta(i=m)\delta(b=b_t) + \sum_{n=1}^{N} e_i(b, t-1, n)\ a_{nm}\ e_m(b_t)$$

Finally, by the end of the recurrence, we marginalize the final state m out of $e_i(b,T,m)$ and estimate the emission parameters through normalization

$$(7.56) \qquad e_j(b) = \frac{\sum_{m=1}^{N} e_i(b,T,m)}{\sum_{\gamma=1}^{D} \sum_{m=1}^{N} e_i(b,T,m)},$$

The forward sweep takes $O(TNQ_{max})$ time, where only the values of $f_{i(t-1)}$ for $1 \leq i \leq N$ are needed to evaluate f_{it}, thus rendering memory requirement to $O(N)$ for the forward algorithm. Computing $e_i(b,t,m)$ takes $O(NED)$ previous probabilities of $e_i(b,t-1,m)$ for $1 \leq m \leq N$, $1 \leq i \leq E$, $1 \leq b \leq D$. Recurrent updating of each $e_i(b,t,m)$ probability elements takes $O(Q_{max})$ summations, totaling $O(TNEDQ_{max})$.

7.8 GHMMs: Distributable Viterbi and Baum-Welch Algorithms
Distributed HMM processing via 'Viterbi-overlap-chunking' with GPU speedup
In HMM signal processing latency becomes very prohibitive when attempting to increase device bandwidth or when input datasets are large. Described in what follows are results from performing HMM algorithms in a distributed manner by breaking the full HMM table computation into overlapping chunks and leveraging the Markovian assumption underlying the HMM to help arrive at a chunk to full table reconstruction. The pathological instances where the distributed merges can fail to exactly reproduce the non-distributed HMM calculation can be made as least likely as desired with sufficiently strict, but not computationally expensive, segment join conditions. In this way, the distributed HMM provides a feature extraction that is equivalent to that of the sequentially run, general definition HMM, and with a speedup factor approximately equal to the number of processes (threads) operating on the data. The Viterbi most probable path calculation and the Expectation/Maximization (EM) calculation can both be performed in this distributed processing context.

The linear memory implementation described previously (and in [100]) was optimized according to the observation that Viterbi traceback paths in the Viterbi procedure typically converge to the most likely state path and travel together to the beginning of the decoding table – the picture being much like a river with minor tributaries backtracking onto that river, and maybe those 'tributaries' themselves have more minor state paths converging into them, etc. But the trait that is most notable in the convergence-durations to the 'main-tributary', or what is to be the most likely (Viterbi) path, is that it is usually a modest number of columns for many data types. This backwards Markovian memory loss on a tributary with respect to its origin (said to occur when backtracked and mixed with the main, Viterbi, convergence path of the tributaries) is hypothesized to be an indicator of the span of overlap sequence needed to have Viterbi path probabilities in a given column that have settled into their properly ordered relative probabilities in that column. Further column processing refinement to bring the relative values of the Viterbi-path probabilities into better estimation is then possible. In distributed processing efforts, this "Viterbi relaxation time" is a key parameter that can be used to design an optimally overlapping chunking of the data sequence in a distributed speed-up on the sequence analysis. For further details see [1,6].

A distributed signal processing test of some basic chunk reconstruction heuristics was performed on 5 computers with 300 signals in the study in [1,6]. Each signal had 5000 samples. The resulting Viterbi paths matched between the distributed HMM and standard HMM on a 10-column segment. For the standard HMM, EM training (5 loops) the Viterbi algorithm took 272 seconds. For distributed HMM with 5 CPU's, the computational time was reduced to 69 seconds. So using 5 computers, we had a speedup of 3.94. A perfect de-segmentation was performed with an N=10 match window as indicated, initially, but it was found that a perfect re-stitching of segments was also possible simply with N=1 (see Fig. 7.14), due to the implicit stringency of the simultaneity condition (the overlap match, at the one position corresponding to N=1, must globally index to the same observation data index for both segments). The multi-chunk re-stitching makes use of the Viterbi path and the entire set of Viterbi traceback pointers in a given overlap set of columns.

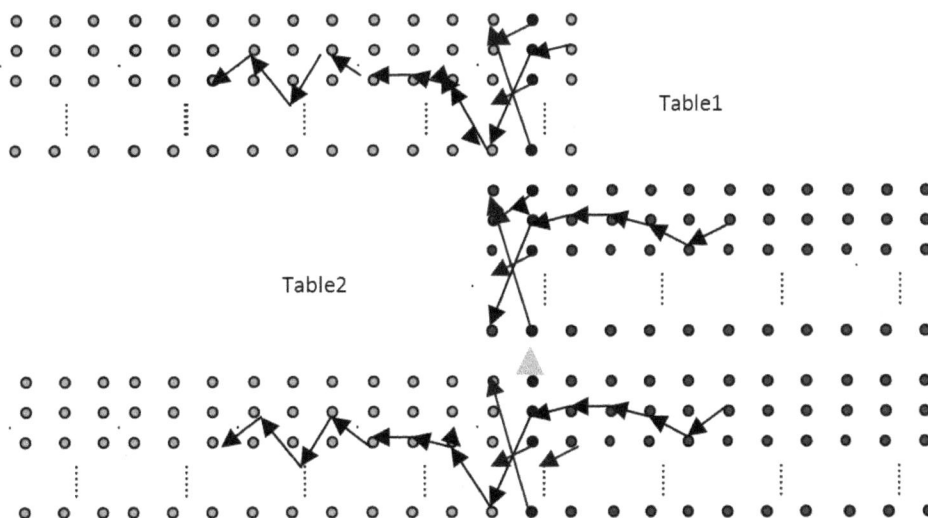

Figure 7.14. Viterbi column-pointer match de-segmentation rule. Table1 and Table2 (in figure) are overlapped. And their blue columns have the same

pointers. Then the index of this blue column becomes the joint. The black pointers form the final Viterbi path.

Relative Entropy and Viterbi Scoring

Sometimes tFSA methods can identify possible signal regions, but not all such regions contain true signals or good signals. This is simply because anomalous signal may come in multiple forms, some 'good' in the sense that it is usable, some 'bad' in that the signals aren't sufficiently stable for use (and should be dropped from the analysis, like dropping 'weak' confidence signals in SVM analysis [1]). Having an objective, minimally informed, process for evaluating good or bad signals is needed. In this context relative entropy comparison on newly captured signal with known good signals can be used to determine if the unknown newly acquired signal is sufficiently useful. Relative entropy is the natural measure for comparison in this setting as the HMM priors, emissions, and transition probabilities, lead to a comparison between discrete probability based feature vectors (such as that used in [1]). The proper measure for comparison of discrete probabilities is relative entropy [1] (not Euclidean distance). The priors, transitions, and emissions obtained on a particular signal region can have strong characterization by use of the Baum-Welch algorithm to re-estimate these parameters such they very closely reflect the attributes of the signal acquisition in question. In addition to the HMM feature extraction in terms of emission and transition probabilities, and the priors from the transitions, another set of feature components is the Viterbi path state frequencies (similar to the priors).

It is possible to have a good-state confidence test simply in terms of the relative entropy between the acquired signals prior probabilities and that of the known 'good' signal class. The weakness of this approach is that the priors entirely miss the transition structure, which might be highly distinctive, unless the prior states are actually dimer states or higher order footprint states thereby encapsulating the transition probabilities anyway [1]. In the examples in [1], the dimer and footprint states are introduced in analyzing genomic data for gene structure discovery, and the methods can be used, practically speaking, due to the low order of the genomic states. In channel current studies, and power signal analysis in general, there are typically too many states with the generic HMM. This problem can be overcome by use of EVA-projection on the acquired signal to project the noisy signal onto the dominant blockade states, however, resulting in a much smaller set of EVA-projected blockade states, often as few as four as with the genomic analysis, and in this setting the higher order states can be introduced and used in the higher-order-state prior comparisons.

7.9 Martingales and the Feasibility of Statistical Learning

Martingale Definition

A stochastic process $\{X_n; n=0,1, \ldots\}$ is martingale if, for $n=0,1, \ldots$,

1. $E[|X_n|] < \infty$
2. $E[X_{n+1}|X_0, \ldots, X_n] = X_n$

Def.: Let $\{X_n; n=0,1, \ldots\}$ and $\{Y_n; n=0,1, \ldots\}$ be stochastic processes. We say $\{X_n\}$ is martingale with respect to (w.r.t) $\{Y_n\}$ if, for $n=0,1, \ldots$:

1. $E[|X_n|] < \infty$

168

2. $E[X_{n+1}|Y_0, ..., Y_n] = X_n$

Examples of Martingales:

        (a) Suns of independent random variables: $X_n = Y_1 + ... + Y_n$.

        (b) Variance of a Sum $X_n = (\sum_{k=1}^{n} Y_k)^2 - n\sigma^2$

        (c) Have induced Martingales with Markov Chains! ....

        (d) For HMM learning, sequences of likelihood ratios are martingale....

The asymptotic equipartition theorem (AEP) and Hoeffding Inequalities (critical in Ch. 11) have both been generalized to Martingales.

Induced Martingales with Markov Chains

Let $\{Y_n ; n=0,1, ...\}$ be a Markov Chain (MC) process with transition probability matrix $P=\|P_{ij}\|$. Let f be a bounded right regular sequence for P:

$f(i)$ is non-negative and $f(i)=\sum_{k=1}^{n} P_{ij} f(j)$. Let $X_n = f(Y_n)$ → $E[|X_n|]< \infty$ (since f is bounded).

Now have:

$E[X_{n+1}|Y_0, ..., Y_n]$

  $= E[f(Y_{n+1})|Y_0, ..., Y_n]$

  $= E[f(Y_{n+1})|Y_n]$ (due to MC)

  $= \sum_{k=1}^{n} P_{Y_n, j} f(j)$ (def . of P_{ij} and f)

  $= f(Y_n)$

  $= X_n$

In HMM learning have sequences of likelihood ratios, which is a martingale, proof:

Induced Martingales with Sequences of Likelihood Ratios

Let $Y_0, Y_1, ...$ be iid rv.s and let f_0 and f_1 be probability density functions. A stochastic process of fundamental importance in the theory of testing statistical hypotheses is the sequence of likelihood ratios:

$$X_n = \frac{f_1(Y_0)f_1(Y_1)...f_1(Y_n)}{f_0(Y_0)f_0(Y_1)...f_0(Y_n)}, n = 0,1, ...$$

Assume $f_0(y) > 0$ for all y:

$$E[X_{n+1} | Y_0, ..., Y_n] = E[X_n \left(\frac{f_1(Y_{n+1})}{f_0(Y_{n+1})}\right) | Y_0, ..., Y_n] = X_n E[\frac{f_1(Y_{n+1})}{f_0(Y_{n+1})}]$$

When the common distribution of the Y_k's (used in the 'E' function) has f_0 as its probability density, have:

$$E[\frac{f_1(Y_{n+1})}{f_0(Y_{n+1})}] = 1$$

So, $E[X_{n+1} | Y_0, ..., Y_n] = X_n$. So likelihood ratios are martingale when the common distribution is f_0.

7.10 HMM Implementation for Viterbi in C

```c
int init_state_priors(int state_cardinality, double *state_prior, int *data_quant,
                      int total_pts, int stepsize, FILE *sigfile_hmm,int *state_count,
                      int total_state_count, int j) {

    int print_quant_profile=0;
    int print_priors_profile=0;
    int prior_psuedocount=1;
    int k;
    double low_bound_cutoff = 0.05;
    double high_bound_cutoff = 0.05;
    double prior_test = 0.0;

    for (k=0;k<state_cardinality;k++) {
        state_count[k]=prior_psuedocount; // init psuedocounts
    }
    total_state_count = prior_psuedocount*state_cardinality; // init value
    for (k=0;k<total_pts/stepsize;k++) {
        state_count[data_quant[k]]++;
        total_state_count++;
    }
    for (k=0;k<state_cardinality;k++) {
        state_prior[k] = (double) state_count[k]/total_state_count;
        prior_test += state_prior[k];
    }

    // prior test
    if (prior_test>1.00001 || prior_test<0.99999) {
        printf("error: prior_test=%7.5f\n",prior_test);
        j++;
        return 1;
    }
    return 0;
}


void init_emissions(int state_cardinality, double **emission_prob,  int *state_count){
    int i,k;
    double variance[state_cardinality];
    double em_prob_Z[state_cardinality];
    double rayleigh_var = 1.0;
    double emission_prob_test;
    for (i=0;i<state_cardinality;i++) {
        variance[i] = rayleigh_var;
    }
    for (i=0;i<state_cardinality;i++) {
        em_prob_Z[i] = 0.0;
        for (k=0;k<state_cardinality;k++) {
            emission_prob[i][k] = exp(-(k-i)*(k-i)/(2*variance[i]));
            em_prob_Z[i] += emission_prob[i][k];
        }
        for (k=0;k<state_cardinality;k++) {
            emission_prob[i][k] = emission_prob[i][k]/em_prob_Z[i];
        }
        emission_prob_test = 0.0;
        for (k=0;k<state_cardinality;k++) {
            emission_prob_test += emission_prob[i][k];
        }
        if (emission_prob_test>1.01 || emission_prob_test<0.99) {
            printf("error: emission_prob_test failure\n");
        }
    }
}


void init_transitions(int state_cardinality, int *data_quant, double **trans_prob,
                      int total_pts, int stepsize, double **emission_prob) {
    int i,k,l;
    int projection_init = 1;
    int trans_psuedocount = 3;
```

```
    int trans_count[state_cardinality][state_cardinality];
    int trans_count_total[state_cardinality];
    double trans_total[state_cardinality];
    double trans_prob_sum[state_cardinality];
    double test_total;
    double weight_total;
    double weight[state_cardinality][state_cardinality];
    int in_state,out_state;
    int shift = 10;
    int steps = 15; //by two
    int steplength = 2;
    int loop;
    int loop_max = 10;
    double weight_old[steps][steps];
    double weight_new[steps][steps];

    if (projection_init) {
        for (i=0;i<state_cardinality;i++) {
            for (k=0;k<state_cardinality;k++) {
                trans_prob[i][k] = 0.0;
            }
        }
        for (l=0;l<total_pts/stepsize-1;l++) {
            in_state = data_quant[l];
            out_state = data_quant[l+1];
            for (i=0;i<state_cardinality;i++) {
                trans_total[i] = 0.0;
                for (k=0;k<state_cardinality;k++) {
                    trans_prob[i][k] += emission_prob[i][in_state]
                                    *emission_prob[k][out_state];
                    trans_total[i] += trans_prob[i][k];
                }
            }
        }
        for (i=0;i<state_cardinality;i++) {
            test_total = 0.0;
            for (k=0;k<state_cardinality;k++) {
                trans_prob[i][k] = trans_prob[i][k]/trans_total[i];
                test_total += trans_prob[i][k];
            }
            if (test_total>1.01 || test_total<0.99) {
                printf("error: trans_prob[%d][summed]=%6.4f\n",i,test_total);
            }
        }
    }
// omitted options ..........
}

void calculate_forward_backward(int state_cardinality, double **forward,
            double **backward, int total_pts, int stepsize, double **emission_prob,
            double **trans_prob, int *data_quant, double *state_prior) {
    double scale[total_pts/stepsize];
    int i,k,l;
    double log_sig_prob;
    double fb_identity;

    //// calculate forward/backward variables (scaled versions)
    scale[0] = 0.0;
    for (i=0;i<state_cardinality;i++) {
        forward[0][i] = emission_prob[data_quant[0]][i]
                        *state_prior[i];
        scale[0] += forward[0][i];
    }
    // rescale forward vars
    for (i=0;i<state_cardinality;i++) {
        forward[0][i] = forward[0][i]/scale[0];
    }
    for (i=1;i<total_pts/stepsize;i++) {
        scale[i] = 0.0;
        for (k=0;k<state_cardinality;k++) {
            forward[i][k] = 0.0;
            for (l=0;l<state_cardinality;l++) {
                forward[i][k] += forward[i-1][l]*trans_prob[l][k];
            }
            forward[i][k] = forward[i][k]
```

```
                              *emission_prob[data_quant[i]][k];
                scale[i] += forward[i][k];
            }
            // rescale forward vars
            for (k=0;k<state_cardinality;k++) {
                forward[i][k] = forward[i][k]/scale[i];
            }
        }
        log_sig_prob = 0.0;
        for (i=0;i<total_pts/stepsize;i++) {
            log_sig_prob += log(scale[i]);
        }
        printf("-log_sig_prob=%9.7f\n",-log_sig_prob);
        // now have eval of forward variables

        for (i=0;i<state_cardinality;i++) {
            // without rescale, backward[total_pts-1]=1 is b.c.
            backward[total_pts/stepsize-1][i] = 1;
        }
        for (i=total_pts/stepsize-2;i>=0;i--) {
            for (k=0;k<state_cardinality;k++) {
                backward[i][k] = 0.0;
                for (l=0;l<state_cardinality;l++) {
                    backward[i][k] += backward[i+1][l]*trans_prob[k][l]
                                    *emission_prob[data_quant[i+1]][l];
                }
                backward[i][k] = backward[i][k]/scale[i+1];
            }
        }
        for (i=0;i<total_pts/stepsize;i++) {
            fb_identity= 0.0;
            for (k=0;k<state_cardinality;k++) {
                fb_identity += forward[i][k]*backward[i][k];
            }
            if (fb_identity>1.0001 || fb_identity<0.9999) {
                printf("fb_identity failure\n");
                printf("i=%d:\t%6.4f\n",i,fb_identity);
                exit(0);
            }
        }
        // now have eval of backward variables
        // also passing identity check: forward and backward variables good
}

void get_expected_values(int state_cardinality, int total_pts, int stepsize,
        int *data_quant, double **emission_prob, double **trans_prob,
        double **forward, double **backward,double **expected_emission_count,
        double **expected_trans_count) {
    int i,k,l;
    double min_prob = 0.000000001;
    int in_state,out_state;
    double temp_trans_sum;
    double temp_trans[state_cardinality][state_cardinality];

    for (i=0;i<state_cardinality;i++) {
        for (k=0;k<state_cardinality;k++) {
            expected_emission_count[k][i] = min_prob;
            expected_trans_count[k][i] = min_prob;
        }
    }

    // get expected counts on transitions
    for (i=0;i<total_pts/stepsize-1;i++) {
        in_state = data_quant[i];
        out_state = data_quant[i+1];
        temp_trans_sum = 0.0;
        for (k=0;k<state_cardinality;k++) {
            for (l=0;l<state_cardinality;l++) {
                // recall convention: emission[state][base]
                temp_trans[k][l] =
                    emission_prob[l][out_state]*trans_prob[k][l]*forward[i][k];
                temp_trans_sum += temp_trans[k][l];
            }
        }
        for (k=0;k<state_cardinality;k++) {
```

172

```
                    for (l=0;l<state_cardinality;l++) {
                        expected_trans_count[k][l] +=
                            (temp_trans[k][l]/temp_trans_sum)*backward[i+1][l];
                    }
                }
            }
        // now have expected counts on transitions

        // get expected counts on emissions
        // recall convention: emission[state][base]
        for (i=0;i<total_pts/stepsize;i++) {
            in_state = data_quant[i];
            for (k=0;k<state_cardinality;k++) {
                expected_emission_count[k][in_state] +=
                    forward[i][k]*backward[i][k];
            }
        }

        for (i=0;i<state_cardinality;i++) {
            for (k=0;k<state_cardinality;k++) {
                if (expected_trans_count[i][k]<min_prob) {
                    printf("expected_trans_count error\n");
                    exit(0);
                }
                if (expected_emission_count[i][k]<min_prob) {
                    printf("expected_emission_count[%d][%d]=%20.18f\n",
                        i,k,expected_emission_count[i][k]);
                    exit(0);
                }
            }
        }
    }

void obtain_viterbi_path(int state_cardinality,double **emission_prob,
                        double **trans_prob,int total_pts,int stepsize,
                        int *data_filtered,int *data_quant,
                        double *state_prior, int j)  {
    int i,k,l,penultima_index;
    double log_path_probt;
    int in_state,last_path_state;
    int min_ptr = 100;
    int min_loc = 0;
    int min_state = 0;
    double max_path_value,path_value;
    int back_ptr[total_pts/stepsize][state_cardinality];
    double log_path_prob[total_pts/stepsize][state_cardinality];

    in_state = data_quant[0];
    for (k=0;k<state_cardinality;k++) {
        log_path_prob[0][k] = log(state_prior[k]) +
                        log(emission_prob[k][in_state]);
        back_ptr[0][k] = state_cardinality/2; // arbitrary
    }

    for (i=1;i<total_pts/stepsize;i++) {
        in_state = data_quant[i];
        for (k=0;k<state_cardinality;k++) {
            max_path_value = log_path_prob[i-1][state_cardinality/2]
                        + log(trans_prob[state_cardinality/2][k]);
            back_ptr[i][k] = state_cardinality/2;
            for (l=0;l<state_cardinality;l++) {
                path_value = log_path_prob[i-1][l] + log(trans_prob[l][k]);
                if (path_value > max_path_value) {
                    max_path_value = path_value;
                    back_ptr[i][k] = l;
                }
            }
            log_path_prob[i][k] = log(emission_prob[k][in_state])
                                +max_path_value;
            if (back_ptr[i][k]<min_ptr) {
                min_ptr=back_ptr[i][k];
                min_loc=i;
                min_state=k;
            }
        }
```

```perl
        }
        last_path_state = state_cardinality/2; //arbitrary, just not undef!
        log_path_probt = log_path_prob[total_pts/stepsize-1][0];
        for (l=1;l<state_cardinality;l++) {
            if (log_path_prob[total_pts/stepsize-1][l]>log_path_probt) {
                log_path_probt = log_path_prob[total_pts/stepsize-1][l];
                last_path_state = l;
            }
        }
        data_filtered[total_pts/stepsize-1] = last_path_state;
        penultima_index = (total_pts/stepsize)-2;
        for (i=penultima_index;i>=0;i--) {
            data_filtered[i] = back_ptr[i+1][data_filtered[i+1]];
        }
    }
}
```

```perl
my $Init_State_Priors = sub {
    my ($level_one_ref,$HMM_state_cardinality,$state_shift,
        $pseudocount,$HMM_data_ref,$bin_size) = @_;
    my @HMM_data_array;
    my @state_count = ();
    my $total_instance_count=0;
    if (!$state_shift) { $state_shift = -20; }
    if (!$pseudocount) { $pseudocount = 1; }
    if (!$bin_size) { $bin_size = 1; }

    if ($HMM_data_ref) {
        @HMM_data_array = @{$HMM_data_ref};
        my $prior_training_data_instances = scalar(@HMM_data_array);
        my $training_index;
        for $training_index (0..$prior_training_data_instances-1) {
            my $state = int( ($HMM_data_array[$training_index]+$state_shift)/$bin_size );
            if ($state<0) { $state = 0; }
            $state_count[$state]++;
            $total_instance_count++;
        }
    }
    else { # get pseudocounts from here, if conditional defunct
        my $state;
        for $state (0..$HMM_state_cardinality-1) {
            $state_count[$state]=$pseudocount;
            $total_instance_count+=$pseudocount;
        }
    }

    my @lev1_array = @{$level_one_ref};
    my $training_data_instances = scalar(@lev1_array);
    my $training_index;
    for $training_index (0..$training_data_instances-1) {
        my $state = int( ($lev1_array[$training_index]+$state_shift)/$bin_size );
        if ($state<=0) {
            $state = 0;
#           print "zero state thresholding\n";
        }
        my $max_states = $HMM_state_cardinality;
        if ($state>=$max_states) {
            $state = $max_states-1;
#           print "upper $max_states state thresholding\n";
        }
        $state_count[$state]++;
        $total_instance_count++;
    }

    my $state;
    my $prior_prob_test = 0;
    my @state_prior;
    for $state (0..$HMM_state_cardinality-1) {
        $state_prior[$state] = $state_count[$state]/$total_instance_count;
        $prior_prob_test += $state_prior[$state];
```

174

```perl
        }
        if ($prior_prob_test>1.00001 || $prior_prob_test<0.99999) {
            print "error, prior_prob_test = $prior_prob_test\n";
        }
        my $prior_prob_ref = \@state_prior;
        return $prior_prob_ref;

};


my $Init_Emissions = sub {
    my ($HMM_state_cardinality,$esigma) = @_;

    my $state;
    my $emission_prob_test;
    my @emission_prob;
    my @emission_prob_Z;
    for $state (0..$HMM_state_cardinality-1) {
        $emission_prob_Z[$state] = 0.0;
        my $emission_state;
        for $emission_state (0..$HMM_state_cardinality-1) {
            $emission_prob[$state][$emission_state] = 0.0000001;
            $emission_prob[$state][$emission_state] +=
                            exp(-(($emission_state-$state)**2)/($esigma*2));
            $emission_prob_Z[$state] += $emission_prob[$state][$emission_state];
        }
        $emission_prob_test = 0;
        for $emission_state (0..$HMM_state_cardinality-1) {
            $emission_prob[$state][$emission_state] =
                    $emission_prob[$state][$emission_state]/$emission_prob_Z[$state];
            $emission_prob_test += $emission_prob[$state][$emission_state];
        }
        if ($emission_prob_test>1.01 || $emission_prob_test<0.99) {
            print "error, emission_prob_test = $emission_prob_test\n";
        }
    }

    my $emission_prob_ref = \@emission_prob;
    return $emission_prob_ref;

};

my $Init_Transitions = sub {
    my ($level_one_ref,$HMM_state_cardinality,$state_shift,$HMM_data_ref,
        $emission_prob_ref,$bin_size,$decimation) = @_;
    if (!$bin_size) { $bin_size = 1; }
    if (!$decimation) { $decimation = 1; }

    my @emission_prob = @{$emission_prob_ref};
    my @HMM_data_array;

    my $in_state;
    my $out_state;
    my @transition_prob;
    my @transition_total;
    for $in_state (0..$HMM_state_cardinality-1) {
        for $out_state (0..$HMM_state_cardinality-1) {
            $transition_prob[$in_state][$out_state] = 0.0;
        }
    }

    my @lev1_array = @{$level_one_ref};
    my $training_data_instances = scalar(@lev1_array);
    my $training_index;

    for ($training_index=0; $training_index<$training_data_instances-1;
         $training_index+=$decimation) { # stops one short for out state +1 ref
        $in_state = int( ($lev1_array[$training_index]+$state_shift)/$bin_size );
        if ($in_state<0) { $in_state=0; }
        $out_state = int( ($lev1_array[$training_index+1]+$state_shift)/$bin_size );
        if ($out_state<0) { $out_state=0; }

        my $in_index;
        my $out_index;
        for $in_index (0..$HMM_state_cardinality-1) {
```

```perl
            $transition_total[$in_index] = 0.0;
            for $out_index (0..$HMM_state_cardinality-1) {
                $transition_prob[$in_index][$out_index] +=
                            $emission_prob[$in_index][$in_state]*
                            $emission_prob[$out_index][$out_state];
                $transition_total[$in_index] += $transition_prob[$in_index][$out_index];
            }
        }
    }

    my $in_index;
    my $out_index;
    my $test_total;
    for $in_index (0..$HMM_state_cardinality-1) {
        $test_total = 0.0;
        for $out_index (0..$HMM_state_cardinality-1) {
            if ($transition_total[$in_index] == 0) {
                print "error\n";
            }
            else {
                $transition_prob[$in_index][$out_index] =
                    $transition_prob[$in_index][$out_index]/$transition_total[$in_index];
            }
            $test_total += $transition_prob[$in_index][$out_index];
        }
        if ($test_total>1.01 || $test_total<0.99) {
            print "error in trans_prob[$in_index][] not summing to unity\n";
        }
    }

    my $trans_prob_ref = \@transition_prob;
    return $trans_prob_ref;

};

my $Evaluate_Viterbi_Path = sub {
    my ($level_one_ref,$HMM_states_ref,$prior_prob_ref,$emission_prob_ref,
        $transition_prob_ref,$state_shift,$bin_size,$subsample_size) = @_;
    if (!$bin_size) { $bin_size = 1; }
    my @HMM_states = @{$HMM_states_ref};
    my $HMM_state_cardinality = scalar(@HMM_states);
    my @lev1_array = @{$level_one_ref};
    my @state_prior = @{$prior_prob_ref};
    my @emission_prob = @{$emission_prob_ref};
    my @transition_prob = @{$transition_prob_ref};
    my $limit;
    my $training_data_instances = scalar(@lev1_array);
    if ($subsample_size) { $limit = $subsample_size-1; }
    else { $limit = $training_data_instances-1; }

    my @log_path_prob;
    my @back_ptr;
    my $in_state = int( ($lev1_array[0]+$state_shift)/$bin_size );
    my $in_index;
    for $in_index (0..$HMM_state_cardinality-1) {
        $log_path_prob[0][$in_index] = log($state_prior[$in_index]) +
                            log($emission_prob[$in_index][$in_state]);
        $back_ptr[0][$in_index] = int($HMM_state_cardinality/2);
    # arbitrary, avoiding boundaries
    }


    my $min_ptr;
    my $min_loc;
    my $min_state;


    my $max_path_value;
    my $training_index;
    for $training_index (1..$limit) {
        $in_state = int( ($lev1_array[$training_index]+$state_shift)/$bin_size );
        my $arbitrary_state = int($HMM_state_cardinality/2);
        my $in_index;
        for $in_index (0..$HMM_state_cardinality-1) {
            $max_path_value = $log_path_prob[$training_index-1][$arbitrary_state]
```

```perl
                            + log($transition_prob[$arbitrary_state][$in_index]);
                $back_ptr[$training_index][$in_index]=$arbitrary_state;
                my $out_index;
                for $out_index (0..$HMM_state_cardinality-1) {
                    my $path_value = $log_path_prob[$training_index-1][$out_index]
                                + log($transition_prob[$out_index][$in_index]);
                    if ($path_value > $max_path_value) {
                        $max_path_value = $path_value;
                        $back_ptr[$training_index][$in_index]=$out_index;
                    }
                }
                $log_path_prob[$training_index][$in_index]=
                    log($emission_prob[$in_index][$in_state])+ $max_path_value;
                if ($back_ptr[$training_index][$in_index]<$min_ptr) {
                    $min_ptr = $back_ptr[$training_index][$in_index];
                    $min_loc = $training_index;
                    $min_state = $in_index;
                }
            }
        }
    }

    my $last_path_state = int($HMM_state_cardinality/2); # arbitrary init
    my $log_path_probt = $log_path_prob[$training_data_instances-1][0];

    my $out_index;
    for $out_index (0..$HMM_state_cardinality-1) {
        if ($log_path_prob[$training_data_instances-1][$out_index]>$log_path_probt) {
            $log_path_probt = $log_path_prob[$training_data_instances-1][$out_index];
            $last_path_state = $out_index;
        }
    }

    my @viterbi_path_data;
    $viterbi_path_data[$limit] = $last_path_state;
    my $penultima_index = $limit-1;
    my $index;
    for ($index = $penultima_index; $index >=0; $index--) {
        $viterbi_path_data[$index] = $back_ptr[$index+1][$viterbi_path_data[$index+1]];
    }
    my $viterbi_score = $log_path_probt/$training_data_instances;

    return $viterbi_score;

};


my $Calculate_Forward_Backward = sub {
    my ($level_one_ref, $HMM_states_ref, $state_shift, $prior_prob_ref, $emission_prob_ref,
$transition_prob_ref,$bin_size) = @_;

    my @HMM_states = @{$HMM_states_ref};
    my $HMM_state_cardinality = scalar(@HMM_states);
    my @lev1_array = @{$level_one_ref};
    my @prior_probs = @{$prior_prob_ref};
    my @emission_probs = @{$emission_prob_ref};
    my @transition_probs = @{$transition_prob_ref};
    my $data_instances = scalar(@lev1_array);

    my @rescale;
    my $log_sig_prob;
    my $fb_identity;
    my @forward;
    my @backward;

    $rescale[0] = 0.0;
    my $i;
    my $k;
    my $l;
    for ($i=0; $i<$HMM_state_cardinality; $i++) {
        my $state = int( ($lev1_array[0] + $state_shift)/$bin_size );
        $forward[0][$i] = $emission_probs[$state][$i]*$prior_probs[$i];
        $rescale[0] += $forward[0][$i];
    }

    #rescale forward vars
```
177

```perl
        for ($i=0; $i<$HMM_state_cardinality; $i++) {
            $forward[0][$i] = $forward[0][$i]/$rescale[0];
        }

        for ($i=1; $i<$data_instances; $i++) {
            $rescale[$i] = 0.0;
            for ($k=0; $k<$HMM_state_cardinality; $k++) {
                $forward[$i][$k] = 0.0;
                for ($l=0; $l<$HMM_state_cardinality; $l++) {
                    $forward[$i][$k] += $forward[$i-1][$l]*$transition_probs[$l][$k];
                }
                my $state = $lev1_array[$i] + $state_shift;
                $forward[$i][$k] = $forward[$i][$k]*$emission_probs[$state][$k];
                $rescale[$i] += $forward[$i][$k];
            }
            #rescale Forward vars
            for ($k=0; $k<$HMM_state_cardinality; $k++) {
                $forward[$i][$k] = $forward[$i][$k]/$rescale[$i];
            }
        }
        $log_sig_prob = 0.0;
        for ($i=0; $i<$data_instances; $i++) {
            $log_sig_prob += log($rescale[$i]);
        }
        my $neglog = -$log_sig_prob;
        my $length = scalar(@lev1_array);
        my $renorm = int($neglog/$length);
        print "-log_sig_prob=$neglog\trenorm_log_prob=$renorm\n";
        # have now completed eval of forward vars

        for ($i=0; $i<$HMM_state_cardinality; $i++) {
            # without resclae, backward[$data_instances-1][]=1 is bc
            $backward[$data_instances-1][$i] = 1;
        }
        for ($i=$data_instances-2; $i>=0; $i--) {
            for ($k=0; $k<$HMM_state_cardinality; $k++) {
                $backward[$i][$k] = 0.0;
                for ($l=0; $l<$HMM_state_cardinality; $l++) {
                    my $state = int( ($lev1_array[$i+1] + $state_shift)/$bin_size );
                    $backward[$i][$k] += $backward[$i+1][$l]*$transition_probs[$k][$l]*
                                        $emission_probs[$state][$l];
                }
                $backward[$i][$k] = $backward[$i][$k]/$rescale[$i+1];
            }
        }
        for ($i=0; $i<$data_instances; $i++) {
            $fb_identity = 0.0;
            for ($k=0; $k<$HMM_state_cardinality; $k++) {
                $fb_identity += $forward[$i][$k]*$backward[$i][$k];
            }
            if ($fb_identity > 1.0001 || $fb_identity < 0.9999) {
                print "fb_identity_failure: oneval = $fb_identity\n";
            }
        }
        # now have backward vars, with fb_identity check

        my @ref_array = (\@forward,\@backward,$renorm);
        my $training_refs = \@ref_array;

        return $training_refs;
};

my $Get_Expected_Values = sub {
    my ($level_one_ref, $HMM_states_ref, $state_shift, $prior_prob_ref,
        $emission_prob_ref, $transition_prob_ref, $forward_ref, $backward_ref,
        $bin_size) = @_;

    my @HMM_states = @{$HMM_states_ref};
    my $HMM_state_cardinality = scalar(@HMM_states);
    my @lev1_array = @{$level_one_ref};
    my @prior_probs = @{$prior_prob_ref};
    my @emission_probs = @{$emission_prob_ref};
    my @transition_probs = @{$transition_prob_ref};
    my $data_instances = scalar(@lev1_array);
    my @forward = @{$forward_ref};
```

```perl
    my @backward = @{$backward_ref};

    my $i;
    my $k;
    my $l;
    my $min_prob = 0.000000001;
    my $in_state;
    my $out_state;
    my $temp_trans_sum;
    my @temp_trans;
    my @expected_emission_count;
    my @expected_transition_count;

    for ($i=0; $i<$HMM_state_cardinality; $i++) {
        for ($k=0; $k<$HMM_state_cardinality; $k++) {
            $expected_emission_count[$k][$i] = $min_prob;
            $expected_transition_count[$k][$i] = $min_prob;
        }
    }

    # get expected counts on transitions
    for ($i=0; $i<$data_instances; $i++) {
        $in_state = int( ($lev1_array[$i]+$state_shift)/$bin_size );
        $out_state = int( ($lev1_array[$i+1]+$state_shift)/$bin_size );
        $temp_trans_sum = 0.0;
        for ($k=0; $k<$HMM_state_cardinality; $k++) {
            for ($l=0; $l<$HMM_state_cardinality; $l++) {
                # convention: emission[state][base]
                $temp_trans[$k][$l] = $emission_probs[$l][$out_state]*
                                      $transition_probs[$k][$l]*$forward[$i][$k];
                $temp_trans_sum += $temp_trans[$k][$l];
            }
        }
        for ($k=0; $k<$HMM_state_cardinality; $k++) {
            for ($l=0; $l<$HMM_state_cardinality; $l++) {
                $expected_transition_count[$k][$l] +=
                ($temp_trans[$k][$l]/$temp_trans_sum)*$backward[$i+1][$l];
            }
        }
    }
    # now have expected counts on transitions

    # get expected counts on emissions
    # convention: emission[state][base]
    for ($i=0; $i<$data_instances; $i++) {
        $in_state = int( ($lev1_array[$i]+$state_shift)/$bin_size );
        for ($k=0; $k<$HMM_state_cardinality; $k++) {
            $expected_emission_count[$k][$in_state] +=
                    $forward[$i][$k]*$backward[$i][$k];
        }
    }

    for ($i=0; $i<$HMM_state_cardinality; $i++) {
        for ($k=0; $k<$HMM_state_cardinality; $k++) {
            if ($expected_transition_count[$i][$k] < $min_prob) {
                print "expected_trans_count_error\n";
                die;
            }
            if ($expected_emission_count[$i][$k] < $min_prob) {
                print "expected_emission_count_error\n";
                die;
            }
        }
    }

    my $expected_emission_count_ref = \@expected_emission_count;
    my $expected_transition_count_ref = \@expected_transition_count;
    my @count_ref_array = ($expected_emission_count_ref,$expected_transition_count_ref);
    my $count_ref_array_ref = \@count_ref_array;
    return $count_ref_array_ref;
};

my $Eval_Maxlike_Estimators = sub {
    my ($HMM_states_ref, $emission_prob_ref, $transition_prob_ref,
        $expected_emission_count_ref, $expected_transition_count_ref, $em_loop) = @_;
```

```perl
    if (!$em_loop) { $em_loop = 1; }

    my @HMM_states = @{$HMM_states_ref};
    my $HMM_state_cardinality = scalar(@HMM_states);
    my @emission_prob = @{$emission_prob_ref};
    my @transition_prob = @{$transition_prob_ref};
    my @expected_emission_count = @{$expected_emission_count_ref};
    my @expected_transition_count = @{$expected_transition_count_ref};
    my @transition_probs = @{$transition_prob_ref};

    my $k;
    my $l;
    my @expected_trans_count_sum;
    my @expected_emission_count_sum;
    my @trans_prob_test;
    my $temp_trans_prob;
    my $temp_emission_prob;
    my $min_prob = 0.000000001;
    my $emprob = 1.0;     # disables debug, have redundant error check
    my $transprob = 1.0;# disables debug, have redundant error check

    for ($k=0; $k<$HMM_state_cardinality; $k++) {
        $expected_trans_count_sum[$k] = 0.0;
        $trans_prob_test[$k] = 0.0;
        for ($l=0; $l<$HMM_state_cardinality; $l++) {
            $expected_trans_count_sum[$k] += $expected_transition_count[$k][$l];
        }
        #new transition probabilities defined here
        for ($l=0; $l<$HMM_state_cardinality; $l++) {
            $temp_trans_prob = $expected_transition_count[$k][$l]/
                            $expected_trans_count_sum[$k];
            # error check
            if (abs($transition_prob[$k][$l]-$temp_trans_prob) > 1.0) {
                print "error: transition_prob[$k][$l] = $transition_prob[$k][$l]\t
temp_trans_prob = $temp_trans_prob\n";
            }
            # lower bound to prevent underflow
            if ($transition_prob[$k][$l] < $min_prob) {
                $transition_prob[$k][$l] = $min_prob;
            }
            # error and debug checks
            if (abs($transition_prob[$k][$l]-$temp_trans_prob) > $transprob) {
                print "loop=$em_loop\t transition_prob[$k][$l]=$transition_prob[$k][$l]\t
temp_trans_prob=$temp_trans_prob\n";
            }
            $transition_prob[$k][$l] = $temp_trans_prob;
            $trans_prob_test[$k] += $temp_trans_prob;
        }
        # test on new trans_prob
        if ($trans_prob_test[$k] > 1.01 || $trans_prob_test[$k] < 0.99) {
            print "trans_prob_test[$k] = $trans_prob_test[$k]\n";
            die;
        }
    }

    for ($k=0; $k<$HMM_state_cardinality; $k++) {
        $expected_emission_count_sum[$k] = 0.0;
        for ($l=0; $l<$HMM_state_cardinality; $l++) {
            $expected_emission_count_sum[$k] += $expected_emission_count[$k][$l];
        }
        # new emission probabilities defined here
        for ($l=0; $l<$HMM_state_cardinality; $l++) {
            $temp_emission_prob = $expected_emission_count[$k][$l]/
                                $expected_emission_count_sum[$k];
            # error check
            if (abs($emission_prob[$k][$l]-$temp_emission_prob) > 1.0) {
                print "error: emission_prob[$k][$l] = $emission_prob[$k][$l]\t
temp_emission_prob = $temp_emission_prob\n";
            }
            # lower bound to prevent underflow
            if ($emission_prob[$k][$l] < $min_prob) {
                $emission_prob[$k][$l] = $min_prob;
            }
            # error and debug checks
            if (abs($emission_prob[$k][$l]-$temp_emission_prob) > $emprob) {
```

```
                    print "loop=$em_loop\t emission_prob[$k][$l]=$emission_prob[$k][$l]\t
temp_emission_prob=$temp_emission_prob\n";
                }
                $emission_prob[$k][$l] = $temp_emission_prob;
            }
        }
        # test on new emission_prob
        for ($k=0; $k<$HMM_state_cardinality; $k++) {
            $temp_emission_prob = 0.0;
            for ($l=0; $l<$HMM_state_cardinality; $l++) {
                $temp_emission_prob += $emission_prob[$k][$l];
            }


            if ($temp_emission_prob > 1.01 || $temp_emission_prob < 0.99) {
                print "error: emission_prob[$k][summed] = $temp_emission_prob\n";
                die;
            }
        }
        # pass out re-est probs here........
        my $emission_prob_ref = \@emission_prob;
        my $transition_prob_ref = \@transition_prob;
        my @new_HMMparam_ref_array = ($emission_prob_ref,$transition_prob_ref);
        my $new_HMMparam_ref_array_ref = \@new_HMMparam_ref_array;
        return $new_HMMparam_ref_array_ref;
};


my $Relative_Entropy = sub {
    my ($new_prob_ref,$old_prob_ref) = @_;
    my @new_prob = @{$new_prob_ref};
    my @old_prob = @{$old_prob_ref};
    my $max_index = scalar(@new_prob)-1;
    my $index;
    my $relative_entropy = 0;
    for $index (0..$max_index) {
        if ($new_prob[$index]==0 || $old_prob[$index]==0) {
            print "error:
new_prob[$index]=$new_prob[$index]\told_prob[$index]=$old_prob[$index]\n";
        }
        else {
            $relative_entropy += $new_prob[$index]*log($new_prob[$index]/$old_prob[$index]);
        }
    }
    return $relative_entropy;
};


my $Do_Gaussian_Projection = sub {
    my ($HMM_states_ref,$emission_prob_ref) = @_;

    my @HMM_states = @{$HMM_states_ref};
    my $HMM_state_cardinality = scalar(@HMM_states);
    my @emission_prob = @{$emission_prob_ref};

    my $i;
    my $k;
    my $m;
    my @level_std_dev;
    my @mean;
    my @variance;
    my @em_prob_Z;
    my $eva = 1.0; # no eva projection

    for ($k=0; $k<$HMM_state_cardinality; $k++) {
        $level_std_dev[$k] = 0.0;
        $mean[$k] = 0.0;
        for ($m=0; $m<$HMM_state_cardinality; $m++) {
            $level_std_dev[$k] += $m*$m*$emission_prob[$k][$m];
        }
        for ($m=0; $m<$HMM_state_cardinality; $m++) {
            $mean[$k] += $m*$emission_prob[$k][$m];
        }
        $level_std_dev[$k] -= $mean[$k]*$mean[$k];
        $variance[$k] = abs($level_std_dev[$k]);
        $level_std_dev[$k] = sqrt($variance[$k]);
```
181

```perl
        }
        for ($i=0; $i<$HMM_state_cardinality; $i++) {
            $em_prob_Z[$i] = 0.0;
            for ($k=0; $k<$HMM_state_cardinality; $k++) {
                $emission_prob[$i][$k] = exp(-($k-$i)*($k-$i)/(2*$eva*$variance[$k]));
                if ($emission_prob[$i][$k]<0.000000001) {
                    $emission_prob[$i][$k]=0.000000001;
                }
                $em_prob_Z[$i] += $emission_prob[$i][$k];
            }
            for ($k=0; $k<$HMM_state_cardinality; $k++) {
                $emission_prob[$i][$k] = $emission_prob[$i][$k]/$em_prob_Z[$i];
            }
            my $emission_prob_test = 0.0;
            for ($k=0; $k<$HMM_state_cardinality; $k++) {
                $emission_prob_test += $emission_prob[$i][$k];
            }
            if ($emission_prob_test > 1.01 || $emission_prob_test < 0.99) {
                print "error: emission_prob_test \n";
            }
        }
        my $emission_ref = \@emission_prob;
        return $emission_ref;
    };
```

7.11 Exercises

(Ex. 7.1) Derive the recursive relation for the Viterbi algorithm shown in Sec. 7.1.4 (also see Fig. 7.5).

(Ex. 7.2) Derive the recursive relation for the forward algorithm shown in Sec. 7.1.5.

(Ex. 7.3) Derive the recursive relation for the backward algorithm shown in Sec. 7.1.5.

(Ex. 7.4) Re-derive with more detail the Akl used in estimating akl.

(Ex. 7.5) Re-derive with more detail the Ek(b) used in estimating ekb.

(Ex. 7.6) Implement Adaboost, use to do simple classification tests.

(Ex. 7.7) Implement modified adaboost, use to rank strongest features.

(Ex. 7.8) Derive the P(B,L) equation.

(Ex. 7.9) Verify the result in Eq. 3.7

(Ex. 7.10) Re-do Example One with more detail or explanation, explain significance of overcoming bias towards geometric length distributions by the more informed situation in the example.

(Ex. 7.11) Re-do Example Two with more detail or explanation, explain significance of contrast resolution.

(Ex. 7.12) Rederive result that the standard HMM has geometric length distributions.

(Ex. 7.13) Re-derive 7.4-7.8.

(Ex. 7.14) re-derive the linear memory recursion relations 7.53 and 7.54

(Ex. 7.14) re-derive the linear memory recursion relations 7.55 and 7.56

(Ex. 7.15) show O(TNEDQmax) for the linear memory recursion relations

(Ex. 7.16) implement HMM code shown, apply to gene-finding using annotated genome ata (from genbank) to train test performance.

184

Chapter 8

Cell/Virus Compartmentalization and Nucleic Acid Genomes

8.1 Emergence of cell/virus and standard dogma: DNA→mRNA→protein

8.2 Mobile Nucleic Information Structures

8.3 Cellular Nucleic Information Structures, prokaryotic

8.4 Early transcriptomes and emergence of RNAi & CRISPRi

8.5 Viral eukaryogenesis

8.6 Cellular Nucleic Information Structures, eukaryotic

8.7 Computational Genomics

8.8 Alt-splice gene predictor (AGP)

In this chapter we start with the emergence of Cell and Virus compartmentalizations containing nucleic acid genomes. Genomic descriptions for virus, prokaryote, and eukaryote are given in Sec.s 8.2.1, 8.3.1, 8.6. Sec. 8.4 speaks to the key role of the emergence of RNAi. Sec. 8.5 ties this into the viral eukaryogenesis hypothesis. Sec. 8.7 describes computational genomics results with the meta-HMM and HMMBD described in Ch. 7. Sec. 8.8 describes the preliminary analysis of statistical support for a meta-HMM model that has multiple tracks of possible annotation (to capture alt-splice information). Regarding the latter. In the meta-HMM application described for alternatively spliced gene prediction, preliminary comparative analysis of the alt-splicing structure of genomes indicates a significant evolutionary acceleration in mammals due to greatly increased spliceosomal exon acquisition/growth in genes (discussed in Sec. 8.6.2). An optimally-sized exon is then tokenized in a particular gene, with alt-splicing on additional exons, with increasing overall gene encoding into higher exon count genes via exon acquisition – this appears to be a significant driver of the rapidly branching evolution of the mammalian family.

8.1 Emergence of cell/virus and standard dogma: DNA→mRNA→protein

The classic central dogma of biology describes how information encoding in the form of a DNA polymer (or collection of DNA polymers, e.g., chromosomes) transcribes to messenger RNA (mRNA) polymers, which are then translated to protein using a three-base encoding scheme (see Fig. 8.1 for monocistronic example, for polycistronic see Fig. 9.1, and for a simple informatics detection of the three-base encoding scheme see Ch. 3). The three-base encoding scheme leads to the discovery of anomalously long ORF encodings (see Ch. 3), which is the basis of the ORF-finder algorithm described in Ch.s 3 & 4 (with modifications for use with mRNA or EST data in Ch. 9).

For an organism's genomic DNA information repository the transcription from DNA to mRNA can be done in multiple ways from the *same* section of DNA, e.g., different overlapping reads are possible where different three-base codon framings step across the same DNA encoding region (see Fig. 8.2). For some prokaryotic organisms this overlap encoding can be quite significant [39] (see Ch. 3 for details, and this overlap encoding by frame shift is effectively doubled for duplex DNA genomes (with encoding in the complement strand), as well as duplex RNA genomes, and ssDNA and ssRNA genomes that have an antisense (reverse complement) encoding read-out by way of an intermediate duplex form. So, for prokaryotes a high degree of overlap encoding, for both forward and reverse reads, is already prevalent at the level of the genome, whether the genome is single stranded or duplex, or DNA-based or RNA-based.

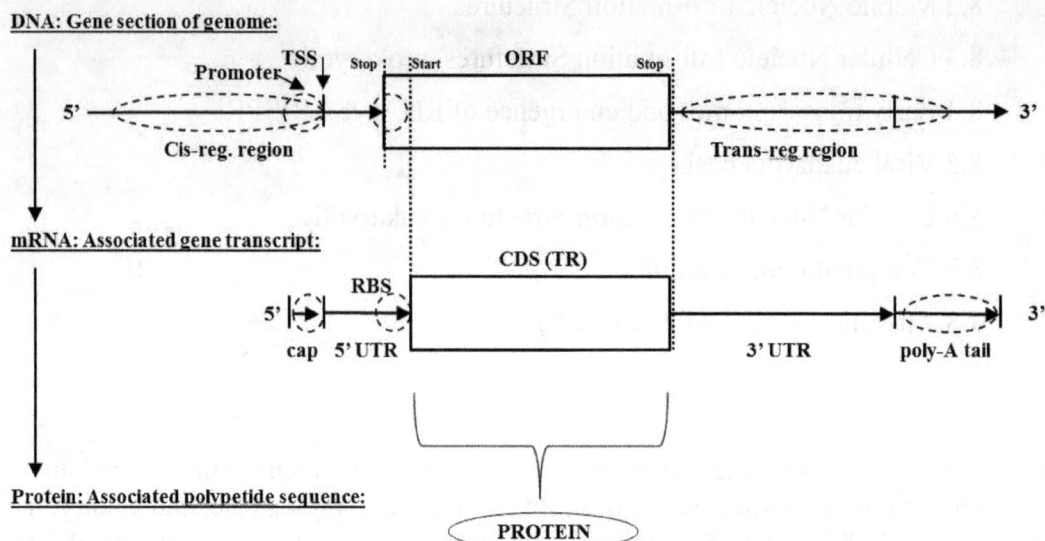

Figure 8.1. Central Dogma: DNA → mRNA → Protein (monicistronic).

In Ch. 3 we see that the *C. trachomatis* genome is half coded on the forward strand and half on the reverse, with very little dual overlap encoding. In Table 1 of [39], for ORFs > 200 bases in the *V. cholera* genome, the percentage with dual encoding is 6.57% (dual occurs when overlapping opposite read directions, with scores like 11000, 12000, and 21000). For Deinococcus radiodurans the amount of dual encoding is 69.4%.

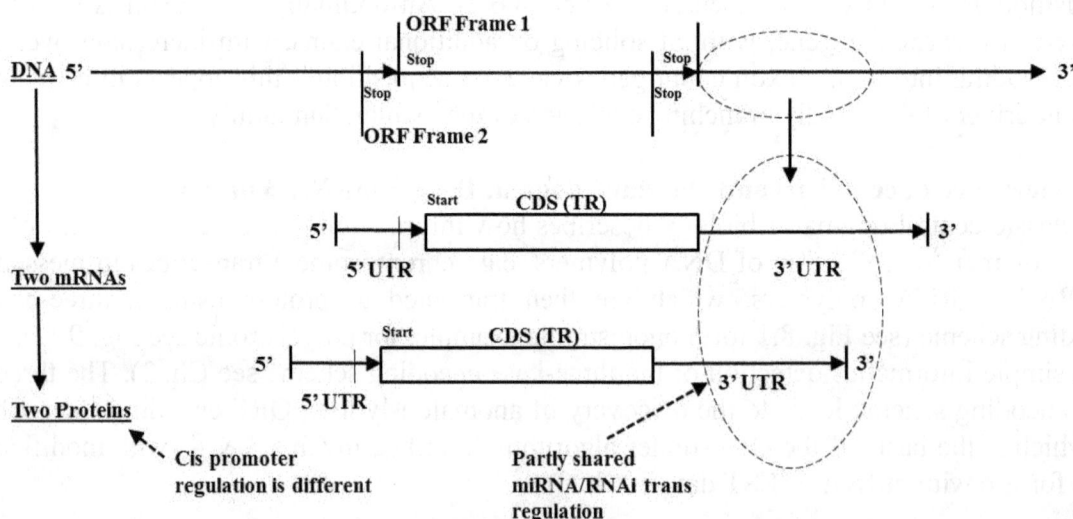

Figure 8.2. mRNA Transcriptome Topology: Overlapping monicistronic

Once the prokaryotic transcription to mRNA is complete a selection for the RNA-based coding region is effectively done, and unique protein products are thereby directly indicated.

There can be multiple protein products because prokaryotes can have polycistronic transcripts, whereby a single mRNA may have multiple, sequentially located (non-overlapping), regions that each encode their own protein product (a.k.a, operons, shown in Fig. 9.1), while eukaryotic transcript processing is more complex due to introns and alternative splicing. Once a eukaryote reaches the same stage of having a 'mature' mRNA, on the other hand, the resulting encoding is typically monocistronic (with cis-regulation governing only one encoding region). Simple eukaryotes, such as *C. elegans*, are known to have both types of encoding (monocistronic with introns and polycistronic without introns) in significant numbers.

The process of DNA→mRNA→Protein production is regulated at both transcription and translation polymerase stages (see Fig. 8.3). *Cis* regulation dominates at the DNA→mRNA polymerase stage, and *trans*-regulation at the mRNA→Protein polypeptide production stage. In the case of the polycistronic encodings, there is one *cis*-regulatory region for multiple coding regions (as indicated in Fig. 9.1). The dominance of trans-regulatory mechanisms at the mRNA→protein stage is significant because all living processes, including viral processes, can be regulated at this stage, and many of the regulatory processes involve simple antisense nucleic acid molecular recognition, indicating a possible common and ancient (RNA World) biomolecular process. In eukaryotes the process of DNA→mRNA→Protein production is also regulated at the spliceosome level (for which a brief background is given in the next section). The main mechanism for *trans* regulation in eukaryotes is RNAi. The role of *trans*-regulation in prokaryotes involves a non-RNAi process *that employs no RdRp for siRNA amplification*, using a method evidently separately evolved: CRISPR/cas.

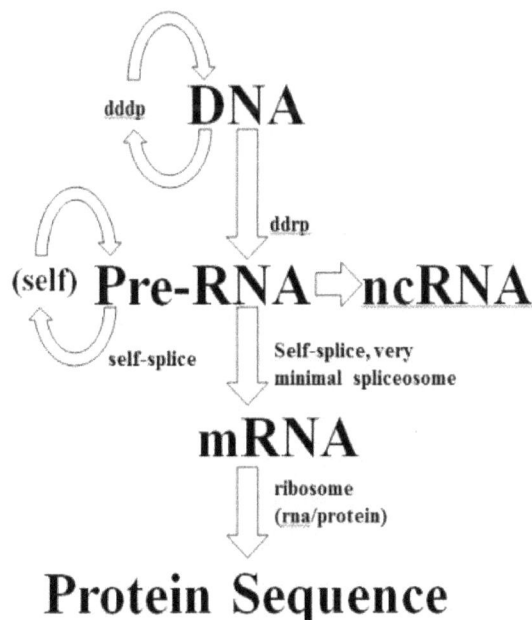

Figure 8.3. Standard Central Dogma for Prokaryotic Cells. Minimal splicesome indicated, zero for many. Early cells eventually lose spliceosome and RdRp, but still have self-splicing introns to some extent.

8.2 Mobile Nucleic Information Structures

Viruses are a well-known exception to the central dogma and have already modified the central dogma when it comes to the role of reverse transcriptase (see Fig. 8.4). Using reverse transcriptase, as the name suggests, it is possible to go back from RNA to DNA, altering the cell's genomic repository of information (in an inheritable way even in multicellular eukaryotes if that genomic DNA happens to be in a gamete cell). Viruses also have their own means for producing (or replicating) RNA information by way of the aforementioned RNA-dependent RNA polymerase (RdRp), while the production of pre-mRNA from DNA in the central dogma is by way of a DNA-dependent RNA polymerase (DdRp). The viral information processing, thus, includes everything in the central dogma up to the protein-production (cytosol) stage, as shown in Fig. 8.4.

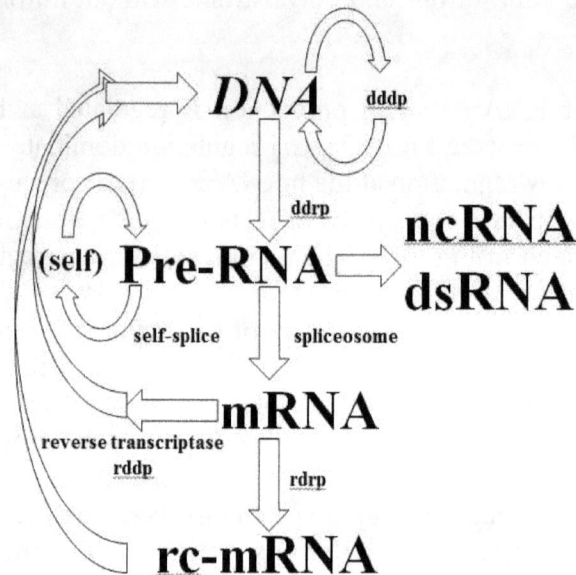

Figure 8.4. Central Dogma for Viruses (have RdRp). Virus has minimal cytosol, no ribosome, no protein production, since this is taken from cell, as is much of the DNA processing. Virus retains RdRp and reverse transcriptase (RdDp, DdDp), RdRp, (so nucleic acid polymerases), and spliceosome.

The typical viral info-flow is RNA → Protein initially, then RNA→mRNA→Protein (capsid). The genomic diversity among viruses, however, appears to have explored the DNA/RNA encoding space in every way conceivable, and that's from the 5000 viral genomes used in an initial study, with hundreds of millions of viral genomes unknown. Genomes can be made from DNA, RNA, or both at different stages in the life cycle. The genomes topology can linear or circular, or segmented into linear and circular components. The DNA or RNA can be single-stranded (ss), double-stranded (ds), or partly both. The sense of translation can either be positive (direct encoding from base sequence, where positive sequence is what is recorded in the genomic databases, unless specified otherwise, by convention), or negative (direct encoding off of RNA-pairing product, e.g., the reverse strand read direction), or ambisense (some ssDNA and ssRNA viruses have some transcription off of the negative strand in their double-stranded replicative intermediates – the geminiviruses, for example).

The smallest virus has 2 proteins and is 2 kilobases in length (circoviridae). One of the largest virus has more than 1,000 proteins and is over 1.2 Mb in length (mimiviruses). All RNA viruses use their own RNA replicase enzyme to create copies of their genome. RNA viruses generally have smaller genomes than DNA viruses. This is consistent with the higher error rate when replicating based off of a RNA template (whether ssRNA or dsRNA), or even a ssDNA template. Stability of dsDNA genomes allows less error, with corresponding increase in genome size allowed. Some evolutionary adaptions were used by the RNA-based genomes to off-set this, including segmentation.

8.3 Cellular Nucleic Information Structures, prokaryotic

8.3.1 prokaryotic cellular genomes

Prokaryotic Genomes can be ssDNA (single stranded DNA) or dsDNA (double-stranded DNA), with linear or circular topology, and possibly segmented (segments referred to as chromosomes). Chromosomes usually only have one or two parts (with the second often only a plasmid). Genes are transcribed from the 5' to the 3' ends by the molecular machinery, where the region preceding the 5' end is the 'cis' regulatory regions, and the region after the 3' end is the 'trans' regulatory region. In prokaryotes one coding region maps to one protein product (see Fig. 8.5).

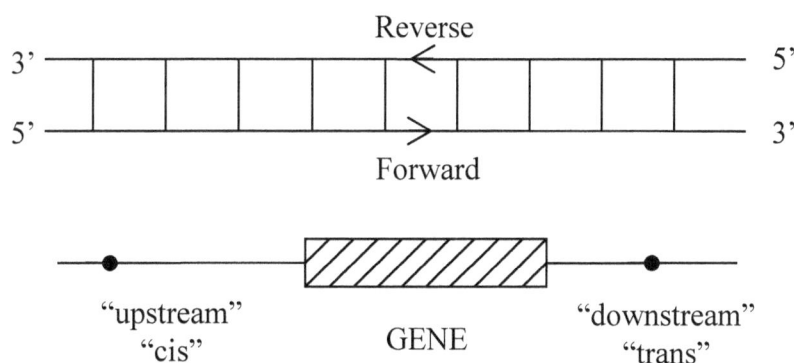

Fig. 8.5. Prokaryotic Genome. Top is the Duplex DNA in a 'ladder' diagram, where the rungs of the ladder mark the hydrogen bonding between Watson Crick base-pairing between the two strands. **Bottom** is the standard one gene region one gene product structure (the initial hypothesis of gene encoding).

The typical prokaryotic coding sequence is shown in Fig. 8.6. The typical gene constructs are: protein coding; RNA specifying; un-transcribed; and pseudo-genes. The core promoter zone is shown in Fig. 8.6 as tatawaw (note: y= c or t; w = a or t; and r = a or g). The consensus Shine-Dalgarno sequence, aaggaa, is shown preceding the transcription start site (TSS), where mRNA transcription begins. Approximately 10 bases of the 5' untranslated region (5' UTR) separate the TSS from the start of coding, with possible presence of secondary (hairpin) structure that is inhibitory. The start of protein coding commences with the atg codon, and the end of protein coding is at the codon prior to the stop codon taa (the taa codes for stop, not for an AA). The region from codon to end of the mRNA transcript is referred to as the 3' UTR.

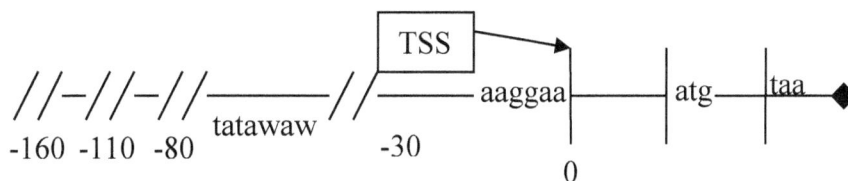

Fig. 8.6. Prokaryotic start-of-coding region.

In prokaryotic genomes genes are often linked under common regulatory control in groups called operons: Common Start – TATA box – TSS – G1 start – G1 stop – G2 start – G2 stop – G3 start – G3 stop – Common Stop. Fig. 8.7 shows such an operon, where individual genes can overlap in their encodings.

Operon encoding:

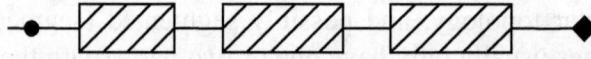

Overlapping Operon encoding:

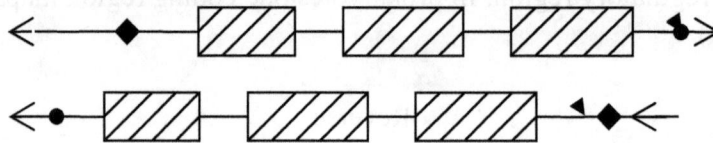

Fig. 8.7. Prokaryotic gene structure.

8.3.2 Two types of membrane

Lipid/proto-metabolic World settles on two cellular membrane compartmentalizations, but with the same nucleic acid encoding scheme and primitive processing. How is this possible unless RNA World precedes the two cellular membrane compartmentalizations (e.g., the non-cellular phase of RNA World)?

8.4 Early transcriptomes and emergence of RNAi & CRISPRi

Although RNAi has been discovered only recently (ca. 1998 [234] and 2001 [235]), and is thought to have only become significant with the introduction of eukaryotes, some aspects of RNAi appear to be ancient and even fit within the RNA world paradigm. RNAi appears to be a universal process used by eukaryotes and their viruses, but not prokaryotes. A key component of the RNAi process is the use of a miRNA that is incorporated into a collection of argonaute proteins in what is known as the RISC complex [235]. The miRNA provides the nucleic acid sequence template that is used in regulating specific antisense-related mRNAs (see Fig. 8.8). The miRNA's guide strand provides an antisense match to its mRNA target and plays a role in regulation or complete inhibition (if the target ssRNA is viral or a transposon). miRNAs may have had an early (RNA World) role as siRNAs given the discovery of a simple biogenesis pathway for miRNAs: 'mirtrons' are introns that once spliced anneal to themselves to form a miRNA. Mirtrons and mirtron-based RNA interference are also consistent with a "follow the introns" analysis that suggests that introns might have been fundamental and ancient. The appearance of RNAi throughout the eukaryotes is an indication of its ancient eukaryotic origin.

RNAi is an RNA interference method that requires formation of a dsRNA intermediate. In the ssRNA gene-silencing experiments in 1998 [234] it was found that dsRNA was not as effective as ssRNA at silencing, and that the ssRNA silencing was "too good" in that a small amount of ssRNA would accomplish complete silencing, indicating an enzymatically catalyzed silencing process. The RNAi process was clarified in 2001 [235] with the description of Dicer and its role in preparing 22bp dsRNA segments for ssRNA template loading into the RNA-induced silencing complex (RISC). RNAi interferes with specificity by using a ssRNA strand that is antisense to the ssRNA target of interest (a mRNA or a retrotransposon RNA intermediate, for example). The current form of RNAi may not have been around with the early eukaryotes. Early eukaryotes may have had a proto-RNAi that was only mirtron based, and may not have had a significant RISC complex developed yet.

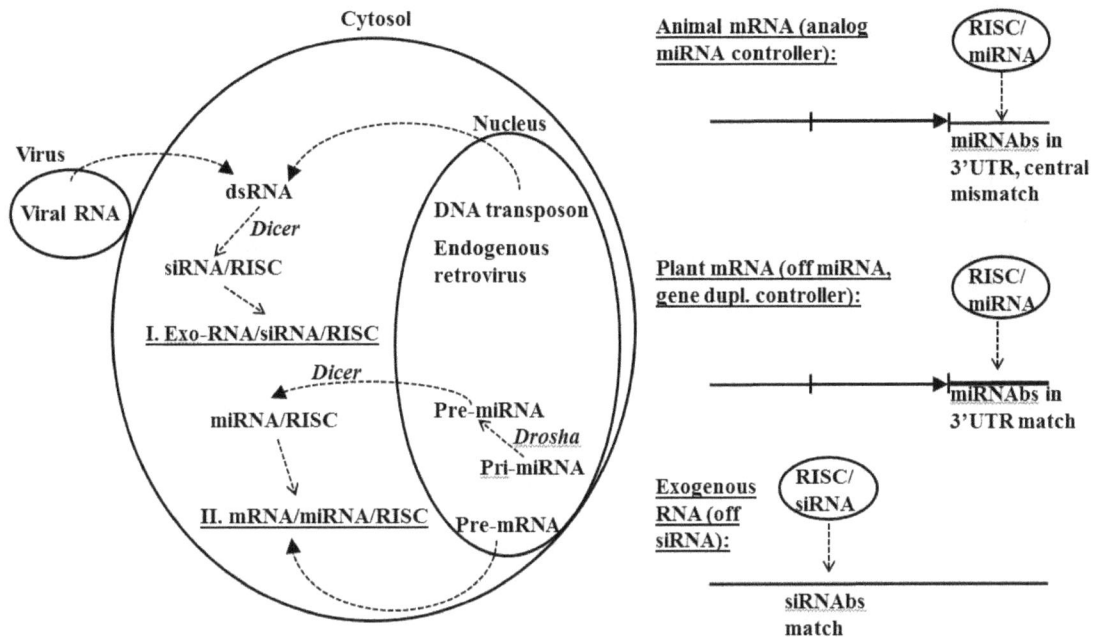

Figure. 8.8. RNA interference (RNAi) defense and expression regulation in eukaryotes. Drosha clips pri-miRNA from mRNA form to the pre-miRNA form for export to Dicer. Dicer targets dsRNA intermediate (transposon , viral, and pre-miRNA) and creates miRNA or siRNA template and recruits RISC complex to hold ssRNA specific-binding template. When RISC complex with template binds RNA target have cleavage or binding according to specificity/stability of template match. A central miRNA template and miRNA binding site (miRNAbs) mismatch leads to gene downregulation, while a perfect match results in a gene or ncRNA knockout. Strong binding site match region is 7-8 bases in length. Strong match, length of match, vs mismatch…Epigenetic machinery of cell is partly regulated by a subgroup of miRNAs known as epi-miRNAs [236].

In the viral eukaryogenesis hypothesis, to be discussed in the next section, we see that an RNAi interference CRISPR/cas precursor is hypothesized to have existed in the archaeon/prokaryote-like cell (possibly with mitochondria) when it is invaded by a membrane-bound viral endosymbiont, where the membrane-bound invasion of the virus involves an RNA interference arms race (whereby the viruses membrane can protect and complete critical mRNA processing prior to release into the prokaryote-like host's cytosol). Thus, the virus endosymbiont may have resulted from a mutually beneficial symbiosis (mutualism) on the basis of RdRp usage and RNAi co-evolution, that eventually resulted in the wholesale adoption of the viral machinery and separate nucleus processing in the hypothesized viral eukaryogenesis.

8.5 Viral Eukaryogenesis
8.5.1 The Last Eukaryotic Common Ancestor (LECA)
The possible ancient viral origin of RNA polymerases is described in [237], where there is a hypothesized loss of RdRp in the ancient cell line that is regained from virus in later eukaryotic cell lines for cytosol RNAi support (via siRNA production). It's possible that the

introduction of RdRp processes into both the cytosol and the nucleus of the proto-eukaryotic cell line was via the viral endosymbiont that is hypothesized to form the proto-eukaryotic nucleus, e.g., RdRp's adoption could be a remnant of the hypothesized viral eukaryogenesis event itself. The origin of many critical nucleic acid processing enzymes, the transfer of nucleic acid processing methods in particular, appears to have been dominated by viruses transferring their methods to cellular hosts and rarely the other way around [238]. Perhaps the spliceosome is viral in origin as well, or at least co-evolved with an ancient archaeon/prokaryote host. If the latter, however, we would expect to see spliceosomal activity in archaeons/prokaryotes, but there is no evidence of such. So simpler is to hypothesize that the list of hypothesized nucleic acid processing methods of viral origin, like RdRp, mRNA capping, and mRNA polyadenylation, also includes spliceosomal machinery. Details in support of this include *spliceosomal* introns (e.g., not the self-splicing Group I and II introns) are not seen in prokaryotes or archaeons, but are seen in viruses large enough to bother with the complexity [239], where the megaviridae class of viruses includes viral genomes larger than some cellular genomes [239-241], and in *Mollivirus* (infects *Acanthamoeba*), for example, has about 4% of its genes with *spliceosomal* introns.

Viral-based biomolecular machinery for passing virus molecules, including the viral genome, into a target nucleus is well-studied as it is a fundamental trait of all eukaryotic viruses [242-248] – the exception being those viruses, usually very small, that attack during mitosis when the nuclear membrane is temporarily disassembled (the parvo virus, for example, is only about 5,000 bases long) [242-248]. So, viral machinery for nuclear transport is well known and it could have been prevalent and co-opted in a mutualism context, where a host cell having multiple large viruses and multiple prokaryotic endosymbionts could have existed in a proto-eukaryote then as it is does in amoeba now. Viral control of access to the present-day eukaryotic nuclear envelope [242-248], or possibly the nuclear-like envelope of another virus in a large cellular host [239], and viral control of the spliceosome [249,250], and viral encoding of spliceosomal molecules [239,251] for optimized processing on viral encoded genes that require spliceosomal processing.[239,251], all lay the groundwork for a possible viral origin for the spliceosome in eukaryotic cells.

The standard hypothesis for the origin of the spliceosome in non-viral eukaryogenesis hypotheses is that it evolved from self-splicing (Group I and II) introns imported from the prokaryotic endosymbionts. And such a non-viral origin for the spliceosome has been suggested in the viral eukaryogenesis context as well [252]. The Results presented here appear to favor a *viral* origin for the spliceosome via the viral eukaryogenesis hypothesis. Results are shown that indicate an operational spliceosome in the proto-nuclear envelope as non-nuclear genomic information was being 'adopted', e.g., the spliceosome was under control of the proto-nucleus during the proto-eukaryote's uptake of the non-nuclear (archaeon and prokaryotic) genomic material. The spliceosome likely evolved from the Group I and II self-splicing introns, as suggested by others [252], but this spliceosome development may have occurred at a much earlier time than viral eukaryogenesis. This is hypothesized to be the case given the sizable percentage of the eukaryotic transcriptomes' (5% to 15% of mRNA *transcripts*) that have overlapped encodings that represent coding artifacts that are 'intronless' in origin, e.g., such as would occur with an archaeon/prokaryote ancestor having dually encoded transcriptome material (imprinted from dually-encoded intron-less genome). Some of the overlap encoding artifacts even appear to be functional given their long ORF encodings (greater than 300 bases) and long 3'UTR regions (greater than 200 bases).

The possible viral origin of the spliceosome, which is beginning to be indicated by results like those in [239], and described here, is relevant to two hypotheses: "Virus World" and "Introns Earliest". The Introns Earliest Hypothesis was mentioned in Ch. 5, so will only be mentioned briefly in what follows. The Virus World Hypothesis suggests that the role of viruses could be significantly underestimated by the standard descriptions. In [253] it is even suggested that DNA and DNA replication may have first appeared in Virus World, from which three RNA cell lineages, each with its own symbiotic DNA virus lineage, could have then led to the cellular domains seen today [254].

Pre-eukaryotes may have co-evolved an early form of RNAi (typical archaeons/prokaryotes have an unrelated form of RNA interference via CRISPR as described in Sec. 8.4) with a mega Virus, where the battle for RNAi control of host, eventually gave rise to the eukaryotic cell via modulation of RNAi. If nothing else, RdRp's have a pervasive role in eukaryotes in defense against foreign nucleic acids, in developmental regulation, in genome maintenance, and in transcriptome modulation [255]. The RNAi transcriptional and post-transcriptional silencing in *Schizosaccharomyces pombe*, for example, is accomplished with a single version of Dicer, RdRp, and Argonaute protein (Ago1) [256]. Some theories of viral eukaryogenesis indicate that the development of RNAi was a critical escalation in the battle for cellular control that led to the viral-nucleus dominated viral eukaryogenesis pathway [237]. Viral eukaryogenesis has been proposed in a variety of forms [1,237,257-259], all consistent with the lack of RdRp in prokaryotes/archaea (as with RNAi), while RdRp is found in eukaryotes and viruses (as is RNAi). Viral eukaryogenesis is also indicated by a number of other recently discovered structural properties, including the ease of membrane vesicle bound transfer of genomic information [260], and an emerging picture of virus complexity and their co-evolving relation with cells [261-265]. So the important role of RdRp for RNAi purposes clearly explains why RdRp would have singular importance to eukaryotes, but is there a non-RNAi role for RdRp as well? In some RdRp RNA productions lengthy anti-sense strands are produced, and this suggests a possible non-RNAi role, as will be discussed later.

As briefly discussed in Sec. 5.5.3, the viral endosymbiosis could have been a very slow transitional process given the likely mutualism 'melting pot' of endosymbionts, including both proteobacteria (eventually leading to mitochondria, etc.) and viruses (including mega viruses) that could have existed at the LECA. This could have existed then since it still exists now, in present day *Acanthamoeba*, which is the host to the megaviruses Mimivirus, Marseillesvirus, and other nucleocytoplasmic large DNA viruses (the NCLDVs), as well as a variety of bacteria [266], often hosting multiple virus and bacterial visitors at the same time. Furthermore, phylogenetic analysis shows that the NCLDV viruses have an ancient relation to eukaryotes, thus the LECA [267-270], placing them in the mutualism context at the time of the hypothesized viral eukaryogenesis. The NCLDV viruses possess their own mRNA capping protein (eIF4E), mRNA capping enzyme, and DdRp, to ensure preferential production of their mRNAs by the host, and eIF4E, at least, is thought to be unique to the virus (not obtained from the host *Acanthamoeba*) [271-273]. The mutualism 'melting pot' environment of the early eukaryote formation is further supported by viral mutualism in the form of favorable RdRp exchange from T7 to the mitochondrial host genome, which is thought to have occurred at the time of the LECA (or earlier) since it is present in all known eukaryotic mitochondria (with only one known exception [266]).

The viral eukaryogenesis theory leaves little opportunity for testing since it relates to a hypothesized ancient historical event, and for this reason testing the viral eukaryogenesis theory has been grouped with other hypothesized endosymbiosis events, such as those endosymbiosis events leading to the mitochondria and chloroplasts [274]. The viral eukaryogenesis hypothesis, however, involves a shift of non-eukaryotic cytosol based genomic data into the newly formed nucleus of the organism, so may leave more evolutionary artifacts in the genomic sequence information than could be obtained in the case of the organelles (see Sec. 8.6 & 8.7).

Antisense encoded mRNA information is known to exist. In Sec. 8.7, however, we see anomalous amounts of *overlapping* antisense encoding, with overlapped transcriptome encoding at percentages seen in some prokaryotes and archaea. Even if the antisense encoding aren't functional mRNAs in their own right, they are artifacts of such, and in sufficient numbers to indicate the non-eukaryotic (non-spliceosomal) genomic information was imported into the proto-eukaryotic nucleus by way of transcriptome adoption, apparently favoring uptake of a dominant transcript. If any of the antisense encodings are functional this would then require use of an RdRp. Such use of RdRp is already well known to exist, however, for shorter, partial transcripts, where it is used to get siRNA for RNAi regulation and control. Thus a role for RdRp that is not RNAi related is suggested, in order to access "ghost" antisense transcripts from the ancient prokaryotic/archaeal ancestor, and to allow for the overlap encoding in general.

To understand the nature of the imprint artifact from the prokaryotic/archaeal genome/transcriptome to the eukaryotic transcriptomes, it helps to first review some background on genome and transcriptome coding topology), and overall classic central dogma for archaeons/prokaryotes. Since archaeons/prokaryotes very rarely exhibit introns (some do have self-splicing introns, however, and also for some viruses too [1]) their transcriptome structure almost directly maps to their genomic structure.

8.5.2 Viral Eukaryogenesis Hypothesis
Given the possibly widespread and thus ancient use of RdRp in eukaryotes, this would indicate that the inception of the proto-eukaryotic cell line would have been marked by the adoption of a native RdRp capability. Consider also that at the inception of the eukaryotic cell line there is the adoption of a nucleus (by definition) with the possible wholesale adoption of a spliceosomal machine protected by the nuclear membrane, as well as any other nucleic acid processing that might be protected by that membrane boundary. For the proto-eukaryote there is also thought to be a more energy-rich metabolic suite of capabilities than is typical for prokaryotes. For this reason the archaeon/prokaryotic-like organism involved in the viral eukaryogenesis may have already adopted a proto-mitochondrial endosymbiont, allowing it to perform significantly more ATP production at the mitochondrial membrane, not the cellular membrane, freeing the cellular membrane to become simpler (e.g., no wall, just a single membrane) allowing greater cellular communication (and greater susceptibility to membrane-bound virus invasion). Now consider the archaeon/prokaryotic-like cell scenario in the co-evolutionary context of an ancient evolutionary battle between virus and cell. As the archaeon/prokaryotic-like cell develops more and more refined RNA interference defenses it forces the co-evolving virus to compensate, by learning how to co-opt those defenses for its own use, and by adoption of a membrane boundary for invasion by internali-

zation and operation as an internal (nuclear) boundary (in some cases, such as for poxviruses [257]) to shield its RNA processing from interference. All that's needed for the host virus system to move towards mutualism is a trade-off, such as the host getting the use of RdRp, where the virus gets the usual access to the host cellular machinery. Viral eukaryogenesis is, thus, hypothesized in this picture as the simplest description given the organisms and their interplay at the time.

In Sec. 8.5 and Ch. 9 a remarkable 'fingerprint' will be shown from the prokaryotic-like precursor's genome/transcriptome in the eukaryotic transcriptomes we see today. This is because the retention of the archaeon/prokaryotic-like genomic information seems to be by way of adoption of the archaeon/prokaryotic-like organism's transcripts, where the transcript that carried a particular gene with an overlap encoding is adopted, with overlap information intact, into the proto-eukaryotic transcriptome processing, and eventually (possibly via reverse transcriptase) gets written into the viral/nuclear dsDNA genome (assuming a dsDNA virus). Thus, the highly compact overlap, operonic, and *dual* encoding found for prokaryotic genes is found imprinted not via genome-genome transfer, but via transcriptome-genome transfer. Given the splicing to arrive at transcript, however, this results in the transcript only producing genomic information from one strand, with the other (dual) information necessarily accessed via RdRp. With the viral mutualism hypothesized already in-place, however, this accessibility of RdRp would have not been a problem.

There are a number of assumptions leading up the specific forms of viral eukaryogenesis hypothesis outlined above. Part of the 'stage that is set' involves the proto-archaeon/prokaryotic cell and ancient virus co-evolution in place at the time. Whether viruses had spliceosome processing already (and it was ancient) or whether nucleic acid splicing was a remarkably late invention, this is another assumption that impacts the viral eukaryogeneis model. In [1] and here, the Intron Earliest hypothesis is posed, such that the viruses arrived at the viral eukaryogenesis with splicesome already present, this being one of the selection pressures for them to protect against RNA interference by adoption of membrane enclosure in their 'trojan horse' endocytosis attack (that eventually leads to endosymbiosis when entering a mutualism relation). In the Intron Earliest hypothesis, the spliceosome processing is itself ancient and carried in the viral line since selection pressure on proto-prokaryotes led to loss of introns (and loss of the need for the spliceosome). RdRp is similarly thought to be ancient and carried in viral line and similarly lost in proto-prokaryotic line as shift to DNA and larger genomes (and host complexity) led to shift to DdRp in cells.

The viral eukaryogenesis theory also suggests a possible origin for meiosis and sex [274], where it is proposed that the mitotic cycle evolved from virus established with a permanent lysogenic presence, and the meiotic cycle (and sex) evolved from the process whereby the virus transferred to new hosts. Also in [274] is discussed the process whereby the viral-nucleus dominated cellular control led to a reorganization of the prokaryotic transcription/translation regime into the typical eukaryotic process whereby mRNA is capped prior to extrusion into the cytoplasm, and where the cap binding protein directs translation of the capped mRNA. Reorganization covers an evolutionary refinement process in the proto-eukaryote where non-nuclear genomic information gets 'lifted' into the nucleus. Perhaps the same proteins that participate in the spliceosomal activity in the nucleus, bind nucleic acid in cytosol on their way from their cytosol production and assembly into the nucleus [249,250], allowing reverse transport, with reverse splicing of introns already occasionally occurring inside the nucleus, reverse transcriptase (RT) would then be all that's needed to pull the 'intronified' transcript information permanently into the viral/nuclear genome. This could easily occur since RTs are a common component of viruses, even the simplest viruses. In the evolutionary lift procedure outlined, an archaeon/prokaryotic host transcript would be mapped to an 'intronified' viral-nucleus genome sequence. This is hypothesized to have occurred given the distinctive statistical artifact that is seen in Sec. 8.5 – e.g., eukaryotic mRNA transcripts are seen with overlap encoding information with respect to their reverse complement reads (tracing back to non-eukaryotic mRNA transcripts with such overlap encoding, which then relates directly to the same overlap encoding at the non-eukaryotic *intron-less* dsDNA genomic level). The results, thus, support a form of the viral eukaryogenesis hypothesis with a genomic uptake via 'intronification', further suggesting that the viral nucleus already had control of the spliceosomal machinery. This also suggests a possibly larger role for RdRp in eukaryotes than purely RNAi-related.

8.6 Cellular Nucleic Information Structures, eukaryotic

There are six chromosomes for Worm (*C. elegans*). As mentioned in Ch.5, for Eukaryotes the Gene → Protein translation is not collinear due to the existence of "introns," as is shown in Fig. 8.9.

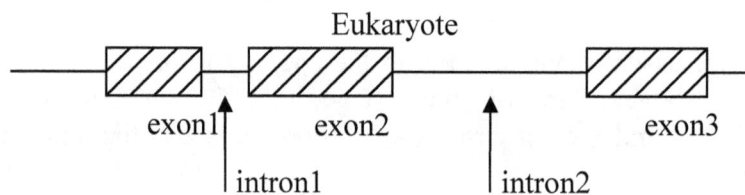

Fig. 8.9. The Exon/Intron structure of a 3-exon eukaryotic gene.

The eukaryotic cell has two separated sets of machinery that work on the nucleic acid information, one to transcribe DNA to mRNA, and one to translate mRNA to protein, the overlapping imprint of structures (motifs) is more complex for this reason. The transcription factor (TF) binding sites (TFBSs) are usually located upstream of the gene (*cis*), and help to modulate the transcription of the downstream gene product. The cat box, tata box, and inr box, are shown in Fig. 8.10, are motifs associated with the interaction with RNA polymerase (promoter signals). Also upstream are CpG methylation sites, where areas rich in GC are modifiable to "turn off" transcription. When the mRNA is transcribed it is given a 5'CAP at position -1. In the 5' UTR, there is typically a motif, the Kozac sequence (GCC G/A CC | ATG G), that is a ribosome binding site.

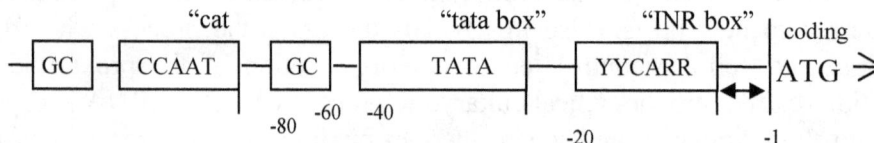

Fig. 8.10. Eukaryotic coding region: the start of coding.

After the start of coding, eukaryotic genes have introns interspersed with incomplete coding elements (exons). There are three types of exons: first, internal, and last (see Fig. 8.11).

196

Internal exon:

```
—————————|..) (...)...(...)(...)(|—————
```

First exon:

```
—————————|(atg) (...)...(...) (...) (|—————
```

Last exon:

```
————————|..) (...) ... (...)(...)(...)|(taa)——
```

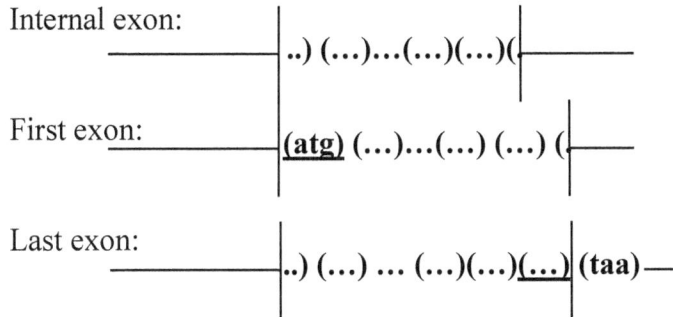

Fig. 8.11. Exons: first, internal, and last.

The ends of introns are highly conserved and some are self-splicing (see Fig. 8.12). Single Nucleotide Polymorphisms (SNPs) usually have only one variant → thus binary (on/off). If in promoter or protein coding, the SNP is very important, if in the intron region, not generally as important (unless at a splice site). The internal schematic for a generic intron is shown in Fig. 8.12 (Y=C or T; N=anything).

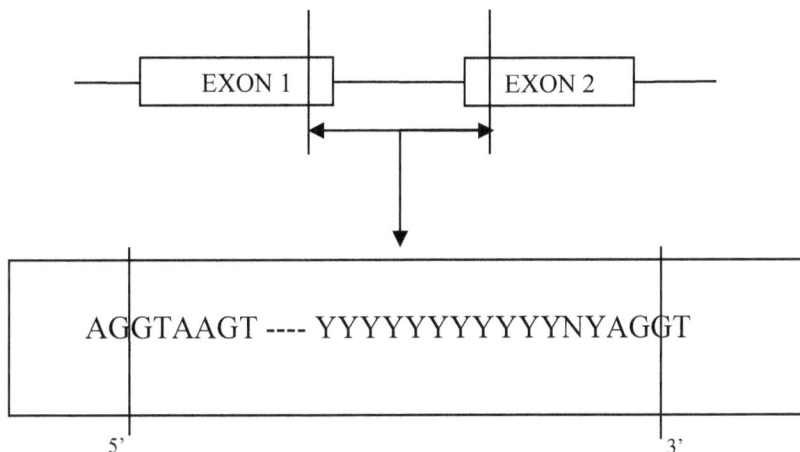

AGGTAAGT ---- YYYYYYYYYYYYNYAGGT

Fig. 8.12. Intron Splice Signals

The non-self-splicing variety of introns have further artifacts indicative of their co-evolution with an enzyme. Here, the motif of interest is known as the branch point, or the adenosine moiety, which typically has length 19-37 nt, with consensus sequence NYTRAY, where the 'A' is very highly preserved. In yeast the consensus is TACTAAC. The branch point is part of the lariat loop (end stuck to itself at branch point) transient complexation/splicing by the spliceosome (see Fig. 8.13).

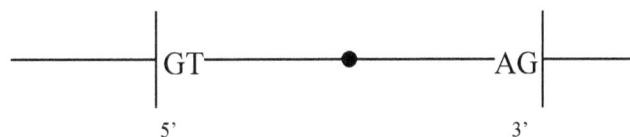

Fig. 8.13. Intron with branch point marked.

To understand the end-of-gene encoding we must backtrack to the transcription stage, where the pre-mRNA → mRNA is complete with cleavage at the polyadenylation site is followed with attachment of the poly-A tail. The poly-A cleavage site typically has a motif AATAAA (see Fig. 4.14) that interacts with the cleavage polyadenylation specifying factor (CPSF) followed by a CPSF stimulation factor (CstF) consisting of 15-25 nucleotides of GT rich region trans to the CPSF motif. The distance from the end of coding to the CPSF can be quite large, on the order of 100 nucleotides.

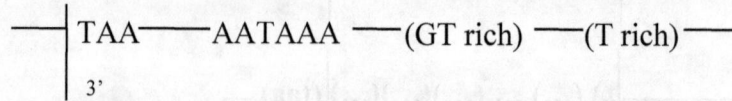

Fig. 8.14. Eukaryotic end-of-coding structure.

It is found that there is a preserved order of exons (synteny) between closely related species. This permits comparative genomics at the mammalian level (see Fig. 8.15), with most differences in the length of the introns.

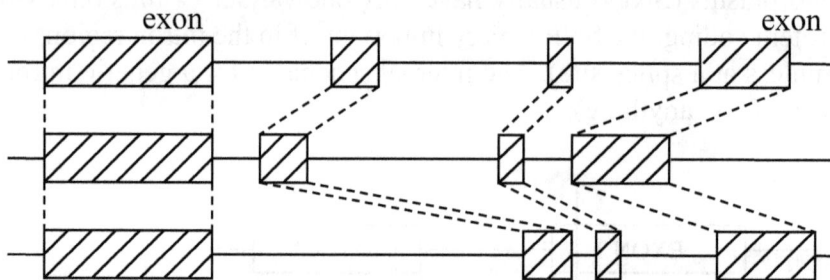

Fig. 8.15. Synteny offers the ability to do extensive comparitive genomics at mammalian level. Introns (and their lengths) can be variable while exons are more conserved. Coding exons are $\approx$ 150 bases, while introns are $\approx$ 500 bases (with some as large as 100,000 bases or more).

The eukaryote *C. elegans* (*Caenorhabditis elegans*) has a genome consisting of $\approx$ 97 million base-pairs of DNA ($\approx$ $^1/_{30}$ human, $\approx$ 8x yeast). C. elegans has 6 chromosomes, denoted: I, II, III, IV, V, X (roman numerals), and its chromosomes have cis- and trans-splicing as well as operon structure (it still has prokaryotic genomic remnants…). An individual gene construct for *C. elegans* is shown in Fig. 8.16. Note the existence of the 'outron' construct for *C. elegans*, essentially an intron on the outside, in front, with a 3' consenses at the start of coding end, but no 5' consensus prior to the INR (in the resulting 5' UTR). Non-gene repeats are thought to aid in signaling at splicing, at borders between AT and GC rich regions.

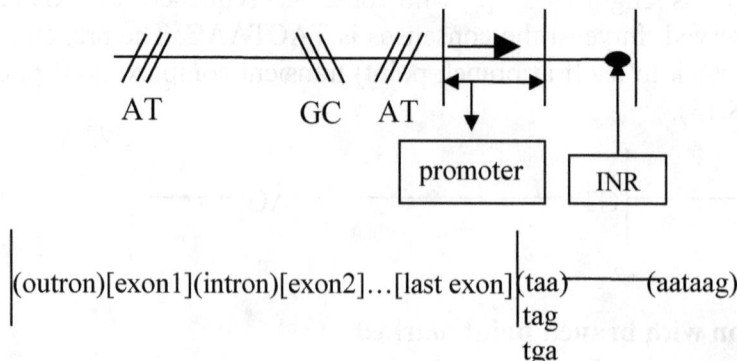

Fig. 8.16. *C.elegans* gene/outron structure.

198

8.7 Computational Genomics

Computational gene-finding dates back to the 1980's [80,275]. The most successful gene-finding tool has been the hidden Markov model, both in statistics intrinsic to the genome under study (*ab initio* gene-finding) [80,275], and in statistical analysis extrinsic to the genome (homology or EST matching) [277]. Matching, or alignment, of query sequences to a known sequence database is typically done using BLAST [82] (which involves a form of HMM seed-alignment, followed by less optimal, but faster, non-HMM seed-alignment extension). BLAST can also be used for gene finding alone, in homology-based programs to identify new genes by sufficiently aligning a query sequence with a known gene or genes [277]. In [278], they combine homology information with intrinsic genomic information (from statistical properties of the genomic sequence data alone). The main drawback of homology-based approaches is that they appear to be very weak at finding new genes, as discussed in [279], and explored in [280]. This is largely because approximately half of the genes in eukaryotic genomes appear to be novel to that genome (such as for *C. elegans*). This is also true for humans, where only about half of the proteins encoded in chromosome 22, for example, are found to be similar to previously known proteins. In [281], the author describes application of the best gene-finders known at the time (c.a. 2004) to gene-finding in novel genomes. From that study it is clear that gene-prediction is species-specific, i.e., an *ab initio* component must operate for any gene-finder to succeed at identifying genes and genomic structures novel to that organism [281].

Beginning c.a. 2000 there was a movement towards consolidation of the intrinsic and extrinsic approaches [280,282], as described in a 2002 review [282] and a 2006 review [283]. Furthermore, in the 2006 review, it was claimed that "improved modeling efforts at the hidden Markov model level are of relatively little value." We describe here a radical improvement in HMM capabilities in gene-finding, and likely a number of other areas of application, by introducing a fundamental new development at the model level. Also beginning c.a. 2000 was specialization to sensor development [284-289] to help supplement the HMM-based structure discovery process. There were sensors for transcription start site prediction [278], transcription initiation sites and polyadenylation signals [290], splice-site recognition [191,292], and identification of 3' ends of exons by EST analysis [293], to list just a few examples.

Since 2000, there has also seen rapid growth in motif-discovery algorithms -- in parallel with the aforementioned sensor specialization (and growing more interdependent). Many of these motif-discovery algorithms are beginning to tie into HMM-based structure identification via referencing regions indicated by the HMM. In [294] and [295], many important TFBS's, promoters, and other regulatory motifs can be identified by their position relative to the start and stop of coding (and other non-self transitions identified by the HMM's optimal Viterbi-path parsing). In [294] they find that the motif finding effort is greatly enhanced by referencing to nearby gene-structure and identifying "peak regions" where motifs can be isolated. Not surprisingly, if separate statistical profiling is performed on the regions just outside (before and after) the transcription region, then gene-finding is improved [1,294]. Motif discovery can be focused onto the *cis*-regulatory regions in particular, and if linked with the HMM discovery, the motif-discovery and gene-discovery efforts are simultaneously strengthened. One of the clear benefits of having a very strong intrinsic HMM formulation as a foundation is that the later pairing with motif discovery and signal-sensor augmentations then arrives at a unified and powerful intrinsic/extrinsic gene and motif discovery platform (as shown for prokaryotes in the bootstrap acquisition analysis in Ch. 4). This is capability is enhanced further if zone-dependent emissions are employed via larger meta-states or via reference to HMMD improvements as indicated in [1,18,19,21]. As mentioned previously, the HMM formulation with HMMD augmentation also provides an optimal means for inclusion of extrinsic statistics (side-information) into the Viterbi optimization (as described in [1]). The 'scaffolding' provided the HMM parsing (via the Viterbi path derivation) defines regions where zone-dependent statistics and zone-restricted motif-discovery can be applied. Many motif-finding methods would benefit from the alignment referencing provided by the HMM's scaffolding of annotation across coding and non-coding regions. With zone-restricted motif discovery, gap and hash interpolated Markov model's [1,39] become powerful tools for motif discovery in a restricted region [296-300].

8.7.1 Primer on specific genome data
In eukaryotes, genes consist of coding segments or exons which are delimited internally by special, intragenic, non-coding segments or introns. The *inter*genic, non-coding regions of bases outside the genes are referred to here as 'junk'.

The process of removing the intermediate introns and reconnecting (possibly variable subsets of, but always order preserving) the resulting exons end-to-end is referred to as *splicing*. Perhaps the most important role of introns is to provide a mechanism for the formation of alternative combinations and/or subsets of the exons contained in a given gene in order to form alternative proteins also used by the organism in question. These alternative combinations are referred to as *alternative splicings*.

The *C. elegans* genome consists of six chromosomes {I,II,III,IV,V,X}, containing approx. 97,000,000 base-pairs of DNA. The 90% base accuracy of our meta-state HMM is sufficient to isolate and resolve outrons (a partial intron construct preceding the first exon) and other structures described in [301], such as the following dozen attributes:
1) Approx. 19,000 genes, so approx. 1 gene per 5,000 bases.
2) Each gene has an average of 5 introns.
3) Tandem repeats account for 2.7% of genome, inverted repeats 3.6%. Repeats have different families on different chromosomes, and are more likely on introns. Common TTAGGC hexamer repeat.
4) 38 dispersed repeat families can potentially be identified via hash interpolated Markov model.
5) Approx. 50% of genome novel.
6) Approx. 80% of genes are trans-spliced to a common spliced leader.
7) Approx. 20% of genes organized as operons.
8) Common occurrence of 'outron' structure: introns-like sequence with no internal 5' consensus that is found before the first exon.
9) Genes with trans-splices are often distinguished from those that are not by the presence of an outron.
10) 3' ends of genes within operons typically signaled by AATAA.
11) Typical translation Initiation: [(A/G)CCATG]
12) Termination (TAA (61%); TAG (17%); TGA (22%))

8.7.2. The meta-HMM for eukaryotic genomics, and data preparation
The generalized clique HMM begins by enlarging the primitive hidden states associated with individual base labeling as exon {e}, intron {i}, or junk {j} on substrings of primitive hidden states or *footprint* states -- 'ieeeeee' for example (also a Cajun exclamation). In

what follows, the transitions between primitive hidden states for coding {e} and non-coding {i,j}, {ei,ie,je,ej}, are referred to as 'eij-transitions', and the self transitions, {ee,ii,jj}, are referred to as 'xx-transitions'. The emissions are likewise expanded to higher order in the fundamental joint probability that is the basis of the generalized-clique, or 'meta-State', HMM. We consider application to eukaryotic gene finding and show how a meta-state HMM improves the strength of eij-transition contributions to gene-structure identification. We will describe situations where the meta-state eij-transition modeling can effectively 're-capture' the exon and intron heavy tail distribution modeling capability as well as manage the exon-start 'needle-in-the-haystack' problem.

The meta-state HMM is higher order in both base-emission Markov order and state-transition Markov order, i.e., the meta-state HMM describes an irreducible joint-probability, or 'clique', generalization. The footprint states created from windows of 13 primitive states (or footprint size F=12, in consecutive overlapping 'dimers') lead to one of our best performing models, with *full-exon* predictive accuracy of 86% on the B&G ALLSEQ data [84] (with data used as both train and test for comparison with GeneID+ and FGENEH). One method, FGENEH, is similar to ours in that it only uses the intrinsic genomic sequence data (not homology searches, etc.). FGENEH's predictive accuracy on the same ALLSEQ data was 64% [84]. One of the best scoring methods on the ALLSEQ data is GeneID+, whose accuracy is 71%, where GeneID+ *does* use external information [84]. The base-level accuracy of our meta-state HMM on the ALLSEQ data is 97%, compared to 86% scoring at the full-exon correct level, indicating that improvement in identification of coding/non-coding transitions would improve results, particularly at start-of-coding. This has been addressed in [26] with the introduction of SVM methods so won't be elaborated upon here.

Other gene finding methods typically involve some degree of pre-processing – as is made clear by how their test-data is often arranged (e.g., the 570 *separate* sequences, each containing one gene, in the B&G ALLSEQ dataset [84]). When examining these datasets, and then turning to applying our methods on large blocks of genomic data, there seems to be a 'contrast' problem in the recognition of the start-of-coding region when working with the standard 1st-order HMM (a 'needle-in-the-haystack' problem). We find in our meta-state HMM approach that the contrast problems are automatically solved, and that many of the beneficial attributes of HMM-with-duration modeling are, remarkably, recovered (the heavy-tail modeling capability on intron and exon length distributions in particular).

In this effort we also wanted to introduce a new dataset that minimally alters the full genome dataset. We want our optimized HMM to also lay the foundation for a multifaceted regulatory motif discovery process as well. The gene prediction, in the end, will not only identify gene-structure, but it will have done so by identifying similar structures and regions in relation to the eij-transitions. The regions around the predicted eij-transitions can, thus, be analyzed using focused motif-finder approaches (like the MI method in [26,39] and [90], to then decipher various aspects of gene-regulation). To this end, our main concern with the raw *C. elegans* genomic data is that the alternatively spliced regions will be harder for the HMM to manage, since it is not part of the modeling in any way, and will be harder to score, since one prediction will exclude an overlapping alternatively-spliced variant, such that to be correct on one you have to be wrong on the other. So our approach is to simply drop the regions of the genome that have alternatively splice genes. More precisely, we drop those segments of the genome corresponding to the transitive closure with respect to overlap of alternatively spliced genes at their beginnings. The alternatively-spliced regions are simply dropped from the working dataset (resulting in dataset *C.elegans* reduced), and the annotation is offset as needed to compensate for the deletions. The alt-splice redacted set of genomic data that we obtain is reduced by 30.5% for Chromosomes I-V (*C. elegans* genome release WS200). We make no use of the sixth chromosome (labeled as X, roman numeral ten, for legacy reasons), where the odd naming convention is the least of the oddities of this chromosome, which has a large contribution from non-protein encoding DNA (tRNA, etc.).

Our alternative-splice redacted *C. elegans* genome has chromosomes I-V concatenated, then split into 67 non-overlapping chunks, which are then evenly distributed (as allowable) amongst five groups ('folds'). Five-fold cross-validation was then performed: where 4-folds are used in learning the HMM parameters, and the other fold used to test, with prediction scored against the annotation on that fold, and this process repeated with other folds held out, then averaged over all five cross-validations to obtain the prediction accuracies detailed in what follows. On the alt-splice redacted genome we have a full-exon prediction accuracy of 74% (with F=20), while the F=2 model, with minimal footprint, has full-exon predictive accuracy of only 61%, in rough agreement with the performance of standard-HMM gene finders with purely intrinsic information (like FGENEH). The base level accuracy at F=20 is 90%, so as with the ALLSEQ data, there is clear room for improvement with better eij-transition recognition.

The Benchmark Data Set ALLSEQ
In [84], the authors performed the following steps to arrive at the ALLSEQ data set:

1)   Select the set of all sequences encoding at lease one complete protein from the vertebrate divisions of GenBank Release 85.0 (October 15, 1994).

2)   From the above discard the following:
   a.   Any sequence encoding at least one incomplete protein.
   b.   Any sequence for which the exact coding regions was not unambiguous.
   c.   Any sequence encoding a protein in the complementary (reverse encoding) strand.
   d.   Any sequence containing a gene or part of a gene associated with other sequences.
   e.   Any sequence encoding a pseudogene [1] (via "CDS Key" value "/pseudo").
   f.   Any sequence encoding more than one gene or alternative splicing of a gene.
   g.   Any sequence encoding a gene without introns.

3)   From the 1410 sequences resulting from the above the following further discards were made:
   a.   Any sequence whose coding segment did not start with the start codon ATG.
   b.   Any sequence whose coding segment did not end with a stop codon (TAA, TAG, TGA).
   c.   Any sequence whose coding segment was not a multiple of 3 in length.
   d.   Any sequence with any intron not beginning with GT and/or ending with AT (sic).
   e.   Any sequence whose coding segment contained an in-frame stop codon.

4)   The following additional discards were made:
   a.   Sequences for immunoglobulins, histocompatibility antigens and additional pseudogenes not discarded using previous criteria.
   b.   3 sequences longer than 50,000 bp.

5)   One final selection was made from the sequences surviving the above in that the sequence's date of entry postdated Release 74 of Genbank (January, 1993) – intended as such to minimize the overlap of the resulting test set with training sets for the programs tested in [84].

As mentioned previously, because the training and testing sets were identical in our case, or close to identical in the Burset and Guigo study [287,84], we consider the ALLSEQ results as a brute force parameter search yielding what to expect in the ideal case and not necessarily a valid test of prediction performance. (The authors in [84] separate the test set from the training set by a date of entry criterion, but there was significant overlap between the testing and training data sets obtained [287] (an inevitable overlap since the ALLSEQ data set consisted of the "vast majority" of vertebrate sequences available at the time). We compare our initial test results with those reported by Burset and Guigo for this reason.

Early gene finding efforts are described in [302-304]. The authors of [287] provide an informative discussion, and references, on exon and intron durations, among other things. In [302], the authors observe "that the in-phase hexamer measure, which measures the frequency of occurrence of oligonucleotides of length six in a specific reading frame, is the most effective" for inclusion in gene finding. Moreover, those authors assembled their own test data set, called HMR195 [287], based on sequences submitted to Genbank after August 1997. We proceed with the results of the clique-parameter search using the ALLSEQ dataset. The ALLSEQ dataset properties are summarized in Table 8.1.

# Bases	Coding Density	Sequences			Introns			Exons		
		Total	BP	Avg. Len.	Total	BP	Avg. Len.	Total	BP	Avg. Len.
2892149	0.15	570	1754950	3078.86	2079	1310452	630.33	2649	444498	167.80

Table 8.1. Properties of the ALLSEQ data set.

Data preparation procedure for non-multiply-coded C. elegans data
The following steps were used in order to prepare the data (described in Tables 8.2 & 8.3) prior to training and testing.

1) The data was scanned for in-frame stops, and ultimately no in-frame stops were detected.

2) The data was scanned for alternative splicing, and 6260 (30.5%) out of a total of 20514 sequences represent alternative splicing – including some forward encoded alternative splicings overlapping with reverse encoded alternative splicings.

3) In order to avoid the complexities involved in the prediction of alternative splicings, the *transitive closure* with respect to overlap of all alternative splicings was deleted from the data and the remaining annotation was appropriately offset in compensation for the deletions. For all branches of all alternative splicing sequences – along with any sequences interfering with them - the following segments, s, were deleted:
   a. s=the 5'- UTR, where (15b< length(s) <=200b) (15=WS/2: See item 7 below)
   b. s=the 3'- UTR, where (15b< length(s) <=3kb), and
   c. s=the entire coding sequence, CDS, including exons and introns

4) In order to avoid both the complexity of segmented prediction as well as any bias toward any specific subset of chromosomes during cross-validation, the following were performed:
   a. Both data and annotation files for all 5 chromosomes were divided into a total of 67 autonomous chunks of nominal size 1Mb and minimum size 500kb.
   b. The resulting 67 chunks were then evenly (as allowable) distributed into five (5) groups for 5-fold cross-validation.

5) Training was performed independently on each of the above chunk groups with a sampling window size of first WS=30, then WS=40.

6) Five-fold cross-validation counts from training on chunk groups 1-4 were combined to form probability estimates used to test on chunk group 5, then training on 2-5 for testing on 1, and so on.

Summary of data reduction in *C. elegans*, Chromosomes I-V						
File	#sequences	# alt.	% alt.	# exons	# alt.	% alt.
CHROMOSOME_I	3537	1306	36.92%	24295	10942	45.04%
CHROMOSOME_II	4161	1316	31.63%	25427	10427	41.01%
CHROMOSOME_III	3277	1220	37.23%	21541	9614	44.63%
CHROMOSOME_IV	3886	1195	30.75%	24390	9509	38.99%
CHROMOSOME_V	5653	1222	21.62%	32135	9122	28.39%
Total	20514	6259	30.51%	127788	49614	38.83%

Table 8.2. Summary of data reduction in *C. elegans*, Chromosomes I-V.

# Bases	Coding Density	Sequences			Introns			Exons		
		Total	BP	Avg. Len.	Total	BP	Avg. Len.	Total	BP	Avg. Len.
67000811	0.24	14255	32547117	2283.2	63919	16371001	256.1	78174	16176057	206.9

Table 8.3. Properties of data set *C. elegans*, Chromosomes I-V (reduced). Note: sequence-BP – (intron-BP + exon-BP) = 59, due to a premature start of the sequence ZK1010.9 of Chromosome III in the annotation provided.

8.7.2.1 The meta-HMM states and structure identification

Exons have a 3-base encoding as directly revealed in a mutual information analysis of gapped base statistical linkages as shown in Ch. 2 (from [39]). The 3-base encoding elements are called *codons*, and the partitioning of the exons into 3-base subsequences is known as the codon *framing*. A gene's coding length must be a multiple of 3 bases. The term *frame position* is used to denote one of the 3 possible positions – 0, 1, or 2 by our convention – relative to the start of a codon. Introns may interrupt genes after any frame position. In other words, introns can split the codon framing either at a codon boundary or one of the internal codon positions.

Although there is no notion of framing among introns, for convenience we associate framing with the intron, as indicated in the example below, as a tracking device in order to ensure that the frame of the following introns-to-exon transition is constrained appropriately. The primitive states of the individual bases occurring in exons, introns, and junk are denoted by:

Exon states = { e_0, e_1, e_2 },
Intron states = { i_0, i_1, i_2 },
Junk state = {j}.

We have three possible intron framings indicated in the following state strings.

jj...je$_0$e$_1$e$_2$...e$_0$**i$_0$i$_0$**...**i$_0$**e$_1$...e$_0$e$_1$e$_2$jj...j   (intron frame 0)
jj...je$_0$e$_1$e$_2$...e$_1$**i$_1$i$_1$**...**i$_1$**e$_2$...e$_0$e$_1$e$_2$jj...j   (intron frame 1)
jj...je$_0$e$_1$e$_2$...e$_2$**i$_2$i$_2$**...**i$_2$**e$_0$...e$_0$e$_1$e$_2$jj...j   (intron frame 2)

There are 15 unique two-label (dimer) transitions: $\{jj, je_0, e_0e_1, e_1e_2, e_2e_0, e_0i_0, e_1i_1, e_2i_2, i_0i_0,$ $i_1i_1, i_2i_2, i_0e_1, i_1e_2, i_2e_0, e_2j\}$. In what follows we split the stop codon into the three possibilities strictly observed $\{e_2j\_TAA, e_2j\_TAG, e_2j\_TGA\}$, for a total of 17 states in our forward encoding model.

Encodings for proteins can be found in both directions along the DNA strand. For some genomes the encodings are sparse, rarely overlapping, and have approximately equal numbers of forward and reverse ('shadow') encodings. The differences in the base statistics in the forward and reverse gene encodings are sufficiently negligible (or disjoint) that their counts can simply be merged in the modeling (data not shown). We incorporate *shadow* states, indicating reverse encoded exons and introns, into the state model of our meta-state HMM, denoted by the primitives by ê and î, respectively. For example, the 3 possible intron framings for the reverse encoding are as follows:

$jj...j\hat{e}_2\hat{e}_1\hat{e}_0...\hat{e}_1\hat{i}_0\hat{i}_0...\hat{i}_0\hat{e}_0...\hat{e}_2\hat{e}_1\hat{e}_0jj...j$ (intron frame 0)
$jj...j\hat{e}_2\hat{e}_1\hat{e}_0...\hat{e}_2\hat{i}_1\hat{i}_1...\hat{i}_1\hat{e}_1...\hat{e}_2\hat{e}_1\hat{e}_0jj...j$ (intron frame 1)
$jj...j\hat{e}_2\hat{e}_1\hat{e}_0...\hat{e}_0\hat{i}_2\hat{i}_2...\hat{i}_2\hat{e}_2...\hat{e}_2\hat{e}_1\hat{e}_0jj...j$ (intron frame 2)

There are 16 reverse encoding state transitions in direct correspondence with the 16 non-jj state transitions for the forward read. The jj transition couples the forward and reverse reads in that a forward encoding can 'end', i.e., transition to a region of junk, then eventually transition to a reverse encoded gene. The total number of state-transition (dimer states) in our model is, thus, 33:

13 xx-type (homogeneous) dimers:
a.   6 Intron-intron – $i_0i_0, i_1i_1, i_2i_2, \hat{i}_0\hat{i}_0, \hat{i}_1\hat{i}_1, \hat{i}_2\hat{i}_2$
b.   6 Exon-exon – $e_0e_1, e_1e_2, e_2e_0, \hat{e}_0\hat{e}_1, \hat{e}_1\hat{e}_2, \hat{e}_2\hat{e}_0$
c.   1 Junk-junk – jj

20 eij-type (heterogeneous) dimers:
d.   6 Exon-intron – $e_0i_0, e_1i_1, e_2i_2, \hat{e}_0\hat{i}_0, \hat{e}_1\hat{i}_1, \hat{e}_2\hat{i}_2$
e.   6 Intron-exon – $i_0e_1, i_1e_2, i_2e_0, \hat{i}_0\hat{e}_1, \hat{i}_1\hat{e}_2, \hat{i}_2\hat{e}_0$
f.   6 Exon-junk – $(e_2j)_{TAA}, (e_2j)_{TAG}, (e_2j)_{TGA}, (\hat{e}_2j)_{TAA}, (\hat{e}_2j)_{TAG}, (\hat{e}_2j)_{TGA}$
g.   2 Junk-exon – $(je_0), (j\hat{e}_0)$

In order to work directly with the above dimer states, or the footprint-state generalization, we need to generalize to a higher order HMM model. The standard HMM has emissions that only dependent on the current state (e.g., we have $P(b_{n-1}|\lambda_{n-1})$ terms). This leads to poor performance in modeling the anomalous statistics in the transition regions between exon, intron, or junk regions. If a transition 'je_0' has occurred, for example, and we are looking at the base emission for the 'e_0' state, we can't account for the prior state with the simple $P(b_{n-1}|\lambda_{n-1})$ conditional probabilities in the standard bare-bones HMM modeling, we minimally need $P(b_{n-1}|\lambda_{n-2}, \lambda_{n-1})$, i.e., state modeling at the dimer-level or higher.

Enumeration of the Footprint States
According to the restrictions just described, footprint states fall into the same two categories or types as dimer states, xx-type and eij-type. Regardless of footprint state type, each footprint state can be considered to be generated by the xx-type dimer that it contains. For xx-

types, it is sufficient to specify the generating dimer only, such as i_0i_0 for the xx-type footprint state $i_0i_0\ldots i_0$. For eij-types, a position must also be specified for the location of the generating dimer within the generated footprint state. The number of xx-type footprint states is identical to the number of xx-type dimers, as enumerated in Table 8.4 below.

Dimer Index	XX-type Generating Dimer	XX-type Footprint State
0	i_0i_0	$i_0i_0\ldots i_0$
1	i_1i_1	$i_1i_1\ldots i_1$
2	i_2i_2	$i_2i_2\ldots i_2$
3	$\hat{i}_0\hat{i}_0$	$\hat{i}_0\hat{i}_0\ldots\hat{i}_0$
4	$\hat{i}_1\hat{i}_1$	$\hat{i}_1\hat{i}_1\ldots\hat{i}_1$
5	$\hat{i}_2\hat{i}_2$	$\hat{i}_2\hat{i}_2\ldots\hat{i}_2$
6	e_0e_1	$e_0e_1\ldots e_{(F)\bmod 3}$
7	e_1e_2	$e_1e_2\ldots e_{(F+1)\bmod 3}$
8	e_2e_0	$e_2e_0\ldots e_{(F-1)\bmod 3}$
9	$\hat{e}_0\hat{e}_1$	$\hat{e}_0\hat{e}_1\ldots\hat{e}_{(F)\bmod 3}$
10	$\hat{e}_1\hat{e}_2$	$\hat{e}_1\hat{e}_2\ldots\hat{e}_{(F+1)\bmod 3}$
11	$\hat{e}_2\hat{e}_0$	$\hat{e}_2\hat{e}_0\ldots\hat{e}_{(F-1)\bmod 3}$
12	jj	$jj\ldots j$

Table 8.4. All 13 xx-type footprint states generated by the xx-type dimmers

As for the eij-type footprint states, each is generated by the non-homogeneous dimer that it contains but is further characterized by the position of the generating dimer within the footprint string, such as e_0i_0 in the right-most position of the eij-type footprint state $e_{(F-2)\bmod 3}e_{(F-1)\bmod 3}\ldots e_0e_0e_0i_0$. As a consequence of this, there are F eij-type footprint states for each corresponding eij-type dimer. Given an eij-type footprint state of length F in dimers, there are precisely F possible positions for the implied eij-type dimer to occur within the footprint state's string of primitives. These dimer positions are labeled 0, …, F-1 and taken in the order of encoding (forward or reverse) in Table 8.5 below. Thus we have the relation: # eij-type footprint states= 20 (F) = (# eij-type dimer states) (F).

Dimer Index	EIJ-type Generating Dimer	EIJ-type Generated Footprint State For Generating Dimer Positions 0, …, F-1		
		0	…	F-1
0	e_0i_0	$e_0i_0\ldots i_0$	…	$e_{(1-F)\bmod 3}e_{(2-F)\bmod 3}\ldots e_0i_0$
1	e_1i_1	$e_1i_1\ldots i_1$	…	$e_{(2-F)\bmod 3}e_{(-F)\bmod 3}\ldots e_1i_1$
2	e_2i_2	$e_2i_2\ldots i_2$	…	$e_{(-F)\bmod 3}e_{(1-F)\bmod 3}\ldots e_2i_2$
3	$\hat{e}_0\hat{i}_0$	$\hat{e}_{(1-F)\bmod 3}\hat{e}_{(2-F)\bmod 3}\ldots\hat{e}_0\hat{i}_0$	…	$\hat{e}_0\hat{i}_0\ldots\hat{i}_0$
4	$\hat{e}_1\hat{i}_1$	$\hat{e}_{(2-F)\bmod 3}\hat{e}_{(-F)\bmod 3}\ldots\hat{e}_1\hat{i}_1$	…	$\hat{e}_1\hat{i}_1\ldots\hat{i}_1$
5	$\hat{e}_2\hat{i}_2$	$\hat{e}_{(-F)\bmod 3}\hat{e}_{(1-F)\bmod 3}\ldots\hat{e}_2\hat{i}_2$	…	$\hat{e}_2\hat{i}_2\ldots\hat{i}_2$
6	i_0e_1	$i_0e_1e_2\ldots e_{(F)\bmod 3}$	…	$i_0\ldots i_0e_1$
7	i_1e_2	$i_1e_2e_0\ldots e_{(F+1)\bmod 3}$	…	$i_1\ldots i_1e_2$
8	i_2e_0	$i_2e_0e_1\ldots e_{(F-1)\bmod 3}$	…	$i_2\ldots i_2e_0$
9	$\hat{i}_0\hat{e}_1$	$\hat{i}_0\ldots\hat{i}_0\hat{e}_1$	…	$\hat{i}_0\hat{e}_1\hat{e}_2\ldots\hat{e}_{(F)\bmod 3}$
10	$\hat{i}_1\hat{e}_2$	$\hat{i}_1\ldots\hat{i}_1\hat{e}_2$	…	$\hat{i}_1\hat{e}_2\hat{e}_0\ldots\hat{e}_{(F+1)\bmod 3}$
11	$\hat{i}_2\hat{e}_0$	$\hat{i}_2\ldots\hat{i}_2\hat{e}_0$	…	$\hat{i}_2\hat{e}_0\hat{e}_1\ldots\hat{e}_{(F-1)\bmod 3}$

12	$(e_2j)_{TAA}$	$(e_2j)_{TAA}jj...j$	$...e_{(-F)mod3}e_{(1-F)mod3}...(e_2j)_{TAA}$
13	$(e_2j)_{TAG}$	(Similar to above)	...(Similar to above)
14	$(e_2j)_{TGA}$	" "	... " "
15	$(\hat{e}_2j)_{TAA}$	$\hat{e}_{(-F)mod3}\hat{e}_{(1-F)mod3}...(\hat{e}_2j)_{TAA}$	$...(\hat{e}_2j)_{TAA}j...j$
16	$(\hat{e}_2j)_{TAG}$	(Similar to above)	...(Similar to above)
17	$(\hat{e}_2j)_{TGA}$	" "	... " "
18	je_0	$je_0e_1...e_{(F-1)mod3}$	$...jj...je_0$
19	$j\hat{e}_0$	$jj...j\hat{e}_0$	$...j\hat{e}_0\hat{e}_1...\hat{e}_{(F-1)mod3}$

Table 8.5. All 20(F) eij-type footprint states generated by the eij-type dimers

We have the following relations:

footprint states = 13 + 20(F)

footprint state transitions = 13 + 20(F+1)

In the model without the minimum length constraint we still have the fundamental set of 33 dimers, beyond that, however, the larger footprints can have arbitrary numbers of state-toggles:

extended states without minimum length assumption $\geq 33 * 2^{F-1}$

extended state transitions without assumption $\geq 33 * 2^{F}$

8.7.2.2 Measures of predictive performance (recap)

The measure of prediction performance was taken in two ways: full exon accuracy and individual base (nucleotide) accuracy, according to the conventions of Burset and Guigo in [84].

Accuracy at the base or nucleotide level, is given by (detailed description in Ch. 4):

$$snsp\_avg = (sn + sp^*)/2,$$
$$\text{where } sn = TP/(TP + FN) \text{ and } sp^* = TP/(TP + FP), \text{ and}$$
$$TP = \text{true positives}; FP = \text{false positives}; FN = \text{false negatives}$$

Note that the authors [84] have used an alternative form of specificity from the usual form

$$sp=TN/(TN+FP).$$

This is done in the context of gene prediction, with typically high concentrations of junk, where the contribution from the quantity TN= true negative (or correctly predicted actual non-coding) can overwhelm FP in what is actually weakly accurate prediction (i.e., scoring is best conveyed in terms of the overlap between predicted positives and actual positives).

We use $(sn + sp^*)/2$ for accuracy, following the conventions of [84], partly to compare with their results, but we also calculate the specificity according to the standard form $sp=TN/(TN+FP)$. The specificity convention $sp^* = TP/(TP + FP)$ has the effect of weighting genes with shorter and fewer exons more heavily in the base and exon level accuracy measurements, respectively. (In the notation to follow, sp will be used in place of sp* if there is no ambiguity.) Moreover, this effect can become extremely pronounced in cases such as both of the cited evaluations, where all DNA sequences tested contain only a *single gene*. In this effort, the number of correct (and incorrect) predictions are first summed over all test sequences and then the measurements were computed from those sums for the exon and base level measurements, respectively. Either method of measurement appears appropriate for the Burset and Guigo data sets, where the data sequences have a single gene via pre-processing (and may be *leveraged* as such in the design of the program being tested). In what is a more realistic context of raw genomic data processing, however, we are likely to encounter two key issues as part of the problem:

1)   We have raw genomic sequences that contain multiple genes.
2)   Scoring at the exon level in effect designates the *exon* as the fundamental unit being counted rather than the *gene*, this avoids weighing more complex genes the same as simpler genes (that have fewer exons).

As indicated above, in each case of the data sets used in this effort, the measurements for both the exon and base level prediction differ somewhat from the method used in the cited evaluations.   Moreover, of the data sets tested in this effort, ALLSEQ is the only data set consisting entirely of single-gene DNA sequences. The results of the meta-state HMM for ALLSEQ in this effort are given in both the cited measure of accuracy [84], as well as standard 'exon-level' scoring.

The accuracy measure at the full exon level presents a much greater challenge as it requires the successful prediction of the entire exon for the exon to be scored as correct. These events include the start and end positions of exons as well as the continuation of the exon at all intermediate introns splicing points. The full exon accuracy is given similarly to that given before at base-level scoring:

$$SNSP\_AVG = (SN + SP^*)/2, \text{ where}$$
$$SN = (\text{number of correct exons})/(\text{number of actual exons}), \text{ and}$$
$$SP^* = (\text{number of correct exons})/(\text{number of predicted exons})$$

Again, SP will be used in place of SP* in what follows if there is no ambiguity. It should be noted that this measure for full exon accuracy does not allow for any improvement due to *partial* exon prediction.   More specifically, the exon level accuracy can only be improved by the precise prediction of one or more *entire* exons – at both start and end positions.

8.7.2.3 meta-HMM results for *C. elegans* genome

All predictions are based on state prior, state transition, and emission probabilities which are estimated directly from counts in the training data without any further refinement.   The meta-state HMM model is interpolated to highest Markov order on emission probabilities given the training data size, and to highest Markov order (subsequence length) on the footprint states (with different values shown in multi-trajectory plots in what follows). The former is accomplished via simple count cutoff rules, the latter via an identification of anomalous base statistics near the coding/noncoding-transitions, initially, followed by direct HMM performance tuning. Allowed footprint transitions are restricted to those that have at most one coding/noncoding-transition, which leads to only linear growth in state number with footprint size, *not geometric growth*, enabling the full advantage of generalized-clique modeling at a computational expense little more than that of a standard HMM.

Algorithmic Complexity of meta-HMM dynamic programming table construction

For comparison with the meta-state HMM, we first consider the complexity of the traditional 1st order HMM. First define 'T' as the length of the testing data set, and 'N' as the number of states. The Viterbi algorithm constructs the table recursively, with computational updates in each cell in a given column only dependent on computations involving each of the cells of the prior column, thus the time complexity involved in the Viterbi algorithm is given by $O(TN^2)$. In the meta-state HMM we have similar growth in number of states, but in the case of the increasing footprint size F this increase in states, *and state transitions*, is linear, with time complexity given by $O(T(F+L+R))$, where linearity in F for fixed L and R is verified in the set of time trials shown in Fig. 8.18.

Results for Benchmark Dataset ALLSEQ

Exon- and base-level accuracy for values of the parameters M, F, L, and R were tested and examined for stability. Fig. 8.19 and Fig. 8.20 below show plots for exon- and base-level maxima, respectively, over the parameters L and R of meta-state HMM's prediction performance. The plots illustrate the enhanced performance of the meta-state HMM over simpler prediction models, including the (null hypothesis result) meta-state HMM for which the base Markov parameter, M=0. (Note: the meta-state HMM uses only the *intrinsic* information in the data – making no use of *extrinsic* information, such as EST's, protein homology, etc.)

In comparing the results of this data set to the other results in this effort, the quality of the best result can be attributed to the increased size of the training data set (despite the decreased coding density) as well as adherence among the donor and acceptor splice sites to the consensus sequences, gt and ag, respectively. Fig.s 8.19 & 8.20 also show the best performing predictors from the original benchmark study, FGENEH and GeneID+, that use intrinsic and extrinsic genomic information, respectively. At both the full exon- and base-levels, the meta-state HMM outperforms standard HMM approaches by a discernable margin.

Results for C. elegans Dataset

The results shown in Fig.'s 8.21 & 8.22 indicate that a local maximum for the exon and base level predictions was attained at F=12, with a plateau for F>12 extending to F=20, with exact exon prediction accuracy 74% and base accuracy 90%. In comparing the results of this data set to the other results in this effort, the reduced performance at full exon level for M=8 compared to that for M=5 is an indication of insufficient training size reflected in lack of support for M=8 probability estimates at splice sites.

The degree of preconditioning in our data set is minimal, such that there is allowance in the data for disagreement with the consensus dinucleotide introns sequences, gt and ag, as well as the incorporation of reverse encodings. As mentioned previously, we arrive at a base accuracy of 90%. The prospects for improving this result further are many, starting with simply enlarging the training dataset by including similar genomes from other nematodes, *C. Briggsiae* in particular.

The top performing results from the evaluations performed in [84] and [287] are included in Table 8.6 & 8.7 below (where they predict on data that has much greater preprocessing, not raw genome), including values for the (nucleotide) base level accuracy converted from the AC measurement to E[(sn+sp)/2].

Table 8.8 shows the top results of the meta-state HMM for the data sets and parameter values tested in this effort, including in each case the optimum values for the parameters M, F, L and R. Recall that the method of measurement used in this effort differs slightly from that of the cited evaluations. For additional reference, Table 8.9 shows the maximum accuracy specifically for the ALLSEQ data set at both the base and exon levels using the method of measurement in the cited evaluations, as well as our own.

Software	Nucleotide level				Full Exon Level		
Name	E[sn]	E[sp]	AC	E[(sn+sp)/2]	E[SN]	E[SP]	E[(SN+SP)/2]
FGENEH	0.77	0.88	0.78±0.26	0.825	0.61	0.64	0.64±0.33
GeneID+	0.91	0.91	0.88±0.16	0.91	0.73	0.70	0.71±0.29

Table 8.6. Top 2 performers in the evaluation by Burset and Guigo testing with **ALLSEQ**.

Software	Nucleotide level				Full Exon Level		
Name	E[sn]	E[sp]	AC	E[(sn+sp)/2]	E[SN]	E[SP]	E[(SN+SP)/2]
Genie	0.91	0.90	0.89±0.16	0.905	0.71	0.70	0.71±0.30
Genscan	0.95	0.90	0.91±0.12	0.925	0.70	0.70	0.70±0.32
HMMgene	0.93	0.93	0.91±0.13	0.93	0.76	0.77	0.76±0.30

Table 8.7. Top 3 performers in the evaluation by Rogic, et al., testing with HMR195 [288].

The meta-state HMM's performance on the ALLSEQ dataset clearly exceeds that of the top performing program, GeneID+, cited in [84], by substantial margins, 6.5% and 17%, at the base- and exon-levels, respectively. GeneID+ also uses *extrinsic* information via "amino acid similarity searches" in the process of forming its prediction, whereas the meta-state HMM in this effort uses only the *intrinsic* information contained in the DNA sequence data alone.

Dataset	Nucleotide level					Full Exon Level				
Name	sn	sp	(sn+sp)/2	M	F	SN	SP	(SN+SP)/2	M	F
ALLSEQ	0.978	0.954	0.966	8	4	0.919	0.803	0.861	8	12
Chr. I-V	0.938	0.864	0.901	5	12	0.775	0.711	0.743	2	20

Table 8.8. Maximum accuracy of meta-state HMM for the parameter values tested.

Dataset	Nucleotide level					Full Exon Level				
Name	E[sn]	E[sp]	E[(sn+sp)/2]	M	F	E[SN]	E[SP]	E[(SN+SP)/2]	M	F
ALLSEQ	0.987	0.961	0.974	8	12	0.917	0.847	0.882	8	12

Table 8.9. Maximum accuracy of meta-state HMM for ALLSEQ using the cited method of measurement

The question naturally arises on how we might do better, and we are proceeding in three directions: (1) verifying that HMMD offers little improvements due to the recovery of the heavy tail attribute see [1,2]; (2) work involving pMM/SVM sensors [26]; (3) work involving alternative-splice state structures [18] (also Sec. 8.8); and (4) use of large footprints of HMMD scaffolding to employ zone-dependent statistics to capture *cis*-regulatory signaling, in particular, in the generalized meta-HMMD model. In this effort we tried to mainly draw comparisons with other methods similarly based solely on intrinsic genomic statistics. The method presented here will benefit from extrinsic genomic information 'add-ons' for boosting performance via use of homology matching, or EST alignment, for example [305].

Meta-HMM performance for different meta-state definition HMMs is analyzed next (with results). The model involves both observations and states of extended length in a generalized clique structure, where the extents of the observations and states are incorporated as parameters in the new model. This clique structure was intended to address the following 2-fold hypothesis.

1) The introduction of extended observations would take greater advantage of the information contained in higher order, position-dependent, signal statistics in DNA sequence data taken from extended regions surrounding coding/noncodong sites; and
2) The introduction of extended states would attain a natural boosting by repeated look-up of the tabulated statistics associated in each case with the given type of coding/non-coding boundary.

We find that our meta-state HMM approach enables a stronger HMM-based framework for the identification of complex structure in stochastic sequential data. We show an application of the meta-state HMM to the identification of eukaryotic gene structure in the *C. elegans* genome in what follows, where the performance of the meta-state HMM-based gene-finder performs comparably to three of the best gene-finders: GENIE, GENSCAN and HMMgene [1]. The method shown here, however, is the bare-bones HMM implementation without use of signal sensors to strengthen localized encoding information, such as splice site information. An SVM-based improvement, to integrate directly with the approach introduced here, is described in [26], and given the successful use of neural-net discriminators to improve splice-site recognition in the GENIE gene finder [306], there are clear prospects for further improvement in overall gene-finding accuracy with the meta-state HMM foundation described in this paper.

In the meta-state HMM we have linear growth in number of states with linear increase in footprint size F, with computational time complexity given by O(T(F+L+R)), where linearity in F for fixed L and R is verified in the set of time trials shown in Fig. 8.18.

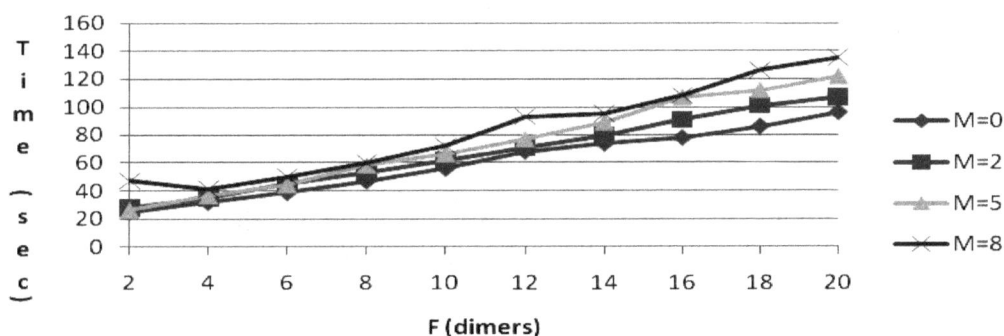

Fig. 8.18. Meta-state HMM test times for test data length 1Mb

Exon- and base-level accuracy for values of the parameters M, F, L, and R were tested and examined for stability. Fig. 8.19 below shows plots for exon- and base-level maxima, respectively, over the parameters L and R of meta-state HMM's prediction performance. The plots illustrate the enhanced performance of the meta-state HMM over simpler prediction models, including the (null hypothesis result) meta-state HMM for which the base Markov parameter, M=0. (Note: the meta-state HMM uses only the *intrinsic* information in the data – making no use of *extrinsic* information, such as EST's, protein homology, etc.) Fig. 8.19 also shows the best performing predictors from the original benchmark study, FGENEH and GeneID+, that use intrinsic and extrinsic genomic information, respectively. At both the full exon- and base- levels, the meta-state HMM outperforms standard HMM approaches by a discernable margin.

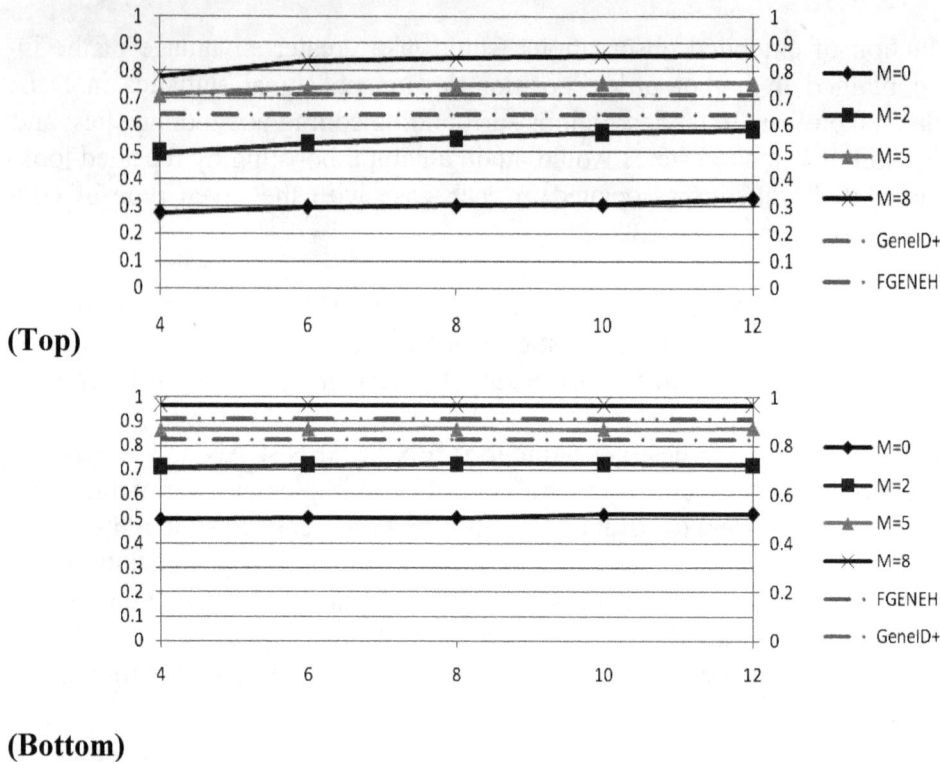

(Top)

(Bottom)

Fig. 8.19. Top. Maximum full exon meta-state HMM performance for data ALLSEQ. Bottom. Maximum base level meta-state HMM performance for data ALLSEQ.

The results shown in Fig. 8.20 (F-view, with Fig. 8.21 showing 'M-view') indicate that a local maximum for the exon and base level predictions was attained at F=12, with a plateau for F>12 extending to F=20, with exact exon prediction accuracy 74% and base accuracy 90%. In comparing the results of this data set to the other results in this effort, the reduced performance at full exon level for M=8 compared to that for M=5 is an indication of insufficient training size reflected in lack of support for M=8 probability estimates at splice sites. The degree of preconditioning in our data set is minimal, such that there is allowance in the data for disagreement with the consensus dinucleotide introns sequences, gt and ag, as well as the incorporation of reverse encodings. As mentioned previously, we arrive at a base accuracy of 90%. An overview of the data-processing architecture and code implementation is shown in Fig. 8.22. The prospects for improving this result further with the foundation in place are many, starting with simply enlarging the training dataset by including similar genomes from other nematodes, *C. Briggsiae* in particular.

(Top)

(Bottom)

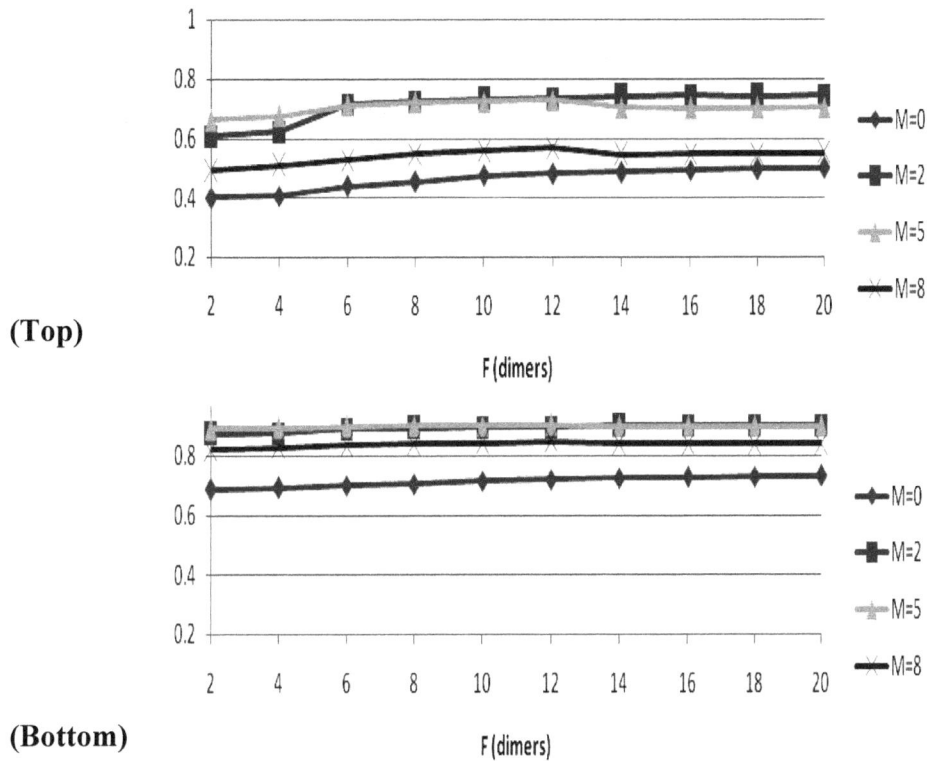

Fig. 8.20, F-view. Top. Full exon level accuracy for *C. elegans* with 5-fold cross-validation. **Bottom.** Base level accuracy for *C. elegans* with 5-fold cross-validation.

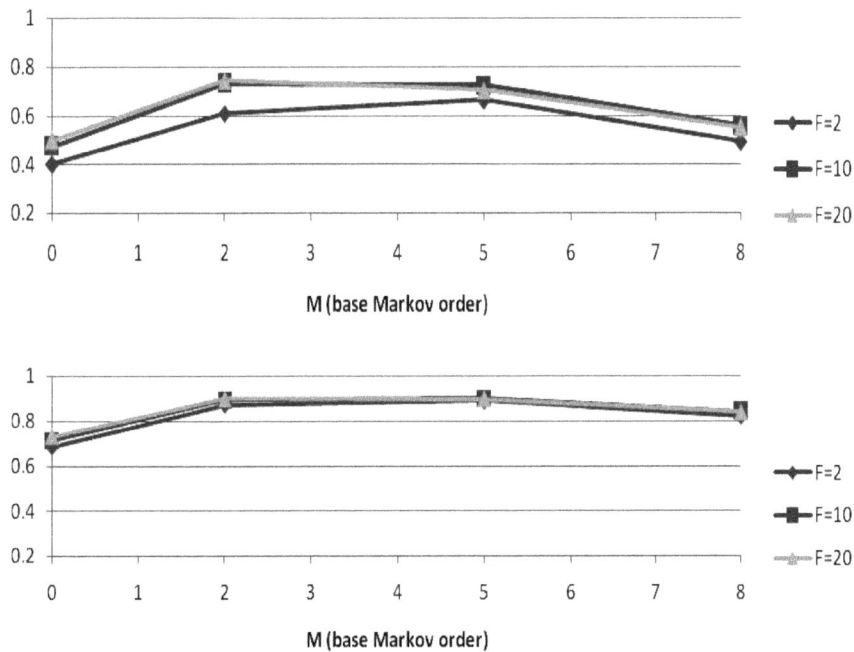

Fig. 8.21, M-view. Top. Full exon level accuracy for *C. elegans* 5-fold cross-validation. **Bottom.** Base level accuracy for *C. elegans* 5-fold cross-validation.

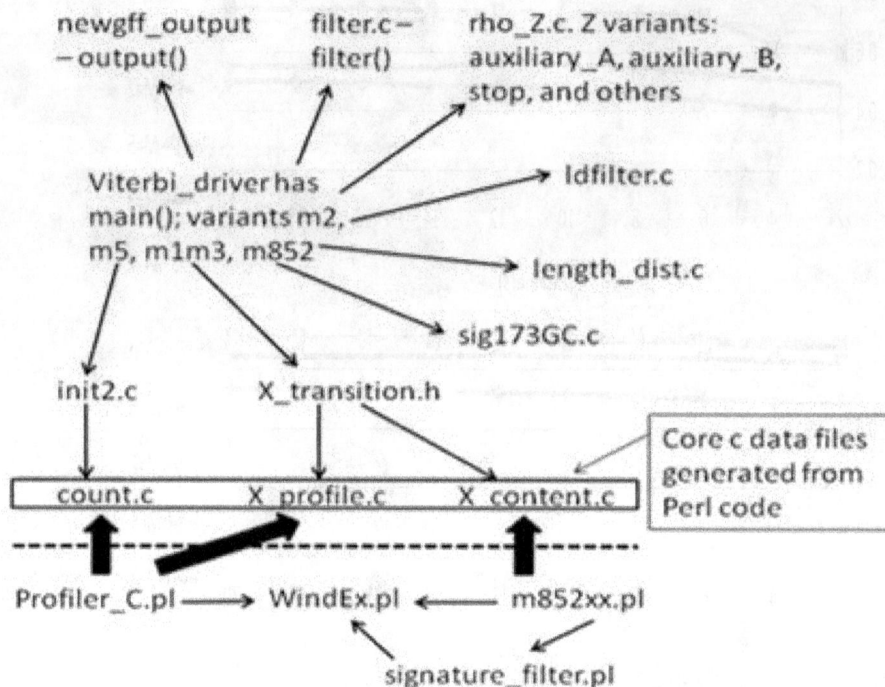

Fig. 8.22. HOHMM Gene-predictor code-base._**WindEx.pl** (previously Window_Extractor.pl) – extracts windows around features defines according to GFF-annotated data (uses GFF.pm).

For the gene-predictor shown in Fig. 8.22: **signature_filter.pl** – validation of annotation attributes can be performed or enforced. **m852xx.pl** → produces X_content.c, where X is a model-dependent set (given as sig173GC.c for the implementation shown in the diagram; which is the footprint F=8 model described in the model synopsis that follows). **Profiler_C.pl** → produces count.c and X_profile.c. **Viterbi_driver** has main() → variants depending on strength of representation in dataset (m2, m5, m1m3, m852) [part of the core HOHMM implementation]._**newgff_output** (previously gff_output.c) has output() which outputs results in a format such that it can be easily slurped up by BGscore.pm and other scoring algorithms)._**X_transition.h** [core HOHMM implementation; X is a model-dependent set given in sig173GC.c]._**init2.c** (previously initialization.c). **sig173GC.c** (the implementation for the footprint F=8 theoretical model described the synopsis that follows). **ldfilter.c** → calls length_dist.c (an approximate HMM with duration implementation). **rho** has rho() → variants depending on use of possible approximations, re-estimations; main attribute, however, is a reduction of the HMM algorithm to a series of data table look-ups, where those data tables are produced carefully, in clear Perl meta-language code to produce the data-table C-code, and directly loaded into RAM as part of the core HMM C program. This is a highly optimized arrangement on most machines automatically, so permits hetergenous network distribution very easily when distributed Perl training and C HMM/Viterbi operations are performed. **Bad_exon.pl** → a bad exon filter. **Cleaner.pl** → a cleaned dataset creator according to specification on filters. **(various datarun scripts).**

8.7.3 HMMBD+pde+zde
Zone Dependent Emission (ZDE) modeling

The vicinity around the transitions between exon, intron and junk usually contains rich information for gene identification. The junk to exon transition usually starts with an ATG; the exon to junk transition ends with one of the stop codons {TAA, TAG, TGA}. Nearly all eukaryotic introns start with GT and end with with AG (the AG-GT rule). To capture the information at these transition areas we build a position- dependent emission (pde) table for base positions around each type of transition point. It is called 'position-dependent' since we make estimation of occurrence of the bases (emission probabilities) in this area according to their relative distances to the nearest non-self state transition. For example, the start codon 'ATG' is the first three bases at the junk-exon transition. The size of the pde region is determined by a window size parameter centered at the transition point (thus, only even numbered window sizes are plotted in what follows). We use four transition states to collect such position-dependent emission probabilities ie; je0; ei; e2j: Considering the framing information, we can expand the above four transition into eight transitions i2e0; i0e1; i1e2; je0; e0i0; e1i1; e2i2; e2j: We make i2e0; i0e1; i1e2 share the same ie emission table and e0i0; e1i1; e2i2 share the same ei emission tables. Since we process both the forward-strand and reverse-strand gene identifications simultaneously in one pass, there is another set of eight state transitions for the reverse strand. Forward states and their reverse state counterparts also share the same emission table (i.e., their instance counts and associated statistics are merged). Based on the training sequences' properties and the size of the training data set, we adjust the window size and use different Markov emission orders to calculate the estimated occurrence probabilities for different bases inside the window (e.g., interpolated Markov models in [39]).

The regions on either side of a pde window often include transcription factor binding sites, etc., such as the promoter for the je window. Statistics from these regions provide additional information needed to identify start of gene coding and alternative splicing. The statistical properties in these regions are described according to zone-dependent emission (zde) statistics. The signals in these areas can be very diverse and their exact relative positions are typically not fixed positionally. We apply a 5th-order Markov model on instances in the zones indicated (further refinements with hash-interpolated Markov models [39] have also met with success but are not discussed further here). The size of the 'zone' region extends from the end of the position-dependent emission table's coverage to a distance specified by a parameter. For the dataruns shown in what follows, this parameter was set to 50.

There are eight zde tables:{ ieeeee, jeeeee, eeeeei, eeeeej, eiiiii, iiiiie, ejjjjj, jjjjje}, where ieeeee corresponds to the exon emission table for the downstream side of an ie transition, with zde region 50 bases wide, e.g., the zone on the downstream side of a non-self transition with positions in the domain (window, window+50].We build another set of eight hash tables for states on the reverse strand. We see 2% performance improvement when the zde regions are separated from the bulk dependent emissions (bde), the standard HMM emission for the regions. When outside the pde and zde regions, thus in a bde region, there are three emission tables for both the forward and reverse strands exon, intron, and junk states, corresponding to the normal exon emission table, the normal intron emission table and the normal junk emission table. The three kinds of emission processing are shown in Fig. 8.23.

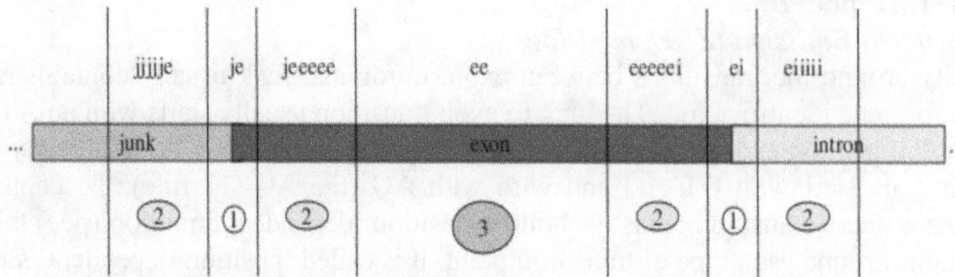

Fig. 8.23: Three kinds of emission mechanisms: (1) position-dependent emission; (2) hash- interpolated emission; (3) normal emission. Based on the relative distance from the state transition point, we first encounter the position-dependent emissions (denoted as (1)), then we use the zone-dependent emissions (2), and finally, we encounter the normal state emissions (denoted as (3)).

The model contains the following 27 states in total for each strand, three each of {ieeeee, jeeeee, eeeeei, eeeeej, eeeeee, eiiiii, iiiiie, iiiiii}, corresponding to the different reading frames; and one each of {ejjjjj, jjjjje, jjjjjj}. As before, there is another set of corresponding reverse-strand states, with junk as the shared state. When a state transition happens, junk to exon for example, the positional-dependent emissions inside the window (je) will be referenced first, then the state travels to the zone-dependant emission zone (jeeeee), then travels to the state of the normal emission region (eeeee), then travels to another state of zone-dependent emissions (eeeeei or eeeeej), then to a bulk region of self-transitions (iiiiiii or jjjjjj), etc. The duration information of each state is represented by the corresponding bin assigned by the algorithm, according to [21]. For convenience in calculating emissions in the Viterbi decoding, we pre-compute the cumulant emission tables for each of 54 sub-states (states of the forward and reverse strand), then as the state transitions, its emission contributions can be determined by the differences between two references to the pre-computed cumulant array data.

The occurrence of a stop codon (TAA, TAG or TGA) that is in reading frame 0 and located inside an exon, or across two exons because of the intron interruption, is called an 'in-frame stop'. In general the occurrences of in-frame stops are considered very rare. We designed our in-frame stop filter to penalize such Viterbi paths. A DNA sequence has six reading frames (read in six ways based on frames), three for the forward strand and three for the reverse strand. When pre-computing the emission tables in the above for the sub-states, for those sub-states related to exons we consider the occurrences of in-frame stop codons in the six reading frames. For each reading frame, we scan the DNA sequence from left to the right and whenever a stop codon is encountered in-frame we add to the emission probability for that position a user defined stop penalty factor. In this way, the in-frame stop filter procedure is incorporated into the emission table building process and does not bring the additional computational complexity to the program. The algorithmic complexity of the whole program is O(TND*) where N = 54 sub-states and D* is the number of bins for each sub-state, and the memory complexity is O(TN), via the HMMBD method described in [21].

HMMBD+pde+zde results for C. elegans genome

We take advantage of the parallel presentation in [29] to start the tuning with a parameter-set that is already nearly optimized (i.e., the Markov emissions, window size, and other genome-dependent tuning parameters is already close to optimal). For verification purposes, we first do training and testing using the same folds, the results for each of the five folds indicated above are very good, a 99%-100% accuracy rate (not shown). We then do a 'proper' single train/test fold from the five-fold cross-validation set (i.e., folds 1-4 to train, and the 5th fold as test), and explore the tuning on Markov model and window size as shown in Fig.'s 8.24-8.27. We then perform a complete five-fold cross-validation with the five folds for the model identified as best (i.e., train on four folds, test on one, permute over the five hold-out test possibilities and take their average accuracies of the different train/tests as the overall accuracy).

In Fig.s 8.24 & 8.25 we show the results of the experiments where we tune the Markov order and window size parameters to try to reach a local maximum in the predication performance for both the full exon level and the individual nucleotide level. We compare the results of three kinds of different configurations. In the first configuration, shown in Fig.'s 8.24 & 8.25, we have the HMM with binned duration (HMMBD) with position-dependent emissions (pde's) and zone dependent emissions (i.e., HMMBD+pde+zde).

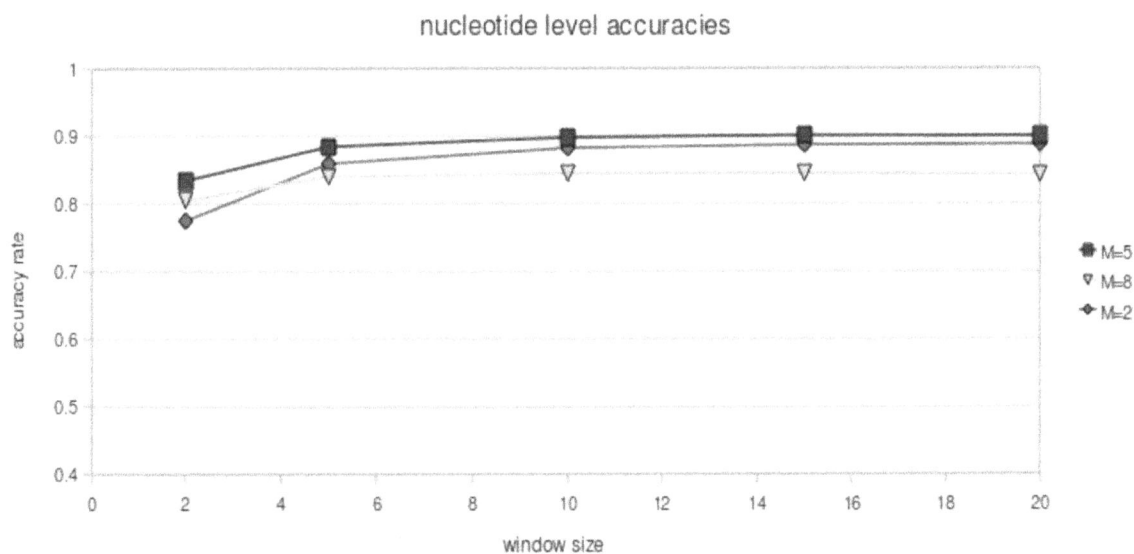

Fig. 8.24. Nucleotide level accuracy rate results with Markov order of 2, 5, 8 respectively for *C. elegans*, Chromosomes I-V.

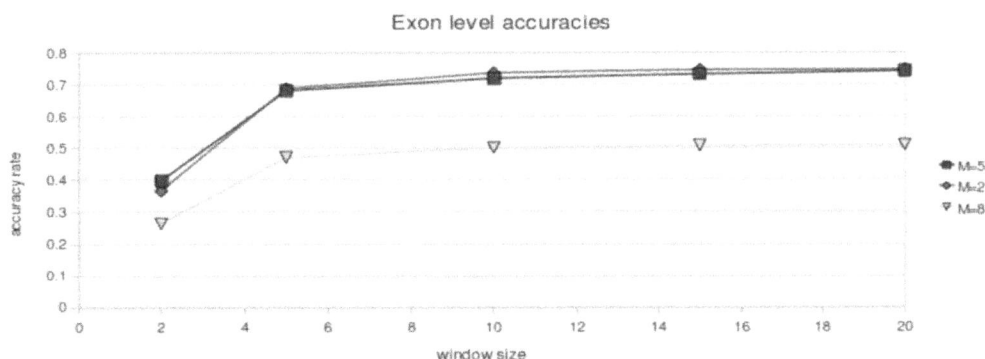

Fig. 8.25. Exon level accuracy rate results with Markov order of 2, 5, 8 respectively for *C. elegans*, Chromosomes I-V.

In the second configuration, we turn off the zone dependent emissions (so, HMMBD+pde), the resulting accuracy suffers a 1.5-2.0% drop as shown in Fig.s 8.26 & 8.27. In the third setting, we use the same setting as the first setting except that we now use the geometric distribution that is implicitly incorporated by HMM as the duration distribution input to the HMMBD (HMMBD+pde+zde+Geometric). The purpose is have an approximation of the performance of the standard HMM with pde and zde contributions. As show in Fig.s 8.26 & 8.27, the performance of the result has about 3% to 4% drop (conversely, the performance improvement with HMMD modeling, with the duration modeling on the introns in particular, is improved 3-4% in this case, with a notable robustness at handling multiple genes in a sequence – as seen in the intron submodel that includes duration information in [305]) . When the window size becomes 0, i.e., when we turn off the setting of position-dependent emissions, the performances of the results drop sharply as shown in Fig.s 8.26 & 8.27. This is because the strong information at the transitions, such as the start codon with ATG or stop codons with TAA, TAG or TGA, etc., are now 'buried' in the bulk statistics of the exon, intron, or junk regions.

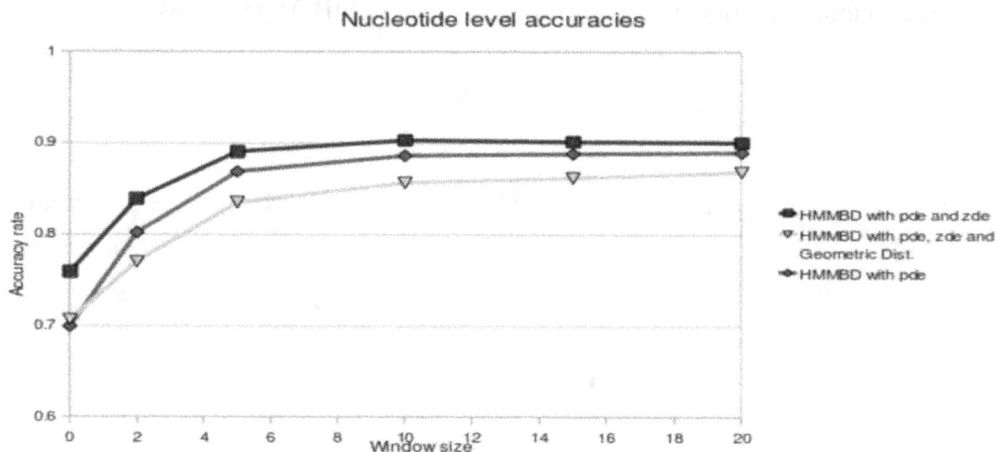

Fig. 8.26. Nucleotide level accuracy rate results for three different kinds of settings.

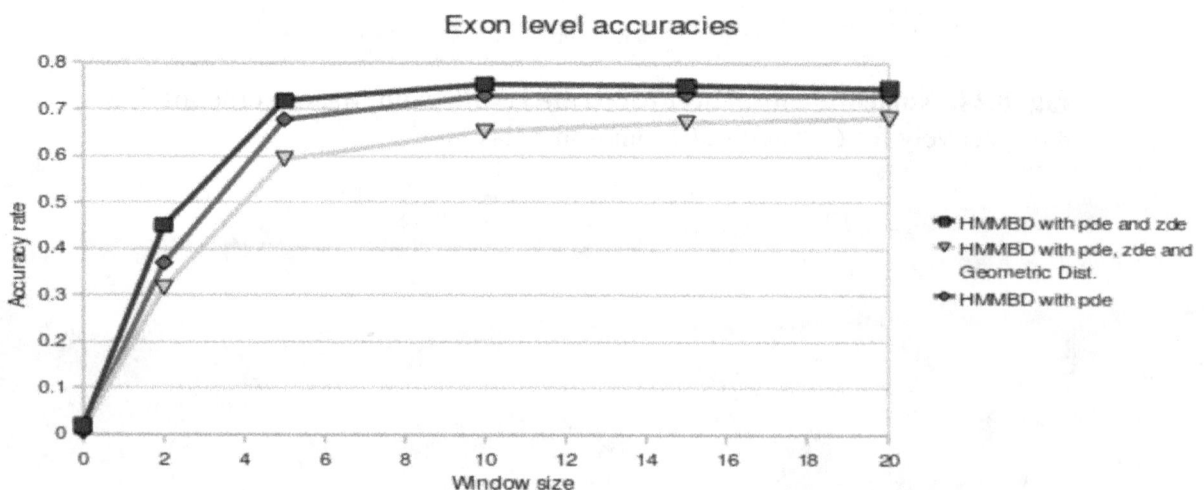

Fig. 8.27. Exon level accuracy rate results for three different kinds of settings.

A full five-fold cross validation is performed for the HMMBD+pde+zde case, as shown in Fig.s 8.28 & 8.29. The fifth and second order Markov models work best, with the fifth order Markov model having a notably smaller spread in values consistent with [1] and validating the rapid tuning performed in Fig.s 8.24-8.27 (that proceeded with analysis using only one fold). The best case performance was 86% accuracy at the nucleotide level and 70% accuracy at the base level (compared with 90% on nucleotides and 74% on exons on the exact same datasets in the meta-HMM described in [1]).

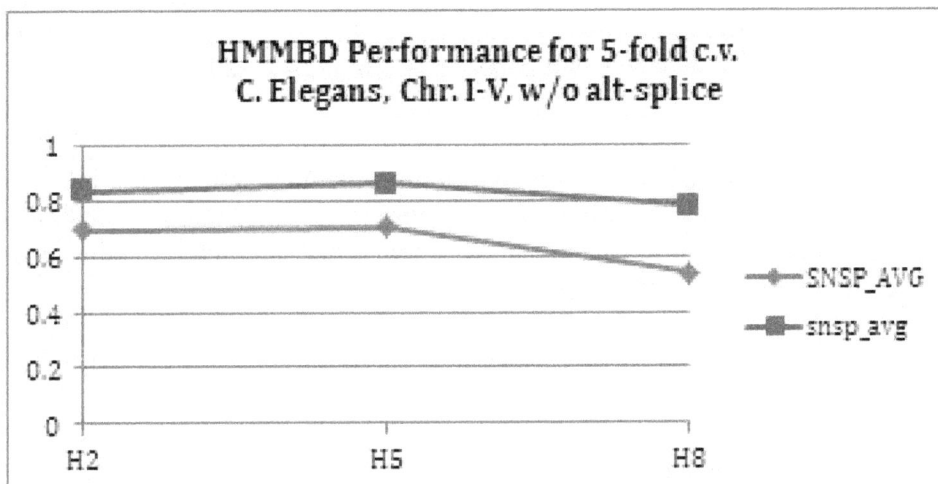

Fig. 8.28. Nucleotide (red) and Exon (blue) accuracy results for Markov models of order: 2, 5, and 8, using the 5-bin HMMBD (where the AC value of the five folds is averaged in what is shown).

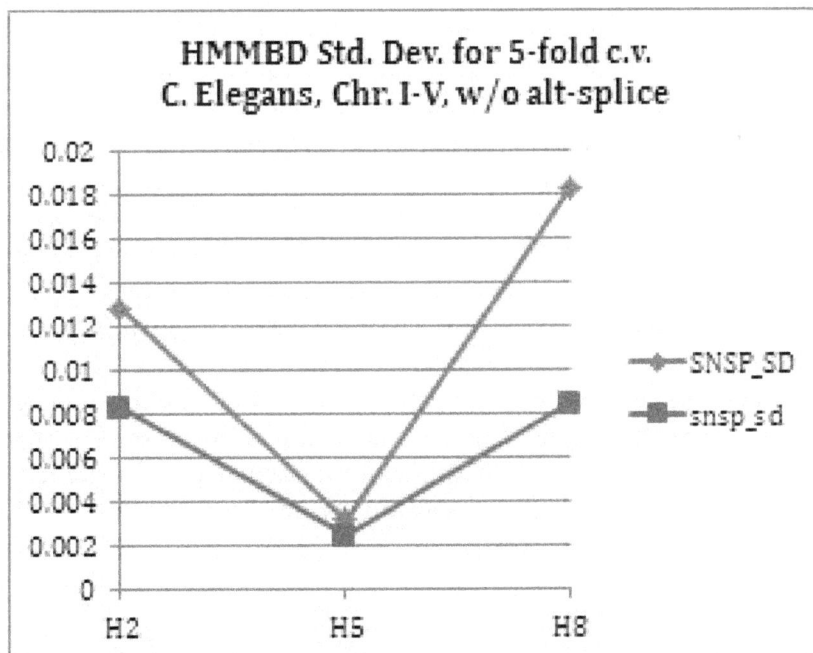

Fig. 8.29. Nucleotide (red) and Exon (blue) standard deviation results for Markov models of order: 2, 5, and 8, using the 5-bin HMMBD (where the standard deviation of the AC values of the five folds is shown).

The gap and hash interpolating Markov Models (gIMM and hIMM) [39] will eventually be incorporated into the model since they are already known to extract additional information that proves useful, particularly in the zde regions where promoters and other gapped motifs exist. This is because promoters and transcription factor binding sites often have lengthy overall gapped motif structure, and with the hash-interpolated Markov models it is possible to capture the conserved higher order sequence information in the zde sample space. The hIMM and gIMM methods will not only strengthen the gene structure recognition, thus the gene-finding accuracy, they can also provide the initial indications of anomalous motif structure in the regions identified by the gene-finder (in a post-genomic phase of the analysis) [39].

In this section we have presented a novel formulation for inclusion of side information, beginning with treating the state-duration as side-information and thereby bootstrapping from an HMM to a HMMD modeling capability. We then apply the method, using binned duration for speedup, HMMBD [21], to eukaryotic gene-finding analysis and compare to the meta-HMM [1,39]. In further work we plan to merged the methods to obtain a meta-HMMBD+zde that is projected to have at least a 3% improvement over the meta-HMM at comparable time complexity.

8.8 Alt-splice gene predictor (AGP)

One of the main limitations of the typical HMM implementation for gene structure identification is that a single structure is identified on a given sequence of genomic data – i.e., identification of overlapping structure is not directly possible, and certainly not possible within the confines of the optimal Viterbi path evaluation. This is a huge limitation given that we now know that significant portions of eukaryotic genomes, particularly mammalian genomes, are alternatively spliced, and, thus, have overlapping structure in the sense of the mRNA transcripts that result. Using the general meta-state HMM approach developed in prior work, however, more than one 'track' of annotation can be accommodated, thereby allowing a direct implementation of an alternative-splice gene-structure identifier. In this section we examine the representation of alternative splicing annotation in the multi-track context, and show that the proliferation on states is manageable, and has sufficient statistical support on the genomes examined (human, mouse, worm, and fly) that a full alt-splice meta-state HMM gene finder can be implemented with sufficient statistical support. In the process of performing the alternative splicing analysis on alt-splice event counts we expected to see an increase in alternative splicing complexity as the organism becomes more complex, and this is seen with the percentage of genes with alt-splice variants increasing from worm to fly to the mammalian genomes (mouse and human). Of particular note is an increase in alternative splicing variants at the start and end of coding with the more complex organisms studied (mouse and human), indicating rapid new first and last exon recruitment that is possibly spliceosome mediated. This suggests that spliceosome-mediated refinements (acceleration) of gene structure variation and selection, with increasing levels of sophistication, has occurred in eukaryotes and in mammals especially.

The shortcomings of the HMM due to algorithmic definitions, such as lack of state-duration modeling, are readily apparent (with fixes as described in [1,39]). The shortcomings of the HMM due to choice of model definition and related implementation, are more subtle. In an HMM implementation the number of look-ups to a particular emission or transition probability table will show how that table's anomalous statistics influence the overall computation (where the count on use of a particular *component* in the table is precisely what provides an estimation in the HMM Baum-Welch algorithm). Standard HMM's lead to a model that strongly de-emphasizes (with low table usage) the anomalous statistics known to exist around non-self transitions, and restricts to transition probabilities that are not sequence dependent. In [1,39] it is shown that use of transition probabilities that are sequence dependent, via use of a constrained set of 'meta-states', is possible with comparable computational complexity to the standard HMM. There is, thus, a 'model primitive' shortcoming underlying the standard HMM implementation that is resolved in the meta-state HMM description [1,39].

Using the general meta-state HMM approach more than one 'track' of annotation can be accommodated, thereby allowing a direct implementation of an alternative-splice gene-structure identifier. There is still the necessity, however, for there to be sufficient statistical support (e.g., samples) on the non-self transitions to have a reliable profile HMM developed (e.g., establish the bare-bones HMM sensors). This can only succeed, practically speaking, if the multi-track annotation describing the alternative splicing can be represented with a manageable number of multi-track transition states, where the intrinsic genomic statistics on these multi-tack states has sufficient support to properly model the proliferation in meta-states that results.

In this section we examine the representation of alternative splicing annotation in the multi-track context, and show that the proliferation on states is manageable, and has sufficient statistical support on the Genbank annotated genomes examined (human, mouse, worm, fly) that a full alt-splice meta-state HMM gene finder can be implemented using an analysis only based on the intrinsic statistical information of the genome studied. The four organisms selected in this study are all animals, thus our focus is on eukaryotes that are animals and not plants or protists (or single-celled anything).

8.8.1 HMM states for AGP gene-structure identification

The codon structure in exons is directly revealed in a mutual information analysis of gapped base statistical linkages as shown in [39] and in Ch. 2. Part of what follows re-iterates Sec. 8.7.2.1 material in greater detail relevant to this domain. Denote the primitive states of the individual bases, described as exon, intron, or junk, by:

> Exon states = { e_0, e_1, e_2 }, where frame label is 'real', i.e., there are three emission tables;

> Intron states = { i_0, i_1, i_2 }, where frame label is a convenient implementation artifact (so one em table);

> Junk state = {j}. the non-coding (non-exonic) nucleotides in the intergenic regions, while the non-coding nucleotides in the intragenic regions are the aforementioned introns.

While 'emitting' the base sequence observed, the 'real' exon framing subscript 'cycles' over states corresponding to the frame position as expected, while the intron framing info stays the same and 'transmits' framing information thereby to the end of the intronic region (purely for the convenience in the HMM implementation). We thus have three possible intron 'framings' indicated in the following state strings (with exon framing shown cycling):

jj...je$_0$e$_1$e$_2$...e$_0$i$_0$i$_0$...i$_0$e$_1$...e$_0$e$_1$e$_2$jj...j   (intron follows exon base with frame 0)
jj...je$_0$e$_1$e$_2$...e$_1$i$_1$i$_1$...i$_1$e$_2$...e$_0$e$_1$e$_2$jj...j   (intron follows exon base with frame 1)
jj...je$_0$e$_1$e$_2$...e$_2$i$_2$i$_2$...i$_2$e$_0$...e$_0$e$_1$e$_2$jj...j   (intron follows exon base with frame 2)

Using the base-level state labeling, consider the 'toy' gene shown in Fig. 8.30 that has only two exons. The label information is shown consistent with this, and an 'arrow' notation is introduced in the figure to show how the arrow demarks the boundary of the intragenic region that will be used in the figures to follow.

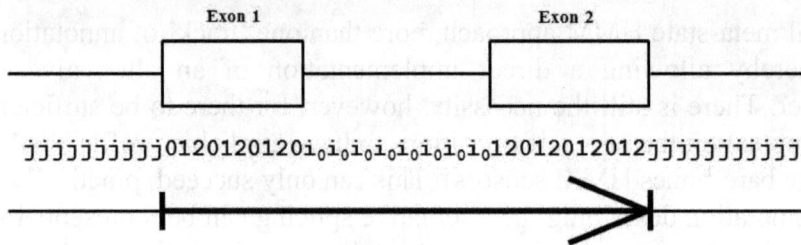

Fig. 8.30 The standard forward-read Gene Predictor with 5 state labels: j, i, 0, 1, 2; and 13 state transitions: jj, j0, 2j, 01, 12, 20, 0i, 1i, 2i, i0, i1, i2, ii. The arrow covers the extent of the exon bounded region.

Although there is no notion of framing among introns, for convenience we associate framing with the intron for use in code implementation, as indicated in Fig. 8.30, as a tracking device in order to ensure that the frame of the following intron-to-exon transition is constrained appropriately.

In [18], the 13 state transitions are not only extended to 15 to incorporate the above frame-tracking across introns, but further extended to 17 states to incorporate stop codon recognition/validation directly into the end-of-coding transition. The 17 two-label (dimer) forward transitions are: {jj,je$_0$, e$_0$e$_1$, e$_1$e$_2$, e$_2$e$_0$, e$_0$i$_0$, e$_1$i$_1$, e$_2$i$_2$, i$_0$i$_0$, i$_1$i$_1$, i$_2$i$_2$, i$_0$e$_1$, i$_1$e$_2$, i$_2$e$_0$, e$_2$j_TAA, e$_2$j_TAG, e$_2$j_TGA}. See Table 8.4 and 8.5 for details on the 33-state model for the forward and reverse encoding together, to be described next.

There is further complexity in that the encodings for proteins can be found in both directions along the duplex DNA strand, where the forward and reverse encodings are found to be present in approximately equal numbers. Furthermore, the differences in the base statistics in the forward and reverse gene encodings are sufficiently negligible (or disjoint) that their counts can simply be merged in the modeling (data not shown). To see the application, consider using the above 17 transition model on dsDNA genomic data, a genome would then be analyzed by doing two passes on the genomic data reference strand provided, a forward pass and a reverse pass (see Fig. 8.31).

Fig. 8.31. The standard two-pass gene predictor. A forward pass is used to catch forward reads, followed by a reverse complement pass to catch reverse reads.

The problem with the decoupling of parsing on forward reads and reverse reads is that a forward read in a reverse coding region can encounter non-standard base statistics for 'non-coding' (since it's the statistics of a reverse coding region), which can lead to error (see Fig. 8.32).

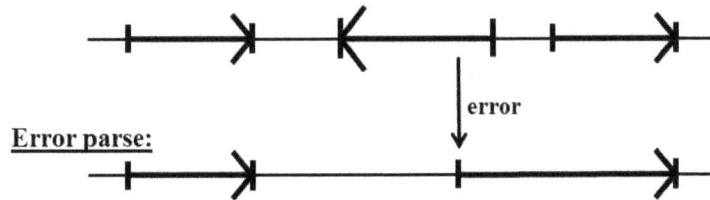

Fig. 8.32. The problem with the standard two-pass gene predictor. Confusion can result in the forward pass across reverse read regions, as shown, that can obscure the true start of other, valid, forward reads.

One possible solution to this, for the case where the forward and reverse gene encodings do not overlap is to capture both in a single pass involving state transitions describing both forward transitions and reverse transitions. There are nine states: j, i, I, 0, 1, 2, A, B, C; where A, B, C are the primitive labels on the reverse read coding bases, and I is for the reverse read intronic bases. The reverse-read codon is 'CBA'. Accordingly, there are 25 state transitions: jj, j0, jC, 2j, Aj; 01, 12, 20, BA, CB, AC, 0i, 1i, 2i, i0, i1, i2, AI, BI, CI, IA, IB, IC, ii, II. In Fig. 8.33 is shown two forward gene encodings on track 1 and one reverse encoding on track 2, where the forward and reverse encodings do not overlap. In the bottom part of Fig. 8.33 is shown the forward and reverse (non-overlap) encodings on a single track using the arrow notation.

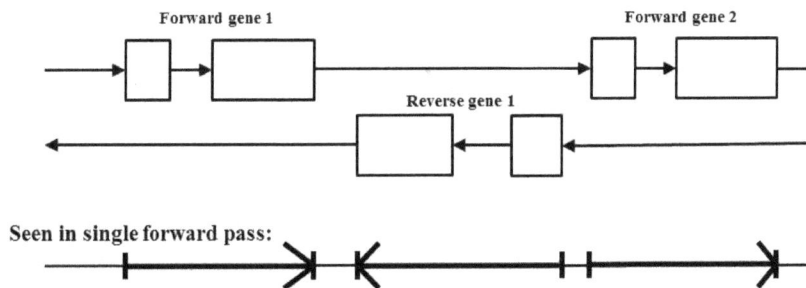

Fig. 8.33. The single-pass forward/reverse coding Gene Predictor with non-overlapping encoding. Top: the forward and reverse reads shown on two separate tracks. Bottom: the forward and reverse reads on a single forward-scan pass on an enlarged state and transition model (shown without refinement involving intron frame-pass and end-of-coding stop codon validation states).

Using a single-pass forward/reverse coding Gene Predictor, and using the previously mentioned refinements involving intron frame-pass and end-of-coding stop codon validation states, it is possible to work directly with both forward and reverse states. This type of HMM implementation has been done in [18] and results in a 33-element transition model (see Table 8.4 and 8.5 for details). The 33 transitions can be taken as the states themselves (two-element meta-states, or 'dimer' states, or length 2 footprint states according to the terminology in [18] and in what follows).

223

In order to work directly with the above dimer states, or the footprint-state generalization, we need to generalize to a higher order HMM model (see Fig.s 1 and 2, and performance results in Fig. 8.18-8.22). The standard HMM has emissions that only depend on the current state (e.g., we have $P(b_{n-1}|\lambda_{n-1})$ terms). A simple HMM with single-base state representation has poor performance in modeling the anomalous statistics in the transition regions between exon, intron, or junk regions without additional side-rules that break with a purely HMM implementation. If a transition 'je$_0$' has occurred, for example, and we are looking at the base emission for the 'e$_0$' state, we can't account for the prior state with the simple $P(b_{n-1}|\lambda_{n-1})$ conditional probabilities in the standard bare-bones HMM modeling, we minimally need $P(b_{n-1}|\lambda_{n-2}, \lambda_{n-1})$, i.e., state modeling at the dimer-level or higher.

Even with the 33-state dimer footprint model above we still can't handle overlapping encodings (alternative splicing or overlap with a reverse coding region). This wasn't a significant problem in the C. elegans genome analysis in [18], but when moving to human, where alternative-splicing is much more common (see Fig. 8.34), the resulting HMM modeling will not perform as well as desired.

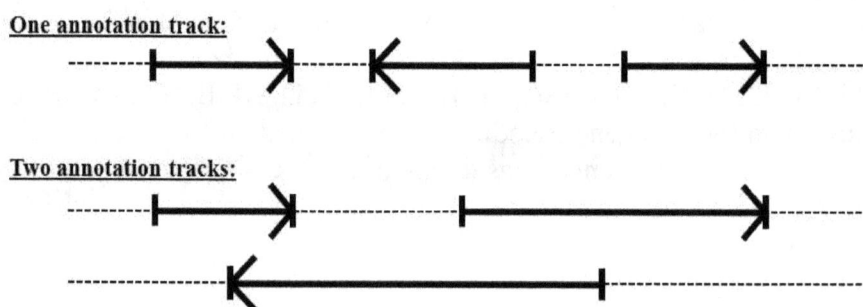

Fig. 8.34. Overlapping encoding requires more than one annotation track if using a single forward-pass gene-structure identifier.

Adding further complication is the fact that it is possible to have higher order overlaps requiring more tracks than two. Fortunately for the alt-splice gene prediction (AGP) modeling sought here this is much less common. Two tracks will be shown to not only provide an excellent statistical representation of the forward/reverse overlap encodings, but also alternative splicing alternate encodings where the same issue of occasional very highly alternatively splices section of genomes are known to exist (but are very rare, with typical alternative splicing giving one alternative). Thus, there is the use of 'two tracks' only in what follows, not three, or more.

In the genome annotations studied, forward and reverse transcripts often overlap, but often with their coding regions (exons) in the other transcript's intronic regions (Fig. 8.35). With the two-track annotation on states we can now introduce the notion of vertical (V) state labels (see Fig. 8.35): $\binom{j}{A}$... also denoted as a 'jA' V-state, and V-transitions: $\binom{ii}{CB}$... also denoted as a 'iiCB' V-transition.

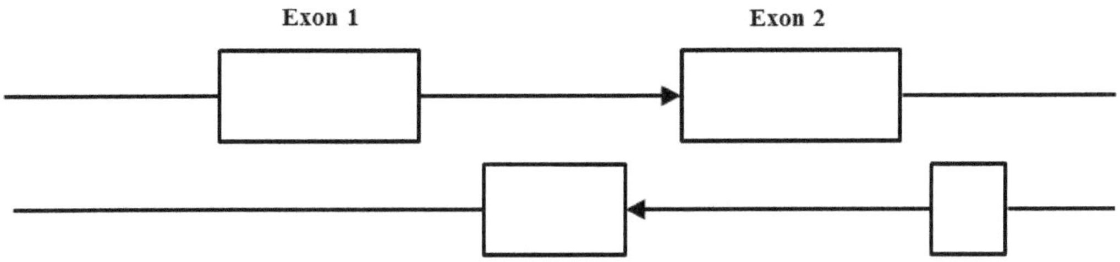

Exon 1   Exon 2

jjjjjjjjjj0120120120$i_0 i_0 i_0 i_0 i_0 i_0 i_0 i_0 i_0$12012012012jjjjjjjjjjj

jjjjjjjjjjjjjjjjjjjjjjjjCBACBACB$i_A i_A i_A i_A i_A i_A i_A i_A i_A$ACBAjjjjj

Fig. 8.35. Overlap of coding with reverse intronic regions, with individual base states shown below for the two tracks.

For alt-splice annotation representation with two tracks we have both reads in the same direction and the exon overlap with an intron region represents alternatively spliced transcripts where the exon has been, alternatively, spliced out (see Fig.s 8.36 and 8.37).

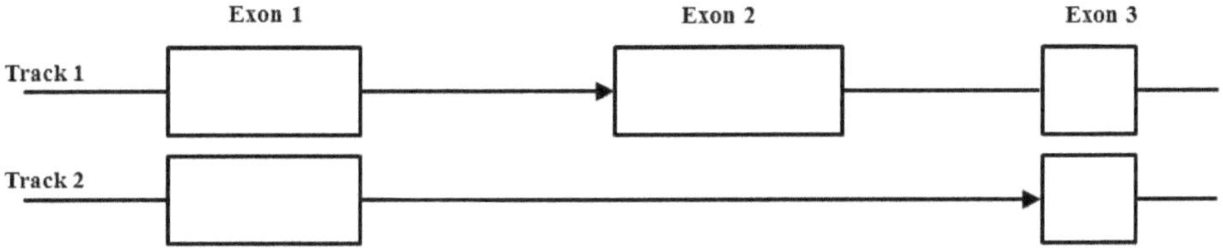

Track 1   Exon 1   Exon 2   Exon 3

Track 2

jjjjjjjjjj0120120120$i_0 i_0 i_0 i_0 i_0 i_0 i_0 i_0$120120120120$i_0 i_0 i_0 i_0 i_0 i_0$012012jjj

jjjjjjjjjj0120120120$i_0 i_0 i_0 i_0 i_0 i_0 i_0 i_0$iiiiiiiiiiiiiiii$i_0 i_0 i_0 i_0 i_0 i_0$012012jjj

Fig. 8.36. Alt-splice overlap encoding with alternatively spliced exon present on track 1. We find V-state labels: $\binom{0}{i}$, etc., and V-transitions: $\binom{i1}{ii}$, compactly denoted 'i1ii', shown. Other 3-prime splice-site, intron-exon (ie), overlap with intron (ii) transitions include 'i0ii' and i2ii. We also have V-transitions: $\binom{0i}{ii}$, denoted '0iii', for 5-prime splice-site, exon-intron (ei), overlap with intron (ii) transitions (other 5-prime ei overlap V-transitions include '1iii' and 2iii').

Less common than exon overlap with intron is partial exon overlap with intron/exon as shown in Fig. 8.38, where a 3-prime splice site overlap with alternative splice intron region is shown, denoted (3'|i). The total count on the 12 (3'|i) types will be shown for four genomes in the comparative analysis that follows. Also shown in Fig. 8.38 is a 5-prime splice site overlap with alternative splice intron region, denoted (5'|i). The total count on the 12 (5'|i) types will also be shown for four genomes in the comparative analysis that follows.

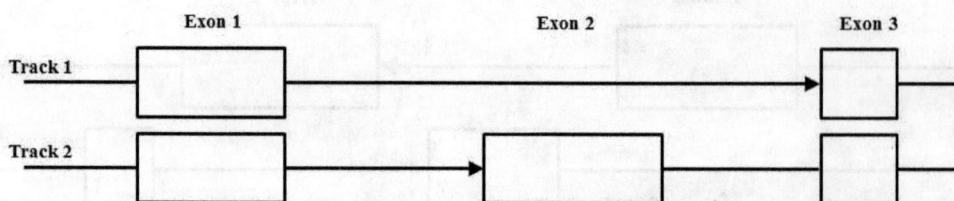

Fig. 8.37. Alt-splice overlap encoding with alternative exon on track 2. The first track describes a transcript with an exon spliced-out with respect to the encoding on track 2.

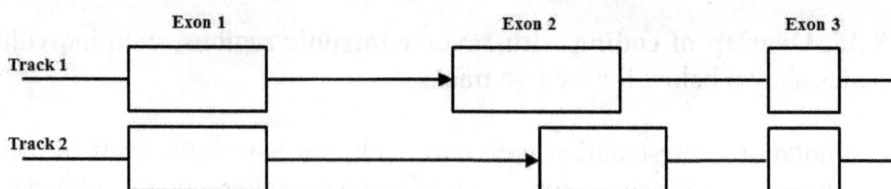

jjjjjjjjjj0120120120120$i_0i_0i_0i_0i_0i_0i_0i_0i_0$120120120120$i_0i_0i_0i_0i_0i_0$012012jjj

jjjjjjjjjj0120120120120$i_0i_0i_0i_0i_0i_0i_0i_0i_0$iiiiiii120120120$i_0i_0i_0i_0$012012jjj

Fig. 8.38. Alt-splicing involving different exons. V-transitions: $\binom{01}{i1}$... '01i1' shown. The 3-prime splice-site, intron-exon (ie), overlap with exon (ee) transitions, for both track placements and read directions, denoted (3'|e), are: 01i1,12i2, 20i0, i020, i101, i202, AIAC, BIBA, CICB, BABI, CBCI, ACAI. Counts on (3'|e) group to follow. V-transitions: $\binom{0i}{01}$... '0i01' also shown. The 5-prime splice-site, exon-intron (ei), overlap with exon (ee) transitions, for both track placements and read directions, denoted (5'|e), are: 0i01,1i12, 2i20, 010i, 121i, 202i, IABA, IBCB, ICAC, BAIA, CBIB, ACIC. Counts on (5'|e) group to follow.

8.8.2 HMM AGP training data for collection of genomes
8.8.2.1 Genome Versions used in AGP Analysis

Table 8.10 shows Genome Versions used in data analysis (all from www.ensembl.org):

Species	Release	GTF File
Human (Homo sapiens)	75	Homo_sapiens.GRCh37.75.gtf
Mouse (Mus musculus)	81	Mus_musculus.GRCm38.81.gtf
Worm (Caenhorhabditis elegans)	83	Caenhorhabditis_elegans.WBcel235.83.gtf
Fly (Drosophila melanogaster)	75	Drosophila_melanogaster.BDGP5.75.gtf

Table 8.10. Genome versions.

8.8.2.2 Pre-partitioning training data, distributed solutions

Starting with the ensemble GTF file of a particular organism, we run a script to identify the number of chromosomes, and any other discrete genomic elements present, according to the annotation listings, and these genomic elements are listed in a log file. The user is then allowed to edit this log file before further processing to delete out entries for chromosomes or other genomic elements on the list, and thereby exclude those deleted entries from the analysis that follows. If nothing is deleted (the file isn't modified), then all of the chromosomes in the genome are used in the analysis, as was the case for the genomes examined here.

Each chromosome that is examined is modelled with a two-label-track annotation scheme that is derived from the ('single-track') GTF file annotations, where the two-track conversion scheme is described in Fig.s 8.39. The general implementation of the HMM modelling software allows for arbitrarily many tracks, so three or more tracks could have been accommodated if necessary, but this turns out to not be the case for the genomes examined (fortunately, as there is then sufficient support from an *ab initio* analysis of the genomes examined for a two-track label scheme, but only barely for the rarest transition states, as will be shown). Due to the potentially high overhead of multi-track labeling, and for the speedup on distributed processing regardless, the implementation is developed for pre-processing of the chromosome training data into chunks. A naïve training data partitioning could easily result in a chunk partition cutting a gene region, so the partition algorithm is designed to offer chunks of approximately the indicated size, but with boundaries moved such that they don't result in a chunking that cuts a gene. This is a non-trivial partitioning task in organisms with dense or extended (operon or many exon) gene structures.

On each chunk of a given Chromosome being processed, two-track feature counts are then done in order to design the HMM, e.g., identify good states and transitions, or train the HMM, e.g., obtain prior probabilities on the various states and transitions, and profile HMMs for the bases emitted by those states and transitions. The pseudocode for counting on the different states and transitions found in the chunk under analysis is shown below:

```
Pseudocode for genome-wide two-track annotation and
state/transition count based on GTF files from ensemble.org.

1. Obtain a genome annotation file in standard GTF format.
2. Perform a smart-partitioning of the genome annotation:
      2.1 Decide on a annotation chunk size (100,000-length base
          segments are used as default).
      2.2 Repeat: attempt a partition 'cut' at position one chunk
          size from last cut (or beginning of annotation
          sequence, whichever is nearer):
          2.2.1 If cut falls outside of any gene family elements
                2.2.1.1 Make cut, goto 2.2.
                2.2.1.2 Else, advance attempted cut position 1%
                        of chunk size (default 1,000), goto 2.2.1.
3. For each chunk that is partitioned:
      3.1 Perform mapping of 'single-reference track' standard
          GTF annotation (with overlapping annotation references
          on that single track) to 'two-track' annotation where
          each track has only a single annotation:
          3.1.1 If not ordered, order the GTF forward reads with
                ascending index number, followed by GTF reverse
                reads with ascending index number.
          3.1.2 Repeat: In the order of first appearance of any
                gene-labeled annotation, that gene gets placed
                ('painted') on track one if no collision with
                another gene annotation region already placed
                there, otherwise placed on track two, unless
                still a collision, in which case abandon the gene
                colliding on both track one and two but list it
                in a 'rejects' logfile (found to be typically
                less than 1% of cases). When a gene region is
                'painted' on an annotation track, it does so from
                the first indexed annotation for the indicated
                gene to the last indexed annotation position for
                that gene.
      3.2 Scan the two-track annotation from 3.1 in terms of two-
          track states and their transitions (referred to as
          'vertical' V-states and V-transitions) and collect
          counts on the various V-states and V-transitions
          encountered.
4. Merge counts on V-states and V-transitions for all of the
chunks.
```

Pseudocode for two-track annotation conversion from GTF, together with counting on two-track states and transitions.

8.8.2.3 Two-track state annotation and counting

Fig. 8.39 shows the two-track annotation conventions, where placement on track 1 is for the entirety of the first transcript from the GTF annotation file, and if another transcript has overlap with the first transcript it is placed on track 2. If further overlap occurs (requiring a third track) there are two conventions: (i) ignore third and higher overlapping transcript annotations, but record the location of the higher than 2nd order alt-splicing region, and (ii) mask the transcripts that have more than two overlaps and exclude from the counting analy-

228

sis entirely. Since the occurrence of higher overlap order than two transcripts is rare (generally less than 5% in general, typically less than 1%), either convention works about the same insofar as the meta-state counts are concerned. In what follows, convention (i) is used.

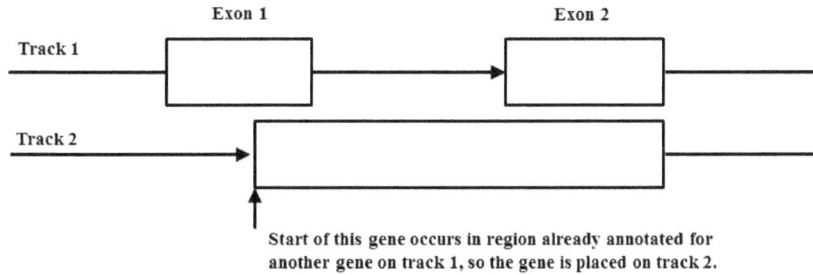

Fig. 8.39. Track annotation conventions.

Track placement info taken by itself can't be used without trivial artifacts resulting from the ordering of the annotation information. Thus the need to pool counts with transitions from both track 1 and track 2. In other words, the V-transition counts on 'ieii' and 'iiie' (where 'e' is 0,1,or 2), both describe ie overlap with ii and are pooled. Similarly for reverse reads, there is a further doubling of transitions when considering the reverse complement versions of the 3-prime -splice-site (ie → EI) overlap with alternative intronic (II).

8.8.3 HMM AGP training data results for collection of genomes

In Table 8.11 and Fig. 8.40 are shown the results for the different types of alternative splicing described, along with the counts on start-of-coding, with extent of alternative splicing in the genome captured in terms of the ratio of alternative splicing events to the number start-of-coding events (the latter being the approximate number of genes). In Table 8.11, the V-transitions contributing to the counts on the different splice types are grouped as follows:

(3'|i) V-transitions: i0ii, i1ii, i2ii, iii0, iii1, iii2, AIII, BIII, CIII, IIAI, IIBI, IICI.
(5'|i) V-transitions: 0iii, 1iii, 2iii, ii0i, ii1i, ii2i, IAII, IBII, ICII, IIIA, IIIB, IIIC.
(3'|e) V-transitions: 01i1,12i2, 20i0, i020, i101, i202, AIAC, BIBA, CICB, BABI, CBCI, ACAI.
(5'|e) V-transitions: 0i01,1i12, 2i20, 010i, 121i, 202i, IABA, IBCB, ICAC, BAIA, CBIB, ACIC.

Table 8.11 also summarizes the fraction of gene transcripts that have alternative splicing in the 'Alt/j0' column, where the # transcripts with alt-splicing is given in relation to the # transcripts total.

species	j0+Aj	(5'|i)	(5'|e)	(3'|i)	(3'|e)	altsum	Alt/j0
worm	25,462	809	809	1,438	653	4,283	0.175
fly	18,730	768	768	1,501	699	4,385	0.234
mouse	33,561	2,260	2,260	7,922	1,540	18,473	0.550
human	36,620	12,075	3,186	14,317	2,002	31,580	0.862

Table 8.11. Counts on start-of-coding (j0 and Aj dimers) and on the different splice-sites. Altsum is the sum total of the different splice types (5'|i, 5'|e, 3'|i, and 3'|e). The last column 'Alt/j0' is the ratio of altsum to the {j0+Aj} counts.

229

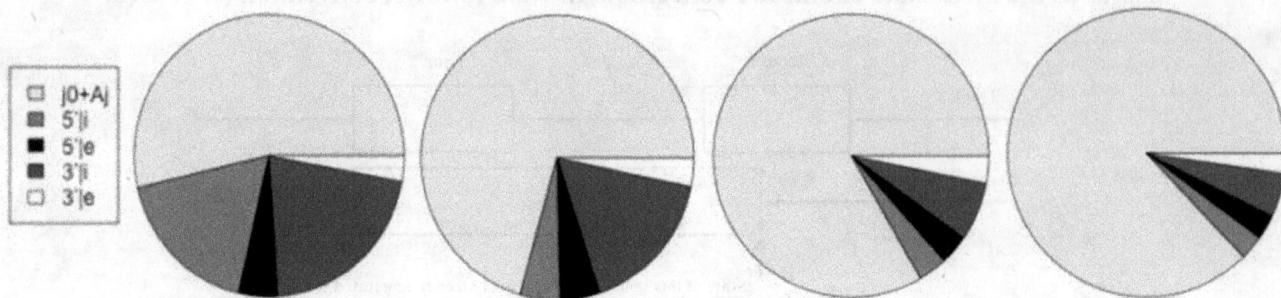

Fig. 8.40. The relative number of counts on start-of-coding (j0 and Aj dimers) and on the different splice-sites are shown in relation to each other. The charts, from left-to-right, are for the human, mouse, fly, and worm genomes.

In Table 8.12 and Fig. 8.41 are shown the counts for the different types of alternative splicing at the start of coding. Further discussion of the notation and results is in the Discussion section. In the table, {j0jj+jjj0}/j0 is the ratio of non-alt-splice starts to all starts. This partly captures the increased overall occurrence of alternative splicing since this would lead to more j0j0 counts and fewer j0jj.The start V-transitions marked with an '*' have encumbered base-profiles in that the base statistics must be consistent with two types of consensus sequence, especially in the case of 'j0i0'. Unencumbered starts would be: j0jj, j0j0 (overlapping starts, but both have same consensus), j0ii, j0II.

V-trans	human	mouse	fly	worm
H-trans j0	18,911	16,899	9,389	12,938
{j0jj+jjj0}	4,208	6,112	4,334	8,323
j0j0	5,892	4,623	2,178	1,750
{j001+01j0}*	106	32	10	4
{j012+12j0}*	65	14	0	2
{j020+20j0}*	1,695	888	251	686
{j0i0+i0j0}*	88	55	6	32
{j0ii+iij0}	873	490	237	204
{j0II+IIj0}	118	59	193	181
{j0jj+jjj0}/j0	0.223	0.362	0.462	0.643
/non-	0.176	0.088	0.038	0.069

Table 8.12. Counts on alternative splicing at the start-of-coding.

230

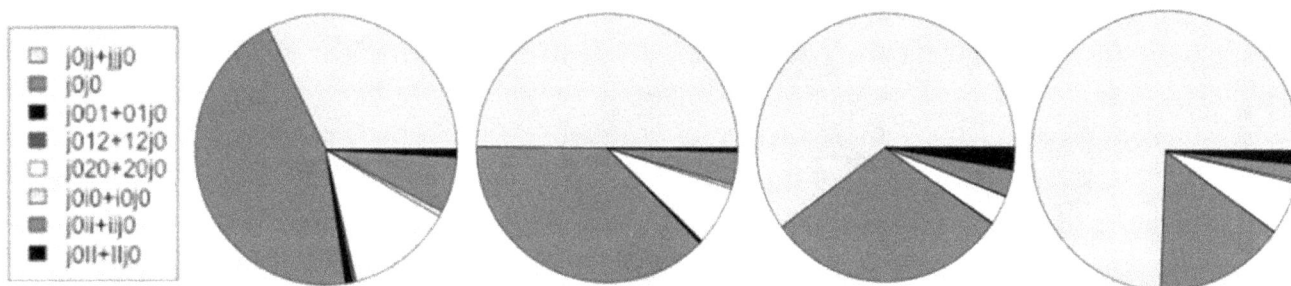

Fig. 8.41. The relative number of counts on alternative start-of-coding.
The charts, from left-to-right, are for the human, mouse, fly, and worm genomes.

In Table 8.13 and Fig. 8.42 are shown the counts for the different types of alternative splicing at the end of coding. Further discussion of the notation and results is in the Discussion section. In the table, {2jjj+jj2j}/2j is the ratio of non-alt-splice ends to all ends. This partly captures the increased overall occurrence of alternative splicing since this would lead to more 2j2j counts and fewer 2jjj. The start V-transitions marked with an '*' have encumbered base-profiles in that the base statistics must be consistent with two types of consensus sequence, as before. Now see spliceosome mediated end variation as very common ({2jii+ii2j}=2,749 vs 2j2j=3,442, so almost half of the alternative spliced genes in human have different ends) .

V-trans	human	mouse	fly	worm
H-trans 2j	19,040	16,727	9,409	12,955
{2jjj+jj2j}	6,641	7,347	4,355	7,843
2j2j	3,442	3,359	2,163	2,249
{2j01+012j}*	926	383	48	46
{2j12+122j}*	908	406	39	79
{2j20+202j}*	704	339	70	5
{2j2i+2i2j}*	51	55	0	3
{2jii+ii2j}	2,749	1,371	378	306
{2jII+II2j}	156	117	192	175
{2jjj+jj2j}/2j	0.349	0.439	0.463	0.605
/non-	0.199	0.097	0.022	0.013

Table 8.13. Counts on alternative splicing at the end-of-coding.

231

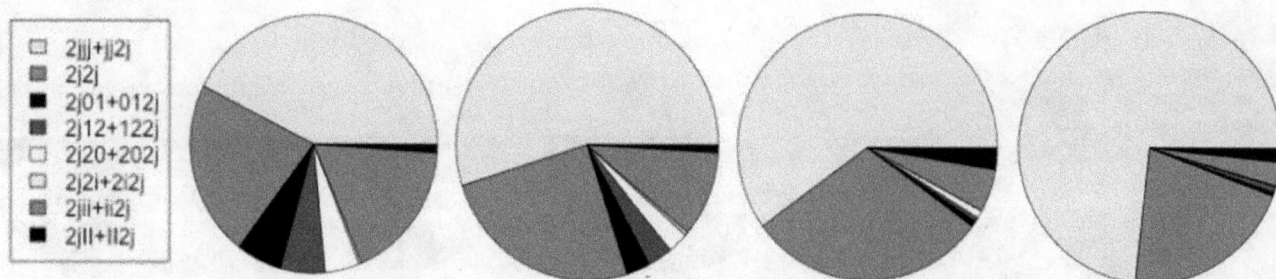

Fig. 8.42. The relative number of counts on alternative end-of-coding. The charts, from left-to-right, are for the human, mouse, fly, and worm genomes.

8.8.4 AGP state structure and transition rules

In the counting on states shown, and discussed in what follows, we are working with the 25-transition (dimer state) model based off of the nine 'primitive' state model: j, i, I, 0, 1, 2, A, B, C. The 25 transitions that then follow are: jj, j0, jC, 2j, Aj; 01, 12, 20, BA, CB, AC, 0i, 1i, 2i, i0, i1, i2, AI, BI, CI, IA, IB, IC, ii, II. For vertical transitions (V-transitions) across tracks 1 and 2 there are thus 25 x 25 = 625 possible meta-states since there is no explicit constraint between tracks. Far fewer are seen in practice, however, due to the consistency constraints on overlapping splice-site signals, etc. Transitions overlapping with junk or intron are clearly allowed, so (25)jj, jj(25), ii(25), (25)ii, II(25), and (25)II, states are allowed (150 total) and the 4x12=48 transitions described in what follows for alt-splices overlapping with exon or intron, denoted (5'|e), (3'|e), (5'|i), and (3'|i) previously, are allowed, so expect to see at least 198 V-transitions. Of the 625 possible V-transitions many are never seen, however, and others are seen extremely rarely. This gives rise to 5 rules on allowed V-transitions involving splice sites, three rules on allowed V-transitions involving start-of-coding transitions, and two rules for the allowed V-transitions involving end-of-coding transitions:

(1) Approximate frame agreement rule: j0 on track 1 can't overlap 2j,0i,1i,i1,i2 on track 2, and only rarely overlap with 01 or 12 on track 2 (a consensus agreement rule). {j0,jC,2j,Aj} similar, so excluding 4 x 5 =20. Similarly with 01 track 1 not overlapping with 12,20,1i,2i,i0,i2 on track 2 (rarely with j0 and 2j as noted). {10.12.20.BA,CB,AC} similar, so excluding 6 x 6 = 36 V-transitions. Similarly 0i on track 1 can't overlap with j0,2j,12,20,1i,2i,i0,i2 on track 2. {0i,1i,2i,i0,i1,i2,AI,BI,CI,IA,IB,IC} similar, so excluding 12 x 8=96 V-transitions.

(2) No 'eiie' or 'ieei' rule (a consensus agreement rule): 0i on track 1 can't overlap with i1. {0i,1i,2i,i0,i1,i2,AI,BI,CI,IA,IB,IC} similar, so excluding 12 x 1 = 12 V-transitions.

(3) No exon boundary overlap with reverse coding region rule, where j0 can't overlap BA, CB, AC, for example. {j0,jC,2j,Aj} similar, so excluding 4 x 3 =12. Similarly 0i can't overlap BA,CB,AC, and there are 12 splice types, so excluding 12 x 3 = 36. And, 01 can't overlap jC,Aj,AI,BI,CI,IA,IB,IC, so 6 x 8 = 48 more exclusions. This appears to be a rule that shows that a coevolutionary linkage between cis or trans regulatory regions and reverse coding regions is highly unfavorable.

Of the 625 V-transitions possible, rules (1)-(3) reduce the types of V-transitions seen by 20+ 36+ 96+ 12+ 12+ 36+ 48 = 260, so down to 625-260 = 365 V-transitions thus far.

Since consensus agreement on overlapping signal types is a strong constraint, the question naturally arises as to when there is consensus agreement. Fig. 8.43 shows examples of how eij0 and ie2j types of V-transitions can have consistent consensus sequences, thus giving rise to allowed V-transitions for these types of overlaps (and similarly for the reverse-read state transitions).

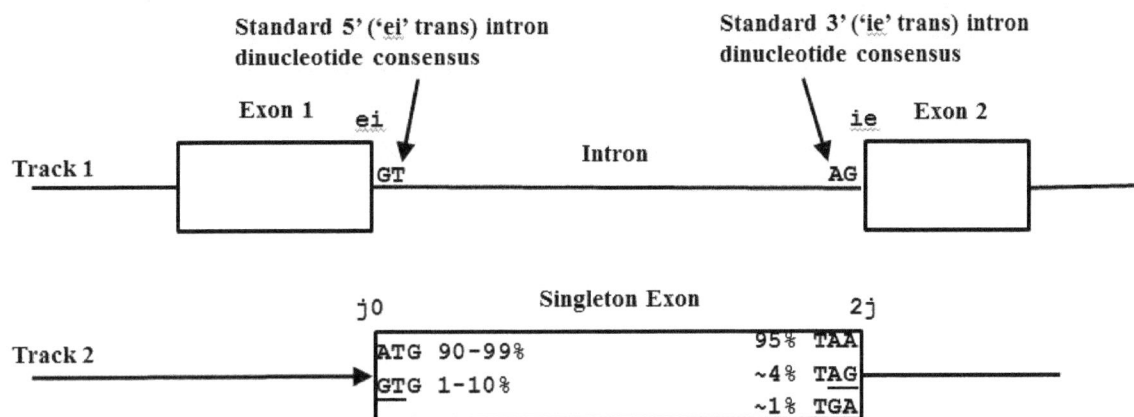

Fig. 8.43. The eij0 and ie2j types of V-transitions can have consensus agreement in their overlap, thus are allowed.

(4) Start/End consensus disagreement rule: Fig. 8.43 shows how consensus agreement is possible for 'eij0' and 'ie2j', but not for flipped consensus EIj0 or IEj0 or IE2j or EI2j (so twelve cases). When treating Aj and jC similarly to j0 and 2j, get another 12, for 24 V-transition exclusions total.

(5) Avoid forward/reverse splice signal overlap. '0i' can't overlap AI, BI, CI; and would generally not favor overlap with IA, IB, IC. There are 12x6 = 72 similar exclusions.

Starting from the 625 V-transitions possible, rules (1)-(5) reduce to 269 'likely' V-transitions (although many are very rare, possibly with zero counts, as will be seen). Focusing on the start-of-coding and the end-of-coding allowed V-transitions as seen in the count data, further elaboration on the allowed V-transitions can be given. The start-of-coding ('j0') consensus rules, as seen in count data, appear to occur in three forms:

(i) Zero counts found for: j0jC, j02j, j0Aj, jCj0, 2jj0, Ajj0 → non-overlap with other start/end rule
(ii) Zero counts found for j0 overlap with reverse transitions except for II.
(iii) Zero counts found for j0 overlaps with forward splice unless 3' (dominated by base-frame 0 to be in agreement with 0 frame in 'j0').

As alternative splicing increases in usage across the genomes, expect both unencumbered alternative splicing (j0j0) and encumbered splicing (such as j0i0 and j020) to increase. Notably, the increase in j0i0 and j020 in more complex mammalian genomes, like mouse and human, indicates gene-growth that is probably spliceosome mediated by way of new first exon recruitment, as shown in Fig. 8.44.

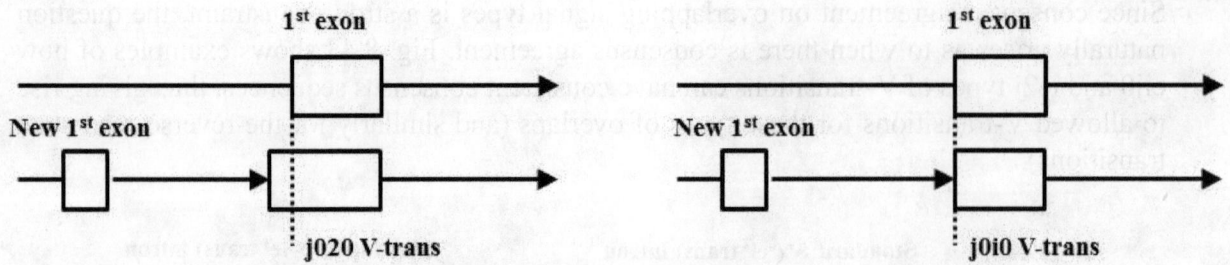

Fig. 8.44. Possible gene growth by way of new first exon recruitment.

The end-of-coding ('2j') consensus rules, as seen in count data, appear to occur in two forms:

(I) Zero counts found for: j2j0,j20i,j21i,j2i0,j2i1,j2i2, indicating a non-overlap with other start/end or splice rule, except for 2j2i (end overlap with 5'splice appearing in more spliced genomes, and only in-frame, showing a slower growth in encumbered 2j versus encumbered j0, as with j0, have indications of spliceosomally driven alt-splice gene extension via exon recruitment from the trans-side of the gene).

(II) Zero counts found for 2j overlap with reverse transitions except for II.

To a much smaller extent than seen at the start-of-coding cis region, spliceosome mediated growth also appears to occur directly via new terminus exon recruitment (shown as the alt-splice variant in the bottom-most annotation sequence shown in Fig. 8.45).

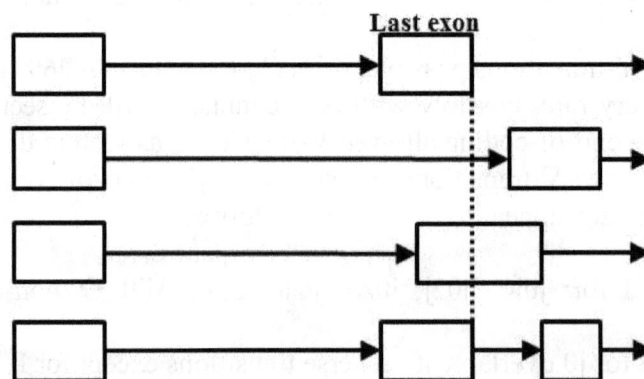

Fig. 8.45. End-of-coding alternative splicing, with the last case shown (bottom track) indicative of a process (possibly spliceosome mediated) for gene growth by way of new last exon recruitment.

In practice we see a small number of annotation errors, for example, in worm, the number of (normal) transition types seen is 31 (not the 25 theoretically possible), with the extra six

234

(annotation error) transitions having very low counts: 1j=7, ij=14, 0j=4, j1=4, ji=28, j2=7 (where the smallest count on valid 25-group transitions is for Aj=12524=jC). For worm, 251 non-zero count V-trans are seen, where the 31 base-state transitions are observed. Similarly, for fly 230 V-transitions are seen, with 33 base-state transitions; for mouse 324 V-transitions are seen, with 35 base-state transitions; and for human 351 V-transitions are seen, with 36 base-state transitions.

Of the 251 non-zero count V-transitions seen for worm, 61 are in the exclusion categories mentioned or involving non-25 transitions, all with extremely low counts, corresponding to annotation errors at a rate ~1/100,000. So only 190 'valid' or non-exclusion V-transitions are seen for worm, some with very low counts, and some, evidently, zero due to 'small' sample size (e.g., 79 of the allowed, but very rare, 269 V-trans have 0 counts for worm). The larger genome sizes for mouse and human, on the other hand, appear to complete the sampling over likely transitions. If all 269 likely transitions are found in the human genome, this leaves 82 non-zero (but very low) counts in exclusion and annotation error categories.

A meta-state HMM implementation with 269 Vertical transitions, or two-track dimer states, is thus shown to suffice for performing a single-pass gene-structure identification that would capture (predict) almost all alternative splicing variants. Since roughly 70 of the possible V-transitions typically have either zero counts, or very low counts, modeling appears possible with only 200 two-track dimer states. The meta-HMM implementation described in [18] explored implementations with more states than this when working with larger footprint states, and did so using only a single workstation or laptop. Thus it is shown to be feasible to implement a meta-state HMM for alternative-splice gene structure identification without special computational requirements, and with sufficient statistical support (using roughly 200 two-track dimer states) for a strong model.

An analysis of the alternative splicing in a comparative genomics context reveals the expected increase in alternative splicing complexity as the organism becomes more complex, with the percentage of genes with alt-splice variants increasing from worm to fly to the mammalian genomes (mouse and human). Of particular note is an increase in alternative splicing variants at the start and end of coding with the mammalian genomes studied (mouse and human), allowing for new first exon and new last exon recruitment that is possibly spliceosome mediated. This suggests a possible mechanism for accelerated gene structure variation and selection in the mammals that is spliceosome mediated.

236

Chapter 9

Transcriptomes and their Co-regulation

9.1 From genome to transcriptome

9.2 Transcriptome Analysis

The process of DNA→mRNA→Protein production is regulated at both transcription and translation polymerase stages (see Fig. 9.1, reproduced from Ch. 8, and Fig. 9.2). *Cis* regulation dominates at the DNA→mRNA polymerase stage, and *trans*-regulation at the mRNA→Protein polypeptide production stage. In the case of the polycistronic encodings, there is one *cis*-regulatory region for multiple coding regions (as indicated in the first section). The dominance of *trans*-regulatory mechanisms at the mRNA→protein stage is significant because all living processes, including viral processes, can be regulated at this stage, and many of the regulatory processes involve simple antisense nucleic acid molecular recognition, indicating a possible common and ancient (RNA World) biomolecular process. In eukaryotes the process of DNA→mRNA→Protein production is also regulated at the spliceosome level (for which a brief background is given in the next section). The main mechanism for *trans* regulation in eukaryotes is RNAi. The role of *trans*-regulation in prokaryotes involves a non-RNAi process *that employs no RdRp for siRNA amplification*, using a method evidently separately evolved: CRISPR/cas. Fig. 9.2 shows a modified Central Dogma with reverse transcriptase and RdRp accessible to the system.

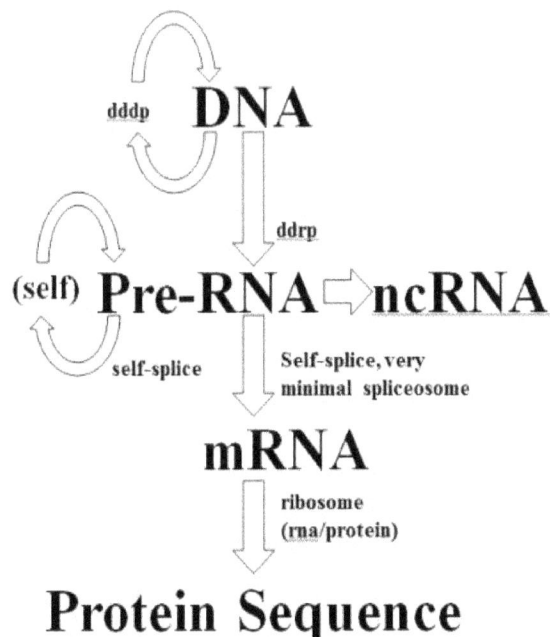

Figure 9.1. Standard Central Dogma for Prokaryotic Cells. Minimal splicesome indicated, zero for many. Early cells eventually lose spliceosome and RdRp, but still have self-splicing introns to some extent.

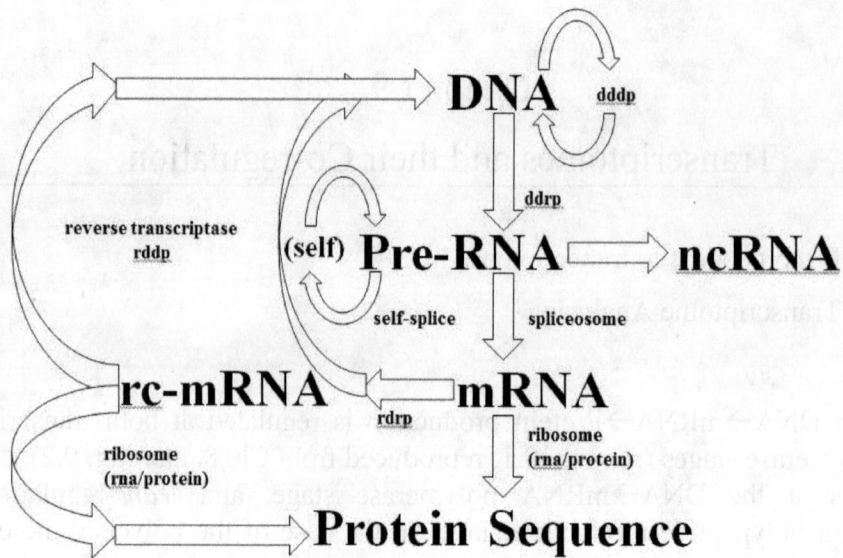

Figure 9.2. Modified Central Dogma (with reverse transcriptase and RdRp). Shows the modified central dogma with both reverse transcriptase and RdRp present in the evolutionary process, early cells are hypothesized to have lost their spliceosome and RdRp processes to arrive at the familiar pro-karyotic cell, as shown in Right.

9.1 From genome to transcriptome

The classic central dogma for the simplest, monicistronic, encoding was presented in Sec. 8.1 (and Fig. 9.1). Here we have the modified central dogma (above Fig. 9.2) and a diagram for the polycistronic case (Fig. 9.3 & 9.4 below):

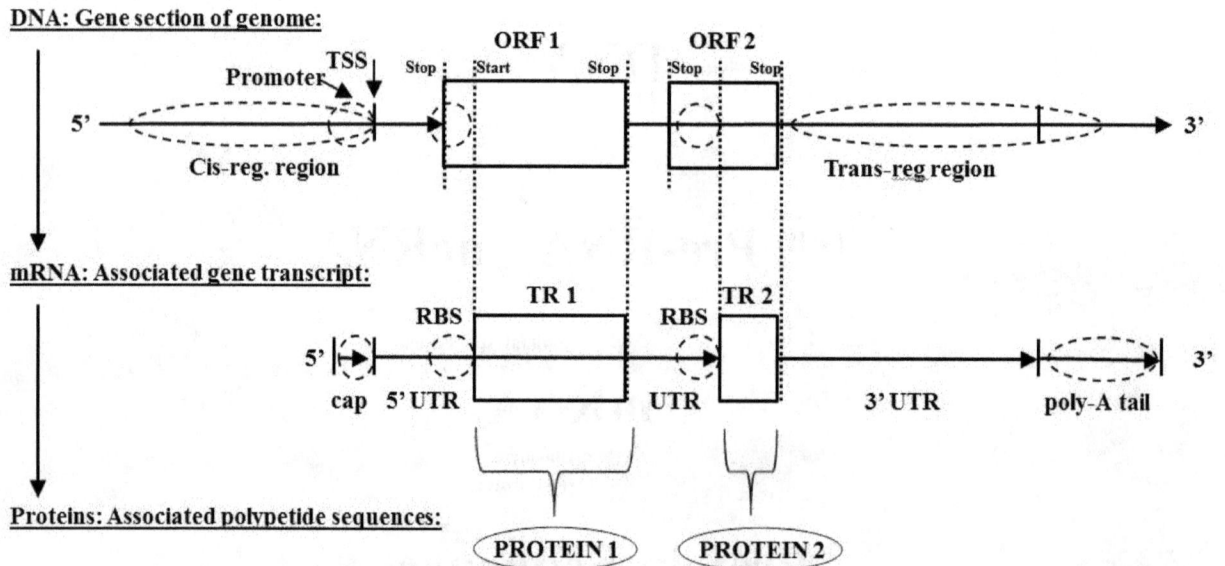

Fig. 9.3. Classic Central Dogma, operon (polycistronic): DNA→mRNA→Protein Set.

Monocistronic:

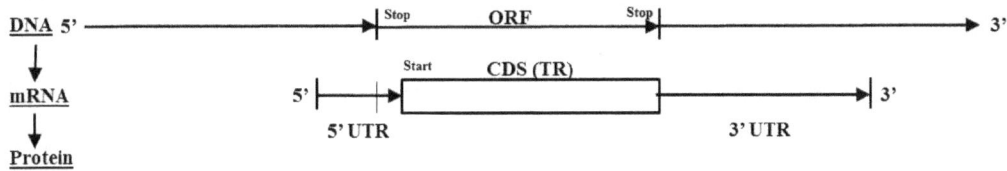

Polycistronic:

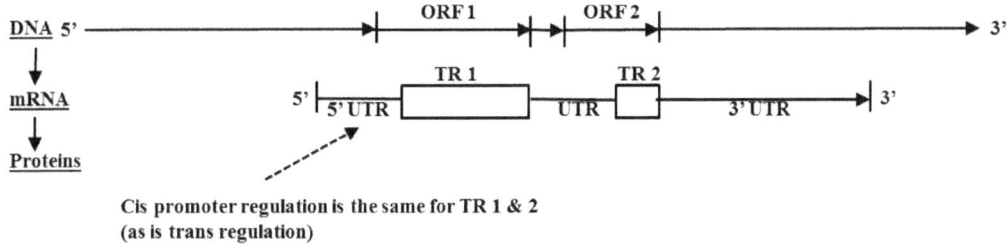

Cis promoter regulation is the same for TR 1 & 2
(as is trans regulation)

Fig. 9.4. mRNA Transcriptome Topology: monocistronic and polycistronic

A long ORF can overlap with another ORF that has a different framing (since the codon has length three bases, there are three possible framings). When working with dsDNA genomes both strands encode, so with reference to one strand listed in genbank, say, one needs to perform three frame passes in the normal 'forward' direction, then three frame passes on the reverse complement of the reference strand, in order to identify all ORFs >= 300 bases. Once this is done it is found that many of the ORFs overlap. An accounting of this overlap 'topology' is indexed and plotted as shown in Ch. 3 and 4 .

9.2 Transcriptome Analysis

Once the anomalous ORF structure is identified, nearby associated encoding anomalies are discovered (which in turn serve as validators), such as transcription start site recognition, in case of genomic sequence, or start/end of coding region recognition, in case of genomic or transcriptomic sequence information. The *cis-* and *trans-*regulatory regions are shown in Fig. 9.3, with *cis-*regulation via protein transcription factors dominating for DNA→mRNA regulation, and miRNA template strand recognition (via RNAi) regulation dominating mRNA→ protein processing.

A transcriptome-wide study is done on numerous species of fish (as well as worm and mouse and a few other species, see Table 9.1). For a given species, the length distribution on their 3'UTR regions is examined, with specific plots shown for three species of fish in Sec. 9.2.1.2, where the selection of >300 ORF and >200 3'UTR is made in the initial data handling (as summarized in Table 9.1 in Sec. 9.2.1 to follow).

9.2.1 Sustainability/Eco-collapse analysis on Fish: A case study

The mRNA data used in the transcriptome analysis is from the NCBI Genbank entries with the download dates indicated. The files are downloaded from www.ncbi.nlm.gov, where the mRNA database is selected, with search on the indicated organism, and download as file option selected. For the tuna and salmon data, the entire collection of sequences available on that day were used in the analysis (Tuna only had 10163 transcripts on 7/5/2016.) See Table 9.1 for dataset download dates/versions. For the mouse and worm data, both involving test subsets of the full mRNA dataset available (from the most recent mRNA listings), where the number of sequences used in the analysis is as shown. For mouse, the actual full set of mRNAs number about 50 times more than that examined, and a more comprehensive analysis is to follow. For worm, the test chunk was also a small fraction of the mRNAs available, and was mainly done to see how the acquisition of 3'UTR regions is expected to fail as richer operon structure, with ORFs frequently shorter than 300 bases, begins to become prevalent (as in worm). The results for worm indicate a very simple fix via a second pass of processing (but this is part of a separate analysis). A more extensive survey of all eukaryotes and a transcriptome ORF overlap topology analysis is being done to provide a comparative transcriptomics analysis, similar to the comparative genomics analysis done for prokaryotic ORF overlap topology in [39].

Species	#mRNAs	Download Date	Source
Mus musculus (Mouse)	98484	8/19/2016	NCBI genbank
Thunnus Thynnus (Tuna)	10163	7/5/2016	NCBI genbank
Salmo salar (Atlantic Salmon)	498523	7/7/2016	NCBI genbank
Caenorhabditis elegans (Worm)	8327	8/18/2016	NCBI genbank

Table 9.1. mRNA dataset download dates/versions.

9.2.1.1 Current Fish Stock assessment methods

Fisheries stock assessment refers to the analysis of the past and current status of a group of fish that live in the same geographic area, in order to learn more about the effects of fishing and other factors. The information obtained from stock assessments helps fisheries managers make sustainable decisions.

Stock assessments are done using models which rely on three different types of data: catch, abundance and biology. Catch data is simply the amount of fish taken from a stock of fish by fishing. There are many ways fisheries managers can obtain this data, including dockside monitoring, logbooks from commercial fishermen, observers that go to sea with commercial fishermen, and sampling the catch of recreational anglers. Abundance data is a measure or representation of the amount of fish that are actually in the stock. This type of information usually is generated by a statistical model which analyzes sampling data from fishery-independent surveys. These surveys take place on research vessels or contracted fishing vessels and use standardized sampling methods. Biology data adds the aspect of individual fish growth and mortality into the model. Some aspects of biological data that are incorporated can include growth rates, reproductive rates and movement.

The models which are used to conduct stock assessment differ among different commercial fisheries, and are limited by the amount and type of data available to use. Many other factors are also often incorporated into these models. A species' position in its larger food web, competition between other species, habitat and physical environmental conditions are all other aspects that can be taken into account. While some fisheries are very well maintained, others may need some work to better the way in which they are maintained.

9.2.1.2 Characterization of fish stock diversity via EST-based miRNA trans-regulation profiling

Many current fishery stock assessment methods strongly rely on the amount of fish harvest reported at the dock by fishermen. We seek a method for fish stock assessment that is based on transcriptome measures. In this study we were interested in the correlation between transcriptome level diversity and changes in the phenotype expression ability of commercially targeted fish. By analyzing the complexity of miRNA/RNAi 7mer binding sites in the 3'UTR regions, inferences are made as to the accessible repertoire of phenotypes for the organism. If fewer phenotypes are available, for use in response to environmental change, or for use in extending habitable niche, such as by 'schooling', then significant loss of fishery stock may result. Preliminary results indicate *Gadus Morhua* (Atlantic Cod) has undergone such a loss in transcript regulatory complexity, which appears to be associated with the collapse of the Cod fishery in the Gulf of Maine.

Studies of individual regulatory elements in a variety of species have demonstrated the prevalence of functional motif conservation without sequence conservation. This would indicate that the sequence meta statistics, such as on distributions of anomalous regulatory motif counts, might remain the same, while the individual sub-sequences with anomalously high counts, for example, might be significantly changed from one species to the next. Where strong sequence conservation does hold, there is often associated some constraint on the encoding that prevents neutral drift to another motif sequence (such as with the overlap encoding regions).

Cleavage stimulatory factor (CstF), is a 200kDA heterotrimeric protein which assembles onto the 3' end of a pre-mRNA (probably as a dimer). CstF binding promotes the polyadenylation process. Once polyadenylated, the mature mRNA is ready for export outside the nucleus. Not surprisingly, the amount of CstF depends on cell cycle. CstF is also known to play an active role in response to DNA damage, where it has been found that cells with lower levels of CstF have less viability for survival following UV exposure. CstF is seen to play a critical role in tumor cells as well. Many tumors have been found to have a mutated p53 gene (the most commonly mutated gene in human tumors). Recent studies of p53 show that it inhibits mRNA 3' processing via interaction with CstF. P53 is also known to transactivate miRNAs, allowing large changes in expression for miRNA targeted genes in later post-translational processing. P53 and CstF together are at the nexus of a critical regulatory control via 3' processing. Not surprisingly, as we will show, the motif 'footprints' of the CstF binding site are one of the most statistically strong motifs (high count anomalous) in the 3' region of mRNAs. The prevalence of the CstF motif seen in the 'healthy' species is found to be reduced and less varied in damaged fish stocks (as will be shown), and is associated with reduced, less targeted, CstF binding.

Transcriptome-wide comparisons have been done via SNP profiling, where identification and use of SNP markers permit a fine-scale stock identification and tracking, and could eventually allow a deeper understanding of ecotype divergence. In a study of pacific herring almost 11,000 potential SNPs were identified, of which 96 were directly tested. Of those 96, six were found to provide excellent sub-population biomarkers. SNP discovery is more scalable than SNP validation. SNP validation is inherently more difficult than motif validation in that the single nucleotide has no additional implicit information than the 'one bit' of information typically encoded in a two-state SNP. A motif that is 10 bases long, on the other hand, has $4^{10}=2^{20}\sim=10^6$ possibilities, of which some can occur with anomalously high counts, allowing for six orders of magnitude greater internal or 'implicit' information content. This allows a preliminary validation process to be done much more in the computational (scalable) realm, if not entirely computational if referring to a meta-level statistical analysis as we will be being done here.

An investigation into transcriptome diversity is described next, and associated phenotype expression ability, of commercially targeted fish. This is done by analyzing the complexity of miRNA/RNAi 7mer-based regulatory motif footprints in the 3' untranslated region (3'UTR) of protein coding transcripts. There appears to be a 'normal' 7mer count distribution profile. The hypothesis is that a reduction (or significant deviation from normal) in these motif footprints correlates with loss of transcriptome diversity and a less abundant stock.

The transcriptome/EST data analysis is done using on ORF-finder program. EST 3'UTRs are identified, wherein anomalously recurring 7-base sequences, known as "7mers," are sought. By analyzing the distribution on 7mers, a crude assessment of transcriptome regulatory diversity is inferred, with possible implications for fish stock assessments.

9.2.2 Computational methods for transcripts (from prokaryotic genomics toolset)

A computer program is used to process each mRNA entry with an ORF-finder with three forward frame passes and three reverse complement frame passes. The mRNA entries are filtered to keep only those with at least one ORF >= 300 bases in length, where the 3'UTR regions indicated by the ORF's right boundary are at least 200 bases in length, and begin with a unique 35-base initial 3'UTR sequence for a given prior ORF-length (allows for alt-splice variants to pass). The method only works with operon encoded transcripts if the last ORF in the operon is >=300. Thus it is meant to be applied to genomes with low operon percentage (which favor longer ORFs) to minimize operon recognition failure errors. In the Results is shown how the 3'UTR identification problem occurs in the *C. elegans* (worm) transcriptome, as anticipated, due to the high operon percentage, and this is found to be the case for axolotl to a smaller extent (not shown), for similar reasons. For the case of the worm and axolotl a simple algorithmic fix is used to reprocess the transcripts passed with ORFs>=300, rescanning their 3'UTRs for ORF>=50, thereby eliminating most of the missed operon structure that is below 300 bases in length that is interfering with the proper delineation of the 3'UTR regions (after the last ORF in the properly identified collection of ORFs in the operon structure). This description isn't focused on worm and axolotl, however, so those results aren't presented. The software for the ORF overlap topology tabulation is described in Ch. 2-4.

The analysis in what follows focuses on data presented at the transcriptome level, particularly that from EST processing. This allows analysis to be done at the earliest opportunity since EST generation is an essential first step in genome construction, SNP discovery, and microarray design. Assuming the collection of transcripts has already been filtered such that each transcript has at least one ORF length greater than or equal to 300 nucleotides, we now filter further according to retaining those transcripts with 3'UTR regions 200 nucleotides in length or greater (se Fig. 9.3), with results as shown in Table 9.2.

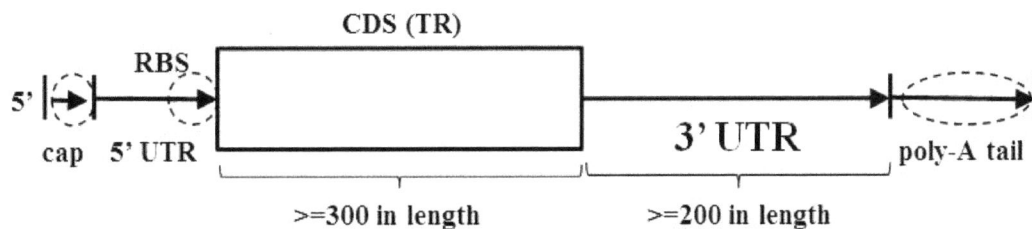

Fig. 9.3. Transcript selection: >=300 length ORF regiona and >=200length 3'UTR region.

Referring to Salmon from Table 9.2 as an example: there are 498,523 EST transcripts from Genbank that are validated via a high-confidence BLAST score alignment to a Genbank-annotated protein coding mRNA. These EST transcripts are scanned with six ORF-finder passes: three ORF passes in the forward direction, for the three positive strand ORF frame-passes, and three ORF frame-passes on the reverse-compliment strand for the negative DNA strand genes. (There are three frame passes because the codon encoding element is three bases long, such that a tiling over the sequence with codons is possible with three different codon 'frame' conventions.) We restrict to transcripts for which at least one ORF>=300 bases in length is found according to any of the six aforementioned frame-passes. Of the ORF>=300 sequence, we restrict further to those having 3'UTR regions greater than 200 bases.

Species	Genbank ESTs	uniq_ORF>=300	3UTR>=200
Tuna	10,163	5,366	1,739
Salmon	498,523	232,014	96,084
Cod	257,255	117,443	41,673
Catfish	139,475	60,094	24,558
Pufferfish	26,069	11,274	2,599
Cyprinus	47,738	26,579	10,166
Dicentrarchus	55,837	25,929	9,904
Disso	37,104	17,371	4,803
Hippoglossus	20,836	15,066	5,659
Osmerus	36,788	28,693	16,040
Sparus	29,216	38,034	8,710
Zebrafish	1,488,339*	121,554	44,253
Astyanax	189,864	118,036	43,094

Table 9.2. Preprocessing of mRNA/ESTs → unique strands with ORFs>=300 → also with 3UTRs>=200. *first 20% of genbank sequences for zebrafish.

The cutoff of >=200 3'UTR length is justified on a similar basis to the ORF cut-off that is typically used (mentioned earlier). As with the ORF length distribution, the 3'UTR distributions reveal a clear deviation from geometric fall-off on length (as might be expected from a random process), and if sufficiently far into the heavy tail region (with non-zero counts), where the geometric distribution fit would indicate a zero count, then all such instances have

243

a high likelihood of pertaining to a biological encoding. The 3'UTR length histograms for three species of fish are shown in Fig. 9.4.

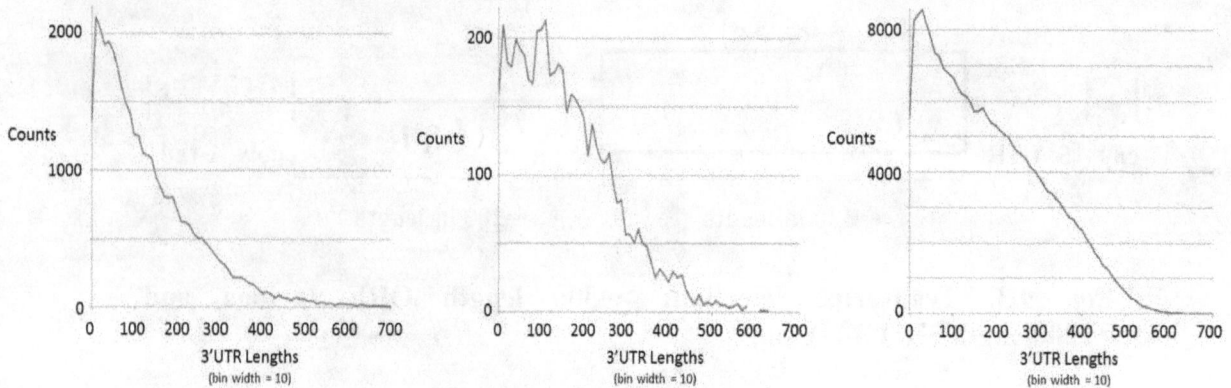

Fig. 9.4. 3'UTR Length Distribution Profiling/Validation. Length distribution on 3' UTR regions for tuna, salmon, cod (from left to right).the ORFs selected as indicated in Table 9.2.

In each instance in Fig. 9.4, a fit to a geometric distribution can be based on the short 3'UTR lengths (just as with short ORF lengths) to estimate the random approximately geometric distribution, from which the deviation of the actual length distribution is can be estimated. For the species shown in Fig. 9.4 and also listed in Table 9.2, the deviation is notable for lengths >= 200, thus the choice of cut-off. What is perhaps even more notable is that species-wide uniformity in the maximal 3'UTR lengths. Notice in Fig. 9.4 that there are no 3'UTR regions greater than 600 bases, with very few greater than 400 bases. The same is also found to hold for the other fish in Table 9.2, and for human, moue and a number of other organisms (not shown). A heavy tail 3'UTR distribution with strict fall-off to zero at 600 length or longer serves as a further validation on acquisition as well, since it appears to be a universal.

9.2.3 Transcriptome analysis results: Dually encoded mRNA's

mRNA data for the mouse, tuna, salmon, and worm transcriptomes is examined with six-pass ORF processing: three ORF passes for the different codon framings possible on the ssRNA transcript, and three passes repeated on the reverse complement of the ssRNA sequence. The transcripts with ORF lengths greater than or equal to 300 bases are selected. The ORFs identified from the different ORF passes are then incorporated into a multitrack indexing scheme, as used in [39], whereby the ORF overlap topology can be quantified. The non-overlapping ORFs can also be used to ascertain the amount of operon encoding. Once the operon encoding is resolved, the 3' UTR regions can be identified as the remainder of the transcript after the last ORF of the operon (for a polycistronic transcript), or simply after the (single) ORF in the transcript read to be performed (for a monicistronic transcript). Further selection is then performed at this juncture to restrict to transcripts with 3' UTR regions with lengths at least 200 bases. Like ORF-length, 3'UTR lengths have heavy-tailed distributions, where the heavy tail regions are where the genes (if ORFs) or miRNA regulatory regions (if 3'UTR) often reside. See Table 9.3 for details. The plot of the length distribution on 3' UTR regions so identified is given in Fig. 9.4, and is used to help guide the choice of the length 200 cut-off to be where the tail of the distribution is entered, where significant deviance from randomness for all events begins to occur.

Species	#mRNAs (Genbank)	#ORFs>300 (and unique 35_length)	#ORFs (tranlen >=200)	#Uniq mRNAs	%mRNAs Dual	% ORFs Operon	% ORFs Forward Overlapping
Mouse	98484	36654	8907	7303	12.7	0.70	15.0
Tuna	10163	5366	1739	1541	9.5	0.63	11.8
Salmon	498523	232014	96084	82007	8.0	0.86	13.5
Worm	8327	13864	8590	4660	30.4	12.9*	-----

Table 9.3. The number of mRNAs used in the transcriptome analysis and their ORF topology characteristics. *Worm result greatly underestimates extent of operon due to ORF>=300 constraint.

It is easy to imagine how each strand with ORF>=300 encoding might have a partially over-lapping ORF >=300 encoding with different framing (as described in the Background), the percentage of such ORF overlaps in a given transcriptome sample is as shown in Table 9.3 (with accounting for both transcript and reverse complement transcript in the frame-shift overlap analysis). Some ORFs on a given strand do not overlap, necessarily the case if with same global framing, or with separability on other codon framing (from one of the other two codon framing passes). ORFs on the same strand (the transcript sequence 'as is' or the reverse complement of the transcript sequence) that do not overlap can be grouped as hypothesized "operons". This is done in the estimated accounting shown. This results in an upper bound estimate on the true operon percentage, shown in the Table 9.3. It is an estimate since some ORFs may not fit on one operon grouping since it's only their coding region and small untranslated regions that must fit, i.e., the ORF pieces are generally trimmed on their left ends when it comes to fitting the segments together to have an operon. A quick analysis on ORF track placement for various degrees of left ORF boundary 'trimming' allows a means for the operon percentage to be upper bounded, and it is found that the estimates of less than 1% operon structure in the >=300 ORF transcripts are at most 1.5%. This is assuming, however, that the end of any operon structure is being properly identified when the ORFs < 300 bases in length are themselves being ignored. From 3'UTR distribution data in Fig. 9.4 we see that this is the case for the genomes with low operon structure, which all show very few occurrences of 3'UTR regions greater than 600 bases.

Any missed last ORFs in an operon would greatly add to the length of the 3'UTR region thereby falsely arrived at, and would lead to a distortion in the length distribution of the 3'UTR regions, with the first tell-tale sign of operon recognition failure being in the cutoff on maximum 3'UTR starting to slip to larger values than 600 bases (where other genomes, not shown, also share the trait that 3'UTR regions typically are very rarely greater than 600 bases in length). With worm, however, we expect the operon handling to be insufficient since it is operon rich, which together with the possible occurrence of ORFs<300 length are now much more significant source of error. The length distribution profile for worm has 3'UTR lengths in significant numbers out to about 1200 bases in length (see Fig. 9.5), indicating an operon boundary identification failure due to filtering out ORFs<300 that are trans to an identified ORF>=300 that is selected in the analysis. For this reason some of the numbers for worm in the table are omitted as entirely invalid, or marked as a lower bound when only providing an estimate of some sort.

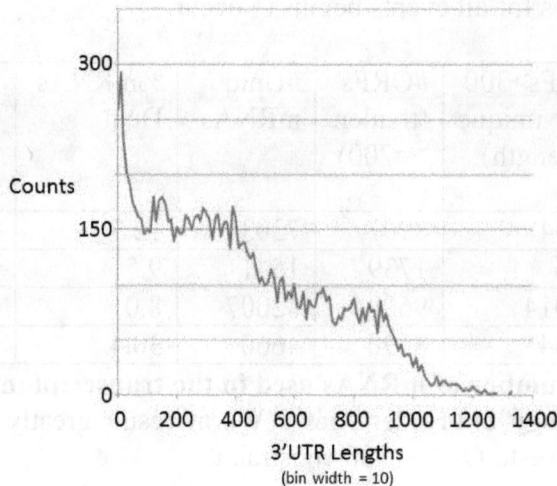

Fig. 9.5. Length distribution on 3' UTR regions for worm.

The ORF>=300 and 3'UTR>=200 overlapping constructs for the non-operonic transcriptomes are thus strongly validated as functional given their anomalously long ORF and 3'UTR regions. Consider now that the same analysis has been applied to the reverse complement of the transcript with selection for any coding constructs passing the same stringent cut-offs applied there as well. The transcripts having functional encodings both directly and on their reverse complement are referred to as 'dually encoded' in Table 9.3, with the percentage of transcripts with dual encodings between 8% and 13% as shown. The failure of the operon recognition with the worm transcriptome analysis does not directly impact the percentage dual mRNAs similarly revealed, allowing an estimation to be done, and the dual encoding on 3'UTR>=200 transcripts in worm is approximately 30%. Keep in mind this is not a result that would necessarily hold true as a percentage of the *entire* worm transcriptome (similarly for the other transcriptomes) since there is the restriction to 3'UTR>=200 transcripts. Regardless, whether the amount of dual encoding is 8% or 30% it is still significant and the problem is there is no standard RdRp-like mechanism for accessing the dual genes indicated, or examination of their possible unique disease associations (as a possibly more precariously regulated group). Thus, an active, more significant non-RNAi role for RdRp is hypothesized for eukaryotes. This modifies the central dogma of biomolecular processing (DNA→mRNA→protein) to now account for more paths when RdRp is considered (analogous to the extension of the standard model that was made when reverse transcriptase was adopted to allow a path from mRNA back to DNA). Both RdRp and reverse transcriptase are thought to be of viral origin, and the accumulation of both such viral attributes in eukaryotes, but not prokaryotes, leads to a reiteration of the viral eukaryogenesis hypothesis in light of this new information, and this will be discussed in the sections that follow.

What is remarkable is the appearance of coding-overlap structures in eukaryotic transcripts, with either forward overlapping or, especially, dual overlapping, that are similar to the coding-overlap structures that appear in prokaryotic transcripts (that derive from a dsDNA genome, say, that is dually encoded). It's as if the endosymbiosis of a viral nucleus left the prokaryote-like genomic information to be 'lifted' into the viral-based proto-nucleus over time via their mRNA transcripts, where the reverse complement information is available via RdRp.

As a further validation on the transcripts used in the analysis, that are restricted with selection for ORFs>=300 and 3'UTRs>=200, an analysis of the 7mer motif statistics in the 3'UTR regions is performed (see Table 9.4). The 7mer motif counts are expected to be a richly structured statistic due to the selection pressure from RNAi that uses 7mer miRNA/RISC binding site motifs as loci for RNAi control in the 3'UTR regions. An examination of the 16,384 possible 7mer counts reveals an average count and standard deviation on counts for the various 7mers as shown for mouse, tuna, salmon, and cod. Atlantic cod, has very few high-frequency 7mer structures (less than half that of the others including mouse), strongly indicating a damaged transcriptome for Atlantic cod , which would be consistent with the known overfishing and long-term collapse of the cod fishery in the north Atlantic. For the results in this paper, however, the 7mer results will merely serve to further validate the transcriptome sampling process, especially the very large sample-size Atlantic Salmon data, making the conclusion of significant dual encoding, *at the transcriptome level*, clear.

Species	Average nonzero count (μ)	Standard Deviation (σ)	σ/μ
Mouse	162	118	0.728
Tuna	30.7	22.9	0.745
Salmon	1821	1280	0.703
Cod	794	919	1.157

Table 9.4. 7mer statistical profile validation on 3'UTR.

An analysis of mRNA data reveals that mRNA transcripts passing stringent validation conditions, having at least one ORF with length >=300 nucleotides in length and with 3'UTR length >=200 nucleotides, have a significant amount of overlapping reverse complement encoding structure passing similar stringency tests. The overlap encoding revealed for the ssRNA is what might result if a reverse complement mRNA could be generated, such as by RNA-dependent RNA polymerase (RdRp), and is analogous to the overlap encoding that might exist on a prokaryotic dsDNA genome. This is indicative of three things: (i) RdRp might play a larger role in eukaryotes than to support RNAi, with associated changes to the central dogma; (ii) ancient remnants of the imprinting of an archaeon/prokaryotic overlap encoding at the genome/transcriptome level appear on the proto-eukaryotic transcriptome with resulting overlap encoding at transcriptome level in eukaryotes; (iii) a specific form of viral eukaryogenesis hypothesis is suggested, where the viral ancestor provided both RdRp and the spliceosome.

9.2.3.1 encoding artifacts in eukaryotic transcriptomes

Analysis of eukaryotic transcriptomes is done using BLAST-validated mRNAs from Genbank. Each mRNA transcript is traversed with a simple ORF-finder with three frame passes on forward reads and three frame passes on reverse compliment reads. In doing so we arrive at an encoding overlap-topology analysis of eukaryotic nucleic acid (transcriptome) sequences that parallels a previous analysis of prokaryotic nucleic acid (dsDNA genome) sequence (summarized in the Supplement). A reverse frame pass for the prokaryotic genome was necessary because the sequence information is only the reference ssDNA strand, requiring a second three-way frame pass for the reverse compliment ssDNA that completes the actual dsDNA prokaryotic genome. When the reverse frame pass is also done for the eukaryotic transcripts there is seen an overlap encoding topology like that seen in the intron-less prokaryotic genome. Even if the antisense overlap encoding in the eukaryotic transcripts is entirely non-functional, it indicates an intron-less archaeon/prokaryotic evolutionary artifact consistent with the viral eukaryogenesis hypothesis (summarized in the Supplement). In the Discussion, some of the eukaryotic reverse complement transcript encodings are thought to be functional given their lengthy miRNA signaling regions, suggesting a possible non-RNAi role for RNA-dependent RNA polymerase in eukaryotes.

Healthy eukaryotic cells are known to have RNA-dependent RNA polymerases (RdRp's) [237,307-311,312,313]. The native role of specialized RdRp's in production of siRNAs is already widely understood [307-310], especially in the analysis of plant transcriptomes [307,309,310]. Plants are found to regularly use RdRp to amplify siRNA for RNAi defense processes [310] (possibly an essential mechanism for transposon control). A sophisticated role for RdRp-control in post-transcriptional gene-silencing (as a rate-limiting factor) has also been demonstrated, such as with *N. crassa* and *D. melanogaster* [314-316]. The study of RdRp in eukaryotes has been complicated since the early 1980's, however, since in many cases their source could simply be attributed to viral origins [317].

Part of the mystery of the eukaryotic source for RdRp in some organisms is found to be simply a matter of RdRp being induced from an existing DNA-dependent RNA polymerase (DdRp), as is found to exist in a growing number of organisms [307] (there are also situations where RdRp can act as DdRp via transcription factor control [308]). Pol II is an example of a DdRp that can shift to being an RdRp, as seen in plants. In humans Pol II RdRp activity allows for novel regulation mechanisms [318]. In yeast (*S. cerevisiae*) Pol II is even involved in gene loop topologies in the complex early stages of transcriptional activation, where the Pol II DdRp binds and juxtaposes promoter and terminator ends of transcription at activation – indicating both ends of the transcriptional unit must be properly recognized by entering a loop-configuration with Pol II at initiation of transcription [319].

The role of RdRp may be critical to eukaryotes in a variety of ways, including robust development, where [309] show that some plants require their RdRp for healthy, competitive growth. Likewise, yeast (*S. pombe*, *N. crassa*, *S. cerevisiae*) and lower eukaryotes (*C. elegans*, *A. thaliana*, *D. melanogaster*) are well-known to have RdRp activity [314-316]. RdRp activity has also been reported in rat brain cells [320] and rabbit reticulate cells [321]. In a study of axolotl [313], an evolutionarily conserved enzyme activity with properties of RdRp, but not RdRp II or III, is observed. In bats there even appears to be an instance of 'recent' RdRp gene adoption from virus [311]. Even if the previous Bat RdRp was of non-viral origin, numerous instances are thought to exist where enzymes in eukaryotes are replaced by (better) viral counterparts [238].

Extensive RdRp activity has been documented in *Trypnosoma brucei* (the unicellular parasitic kinetoplastid that causes African sleeping sickness) [322,323]. In *T. brucei* there are found *the negative strands* of the mRNAs of a number of genes, including: cytochrome b, cytochrome oxidase I, cytochrome oxidase III, and MURF 2 [323], indicating significant RdRp activity resulting in antisense transcript production. This is an example where the antisense encoding overlaps with a transcript produced with a positive sense encoding already present. Further indication of use of negative sense strands, e.g., reverse complement encodings with respect to a reference 'positive' transcript, are described in what follows. The implications of this for RdRp processing, spliceosome processing, and viral origins (whereby both of the prior methods may have been introduced), are discussed next.

9.2.3.2 Indications of noninfectious and non-RNAi RdRp role in eukaryotes

The results described in here suggest endogenous viral-like RNA-dependent RNA polymerase (RdRp) enzymatic processing in eukaryotes at the level of mature mRNA products, such that reverse compliment mRNA transcripts are generated. Once again there appears to be a critical role for certain nucleic acid processing enzymes, such as transposase, when their most common incarnation, or initial discovery, is of viral origin. Such processing could have been introduced via gene transfer from a bacteriophage into a prokaryotic ancestor that eventually branched into the eukaryotic group of organisms. RdRp could have been introduced into eukaryotes, for example, via a viral eukaryogenesis process (discussed in Ch. 5), via a gradual evolutionary process whereby viral-infected archaeons/prokaryotes could have been selected for commensalism, then mutualism, and then for an endosymbiotic viral-archaeon/prokaryote relationship involving adoption of the viral type of RdRp.

Endosymbiosis of a membrane-bound organism results in an organelle, as with the mitochondrion or chloroplast, while endosymbiosis of a selfish gene organism (virus or transposon) without encapsulation results in adoption of a gene or selfish genomic construct. The latter case is seen in the many endogenous retroviruses that have been identified, which, if nothing else, offer benefit by providing a competitive inhibition against parasitic exogenous retroviral attacks. What is proposed here is that the endosymbiosis that led to eukaryotic adoption of RdRp could have established the mutualism with a membrane-bound virus that eventually led to a viral endosymbiosis with viral membrane *included*, the viral membrane then becoming the nuclear membrane of the proto-eukaryotic cell (discussed further in Ch. 5).

If RdRp is part of a eukaryotic organism's inheritable complement of biomolecular information processing, then a further modification to the central dogma is needed as shown in Fig. 9.6, where more explicit notation of the critical spliceosome stage is shown as well.

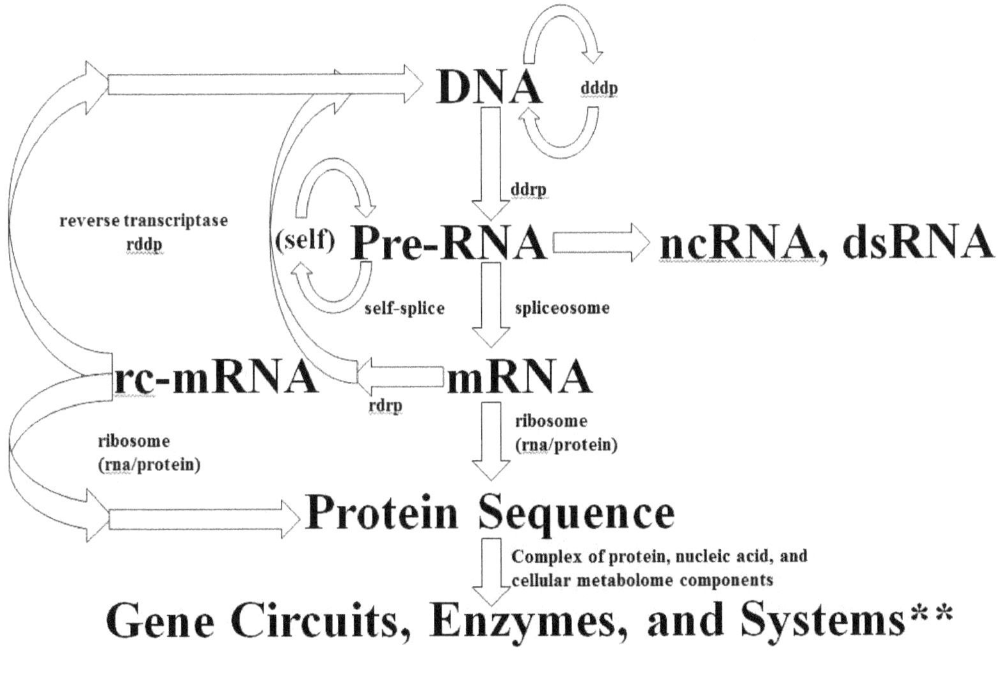

Figure 9.6. Central Dogma for familiar RNA/DNA/Protein World information processing. Depending on when the development of cellular encapsulation occurs in relation to development of the ribosome and other key

enzymes, RNA/DNA/Protein World could have had a pre-cellular phase. Cellular encapsulation could have greatly accelerated the switch (optimization) from ribozyme to enzyme, so once you have a Cell (and virus) you might arrive at the familiar RNA/DNA/Protein information encoding scheme. The full diagram above might apply to an early universal precursor cell (ancestor to prokaryote and eukaryote), while the same diagram without the last two stages would describe an early universal precursor virus (where the last two stages are implemented for the virus using the host's cytosol). The selection for more optimized cells and viruses is accelerated via their co-evolution, so co-evolution is itself effectively selected. ** By Systems we mean any situation that can give rise to emergent phenomena (or phenotypes) at 'system' level, where the role of noise can be one such phenotype.

9.2.4 Transcriptome analysis results: Species eco-collapse biomarker identification

In Sec. 9.2.3.1 we describe how Genbank mRNA/EST data is downloaded, filtered, and rudimentary validation is done. In this process all of the fish 3'UTR regions shared similar meta-statistical features as already mentioned. In Table 9.5 is shown further transcriptome-wide processing for the fish species described in Table 9.2. The first column describes the transcripts obtained after the aforementioned ORF>=300 and 3'UTR>=200 filters, plus the added filter of requiring that the first 35 bases in a 3'UTR region be unique (otherwise take the longer transcript and discard the other). The transcripts meeting the various filters indicated are then passed through a prokaryotic gene-finding program that does three ORF passes in the forward direction then three ORF passes on the reverse complement read of the sequence. The six ORF passes filter according to the ORF>=300, 3'UTR>=200 and '35uniq', and their overlap topology is noted as done in previous work [39]. If a transcript has both forward and reverse encoding, each of which meets the strict filtering criteria (ORF>=300, etc.) then the transcript is referred to as 'dual;' in Table 9.5. The extent of dual encoding revealed at this stage of the transcriptome-wide validation process was a surprising result -- a universal amount of 'duality' appears to occur in the 7%-15% range (and this is seen to hold for human and mouse and other transcriptomes as well). The amount of same read direction overlap encoding is also significant, and also typically falls in a range (between 11% and 18%) that can serve to validate acquisition.

Perhaps the most concerning 3'UTR acquisition validation statistic in Table 9.5 is the percentage of ORFs recognized as being part of an operon. As mentioned in the methods, there is no direct handling on operon structure (if present) with the simple algorithm used. Rather, operon handling is done via the iterative bootstrap process mentioned earlier. In the fish analysis a crude operon recognition was done for any transcript that had multiple ORFs non-overlapping, where those ORFs would all be considered part of a single operon, for which a single 3'UTR region is indicated (to the right of the rightmost ORF in the operon). An operon is a cluster of coding regions under common cis-regulation, where the ORFs enclosing those coding regions may overlap to a small extent, such that the operon construction algorithm based on sets of disjoint ORFs (with results shown in Table 9.6) only captures part of the operon structure (providing an estimate). In practice, tuning on allowed overlap amounts reveals an upper bound on percentage of operon structure that is roughly twice that shown in Table 9.5, for most species, but less than 3% for all. Since the upper bound on operon structure is 3% of the filtered data obtained thus far, this means that we have at most a 3% source of count errors in the 3'UTR 7mer motif analysis. This level of error can be tolerated with the motif-type signal analysis that follows, given the cutoffs that are employed,, so further efforts to deal with the operons will be left to when it is necessary.

Species	# sequences with ORF >=300, 3UTR >=200, & uniq35start	% column1 mRNA/EST sequences dual	% ORFs from column1 sequences that are in operons	% ORFs from column1overlapping with same read direction:
Bluefin Tuna **Thunnus thynnus**	1541	9.5	0.63	11.8
Atlantic Salmon **Salmo Salar**	82007	8.0	0.86	13.5
Atlantic Cod **Gadus Morhua**	34069	10.1	1.17	17.0
Blue Catfish Ictalurus Furcatus	20727	8.7	2.06	13.7
Japanese Pufferfish Takifugu Rubripes	2313	6.5	0.19	12.2
Carp **Cyprinus Carpio**	8275	12.4	1.50	14.6
European Bass **Dicentrarchus Labrax**	8372	9.8	0.97	13.1
Antarctic Toothfish **Dissostichus mawsoni**	4151	7.1	0.40	14.2
Atlantic Halibut **H. Hippoglossus**	4579	10.9	0.51	14.7
Rainbow Smelt **Osmerus Mordax**	12409	14.3	2.03	17.9
Gilt-head Bream **Sparus Aurata**	13830	9.8	1.15	12.7
Zebrafish **Danio Rerio**	37844	7.4	0.62	13.9
Blind Cave Fish **Astyanax Mexicanus**	37,695	7.2	0.23	12.8

Table. 9.5. 3'UTR Sample Selection and associated ORF topology. The number of ESTs used in the transcriptome analysis and their ORF topology.

At this point we have a set of transcriptome-wide 3'UTR extracts for several species of fish that is highly vetted. Let's now examine these sets of 3'UTR regions for their 7mer count statistics at a meta-statistical level (see Table 9.6), without reference to specific sequence information, and then at a direct statistical level as relates to particular signaling motifs that have been identified. In Table 9.6 is shown the transcriptome-wide 3'UTR 7mer count statistics, including the mean count and standard deviation on counts, etc., for each species.

Species /7mer_counts	μ (mean)	σ (std.dev)	σ/μ	#>μ+3σ	#>μ+1σ	% '>μ+1σ' with no4	7A-mer counts	#7A/μ
Bluefin Tuna **Thunnus thynnus**	30.6	22.87	0.745	177	2005	**42.3**	920	*30*
Atlantic Salmon **Salmo Salar**	1820	1280	0.703	172	2211	**45.7**	28940	*16*
Atlantic Cod **Gadus Morhua**	794	919	1.157	70	767	**15.0**	88430	*111*
Blue Catfish Ictalurus Furcatus	478	442	0.925	107	1348	**32.3**	30647	*64*
Japanese Pufferfish Takifugu Rubripes	43	38	0.883	247	1673	**55.9**	1796	*42*
Carp **Cyprinus Carpio**	202	170	0.842	114	1684	**40.6**	12078	*60*
European Bass **Dicentrarchus Labrax**	190	152	0.800	143	2047	**44.9**	6152	*32*
Antarctic Toothfish **Dissostichus mawsoni**	86.5	87.7	1.014	118	1497	**38.3**	6830	*79*
Atlantic Halibut **H. Hippoglossus**	104.1	72.8	0.699	233	2320	**58.6**	913	*9*
Rainbow Smelt **Osmerus Mordax**	348.6	234.0	0.671	191	2238	**47.1**	3554	*10*
Gilt-head Bream **Sparus Aurata**	329.6	308.3	0.935	107	1628	**42.1**	22283	*68*
Zebrafish **Danio Rerio**	816	1249	1.531	61	652	**28.4**	133791	*164*
Blind Cave Fish **Astyanax Mexicanus**	753.0	680.5	0.904	185	1778	**44.3**	26716	*35*

Table 9.6. 7mer count statistics. Noisy ESTs show as significant overcounting in 'aaaaaaa' 7mers, which, via #polyA/mu, is used as a gauge of the noise in the dataset in the table.

If $\sigma/\mu < 1.0$ we have more of a Gaussian structure emerging for k-mer count distributions, with easily identifiable "heavy-tail" statistical anomalies, while $\sigma/\mu > 1.0$ indicates a more uniform distribution. The $\sigma/\mu > 1.0$ of the Cod 7mer distribution is partly an artifact of the high poly-A 7mer counts distorting the count statistics, however, as other species transcriptome data with $\sigma/\mu > 1.0$ also had high #7A/u. So $\sigma/\mu > 1.0$ is not a distinguishing characteristic. If we look further at the types of motifs, however, we find that the high-count 7mers typically fall into two categories: 4 or more bases the same, or no more than 3 bases the same ("no4"). If we consider the percentage of high-count anomalous 7mer with no more than 3 bases of the same type we see that Atlantic Cod is singled out. If we look further, into the list of high-count sequences we see that there is a group of 4-or-mor-bases-the-same motifs missing as well, many of them variants of the CstF motif. Thus Atlantic Cod has a notably reduced TF binding site strength for CstF and is lacking a large number of "no4" 7mer miRNA targets. This is discussed further in the Discussion, but the main result is seen here in the statistics. In these results we are seeking a trans-regulation diversity biomarker (that is meta-statistics based) and the no4 statistic appears to suffice in this role by singling out atlantic cod where fishery collapse has occurred from numerous other species not suffering from such as drastic niche failure.

To recap, first recall the typical eukaryotic 3'UTR signaling (starting with the stop codon at the left):

---|TAA-------(T-rich)-----(*)-----AATAAA-----(poly-A site)----(T/GT rich)----

So, we expect to see in the list of most frequent 7mers in the 3'UTR:
(1)   7mers that are T-rich: tttttt, ttatttt, tttattt, etc.
(2)   7mers that are A-rich and poly-A with very high counts,
(3)   7mers that have 'AATAAA'
(4)   7mers that are GT-rich for alt-polyA via (*)=(GT rich) signal

All of which is seen. (Note how all of the 3'UTR signaling related to mRNA production processing have multi-target repeat type signals.)

Atlantic Cod, however, is found to have significantly less 'diffuse GT' motif than other species of fish (not shown), the motif involved in CstF recruitment and related poly-A cleavage site selection: e.g., g(tg)(tg)(tg) motifs are seen in cod, but not c(tg)c(tg) or c(tg)tc(tg). Damaged CstF activity is associated with disease and enhanced (detrimental) sensitivity to environmental stimulus – yeast cells with reduced levels of CstF display an enhanced sensitivity to UV treatment, for example.

We expect to see 7mers with high frequencies when they associate with miRNA binding sites. It is known that many miRNA 7mer binding sites are controlled with high-specificity (i.e., the 7mer-target has no repeating elements that would allow multiple targeting miRNAs), while other miRNA targeting is meant for multiple binding sites (with 7mer binding sites with repeats). We can 'lock' onto the high-specificity miRNA signaling by focusing on 7mers with low motif-pattern repetition – this is accomplished by focusing on 7mers that have no more than three bases of the same type (the 'no4' 7mers). The notably less informed (Shannon entropy greater) 7mer count distribution for Cod is hypothesized to relate to a reduced complexity in 7mer-based miRNA/RNAi regulatory capabilities.

If Cod has less trans-regulatory capabilities, resulting in a less diverse selection of phenotypes needed in order to robustly respond to environmental change, then it will become endangered as a species from much more minor environmental changes, as appears to be the case since the collapse of the Cod fisheries in the Northeast. The loss of trans-regulatory diversity may provide a new indicator of overfishing and environmental strain (due to shift in feeding areas further from spawning areas for example), and may provide an early transcriptome-based indicator of fishing stock damage for commercial fisheries.

Atlantic Cod appears to have significantly less 'diffuse GT' motif in its 3'UTR transcripts, indicative of compromised CstF recruitment. Damaged CstF activity is associated with disease and enhanced (detrimental) sensitivity to environmental stimulus – enhanced sensitivity to UV for example. Atlantic Cod also appears to have significantly less trans-regulatory high-specificity ('no4') miRNA complexity than other fish. Less trans-regulatory complexity will lead to less diverse mRNA trans-regulation control of phenotypes, leading to less robust response to environmental change. These results identify a meta-statistical transcriptome-based stock assessment biomarker for potential or occurring ecotype collapse. The biomarker correctly identifies Atlantic Cod as a species at risk from a set including twelve other fish species not thought to be at risk.

Chapter 10

Proteomics, Nanomachines, and Gene Circuits

In Sec. 10.1 a summary is given of the amazing functional roles of protein. In Sec. 10.2 elaboration is given on how highly optimized the protein information is on multiple levels, from hydrophobicity gematria encoding to the Immune Repertoire (and individual characterization). In Sec. 10.3 an elaboration is given on the protein complexity due to post-translational modification (PTM), such as glycosylation. Sec. 10.4 describes protein complexity in terms of dynamic conformational state. Sec. 10.5 describes critical role of proteins as typical feedback elements in gene circuits, giving rise to the need to track individual classes of proteins during cellular operation (to be discussed further in Ch. 14). Tracking protein information flow in a gene circuit with feedback is immensely difficult. Fortunately we know how to do this in electrical feedback circuits with use of the extra element theorem (EET) [324], which is amenable to the gene-circuit problem on short timescales (when components can be modeled linearly, albeit with strong shot noise effects). Sec. 10.5 describes gene circuits and the use of a Nanoscope as gene circuit 'voltmeter' (with further detail in Ch. 14, in the biological Extra-Element-Theorem (bEET) analysis [10]). Sec. 10.6 describes protein assays in this context.

10.1 Protein Nanomachines

The study of protein nanomachines as a new field of physics was suggested by Nobel Prize winner R.P. Feynman in lectures presented in 1959, and published shortly thereafter [325]. The main idea was that *individual* molecules might eventually be identified, observed, modulated, and utilized in a variety of ways. One of the most notable ways this has come to fruition is in the Nanopore detector described in Ch. 14, and [1], and in the Nanoscope described in [54]. Also anticipated in Feynman's 1959 lectures was a new physics of bionano-technology, starting from molecular 'nanomachines', but not made 'from scratch', rather from re-use of existing, biologically selected/optimized, protein nanomachines (as is accepted practice today).

Virtually all protein function involves specific binding to other molecules. The molecule bound by the protein is known as a 'ligand'. Anything can be the binding target or ligand, including small molecules, lipids, sugars, DNA, peptides, and other proteins. If the protein is an enzyme then the substrate is the ligand, for example.

Specific binding is possible due to the specific complementary pocket-like shape and interaction of the protein's 'active site' to its ligand target. This specific binding structure is critical to the functional role of the protein. Protein polymer is connected via peptide bonds. The peptide bond imparts critical rigidity and leads to the alpha helix and other stable conformational structures. A critical bond hybridization leads to planar peptide bond, leaving the polymer's conformational degrees of freedom largely simplified to the two orientation angles along the backbone at each C-alpha (see Fig. 10.1).

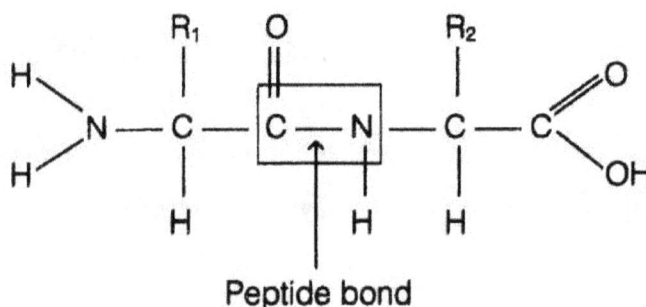

Peptide bond

Fig. 10.1. The peptide bond.

As mentioned previously, DNA encodes for the 20 'standard' amino acids, and a 21st (selenocysteine) and 22nd (pyrrolysine) are known to be in use as well (in simple, archaic, organisms). A protein is a polypeptide biomolecule in stable 3-D conformation. (Folding typically produces a globular shape, with a hydrophobic core and a surface that is hydrophilic dominated, sometime according to specific waters of hydration.) A polypeptide is any length, but implies lacking in defined 3-D conformation. A peptide is a short amino acid oligomer often lacking defined 3-D conformation. After translation, the residues of a protein are often modified by posttranslational modifications (glycations, etc.). After release of synthesized polypeptide, the molecule is selected for its ability to form a 3-D conformation with sufficient rigidity and surface attributes to have function.

It is interesting to note that a 22 amino acid alphabet is in use in encoding protein information, similar to a number of alphabets with 22 letters, where words based off of an alphabet with 22 letters are thought to be theoretically optimal for maximal information transmission in certain circumstances [4], so this is probably not a coincidence.

Although the emphasis on the protein structure-function relation is well warranted, it has also been over-used. In addition to molecular function, much of a protein's role is governed by location (cellular compartment) and timing (e.g., role in biological process). A protein of interest can be targeted with a chimeric molecule that includes (green) fluorescent protein, allowing the location of protein to be 'lit up' under fluorescent illumination. Protein that resides in the membrane will be clearly shown at the cell membranes, thereby outlining the boundaries of the cellular network like a voronoi tessellation. Protein that is more distributed in the cytosol, or concentrated in the nucleus (if there is one) are other obvious compartmentalizations that could be revealed upon immunofluorescent protein tagging.

Ascertaining the function of protein can often best be done by 'knocking out' the protein and seeing what function is lost (the classic loss of function, with regain of function, family of experiments). Although highly informative, the individual nature of the knock-out analysis, as with the individual nature of the immunofluorescent tagging, leads to a process that won't scale well as the number of proteins of interest grows into the hundreds of thousands and beyond. In well-studied single-cellular yeast cells, however, there is an example of a partly-scalable knock-out analysis by use of transposons with a β-galactosidase payload. If the transposon successfully inserts at the start of a gene, it does so by knocking out the gene with an active payload. In this instance, the β-galactosidase, which if produced, turns a substrate blue, thereby indicating a mutant cell (with a knock-out) is present. The mutants can be isolated and grown (in colonies) such that genome sequence can be obtained, to reveal which gene, thus protein, has been knocked-out. Studies of the knockout strains are then done. This process is still immensely labor intensive, and requires some repetition, so is only partly scalable.

If we turn to the structure-function paradigm to help us with understanding protein function, we are again faced with an established approach, crystallography-based structure identification, that is non-scalable for large numbers of proteins. Worse than that, the approach isn't even scalable to proteins that are 'large' (greater than 200 amino acids in length). As the name suggests, the method requires the object of study to be convertible to a crystalline form. Therein lies the rub, since to achieve crystalline form requires a dominant conformer structure (the repeating configuration sub-unit of the crystal) that is solution soluble. This poses significant complication for any membrane-bound protein due to their hydrophobic components not being solution soluble, requiring detergents to be introduced to bind the hydrophobic parts allowing the molecule to be lifted into solution, preferably with a single conformer. Often molecules need to be broken and crystallized in parts, and this is even more typical (whether soluble protein or not) for proteins greater in size than 200 amino acids. The production of the crystals themselves can often take significant time (up to months, while for photorefractive crystals used in optics it's up to two years). For these reason, although the gold standard for their remarkable precision, the crystal-based diffraction methods do not scale for the genomic era.

Often a protein can have more than one structure, in which case the crystal analysis would need to identify situations where each structure dominated, to get a monoconformer collection for each structure, and thus get two crystal types for the diffraction analysis.

To get an idea how important a protein's choice of configuration is, with just two possibilities, say, consider the famous prions. What would happen if a protein has a conformation that induces other proteins of that type to take on that same conformation? – an infectious conformation as it were. If the protein shape thereby catalyzed also allows crystalline structures to form in vivo, then a disease condition results (Jakob-Creutzfeld in humans, bovine spongiform encephaly in cows, aka Mad cow disease). The discovery of prions as an infectious agent was quite a novelty, and the first discovery of an infectious agent that did not involve nucleic acid (Stanley Prusiner got the Nobel Prize for this). Prions as an infectious agent are fundamentally different for this reason (they can't be destroyed by heat, e.g. cooking, as in nucleic acid based infectious agent). The thought that a single prion molecule exposure could initiate a lethal crystallization (in brain tissues years later) is so fantastical as to be reminiscent of Kurt Vennegut's "Ice 9" (a humorous satire where water crystallization above freezing was sought, the Ice 9 conformer, to allow tanks to drive over mud frozen to hardness – in the end the Ice 9 gets out and freezes the whole world and everyone dies).

This is not to say the prions occurring in nature are entirely associated with disease conditions. There is a prion-like protein in yeast (Sup35p) that binds ribosome to induce loss of fidelity on recognizing stop codons. This results in a flurry of protein production that is non-standard, and in some cases appears to offer antibiotic resistance. The infectious protein is inheritable from mother cell to daughter cell, thus selection pressure reveals the benefits of Sup35p in such situations.

10.1.1 Enzymes
Cellular life requires a huge number of chemical reactions to occur, in a non-interfering manner, on timescales ranging from milliseconds to nanoseconds, where those chemical interactions would normally occur on the timescale of up to hundreds of years. This is accomplished by having virtually all biological reactions catalyzed. It has long been noted how simple metals can aid in catalysis, but this occurs non-specifically (thus interfering), so what is required is an enormous collection of special catalysts for basically every biological reaction, where their catalytic activity is highly specific (thus non-interfering). This collection of catalysts is almost entirely protein-based (e.g., enzymes), but vestiges of nucleic acid based catalysts, indicative of an RNA World precursor, still remain (the ribosome being the most notable example).

The immense variety and complexity of modern protein-based catalysis is unlikely to have ever been matched by RNA World constructs. In fact, RNA World may have not allowed membrane channels to develop, significantly, due to their lack of hydrophobic domains (further details in the next sub-section). For this reason, the primary cellular expansion in the biosphere may not have occurred until in-step with the protein catalyst-takeover revolution, such that familiar basic cellular constructs, like channels, could be present.

The basic idea of a catalyst is that it lowers the potential barrier for a biological reaction to proceed (in a timely manner). It also needs to do this in manner that is non-destructive to the catalyst as well, such that a single catalyst can catalyze hundreds of interactions in the fraction of a second. But there's more to it than that. The rate of catalysis for an individual catalytic molecule is not found to be the same even in identical buffer, for which two main causes are attributed: (1) the exact same molecule can have slightly different conformational state, each with different catalytic rates; and (2) the same protein sequence molecule can have different post–translational modification, such as with glycosylation. In the case of (1), the catalyst can be modulated as to its catalytic strength according to secondary molecules (also protein or peptide) that serve to lock the catalyst into one conformation or another (with associated modulation of catalytic activity).

Proteins, such as enzymes, can have a high degree of variability. It has been demonstrated that enzyme turnover rate, for example, can differ at the single molecule level [326-328], with a single enzyme observed with one constant turnover rate, while another enzyme, differing only in conformation, or possibly by a difference in glycation, has a different, but still constant, substrate processing rate. And this is a simple example where there is only one interaction region and it is (mostly) unchanging in its conformation for the individual protein examined. Some allosteric proteins, on the other hand, with multiple binding sites for a particular target, change their binding affinity according to how many ligands they have bound. Antibodies are known to change conformation during binding to one (or two) antigens in such a significant manner that this is the basis for activation of the complement cascade of the adaptive immune response.

10.1.2 Channels and Transport Proteins
As mentioned in the prior section, it's hard to imagine cellular life really taking off without a rich assortment of membrane channels and transporters with which to regulate the chemical composition of the cell. In practice, proteins embedded in the cells plasma membrane are found to operate in a very highly regulated manner (where most variations are associated with a disease condition). Some proteins provide very narrow channels, allowing highly selective transport even on small ions. Channels even exist just for transport of water molecules (aquaporins) in a highly controlled 'ratchet' process that prevents a capillary entrainment catastrophe on water-transport. Channels exist for transport of specific larger molecules also, such as maltoporin. If transport can occur down an electro-chemical gradient, e.g. unaided, then it's referred to as passive transport via the indicated channel or transport mechanism. If energy is required to transport the molecule across the cell membrane, it's referred to as active transport. The standard supply of energy via ATP is used form many active transport situations. Sometimes, however, the transporter molecule, when bound to transport target, provides an autocatalytic transport activity.

The typical membrane channel formation is an ATP driven process. In the case of cellular pathogens, however, their pore-forming toxins would not be expected to knock on the cells fortress walls and request some ATP to aid in breaching said walls. Thus, pathogen-based pore-forming toxins provide an excellent set of candidates for autocatalytic channel-formation. This is a key attribute used for the channel-forming toxin (alpha-hemolysin) central to the nanopore detector construction described in Ch. 14.

10.1.3 Receptors and Messengers (Primary and Secondary)
Cells are easy units of selection, so it's easy to imagine that other membrane constituents, than for 'basic' maintenance of chemical composition, might be developed. Thus it is not surprising to find that cells communicate, and evidently with selection advantage if they can communicate with each other cleverly (about availability of resources, for example, such as with quorum sensing). The molecular mechanism of cell-cell communication involves what are referred to as messenger molecules. Messenger molecules typically involve certain short proteins, referred to as peptides, that specifically bind (the primary messenger) to cell-surface receptors. Once bound, the cell-surface receptor relays the 'message' into the cell interior, often by activating enzymatic activity (with substrate the secondary messenger) or by means of releasing or binding a short protein or peptide on the cell interior (a more complex secondary messenger). The secondary messenger, in turn, can lead to cell growth, division, or death. The secondary messenger can also trigger production of particular molecules (of great interest from a biotechnology perspective). One of the most common cell-surface receptors is the G-protein coupled receptor (GPCR), to which about 40% of medica-

tions are targeted. (The G-protein is a heterotrimeric protein and occur in the context of the genome structure of operons).

Not all cell receptors need be on the surface, especially those that modulate gene expression. In these cases, the transport of the messenger to the receptor in the cell interior can happen by a variety of means, and once bound to receptor, an activated receptor message or action (binding or enzymatic, for example) then ensues. The typical peptide hormone or neuro-transmitter 'first messenger' is hydrophilic, so cannot cross the cell membrane barrier. The steroid hormones are an example of first messenger that can cross the membrane barrier and directly interact with an interior receptor.

The step going from primary messenger to secondary messenger can be one-to-many, and can lead to further downstream catalytic cascades in the cell interior. Thus, there are multi-ple stages at which signaling amplification can occur.

Not all primary messengers need be protein or peptide based. Perhaps the most famous non-protein system is the endocannabinoid system, which is comprised at two endocannabinoid receptors (CB1 and CB2) and two GPCRs (so far), and a variety of endogenous arachi-donate-based lipids (ancient lipids in the plant kingdom) that interact with these receptors, known as endocannabinoids. Famous endocannabinoids from exogenous sources include THC from the cannabis plant.

10.1.4 Co-factors and Prosthetic Groups
Sometimes protein function requires hetero-atom configurations, where additional elements are incorporated, such as simple metals (co-factors) or small organic molecules (co-enzymes if protein and enzyme). Together with PTM, this allows diverse function not easily obtained by pure amino acid sequence otherwise, such as: photo-activation, charge transfer, and elec-trostatic stabilization, to name a few.

If the added small organic molecule is meant to bind to the protein at all times to achieve a stabilized/modified 3D structure, then it is known as a prosthetic group. The ribosome, a nu-cleoprotein, is an excellent example of the latter, where more archaic organisms have ribosomes predominantly nucleic acid based, with a small number of protein prosthetics. While later organisms, eukaryotes and multicellular, for example, exhibit more and greater sophistication of prosthetics, such that the ribosome becomes a more protein-based assem-blage (although the active sites remain in the ancient nucleic acid portions).

10.1.5 Structure-Function Paradigm
The classic structure-function paradigm has been a critical part of the understanding and ex-ploration of protein function for over 100 years (since the advent of x-ray crystallography at the start of the 20th Century). The gold-standard for structure understanding has been crystal-lography-based for all of this time, and has been critical to understanding proteins. There are problems with the crystallography-based approaches, however, first you have to have a crys-tal, which means you have to start with something solution-soluble. Furthermore, the crystal conformer-structure can't be too different from native conformation or the effort to identify structure is wasted. This is more complicated than it sounds, consider first the non-solution soluble (membrane-bound) proteins, their structure requires locking with a molecule to draw it into a soluble state (a detergent, essentially), such that the detergent-bound form is what is

crystallized. If that form is carefully selected to be close to native then all is good, but this can take several attempts, each requiring many months. Consider also, that the solution soluble conformer structure works well as a clearly defined object, without significant variation, only for proteins consisting of roughly 200 amino acids or less, thus the larger molecules must be broken and crystallized in parts. This latter complication does not bode well for understanding multiple conformations of the (allosteric) molecule at different instances in time when we can't even get a clear picture of the entire molecule at a single instant in time. Another complication of the protein structure approach is that identifying any structure by this process is expensive and time consuming, and simply doesn't scale to the rapidly growing task given the rate of new protein discovery. If may be that a multi-nanoscope assayer, leveraging existing multi-well reactor sophistication (such as with ZMW sequencing), would allow scalable protein function analysis, but in doing so we would of necessity move from a structure-function paradigm to a *binding-state* function paradigm.

10.1.6 Changing Structure – Proteins as Dynamic entities

For many proteins, their dynamics is critical to their function. This is most notably the case for allosteric enzymes, for which binding analyte induces conformational change, which changes the enzymes function, and possible further binding (if it has multiple binding sites, such as for the quaternary structured hemoglobin or streptavidin molecules). Often it's the natural dynamics of the protein that is modulated by co-factors, or other molecules. Given this critical new information, and the need for characterizing more complex molecules and mixtures, such as complex glycoprotein mixtures (well beyond the scope of a crystallography effort), we see the need for a radically new approach.

10.1.7 State-Function Paradigm (via Nanoscope)

The Nanoscope, to be detailed in Ch. 14 (and extensively in [1,198,54]), may provide a key way forward in the 'post-genomic' era, where scalable inexpensive procedures are needed to assay complex mixtures. One of the key benefits may be realized by a shift from the protein structure-function paradigm, where we know the structure and infer the function to a "binding state"-function paradigm, where we know the binding state and infer the function (where binding state is knowledge that can be obtained via a scalable process).

10.2 Optimized proteins

There is a recent and bizarre connection from mathematical communications theory [2,3,15] that should be mentioned, so first a mathematical interlude.

In mathematics papers on information propagation [2,3,15] we find that maximal information can be propagated (with unitary property maintained) building from the standard 8-dimensional octonion, but with two more dimensions via chiral extensions (into the sedenions and trigintaduonions). This is, thus, describing a 10-dimensional propagation in a 32-dim. space, meaning that propagation in 22 of the 32-dim. does not occur, giving rise to 22 emergent parameters instead.

Thus information propagates with two chiralities, thus 2x2=4 'types', and does so in a context where 22 parameters are emergent in describing that propagation. Any highly optimized (proven effective via usage) information encoding scheme will, arguably, begin to take on

261

the aforementioned structure for maximal transmission of information. For the connections to Physics, see the papers [2,3,15] and a forthcoming book [55]. For the connections to written language (text analytics, Babylonian gematria, kabbala, tarot) see a forthcoming book on Informatics and Advanced ML [53]. It bears mentioning here, however, that the ancient written languages all had 22 letters, in analysis of thought (sequences) there are 22 standard Jungian archetypes, and in Tarot readings, seen as a story generation mechanism, there is a deck with 22 major arcana (and 52 minor arcana). Words and 'stories' are derived from sequences of these 22 letters, archetypes, or arcana. Is there an optimal word 'size'? In Babylonian and gematria the answer is yes, where size is determined by a letter weighting scheme with optimal weighting determined to be ~137 (this same optimal is proven to exist mathematically [2,3,15] and in Physics, where in inverted form, it is known as the famous alpha = 1/137 parameter).

Now, let's return to proteins seen as a sequence of (22) amino acids, an encoding scheme that has been selected after billions of years of optimization (with a massively parallel Avogadro number, 10^{23}, of parallel chemical processes in every water drop). Arguably the fact that it would allow maximal information transmission with 22 letters (amino acids) in making up its words could be a coincidence….. But the coincidence continues: there are 4 (chiral) modes of information transmission, or in the case of proteins, there are thus four protein families thereby indicated – which is the case [331]. Also, the obvious 'tokenization' of protein coding in terms of exons has remained a mystery for decades. Originally it was thought that proteins would have some structural or functional modularization according to their exon 'chunks', but it turns out this is often not the case – the size and composition of exons appears to obey rules, but we don't know those rules. In the context of optimal information transmission we may finally have an answer, it may be that there is an optimization on 'protein-gematria' score (to be 137 in some amino acid weighting scheme), that is evaluated on the exons as regular gematria evaluates on individual words. The (unknown) protein gematria scoring is probably closely related to hydrophobicity 'scoring' (that is sometimes done), and probably relates to an optimality that gives rise to a globular protein shape with mostly neutral charge and balanced hydrophobicity (hydrophobicity more on interior of protein and hydrophobic residues more prevalent on the surface of the protein).

Encoding

So, suppose you're a clever organism that's settled on a DNA-based information encoding scheme (with four letters and a wobbly phosphodiester bond formation to polymerize). As suggested by the above, to have more and more functionalization of a protein 'helper', a new amino-acid (AA) based polymer space would be explored, one that might eventually settle on an encoding with a 22-element (AA) alphabet (where now the polymerization linker is the rigid peptide bond – allowing easier reproducibility and stability of complex structures). At this point, we would then need a mapping from a 4-base encoding polymer to a 22-base functionalizable polymer. Two nucleic acid bases could encode 4x4=16 possible AA's, not enough, so we must go to a 3 nucleic acid encoding scheme (the codon) with its unavoidable degeneracy of 64 mapping to 22. One of the codon's, the stop, is exclusively coding for "stop' an action on the translation, not an encoding mapping. Organisms only using the core 20 AA's have three stop codon types (in terms of DNA alphabet they are: TAA, TAG, TGA), thus the mapping is from 61 codons into the 20 AA's (shown in Table 10.1 below, reproduced from Fig. 5.1 in Ch. 5). More ancient (single celled) organism can have the full 22 AA's set, with the same exact encoding scheme for the 20 AA's, but now two of the three 'stop' codons are switched to encoding for the 21st and 22nd AA's.

	U (middle)	C(middle)	A(middle)	G(middle)	
U (5' base)	phe	ser	tyr	cys	U (3' base)
U (5' base)	phe	ser	tyr	cys	C (3' base)
U (5' base)	leu	ser	stop	stop	A (3' base)
U (5' base)	leu	ser	stop	trp	G (3' base)
C (5' base)	leu	pro	his	arg	U (3' base)
C (5' base)	leu	pro	his	arg	C (3' base)
C (5' base)	leu	pro	gln	arg	A (3' base)
C (5' base)	leu	pro	gln	arg	G (3' base)
A (5' base)	ile	thr	asn	ser	U (3' base)
A (5' base)	ile	thr	asn	ser	C (3' base)
A (5' base)	ile	thr	lys	arg	A (3' base)
A (5' base)	met (start)	thr	lys	arg	G (3' base)
G (5' base)	val	ala	asp	gly	U (3' base)
G (5' base)	val	ala	asp	gly	C (3' base)
G (5' base)	val	ala	glu	gly	A (3' base)
G (5' base)	val	ala	glu	gly	G (3' base)

Table 10.1. The codon assignment for the 64 codons. Standard amino acid (AA) abreviations shown for the 20 (main) AA's. The stop codon (UGA) sometimes codes for selenocysteine, a 21st AA. The stop codon (UGA) codes for a 22nd AA, pyrolysine.

10.3 Glycoproteins and PTMs

Determining the glycosylation profile of antibodies, and Fc glycosylation in particular, is critical to understanding antibody efficacy and blood circulation half-life, so the nanopore platform and the same signal processing methods for understanding NTD transducers can be directly applied to profiling antibody glycosylation blockade signals where the antibody is treated as an NTD transducer in and of itself. Direct antibody profiling would likely only work for part of the glycosylation (or glycation) profile, however, since the Fab N-terminus neutral glycosylation and glycations would probably still need to be assayed by use of antibody intermediates (as with the standard HbA1c test).

Antibodies are the secreted form of an associated B-cell receptor, where the difference between receptor and secreted forms is in the C-terminus of the heavy chain region. Fig. 10.1 shows the standard antibody schematic and a typical antibody N-glycosylation (exact example for equine IGHD [329]). The main non-enzymatic glycations occur spontaneously at lysines ('K') in proteins in the blood stream upon exposure to glucose via the reversible Maillard reaction to form a Schiff Base (cross-linking and further reactions, however, are irreversible and associated with the aging process).

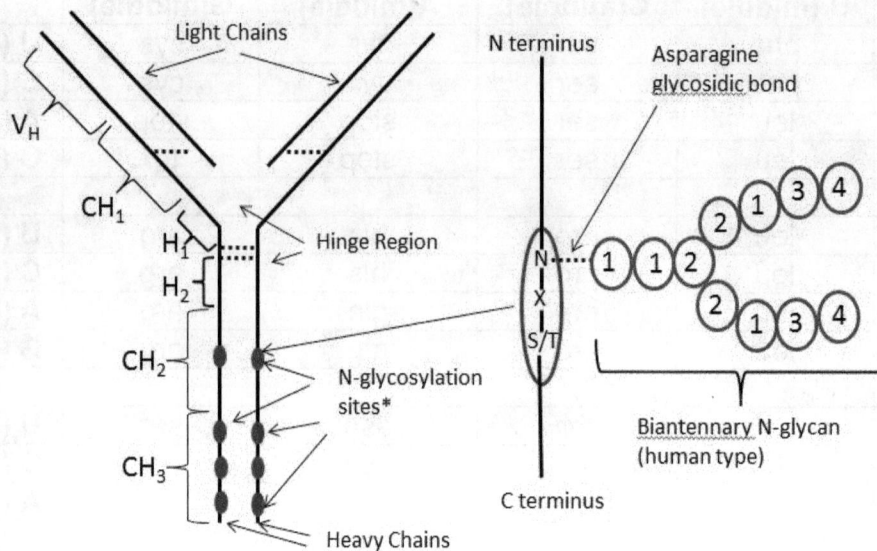

Figure 10.1. The standard antibody schematic and a typical (human) antibody N-glycosylation.

The C-termini and Fc glycosylations of an antibody's heavy chain, especially for IgG, is a highly selected construct that appears to be what is recognized by immune receptors, and is evidently what is recognized as distinct channel modulator signals in the case of the NTD (mAb channel blockade signals are shown in Ch. 14). Using NTD we can co-opt the opsonization receptor-binding role of the Fc glycosylations (and mAB glycations and glycosylations in general), and C-terminus region, to be a channel modulating role. This may also permit a new manner of study of the critical opsonization role of certain classes of antibodies (and possibly differentiate the classes in more refined ways) by use of the nanopore detector platform. The channel may provide a means to directly measure and characterize antibody Fc glycosylations, a critical quality control needed in antibody therapeutics to have correct human-type glycosylation profiles in order to not (prematurely) evoke an immunogenic response. Some of the antibody blockade signals are deep blockades like the nine-base-pair DNA hairpin blockades. Working with these very clear signals, that have stable modulating blockades that go for hours, experiments were done with addition of small amounts of antigen [330]. One of the largest human-type Fc glycosylations, G2-A2+Bi+F, has a molecular weight about 2.7 kDa, which is about half the molecular weight of the eight base-pair hairpin, so ballpark similar size for similar blockade. It would appear that a variety of C-terminus modifications and Fc glycosylations would be appropriately sized and charged for channel capture, and this is what is seen in practice (see Ch. 14 for results).

10.4 conformation and individual-aspect – isomer resolution role for the Nanoscope

Every conformation and functionalization, thus interactivity, is explored in the 3-D protein space. There are an estimated 10^4 protein structure families [331], together with an average number of structures per family at 10^2 (this is in a power-law distribution so have extremes of only a few in a family to thousands). There are thus and estimated 10^6 uniquely functionalized protein structures.

Another family of protein-based conformations/functionalizations is that provided by the immune system's generation of immunoproteins. The variety of immunoproteins, the "immune repertoire" [332,333], appears to be a measure of health and overall age. In a healthy young adult, the immune repertoire is estimated to be as many as 10^6 uniquely functionalized protein structures (in agreement with the general protein structure-space count mentioned above). In older and sickly patients the immune repertoire can be as little as 10^3 to 10^4 structural variants (thus less effective immune response with age or disease). Having the means to effectively profile the immune repertoire of a patient may provide a strong method for overall immune system health evaluation in the tests of the future (see further discussion in the context of the Nanoscope in Ch. 14).

Resolving the up to 10^6 structural variants appears to be impossible, but the problem can be reduced by understanding the generation of these biomolecules. In other words, the information on the mix of 10^6 structural variants is related to the genomic-level information that precedes. The genome information is only part of the information used in identifying the protein families, but assume this and other information allows the 10^6 structural variants to be split back into their 10^4 protein structure families (of roughly 10^2 unique structures each). In this case the problem is reduced (with some initial genome-level family characterization, etc.) to separating roughly 10^2 unique structures. Unfortunately, albeit unique, the 10^2 unique structures are part of the same family and thus very similar (insofar as active-site conformation). The problem of resolving a family of 100-200 very similar biomolecules (even isomers) is not just encountered here in the context of immunoproteins, but also in the attempts to assay the different cannamimetic compounds present in medicinal marijuana (an assay on small, 21 carbon, biomolecules). The main tool for doing this does not exist, but possible applications of the Nanoscope for this purpose is described in Ch. 14.

10.5 Gene Circuits and the Nanoscope biosystem 'voltmeter'

Biosystem circuits come in a variety of forms: (i) metabolic cycles; (ii) info/metabolic such as cycles mRNA→protein (where protein state/dynamics enumerates functionality); and (iii) info cycles: DNA → mRNA (typically involving DdRp, DdDp, RdRp, or RdDp).

The system biologist is currently lacking a general-use method for a biosystem circuit or gene circuit 'voltmeter' or biosystem algorithm 'print statement'. What is needed is a non-destructive, carrier non-modifying, means of testing 'live' biological systems at the single-molecule level. A method using the nanopore transduction detector (NTD) is demonstrated for single-molecule characterization in some situations, so may provide what is lacking. An important aspect of this approach is that use can be made of inexpensive antibody, protein, aptamer, duplex nucleic acid, or nucleic acid annealing molecules (for miRNA and viral monitoring) that have *specific* binding to the system component of interest. The NTD transducer's specific binding can also be designed to have low affinity binding as needed, such that there can be a 'catch and release' on low copy-number molecular components, such that there is not a disruption to the molecular system under study. NTD transducers are typically constructed by linking a binding moiety of interest to a nanopore current modulator, where the modulator is designed to be electrophoretically drawn to the channel and partly captured, with its captured end distinctively modulating the flow of ions through the channel. Using inexpensive (commoditized) biomolecular components, such as DNA hairpins, this allows for an easily constructed, versatile, platform for biosensing. High specificity high affinity binding also allows a very versatile platform for assaying at the single molecule level, even down to the single isoform level, including molecular substructure profiling, such as glycosylation profiling in antibodies. An inexpensive commoditized pathway for constructing nanopore transducers is demonstrated. Nanopore transduction detector based reporter/event-transducer molecules may serve as a means to perform multicomponent mRNA-miRNA-protein and protein-protein systems analysis in general settings.

A growing number of questions facing molecular and medicinal biology experts are systems biology questions, where the complex interaction of genes, mRNAs, proteins, miRNAs, and various metabolites is described at the 'system level'. System level problems are often described in terms of 'gene circuits' or 'metabolic algorithms'. These comparisons to system descriptions in electrical engineering and computer science offer some insights due to actual parallels, and some misleading comparisons due to oversimplification in comparison to actual biological systems.

A reductionist analysis of a biological system, not surprisingly, reveals that the sum is greater than its parts. But this is actually found to be the case in electrical circuits as well, where emergent properties, especially emergent noise and communications properties, are often found in circuits with feedback. Even simple physical systems involving just three bodies in classical orbital dynamics gives rise to chaotic behavior, which was not expected in early physics, where the sum was originally NOT thought to be greater than its parts. Iterative dynamical systems in general are found to exhibit chaotic behavior and emergent constructs such as strange attractors and limit cycles. Systems with feedback, thus, can do surprising things, and biological systems definitely have done some surprising things ranging from living systems in their amazing variety to complex phenomena such as intelligence, language, and consciousness.

The nanopore transduction detector (NTD) method is typically based on a single protein-channel biosensor implemented on a lipid bilayer (synthetic cell membrane), but it could also be implemented as a live cell assay by using the original patch clamp protocol for measuring current through a channel on a live cell [3] (the invention of the patch clamp amplifier resulted in the Nobel Prize for Medicine or Physiology in 1991 [335]). In order for the NTD 'voltmeter' operating on the biological system to work, cell-based or not, the normal operational buffer of the NTD must accommodate a change to the physiological or cellular buffer environment of the biological system of interest, and, if cell-based, the 'carrier signal' that is the basis of the analysis can no longer be channel-current based, but channel-noise based with use of laser modulations for noise state excitation. Work with robust NTD operation with a variety of buffer pH and in the presence of high concentrations of interference agents reveals that operational stability with a wide range of buffers has been achieved [14]. Laser modulations have also been introduced to improve the NTD mechanism to have more general applicability [36], and for purposes of establishing an improved 'stochastic carrier wave' molecular state tracking capability [1], so many of the complications with returning to the single-cell application are mostly solved. What remains to be resolved for general applicability of the NTD system analyzer method, for both *in vitro* and an possible *in vivo* studies, is a standardized method for NTD transducer construction and operation (see Ch. 14 and [9]), and progress along these lines will be shown in Ch. 14. An inexpensive method for a NTD-based biological system 'voltmeter' is thus possible for both *in vivo* and *in vitro* applications.

10.5.1 Electrical/Biological circuits: the biosystem extra element theorem (BEET)

A reductionist analysis of electrical circuits involves a reduction to circuit elements that have linear responses. In this regard biology only compares weakly, as the components of a biological circuit are generally non-linear over much of their operational range. Even so, for some biological system settings sufficiently small perturbations in the biological components can often be made such that they provide a linear system response. Given the complexity of the biological feedback systems, however, this might seem to be small progress. It is very significant, however, given the existence of a sophisticated method from advanced circuit design and analysis that is applicable for linear response systems known as the 'extra element theorem' [324]. It interesting to note that this important circuit method from electrical system theory has not been imported into biological system discussions given its likely significant role in molecular evolutionary theory. The extra element theorem from electrical circuit theory allows simpler circuits, that are more easily understood, to have new components added (the 'extra' element), and if the new component happens to create a feedback loop, then the complexity of the feedback loop analysis can be much more easily evaluated and understood directly by way of the extra element theorem. In practice, very complex electrical amplifier circuits can be built-up and analyzed in this way, by repeated use of the extra element theorem. This offers the means to have a reductionist analysis while capturing the growing complexity of holistic irreducible systems. For a biological variant of the extra element theorem a patchwork of linear response regimes could be used in understanding a particular biological system.

The 'messengers' in biological and electrical systems differ greatly in many respects, which can make some gene circuit intuition entirely misguided. The carriers in an electrical circuit, for example, are remarkably simple by comparison with biological system signal carriers. Electrical charge moves through wires like a fluid. Granted, the electrical charge moves at a sizable fraction of the speed of light, but it is so like a fluid flow that some current flow discussions are basically plumbing discussions, where the description of the current flow is often compared to flow of water through pipes where pipe narrowness is akin to resistance, etc. The flow/interaction topology of electrical current is also self-evident in the connectivity that can be seen in the wiring of the circuit diagram. If the biological system is too interconnected in this comparison this is often where the analogy is shifted to discussions of a gene system *algorithm*. The electrical messengers, or charge carriers, are also vastly simpler than the biological system messengers. Electrical current carriers are of only one type (electrons), and don't have attractive self-interaction molecular carriers (as with dimerization … unless you are talking superconductivity), and don't have internal state (in the sense of the circuit model) like with biological secondary messengers. Biological system messengers, on the other hand, come in a huge variety, operate at the single molecule level, and depending on perspective, everything in the biological system might be considered a system messenger in a massive, living, autocatalytic cascade. The biological system carriers or messengers are also much fewer in number compared to their electrical counterparts. This actually makes things more complicated. In electronics having small currents is modelled as a noise source, where once the discreteness of the charge carriers begins to be discernible this puts one in the realm of stochastic 'shot' noise. In the biological comparison this stochastic underpinning, if significant, again favors a shift to the 'algorithm' analogy instead of the circuit analogy. To further complicate matters, the biological carriers of the system interactions interact with each other, and typically have internal states (e.g., proteins and riboswitches often have conformational states), so the picture of the carriers for biology introduces vastly greater complexity and interaction interconnectivity.

In electrical circuit analysis a good voltmeter is something that will not significantly 'load' or alter the circuit while measuring a particular component's voltage drop. Likewise, in analyzing a computer program, or resolving a runtime error (the closest analogy to analyzing a 'live' biological algorithm), one of the best tools available is to simply introduce a 'print statement' to track any internal state behavior of interest in the program. This is where the weakness of the circuit or algorithm analogy in biological systems is most profound. The system biologist doesn't have a gene circuit voltmeter or gene system algorithm print statement. Some of the closest biochemistry methods to offer such capabilities are fluorescence based, and in certain specialized applications remarkable results have been obtained along these lines, but they typically involve the introduction of constructs with a great deal of effort that won't scale well to the vast number of biological systems that need to be studied in the post-genomic era. What is needed is a non-destructive, carrier non-modifying, means of testing 'live' biological systems, possibly in their native cellular environment.

10.5.2 Validation of miRNA's and miRNA binding sites using a nanopore transduction nanoscope

The discovery of the RNA interference (RNAi) immune response and translational regulation mechanism has led to an explosion in the number of identified microRNAs (miRNAs) and their mRNA binding sites. An understanding of miRNAs and their binding sites, typically in the 3' untranslated region (3' UTRs) of mRNAs, is helping to explain a wide range of complex phenomena, ranging from latency control by viruses during infection (such as with HIV) [336], to complex regulation in system syndromes such as in diabetes and in the effects of aging [337], to the general trans-regulation of mRNAs at the translational level (complementing transcription factor and promoter cis-regulation at the transcriptional level) [338]. The examination of miRNAs, and especially miRNA binding sites, is confounded by the small size of the miRNAs, however: 21-25 nucleotides in length for typical mature miRNAs, and only 7-8 base ssRNA seed regions in the guide-strand RNA incorporated into the RNAi's RISC complex for actual binding/repression to complementary 7-8 base sequence in the 3'UTR region of the target mRNA [339]. For the latter case of verification for miRNA/RISC derived sequence binding with a 7 base sequence in a mRNA's 3'UTR there is further complication given possible posttranscriptional modifications, such as via inosine substitution for adenosine due to adenosine deaminases with inosine recognition as guanine in terms of base-pairing that can alter the actual target sequence of the miRNA/RISC binding [340]. This is in addition to the obvious complication of identifying the presence of RNA annealing when the annealing only involves 7 bases of RNA.

Preliminary work with NTD-based detection on short DNA annealing suggests a possible means to examine the miRNA/RISC binding to target 3'UTR region with or without the RISC complexes argonaute proteins intact, where results are expected to improve even more upon refinement using locked nucleic acid transducer/reporter probes (see Discussion). NTD based detection of DNA annealing has been demonstrated on DNA sequences as short as 5 bases [28], and in the presence of a variety of interference agents and chaotropes [14]. NTD based detection has also been demonstrated in a variety of buffer conditions so could be established in a buffer conducive to the RISC complex remaining intact and where the annealing to 3'UTR complement sequence occurs with the binding strength found *in vivo*. NTD detection can also operate on small volumes since it makes use of a *single* protein channel interaction, thereby inherently operating at the single-molecule interaction level. NTD detection can, thus, identify single-molecule binding events in a non-destructive manner that may be conducive to the 'live' characterization of many critical, transient, interactions.

For biosensing or bioassays applications in general, not all miRNA or miRNA binding site analyses need be in cellular or physiological buffer either. In a 'destructive setting' more forceful miRNA validation assays, and analysis of annealing-based events, can be pursued by use of chaotropes such as urea. Clearer identification of collective binding events, such as for highly complementary annealing interactions, is found to occur upon introduction of chaotropes that eliminate non-specific DNA interactions, and many 'simple' binding interactions, not involving collective interactions of many components as with annealing [27].

10.6 Single-molecule protein assays and protocols – another role for the Nanoscope
Scalable Protein Assays are sought. At present there is a non-scalable problem when protein described according to the standard structure-function paradigm, since structure cannot be sufficiently well-determined via scalable structure resolution methods (the gold-standard for structure determination, x-ray crystallography, is not scalable). Structure determines the function, but we can have information that maps out that function without determining the structure. If that function information, or information gathering process, is scalable, then we finally can have a scalable approach to protein studies.

Note that if the 'protein' is sufficiently small, too small for a fold structure like that found in lengthier AA sequences, then it is referred to as a peptide, and peptides are used as secondary messengers, among other things. Also in this group, of small critically functionalized molecules (such as the peptides), are other small signaling molecules, often derived from the secretory pathways of the cell (ER and Golgi PTM, if protein or peptide, alpha acids, beta acids, cannabinoids, terpenes, pyrethrins). How to assay the presence of such small molecules, especially when they are very similar, if not isomers, of each other? We know we can preferentially bind (and signal this binding) molecules only differing by isomer configuration. A universal platform to take a specific binder (antibody or aptamer) for a specific target and leverage it into a biosensor for that target is what is needed. So whether mapping binding function on larger proteins or specifically binding molecular features on smaller or similar molecules (to collectively differentiate isomers, for example), a Nanoscope approach could be used to solve the problem – see Ch. 14.

Biosensing by way of specific binders, one for each individual molecule to track, cannot scale well when the number of specific targets grows too large (beyond the 100 or so specific signals that can be resolved in a given experimental setup). So, specific binders are needed that effectively bind onto less unique sub-structures or folds of the molecules. A collection of these less-specific binders then profiles what is present and may be able to detect on 100 to 1000s of molecular targets with only 10 or so biosensing binders. So scalable protein analysis appears to be within reach using the Nanoscope platform.

Chapter 11

Classification and Clustering

A classifier is typically a simple rule whereby a class determination can be made, such as a decision boundary. Learning the decision rule, or a sufficiently good decision rule, especially if simple (and elegant), is the implementation aspect of a classifier, and can be difficult and time consuming. Even so, this is usually manageable because at least you have data to 'learn from', e.g., supervised learning, where you have instances and their classifications (or 'labels'). Learning for classification can be done very effectively using Support Vector Machines (SVMs), as will be described in what follows. With clustering efforts, or unsupervised learning, on the other hand, we don't have the label information during training. In what follows SVMs will also be shown to be incredibly effective at clustering when used with metaheuristics to recover label information in a bootstrap learning process. Also shown will be implementation details for distributed SVM training, and other speedup optimizations, for practical deployment of the powerful SVM classification and clustering methods in real-time operational situations (as will be demonstrated with results on a nanopore detector experiment in Ch. 14).

Support Vector Machines (SVMs) are variational-calculus based methods that are constrained to have structural risk minimization (maximum margin optimization), unlike neural net classifiers or perceptrons, such that they provide noise tolerant solutions for pattern recognition [1,37,114-125]. An SVM determines a hyperplane that optimally separates one class from another, while the structural risk minimization (SRM) criterion manifests as the hyperplane having a thickness, or "margin," that is made as large as possible in the process of seeking a separating hyperplane (see Fig. 11.1 below).

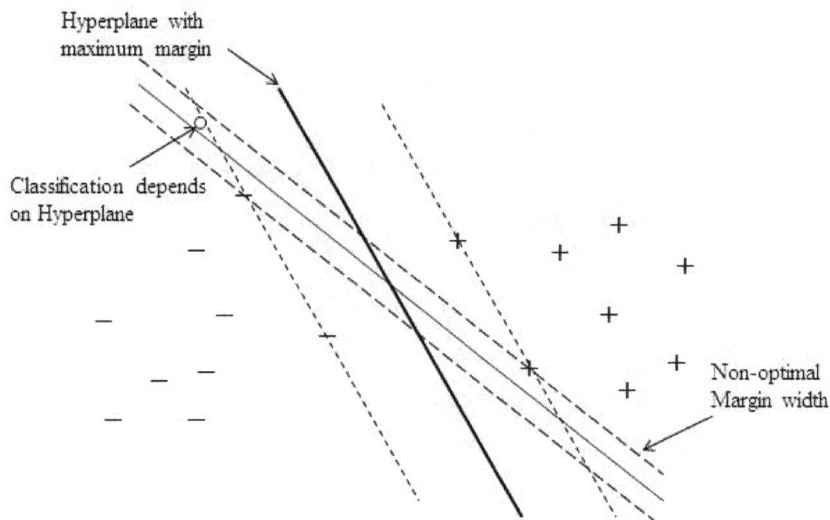

Fig. 11.1. Supervised Learning: Separability and Maximum Margin.
Shown in the figure is data separable by a line. With obvious generalization to a plane in 3-D, and in higher dimensions, etc. We have thereby a (manifold) notion of separability on two datasets. Of all of the separating hyperplanes, it would appear to be optimal to choose one that could be made as 'thick' as possible and still be a separating hyperplane. The thickness is known as the margin, so we are seeking a maximal margin hyperplane, as shown. Also shown is a non-optimal margin hyperplane.

A benefit of using SRM is much less complication due to over-fitting. Once learned, the hyperplane allows data to be classified according to the side of the hyperplane in which it resides. The SVM approach encapsulates a significant amount of model-fitting information in its choice of kernel. The SVM kernel also provides a notion of distance in the neighborhood of the decision hyperplane. SVM binary discrimination outperforms other classification methods with or without dropping weak data. SVMs have a built parameter to assess confidence in a signal classification (related to the kernel distance from the separating hyperplane), thus have a built-in notion of weak data. Other classifier methods, if they have a notion of weak data, often introduce it as a separate evaluation that must itself be tuned and analyzed in order to be trusted. SVM multiclass discrimination and SVM-based clustering are also possible [1,6,7,31,37,122,124]. In the SSA protocol SVMs play a central role in performing classification and clustering tasks.

Most SVM uses are restrictive in both training-set size and number of different classes, where most SVM applications involve datasets with fewer than 10,000 training instances and only two classes (the binary SVM). There are SVM implementations, however, that have no such limit on the number of training instances or the number of classes. Efficient new methods have been discovered for multiclass SVM, both internal to the optimization (multi-hyperplane) and external (decision tree and decision forest) [1,37]. In cases where the SVM training set is much larger than 10,000 instances, or when repeated training over the same training set is needed, significant SVM training computations are necessary. For this reason, distributed/GPU-optimized SVM training processes have been implemented [1,124].

There is a new approach to unsupervised learning that is based on use of supervised Support Vector Machine (SVM) classifiers. A fundamentally novel aspect of the proposed method is that it provides a non-parametric means for clustering (unsupervised learning) and partially-supervised clustering. In preliminary work the SVM-based clustering method appears to offer prospects for inheriting the very strong performance of standard SVMs from the *supervised* classification setting. This offers a remarkable prospect for knowledge discovery and enhancing the scope of human cognition – the recognition of patterns and clusters without the limitations imposed by explicitly assuming a parametric model, where resolution of the identified clusters can be at an accuracy comparable to a supervised learning setting.

11.1 The SVM Classifier – an Overview
With an SVM 'learning' process, once convergent to solution, what is learned, among other things, is the set of "support vectors" that define the thickness boundary of the separating hyperplane (see Fig. 11.2).

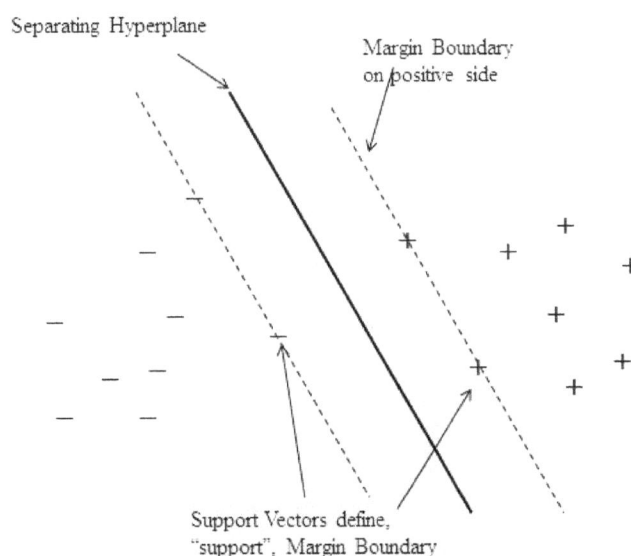

Fig. 11.2. Support Vectors on Margin boundary.

So far we are implicitly describing a two-class problem, a "binary classifier", but what of multiple classes, can this be handled? Yes. Two broad categories of ways to handle this: (i) external refinement, such as via decisions trees (and forests) made from Binary classifier nodes (so more of what we've already got, to be discussed later); and (ii) internal refinement, such as via multiple hyperplanes (now inherently different, so discussed later).

So far we have been explicitly working with data that was separable. What if it isn't? See Fig. 11.3 Left for example where the data is not linearly separable. It is separable with a curve (or connected line segment as shown in Fig. 11.3 Right).

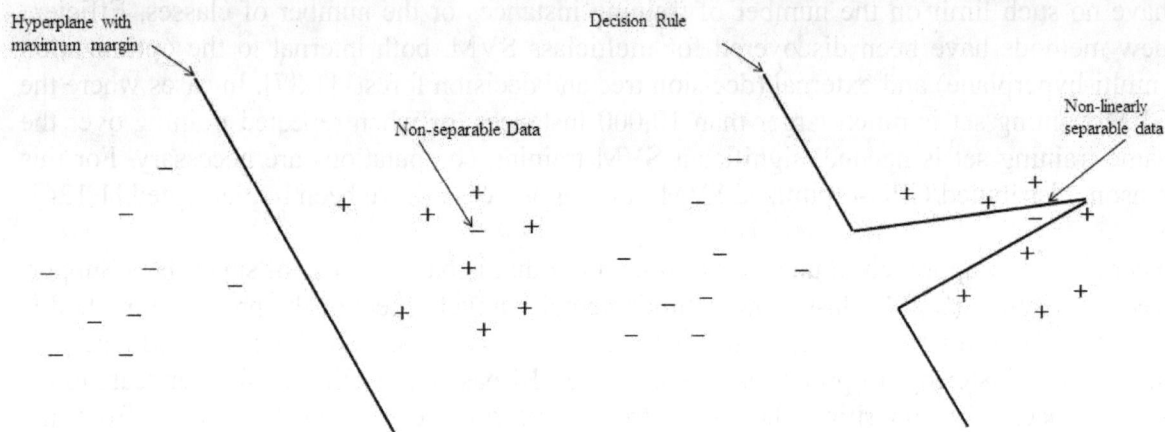

Fig. 11.3. Left. One of the former positives (central to the positive cluster) is now flipped to have a negative label. The data is now non-separable with a (single) straight line. **Right.** The data is shown separable with a curve that happens to be a connected line segment.

11.2 Introduction to Classification and Clustering

In finding a separable solution (Fig. 11.4, with maximum margin shown) we could also change the problem to separability on *most* of the data, with adjustments to account for those instances not consistent with the decision rule by way of a penalty term (according to how much 'wrong', perhaps). Alternatively, we could establish separability with a non-linear discriminant by mapping the feature vector data to a higher dimensional space (e.g., introduction of the Kernel map and overall generalization), where linear separability would almost always be possible (almost provably always the case, due to hypersphere shattering in sufficiently high dimensions – something used to obtain an initial convergence in SVM clustering in Sec. 11.8)

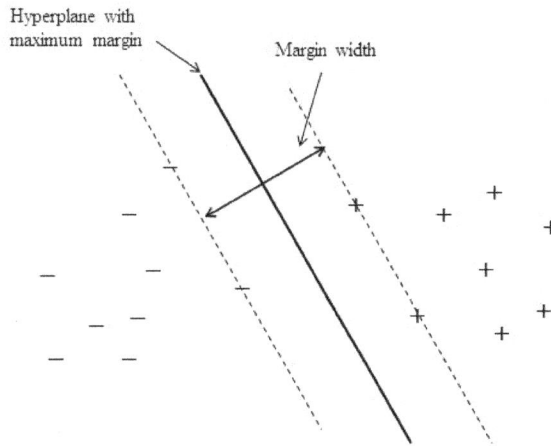

Fig. 11.4. Separable solution with maximum width margin.

Once training is done (have decision rule), we can then do classification (see Fig. 11.5). Using the classifier (training data still shown), we simply classify according to which side of hyperplane (decision surface). Since we know the actual classes of the test data (used in the training/validation), we can score the performance of our classifier – this information, in turn, allows the classifier to be tuned for optimal performance.

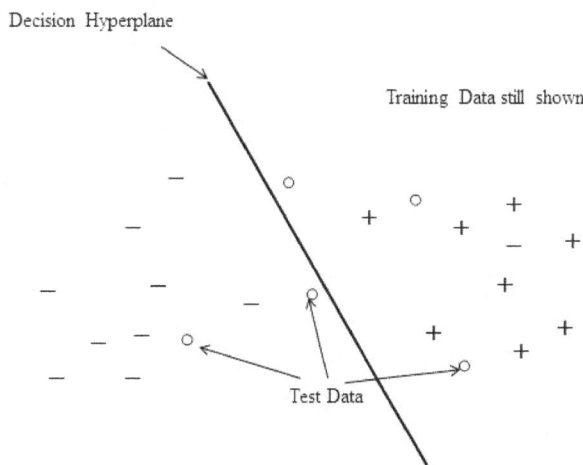

Fig. 11.5. Post-training, have Decision Hyperplane. Now test data (circles in figure) can be introduced and classified according to which side of the hyperplane that they are on. Test data is usually held out from the original training data according to an N-fold cross-validation arrangement. So for analysis on one such fold, the test data used is data for which we "know" the answer ahead of time, but it presented without the knowledge as a test. If the test data is classified positive and it was truly a positively labeled data, then it's a true positive (TP), and similarly for FP, TN, FN.

So far we discussed the problem of learning to classify (with two class data: positive and negative), and we will find that we can solve any of the classification problems mentioned, whether extending to multiple classes or significantly non-separable. We have robust methods to do classification with SVMs and some other methods (carefully managed Neural Nets, for example). So what happens if we take away the label information and want to recover the identification of the positive and negative classes (assuming two classes)? Essentially, we've arrived at the classic clustering problem, where we want to identify clusters in the data. (Clustering is sometimes called unsupervised learning where the lack of label information is related to lack of 'supervision'.) It turns out that clustering is much more difficult than classification since we don't even have a definition for a 'cluster'.

What is a cluster? Vague Rule #1 is indicated in Fig. 11.6, where Inter-cluster distance is required to be greater than intra-cluster distance, and significantly so for good clustering (this fails for two parallel line of dots, for example).

Clustering is qualitative, thus lacks the same level of 'well-definedness' as classification. Having successfully obtained a clustering solution, you can then provide a labeling to the data, and revisit (bootstrap) in a supervised learning scenario to train a classifier....

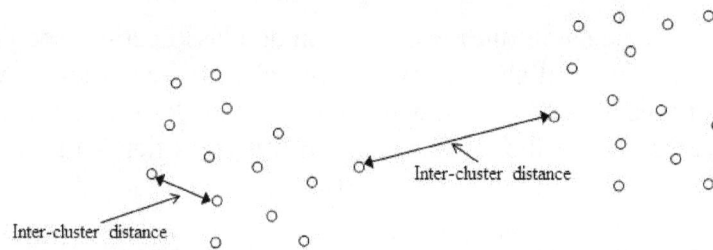

Fig. 11.6. Two clusters, roughly, shown, with intra-cluster distance shown on right and inter-cluster distance shown between the edges of the two clusters.

Instead of bootstrapping from clustering into classification (with addition of label information), can we bootstrap from classification into clustering? By throwing any, random, label info, and having a learning process on the labels? That way we play to our strength, since classification as a learning process is on very form ground, both theoretically and in terms of efficient implementation. This would seem to indicate that a classification → clustering bootstrap solution could be done, but it would also require beginning the initial classification bootstrap run with randomly data. Is this possible for any classifier to manage? The answer is yes, for the SVM, but only for certain choices of SVM kernel that are identified in Sec. 11.5. A schematic for the SVM-classifier based clustering method is shown in Fig. 11.7.

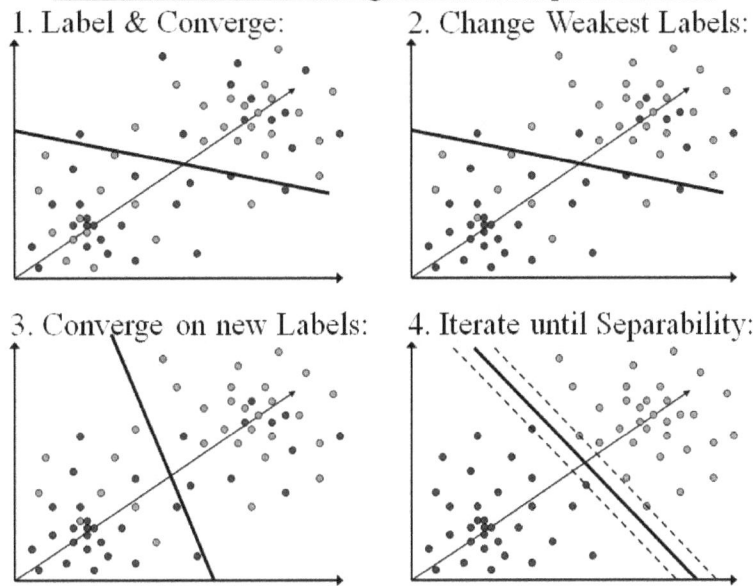

SVM-based Clustering (via multi-pass SVM)

1. Label & Converge: 2. Change Weakest Labels:

3. Converge on new Labels: 4. Iterate until Separability:

Fig. 11.7. Schematic for SVM-based clustering, starting with randomly labeled data for which an SVM 'learning' solution is sought (randomly labeled means extremely non-separable, typically). Remarkably, for certain kernels, convergence is possible.

Suppose you've got a clustering solution. How can you do an objective measure of that cluster solution? One idea is to compute the total of the sum of the distances squared from the "center point" of the clusters

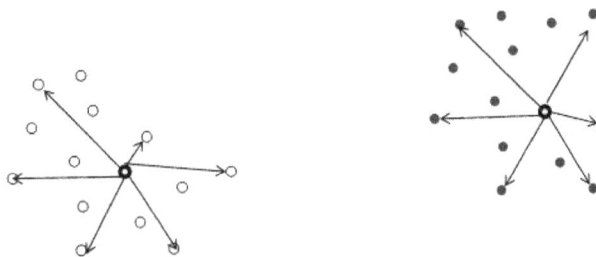

Fig. 11.8. Sum of Squared Error (SSE) Scoring. SSE = the total of the sum of the distances squared from the "center point" of the clusters.

Sum of Squared Error (SSE) Scoring

The sum of squared error (SSE) score for a cluster is the sum of the distances squared from the "center point" of the cluster (see Fig. 11.8). The center point can be identified either as the most central data-point in the indicated cluster, or as the average data-point, i.e. centroid, that may not correspond with an actual data-point in the data-set. If you were hoping for more mathematical detail, that is covered in the sub-section that follows on K-means clustering (one of the most popular clustering methods). It turns out that the central idea of the K-means clustering effort is an effort to minimize the SSE on the solution. For this reason, SSE scoring can't be used (as effectively) for scoring K-means, since a different cluster evaluation would be needed to not be systematically blind to poor cluster solutions.

11.2.1 K-Means clustering (unsupervised learning)

K-means is a simple algorithm for clustering a set of un-labeled feature vectors X: $\{x_1, \ldots, x_n\}$ that are drawn independently from the mixture density $p(X|\theta)$ with a parameter set θ. At the heart of the K-means algorithm is optimization of the sum-of-squared-error function (SSE), J_i defined in definition SSE below.

Definition SSE (Sum-of-squared-error): Given a cluster χ_i, the sum-of-squared, J_i is defined by:

$$J_i = \Sigma_x \|x - m_i\|^2, \, x \in \chi_i,$$

and where m_i is the mean of the samples belonging to χ_i. The geometric interpretation of this criterion function is that for a given cluster χ_i the mean vector m_i is the centroid of the cluster by minimizing the length of the vector $x - m_i$. This can be shown by taking the variation of J_i with respect to the "centroid" m_i and setting it zero,

$$\partial/\partial m_i \, J_i = \partial/\partial m_i \, \Sigma_x \, (x - m_i)\mathrm{T} \, (x - m_i) = 2\Sigma_x \, (x - m_i) = 0$$

with minimum when equal to zero, where $x \in \chi_i$ in the sums, and solving for m_i:

$$m_i = 1/\mathrm{n}_i \, \Sigma_x x$$

where $\mathrm{n}_i = |\chi_i|$ is the number of feature vectors belonging to χ_i. The total SSE for all of the clusters, J_e is the sum of SSE for individual clusters. The value of J_e depends on the cluster membership of the data, (i.e. the shape of the clusters), and the number of clusters. The optimal clustering is the one that minimizes J_e for a given number of clusters, k, and K-means tries to do just that.

Kernel K-means [139] is a natural extension of K-means. Denote M_{iv} to be the cluster assignment variables such that $M_{iv} = 1$ if and only if x_i belongs to cluster v and 0 otherwise. As for K-means, the goal is to minimize the J_v for all clusters, v in feature space, by trying to find k means $\Phi(m_v)$ such that each observation in the data set when mapped using Φ is close to at least one of the means. Since the means lie in the span of $\Phi(x_1)$, ..., $\Phi(x_n)$, we can write them as:

$$\mu_v \equiv \Phi(m_v) = \Sigma_j \, \gamma_{vj}\Phi(x_j)$$

We can then substitute this in the J_i of definition (10) to obtain,

$$J_v = \Sigma_x \|\Phi(x) - \mu_v\|^2 = \Sigma_x \|\Phi(x) - \Sigma_j \, \gamma_{vj}\Phi(x_j)\|^2$$
$$= K(x, x) - 2 \, \Sigma_j \, \gamma_{vj}K(x, x_j) + \Sigma_{ij} \, \gamma_{vi}\gamma_{vj}K(x_i, x_j),$$

where $x \in \chi_i$ in Σ_x, $j \in 1..n$ in Σ_j, and $i, j \in 1..n$ in Σ_{ij}. We initially assign random feature vectors to means. Then Kernel K-means proceeds iteratively as follows: each new remaining feature vectors, x_{t+1}, is assigned to the closest mean μ_α:

$M_{t+1,\alpha} = 1$ if for all $\nu \neq \alpha$, $\|\Phi(x_{t+1}) - \mu_\alpha\|^2 < \|\Phi(x_{t+1}) - \mu_\nu\|^2$,

$M_{t+1,\alpha} = 0$ otherwise. Or, in terms of the kernel function,

$M_{t+1,\alpha} = 1$ if for all $\nu \neq \alpha$, $\sum_{ij} \gamma_{\alpha i}\gamma_{\alpha j}K_{ij} - \sum_j \gamma_{\alpha j}K_{t+1,j} < \sum_{ij} \gamma_{vi}\gamma_{vj}K_{ij} - \sum_j \gamma_{vj}K_{t+1,j}$,

$M_{t+1,\alpha} = 0$ otherwise, where $K_{i,j} \equiv K_{ij} \equiv K(x_i, x_j)$. The update rule for the mean vector is then given by,

$$\mu_{t+1,\alpha} = \mu_{t,\alpha} + \Delta(\Phi(x_{t+1}) - \mu_{t,\alpha}), \text{ where, } \Delta \equiv M_{t+1,\alpha} / \sum_{1..t+1} M_{i\alpha}$$

A code sample in perl for performing K-means is shown below:

```perl
#!/usr/bin/perl

use strict;
use FileHandle;

my $train_fh = new FileHandle "9GC9TA.train";
my $test_fh = new FileHandle "9GC9TA.test";

my $index=0;
my @train_data;
my $comp_length;
while (<$train_fh>) {
    my ($label, @comps) = split;
    $comp_length = scalar(@comps);
#    @{$train_data[$index]} = ($label,@comps);
    @{$train_data[$index]} = @comps;
    $index++;
}
my $train_count = $index;

my ($K) = @ARGV;
if (!$K) { $K = 2; }

print "K=$K\n";

# initialize via random choice of data instances
my %ran_index_hash;
my @centroid;
my $index=0;
FOR: for $index (0..$K-1) {
    my $ran_index = int($train_count*rand() );
    print "$ran_index\n";
    if ($ran_index_hash{$ran_index}) {
        print "collision\n";
        $index--;
        next FOR;
    }
    else {
        $ran_index_hash{$ran_index}=1;
    }

    @centroid[$index] = @train_data[$ran_index];
}

if (0) { #### if0
my $index=0;
for $index (0..$train_count-1) {
    my $comp_index=0;
    for $comp_index (0..$comp_length-1) {
        print "$train_data[$index][$comp_index]\t";
    }
    print "\n\n";
}
} # endif0
```

```perl
if (0) { #### if0
my $index=0;
for $index (0..$K-1) {
    my $comp_index=0;
    for $comp_index (0..$comp_length-1) {
        print "$centroid[$index][$comp_index]\t";
    }
    print "\n\n";
}
} # endif0

my $old_first_diff=100;
my $first_diff=100;
# iterator loop
while (1) {

# have centroids, now evaluate distances of instances to centroids
my @distances;
my @min_distance_labels;
my @min_distance_vals;
my $index=0;
for $index (0..$train_count-1) {
    my $j=0;
    my $min_dist_val=1000000;
    for $j (0..$K-1) {
        $distances[$j][$index]=0;
        my $comp_index=0;
        for $comp_index (0..$comp_length-1) {
            $distances[$j][$index] += ($centroid[$j][$comp_index]-
$train_data[$index][$comp_index])**2;
        }

        if ($distances[$j][$index]<=$min_dist_val) {
            $min_dist_val=$distances[$j][$index];
            $min_distance_labels[$index]=$j;
#           print "$j loop: min_distance_labels[$index]=$j\n";
        }

#       print "index=$index\t j=$j\t distances[$j][$index]=$distances[$j][$index]\n";
    }
    my $mdl = $min_distance_labels[$index];
#   print "index=$index\t mdl=$mdl\t distances[$mdl][$index]=$distances[$mdl][$index]\n";
}

my @old_centroid;
#copy and reset centroid array
my $j=0;
for $j (0..$K-1) {
    my $comp_index=0;
    for $comp_index (0..$comp_length-1) {
        $old_centroid[$j][$comp_index] = $centroid[$j][$comp_index];
        $centroid[$j][$comp_index] = 0;
    }
}

# calculate new centroids
my @cent_count;
my $j=0;
for $j (0..$K-1) {
    $cent_count[$j]=0;
}

my $index=0;
for $index (0..$train_count-1) {
    my $comp_index=0;
    for $comp_index (0..$comp_length-1) {
        $centroid[$min_distance_labels[$index]][$comp_index]+=
$train_data[$index][$comp_index];
    }
    $cent_count[$min_distance_labels[$index]]++;
}

my $j=0;
for $j (0..$K-1) {
    my $comp_index=0;
```

```perl
        for $comp_index (0..$comp_length-1) {
            $centroid[$j][$comp_index] /= $cent_count[$j];
        }
    }


    # if (0) { # if0
    # print new centroids
    my $index=0;
    for $index (0..$K-1) {
        my $comp_index=0;
        for $comp_index (0..$comp_length-1) {
            print "$centroid[$index][$comp_index]\t";
        }
        print "\n\n";
    }
    # } # if0

    $old_first_diff = $first_diff;

    # test for movement of first centroid:
    $first_diff=0;
    my $comp_index=0;
    for $comp_index (0..$comp_length-1) {
        $first_diff += ($centroid[0][$comp_index]-$old_centroid[0][$comp_index])**2;
    }
    print "old_first_diff = $old_first_diff\n";
    print "first_diff=$first_diff\n";
    my $df = abs($old_first_diff - $first_diff);
    print "$df\n";
    my $epsilon = 0.000000001;

    if ($df<$epsilon) {
        print "exiting with no change in centroid 1 position\n";
        my $index=0;
        for $index (0..$train_count-1) {
            print "$index\t$min_distance_labels[$index]\n";
        }
        exit;
    }

    print "end of loop, with new centroid evaluation, starting next loop\n";
} # no indent
```

11.2.2 k Nearest Neighbors classification (supervised learning)

Classification is generally easier than clustering, and that is often reflected in a simpler classification algorithm. Case in point is the classic k nearest neighbors (k-NN) classification algorithm, where, as the name suggest, classification is based on the k nearest neighbors to instances in some given reference 'training' set (where the data is labeled). To keep this simple, k is often chosen to be an odd number, such that a simple majority vote of the neighbors according to their class will then determine the class of the unlabeled instance presented.

A code sample in perl for performing k-NN is shown below:

```perl
#!/usr/bin/perl
use strict;
use FileHandle;
my ($K) = @ARGV; # the K in K-nn
if (!$K) { $K = 5; }
# hardcoded data-file entries
my $train_data = "9GC9TA.train";
my $test_data = "9GC9TA.test";
my $train_fh = new FileHandle "$train_data";
my $test_fh = new FileHandle "$test_data";
my $index=0;
my @train_data;
while (<$train_fh>) {
    my ($label, @comps) = split;
    @{$train_data[$index]} = ($label,@comps);
```

281

```perl
        $index++;
}
my $train_count = $index;
my $index=0;
my @test_data;
while (<$test_fh>) {
        my ($label, @comps) = split;
        @{$test_data[$index]} = ($label,@comps);
        $index++;
}
my $test_count = $index;

my ($TP,$TN,$FP,$FN) = (0,0,0,0);
my $test_index;
for $test_index (0..$test_count-1) {
        my ($test_label,@test_comps) = @{$test_data[$test_index]};

        my @min;
        my @ind;
        my @lab;
        my $k_loop;
        for $k_loop (0..$K-1) {
                $min[$k_loop] = 100;
                $ind[$k_loop] = 0;
                $lab[$k_loop] = 0;
        }

        my $train_index;
        for $train_index (0..$train_count-1) {
                my ($train_label,@train_comps) = @{$train_data[$train_index]};
                my $comp_count = scalar(@train_comps);
                my $square_distance=0;
                my $comp_index;
                for $comp_index (0..$comp_count-1) {
                        $square_distance += ($test_comps[$comp_index]-$train_comps[$comp_index])**2;
                }
                KFOR: for $k_loop (0..$K-1) {
                        if ($square_distance<$min[$k_loop]) {
                                my @min_shift = @min[$k_loop..($K-2)];
                                my @ind_shift = @ind[$k_loop..($K-2)];
                                my @lab_shift = @lab[$k_loop..($K-2)];

                                $min[$k_loop] = $square_distance;
                                $ind[$k_loop] = $train_index;
                                $lab[$k_loop] = $train_label;

                                @min = (@min[0..$k_loop],@min_shift);
                                @ind = (@ind[0..$k_loop],@ind_shift);
                                @lab = (@lab[0..$k_loop],@lab_shift);

                                last KFOR;
                        }
                }
        }
        # get majority vote of k nearest neighbors
        my $vote=0;

        for $k_loop (0..$K-1) {
                $vote += $lab[$k_loop];
        }

        my $test_predict;
        if ($vote>0) { $test_predict = 1; }
        elsif ($vote<0) { $test_predict = -1; }
        else { print "whoaaa!\n"; }

        if ($test_predict == $test_label && $test_predict == 1) {
                $TP++;
        }
        elsif ($test_predict == $test_label && $test_predict == -1) {
                $TN++;
        }
        elsif ($test_predict != $test_label && $test_predict == 1) {
                $FP++;
        }
```

```
    elsif ($test_predict != $test_label && $test_predict == -1) {
        $FN++;
    }


}
print "K-nn with K=$K:\tTN=$TN\t TP=$TP\t FN=$FN\t FP=$FP\t\t";
print "traindata=$train_data\ttestdata=$test_data\n";
```

11.2.3 The Perceptron

The classic machine learning neural net classifier is known as the perceptron. Let's consider this tool in a credit approval context (Notes from "Learning from Data" by Y.S. Abu-Mostafa [64]):

Let $X = R^d$ be the input space: (salary, debt, etc....) for example. Let $Y = \{+1,-1\}$ be the output space (which denotes a yes/no decision in the credit approval context).

We will want to be able to adjust weight on the importance of different features in the input space in arriving at a credit decision, and then have a simple threshold rule to make that decision:

$$\text{Approve if } \sum_{i=1}^{d} w_i x_i > \theta$$
$$\text{Deny if } \sum_{i=1}^{d} w_i x_i \leq \theta$$

Let's treat the threshold value as a weight $w_0 = b$ and associate it with an added X coordinate, $x_0 = 1$. Let's also make use of the sign function: sign(s) = 1 if s>0, and sign(s) = -1 if s<0. The decision function h(x) is 1 if approved and -1 if denied:

$$h(x) = \text{sign}(w \cdot x)$$

The classic perceptron learning algorithm then goes as follows (Fig. 11.9 below):

Suppose at the current iteration, t, of the learning algorithm, we have weight vector w(t). If we haven't already arrived at a solution then some of the $(x_1, y_1)...(x_N, y_N)$ will be misclassified, i.e., $h(x_k) \neq y_k$ for various k values, and one of these misclassifications will be used in the **update rule**:

$$w(t+1) = w(t) + y(t)x(t)$$

Note: $y(t)[w(t) \cdot x(t)] < 0$ for each update (y has different sign than w.x)
Note: $y(t)[w(t+1) \cdot x(t)] > y(t)[w(t) \cdot x(t)]$ (so move towards positivity)
Last follows from $y(t)[w(t+1) \cdot x(t)] = y(t)[w(t) \cdot x(t)] + [y(t)]^2 [x(t) \cdot x(t)]$

283

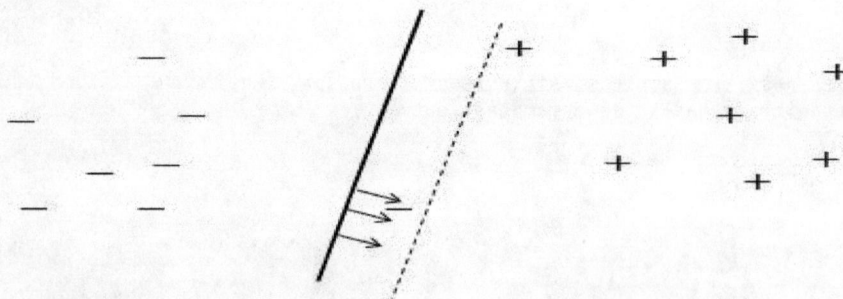

Fig. 11.9 Perceptron update. The update rule shifts the position of the separating hyperplane such that classification errors eventually reduced to zero (assuming separable and that it doesn't get stuck in a local minimum of the minimization process).

Within the infinite space of all weight vectors, the perceptron algorithm finds a weight vector that works. This means that an infinite hypothesis space has been searched in a finite number of steps, so finite time, to find a solution. This search of an infinite hypothesis space in finite time will be one of the hallmarks of the Feasibility of Learning Proof (the "First Law of Machine Learning").

To recap, the components of the Perceptron Learning Problem are:
1. There is an input x.
2. There is an unknown target function f:X→Y (the ideal formula for credit approval in the credit problem).
3. There is a data set D of (input, output) examples $(x_1,y_1),...,(x_N,y_N)$, where $y_n=f(x_n)$.
4. There is a learning algorithm that uses dataset D to pick a formula g:X→Y that approximates f.
5. The algorithm chooses g from a set of candidate formulas under consideration, which we call the hypothesis set H.

In the case of the perceptron, h(x)=sign(w·x), h∈H.

11.3 Lagrangian Optimization and Structural Risk Minimization (SRM)
11.3.1 Decision Boundary and SRM Construction using Lagrangian
In Fig. 11,10, a decision boundary is shown as the solid line for a 2-D domain, where separating hyperplane generalizations to planes in 3-D and hyperplanes in higher dimensional domains are also possible (with in any orientable hyperplane manifold). The notion of a separating hyperplane is not unique to the SVM approach, but it is with use of further Strucutral Risk Minimization (SRM) constraints via maximizing a margin around the decision hyperplane. The margin is shown as the region around the decision boundary in Fig. 11.10 that is between the dotted lines on either side of the decision hypersurface. Generalizations to compact (or circular) or multiple decision surfaces (e.g., multiple lines in 2-D case) are also possible.

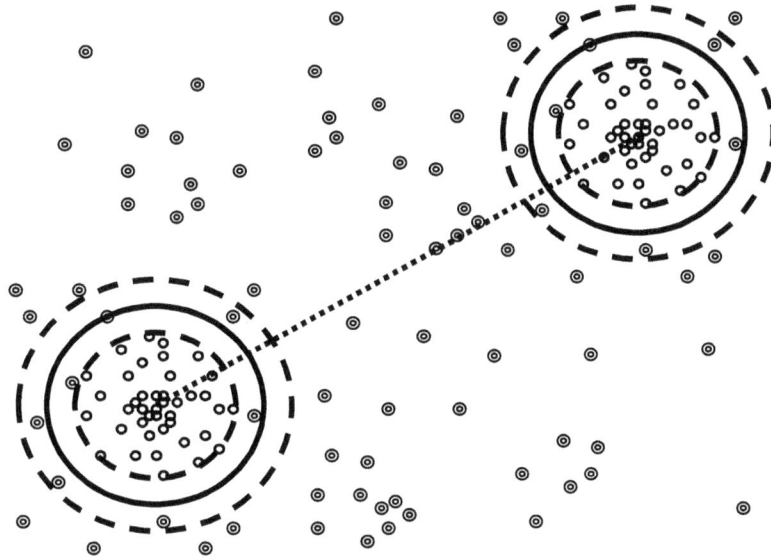

Fig. 11.12. A possible modeling configuration for two-cluster explicit situation. In the case of the enclosing boundary method the hyperspherical clustering can map back to topologically disconnected components, such as that shown as the two cluster groupings shown in the feature space, but the model freedom is restricted and difficult to manage, so, again, separate approaches may be more useful to consider, to some extent for arriving at a computationally efficient solution.

It is conceivable to have a properly coded SVM but to initiate training with model parameters, such as the kernel or kernel parameter, that are so far out of the operational regime that no convergence is obtained in training. So training must be repeated, with tuning on SVM parameters, to optimize. For some feature vectors, such as probability vectors, this can partly be done automatically with choice of kernel. Overall, in many situations the SVM tuning can be done quickly, manually, and to some extent automatically with simple range testing, where only small, separated, subsets of the training data are used in the tuning tests, before performing SVM training on the full dataset minus the tuning data. Sometimes, however, and most certainly for the SVM applications in clustering that will be described, more automated tuning procedures are needed. Tuning is a form of optimization, and excellent metaheuristics are known for identifying optimal solutions when a scoring function (a fitness function) can be identified (such as for the SVM sensitivity and specificity score). Metaheuristic optimization includes genetic algorithms, simulated annealing, swarm intelligence, ACO, steepest ascent hill-climbing, among others (as described in Ch. 12). Applications of many of these methods are shown in the results involving SVM-external clustering in Sec. 11.8.1.

In setting up an SVM Classifier you need to have training data in the form of feature vectors, where all of the feature vectors are the same length. You then need to specify a choice of kernel and kernel parameter (and possibly other parameters), and therein lies the rub. The SVM may not converge with your specification. SVMs have a surprising amount of practical functionality, as will be shown, so it turns out to be fairly easy to tune them, in many cases, by simply using a default set of kernel's and parameter ranges. In the SVM applications to bootstrap a Clustering solution, on the other hand, there is more sensitivity to kernel and kernel parameter, and more sophisticated tuning methods will clearly be helpful, as will be described further in Sec. 11.8.2 & 11.8.3.

The ability to do fast SVM training (with distributed chunking and, possibly, GPU enhancements) means that *online* SVM learning can be managed in a brute-force fashion, with re-tuning on kernels periodically, and directly re-training on a moving window of data.

We describe a new form of clustering, via use of the SVM convergence process. Single-convergence initialized clustering methods, involving label-flipping between SVM convergence training runs, have been studied and will be detailed first. The single-convergence methods outperform other methods on the test sets considered, but in examining the clustering failures (albeit fewer than with parameterized methods), there appears to be room for improvement. Efforts to handle this with more sophisticated tuning have met with initial success, as will be related in what follows. But before proceeding further with efforts along these lines there is one other form of initialization to mention that may be adopted and modify the overall approach, probably to its betterment and reduction in complexity. That different approach is to initialize with information from *multiple* SVM convergences, with selection on training data based on algorithmic methods that leverage the clustering groupings indicated (from the "steepest ascent" multiple convergence data) to more effectively cluster, or simply cluster with less sophistication needed in the overall tuning requirements, and this will be discussed in Sec. 11.8.4.

In application to channel current signal analysis there is generally an abundance of experimental data available, if not, the experimenter can usually just take more samples and make it so. In this situation it is appropriate to seek a method good at both classifying data and evaluating a confidence in the classifications given. In this way, data that is low confidence can simply be dropped. The structural risk minimization at the heart of the SVM method's robustness *also provides a strong confidence measure*. For this reason, SVM's are the classification method of choice for channel current analysis, as they have excellent performance at 0% data drop, and as weak data is allowed to be dropped, the SVM-based approaches far exceed the performance of most other methods known as shown in what follows.

The applications of the SVM methods not only include classification and clustering, but also impacts feature extraction and identification in HMM-based methods, using an HMM/SVM vectorization/classification boost [26] (see Ch. 7).

11.3.2 The theory of classification
The formal description of the problem of classification is to find a general rule to match a set of objects, or observations, to their appropriate classes. In one form the binary classifier's task is to estimate a function $f: \mathbf{R}^N \to \{\pm 1\}$, given examples and their $\{\pm 1\}$ classifications:

$$(\mathbf{x_1}, y_1), \ldots, (\mathbf{x_n}, y_n) \in \mathbf{R}^N \times Y, Y = \{\pm 1\},$$

where $(\mathbf{x}, y)$ are assumed to be independent and identically distributed training data drawn from (unknown) probability distribution $\mathbf{P}(\mathbf{x}, y)$. f perfectly classifies if y = +1 when $f(\mathbf{x}) \geq 0$, with y = -1 otherwise, where this holds for all of the *n* training instances.

In the loss-function formalism, the optimal f is obtained by minimizing the *expected risk* function (expected error) [117]:

$$R[f] = \int l(f(x), y) \mathrm{d}P(x, y)$$

where l is a suitable loss function. For instance, in the case of "0/1 loss"

$$l(f(x), y) = \Theta(-yf(x))$$

where Θ is the Heaviside function ($\Theta(z) = 0$ for $z < 0$ and $\Theta(z) = 1$ otherwise; and where the argument chosen relates to the KKT relations in what follows) In most realistic cases $P(x, y)$ is unknown and therefore the risk function above cannot be used to find the optimum function f. To overcome this fundamental limitation one has to use the information hidden in the limited training examples and the properties of the function class F to approximate this function. Hence, instead of minimizing the expected risk, one minimizes the ***empirical risk***

$$R_{emp}[f] = 1/n \sum l(f(x_i), y), \text{ with sum on } i \in 1..n.$$

The learning machine can ensure that for n→∞ the empirical risk will asymptotically converge to expected risk, but for a small training set the deviations are often large. This leads to a phenomenon called "over-fitting," where a small generalization error can't be obtained by simply minimizing the training error. One way to avoid the over-fitting dilemma is to restrict the complexity of the function class [115]. The intuition, which will be formalized in the following, is that a "simple" (e.g., linear) function that explains most of the data is preferable to a complex one (i.e., an application of Occam's razor). This is often introduced via a regularization term that limits the complexity of the function class used by the learning machine [126].

A specific way of controlling the complexity of a function class is described by the Vapnik-Chervonenkis (VC) theory and the structural risk minimization (SRM) principle [115,116]. Here the concept of complexity is captured by the VC dimension **h** of the function class F from which the estimate f is chosen. The following set of definitions indicate the role of structural risk minimization (SRM) -- in the SVM construction that follows SRM is implemented via maximum margin separation (and clustering).

Definition 1 (Shattering) A Learning Machine f can shatter a set of points $x_1, x_2, \ldots, x_n$ if and only if for every possible training set of the form $(x_1, y_1), \ldots, (x_n, y_n)$ there exists some parameter set that gets zero training error.

Definition 2 (VC Dimension) Given a learning machine f, the VC-dimension **h** is the maximum number of points that can be arranged so that f shatter them. Roughly speaking, the VC dimension measures how many (training) points can be shattered (i.e., separated) for all possible labelings using functions of the class. Constructing a nested family of function classes $F_1 \subset \ldots \subset F_k$ with non-decreasing VC dimension the SRM principle proceeds as follows:

Definition 3 (SRM Principle) Let $f_1, \ldots, f_k$ be the solutions of the empirical risk minimization in the function classes F_i. SRM chooses the function class F_i (and the function f_i) such that an upper bound on the generalization error is minimized which can be computed making use of theorems such as the following one.

Theorem 4 (Expected Risk Upper bound) Let **h** denote the VC dimension of the function class **F** and let R_{emp} be defined by using the "0/1 loss." For all delta > 0 and $f \in F$ the inequality bounding the risk

$$R[f] \leq R_{emp}[f] + [(\mathbf{h}/n)(ln\,(2n/\mathbf{h}) + 1) - (1/n)\,ln\,(\delta/4)]^{1/2}$$

holds with probability of at least $1-\delta$ for n > **h** ([115,116]). For a derivation of this relation see Sec. 11.3.3. Note: this bound is only an example and similar formulations are available for other loss functions [116] and other complexity measures [127].

Thus, in the effort to minimize the generalization error $R[f]$ two extremes can arise: i) a very small function class (like F_1) yields a vanishing square root term, but a large training error might remain, while ii) a huge function class (like F_k) may give a vanishing empirical error but a large square root term. The best class is usually in between, as one would like to obtain a function that explains the data quite well and to have a small risk in obtaining that function. This is very much in analogy to the bias-variance dilemma scenario described for neural networks (see, e.g., [128]).

What these bounds universally indicate is that the minimized generalization error is bounded by a balance between training error and size of function class (i.e., structural risk). The standard SVM formulation (described in Sec. 11.4) directly implements such an optimization problem by balancing such terms using a Lagrangian formalism, and allowing for kernel selection model fitting via choice of kernel parameter selected according to minimal generalization error.

11.3.3 The Mathematics of the Feasibility of Learning
The question of whether D tells us anything outside of D that we didn't know before has two different answers: D cannot tell us something outside of D with certainty, but D can tell us something *likely* about f outside of D.

It is in a probabilistic view (not deterministic) that we can show the feasibility of learning. The only assumption in the probabilistic framework is that the examples in D are generated independently (or, minimally, exchangeably).

11.3.3.1 The Hoeffding Inequality

Here's a form of the Hoeffding Inequality used in what follows:

(11.1) $$P(\,|\bar{X}\text{-}E[\bar{X}]| \geq k) \leq 2e^{-2nk^2}$$

This can be understood in relation to the classic problem of drawing N samples from a Bin containing red and green marbles (Fig. 11.13).

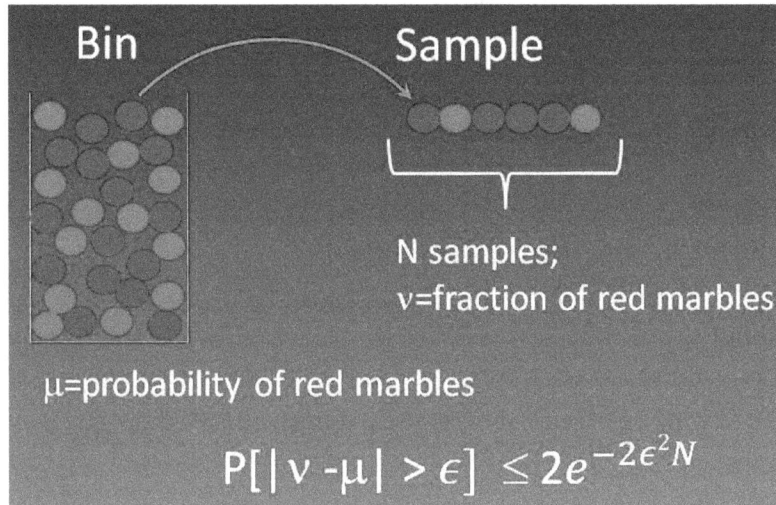

Fig. 11.13. The Hoeffding Inequality can be reduced to $P[|v - \mu| > \epsilon] \leq 2e^{-2\epsilon^2 N}$, where this is the version of the Hoeffding inequality with range $[0,1]$, and values $\{0,1\}$, where red is '1'. The bin can be large, small, finite, or … infinite.

11.3.3.2 Hoeffding inequality is related to Chebyshev Inequality

1853/1867 Bienayme/Chebyshev: $P(|X-E(X)| > k) \leq Var(X)/k^2$.

1963 Wassily Hoeffding: $P(|\bar{X}-E[\bar{X}]| \geq k) \leq 2e^{-2nk^2}$

More Formally: Let $X_1,\ldots,X_n$ be independent random variables. Assume that the X_i are almost surely bounded: $P(X_i \epsilon [a_i,b_i])=1$. Define the empirical mean of the sequence of variables as: $\bar{X} = \frac{1}{n}(X_1+\ldots+X_n)$.

Hoeffding [59] proves the following (relations critical to the theory underpinning SVMs, the entire field of classifiers, statistical learning (below), and is used in the proof of the feasibility of learning – further details in App. C):

$$P(\bar{X}-E[\bar{X}] \geq k) \leq \exp(-\frac{2n^2 k^2}{\sum_{i=1}^{n}(b_i-ai)^2})$$

$$P(|\bar{X}-E[\bar{X}]| \geq k) \leq 2\exp(-\frac{2n^2 k^2}{\sum_{i=1}^{n}(b_i-ai)^2})$$

For each X almost surely bounded have another relation if E(X)=0 known as the Hoeffding Lemma:

$$E[e^{\lambda X}] \leq \exp(\frac{\lambda^2 (b-a)^2}{8})$$

11.3.3.3 Sample Error

In-Sample Error ("v"): $E_{in}(h)$ = (fraction of D where f and h disagree)

$$= \frac{1}{N} \sum_{n=1}^{N} [h(x_n) \neq f(x_n)],$$

where "[...]"=1 if true, else = 0.

Out-of-Sample Error ("μ"): $E_{out}(h) = P[h(x) \neq f(x)]$.

So, from Hoeffding:

(11.2) $\qquad P(\ |E_{in}(h)- E_{out}(h)| \geq \epsilon) \leq 2e^{-2N\epsilon^2}$, for any $\epsilon > 0$.

This result is for one hypothesis h from H={h_1,...,h_M}. Instead of Hoeffding in terms of generalization error on some h in H, want in terms of error on g, the final hypothesis based on D, where g has to be one of the h_M. Using the union-bound property we can obtain an error bound for g:

$$|E_{in}(g)- E_{out}(g)| > \epsilon \Rightarrow |E_{in}(h_1)- E_{out}(h_1)| > \epsilon \text{ OR .....OR } |E_{in}(hM)- E_{out}(h_M)| > \epsilon$$

Note: If $X \Rightarrow Y$ ("X implies Y"), then $P[X] \leq P[Y]$.
Union Bound Rule: $P(X \text{ or } Y \text{ or } ... \text{ or } Z) \leq P[X] + P[Y] + ... + P[Z]$ (weak bound since it doesn't count overlapping). Thus:

(11.3) $\qquad P(\ |E_{in}(g)- E_{out}(g)| > \epsilon) \leq 2Me^{-2N\epsilon^2}$

where M can be thought of as a measure of the complexity of the hypothesis set H.

11.3.3.4 The Generalization Bound (establishes 1st ML Law for |H|<∞)

If M is a measure of the complexity of the hypothesis space, then the relation:

(11.4) $\qquad P(\ |E_{in}(g)- E_{out}(g)| > \epsilon) \leq 2Me^{-2N\epsilon^2}$

tells us about a hypothesis-complexity/generalization-error-minimization trade-off in the hypothesis space selection: the more complex the H, the better (smaller) the $E_{in}(g)$, but the greater its complexity M. So seek the lowest complexity hypothesis space that still has small $E_{in}(g)$, to obtain a small $E_{out}(g)$..... This is, in this context, basically a restatement of Occam's Razor (*lex parsimoniae*, ~1200AD, the law of parsimony, also traces to Ptolemy and Aristotle).

The probabilistic form of the relation is not clear, so let's restate it as:

With probability at least $(1-2Me^{-2N\epsilon^2})\equiv(1-\delta)$ have $|E_{in}(g)-E_{out}(g)| \leq \epsilon$, and in terms of δ:

$$(11.5) \qquad E_{out}(g) \leq E_{in}(g) + \sqrt{\frac{1}{2N}\ln\frac{2M}{\delta}}$$

This bound on the generalization error is often referred to as the "generalization bound". Now the trade-off is clearer, to have $E_{out}(g)$ small we simultaneously need $E_{in}(g)$ to be small and M to be not so huge that its log can't be eliminated with a 'reasonable-sized' sample N. For most cases of interest, however, $|H|=\infty$, even the simple perceptron...... the problem is the union bound has grossly overestimated by assuming no overlap (e.g., complete independence) between the hypotheses in the hypothesis set (an infinitesimal shift in the perceptron's decision hyperplane is counted as an entirely non-overlapping hypothesis...).

11.3.3.5 The VC Generalization Bound (establ. 1st ML Law for $|H|=\infty$)
When accounting for overlapping (non-independent) hypothesis, does the value 'M' still go to infinity? Typically it does not. To account for the overlaps with the binary classifier consider the following notation:

Define the 'growth function' for the binary classifier $(h(x)\rightarrow\{\pm1\})$:
$m_H(N) = \max_{x_1,...,xN\in x} |H(x_1,...,xN)|$, where the "$|...|$" operation is set cardinality.
So, have $m_H(N) \leq 2^N$. The question becomes, does the growth function continue to grow exponentially as $N\rightarrow\infty$? Here's a promising step in that direction. It is found that any growth function with a break point (k in what follows) is bounded by a polynomial:
If $m_H(k) < 2^k$ for some value k, then

$$m_H(N) \leq \sum_{i=1}^{k-1}\binom{N}{i}, \forall N, \text{ where N choose I in this context has degree k-1.}$$

Definition: The Vapnik-Chervonenkis dimension of a hypothesis set H, denoted by $d_{VC}(H)$, or just d, is the largest value of N for which $m_H(N) = 2^N$. Since k= d+1, can simplify $\sum_{i=1}^{d}\binom{N}{i}$ to N^d+1, and can then write:
$$(11.6) \qquad m_H(N) \leq N^d+1$$

The VC Dimension and Generalization
The VC dimension of the perceptron is only 3, because only up to three points in the plane, with arbitrary labels, will always be separable by a line, e.g., with four or more points can have non-separable situations. So can we just use $m_H(N)$ in place of M now that we know it is generally polynomial bound? It turns out there are some subtleties that lead to some of the constants involved changing, but otherwise, YES (for exact derivation see the App. in the book by Abu-Mostafa et al. [64]). WE thus arrive at the following:

For any tolerance $\delta > 0$ have $E_{out}(g) \leq E_{in}(g) + \sqrt{\frac{8}{N} \ln \frac{4m_H(2N)}{\delta}}$,

Where $m_H(N)$ is polynomially bound, so $\frac{1}{N} \ln(poly\ N) \rightarrow 0$ as $N \rightarrow \infty$, have feasibility of learning with infinitely large hypothesis spaces H.

11.3.4 Lagrangian Optimization

The margin width can be easily determined by simply using a point on H_+ (the positive support vector boundary – e.g., the positive face of the hyperplane) as reference and taking the nearest point on H_- (similarly for negative face) (Fig.11.15 will have further details). Consider $x_i^{(+)}$ a feature vector from x_i that has $y_i = +1$, and that resides on ("supports") the H_+ boundary (e.g., a support vector). Likewise for the $x_i^{(-)}$, that is orthogonally positioned, will have $(x_i^{(+)} - x_i^{(-)}) \bullet \omega = 2$.

Since $(x_i^{(+)} - x_i^{(-)})$ is perpendicular to the hyperplane the distance between the hyperplanes is given by $d = \| (x_i^{(+)} - x_i^{(-)}) \| = 2/\| \omega \|$.

A variational derivation of the result $d = 2/\| \omega \|$, the distance between hyperplanes H_+ and H_- will be instructive for those not familiar with Lagrangians, and will be shown next. The variational derivation will provide a refresher on methods to be used in what follows. In Fig. 11.14 we show a line in 2-D space.

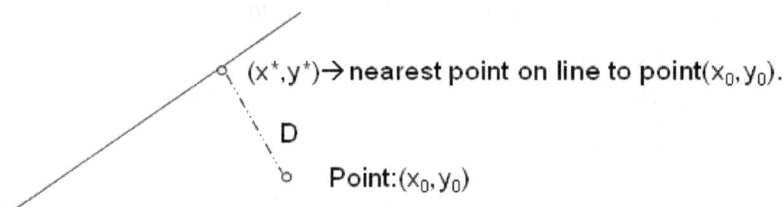

Fig. 11.14. Line Ax+By+C=0 and a nearby point. $D = \sqrt{(x^* - x_0)^2 + (y^* - y_0)^2}$

Want to minimize D subject to constraint $Ax^* + By^* + C = 0$ (i.e., that the nearest point to (x_0, y_0) reside on the line. This suggests the following Lagrangian formulation:

(11.7) $\qquad L(x^*, y^*, \alpha) = D(x^*, y^*) + \alpha\ [Ax^* + By^* + C]$

The Lagrangian solution is obtained by minimizing L on choice of $\{x^*, y^*\}$, i.e., minimize $D(x^*, y^*)$, but subject to the constraint $Ax^* + By^* + C = 0$ (encapsulated in the term with the Lagrange Multiplier):

$\frac{\partial L}{\partial \alpha} = [Ax^* + By^* + C]$, requiring $\frac{\partial L}{\partial \alpha} = 0$ then restores constraint, other variations yield:

$$0 = \frac{\partial L}{\partial x^*} = \frac{(x^* - x_0)}{D} + \alpha\ A; \qquad 0 = \frac{\partial L}{\partial y^*} = \frac{(y^* - y_0)}{D} + \alpha\ B$$

$$\frac{(x^* - x_0)^2}{D^2} = \alpha^2 A^2; \qquad \frac{(y^* - y_0)^2}{D^2} = \alpha^2 B^2 \Rightarrow 1 = \alpha^2 (A^2 + B^2)$$

And, with other set of equations from grouping extremal equations multiplied by A (or B) instead of squaring, it is then possible to solve to get:

(11.8)
$$D = \frac{Ax_0 + By_0 + C}{\sqrt{A^2 + B^2}}$$

Generalization from 2-D space to m-D space is to $|Ax_0 + By_0 + C| \rightarrow |\omega \bullet x - b|$ which will be $|\omega \bullet x - b| = 1$ for the geometries we have described, so simplifies significantly. For the 'ω' parameters in H_0 (same as in H_+) have:

$$\sqrt{A^2 + B^2} \rightarrow \sqrt{\sum_k w_k^2} == \|\omega\|$$

So, $D = 1/\|\omega\|$ from H_+ to H_0, and thus twice that for H_+ to H_-; and, thus, $d = 2/\|\omega\|$ as before.

11.3.5 The Support Vector Machine (SVM) – Lagrangian with SRM

A Support Vector Machine (SVM) is a machine learning classification method with robust learning and minimal overtraining concerns. SVMs can also be used for bootstrap clustering. A fundamental constraint on SVM learning is the management of the training set. This is because the order of computations during the learning process typically goes as the square of the size of the training set. In Ch. 14 we examine experimental data involving a nanopore detector, where 150-component feature data is gathered on individual molecules (that are drawn into the nanopore). SVM training data can be produced by the nanopore detector in prodigious amounts, to arrive at a set of 150-component feature vectors that number from 10,000 to 100,000, depending on the number of molecular classes being examined for a particular application. For the 150-component feature data examined here, training sets of 1000 (500 positives and 500 negatives, for example) can be managed on a PC without hard-drive I/O thrashing. Training sets of 10,000 or more, however, can't be managed with a single PC-based resource. For this reason most SVM implementations must contend with some kind of *chunking* process to learn parts of the data at a time. In later sections, results show that chunk aliasing and outlier accumulation may pose problems for distributed SVM learning. The results also present new methods and how they offer a stable learning solution to these problems at minimal cost. One of those methods extends the learning process with modified alpha-selection heuristics that enable a support-vector reduction phase. What is not as commonly discussed about *distributed* SVM learning are the details of the distributed, or approximately parallel, chunk processing methods. The distributed SVM described here was implemented using Java RMI, and was developed to run on a network of multi-core computers.

As mentioned previously Support Vector Machines are discriminators that use structural risk minimization to find a decision hyperplane with a maximum margin between separate groupings of feature vectors [115]. When SVMs were first implemented in 1995, a quadratic programming algorithm was used [114]. This was slow and only small datasets could be run with them. In 1998, Platt implemented sequential minimal optimization (SMO), which is an algorithm that uses incremental (minimal) learning steps in a Lagrangian implementation to bypass having to use a quadratic algorithm (to be implemented in Sec. 11.4.1) [118,119]. The SMO SVM iterates through the dataset comparing and updating the Lagrange multipliers two at a time. SMO typically provides a significant increase in the speed of learning (once trained, SVM classification is at the speed of computation for an inner-product calculation on the features vectors, here amounting to 150 multiplications). If a GPU is used this can be reduced further, to the time of computing one multiplication (where the inner product multiplications are done in parallel). Although the SMO implementation did much to advance the feasibility and ease-of-use of SVM classifiers, there has still been the key constraint of computing the kernel matrix, which is quadratic in the size of the training data. In the sections that follow we introduce (i) the standard binary SVM; kernel variants; (iii) alpha-selection-variants (including simple chunking); chunking methods; and a synopsis of previous work with a multiclass SVM formulation. The work with the multiclass formulation provides a clear example of the importance of managing and tracking SV's (and other feature vector categories) during the learning process. The importance of tracking the SV's during the learning process will be revisited in the distributed learning results presented in the Results section..

Kernel modeling and other Tuning

The so-called curse of dimensionality from statistics says that the difficulty of an estimation problem increases drastically with the dimension N of the space, since in principle as N increases, the number of required patterns to sample grows exponentially. This statement may cast doubts on using higher dimensional feature vectors as input to learning machines. This must be balanced with results from statistical learning theory [129], however, that show that the likelihood of data separability by linear learning machines is proportional to their dimensionality.

Thus, instead of working in the R^N, one can design algorithms to work in feature space, F, where the data has much higher dimension (but with sufficiently small function class). This can be described via the following mapping

$$\Phi: R^N \rightarrow F ; x \rightarrow \Phi(x).$$

Consider the prior training description with data $x_1, \ldots, x_n \in R^N$ is mapped into a potentially much higher dimensional feature space F. For a given learning algorithm one now considers the same algorithm in F instead of R^N. Hence, the learning machine works with the following:

$$(\Phi(x_1), y_1), \ldots, (\Phi(x_n), y_n) \in F \times Y, Y = \{\pm 1\}$$

It is important to note that this mapping is also implicitly done for (one hidden layer) neural networks, radial basis networks [130] and boosting algorithms [65,131] where the input data is mapped to some representation given by the hidden layer, the radial basis function (RBF) bumps or the hypotheses space, respectively.

As mentioned above, the dimensionality of the data does not detract us from finding a good solution, but it is rather the complexity of the function class F that contributes the most to the complexity of the problem. Similarly, in practice, one need never know the mapping function Φ. Therefore, the complexity and intractability of computing the actual mapping is also irrelevant to the complexity of the problem of classification. To this end, algorithms are transformed via a kernel generalization to take advantage of this aspect of the method.

Kernel construction using polarization

The kernels used in the analysis are based on a family of previously developed kernels [37,45], here referred to as 'Occam's Razor', or 'Razor' kernels. As will be seen, the Gaussian kernel is included in the family of Razor kernels. All of the Razor kernels examined perform strongly on the channel current data analyzed, with some regularly outperforming the Gaussian Kernel itself. The kernels fall into two classes: regularized distance (squared) kernels; and regularized information divergence kernels. The first set of kernels strongly models data with classic, geometric, attributes or interpretation. The second set of kernels is constrained to operate on $(R^+)^N$, the feature space of positive, non-zero, real-valued feature vector components. The space of the latter kernels is often also restricted to feature vectors obeying an L_1-norm = 1 constraint, i.e., the feature vector is a discrete probability vector.

Given any metric space (X, d) one can build a positive-definite kernel of the form $e^{-\lambda d^2}$. Conversely, any positive definite kernel with form $e^{-\lambda d^2}$ must have a 'd' that is a metric (this is Mercer's condition in another form). This suggests that the 'simplest' kernel is the Gaussian kernel, since the 'simplest' distance, the Euclidean distance, is used. Functional variations on the Gaussian kernel are described in what follows (see [37] for further details), including variations that are no-longer represented as distances (non-metric), but that operate on a constrained domain and provide a positive definite kernel (or close enough). In what follows a quick synopsis is given of the novel kernels that are used – two of these kernels regularly outperformed the Gaussian kernel (and all other kernels), as will be shown in the following.

Tuning is needed to optimize the choice of kernel & kernel-parameter used by the SVM. This is often handled simply by ranging over a collection of roughly 10 kernel types and each at roughly 10 kernel parameter setting (where each is single-parameter kernel), and to do this only on smaller test sets in the training data, where the time complexity of the SVM training is directly tied to the training-kernel computation, which is quadratic in the number of training instances. Although caching can modify the assumptions on time-complexity, there is generally an approximately quadratic time-complexity in the size of the training instances regardless. Chunking must be used to break past this, or more extensive use of GPU capabilities (still need to eventually do chunking). Chunking algorithms will be shown to be effective, but susceptible to training-failure pathologies if certain safeguards aren't observed, as will be discussed.

Once the small test set is done on the initial kernel screening indicated above, a sub-set of kernels will emerge as best, and these are considered again with larger training sets, eventually allowing selection of a good choice of kernel and kernel parameter. More directed tuning paradigms typically involve simulated annealing in this setting (to be shown later). Algorithmic and implementation parameters can also be considered in the tuning, which means we now have a collage of different parameter types in a coupled optimization task. For this type of generalization, genetic algorithms have been applied with amazing success (but not shown in what follows). These more sophisticated tuning methods may not always be necessary in the SVM classification applications but will allow for successful classifications in some situations where simple methods do not, and in the SVM-based clustering methods to be described in what follows these tuning methods generally play an important role. Further details on the tuning methods themselves are described in Ch. 12.

In [45], novel, information-theoretic, kernels were introduced for notably better performance over standard kernels – especially when discrete probability distributions or other constrained feature vectors were used as the feature vector data. The use of probability vectors, and L_1-norm feature vectors in general, turns out to be a very general formulation, wherein feature extraction makes use of signal decomposition into a complete set of separable states that can be interpreted or represented as a probability vector (or normalized collection of such, or concatenation, then normalization, etc.). A probability vector formulation also provides a straightforward hand-off to the SVM classifiers since all feature vectors have the same length with such an approach. What this means for the SVM, however, is that geometric notions of distance are no longer the best measure for comparing feature vectors. For probability vectors (i.e., discrete distributions), the best measures of similarity are the various information-theoretic divergences: Kullback–Leibler, Renyi, etc. By symmetrizing over the arguments of those divergences a rich source of kernels is obtained that works well with the types of probabilistic data obtained, as shown in [1].

The SVM Lagranigian formulation and kernel incorporation are described in what follows. The SVM discriminators are trained by solving their KKT relations using the Sequential Minimal Optimization (SMO) procedure [18,119], shown in what follows. Multi-class SVM training is also explored and involves thousands of blockade signatures for each signal class. A chunking variant of SMO (similar to [134,135]) also is employed to manage the large SVM training task. Data rejection heuristics are also explored.

For the binary SVM and 'single-class' SVM, SRM can be simply implemented via a maximal margin on the boundaries indicated, for the multiclass SVM there is the additional constraint used in the multiclass method in Sec. 11.7 that the decision hypersurface distances to a common origin be minimized (this remarkable and practical constraint allows the optimization equations to decouple, and the *multiclass* SVM to be easily implemented on a computer). This can be implemented with a variety of variations, including simply requiring a square term to be minimized that will do the necessary decoupling.

11.3.6 SVM Binary Classifier Derivation
Support Vector Machines (SVMs) use a Lagrangian formulation to construct a separating hyperplane (see Fig. 11.15), surrounded by the thickest margin, using a set of training data represented as feature vectors. Prediction is made according to some measure of the "distance" between the test data and the hyperplane. Complex pattern-classification problems can be transformed into a new feature space where the patterns are more likely to be linearly separable, provided that the transformation itself is nonlinear and that the feature space is in a high enough dimension [133]. The SVM construction described in what follows achieves such a transformation by choosing a qualified kernel.

Linear Binary SVM: N training data "points" (feature vectors with binary labels), are denoted:

$$\{(\vec{x}_1, y_1), (\vec{x}_2, y_2), ..., (\vec{x}_n, y_n)\}, \ \vec{x}_i \in \Re^m, \mathbf{y_i = \pm 1}$$

One possible assumption to proceed: The positive and negative labeled data ($\mathbf{y_i = \pm 1}$) is sufficiently separable and grouped as positives and negatives, that notions such as positive and negative data clusters, and a hyperplane separating them, are meaningful. This is accomplished by finding a separating hyperplane between positives and negatives, $y_i = \pm 1$ (see Fig. 11.15), where we assume full separability possible with choice of feature vector ($f.v.$) components:

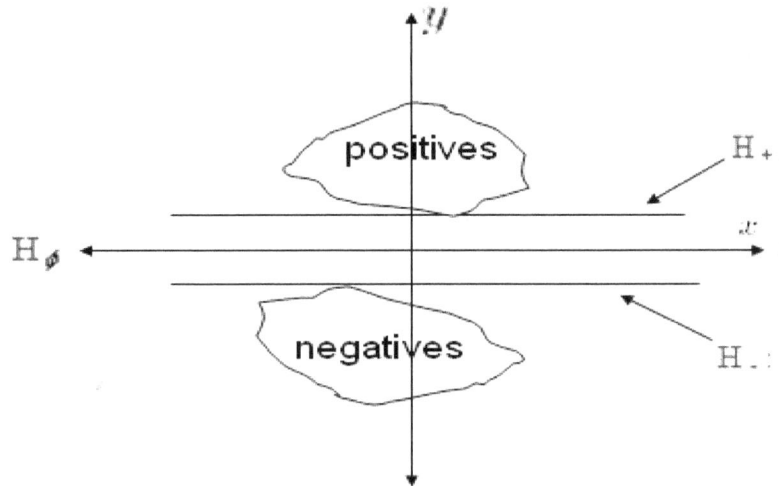

Fig. 11.15. Hyperplane Separability. H_ϕ : $y = \bar{\omega} \cdot \bar{x} - b = 0$

All horizontal hyperplanes in Fig. 11.15 are parallel, $H_\phi \| H_+ \| H_-$ so all have hyperplanes proportional to $\bar{\omega}$. So, have without loss of generality:

$$H_+: \quad y = \bar{\omega} \cdot \bar{x} - b_+ = 0$$
$$H_-: \quad y = \bar{\omega} \cdot \bar{x} - b_- = 0$$

Again, rescaling, to bring into the form for fully separable binary data ($\bar{x}_i, y_i$):

(11.9)
$$\bar{\omega} \cdot \bar{x} - b \geq +1 \text{ for } y_i = +1$$
$$\bar{\omega} \cdot \bar{x} - b \leq -1 \text{ for } y_i = -1$$

Or, unifying:

(11.10)
$$y_i (\bar{\omega} \cdot \bar{x} - b) - 1 \geq 0 \ \forall i$$

This is the constraint that must be satisfied for separable (binary) data (in this formulation).

In the binary SVM implementation described in what follows we follow the notation and conventions used previously [37]. Feature vectors are denoted by x_{ik}, where index i labels the feature vectors ($1 \leq i \leq M$) and index k labels the N feature vector components ($1 \leq k \leq N$). For the binary SVM, labeling of training data is done using label variable $y_i = \pm 1$ (with sign according to whether the training instance was from the positive or negative class). For hyperplane separability, elements of the training set must satisfy the following conditions: $w_\beta x_{i\beta} - b \geq +1$ for i such that $y_i = +1$, and $w_\beta x_{i\beta} - b \leq -1$ for $y_i = -1$, for some values of the coefficients $w_1, ..., w_N$, and b (*using the convention of implied sum on repeated Greek indi-*

ces). This can be written more concisely as: $y_i(w_\beta x_{i\beta} - b) - 1 \geq 0$. Data points that satisfy the equality in the above are known as "support vectors" (or "active constraints").

Once training is complete, discrimination is based solely on position relative to the discriminating hyperplane: $w_\beta x_{i\beta} - b = 0$. The boundary hyperplanes on the two classes of data are separated by a distance $2/w$, known as the "margin," where $w^2 = w_\beta w_\beta$. By increasing the margin between the separated data as much as possible the optimal separating hyperplane is obtained. In the usual SVM formulation, the goal to maximize w^{-1} is restated as the goal to minimize w^2. The Lagrangian variational formulation then selects an optimum defined at a saddle point of

$$(11.12) \qquad L(w, b; \alpha) = \frac{w_\beta w_\beta}{2} - \alpha_\gamma y_\gamma (w_\beta w_{\gamma\beta} - b) - \alpha_0 \; ,$$

$$\text{where } \alpha_0 = \sum_\gamma \alpha_\gamma \; , \; \alpha_\gamma \geq 0 \quad (1 \leq \gamma \leq M)$$

The saddle point is obtained by minimizing with respect to $\{w_1,...,w_N,b\}$ and maximizing with respect to $\{\alpha_1, ..., \alpha_M\}$. If $y_i(w_\beta x_{i\beta} - b) - 1 \geq 0$, then maximization on α_i is achieved for $\alpha_i = 0$. If $y_i(w_\beta x_{i\beta} - b) - 1 = 0$, then there is no constraint on α_i. If $y_i(w_\beta x_{i\beta} - b) - 1 < 0$, there is a constraint violation, and $\alpha_i \to \infty$. These three relations are known as the Karush-Kuhn-Tucker, or KKT, relations. If absolute separability is possible, the last case will eventually be eliminated for all α_i, otherwise it is natural to limit the size of α_i by some constant upper bound, i.e., $\max(\alpha_i) = C$, for all i. This is equivalent to another set of inequality constraints with $\alpha_i \leq C$. Introducing sets of Lagrange multipliers, ξ_γ and $\mu_\gamma (1 \leq \gamma \leq M)$, to achieve this, the Lagrangian becomes:

$$(11.13) \quad L(w, b; \alpha, \xi, \mu) = \frac{w_\beta w_\beta}{2} - \alpha_\gamma [y_\gamma (w_\beta x_{\gamma\beta} - b) + \xi_\gamma] + \alpha_0 + \xi_0 C - \mu_\gamma \xi_\gamma$$

$$\text{where } \xi_0 = \sum_\gamma \xi_\gamma \; , \; \alpha_0 = \sum_\gamma \alpha_\gamma \text{ and } \alpha_\gamma \geq 0 \text{ and } \xi_\xi \geq 0 \quad (1 \leq \gamma \leq M)$$

At the variational minimum on the $\{w_1,...,w_N,b\}$ variables, $w_\beta = \alpha_\gamma y_\gamma x_{\gamma\beta}$, and the Lagrangian simplifies to:

$$(11.14) \qquad L(\alpha) = \alpha_0 - \frac{\alpha_\delta y_\delta x_{\delta\beta} \alpha_\gamma y_\gamma x_{\gamma\beta}}{2} \; ,$$

with $0 \leq \alpha_\gamma \leq C \quad (1 \leq \gamma \leq M)$ and $\alpha_\gamma y_\gamma = 0$, where only the variations that maximize in terms of the α_γ remain (known as the Wolfe Transformation).

Thus, the Wolfe Dual Calculations, with or without slack variable, have the form (with sums explicit):

$$(11.15) \qquad \tilde{L}(\alpha) = \sum_i \alpha_i - \frac{1}{2}\sum_{i,j} \alpha_i \alpha_j y_i y_j \bar{x}_i \cdot \bar{x}_j \; , \; \alpha_i \geq 0$$

where we want to find the α's that maximize L(α). Similarly, for the L_σ Dual:

$$(11.16) \qquad \tilde{L}_\sigma(\alpha) = \sum_i \alpha_i - \frac{1}{2}\sum_{i,j} \alpha_i \alpha_j y_i y_j \bar{x}_i \cdot \bar{x}_j \; , \; C \geq \alpha_i \geq 0$$

So, the duals are the same, with or without start variable, aside from the $C \geq \alpha_i$ (max $(\alpha) \leq C$) constraint.

In the Wolfe Dual form the computational task can be greatly simplified. By introducing an expression for the discriminating hyperplane: $f_i = w_\beta x_{i\beta} - b = \alpha_\gamma y_\gamma x_{\gamma\beta} x_{i\beta} - b$, the variational solution for $L(\alpha)$ reduces to the following set of KKT relations:

(11.17)
$$\begin{aligned} &(i) \ \alpha_i = 0 \, , \, y_i f_i \geq 1 \\ &(ii) \ 0 < \alpha_i < C \, , \, y_i f_i = 1 \\ &(iii) \ \alpha_i = C \, , \, y_i f_i \leq 1 \end{aligned}$$

When the KKT relations are satisfied for all of the α_γ (with $\alpha_\gamma y_\gamma = 0$ maintained) the solution is achieved. The constraint $\alpha_\gamma y_\gamma = 0$ is satisfied for the initial choice of multipliers by setting the α's associated with the positive training instances to $1/N(+)$ and the α's associated with the negatives to $1/N(-)$, where $N(+)$ is the number of positives and $N(-)$ is the number of negatives. Once the Wolfe transformation is performed it is apparent that the training data (support vectors in particular, KKT class (ii) above) enter into the Lagrangian solely via the inner product $x_{i\beta} x_{j\beta}$. Likewise, the discriminator f_i, and KKT relations, are also dependent on the data solely via the $x_{i\beta} x_{j\beta}$ inner product.

Generalization of the SVM formulation to data-dependent inner products other than $x_{i\beta} x_{j\beta}$ are possible and are usually formulated in terms of the family of symmetric positive definite functions (reproducing kernels) satisfying Mercer's conditions [15].

To see the origin of the KKT relations more clearly, consider the SVM Lagrangian with multipliers for the collection of separability constraints on solutions: $y_i(\omega \bullet x - b) - 1 \geq 0 \ \forall i$. For SRM we then need to maximize $d = 2/\|\omega\|$, or minimize $\|\omega\|^2$, which is chosen due to simplifications in the formalism that follows (i.e., if we max $2/\|\omega\|$ by min on $\|\omega\|$, it could just as well be done with min on $\|\omega\|^2$). The Lagrangian formulation then should have one multiplier constraint for each training instance, where $y_i(\omega \bullet x - b) - 1 \geq 0$, and minimize on $\|\omega\|^2$ overall, so:

(11.18)
$$L(\bar{\omega}, b, \bar{\alpha}) = \frac{1}{2} \|\omega\|^2 - \sum_i \alpha_i [y_i(\omega x_i - b) - 1], \alpha_i \geq 0$$

As with the practice Lagrangian described earlier, we seek to minimize L on $\{\bar{\omega}, b\}$ and to extremize (maximize in this case) L on $\{\bar{\alpha}\}$, i.e., what results is a minimization -- maximization saddle-point optimization for the solution. Note how the inequality constraints above differ from the distance-to-line problem. In the latter case, the constant was an exact equality ($Ax^* + By^* + C = 0$) (as with the common holonomic constraints in theoretical physics), and the term entering the Lagrangian was: "$\alpha [Ax^* + By^* + C]$", and the recovery of the constraint from $\partial L / \partial \alpha = 0$ was straightforward. Now, however, the Lagrange multipliers are no longer free to be negative (recall the $\alpha = \pm (A^2 + B^2)^{-1}$ solution before). Now the α's are restricted to be positive, and the term entering the Lagrangian has an overall negative in front: "$-\alpha_i [y_i(\omega_i x_i - b) - 1]$". To understand the inequality constraint recovery, and with it the

Karush-Kuhn-Tucker (KKT) relations, we must consider the overall influence on the Lagrangian in its saddle-point approximation when three possibilities are considered:

- If $[y_i(\omega \cdot x_i - b) - 1] > 0$ (constraint satisfied), then maximization (on α_i's) for $\sum_i \alpha_i [y_i(\omega x_i - b) - 1]$ is achieved for $\alpha_i \to 0$ (since $\alpha_i \geq 0$ constraint).

- If $[y_i(\omega \cdot x_i - b) - 1] = 0$ (constraint satisfied, a support vector), then there is no constraint on α_i.

- If $[y_i(\omega \cdot x_i - b) - 1] < 0$, then $\alpha_i \to \infty$.

The last case, $[y_i(\omega \cdot \bar{x}_i - b) - 1] < 0$, is an example of where the constraint is not satisfied. For completely separable data this case will not occur in the solution, but may occur when incrementally optimizing to achieve that selection. As we shall see, non-separable (perfectly) data can have constraint violations in the solution. How is this managed if the Lagrangian optimization will drive the associated Lagrange multipliers to larger and larger positive values ($\alpha_i \to \infty$)? The answer is to establish a max α cut off: $\max(\alpha_i) = C$. In practice, the max α cut off is usually imposed whether or not you have separable or non-separable data, and thus we have:

(11.19) $\quad L = \frac{1}{2}\|\omega\|^2 - \sum_i \alpha_i [y_i(\omega x_i - b) - 1], \alpha_i \geq 0, \alpha_i \leq C \quad (C - \alpha_i \geq 0)$

The $(C - \alpha_i \geq 0)$ constraint can itself be absorbed into the Lagrangian:

(11.20) $\quad L = \frac{1}{2}\|\omega\|^2 - \sum_i \alpha_i [y_i(\omega x_i - b) - 1] + \sum \sigma(C - \alpha_i), \sigma_i \geq 0, \alpha_i \geq 0$

This can be rewritten where the role of the new Lagrange multiplier is much more apparent:

(11.21) $\quad L = \frac{1}{2}\|\omega\|^2 - \sum_i \alpha_i [y_i(\omega \cdot x_i - b) - 1 + \sigma_i] + C\sum \sigma_i, \sigma_i \geq 0, \alpha_i \geq 0$

The revised form relates back to an initial formulation with constraints:

(11.22)
$$\omega \cdot x_i - b \geq 1 - \sigma_i \text{ for } y_i = +1$$
$$\omega \cdot x_i - b \leq -1 + \sigma_i \text{ for } y_i = -1$$

So, the Lagrange multiplier σ_i, introduced to deal with the $\max(\alpha_i) = C$ constraint, can be interpreted as a "slack variable" (see Fig. 11.16):

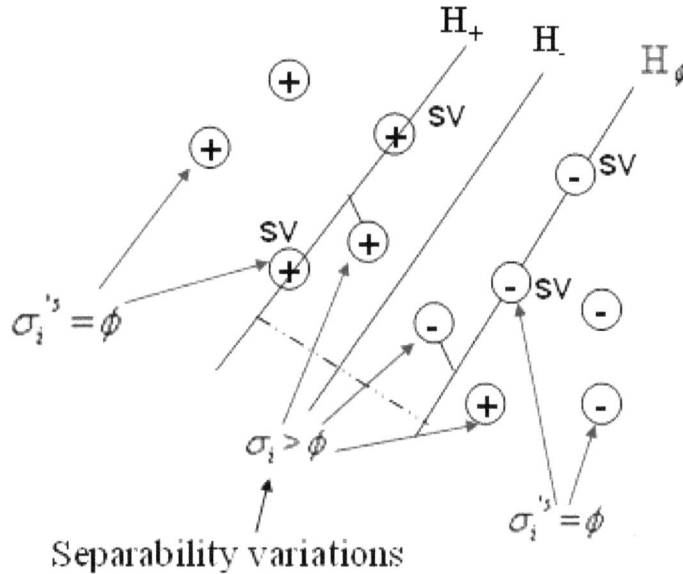

Separability variations

Fig. 11.16. If C>α_i,$\sigma_i \rightarrow \phi$; If C=α_i,σ_i free($\geq \phi$) ; If C<α_i,$\sigma_i \rightarrow \infty$

With the $\alpha^{'s}$ we have more control with$[y_i(\omega \cdot x_i - b) - 1]$, where previously $\alpha_i \rightarrow \infty$ resulted. Can now avoid with C<α_i condition by establishing initial conditions without C<α_i and maintaining those conditions as the Lagrangian optimization goes forward.

To recap, the Wolfe Dual Calculations, with or without slack variable, have the same form:

$$(11.23)\ L = \frac{1}{2}\|\omega\|^2 - \sum_i \alpha_i[y_i(\omega \cdot x_i - b) - 1]\ ,\ \alpha_i \geq 0$$

$$(11.24)\ L_\sigma = \frac{1}{2}\|\omega\|^2 - \sum_i \alpha_i[y_i(\omega \cdot x_i - b) - 1 + \sigma_i] + C\sum \sigma_i\ ,\ \sigma_i \geq 0, \alpha_i \geq 0$$

$$0 = \frac{\partial L}{\partial \omega_j} = \omega_j - \sum_i \alpha_i y_i(x_i)_j\ \forall_j \Rightarrow\ \bar{\omega} = \sum_i \alpha_i y_i \bar{x}_i$$

$$0 = \frac{\partial L}{\partial b} = \sum_i \alpha_i y_i \Rightarrow\ \sum_i \alpha_i y_i = \phi$$

$$\tilde{L} = \frac{1}{2}\sum_j (\sum_i \alpha_i y_i(x_i)_j)^2 - \sum_i \alpha_i y_i (\sum_j (\sum_i \alpha_i y_i(x_i)_j)(x_i)_j) + \sum_i \alpha_i$$

$$(11.25)\ \tilde{L}(\alpha) = \sum_i \alpha_i - \frac{1}{2}\sum_{i,j} \alpha_i \alpha_j y_i y_j \bar{x}_i \cdot \bar{x}_j\ ,\ \alpha_i \geq 0$$

where we want to find the $\alpha^{'s}$ that maximize L(α). Similarly, for the L_σ Dual:

$$L_\sigma \rightarrow \tilde{L}(\sigma, \alpha) = \sum_i \alpha_i - \frac{1}{2}\sum_{i,j} \alpha_i \alpha_j y_i y_j \bar{x}_i \cdot \bar{x}_j - \sum \sigma_i(\alpha_i - C)\ ,\ \sigma_i \geq 0, \alpha_i \geq 0$$

$$(11.26)\ \tilde{L}_\sigma(\alpha) = \sum_i \alpha_i - \frac{1}{2}\sum_{i,j} \alpha_i \alpha_j y_i y_j \vec{x}_i \cdot \vec{x}_j, \ C \geq \alpha_i \geq 0$$

So, the duals are the same aside from the $C \geq \alpha_i$ ($\max(\alpha) \leq C$) constraint.

11.4 SVM Binary Classifier Implementation
11.4.1 Sequential Minimal Optimization (SMO)

The SVM discriminators are trained by solving their KKT relations using the SMO procedure of [118,119]. The method described here follows the description of [118,119] and begins by selecting a pair of Lagrange multipliers, $\{\alpha_1, \alpha_2\}$, where at least one of the multipliers has a violation of its associated KKT relations. For simplicity it is assumed in what follows that the multipliers selected are those associated with the first and second feature vectors: $\{x_1, x_2\}$. The SMO procedure then "freezes" variations in all but the two selected Lagrange multipliers, permitting much of the computation to be circumvented by use of analytical reductions:

$$(11.27)\ \tilde{L}_\sigma(\vec{\alpha}) = \tilde{L}_\sigma(\alpha_1, \alpha_2; \alpha_3, ... \alpha_n) = (\alpha_1 + \alpha_2 + \sum_{i\geq 3} \alpha_i) - \frac{1}{2}(\alpha_1^2 k_{11} + \alpha_2^2 k_{22} + 2\alpha_1\alpha_2 s k_{12})$$

$$-\frac{1}{2}(2\alpha_1 y_1 \sum_{j\geq 3} \alpha_j y_j k_{1j} + 2\alpha_2 y_2 \sum_{j\geq 3} \alpha_j y_j k_{2j}) - \frac{1}{2}\sum_{j\geq 3, i\geq 3} \alpha_i \alpha_j y_i y_j k_{ij}$$

where $s = y_1 y_2$. Let $v_i = \sum_{j\geq 3} \alpha_j y_j k_{ij} = \vec{\omega} \cdot \vec{x}_i - \alpha_1 y_1 k_{i1} - \alpha_2 y_2 k_{i2}$

$$(11.28)\quad \tilde{L}_\sigma(\vec{\alpha}) = \alpha_1 + \alpha_2 - \frac{1}{2}(\alpha_1^2 k_{11} + \alpha_2^2 k_{22} + 2\alpha_1\alpha_2 s k_{12}) - \alpha_1 y_1 v_1 - \alpha_2 y_2 v_2$$

$$+\sum_{i\geq 3} \alpha_i - \frac{1}{2}\sum_{j\geq 3, i\geq 3} \alpha_i \alpha_j y_i y_j k_{ij}$$

Or, in shorthand notation:

(11.29)

$$L(\alpha_1, \alpha_2; \alpha_{\beta'\geq 3}) = \alpha_1 + \alpha_2 - \frac{(\alpha_1^2 K_{11} + \alpha_2^2 K_{22} + 2\alpha_1\alpha_2 y_1 y_2 K_{12})}{2} - \alpha_1 y_1 v_1 - \alpha_2 y_2 v_2$$

$$+\alpha_{\beta'} U_{\beta'} - \frac{\alpha_{\beta'} \alpha_{y'} y_{\beta'} y_{y'} K_{\beta'y'}}{2},$$

with $\beta', \gamma' \geq 3$, and where $K_{ij} \equiv K(x_i, x_j)$, and $v_i \equiv \alpha_{\beta'} y_{\beta'} K_{i\beta'}$ with $\beta' \geq 3$. U projects the sum on $\alpha_{\beta'}$ for $\beta' \geq 3$. Due to the constraint $\alpha_\beta y_\beta = 0$, we have the relation: $\alpha_1 + s\alpha_2 = -\gamma$, where $\gamma \equiv y_1 \alpha_{\beta'} y_{\beta'}$ with $\beta' \geq 3$ and $s \equiv y_1 y_2$.

Now consider variational parameters other than $\{\alpha_1, \alpha_2\}$ to be fixed in the $\{\alpha_1, \alpha_2\}$ variational optimization. Furthermore:

$$\sum_i y_i \alpha_i = 0 \Rightarrow y_1 \alpha_1 + y_2 \alpha_2 = -\sum_{i \geq 3} y_i \alpha_i \; ; \; (\alpha_1 + s\alpha_2) = \gamma$$

$$\gamma = -y\sum_{i \geq 3} y_i \alpha_i \; ; \quad \alpha_1 = \gamma - s\alpha_2$$

(11.30)

$$L(\alpha_2; \alpha_3, \dots \alpha_m) = (\gamma - s\alpha_2) + \alpha_2 - \frac{1}{2}((\gamma - s\alpha_2)^2 k_{11} + \alpha_2^2 k_{22} + 2\alpha_2(\gamma - s\alpha_2)sk_{12})$$

$$- (\gamma - s\alpha_2)y_1 v_1 - \alpha_2 y_2 v_2 + [\text{terms independent of } \{\alpha_1, \alpha_2\}]$$

$$0 = \frac{\partial L}{\partial \alpha_2} = (1-s) - \alpha_2^*(k_{11} + k_{22} - 2k_{12}) + s\gamma k_{11} - s\gamma k_{12} + sy_1 v_1 - y_2 v_2$$

Let: $-\eta = k_{11} + k_{22} - 2k_{12}$

α_2^*: new α , the optimization solution:

(11.31)
$$\alpha_2^* = \alpha_2 - y_2[\vec{\omega} \cdot x_1 - y_1 - (\vec{\omega} \cdot x_2 - y_2)]/\eta$$

Rewriting, and explicitly relating the new alpha to the old:

(11.32)
$$\alpha_2^{new} = \alpha_2^{old} - \frac{y_2((w_\beta x_{1\beta} - y_1) - (w_\beta x_{2\beta} - y_2))}{\eta}$$

Once α_2^{new} is obtained, the constraint $\alpha_2^{new} \leq C$ must be re-verified in conjunction with the $\alpha_\beta y_\beta = 0$ constraint. If the L ($\alpha_2; \alpha_{\beta'} \geq 3$) maximization leads to a α_2 new that grows too large, the new α_2 must be "clipped" to the maximum value satisfying the constraints. For example, if $y_1 \neq y_2$, then increases in α_2 are matched by increases in α_1. So, depending on whether α_2 or α_1 is nearer its maximum of C, we have max $(\alpha_2) = \text{argmin}\{\alpha_2 + (C - \alpha_2) ; \alpha_2 + (C - \alpha_1)\}$. Similar arguments provide the following boundary conditions:
(i) if s = -1, max(α_2) = argmin$\{\alpha_2 ; C + \alpha_2 - \alpha_1\}$, and min($\alpha_2$) = argmax$\{0 ; \alpha_2 - \alpha_1\}$, and (ii) if s = +1, max(α_2) = argmin$\{C ; \alpha_2 + \alpha_1\}$, and min($\alpha_2$) = argmax$\{0 ; \alpha_2 + \alpha_1 - C\}$.

In terms of the new $\alpha_2^{new, \, clipped}$, clipped as indicated above if necessary, the new α_1 becomes:

(11.33)
$$\alpha_1^{new} = \alpha_1^{old} + s(\alpha_2^{old} - \alpha_2^{new, \, clipped}),$$

where s $\equiv y_1 y_2$ as before. After the new α_1 and α_2 values are obtained there still remains the task of obtaining the new b value. If the new α_1 is not "clipped" then the update must satisfy the non-boundary KKT relation: $y_1 f(x_1) = 1$, i.e., $f^{new}(x_1) - y_1 = 0$. By relating f^{new} to f^{old} the following update on b is obtained:

(11.34)
$$b_1^{new} = b - (f^{new}(x_1) - y_1) - y_1(\alpha_1^{new} - \alpha_1^{old})K_{11} - y_2(\alpha_2^{new, \, clipped} - \alpha_2^{old})K_{12}$$

If α_1 is clipped but α_2 is not, the above argument holds for the α_2 multiplier and the new b is:
(11.35)

$$b_2^{new} = b - (f^{new}(x_2) - y_2) - y_2(\alpha_2^{new} - \alpha_2^{old})K_{22} - y_1(\alpha_1^{new,clipped} - \alpha_1^{old})K_{12}$$

If both α_1 and α_2 values are clipped then we don't have a unique solution for b. The Platt convention was to take:

(11.36)
$$b^{new} = \frac{b_1^{new} + b_2^{new}}{2}$$

and this works well much of the time. Alternatively, Keerthi [140] has devised an alternate formulation without this lacuna, as have Crammer and Singer [136], with the latter described in the multiclass SVM section. Perhaps just as good as any exact solution for 'b' in the double-clipped scenario is to manage this special case by rejecting the update and picking a new pair of alphas to update (in this way only unique 'b' updates are made). Alpha-selection variants are briefly discussed next.

11.4.2 Alpha-selection Variants
In the standard Platt SMO algorithm, $-\eta = k_{11} + k_{22} - 2k_{12}$, and speedup variations are described to avoid calculation of this value entirely. A middle ground is sought with the following definition "$\eta = 2k_{12} - 2$; if ($\eta >= 0$) {$\eta = -1$;}" (in [37], where underflow handling and other details differ slightly, and non-standard kernels are explored).

A comparison of some of the SVM Kernels of interest, with "regularized" distances or divergences, where they are regularized if in the form of an exponential with argument the negative of some distance-measure squared ($d^2(x,y)$) or symmetrized divergence measure ($D(x,y)$), the former if using a geometric heuristic for comparison of feature vectors, the latter if using a distributional heuristic. Results are shown in Fig. 11.17 for the Gaussian Kernel: $d^2(x,y)=\Sigma k(x_k-y_k)^2$; for the Absdiff Kernel $d^2(x,y)=(\Sigma k|x_k-y_k|)^{1/2}$; and for the Symmetrized Relative Entropy Kernel $D(x,y)= D(x\|y)+D(y\|x)$, where $D(x\|y)$ is the standard relative entropy.

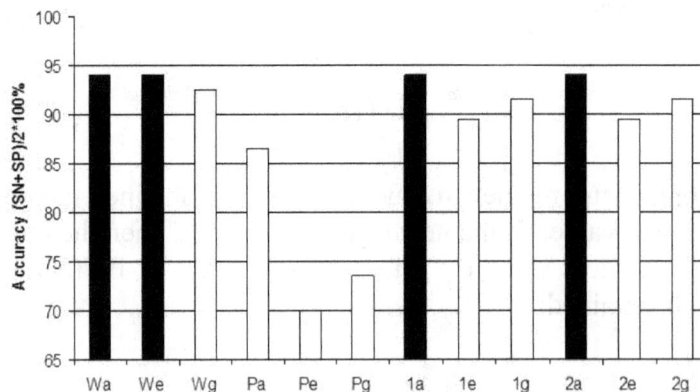

Figure 11.17. Comparative results are shown on performance of Kernels and algorithmic variants. The classification is between two DNA hairpins and uses thousands of samples (in terms of features from the blockade signals they pro-

duce when occluding ion flow through a nanometer-scale channel). Implementations: WH SMO (W); Platt SMO (P); Keerthi1 (1); and Keerthi2 (2). Kernels: Absdiff (a); Entropic (e); and Gaussian (g). The best algorithm/kernel on this and other channel blockade data studied has consistently been the WH SMO variant and the Absdiff and Entropic Kernels. Another benefit of the WH SMO variant is its significant speedup over the other methods (about half the time of Platt SMO and one fourth the time of Keerthi 1 or 2).

11.4.3 Chunking on large datasets: $O(N^2) \rightarrow n\ O(N^2/n^2) = O(N^2)/n$

SVM chunking provides an alternative method to running a typical SVM on a dataset by breaking up the training data and running the SVM on smaller chunks of data. In the chunking process feature vectors associated with strong data points are retained from chunk to chunk, while weak data points are discarded.

The variable projection method (VPM) is developed in [341] for training SVMs in parallel. This method is based off of the SVM light decomposition techniques [135] which delve further into the inner workings of the SMO algorithm [118,119]. In the latter, the feature vector indices are divided into two categories, the free and fixed sets based upon their 'alphas' (Lagrange multipliers). The free set represents the KKT violators which need to be further optimized while the fixed set is comprised of the alphas that already fulfill the KKT equations. An alpha from each set is used to solve each quadratic sub problem in order to optimize the free set alphas until convergence. VPM provides a parallel solution to computing the kernel matrix which is the most memory intensive part of the SVM. The kernel calculations are spread among several processing elements and the rows of the matrix are spread and usually duplicated across the memory of those processing elements. Since the rows are duplicated, they must be synchronized after each local computation. VPM is implemented using standard C and MPI communication routines.

In [121] is shown the Cascade SVM method to parallelize SVMs. This method begins by breaking the large dataset into chunks. The SVM is run on each separate chunk in the first layer. When the SVMs have all converged, new chunks are created from the resulting support vectors from the pairs of first layer chunks which make up the second layer of chunks. This occurs until a final chunk is reached. The final set of support vectors is then fed back into each first layer chunk. If further optimization is possible and needed, the entire process is rerun until the global optimum is met. This method seems intuitive, but after testing we have found that passing 100% of support vectors down to the next set of chunks, without also passing non support vectors or using the SVR method, typically results in systematic convergence failure (with the various 150-component DNA feature datasets examined). The data run never finishes, in other words, since it cannot sufficiently reduce the support vectors to converge (see Fig. 11.18). The weakness of the method, not apparent at first sight, is not simply that the SVs from different chunks might be sufficiently different to pose complications. The added subtlety is to prevent the accumulation of outliers during the distributed learning/merging of the SVM with chunking.

Chunking becomes a necessity when classifying large datasets. The number and size of the chunks depends on the size of the dataset to be trained. In the Java implementation used here, the user specifies the size of each chunk and the chunks are broken up accordingly. If the chunks don't divide evenly, which is the case most of the time, the few remaining feature vectors are added to the last chunk. When training on the chunk is complete, the resulting trained feature vectors split into distinct sets (support vectors, polarization set, penalty set, and KKT violator). If the SVM learning is done well, the largest set consists of the support and polarization feature vectors. The polarization set consists of the feature vectors that have been properly classified. These feature vectors pass the KKT relations and have an alpha coefficient equal to zero. The penalty set consists of the feature vectors which pass the KKT relations and have alpha coefficients equal to C (the max value). The KKT violators make up another set consisting of feature vectors that violate one of the KKT relations. (The KKT violator set is usually zero at the end of the training process, unless some minimal number of violators is allowed upon learning completion.). These sets give the user different categories of feature vectors that they can pass to the next chunk(s). To keep the SVM converging to a better solution on the next chunk run, however, support vectors (and sometimes some of the polarization set) are passed to the next chunk(s). The optimal pass-percentages of each feature vector set depend on which kernel is used, the dataset, and the manner of merging information from different chunks.

There are different methods of extracting the feature vectors from the different sets. The specified percentages of feature vectors are typically randomly chosen from each of the sets, except for one. *The support feature vectors extraction method differs since it extracts the support vectors that are nearest to the decision hyperplane.* In the results we choose feature vectors whose scores are closer to the hyperplane in order to pass a tighter hyperplane on to the next chunk(s), and to manage accumulation of outliers.

The chunk learning topology used in our distributed approach is slightly different from the Binary Tree splitting described in the Cascade SVM presented in [121]. As discussed above, the large dataset is broken into smaller chunks and the SVM is run on each separate chunk. Instead of bringing the results of paired chunks together, all chunk results are brought together and re-chunked as occurred in the first layer. This process occurs until the final chunk is calculated which gives the trained result. At each training stage, the user has the option to tune the percentage of support vectors and non support vectors to pass to the next set of chunks. Additionally, passed support vectors can be chosen to satisfy some max value (approx. C/10 in cases examined) to produce a tighter hyperplane to better distinguish the polarization sets and eliminate outliers. We also incorporate SVR post-processing in some of the dataruns (method below), where SVR runs as part of the core SVM learning task on each chunk. It uses a user-defined alpha cutoff value for further tuning and can significantly reduce the number of support vectors passed to the next set of chunks (with bias towards elimination of outliers and the large non-boundary alphas). These additional steps reduce the size of the chunks, thus making the algorithm run faster without loss of accuracy. The SVR post-processing also appears to offer similar immunity to the convergence pathology (noted previously for 100% SV passing on distributed learning topologies).

Four sets of results are now described. The first two sets concern the optimal performance/learning-rate configurations for feature vector passing ("pass-tuning"), where the SVM training is performed using chunking with different learning topologies (sequential, partially-sequential distributed). The experiments are: (Sec. 11.4.3.1) SV/non-SV pass-tuning on binary subsets of {9AT,9TA,9CG,9GC,8GC}; and, (Sec. 11.4.3.2) SV/non-SV pass-tuning for binary classification of (9AT,9TA) vs (9CG,9GC).

There appear to be instabilities when learning on distributed topologies, and there are a couple of new approaches that appear to be robust in addressing these instabilities. In turn, this allows the hopes of a distributed speedup to be directly realized. The Support Vector Reduction (SVR) Method described in Sec. 11.4.4 uses a post-processing phase: after all KKT violators have been eliminated, the SV alpha's near the boundaries are coerced to their boundary sets (i.e., to the polarization set at alpha=0 or the penalty set at alpha=C). Results on this method are shown in the third section (Sec. 11.4.4.1). . The fourth and last section of the Results shows the combined operation of various methods for comparative purposes, and shows how robust distributed SVM learning may be possible (Sec. 11.4.4.2): Distributed SVM with pass-tuning and SVR.

Distributed SVM Processing (Chunking)

There are a variety of ways to avoid the pure SV training-set pathology [6,37]. Since we are interested in training set reduction overall, we consider the possibility of simply reducing the SV set. This appears to work in preliminary tests on well-studied datasets of interest (see Table 11.1), where the SV's nearest to the decision hyperplane (most supporting the hyperplane) are retained. For the channel current data examined in, with 150-component feature vectors, we find that 30% SV passing is optimal on distributed learning topologies. The low SV-passing percentage that is found to work in *distributed* chunking might fundamentally be an issue of outlier control during distributed learning. Further reduction of SV passed is possible with dropping SV's with confidence values at the other extreme, near zero (i.e., those nearest and most strongly supporting the hyperplane). This entails a additional Support Vector reduction (SVR) process that is run right after the SVM learning step is complete, where we further reduce the support vector set according to some confidence cut-off (actually imposed via cut-off on associated Lagrange multiplier in the SVM/SMO implementation). By reducing the number of support vectors propagated into the next round, we further accelerate the chunked processing. In this way, a strongly performing distributed chunk-training process is possible, with speedup by ~10 in the example shown in the table shown in Table 11.1 (with no significant loss in accuracy). It appears possible to automate the tuning & selection procedures. To achieve this, it is necessary to examine the stability of the algorithmic parameters such as the pass percentages on the different types of learned data (e.g., see Table 11.1 for pass percentages indicated). Further results on distributed SVM learning is given in [6,37].

SVM Method	Sensitivity	Specificity	(SN+SP)/ 2	Time (ms)
SMO (non-chunked)	0.87	0.84	0.86	47708
Sequential Chunking	0.84	0.86	0.85	27515
Multi-threaded Chunking	0.88	0.78	0.83	7855
SMO (non-chunked) with SV Reduction	0.91	0.81	0.86	43662
Sequential Chunking with SV Reduction	0.90	0.82	0.86	18479
Multi-threaded Chunking with SV Reduction	0.85	0.83	0.84	5232
Multi-threaded Dist. Chunking with SVR	0.85	0.83	0.84	5973

Table 11.1. Performance comparison table for the different SVM methods. The distributed chunking used three identical networked machines. Dataset = 9GC9CG_9AT9TA (1600 feature vectors). SVM Parameters: Absdiff kernel (with sigma=.5, C = 10, Epsilon = .001, Tolerance = .001). For

chunking methods: Pass 90% of support vectors, Starting chunk size = 400, maxChunks = 2. For SVR methods: Alpha cut off value = 0.15.

To further enhance processing speed, one can not only perform distributed processing as indicated, but can also boost thread-processing speed on a given computer via use of GPU processing. This has already been undertaken, where distributed chunks of SVM training data were processed using a CPU/GPU that, at marginal added cost (a graphics card), provided as much as a 32-fold speedup on the channel current blockade classification [125]. Similar GPU speed enhancements to the other machine learning algorithms are possible as well.

SV/non-SV pass-tuning on train subsets: an outlier-management heuristic

For DNA hairpin feature vector datasets, our observations have shown the best kernels to be the Gaussian, Absdiff, and Sentropic kernels. Of the three kernels indicated, Absdiff and Sentropic produce similar results when measuring accuracy as the average of the Sensitivity (SN) and Specificity (SP) typically significantly outperforms the third best kernel, Gaussian. The Gaussian kernel, on the other hand, is found to be the best performing of the three at keeping the growth in chunk-size as small as possible.

Sequential chunking is a simple form of chunking which is not multi-threaded. This method runs the SVM on the first chunk, and then sends the support feature vectors (SVs) and sometimes non-SVs to be added onto the training data for the next chunk. This continues until the final chunk has been run. When using sequential chunking, feature vector passing can be difficult since passing too many features on to the next chunk can result in training datasets that are too large in the later chunks in the process. For the sequential chunking method, the accuracy with Absdiff kernel (0.898) is shown in Table 11.2, with kernel and chunking parameters: sigma=.5, C = 10, Epsilon = .001, Tolerance = .001, and passing 100% of support vectors. Using the Sentropic kernel we obtain a similar accuracy of 0.891, where the Sentropic kernel and chunking parameters were: sigma=.5, C = 10, Epsilon = .001, Tolerance = .001, and passing 100% of support vectors. Using the Gaussian kernel provides accuracy 0.864, where the Gaussian kernel and chunking parameters were: sigma=.05, C = 10, Epsilon = .001, Tolerance = .001, and passing 100% of support vectors. As noted, in these data runs, 100% of the support vector set was passed to the next set of chunks. The chunking parameters indicated for the table represent the best accuracy for the given chunking method, and all of the parameter selections are verified for stability (via tests confirming that minor changes of tuned parameter setting do not strongly alter classifier accuracy). In each SVM classifier test the positive class is named first, so '8GC9AT' is a SVM training with 8GC data used for positives, and 9AT data used for negatives. Since the 8 and 9 refer different lengths in the molecules, it's not surprising that the best scoring classifications are for telling the 8GC molecule apart from one of the 9 base-pair molecules. The most challenging case was for discriminating between 9GC and 9CG, where an accuracy of only 77.5% was observed (dropping weak data can boost this classification to 99.9% [1,6,37]).

Sequential Chunked SMO			Chunk Size 200 of 800 total feature vectors			
Data	Iterations	# of SVs	SN	SP	(SN+SP)/2	Elapsed Time (ms)
8GC9AT	100	554	0.96	0.95	0.955	12610
8GC9CG	114	557	0.92	0.92	0.92	16901
8GC9GC	58	524	0.94	0.97	0.955	8914
8GC9TA	68	542	0.97	0.95	0.96	10000
9AT9CG	37	727	0.83	0.8	0.815	10936
9AT9GC	23	727	0.83	0.83	0.83	9757
9AT9TA	9	661	0.93	0.93	0.93	7563
9CG9GC	15	751	0.78	0.77	0.775	9218
9CG9TA	41	597	0.92	0.89	0.905	10267
9GC9TA	51	567	0.95	0.92	0.935	9695
Mean	**52**	**621**	**0.903**	**0.893**	**0.898**	**10586**

Table 11.2. Sequential chunking using different DNA hairpin datasets. This table shows the different sequential chunking data runs performed on datasets deriving from pairs of DNA hairpin data. The last line of the table shows the mean of the data runs. The SVM Parameters used: Absdiff kernel with sigma=.5, C = 10, Epsilon = .001, Tolerance = .001, and passing 100% of support vectors.

For the multi-threaded chunking method, the average accuracy of Sentropic is best (0.855) (see Table 11.3). Absdiff (0.854) is very similar in performance, and Gaussian has average accuracy 0.833. In these data runs, 30% of the support vector set was passed to the next set of chunks, with kernel parameters unchanged. If 100% SV-passing is attempted there is typically failure to converge. As with the sequential Results, these chunking parameters chosen represent the best accuracy for the given chunking method, and all of the parameter selections are verified for stability.

Distributed Chunked SMO			Chunk Size 200 of 800 total feature vectors			
Data	Iterations	# of SVs	SN	SP	(SN+SP)/2	Elapsed Time (ms)
8GC9AT	14	221	0.97	0.89	0.93	2667
8GC9CG	30	202	0.91	0.9	0.905	1993
8GC9GC	27	208	0.91	0.93	0.92	2003
8GC9TA	38	208	0.95	0.88	0.915	2017
9AT9CG	8	232	0.79	0.72	0.755	2531
9AT9GC	21	237	0.71	0.8	0.755	2121
9AT9TA	8	234	0.85	0.87	0.86	2318
9CG9GC	9	237	0.74	0.69	0.715	2132
9CG9TA	8	230	0.84	0.94	0.89	2003
9GC9TA	10	224	0.94	0.87	0.905	1945
Mean	**17.3**	**223.3**	**0.86**	**0.849**	**0.855**	**2173**

Table 11.3. Multi-threaded chunking using different DNA hairpin datasets. This table shows the different multi-threaded chunking data runs performed on assortments of DNA hairpin pairs. The last line of the table presents the mean of the data runs. SVM Parameters: **Sentropic kernel** with

sigma=.5, C = 10, Epsilon = .001, Tolerance = .001. <u>Passing 30% of support vectors.</u>

For the multithreaded chunking, the SVs in the final distributed chunk with Gaussian kernel have an average 78% reduction from the original data-set to final chunk SV decision-set, while the Sentropic kernel has a 72% reduction. The SV number in the final sequential chunk had a 22.5% reduction for the Absdiff kernel in the sequential setting, compared with a 44.3% reduction for the Gaussian kernel. So the improved accuracy of the Absdiff and Sentropic kernels, over the standard Gaussian kernels, comes at a minor cost in computational time in the distributed-chunking setting, while it can involve significantly more time in the sequential-chunking setting.

From tuning over the number of SVs to pass, we find that sequential learning topologies strongly benefit from 100% SV passing, whereas distributed learning topologies have a non-optimality at 100% SV passing (and is prone to non-convergence to a solution – see Fig. 11.18), while 30% SV-passing performs as well and with greater stability. There are a variety of ways to deal with the distributed learning instabilities found with passing 'base' SV's, including the solution of pipelining the learning process to always have SV's merge into an untrained chunk to avoid outlier accumulation (and gridlock) in the learning process. In the Discussion we suggest that the low SV-passing percentage that is found to work in *distributed* chunking might fundamentally be an issue of outlier control during distributed learning.

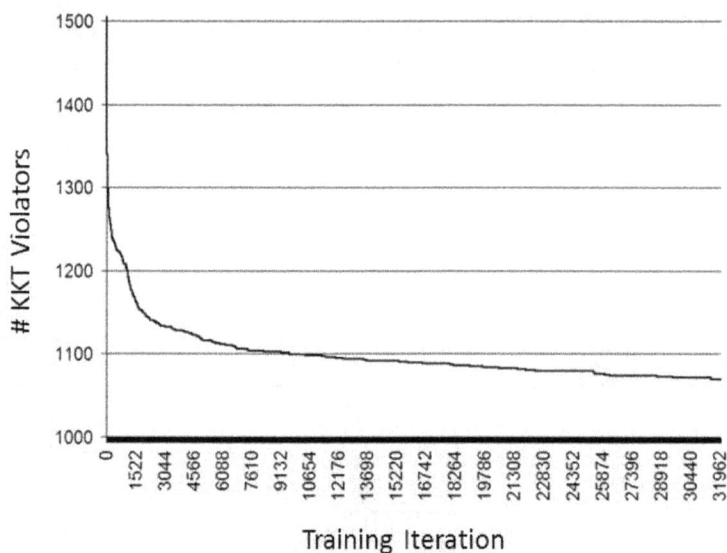

Fig. 11.18. SVM convergence failure seen with 100% SV passing on distributed learning topologies. SVM training dataset reduction with 100% SVs passed on a distributed learning topology.

SV/non-SV pass-tuning on (9AT,9TA) vs (9CG,9GC)

For the DNA hairpin datasets considered in the previous section, and considered here on a larger dataset, we find that the ideal chunking parameter for sequential chunking is 100% of the support vector set. The Absdiff kernel produced the best accuracy (0.855) with stable conditions (see Fig. 11.19). Table 11.4 displays a sample run using Absdiff and the size of each chunk as the algorithm progresses through the chunks. Table 11.4 also shows the fea-

312

ture vector set composition of each chunk. Similar results were obtained when using the Sentropic and Gaussian kernels (not shown).

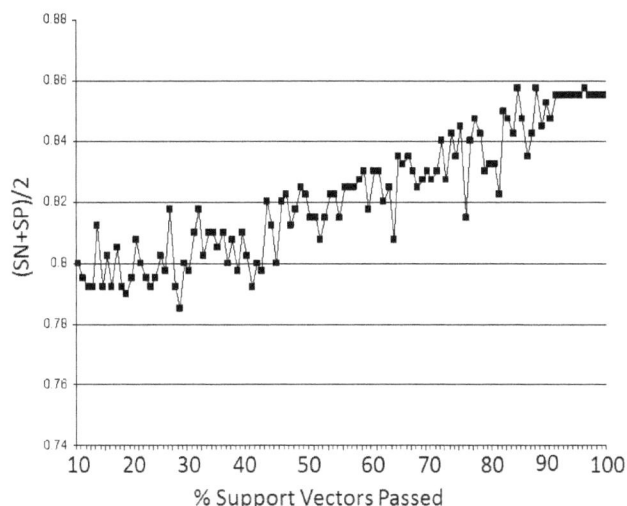

Fig. 11.19. Sequential Learning Topology SV pass-tuning. Dataset = 9GC9CG_9AT9TA (1600 feature vectors). SVM Parameters: Absdiff kernel with sigma=.5, C = 10, Epsilon = .001, Tolerance = .001.

The Fig. 11.19 results show a clear trend for *sequential* chunking when using different support vector and polarization set percentage parameters. (During the tuning operation, every variation of multiples of ten up to 100 was used for each of the two sets. For example, when the SV % parameter was 10, the polarization set % parameter would vary from 10 to 100 in steps of ten.) For most of the data run, especially the more stable part at 100 % SVs, the variation of the small polarization set did not seem to have much effect on the outcome. Table 11.4 shows results for Absdiff kernel passing 100% of support vectors and 50% of polarization set. Final Chunk Performance: {SN, SP} = {.87, .84}. For the Sentropic kernel with sigma=.5, C = 10, Epsilon = .001, Tolerance = .001, passing 100% of support vectors and 50% of polarization set the final Chunk Performance: {SN, SP} = {.875, .82} (table not shown). For the Gaussian kernel with sigma=.05, C = 10, Epsilon = .001, Tolerance = .001, passing 100% of support vectors and 50% of polarization set, the final Chunk Performance: {SN, SP} = {.715, .85}.

	Chunk 1	Chunk 2	Chunk 3	Chunk 4
Total Chunk Size	400	787	1143	1472
Support Vectors	373	700	1002	1320
Polarization Set	27	86	140	152
Penalty Set	0	0	0	0
Violator Set	0	1	1	0
Support Vectors Passed	373	700	1002	
Polarization Set Passed	14	43	70	
Total Passed Set	387	743	1072	

Table 11.4. Sequential chunking with the Absdiff kernel. Dataset = 9GC9CG_9AT9TA (1600 feature vectors). SVM Parameters: Absdiff kernel

with sigma=.5, C = 10, Epsilon = .001, Tolerance = .001. Pass 100% of support vectors and 50% of polarization set. Final Chunk Performance: {SN, SP} = {.87, .84}. A breakdown of each feature vector set is displayed to show how the percentage parameters are used to pass portions of each set to the next chunk.

For the DNA hairpin datasets considered in the previous section, and considered here on a larger dataset, results have shown that the ideal chunking parameter for *distributed* chunking can be as low as 30% of the support vector set. This produced the best accuracy (0.83) with stable conditions (see Fig. 11.20 for results with the Absdiff kernel).

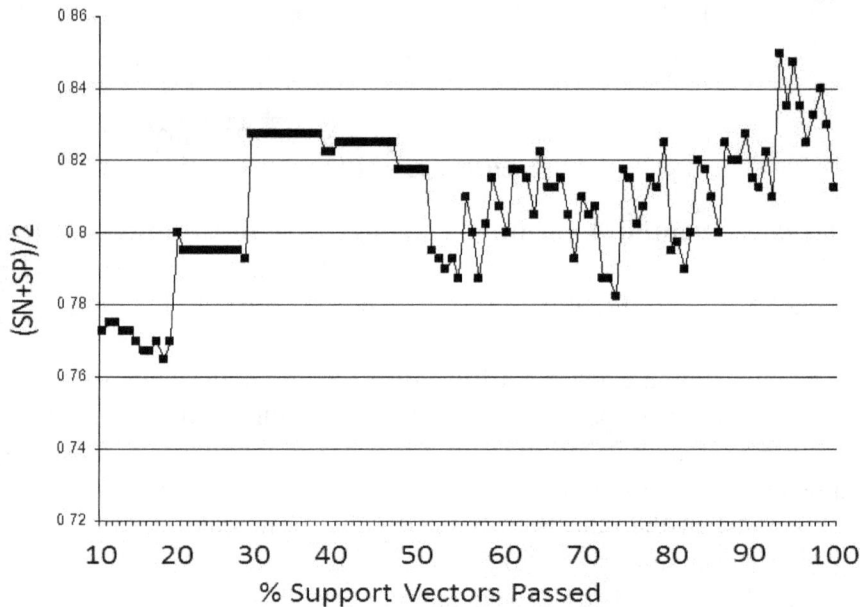

Figure 11.20. Distributed Learning Topology SV pass-tuning. Dataset = 9GC9CG_9AT9TA (1600 feature vectors). SVM Parameters: Absdiff kernel with sigma=.5, C = 10, Epsilon = .001, Tolerance = .001. This shows the trend for multi-threaded chunking when using different support vector and polarization set percentage parameters. (Every variation of multiples of ten up to 100 was used for each of the two sets. For example, when the SV % parameter was 10, the polarization set % parameter would vary from 0 to 100 in multiples of ten.) For most of the data run, especially the more stable part around 30 % SV-passing, the variation of the polarization set did not have much effect on the outcome.

For the *sequential* chunking method, the training process shown in Table 11.4 is optimal when passing 100% of the support vector set and 50% of the polarization set. For *multi-threaded* chunking, with the Absdiff kernel, shown in Table 11.5, on the other hand, good performance was found when passing a wide range of parameters, with results shown for a training run with passing on 80% of the support vector set and 60% of the polarization set. Similar results are found for the Sentropic and Gaussian kernels (Tables not shown). Note that only 30% SV-passing was needed for the best performing multi-threaded learning. With only 30% SV passing there was no weakening of performance or convergence instabilities, and the results shown in Fig. 11.20 reveal this to be a more stable chunk learning parameter

314

for the datasets examined (for discussion on how to implement an SVM with auto-tuning on the kernel and chunking parameters).

-	C1	C2	C3	C4	C5	C6	C7	C8	C9	C10
Total Chunk Size	400	400	400	400	423	423	425	504	504	791
Support Vectors	373	377	378	388	402	402	403	466	460	699
Polarization Set	27	23	22	12	21	21	22	38	43	92
Penalty Set	0	0	0	0	0	0	0	0	0	0
Violator Set	0	0	0	0	0	0	0	0	1	0
Support Vectors Passed	1218	-	-	-	968	-	-	742	-	-
Polarization Set Passed	53	-	-	-	40	-	-	49	-	-
Total Passed Set	1271	-	-	-	1008	-	-	791	-	-

Table 11.5. Multi-threaded chunking with the Absdiff kernel. Dataset = 9GC9CG_9AT9TA (1600 feature vectors). SVM Parameters: Absdiff kernel with sigma=.5, C = 10, Epsilon = .001, Tolerance = .001. Pass 80% of support vectors and 60% of polarization set. Final Chunk Performance: {SN, SP} = {.855, .795}. A breakdown of each feature vector set is displayed to show how the percentage parameters are used to pass portions of each set to the next set of chunks.

For Sentropic kernel with sigma=.5, C = 10, Epsilon = .001, Tolerance = .001, passing 80% of support vectors and 60% of polarization set. Final Chunk Performance: {SN, SP} = {.845, .755} (Table not shown). For Gaussian kernel with sigma=.05, C = 10, Epsilon = .001, Tolerance = .001, passing 80% of support vectors and 60% of polarization set. Final Chunk Performance: {SN, SP} = {.85, .83} (Table not shown).

11.4.4 Support Vector Reduction (SVR)
Support Vector Reduction (SVR) is a process that is run right after the SVM learning step is complete. Instead of going on to testing data against the training results to get accuracy, we further reduce the support vector set. One way to do this is to coerce some alphas to zero which means they would now fall into the polarization set. Converting the smaller alphas to zeros makes the most sense since a larger alpha indicates that the data point is stronger towards its grouping (polarized sign). This is done using a user-defined alpha cut off value. All alpha values that are under the cut off are pushed to zero. It is not entirely trivial since certain mathematical constraints must be met. The constraint that must be met for this method is the linear equality constraint [1,37]:

$$\sum_{i=1}^{N} y_i \alpha_i = 0$$

Therefore, the alpha values not meeting the cutoff cannot just be forced to zero unless the value is retained somewhere else in the set. This is done by first sorting the alpha values of the support vectors. Then for each alpha that does not meet the cut off value, the small left over value is added to the largest alpha of the same polarity. Since the list is sorted it can loop through and evenly distribute the left over values through the larger alphas starting with

315

the largest. The reduction process can cut the number of support vectors significantly, while not significantly diminishing the accuracy. Other observations have shown that the easier the dataset to classify, the larger the reduction via this process.

Support Vector Reduction (SVR) is a process that is run right after the SVM learning step is complete. Instead of going on to merge subsets of feature vectors or to test data against known results, the idea is to further reduce the support vector set. One way to do this is to coerce some alphas to zero which means they would now fall into the polarization set. This process is described further in the Methods.

Figure 11.21 shows the results of the SVR method on the non-chunking SMO SVM. For this dataset, 0.19 was found to be the best cut off value since it retains accuracy while reducing the support vectors. For the 9GC9CG vs 9AT9TA dataset, 140 support vectors (10.5% of total) were dropped without affecting the accuracy.

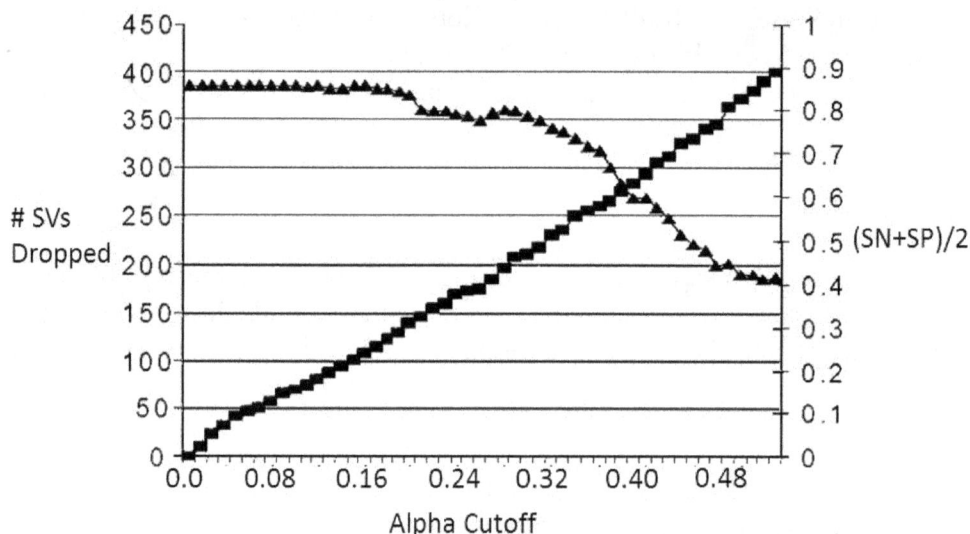

Figure 11.21. SMO (non-chunking) Support Vector Reduction. Dataset: 9GC9CG_9AT9TA (1600 feature vectors). SVM Parameters: Absdiff kernel with sigma=.5, C = 10, Epsilon = .001, Tolerance = .001. This graph shows the rate of support vectors reduced as the alpha cutoff value is increased. The alpha cutoff value 0.19 is chosen as the best since it is the last value before accuracy begins to degrade. This chosen value reduces 140 support vectors.

SVR-enabled data runs using sequential chunking methods (Fig. 11.22) and multi-threaded chunking methods (Fig. 11.23) show similar results. The chunking results tend to be noisier since the SVM algorithm makes some approximations, thus the hyperplane will not be exactly the same for every data run and this behavior is amplified in the chunking methods. Nonetheless, the SVR method cuts down on support vectors and decreases testing time. For sequential chunking (Fig. 11.22), an alpha cut-off value of 0.25 caused 87 support vectors (7.2%) to be dropped without affecting accuracy. For multi-threaded chunking (Fig. 11.23), an alpha cut-off value of 0.22 dropped 26 support vectors (6.2%) while retaining the same accuracy.

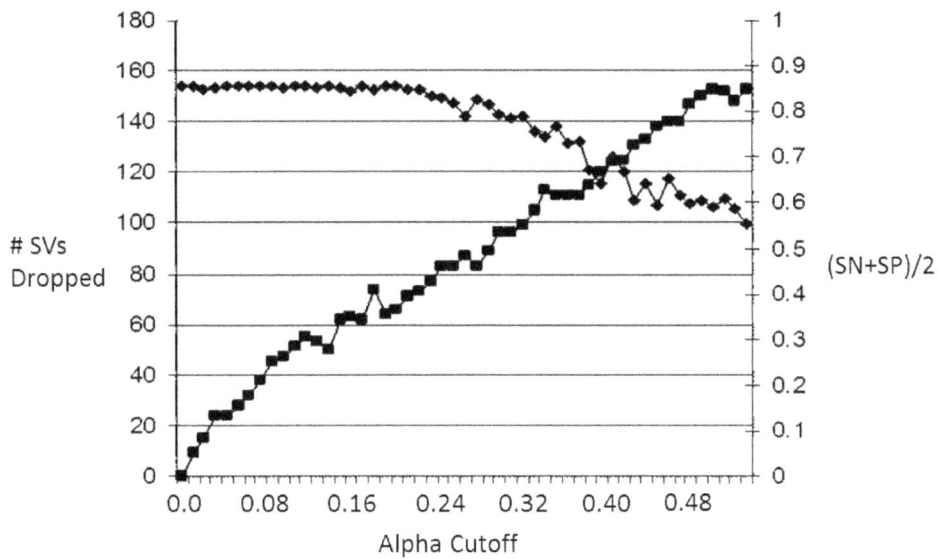

Figure 11.22. Sequential Chunking Support Vector Reduction. Dataset: 9GC9CG_9AT9TA (1600 feature vectors), Starting chunk size=400. SVM Parameters: Absdiff kernel with sigma=.5, C = 10, Epsilon = .001, Tolerance = .001. Passing 100% of Support Vectors. This graph shows the rate of support vectors reduced as the alpha cutoff value is increased. The alpha cutoff value 0.25 is chosen as the best since it is the last value before accuracy begins to degrade. This chosen value reduces 87 support vectors.

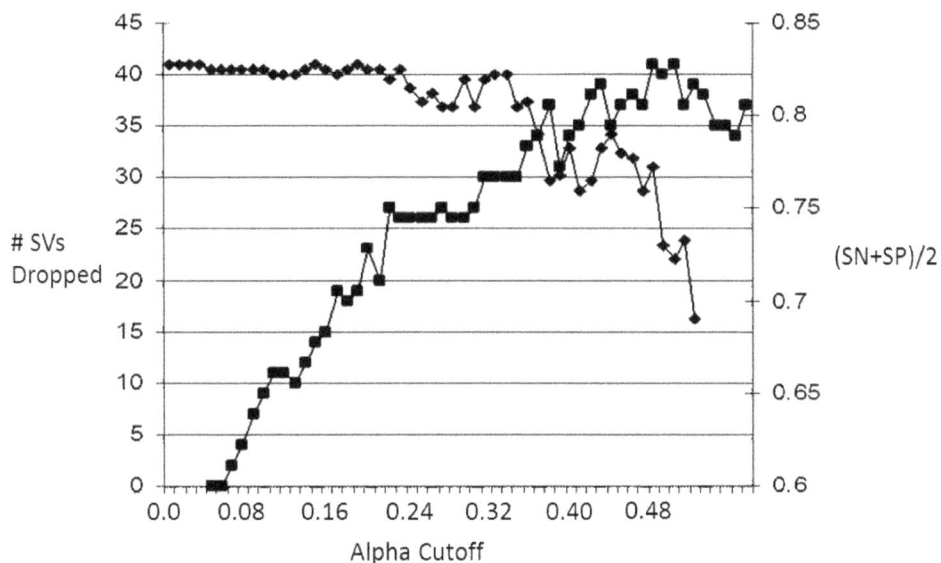

Figure 11.23. Multi-threaded Chunking Support Vector Reduction. Dataset: 9GC9CG_9AT9TA (1600 feature vectors), Starting chunk size=400. SVM Parameters: Absdiff kernel with sigma=.5, C = 10, Epsilon = .001, Tolerance = .001. Passing 30% of Support Vectors. This graph shows the rate of support vectors reduced as the alpha cutoff value is increased. The alpha cut-

off value 0.22 is chosen as the best since it is the last value before accuracy begins to degrade. This chosen value reduces 26 support vectors.

Multi-threaded Chunking with SVR

The multi-threaded chunking method simultaneously runs the chunks using multiple threads. Once all of the threaded chunks are finished training, the chunk results are collected. The same user defined percentages of feature vector sets are used here except this time those percentages of feature vectors are extracted from each chunk. All of the chosen feature vectors to be passed are stored together then re-chunked if the current data set is large enough to be chunked again. Re-chunking occurs when the data set is greater than or equal to twice the specified chunk size. If this is not the case, the final chunk is run alone to get the final result. The main use of the multi-threaded chunking method is with a single computer with multiple processors/cores. Results are shown in Table 11.6.

SVM Method	Sensitivity	Specificity	(SN + SP) / 2	Time (ms)
SMO (non-chunked)	0.87	0.84	0.86	47708
Sequential Chunking	0.84	0.86	0.85	27515
Multi-threaded Chunking	0.88	0.78	0.83	7855
SMO (non-chunked) with SVR	0.91	0.81	0.86	43662
Sequential Chunking with SVR	0.90	0.82	0.86	18479
Multi-threaded Chunking w/ SVR	0.85	0.83	0.84	5232
Multi-thr. Dist. Chunking w/ SVR	0.85	0.83	0.84	5973

Table 11.6. Performance comparison of the different SVM methods. The distributed chunking used three identical networked machines. Dataset = 9GC9CG_9AT9TA (1600 feature vectors). SVM Parameters: Absdiff kernel with sigma=.5, C = 10, Epsilon = .001, Tolerance = .001. For chunking methods: Pass 90% of support vectors, Starting chunk size = 400, maxChunks = 2. For SV Reduction methods: Alpha cut off value = .15.

Multi-threaded Distributed Chunking with SVR

The multi-threaded *distributed* chunking implementation is a multi-server/multi-CPU (core) version of the previous multi-threaded chunking method. Java RMI is used to handle the remote calls between the client and servers. The client program runs multi-threaded remote calls to a user specified set of servers (round robin). Each server and the client machine have an SVM Server listening. When the client program runs, a chunk is passed to each available processor/core in the network until all or as many as possible are training simultaneously. As the chunks finish, the results are passed back to the client. Each "chunk level" may take multiple batches depending on the chunk size and amount of processors/cores available. The final chunk is largest so the client program should be processed on the machine with the most computing power. This not only speeds up the final chunk but allowing larger chunks should produce better final results. The main benefit of this method is a significant decrease in run time for large datasets. As shown in Table 11.6, multi-threaded distributed chunking performs almost as well as non-chunked learning. Network overhead causes it to be slightly slower than the single-server multi-threaded chunking method. With extremely large datasets (i.e. 60,000 feature vectors and larger), the multi-threaded and distributed method is thus shown to work.

Support Vector Machines are extremely useful for classifying data. Since the main weakness of SVMs is the long training time when running large datasets it is only natural to develop multi-threaded distributed SVM training methods, especially since multiple cores/processors are becoming commonplace.

An overall comparison of the SVM with chunking methods is shown in Table 11.6. It is found that sequential chunking has the benefit of holding onto accuracy when compared to running the straight SVM (SMO) but the run times can be inefficient since the method does not run in parallel. Multi-threaded chunking has a significant run time performance improvement, which is further improved when employing the SVR method. The multi-threaded aspect allows training of extremely large datasets which may not be possible using sequential chunking. Additionally, using the multi-threaded distributed method allows users to add machines to make the algorithm train even faster. An instability of the multithreaded approach is found to sometimes occur when the percentage of information passed to later chunks involves 100% of the support vectors, possibly due to outlier accumulation in the chunk-carry set of feature vectors. This instability is eliminated by passing less than 100% of the support vectors, favoring those nearest the decision surface (thereby excluding outliers), and by passing some of the non-support-vector set of data as well. A stable distributed platform for training SVM thus appears possible. With the size of the dataset no longer a significant a limitation in SVM training, many practical applications of SVM methods become accessible in Big Data classification tasks, and in SVM-intensive applications, such as SVM-based clustering mentioned in the Methods.

11.4.5 Code Examples (in OO Perl)

Portions of two OO-PERL programs are shown that perform the SVM computation indicated above. The first is part of a PERL control script, the second is part of a PERL module file.

```
#!/usr/bin/perl

# Perl program Binary_Classifier.pl

use File::Basename;
use lib dirname($0);
use FileHandle;
use SVM_Discriminator;
use strict;
my ($train_file,$label_file,$test_file,$testlabel_file,$output_file,
    $kernel_type,$kernel_param,$bvalue,$Cvalue,$epsilon, $skip_train_loop,
    $class_file,$perm_index,$N,$feature_count) = @ARGV;
my $SVM_Process = new SVM_Discriminator($train_file,$label_file,$output_file,
    $kernel_type,$kernel_param,$bvalue,$Cvalue);
my $signal_count = $SVM_Process->Count_Features();
print "Signal Count = $signal_count\n";
my $badKKT=0;
my $tolerance=0;
if (!$ skip_train_loop) { ### no indent follows
print "Performing Load_Features on Segment $chunk_index\n";
$SVM_Process->Load_Features($feature_count);
print "Performing Eval_Kernel_Matrix\n";
$SVM_Process->Eval_Kernel_Matrix();
print "Performing Initialize_Alphas\n";
$SVM_Process->Initialize_Alphas();
print "Performing Initialize_bvalue\n";
$SVM_Process->Initialize_bvalue($bvalue);
print "Performing Initialize_Disc_Function_Cache\n";
$SVM_Process->Initialize_Disc_Function_Cache();
```

```perl
my @signs = @{$SVM_Process->{signs_ref}};
my @alphas = @{$SVM_Process->{alphas_ref}};
my @kernel = @{$SVM_Process->{kernel_ref}};
my $max_index=scalar(@signs)-1;
my @disc_function = @{$SVM_Process->{disc_function_ref}};


my $datacount = scalar(@signs);
my $looplimit = $datacount*5;
print "Performing Evaluate_KKT to initialize violator lists\n";
my $KKTsatisfied=$SVM_Process->Evaluate_KKT($epsilon); # to init violator lists
print "KKTsatisfied = $KKTsatisfied\n";
my $loopcount=0;
print "Performing Alpha Selections\n";
WHILE: while (!$KKTsatisfied) {
    $loopcount++;
    my $skip_index_default=-1;
    my $nonboundKKT_index =
            $SVM_Process->Select_KKT_nonboundViolator($skip_index_default);
    my $boundKKT_index =
            $SVM_Process->Select_KKT_BoundViolator($skip_index_default);
    my $first_index=-1;
    if ($nonboundKKT_index!=-1) {
        $first_index = $nonboundKKT_index;
    }
    elsif ($boundKKT_index!=-1) {
        $first_index = $boundKKT_index;
    }
    else {
        print "zero nonBound violators or alpha-one selection failure\n";
        $KKTsatisfied=1;
        last;
    }

    my $second_index = $SVM_Process->Select_SecondKKT($first_index);
    print "Performing Update_Cache\n";
    $SVM_Process->Update_Cache($first_index,$second_index);
    print "Performing Evaluate_KKT via KKTsatisfied update\n";

    if ($loopcount>=$looplimit && $loopcount<2*$looplimit) {
        $tolerance = 1+int($datacount/100);  # approx 1% violators
        if ($loopcount==$looplimit) {
            print "KKTlooplimit=$looplimit exceeded, ";
            print "allowing up to $tolerance violators.\n";
        }
        $KKTsatisfied=$SVM_Process->Evaluate_KKT($epsilon,$tolerance);
    }
    elsif ($loopcount>=2*$looplimit) {
        print "Bad KKT convergence, exiting.\n";
        $badKKT=1;
        last WHILE;
    }
    else {
        $KKTsatisfied=$SVM_Process->Evaluate_KKT($epsilon);
    }
}
print "KKT loop count: $loopcount\n";

if (!$badKKT) {
    $SVM_Process->Save($class_file,$perm_index,$N);
    $SVM_Process->Call($test_file,$testlabel_file,$tolerance);
}

#############
} # for skip on train loop
else {
    $SVM_Process->Call($test_file,$testlabel_file,
                        $tolerance,$class_file,$perm_index,$N);
}
```

The Perl module referred to, SVM_Discriminator.pm, is partly given below

```perl
#!/usr/bin/perl
#
# Perl module SVM_Discriminator.pm

package SVM_Discriminator;
use strict;


sub new {
    my ($class,$data_file,$label_file,$output_file,
        $kernel_type,$kernel_param,$bvalue,$Cvalue) = @_;
    my $self = bless {}, $class;
    $self->{data_file}=$data_file;
    $self->{output_file}=$output_file;
    $self->{label_file}=$label_file;
    $self->{kernel_type}=$kernel_type;
    $self->{kernel_param}=$kernel_param;
    $self->{bvalue}=$bvalue;
    $self->{Cvalue}=$Cvalue;

    if (!$kernel_type) {
        $self->{kernel_type}="gaussian";
    }
    if (!$kernel_param) {
        $self->{kernel_param}="1";
    }
    if (!$bvalue) {
        $self->{bvalue}=0;
    }
    if (!$Cvalue) {
        $self->{Cvalue}=100;
    }
    return $self;
}

sub Eval_Kernel_Matrix {
    my ($self) = @_;
    my $kernel_type = $self->{kernel_type};

    my $feature_count = $self->{feature_count};
    print "feature_count = $feature_count\n";
    my $sigma = $self->{kernel_param};
    my @kernel;
    my @data = @{$self->{data_ref}};
    my $index;
    my $max_index=scalar(@data)-1;
    my $count = $max_index+1;
    print "training data count = $count\n";
    my $other;
    my $sqdistance;
    for $index (0..$max_index) {
        if ($index%10==0) {
            print "eval on matrix row $index\n";
        }
        my $start_index;
        $start_index = $index;
        for $other ($start_index..$max_index) {
            $sqdistance=0;
            my $feat;
            for $feat (0..$feature_count-1) {
                my $p = $data[$index][$feat];
                my $q = $data[$other][$feat];
                if ($kernel_type =~ "poly") {
                    $sqdistance += $p*$q;
                }
                elsif ($kernel_type =~ "power") {
                    my ($power) = ($kernel_type =~ /power(\d+\.\d+)/);
                    if (!$power) { $power=1; }
                    $sqdistance += ($p**$power)*($q**$power);
                }
                elsif ($kernel_type =~ "gamma") {
```

321

```perl
                my ($gamma) = ($kernel_type =~ /gamma(\d+\.\d+)/);
                if (!$gamma) { $gamma=1; }
                $sqdistance += ($p**$gamma)*($q**$gamma);
            }
            elsif ($kernel_type =~ "gaussian") {
                my ($power) = ($kernel_type =~ /gaussian(\d+\.\d+)/);
                if (!$power) { $power=1; }
                $sqdistance += ($p**$power-$q**$power)**2;
            }
            elsif ($kernel_type =~ "absdiff") {
                $sqdistance += abs($p-$q);
            }
            elsif ($kernel_type eq "squareexp") {
                $sqdistance += (exp($p)-exp($q))**2;
            }
            elsif ($kernel_type eq "squarelog") {
                $sqdistance += (log($p)-log($q))**2;
            }
            elsif ($kernel_type eq "sentropic") {
                my $minprob = 0.0000001;
                if ($p<$minprob) { $p = $minprob; }
                if ($q<$minprob) { $q = $minprob; }
                $sqdistance += ($p-$q)*(log($p)-log($q));
            }
        }
        if ($kernel_type =~ "poly") {
            my ($poly) = ($kernel_type =~ /poly(\d+\.\d+)/);
            if (!$poly) { $poly=1; }
            $kernel[$index][$other]=$sqdistance**$poly/$sigma;
        }
        elsif ($kernel_type =~ "power") {
            $kernel[$index][$other]=$sqdistance/$sigma;
        }
        elsif ($kernel_type =~ "gamma") {
            my ($gamma) = ($kernel_type =~ /gamma(\d+\.\d+)/);
            if (!$gamma) { $gamma=1; }
            $kernel[$index][$other]=$sqdistance**(1/$gamma)/$sigma;
        }
        elsif ($kernel_type =~ "gaussian" ||
                $kernel_type eq "sentropic" {
            $kernel[$index][$other]=exp(-$sqdistance/(2*$sigma));
        }
        elsif ($kernel_type =~ "absdiff") {
            my ($power) = ($kernel_type =~ /absdiff(\d+\.\d+)/);
            if (!$power) { $power=1; }
            $kernel[$index][$other]=exp(-$sqdistance**$power/(2*$sigma));
        }
        }
    }
    }
    $self->{kernel_ref}=\@kernel;
}

sub Initialize_Alphas {
    my ($self) = @_;
    my @alphas;

    my @signs = @{$self->{signs_ref}};
    my $plus_count=$self->{plus_count};
    my $minus_count=$self->{minus_count};

    my $plus_alpha_init;
    if ($plus_count==0) {
        die "plus_alpha_init=0\n";
    }
    $plus_alpha_init = 1/$plus_count;
    my $minus_alpha_init;
    if ($minus_count==0) {
        die "minus_alpha_init=0\n";
    }
    $minus_alpha_init = 1/$minus_count;

    my $max_index=scalar(@signs)-1;
    my $index;
    for $index (0..$max_index) {
        if ($signs[$index]==1) {
```

322

```perl
            $alphas[$index]=$plus_alpha_init;
        }
        elsif ($signs[$index]==-1) {
            $alphas[$index]=$minus_alpha_init;
        }
        else {
            die "signs[index] error\n";
        }
    }
    $self->{alphas_ref}=\@alphas;
}

sub Initialize_bvalue {
    my ($self,$bvalue) = @_;
    $self->{bvalue} = $bvalue;
    if (!$bvalue) {
        $self->{bvalue} = 0;
    }
}

sub Initialize_Disc_Function_Cache {
    my ($self) = @_;
    my @labels = @{$self->{labels_ref}};
    my @signs = @{$self->{signs_ref}};
    my @data = @{$self->{data_ref}};
    my $plus_count=$self->{plus_count};
    my $minus_count=$self->{minus_count};
    my @alphas = @{$self->{alphas_ref}};
    my @kernel = @{$self->{kernel_ref}};
    my $max_index=scalar(@signs)-1;

    my @disc_function;
    my $index;
    my $other_index;
    for $index (0..$max_index) {
        for $other_index (0..$max_index) {
            $disc_function[$index] += $alphas[$other_index]
                                    *$signs[$other_index]
                                    *$kernel[$index][$other_index];
        }
        $disc_function[$index]+=$self->{bvalue};
    }
    $self->{disc_function_ref} = \@disc_function;
}

sub Evaluate_KKT {
    my ($self,$epsilon,$tolerance) = @_;
    if (!$epsilon) {
        $epsilon = 0.001;
    }
    if (!$tolerance) {
        $tolerance = 0;
    }
    my @KKT_Status;
    my @KKT_violators;
    my @Bound;
    my @Bound_violators;
    my @Nonbound_violators;
    my @Nonbound;
    my @KKT_non_violators;
    my @KKT_supportvectors;
    my @signs = @{$self->{signs_ref}};
    my @alphas = @{$self->{alphas_ref}};
    my $max_index=scalar(@signs)-1;
    my $C = $self->{Cvalue};
    my @disc_function = @{$self->{disc_function_ref}};
    my $index;
    for $index (0..$max_index) {
        $KKT_Status[$index]=0;
        my $score = $signs[$index]*$disc_function[$index];
        if ($alphas[$index]==0 && $score>=1+$epsilon) {
            $KKT_Status[$index]=1;
        }
        elsif ($alphas[$index]>=0 && $alphas[$index]<=$C &&
               $score<1+$epsilon && $score>1-$epsilon) {
```

```perl
        $KKT_Status[$index]=1;
        my $tightness = 5;    # tighten for support vector passing
        my $new_epsilon = $epsilon/$tightness;
        if ($score<1+$new_epsilon && $score>1-$new_epsilon) {
            my $vindex = scalar(@KKT_supportvectors);
            $KKT_supportvectors[$vindex]=$index;
        }
    }
    elsif ($alphas[$index]==$C && $score<=1-$epsilon) {
        $KKT_Status[$index]=1;
    }

    if ($alphas[$index]==0 || $alphas[$index]==$C) {
        my $bound_index = scalar(@Bound);
        $Bound[$bound_index]=$index;
    }
    else {
        my $nonbound_index = scalar(@Nonbound);
        $Nonbound[$nonbound_index]=$index;
    }

    if ($KKT_Status[$index]!=1) { # KKT violators
        my $vindex = scalar(@KKT_violators);
        $KKT_violators[$vindex]=$index;
        if ($alphas[$index]!=0 && $alphas[$index]!=$C) {
            my $nonbound_index = scalar(@Nonbound_violators);
            $Nonbound_violators[$nonbound_index]=$index;
        }
        else {
            my $bound_index = scalar(@Bound_violators);
            $Bound_violators[$bound_index]=$index;
        }
    }
    else {
        my $non_index = scalar(@KKT_non_violators);
        $KKT_non_violators[$non_index]=$index;
    }
}
$self->{KKT_Status_ref} = \@KKT_Status;
$self->{KKT_violators} = \@KKT_violators;
$self->{Bound} = \@Bound;
$self->{Bound_violators} = \@Bound_violators;
$self->{Nonbound} = \@Nonbound;
$self->{Nonbound_violators} = \@Nonbound_violators;
$self->{KKT_non_violators} = \@KKT_non_violators;
$self->{KKT_supportvectors} = \@KKT_supportvectors;

my $violator_count = scalar(@KKT_violators);
if ($violator_count%10==0) {
    print "violator_count = $violator_count\n";
}
print "KKT_violators @KKT_violators\n";
if ($violator_count>$tolerance) {
    return 0;
}
else {
    print "KKT pass obtained\n";
    return 1;
}
}
```

11.5 Kernel selection and Tuning Metaheuristics
11.5.1 The 'stability' kernels

The SVM Kernels of interest are "regularized" distances or divergences, where they are regularized if in the form of an exponential with argument the negative of some distance-measure squared $(d^2(x,y))$ or symmetrized divergence measure $(D(x,y))$, the former if using a geometric heuristic for comparison of feature vectors, the latter if using a distributional heuristic. The Gaussian and Absdiff kernels are regularized distances in the form of an exponential distance measure ($d^2(x,y)$). The Gaussian kernel ($d^2(x,y) = \Sigma_k(x_k - y_k)^2$) is common since it tends to produce good results when used with a wide variety of datasets. The Absdiff ($d^2(x,y) = \Sigma_k(|x_k - y_k|)^{1/2}$) and Sentropic ($D(x,y) = [D(x\|y) + D(y\|x)]/2$) Kernels [1,37] tend to work better with all of the datasets considered here and in other tests not shown. The Sentropic kernel is based on a regularized information divergence ($D(x,y)$) instead of a geometric distance.

The so-called curse of dimensionality from statistics says that the difficulty of an estimation problem increases drastically with the dimension N of the estimate configuration space, since in principle as N increases, the number of required patterns to sample grows exponentially. This statement may cast doubts on using higher dimensional feature vectors as input to learning machines. This must be balanced with results from statistical learning theory [116], however, that show that the likelihood of data separability by linear learning machines is proportional to (and improves with) their dimensionality. The feature space may grow in dimensionality, but does so under constraint to remain in a small (manageable) function class.

The kernels used in the analysis fall into two classes: regularized distance (squared) kernels; and regularized information divergence kernels. The first set of kernels strongly models data with classic, geometric, attributes or interpretation. The second set of kernels is constrained to operate on $(\boldsymbol{R}^+)^N$, the feature space of positive, non-zero, real-valued feature vector components. The space of the latter kernels is often also restricted to feature vectors obeying an L_1-norm = 1 constraint, i.e., the feature vector is a discrete probability vector.

Given any metric space ($\boldsymbol{X}$, d) one can build a positive-definite kernel of the form $e^{-\lambda d^2}$. Conversely, any positive definite kernel with such form must have a 'd' that is a metric (this is Mercer's condition in another form). (The metric appears as a squared entity in the argument, which is the mathematical grouping that satisfies the triangle inequality. It so happens that there ia another set of entities, other than metrics squared, that have a similar relation to the triangle inequality (related by a Lagrange transformation), and these relate to the Bregman divergences, including the information divergences such as relative entropy, in particular, which is the fundamental (simple) divergence, just as Euclideane distance is a fundamental (simple) distance. This suggests that the 'simplest' distance-based kernel is the Gaussian kernel, since the 'simplest' distance, the Euclidean distance, is used. Likewise, this suggests that the simplest that the simplest divergence-based kernel would be the aforementioned entropic kernel.

The use of probability vectors, and L_1-norm feature vectors in general (often in conjunction with the entropic kernel), turns out to provide a very general formulation, wherein feature extraction makes use of signal decomposition into a complete set of separable states that can be interpreted or represented as a probability vector (or normalized collection of such, or concatenation, then normalization, etc.). A probability vector formulation also provides a straightforward hand-off to the SVM classifiers since all feature vectors have the same length with such an approach. What this means for the SVM, however, is that geometric notions of distance are no longer the best measure for comparing feature vectors. For probability vectors (i.e., discrete distributions), the best measures of similarity are the various information-theoretic divergences: Kullback–Leibler, Renyi, etc. By symmetrizing over the arguments of those divergences, the entropic kernels are obtained, where the (symmetrized) Kullbach-Leibler Diveregence is used in the entropic kernel in [1,37,198] and what follows.

Notice how in the Dual reduction the dependence on the training data only appears in the $\vec{x}_i \cdot \vec{x}_j$ inner product term:

$$\sum_{i,j} \alpha_i \alpha_j y_i y_j \vec{x}_i \cdot \vec{x}_j .$$

We can generalize from the simple inner product term in a number of ways, and in doing so arrive at the SVM Kernel generalization. First, however, let's consider re-mapping the feature vectors into some higher dimensional space that is hyperspherically bounded. The volume of a thin shell at the boundary hypersphere dominates at higher dimensions, allowing for the data in the mapping to become approximately unit hyperspherical when the bounded hypershere has its hypershperical bound dilated to be unity by going to higher dimension. I'll proceed then with a new i^{th} feature vector, where the same feature vector label, $\vec{x}_i$, will be used.

If we have $\vec{x}_i \cdot \vec{x}_j = \|\vec{x}_i\| \|\vec{x}_j\| \cos \theta_{ij}$ and $\|\vec{x}_i\| = 1$ $\forall_i$ (unit hyperspherical data), then $\vec{x}_i \cdot \vec{x}_j = \cos \theta_{ij}$. On unit hypersphere, the spherical arc angle between points $\vec{x}_i$ and $\vec{x}_j$ on its surface, for small angle:

$$\cos \theta = 1 - \frac{1}{2}\theta^2 + \dots \quad \text{and} \quad \vec{x}_i \cdot \vec{x}_j \approx 1 - \frac{1}{2}\theta_{ij}^{\,2} .$$

In the Lagrangian the constant term does not matter due to the linear equality constraint:

$$\sum_{i=1}^{N} y_i \alpha_i = 0$$

So, for unit hyperspherical, proximate, feature vectors, arc-length is approximately Euclidean distance, and we have:

$$\vec{x}_i \cdot \vec{x}_j \approx 1 - \frac{1}{2}\theta_{ij}^{\,2} \approx 1 - |\vec{x}_i - \vec{x}_j|^2 .$$

Since there is a conformal angle-preserving mapping (triangle-inequality, so distance square preserving, and divergence preserving) with Lorentz transformation on observation sphere (with generalization to higher dimension, where we can ignore red-shift information, physically, for 4-D (3-D spatial), this occurs in special relativity, the near-lightspeed observer causes more and more to map into the forward view). The point is that we can do another mapping to achieve the small angle approximation on the entire dataset, where the compound mapping preserves the triangle inequality relation that is thought to be important. This specific mapping example is meant indicate what might be argued as existing, however, while in actual implementation the focus is on the kernel function and the mapping need never be known.

For unit hyperspherical data, "$\vec{x}_i \cdot \vec{x}_j \approx 1 - |\vec{x}_i - \vec{x}_j|^2$" can be thought of as measuring a distance that has been regularized in some manner when the distance grows large (i.e. as angular coordinate limitation, or in exponentiation to be seen in what follows), such that it is impossible or harshly penalized to have significantly large distances (equivalent to the original inner product term being close to zero, its contribution in the Lagrangian optimization made irrelevant), while data that is 'near' has its contribution in the Lagrangian optimization set close to one according to $1 - | \bar{x}_i - \bar{x}_j |^2$). What this demonstrates, thus far, is that we can manipulate our feature vectors by some mapping (with inverse) such that $\bar{x}_i \to \Phi(\bar{x}_i)$, and such that the inner product can become $\Phi(\bar{x}_i) \cdot \Phi(\bar{x}_j) \approx \phi(-| \bar{x}_i - \bar{x}_j |^2)$, where $\phi(-| \bar{x}_i - \bar{x}_j |^2)$ is an exponentially regularized distance squared, e.g., the Gaussian Kernel:

$$\phi_G(\bar{x}_i, \bar{x}_j) = \exp(\left. -| \bar{x}_i - \bar{x}_j |^2 \middle/ 2\sigma^2 \right), \text{ and for } \bar{x}_i \approx \bar{x}_j, \phi_G \approx 1 - \frac{1}{2\sigma^2}| \bar{x}_i - \bar{x}_j |^2,$$

which relates to the earlier derivation for kernel parameter (the variance in the case of the Gaussian Kernel) equal one half. It is therefore possible to generalize using $\Phi : \bar{x}_i \mapsto \Phi(\bar{x}_i)$ to obtain:

$$(11.37) \quad \tilde{L}_\sigma(\alpha) = \sum_i \alpha_i - \frac{1}{2}\sum_{i,j} \alpha_i \alpha_j y_i y_j K_{ij}, 0 \le \alpha_i \le C, \text{ where } K_{ij} = \Phi(\bar{x}_i) \cdot \Phi(\bar{x}_j).$$

Kernel functions expressible in this way must have a positive semi-definite kernel, typically tested using what is known as Mercer's condition. Not all kernels satisfy Mercer's condition, and are therefore are not describable in terms of a mapping Φ on feature vectors. Although all kernels examined appear to satisfy Mercer's condition, this will not be taken as a critical limitation, especially if working with algorithmic developments that make use of the KKT relations separate from the originating derivation.

The Mercer test
The kernel is positive definite if and only if:

$$\sum_{i,j} k(\bar{x}_i, \bar{x}_j) C_i C_j \ge 0 \quad \forall \bar{C} \in \mathfrak{R}^m \text{ (for positive semidefinite K)},$$

where C-vectors are randomly generated and tested against the kernel obtained on the training data.

The positive principal minors test
The kernel is positive definite if and only if the determinants of all of the principal minors are positive.

Derivation of 'stability' kernels
For the Gaussian kernel the stability property is exhibited when the log Kernel variation on feature vector components is calculated:
$\partial \ln (K_G(\mathbf{x}_i, \mathbf{x}_j)) / \partial x_i^k = (x_j^k - x_i^k)/\sigma^2$,
where "x_i^k" is the kth component of the ith feature vector and "stability" is indicated by the sign of the difference term $(x_j^k - x_i^k)$, e.g., for

$$(11.38) \quad K_G(\bar{y}, \bar{z}) = \exp(-\| \bar{y} - \bar{z} \|^2 / 2\sigma^2) : \frac{\partial \ln K_G(\bar{y}, \bar{z})}{\partial y_K} = (y_K - z_K)/\sigma^2$$

Clearly, the sign is important, as is a notion of difference. Suppose we generalize on this basis to decouple the sign convention from the "notion of distance", here providing a new kernel expression, for the "variational kernel" by way of an integration factor:

$$(11.39) \qquad \frac{\partial \ln K_G(\vec{y}, \vec{z})}{\partial y_K} = \left(\frac{-1}{2\sigma^2}\right)\left(\frac{\text{sign}(y_k - z_k)}{\sqrt{\sum_k |y_k - z_k|}}\right)$$

$$(11.40) \qquad K_v(\vec{y}, \vec{z}) = \exp\left(-\sqrt{\sum_k |y_k - z_k|}\Big/2\sigma^2\right)$$

The subscript "V" in K_V is meant to denote "variational" kernel (sometimes refered to as "indicator" kernel or "Absdiff" kernel). For suitable choice of tuning parameter σ, the variational kernel offers the best performance on the data sets considered. The regularized distance in K_V is the square root of the "Variational" distance: $V(\mathbf{x}_i \| \mathbf{x}_j) = \sum_k |x_j^k - x_i^k|$. It is found that the variational kernel is usually the best performing kernel on the L_1 normed data considered in the channel current analysis (L_1 norm: $|x| = \sum_k |x_k|$, a discrete prob. dist if $x_k > 0$ also). The argument of the exponential in the variational kernel is a distance squared (which satisifies the triangle inequality, etc.), with $K_v = \exp(-d_v^2/2\sigma^2)$, thus the variational kernel automatically satisfies Mercer's conditions.

Consider now the case where the notion of difference is not arithmetic but multiplicative, i.e., based on $(1 - z_k/y_k)$ rather than $(y_k - z_k)$ (for the Gaussian). In doing so, we must restrict to $y_k \neq 0$ of course. As before, the sign of $(y_k - z_k)$ is information preserved in $(1 - z_k/y_k)$, but the latter is not integrable. However, $\ln(y_k/z_k)$ also provides sign info -- positive when $y_k > z_k$, etc., as before, and also includes a ratio. Which to go with? A combination seems best as this is integrable:

$$(11.41) \qquad \frac{\partial \ln K_G(\vec{y}, \vec{z})}{\partial y_K} = \left(\frac{-1}{2\sigma^2}\right)\left[\left(1 - \frac{z_k}{y_k}\right) + \ln\left(\frac{y_k}{z_k}\right)\right]$$

$$(11.42) \qquad K_\sigma(\vec{y}, \vec{z}) = \exp\left(-[D(y \| z) + D(z \| y)]/2\sigma^2\right)$$

This is usually a close 2nd to the K_v kernel, sometimes out performing. This kernel relates feature vectors via relative entropy terms:

$$(11.43) \qquad D(y \| z) = \sum_k y_k \ln\left(\frac{y_k}{z_k}\right)$$

The doubly novel aspect of the entropic kernel is that it would be the very first guess if one wanted to generalize from kernels based on exponentially regularized, square distances, to exponentially regularized, symmetrized, divergences (beginning with the most fundamental, symmetrized "relative entropy" also known as then Kullback-Leibler information divergence) .

Note that we began with the supposition that sign was important, as was some well-behaved notion of difference (whether it is distance-based or divergence-based, etc.). Remarkably, the entropic kernel K_σ appears to satisfy Mercer's condition, when properly restricted to

328

discrete probability distributions: $y_k > 0, \sum y_k = 1$. This is not established with precise mathematical proof, but tested through exhaustive numerical testing using the Mercer test and the positive principle minors test on test data.

Since the feature vectors can be interpreted as probabilities, and satisfy the probability relation $\sum_k (x_i^k) = 1$, it is, perhaps, not surprising that the symmetric-entropic kernel should be a good performer. There is also an interesting relationship between the Variational distance in the Variational Kernel and the Kullback-Leibler divergence in the Entropic Kernels, known as the Pinsker inequality:

$$(11.44) \qquad\qquad D(\mathbf{x}_i \| \mathbf{x}_j) \geq V(\mathbf{x}_i \| \mathbf{x}_j)^2/2.$$

It may prove possible to generate other such inequalities by use of other integrating factors in the above kernel selection process.

Entropic and Gaussian Kernels relate to unique, minimally structured, information divergence and geometric distance measures

Using the Shannon entropy measure it is possible to derive the classic probability distributions of statistical physics by maximizing the Shannon measure subject to appropriate linear momentum constraints. Constrained variational optimizations involving the Shannon entropy measure can, thus, provide a unified framework with which to describe all, or most, of statistical mechanics. The distributions derivable within the maximum entropy formalism include the Maxwell-Boltzmann, Bose-Einstein, Fermi-Dirac, and Intermediate distributions. The maximum entropy method for defining statistical mechanical systems has been extensively studied [67].

Both statistical estimation and maximum entropy estimation are concerned with drawing inferences from partial information. The maximum entropy approach estimates a probability density function when only a few moments are known (where there are an infinite number of higher moments). The statistical approach estimates the density function when only one random sample is available out of an infinity of possible samples. The maximum entropy estimation may be significantly more robust (against over-fitting, for example) in that it has an Occam's Razor argument that "cuts both ways" – use *all* of the information given and avoid using any information not given. This means that out of all of the probability distributions consistent with the set of constraints, choose the one that has maximum uncertainty, i.e., maximum entropy [67].

At the same time that Jaynes was doing his work, essentially an optimization principle based on Shannon entropy, Soloman Kullback was exploring optimizations involving a notion of probabilistic distance known as the Kullback-Leibler distance, referred to above as the relative entropy [60]. The resulting minimum relative entropy (MRE) formalism reduces to the maximum entropy formalism of Jaynes when the reference distribution is uniform. The information distance that Kullback and Leibler defined was an oriented measure of "distance" between two probability distributions. The MRE formalism can be understood to be an extension of Laplace's *Principle of Insufficient Reason* (e.g., if nothing known assume the uniform distribution) in a manner like that employed by Khinchine in his uniqueness proof, but now incorporating constraints.

In their book *Entropy Optimization Principles with Applications* [66], Kapur and Kesavan argue for a generalized entropy optimization approach to the description of distributions. They believe every probability distribution, theoretical or observed, is an entropy optimization distribution, i.e., it can be obtained by maximizing an appropriate entropy measure, or by minimizing a relative entropy measure with respect to an appropriate *a priori* distribution. The primary objective in such a modeling procedure is to represent the problem as a simple combination of probabilistic entities that have a simple set of moment constraints. Generalized measures of distributional distance can also be explored along the lines of generalized measures of geometric distance. In physics, not every geometric distance is of interest, however, since the special theory of relativity tells us that spacetime is locally flat (Lorentzian, which is Euclidean on spatial slices), with metric generalization the Riemannian metrics. Likewise, perhaps not all distributional distance measures are created equal either. The locally-flat equivalent in information geometry [68-70] is the Kullback-Leibler divergence (e.g., the symmetrized relative entropy used in the entropic kernel). We propose generalization to all exponentially regularized distance squared and information divergence kernels and further generalization to include the larger class of stability kernels and "triangle-inequality" kernels (if not a larger class, then the generalizations consist of metrical and divergence-measure generators).

A comparison of some of the SVM Kernels of interest is shown in Fig. 11.16, with "regularized" distances or divergences, where they are regularized if in the form of an exponential with argument the negative of some distance-measure squared ($d^2(x,y)$) or symmetrized divergence measure ($D(x,y)$), the former if using a geometric heuristic for comparison of feature vectors, the latter if using a information divergence heuristic. Results in Fig. 11.16 are shown for the Gaussian Kernel: $d^2(x,y)=\Sigma_k(x_k-y_k)^2$; for the Absdiff or Variational Kernel $d^2(x,y)=(\Sigma_k|x_k-y_k|)^{1/2}$; and for the Symmetrized Relative Entropy Kernel $D(x,y)= D(x\|y)+D(y\|x)$, where $D(x\|y)$ is the standard relative entropy.

The SVM algorithm variants that have been explored are minimally detailed here: in the standard Platt SMO algorithm, $\eta=2*K_{12}-K_{11}-K_{22}$, while speedup variations are described to avoid calculation of this value entirely. A middle ground is obtained with the following definition $\eta =2*K_{12}-2$; If ($\eta >=0$) {$\eta \geq -1$;} (labeled WH SMO in Fig. 11.16, with underflow handling and other details that differ slightly in the WH-SMO implementation as well).

The best algorithm/kernel in Fig. 11.16, and in other channel blockade data studied, has consistently been the WH SMO variant and the Absdiff and Entropic Kernels. Another benefit of the WH SMO variant is its significant speedup over the other methods (about half the time of Platt SMO and one fourth the time of Keerthi 1 or 2). The alpha handling and other modifications in WH SMO [1,37,198] relate to boundary support vector (BSV) handling (associated with handling on outliers), which is also critical to enhancements to a multiclass SVM solution described in the next section.

11.5.2 Automated kernel selection and tuning

An automated tuning solution for Support Vector Machine (SVM) classifiers is described. This is done by implementing a simulated annealing with perturbation tuning procedure on the SVM's kernel and algorithmic parameters. The SVM performance on training data is used to define a fitness function and the tuning results obtained were as good as or better than those obtained manually. Support Vector Machine (SVM) methods are described for data classification, data clustering, and signal analysis using experimental data obtained from a nanopore detector. The SVM implementations described involve SVM algorithmic variants, SVM kernel variants, and SVM chunking variants, where tuning metaheuristics offer an automated way to obtain a powerful SVM classifier for a given dataset. The SVM discussion is interwoven with application to data involving channel current analysis, with application to the signal processing associated with the nanopore transduction detector (NTD) described in Ch. 14.

.

A classifier is typically a simple rule whereby a class determination can be made, such as a decision boundary. Fig. 11.23 shows labeled training data and a decision boundary with a margin region. Learning the decision rule, or a sufficiently good decision rule, especially if simple and elegant, is the implementation aspect of a classifier, and can be difficult and time consuming. Even so, this is often manageable because at least there is data to 'learn from', e.g., supervised learning, with instances and their classifications (or 'labels'). Learning for classification can be done very effectively using generalized Support Vector Machines (SVMs). With clustering efforts, or unsupervised learning, on the other hand, we don't have the label information during training. In what follows SVMs will also be shown to be incredibly effective at clustering when used with metaheuristics to recover label information in a bootstrap learning process. Also shown will be implementation details for distributed SVM training [6], and other speedup optimizations, allowing practical deployment, with the auto-tuning methods described here, of the generalized SVM classification and clustering methods in real-time operational situations (as demonstrated in applications in nanopore detector experiments).

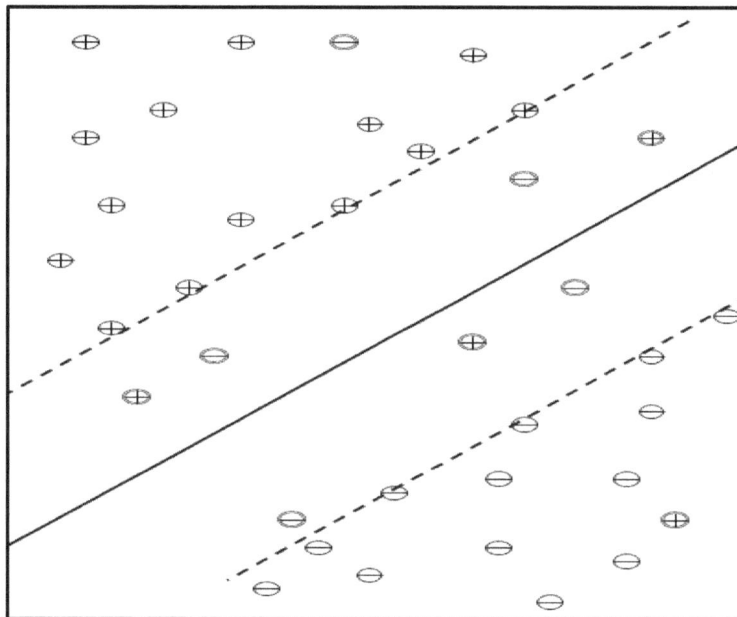

Fig. 11.24. Decision boundary (solid line); with margin (region between dotted lines). Instances are indicated as positive class (+) or negative class (−), where misclassified data on wrong side of hyperplane (or penalized if in margin), is allowed by incurring a penalty in the optimization process. The misclassified or partly penalized margin-region instances are shown with double walled circles.

The SVM-based clustering method that will be described in what follows makes use of the SVM-classifier convergence process. Single-convergence initialized clustering methods, involving label-flipping between SVM convergence training runs, have been studied previously and will be described in detail. The single-convergence methods outperform other methods on the test sets considered, but in examining the clustering failures (albeit fewer than with parameterized methods), there is room for improvement. Efforts to handle this with more sophisticated tuning have met with initial success, as will be related in the following, where multiple convergence processes are examined and scored according to a post-processing sum-of-squared-error (SSE) criterion, where a minimal SSE is sought, to reliably obtain very well-tuned strong SVM performance .

In setting up an SVM Classifier, one must have training data in the form of feature vectors, where all of the feature vectors are the same length. One typically needs to specify a choice of kernel and kernel parameter (and possibly other parameters), and therein lies the rub. The SVM may not converge with your specification. SVMs have a surprising amount of practical functionality, however, as will be shown. It is fairly easy to tune SVMs, in many cases, by simply using a default set of kernel's and parameter ranges. There is more robust performance, however, with more sophisticated tuning. In the SVM applications that attempt to bootstrap a clustering solution, there is more sensitivity to kernel and kernel parameter overall, and more sophisticated tuning methods are clearly needed for the more challenging SVM applications.

Use of SVMs for clustering (unsupervised learning) is possible in a number of different ways. As with the multiclass SVM discriminator generalizations, the strong performance of the binary SVM enables SVM-External as well as SVM-Internal approaches to clustering. Non-parametric SVM-based clustering methods may allow for much improved performance over parametric approaches, particularly since they can apparently be designed to inherit the strengths of their supervised SVM counterparts as will be shown. The 'external' SVM clustering algorithm, to be described in detail, clusters data vectors with no *a priori* knowledge of each vector's class.

It is possible to initiate SVM training with model parameters, such as the kernel or kernel parameter, that are so far out of the operational regime that no convergence is obtained in training. So training must be repeated with tuning on SVM parameters to optimize. For some feature vectors, such as probability vectors, this can partly be done automatically with choice of kernel. In many situations the SVM tuning can simply be done manually, or partly automatically, with simple range testing, where only small, separated, subsets of the training data are used in the tuning tests, before performing SVM training on the full dataset minus the tuning data. Sometimes more elaborate tuning procedures are needed, however, and thus necessary for performance guarantees, and also for the SVM applications in clustering that will be described next. Tuning is a form of optimization, and excellent metaheuristics are known for identifying optimal solutions when a scoring function (a fitness function) can be identified and such is provided by the SVM via sensitivity and specificity scores on training data). Metaheuristic optimizations attempted include genetic algorithms, simulated annealing, and steepest ascent hill-climbing, among others. Applications of many of these methods are shown in the results involving SVM-external clustering.

Our ability to assess a score with SVMs, and thereby assign a fitness, allows for a collection of metaheuristics that basically reduce to 'look around and take the best way forward' via a series of tweaks. This isn't possible for some problems, however, because the 'looking around' part isn't that informative, e.g., the fitness landscape has sections that are at a fixed level (with noise variations about that level, for example). This is the larger problem of the simple globalization algorithm, via random restart: if the fitness landscape or configuration space is too large random restart won't offer a solution (even if it can) in a reasonable amount of time. This is where more clever metaheuristics must be drawn upon to extend to a global optimization algorithm.

One of the weaknesses of the brute force random restart approach mentioned is that the parameter 'tweak' involved is with a *bounded* perturbative change, which may *already* exclude the possibility of reaching the solution sought (given the computational resources and a reasonable amount of time). So one generalization is to allow for tweaks that are unbounded, but in some perturbatively stable way, such as with a Boltzmann factor for regularization, and in doing this we arrive at the Simulated Annealing approach (see Ch. 12 for details).

The global optimization metaheuristics mentioned thus far have worked well, as described in what follows, and suggest more sophisticated configuration selection may benefit further at the component level, on the one hand, and at the population level, on the other hand, especially as further refinements are made to the probabilistic simulated annealing approach. This is because the population and history aspects point to a general metaheuristics that operates on populations of configurations (or populations of 'agents' that interact as intermediaries to determining a configuration selection). The notion of 'history' can be incorporated in various ways, with conveyance of history or learned information internally (such as genome in GA approaches) or externally via 'artifact' (such as via stygmergy in the ACO method). Note that the population based search metaheuristics allow a simple means for distributed computational speedup.

11.6 SVM Multiclass from Decision Tree with SVM Binary Classifiers

The SVM binary discriminator offers high performance and is very robust in the presence of noise. This allows a variety of reductionist multiclass approaches, where each reduction is a binary classification. The SVM Decision Tree is one such approach used extensively with the datasets examined in [37,45], where a collection of SVM Decision Trees (a SVM Decision Forest) can be used to avoid problems with throughput biasing. Alternatively, the variational formalism can be modified to perform a multi-hyperplane optimization situation for a direct multiclass solution [1,37,45], as is described next.

The SVM Decision Tree shown in Fig. 11.25 obtained nearly perfect sensitivity and specificity, with a high data rejection rate, and a highly non-uniform class signal-calling throughput. In Fig. 11.26, the Percentage Data Rejection vs SN+SP curves are shown for test data classification runs with a binary classifier with one molecule (the positive, given by label) versus the rest (the negative). Since the signal calling wasn't passed through a Decision Tree, the way these curves were generated, they don't accurately reflect total throughput, and they don't benefit from the "shielding" shown in the Decision Tree in Fig. 11.25 prototype. In the SVM Decision Tree implementation described in Fig. 11.25 [45], this is managed more comprehensively, to arrive at a five-way signal-calling throughput at the furthest node of 16% (in Fig. 3, 9CG and 9AT have to pass to the furthest node to be classified), while the best throughput, for signal calling on the 8GC molecules, is 75%.

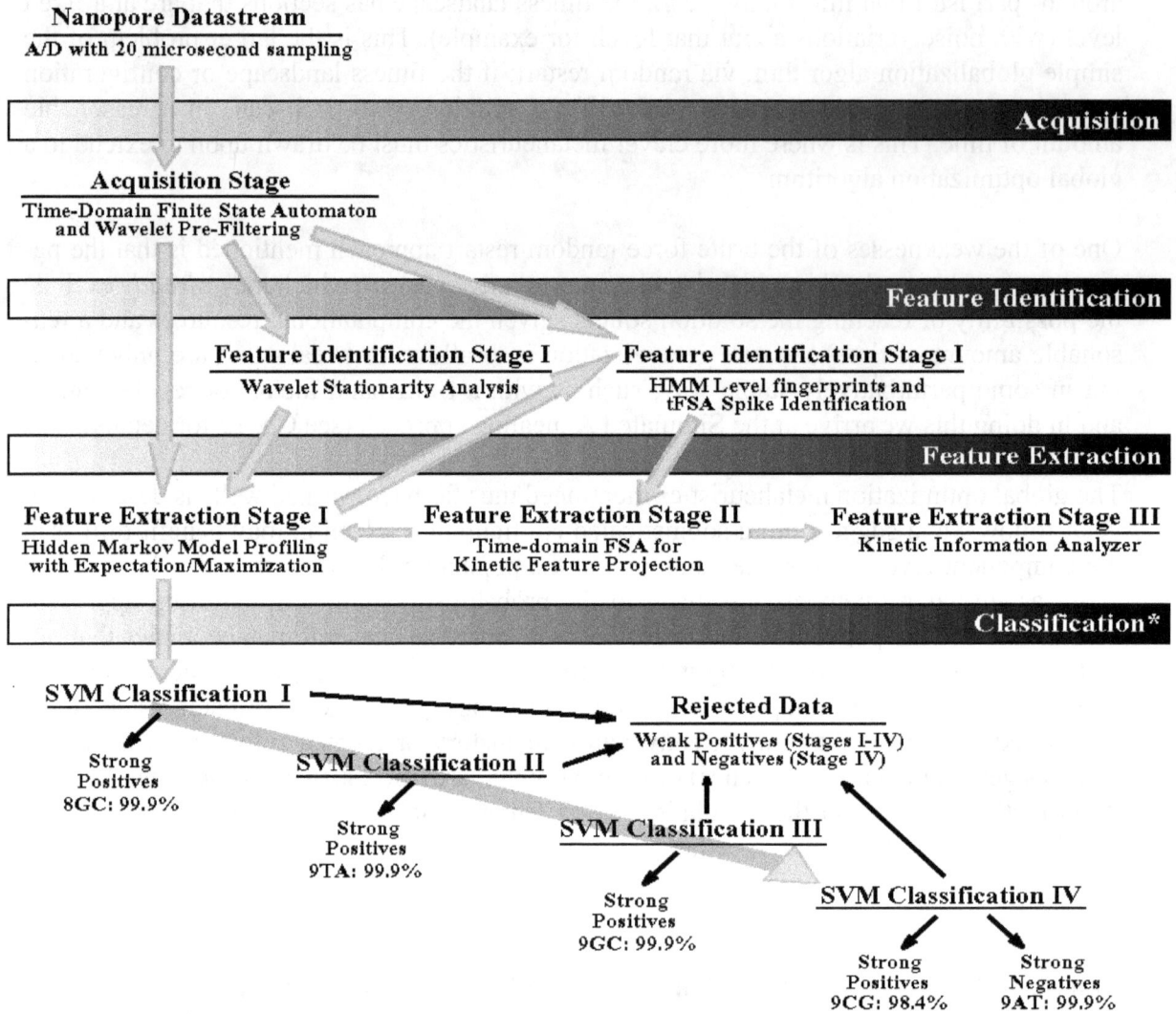

Fig. 11.25. Nanopore Detector signal analysis architecture, with use of an SVM Decision Tree for classification.

The SVM Decision Tree classifier's high, non-uniform, rejection can be managed by generalizing to a collection of Decision Trees (with different species at the furthest node). The problem is that tuning and optimizing a single decision tree is already a large task, even for five species (as in [45]). With a collection of trees, this problem is seemingly compounded, but can actually be lessened in some ways in that now each individual tree need not be so well-tuned/optimized. Although more complicated to implement than an SVM-External method, the SVM-Internal multiclass methods are not similarly fraught with tuning/optimization complications. Fig. 11.27 shows the Percentage Data Rejection vs SN+SP curves on the same train/test data splits as used for Fig. 11.26, except now the drop curves are to be understood as *simultaneous* curves (not sequential application of such curves as in Fig. 11.26). Thus, comparable, or better, performance is obtained with the multiclass-internal approach and with far less effort, since there is no managing and tuning of Decision Trees. Another surprising, and even stronger argument for the SVM-Internal approach to the problem, for many situations, is that a natural drop zone is indicated by the margin.

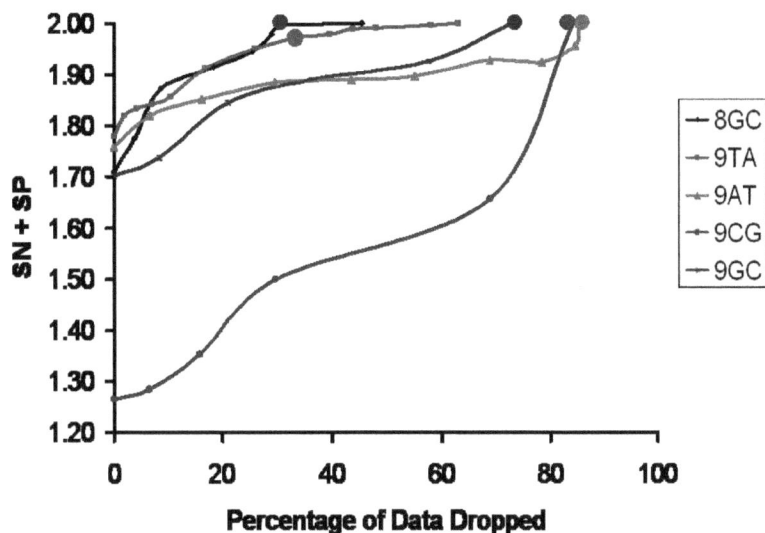

Fig. 11.26. The Percentage Data Rejection vs SN+SP curves are shown for test data classification runs with a binary classifier with one molecule (the positive, given by label) versus the rest (the negative). Since the signal calling wasn't passed through a Decision Tree, it doesn't accurately reflect total throughput, and they don't benefit from the "shielding" shown in the Decision Tree in Fig. 11.25 prototype. The Relative Entropy Kernel is shown because it provided the best results (over Gaussian and Absdiff).

Suppose we define the criteria for dropping weak data as the margin: For any data point x_i; let $\max_m\{f_m(x_i)\} = f_{yi}$, and Let $f_m = \max_m\{f_m(x_i)\}$ for all $m \neq yi$, then we define the margin as: $(f_{yi} - f_m)$, hence data point x_i is dropped if $(f_{yi} - f_m) \leq$ Confidence Parameter. (For this data set using Gaussian, AbsDiff & Sentropic kernel, a confidence parameter of at least $(0.00001)*C$ was required to achieve 100% accuracy.) Using the margin drop approach, there is even less tuning, and there is improved throughput (approximately 75% for *all* species) [1,37].

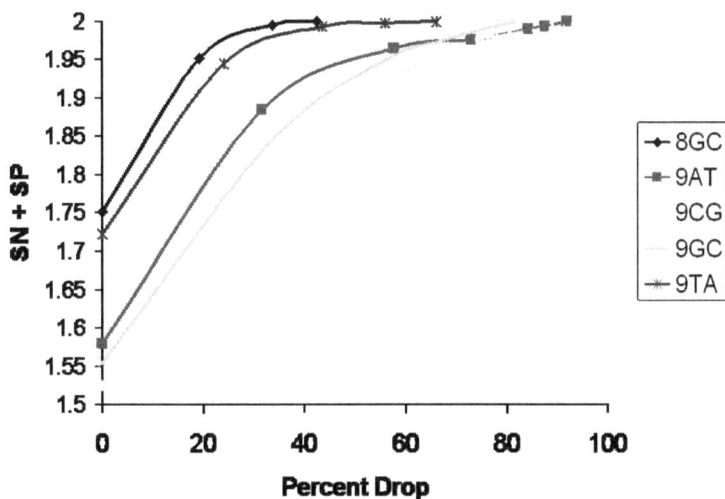

Fig. 11.27. The Percentage Data Rejection vs SN+SP curves are shown for test data classification runs with a *multiclass* discriminator. The following criterion is used for dropping weak data: for any data point x_i; if $\max_m\{f_m(x_i)\} \leq$

Confidence Parameter, then the data point x_i is dropped. For this data set using AbsDiff kernel ($\sigma^2 = 0.2$) performed best, and a confidence parameter of 0.8 achieve 100% accuracy.

11.7 SVM Multiclass Classifier Derivation (multiple decision surface)

In [37] we make use of a variant of a formulation by Crammer & Singer [132]. In the variant [37], the formulation is modified at the Lagrangian level to allow for an analytic decoupling on the constraint equations, permitting a partly analytic solution to the multiclass problem, with significant reduction in algorithmic complexity at the implementation (coding) stage. Using the notation in [37,132]: there are 'k' classes and hence 'k' linear decision functions. For a given input 'x', the output vector corresponds to the output from each of these decision functions. The class of the largest element of the output vector gives the class of 'x'. Each decision function is given by: $f_m(x) = w_m.x + b_m$ for all $m = (1,2,\ldots,k)$. If y_i is the class of the input x_i, then for each input data point, the misclassification error is defined as follows: $\max_m\{f_m(x_i) + 1 - \delta_i^m\} - f_{yi}(x_i)$, where δ_i^m is 1 if $m = y_i$ and 0 if $m \neq y_i$. We add the slack variable ζ_i where $\zeta_i \geq 0$ for all i that is proportional to the misclassification error: $\max_m\{f_m(x_i) + 1 - \delta_i^m\} - f_{yi}(x_i) = \zeta_i$, hence $f_{yi}(x_i) - f_m(x_i) + \delta_i^m \geq 1 - \zeta_i$ for all i, m. To minimize this classification error and maximize the distance between the hyper-planes (Structural Risk Minimization) we have the following formulation:

Minimize: $\sum_i\zeta_i + \beta(1/2)\sum_m w_m^T w_m + (1/2)\sum_m b_m^2$,
where $\beta > 0$ is defined as a regularization constant.
Constraint: $w_{yi}.x_i + b_{yi} - w_m.x_i - b_m - 1 + \zeta_i + \delta_i^m \geq 0$ for all i,m

Note: the term **$(1/2) \sum_m b_m^2$** is added for de-coupling, $1/\beta = C$, and $m = y_i$ in the above constraint is consistent with $\zeta_i \geq 0$, and that periods are being used to denote inner products. The Lagrangian is:

(11.45) $L(w,b,\zeta) = \sum_i\zeta_i + \beta(1/2)\sum_m w_m^T w_m + (1/2)\sum_m b_m^2$
$- \sum_i\sum_m \alpha_i^m(w_{yi}.x_i + b_{yi} - w_m.x_i - b_m - 1 + \zeta_i + \delta_i^m)$

Where all α_i^ms are positive Lagrange multipliers. Now taking partial derivatives of the Lagrangian and equating them to zero (Saddle Point solution): $\partial L/\partial\zeta_i = 1 - \sum_m \alpha_i^m = 0$. This implies that $\sum_m \alpha_i^m = 1$ for all i. $\partial L/\partial b_m = b_m + \sum_i \alpha_i^m - \sum_i\delta_i^m = 0$ for all m. Hence $b_m = \sum_i(\delta_i^m - \alpha_i^m)$. Similarly: $\partial L/\partial w_m = \beta w_m + \sum_i \alpha_i^m x_i - \sum_i \delta_i^m x_i = 0$ for all m. Hence $w_m = (1/\beta)[\sum_i(\delta_i^m - \alpha_i^m)x_i]$ Substituting the above equations into the Lagrangian and after simplification reduces into the dual formalism:

Maximize: $-\frac{1}{2}\sum_{i,j}\sum_m(\delta_i^m - \alpha_i^m)(\delta_j^m - \alpha_j^m)(K_{ij} + \beta) - \beta\sum_{i,m}\delta_i^m\alpha_i^m$
Constraint: $0 \leq \alpha_i^m, \sum_m\alpha_i^m = 1, i = 1\ldots l; m = 1\ldots k$

Where $K_{ij} = x_i.x_j$ is the Kernel generalization. In vector notation:

Maximize: $-\frac{1}{2}\sum_{i,j}(\Delta_{yi} - A_i)(\Delta_{yj} - A_j)(K_{ij} + \beta) - \beta\sum_i\Delta_{yi}A_i$
Constraint: $0 \leq A_i, A_i.1 = 1, i = 1\ldots l$

Let $\tau_i = \Delta_{yi} - A_i$. Hence after ignoring the constant: $-\frac{1}{2}\sum_{i,j}\tau_i.\tau_j(K_{ij} + \beta) + \beta\sum_i\Delta_{yi}\tau_i$, subject to: $\tau_i \leq \Delta_{yi}$, $\tau_i.1 = 0$, $i = 1...l$. The dual is solved (determine the optimum values of all the τs) using the decomposition method.

$$\text{Minimize:} \quad \frac{1}{2}\sum_{i,j}\tau_i^m.\tau_j^m(K_{ij} + \beta) - \beta\sum_{i,m}\delta_i^m\tau_i^m$$
$$\text{Constraint:} \quad \tau_i \leq \Delta_{yi}, \tau_i.1 = 0, i = 1...l$$

The Lagrangian of the dual is:

(11.46) $\quad L = \frac{1}{2}\sum_{i,j,m}\tau_i^m.\tau_j^m(K_{ij} + \beta) - \beta\sum_{i,m}\delta_i^m\tau_i^m - \sum_{i,m}u_i^m(\delta_i^m - \tau_i^m) - \sum_i v_i\sum_m\tau_i^m$;
$\quad$ Subject to $u_i^m \geq 0$

We take the gradient of the Lagrangian with respect to τ_i^m:

$$\blacktriangledown_{\tau i}^m[L] = \sum_i\tau_j^m(K_{ij} + \beta) - \beta\delta_i^m + u_i^m - v_i = 0$$

Introducing $f(\tau) = \sum_i\tau_j^m(K_{ij} + \beta) - \beta\delta_i^m + u_i^m - v_i = 0$ and $f_i^m = \sum_i\tau_j^m(K_{ij} + \beta) - \beta\delta_i^m$, then $f(\tau) = f_i^m + u_i^m - v_i = 0$. By KKT conditions we get two more equations:

(11.47) $u_i^m(\delta_i^m - \tau_i^m) = 0$ and $u_i^m \geq 0$

Case I: if $\delta_i^m = \tau_i^m$, then $u_i^m \geq 0$, hence $f_i^m \leq v_i$. Case II: if $\tau_i^m < \delta_i^m$, then $u_i^m = 0$, hence $f_i^m = v_i$. Note: There is atleast one 'm' for all i such that $\tau_i^m < \delta_i^m$ is satisfied. Therefore combining Case I & II, we get:

(11.48) $\max_m\{f_i^m\} \leq v_i \leq \min_{m: \tau i^m < \delta i^m}\{f_i^m\}$
$\quad$ Or $\max_m\{f_i^m\} \leq \min_{m: \tau i^m < \delta i^m}\{f_i^m\}$
$\quad$ Or $\max_m\{f_i^m\} - \min_{m: \tau i^m < \delta i^m}\{f_i^m\} \leq \varepsilon$

Note: $\tau_i^m < \delta_i^m$ implies that $\alpha_i^m > 0$. Since $\sum_m\alpha_i^m = 1$, for any i each α_i^m is treated as the probability that the data point belongs to class m. Hence we **define KKT violators as:**

(11.49) $\max_m\{f_i^m\} - \min_{m: \tau i^m < \delta i^m}\{f_i^m\} > \varepsilon$ **for all i.**

Decomposition Method to Solve the Dual
Using the method in [178] to solve the Dual, maximize:

$$Q(\tau) = -\frac{1}{2}\sum_{i,j}\tau_i.\tau_j(K_{ij} + \beta) + \beta\sum_i\Delta_{yi}\tau_i; \text{ Subject to: } \tau_i \leq \Delta_{yi}, \tau_i.1 = 0, i = 1...l$$

Expanding in terms of a single 'τ' vector:

$$Q_p(\tau_p) = -\frac{1}{2}A_p(\tau_p. \tau_p) - B_p.\tau_p + C_p$$

Where:

$$A_p = K_{pp} + \beta; B_p = -\beta\Delta_{yp} + \sum_{i\neq p}\tau_i(K_{ip} + \beta); C_p = -\frac{1}{2}\sum_{i,j\neq p}\tau_i.\tau_j(K_{ij}+\beta)+\beta\sum_{i\neq p}\tau_i\Delta_{yi}$$

Therefore ignoring the constant term 'C_p', we have to minimize:

$$Q_p(\tau_p) = \tfrac{1}{2}A_p(\tau_p.\ \tau_p) + B_p.\tau_p;\ \tau_p \leq \Delta_{yp} \text{ and } \tau_p.1 = 0$$

The above equation can also be written as:

$$Q_p(\tau_p) = \tfrac{1}{2}A_p(\tau_p + B_p/A_p).(\tau_p + B_p/A_p) - B_p.B_p/2A_p$$

Substitute $v = (\tau_p + B_p/A_p)$ & $D = (\Delta_{yp} + B_p/A_p)$ in the above equation. Hence, after ignoring the constant term $B_p.B_p/2A_p$ and the multiplicative factor 'A_p' we have to minimize:

$$Q(v) = \tfrac{1}{2}v.v = \tfrac{1}{2}\|v\|^2;\ v \leq D \text{ and } v.1 = D.1 - 1$$

The Lagrangian is given by:

$$L(v) = \tfrac{1}{2}\|v\|^2 - \sum_m \rho_m(D_m - v_m) - \sigma[\sum_m(v_m - D_m) + 1];\ \rho_m \geq 0$$

Hence $\partial L/\partial v_m = v_m + \rho_m - \sigma = 0$. By KKT conditions we have: $\rho_m(D_m - v_m) = 0$ & $\rho_m \geq 0$, also $v_m \leq D_m$. Hence by combining the above in-equalities, we have: $v_m = \text{Min}\{D_m, \sigma\}$, or $\sum_m v_m = \sum_m \text{Min}\{D_m, \sigma\} = \sum_m D_m - 1$. The above equation uniquely defines the 'σ' that satisfies the above equation AND that 'σ' is the optimal solution of the quadratic optimization problem. (Refer to [132] for a formal proof).

Solve for 'σ': We have $\text{Min}\{D_m, \sigma\} + \text{Max}\{D_m, \sigma\} = D_m + \sigma$, hence $\sum_m[D_m + \sigma - \text{Max}\{D_m, \sigma\}] = \sum_m D_m - 1$, or $\sigma = 1/K[\sum_m \text{Max}\{D_m, \sigma\} - 1]$, hence we find σ (iteratively) that satisfies the equation: $|(\sigma_l - \sigma_{l+1})/\sigma_l| \leq$ tolerance. The initial value for 'σ' is set to $\sigma_1 = 1/K[\sum_m D_m - 1]$.

Update rule for 'τ': Once we have 'σ', $\tau_{new}{}^m = v_m - B_p{}^m/(K_{pp} + \beta)$, or:

$$\tau_{new}{}^m = v_m - f_p{}^m/(K_{pp} + \beta) + \tau_{old}{}^m$$

SVM Speedup via differentiating BSVs and SVs

If we track the status of support vectors (SV's) according to whether they are Boundary (penalty) or not, and select accordingly, we can get speedup (even in the binary SVM, where choice of C=100 usually good, but C≥10 typically usually okay too). For the multiclass-internal SVM, on the other hand, the speedup with choice of C can be more significant, as shown in what follows, Fig.s 11.28 & 11.29, where C≥100 typically is needed. Fig. 11.28 shows the percent increase in iterations-to-convergence against the 'C' value. Fig. 11.29 shows the number of bounded support vectors (BSV) as a function of 'C' value.

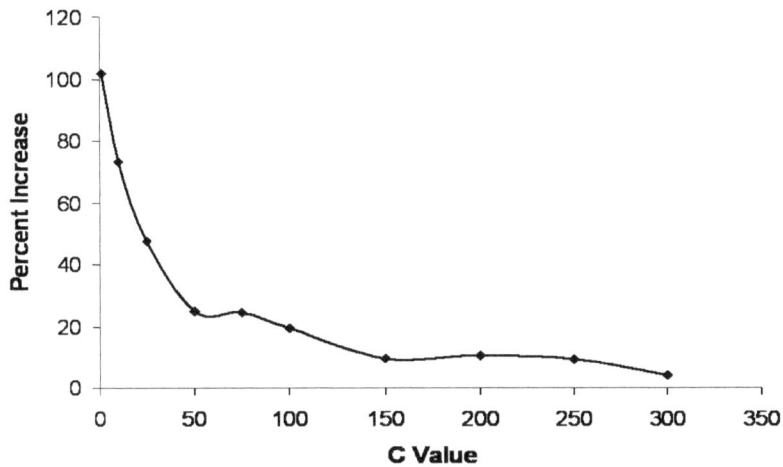

C Value vs Percent Increase in Number of Iterations
5 Classes, 200 Data Points per Class

Figure 11.28. The percent increase in iterations-to-convergence against the 'C' value. For very low values of 'C' the gain is doubled while for very large values of 'C' the gain is low (almost constant for C > 150). Thus we note the dependence of the gain on 'C' value.

Since the algorithm presented in [132] does not differentiate between SV and BSV, a lot of time is spent in trying to adjust the weights of the BSV i.e. weak data. The weight of a BSV may range from [0, 0.5) in their algorithm. In our modification to the algorithm, shown below, as soon as we identify the BSV (as specified by Case III conditions), its weight is no longer adjusted. Hence faster convergence is achieved without sacrificing accuracy.

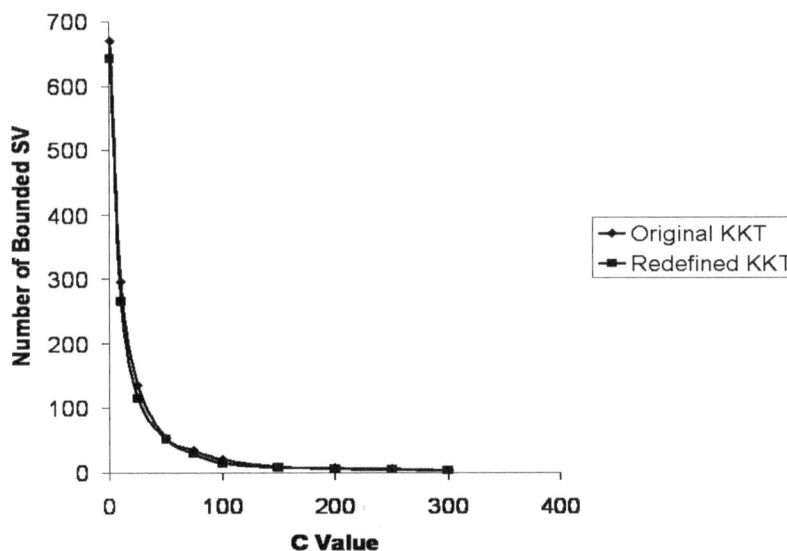

C Value vs Number of Bounded Support Vectors

Figure 11.29. The number of bounded support vectors (BSV) as a function of 'C' value. There are many BSVs for very low values of 'C' and very few

BSVs for large values of 'C'. Thus we can say that the number of BSVs plays a vital role in the speed of convergence of the algorithm.

For the BSV/SV-tracking speedup, the KKT violators are redefined as:
For all $m \neq y_i$ we have:
$\alpha_i^m \{ f_{yi} - f_m - 1 + \zeta_i \} \geq 0$
Subject to: $1 \geq \alpha_i^m \geq 0$; $\sum_m \alpha_i^m = 1$; $\zeta_i \geq 0$ for all i,m
Where $f_m = (1/\beta)[w_m . x_i + b_m]$ for all m

Case I:
If $\alpha_i^m = 0$ for m S.T $f_m = f_m^{max}$
Implies $\alpha_i^{yi} > 0$ and hence $\zeta_i = 0$
Hence $f_{yi} - f_m^{max} - 1 \geq 0$

Case II:
If $1 > \alpha_i^m > 0$ for m S.T $f_m = f_m^{max}$ and $\alpha_i^{yi} > \alpha_i^m$
Implies $\zeta_i = 0$
Hence $f_{yi} - f_m^{max} - 1 = 0$

Case III:
If $1 \geq \alpha_i^m > 0$ for m S.T $f_m = f_m^{max}$ and $\alpha_i^{yi} \leq \alpha_i^m$
Implies $\zeta_i > 0$
Hence $f_{yi} - f_m^{max} - 1 + \zeta_i = 0$
Or $f_{yi} - f_m^{max} - 1 < 0$

11.8 SVM Clustering
The goal of clustering analysis is to partition objects into groups, such that members of each group are more "similar" to each other than the members of other groups. Similarity, however, is determined subjectively as it does not have a universally agreed upon definition. In [129] the author suggests a formal perspective on the difficulty in finding such a unification, in the form of an impossibility theorem: for a set of three simple properties described in [129], there is no clustering function satisfying all three. Furthermore, the author demonstrates that relaxations of these properties expose some of the interesting (and unavoidable) trade-offs at work in well-studied clustering techniques such as single-linkage, sum-of-pairs, k-means, and k-median.

Ideally, one would like to solve the clustering problem given all the known and unknown objective functions. This is provably an NP-Hard problem [342]. This brings us to the work presented here, which seeks to provide a new perspective on clustering by introducing an algorithm that does not require an objective function. Hence, it does not inherit the limitations of an embedded objective function. We propose an algorithm that is capable of suggesting solutions that can be later evaluated using a variety of cluster validators.

11.8.1 SVM-External Clustering
Support Vector Machines (SVMs) provide a powerful method for supervised learning. Use of SVMs for clustering (unsupervised learning) is also possible in a number of different ways. As with the multiclass SVM discriminator generalizations, the strong performance of

the binary SVM enables SVM-External as well as SVM-Internal approaches to clustering. Non-parametric SVM-based clustering methods may allow for much improved performance over parametric approaches, particularly since they can apparently be designed to inherit the strengths of their supervised SVM counterparts as will be shown. Our external-SVM clustering algorithm clusters data vectors with no *a priori* knowledge of each vector's class (Fig. 11.30).

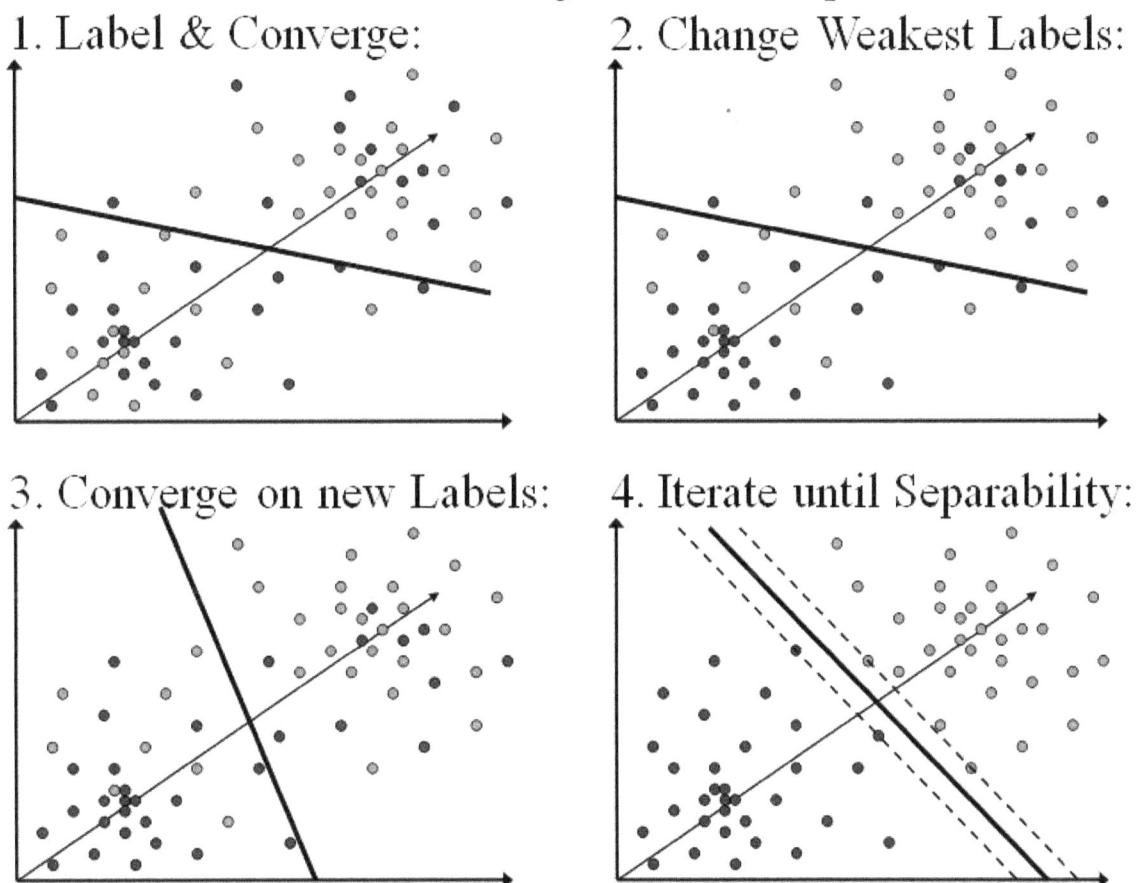

SVM-based Clustering (via multi-pass SVM)

Fig. 11.30. (enlarged version of Fig. 11.7) SVM-external clustering method that uses label flipping with decision making based on the SVM's confidence parameter on classifications.

Single-convergence initialized SVM-clustering: exploration on sensitivity to tuning
The algorithmic variant works by first running a Binary SVM against a data set, with each vector in the set randomly labeled (usually half positives and half negatives), until the SVM converges (Fig. 11.30). Choice of an appropriate kernel and an acceptable sigma value will affect convergence. After the *initial* convergence is achieved, the (sensitivity + specificity) will be low. The algorithm now improves this result by iteratively relabeling the worst misclassified vectors, which have confidence factor values beyond some threshold, followed by rerunning the SVM on the newly relabeled data set. This continues until no more progress can be made. Progress is determined by an increasing value of (sensitivity + specificity).

With sub-cluster identification upon iterating the overall algorithm on the positive and negative clusters identified (until the clusters are no longer separable into sub-clusters), this method provides a way to cluster data sets without prior knowledge of the data's clustering characteristics, or the number of clusters (by iteration on clusters in the binary SVM or direct with merge of multiclass SVM with label flipping algorithms to directly model cluster number without embedded recursion).

Fig.s 11.31 and 11.32 show clustering runs on a data set with a mixture of 8GC and 9GC DNA hairpin data. The set consists of 400 elements. Half of the elements belong to each class. The SVM uses a Gaussian Kernel and allows 3% KKT Violators. The algorithmic variant shown in Fig. 11.32 works by first running a Binary SVM against a data set, with each vector in the set randomly labeled, until the SVM converges. In order to obtain convergence, an acceptable number of KKT violators must be found. This is done through running the SVM on the randomly labeled data with different numbers of allowed violators until the number of violators allowed is near the lower bound of violators needed for the SVM to converge on the particular data set. In practice, the initialization step, that arrives at the first SVM convergence, typically takes longer than all subsequent partial re-labeling and SVM rerunning steps.

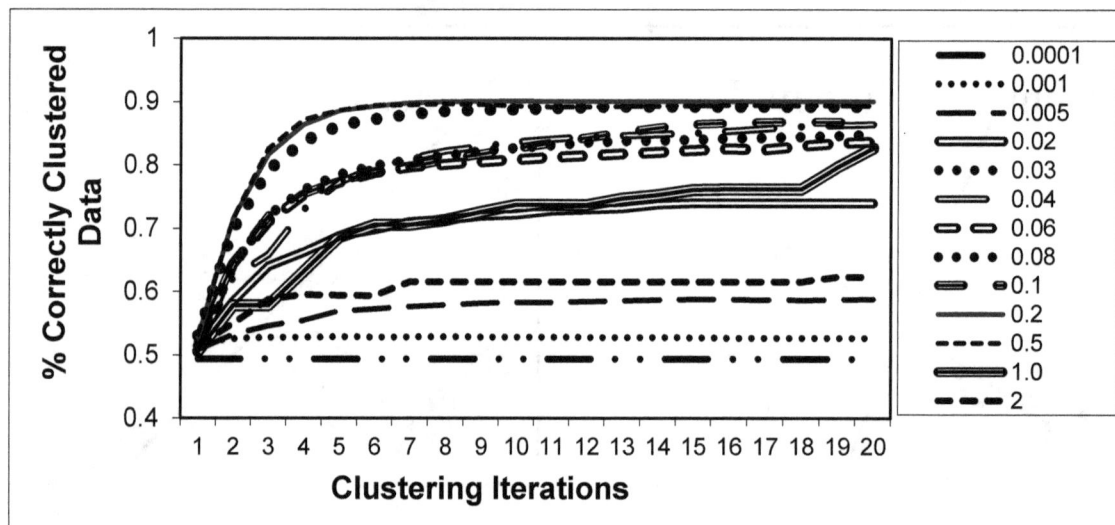

Fig. 11.31. Summary of the degradation in clustering performance for less optimal selection of kernel and tuning parameter – with averages of the five testruns are used as representative curves for that kernel/tuning selection in the above.

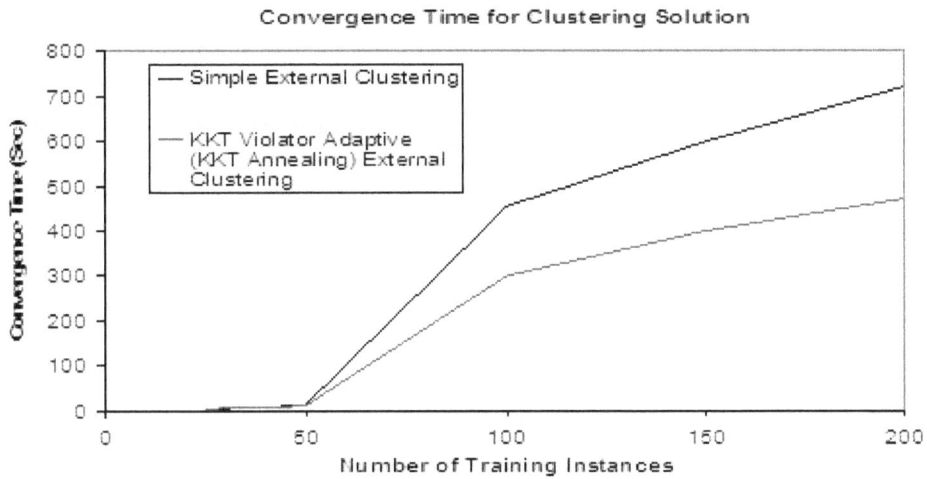

Convergence Time for Clustering Solution

Fig. 11.32. Efforts to use simulated annealing in the number of KKT Violators tolerated on each iteration of the external clustering algorithm, to accelerate the convergence (clustering) process. In results shown, cluster time is approximately halved.

In Fig. 11.33 the decision hyperplane is circular in the feature space. The clustering kernel used in Fig. 11.33 was the polynomial kernel (the linear kernel failed in this case).

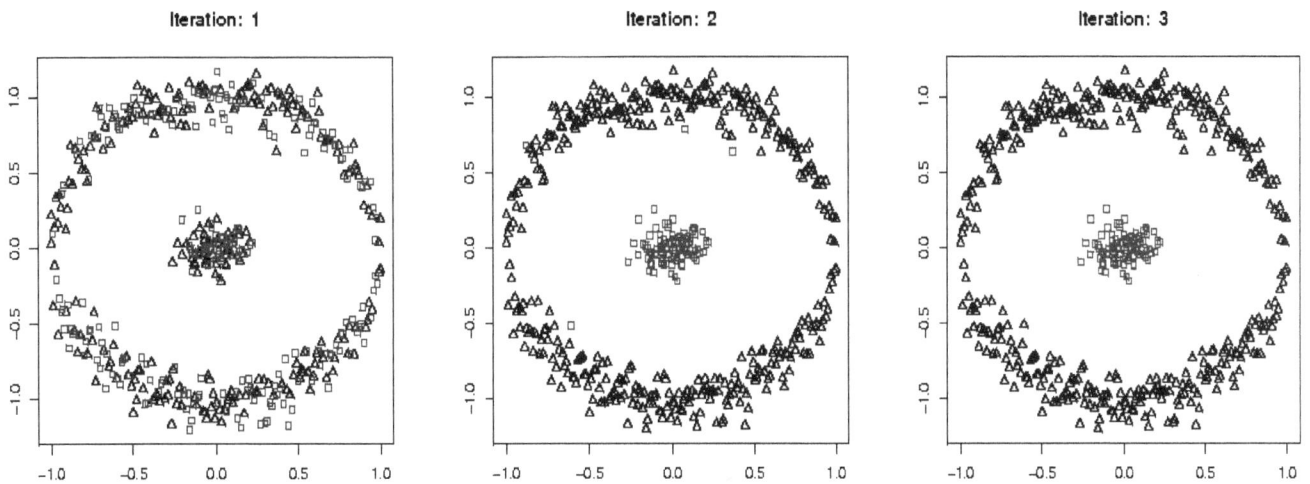

Fig. 11.33. The results of SVM-Relabeler algorithm using a third degree polynomial kernel

Single-convergence SVM-clustering: hybrid clustering
Although convergence is always achieved with the SVM-clustering method in the label-flippings, after the initial convergence, convergence to a *global* optimum is not guaranteed. Fig. 11.34 shows the Purity and Entropy (with the RBF kernel) as a function of Number of Iterations, while Fig. 11.34 (right) shows the SSE as a function of Number of Iterations. The stopping criteria used for the algorithm is based on the unsupervised (external) SSE measure. Comparison to fuzzy c-means and kernel k-means is shown on the same dataset (the solid blue and black lines in Fig. 11.34 left and center).

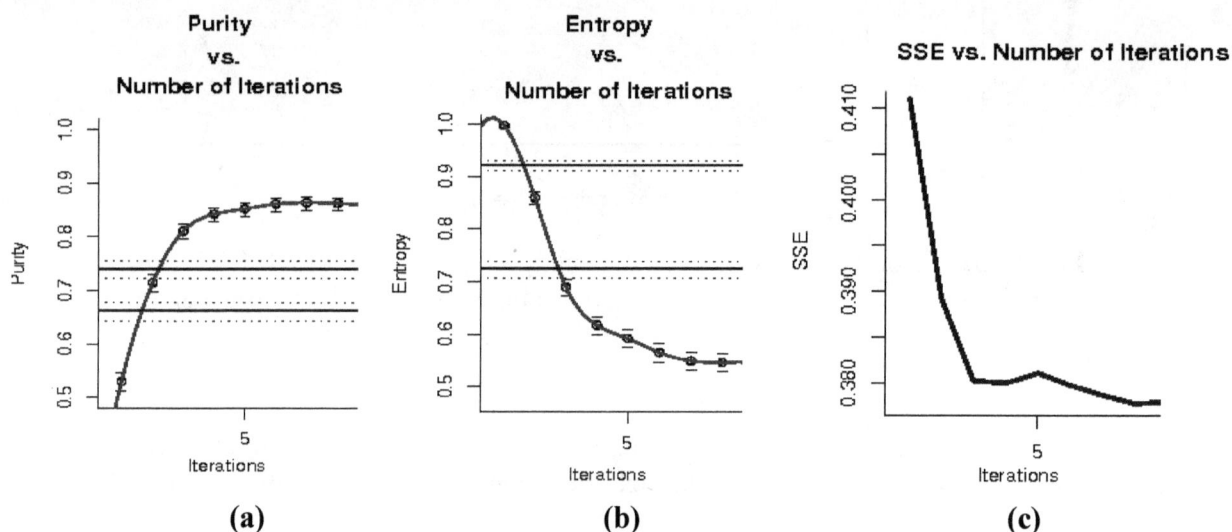

Fig. 11.34. SVM-external clustering results. (a) and (b) show the boost in Purity and Entropy as a function of Number of Iterations of the SVM clustering algorithm. (c) shows that SSE, as an unsupervised measure, provides a good indicator in that improvements in SSE correlate strongly with improvements in purity and entropy. The blue and black lines are the result of running fuzzy c-mean and kernel k-mean (respectively) on the same dataset.

The ability to get stuck in local minima motivates the introduction of perturbations into the methods, as shown in Fig.s 11.35 & 11.36 that follow.

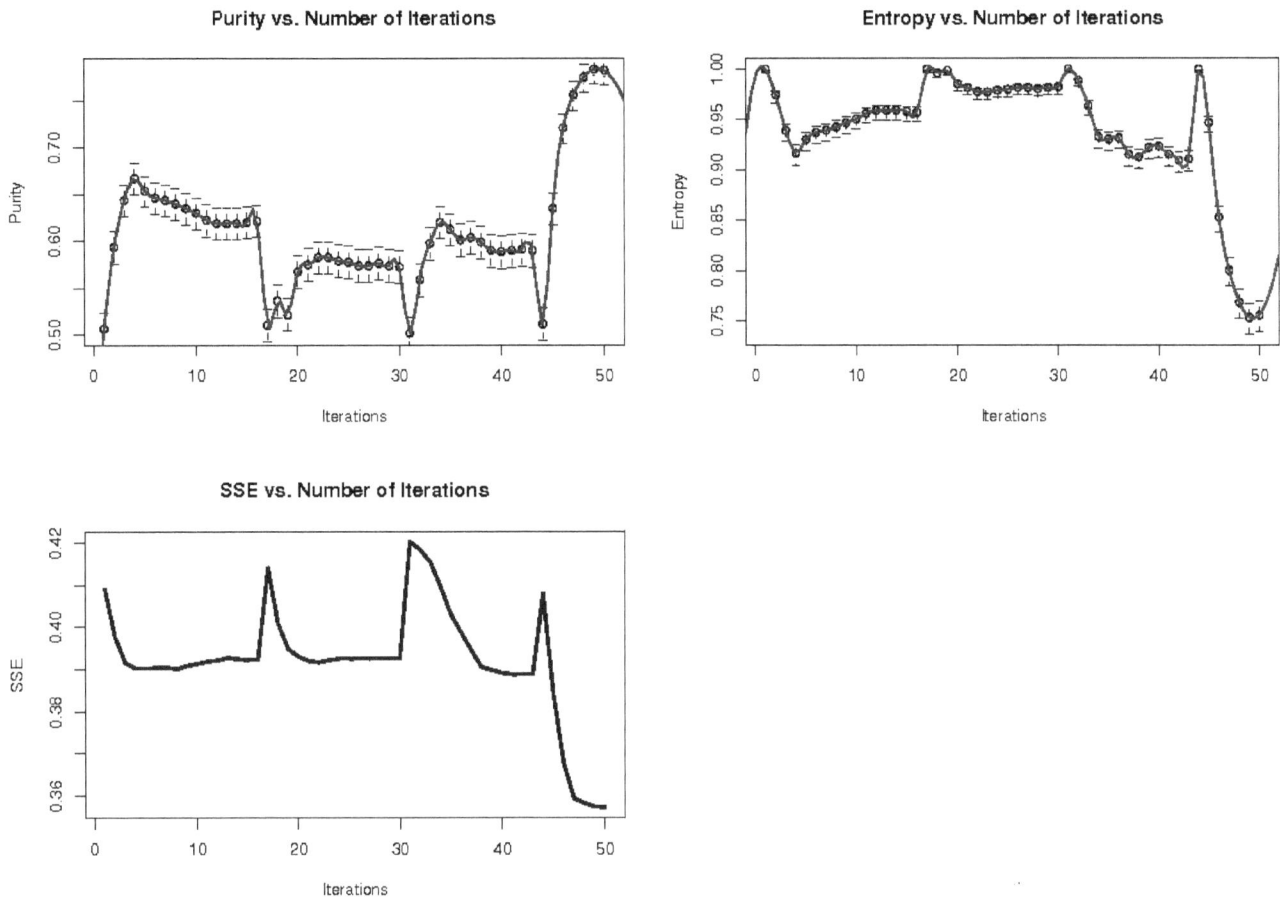

Fig. 11.35. The result of Re-labeler Algorithm with Perturbation. The top plots demonstrate the various Purity and Entropy scores for each perturbed run. The spikes are drops followed by recovery in the validity of the clusters as a result of random perturbation. The bottom plot is a similar demonstration, by tracking the unsupervised quality of the clusters. Note that after 4 runs of perturbation best solution is recovered.

It is found that the result of the Re-labeler algorithm can be significantly improved by randomly perturbing a weak clustering solution and repeating the SVM-external label-swapping iterations as depicted in Fig. 11.36. To explore this further, a hybrid SVM-external approach to the above problem is introduced to replace the initial random labeling step with k-means clustering or some other fast clustering algorithm. The initial SVM-external clustering must then be slightly and randomly perturbed to properly initialize the re-labeling step; otherwise the SVM clustering tends to return to the original k-means clustering solution. A complication is the unknown amount of perturbation of the k-means solution that is needed to initialize the SVM-clustering well -- it is generally found that a weak clustering method does best for the initialization (or one weakened by a sufficient amount of perturbation).

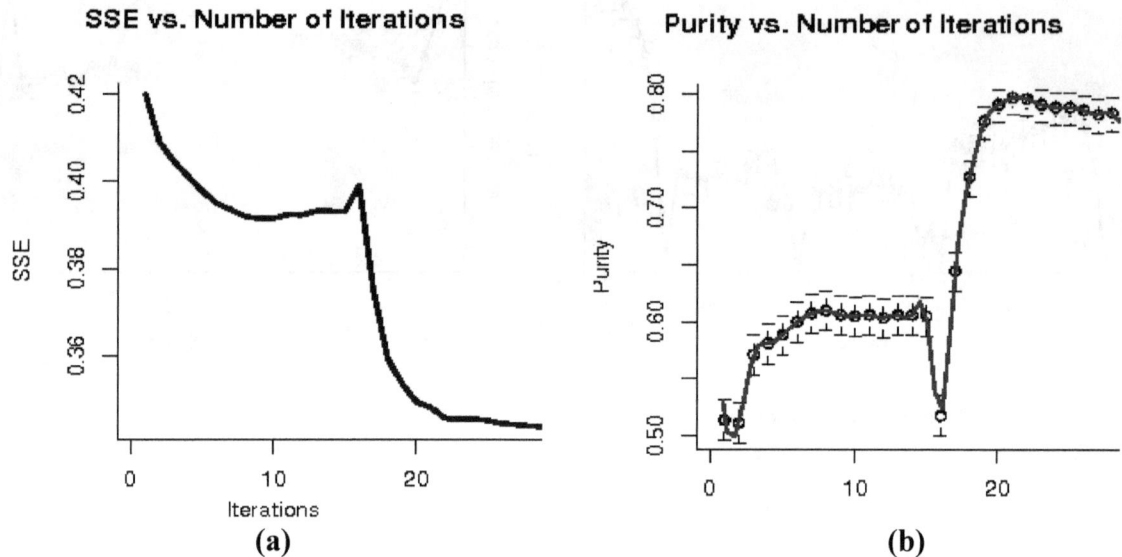

SSE vs. Number of Iterations

Purity vs. Number of Iterations

(a) (b)

Fig. 11.36. (a) and (b) represent the SSE and Purity evaluation of hybrid Re-labeler with Perturbation on the same dataset. Data is initially clustered using k-means to initialize the Re-labeler algorithm. The first segment of the plot (right before the spike at 16) is the result of Re-labeler after 10% perturbation, while the second segment is the result after 30% perturbation. Purity Number of Iterations.

11.8.2 Single-convergence SVM-clustering: comparative analysis

The single-convergence initialized SVM-based clustering algorithm begins by first running a binary SVM classifier against a data set with each vector in the set randomly labelled, this is repeated until an *initial convergence* occurs. The convergence sometimes has to be attempted several times (with different randomized initializations) before a SVM solution is obtained. Once an SVM solution is obtained, however, the strengths of the SVM classifier can be used to full advantage. SVMs are ideal in this effort as they not only classify, but offer a confidence parameter with their classification, and can do so in a generalized kernel space. Once a convergent solution is obtained label-flipping (from positive to negative) can be done for low-confidence labels in an iterative process, with SVM re-training after each round of weak-label changes. At each iteration we can potentially have unequal numbers of positives and negatives changing their labels, thus, asymmetrically sized clusters can be realized from a half-positive/half-negative initialization. This iterative process continues until there is no longer a low-confidence classification by the SVM, or until an external cluster validation, such as the sum-of-squared error (SSE) on each cluster, remains relatively unchanged. There are numerous tuning parameters in the SVM-classification process itself, as well as in the SVM-clustering halting specification, and even tuning choices in the SVM chunk-training (that may be necessary for larger data sets). As shown in Fig. 11.37, SVM-based clustering often outperforms other methods.

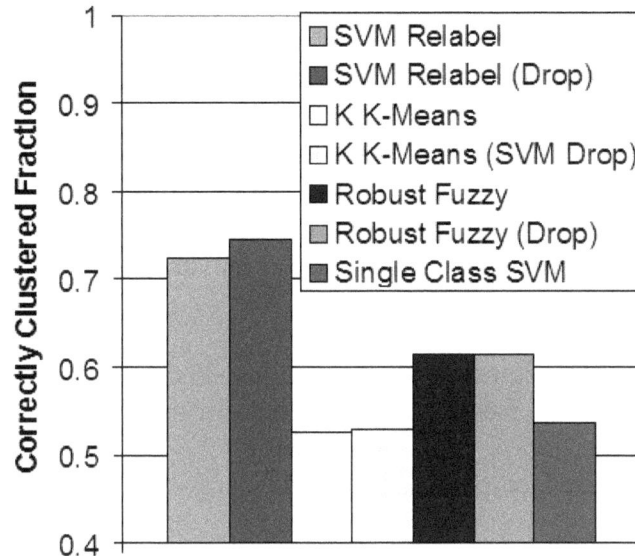

Fig. 11.37. Clustering performance comparisons: SVM-external clustering compared with explicit objective function clustering methods.
Nanopore detector blockade signal clustering resolution from a study of blockades due to individual molecular capture-events with 9AT and 9CG DNA hairpin molecules. The SVM-external clustering method consistently out-performs the other methods. The optimal drop percentage on weakly classified data differed for the different methods for the scores shown: Our SVM relabel clustering with drop: 14.8%; Kernel K-means with drop: 19.8%; Robust fuzzy with drop: 0% (no benefit); Vapnik's Single-class SVM (internal) clustering: 36.1%.

The problem with the single-convergence initiated SVM clustering approach is that it can get stuck in a weak solution or occasionally fail more seriously. Stabilization could be done with numerous repeats of the SVM clustering process, but this is computationally over-kill and more efficient processes, including distributed intelligence tuning (with genetic algorithms, for example) are sought in the label-flipping convergence process, and initializing in a more informed way, with more than one initial convergence required.

SVM 'Internal' Clustering
The SVM-Internal approach to clustering was originally defined by [121]. Data points are mapped by means of a kernel to a high dimensional feature space where we search for the minimal enclosing sphere. The minimal enclosing sphere, when mapped back into the data space, can separate into several components; each enclosing a separate cluster of points. The width of the kernel (say Gaussian) controls the scale at which the data is probed while the soft margin constant helps to handle outliers and over-lapping clusters. The structure of a dataset is explored by varying these two parameters, maintaining a minimal number of support vectors to assure smooth cluster boundaries.

We have used the algorithm defined in [141] to identify the clusters, with methods adapted from [142,143] for their handling. If the number of data points is 'n', then we require n(n-1)/2 number of comparisons. We have made modifications to the algorithm such that we

347

eliminate comparisons that do not have an impact on the cluster connectivity. Hence the number of comparisons required will be less than n(n-1)/2.

In each comparison we sub-divide the line segment connecting the two data points into 20 parts; hence we obtain 19 different points on this line segment. The two data points belong to the same cluster only if all the 19 points lie inside the cluster. Given the cost of evaluating utmost 19 points for every comparison, the need to eliminate comparisons that do not have an impact on the cluster connectivity becomes even more important. Finally we have used Depth First Search (DFS) algorithm for the cluster harvest. The approach to the solving the Dual problem is shown ibelow.

Let $\{x_i\}$ be a data set of 'N' points in R^d. Using a non-linear transformation φ, we transform 'x' to some high-dimensional Kernel space and look for the smallest enclosing sphere of radius 'R'. Hence we have: $\|\varphi(x_j) - a\|^2 \leq R^2$ for all $j = 1,...,N$; where 'a' is the center of the sphere. Soft constraints are incorporated by adding slack variables 'ζ_j':

$$\|\varphi(x_j) - a\|^2 \leq R^2 + \zeta_j \text{ for all } j = 1,...,N; \quad \zeta_j \geq 0$$

We introduce the Lagrangian as:

$$L = R^2 - \sum_j \beta_j (R^2 + \zeta_j - \|\varphi(x_j) - a\|^2) - \sum_j \zeta_j \mu_j + C\sum_j \zeta_j; \quad \beta_j \geq 0, \mu_j \geq 0,$$

where C is the cost for outliers and hence $C\sum_j \zeta_j$ is a penalty term. Setting to zero the derivative of 'L' w.r.t. R, a and ζ we have: $\sum_j \beta_j = 1$; $a = \sum_j \beta_j \varphi(x_j)$; and $\beta_j = C - \mu_j$.

Substituting the above equations into the Lagrangian, we have the dual formalism as:

$$W = 1 - \sum_{i,j} \beta_i \beta_j K_{ij} \text{ where } 0 \leq \beta_i \leq C;$$
with $K_{ij} = \exp(-\|x_i - x_j\|^2/2\sigma^2)$ typically used. Subject to: $\sum_i \beta_i = 1$

By KKT conditions we have: $\zeta_j \mu_j = 0$ and $\beta_j(R^2 + \zeta_j - \|\varphi(x_j) - a\|^2) = 0$.

In the kernel space of a data point 'x_j' if $\zeta_j > 0$, then $\beta_j = C$ and hence it lies outside of the sphere i.e. $R^2 < \|\varphi(x_j) - a\|^2$. This point becomes a bounded support vector or BSV. Similarly if $\zeta_j = 0$, and $0 < \beta_j < C$, then it lies on the surface of the sphere i.e. $R^2 = \|\varphi(x_j) - a\|^2$. This point becomes a support vector or SV. If $\zeta_j = 0$, and $\beta_j = 0$, then $R^2 > \|\varphi(x_j) - a\|^2$ and hence this point is enclosed with-in the sphere.

Solving the Dual (Based on Keerthi's SMO [140])

The dual formalism is: $1 - \sum_{i,j} \beta_i \beta_j K_{ij}$ where $0 \leq \beta_i \leq C$; $K_{ij} = \exp(-\|x_i - x_j\|^2/2\sigma^2)$ is used, also $\sum_i \beta_i = 1$. For any data point 'x_k', the distance of its image in kernel space from the center of the sphere is given by: $R^2(x_k) = 1 - 2\sum_i \beta_i K_{ik} + \sum_{i,j} \beta_i \beta_j K_{ij}$. The radius of the sphere is R = $\{R(x_k) \mid x_k$ is a Support Vectors$\}$, hence data points which are Support Vectors lie on cluster boundaries. Outliers are points that lie outside of the sphere and therefore they do not belong to any cluster i.e. they are Bounded Support Vectors. All other points are enclosed by the sphere and therefore they lie inside their respective cluster. KKT Violators are given as: (i) If $0 < \beta_i < C$ and $R(x_i) \neq R$; (ii) If $\beta_i = 0$ and $R(x_i) > R$; and (iii) If $\beta_i = C$ and $R(x_i) < R$.

The Wolfe dual is: $f(\beta) = \text{Min}_\beta \{\sum_{i,j}\beta_i\beta_jK_{ij} - 1\}$. In the SMO decomposition, in each iteration we select β_i & β_j and change them such that $f(\beta)$ reduces. All other β's are kept constant for that iteration. Let us denote β_1 & β_2 as being modified in the current iteration. Also $\beta_1 + \beta_2 = (1 - \sum_{i=3}\beta_i) = s$, a constant. Let $\sum_{i=3}\beta_iK_{ik} = C_k$, then we obtain the SMO form: $f(\beta_1,\beta_2) = \beta^2_1 + \beta^2_2 + \sum_{i,j=3}\beta_i\beta_jK_{ij} + 2\beta_1\beta_2K_{12} + 2\beta_1C_1 + 2\beta_2C_2$. Eliminating β_1: $f(\beta_2) = (s - \beta_2)^2 + \beta^2_2 + \sum_{i,j=3}\beta_i\beta_jK_{ij} + 2(s - \beta_2)\beta_2K_{12} + 2(s - \beta_2)C_1 + 2\beta_2C_2$. To minimize $f(\beta_2)$, we take the first derivative w.r.t. β_2 and equate it to zero, thus $f'(\beta_2) = 0 = 2\beta_2(1 - K_{12}) - s(1 - K_{12}) - (C_1 - C_2)$, and we get the update rule: $\beta_2^{new} = [(C_1 - C_2)/2(1 - K_{12})] + s/2$. We also have an expression for "$C_1 - C_2$" from: $R(x_1^2) - R(x_2^2) = 2(\beta_2 - \beta_1)(1 - K_{12}) - 2(C_1 - C_2)$, thus $C_1 - C_2 = [R(x_2^2) - R(x_1^2)]/2 + (\beta_2 - \beta_1)(1 - K_{12})$, substituting, we have:

$$\beta_1^{new} = \beta_1^{old} - [R(x_2^2) - R(x_1^2)]/[4(1 - K_{12})]$$

Keerthi Algorithm:
Compute 'C': if percent outliers = n and number data points = N, then: $C = 100/(N*n)$

Initialize β: Initialize $m = \text{int}(1/C) - 1$ number of randomly chosen indices to 'C'
Initialize two different randomly chosen indices to values less than 'C' such that $\sum_i\beta_i = 1$

Compute $R^2(x_i)$ for all 'i' based on the current value of β. Divide data into three sets: Set I if $0 < \beta_i < C$; Set II if $\beta_i = 0$; and Set III if $\beta_i = C$. Compute $R^2\_low = \text{Max}\{R^2(x_i) \mid 0 \leq \beta_i < C\}$ and $R^2\_up = \text{Min}\{R^2(x_i) \mid 0 < \beta_i \leq C\}$.

In every iteration execute the following two paths alternatively until there are no KKT violators:
1. Loop through all examples (call Examine Example subroutine)
2. Keep count of number of KKT Violators.
3. Loop through examples belonging only to Set I (call Examine Example subroutine) until $R^2\_low - R^2\_up < 2*\text{tol}$.

Examine Example Subroutine
a. Check for KKT Violation. An example is a KKT violator if:
b. Set II and $R^2(x_i) > R^2\_up$; choose R^2_up for joint optimization
c. Set III and $R^2(x_i) < R^2\_low$; choose R^2_low for joint optimization
d. Set I and $R^2(x_i) > R^2\_up + 2*\text{tol}$ OR $R^2(x_i) < R^2\_low - 2*\text{tol}$; choose R^2_low or R^2_up for joint optimization depending on which gives a worse KKT violator
e. Call the Joint Optimization subroutine

Joint Optimization Subroutine
a. Compute $\eta = 4(1 - K_{12})$ where K_{12} is the kernel evaluation of the pair chosen in Examine Example
b. Compute $D = [R^2(x_2) - R^2(x_1)]/\eta$
c. Compute $\text{Min}\{(C - \beta_2), \beta_1\} = L1$
d. Compute $\text{Min}\{(C - \beta_1), \beta_2\} = L2$
e. If $D > 0$; then $D = \text{Min}\{D, L1\}$
f. Else $D = \text{Max}\{D, -L2\}$
g. Update β_2 as: $\beta_2 = \beta_2 + D$
h. Update β_1 as: $\beta_1 = \beta_1 - D$
i. Re-compute $R^2(x_i)$ for all 'i' based on the changes in β_1 & β_2

j. Re-compute R^2_low & R^2_up based on elements in Set I, $R^2(x_1)$ & $R^2(x_2)$

11.8.3 Stabilized, single-convergence initialized, SVM-External Clustering

The External SVM Clustering data set is chosen to be an equal positives vs negatives sample of 200 8GC blockade signals and 200 9GC blockade signals (see [1,37,45] for details about these molecules). Each feature vector is 150 dimensional and normalized to satisfy the L_1 (norm = 1) constraint. Features from the 8 and 9 base-pair blockade signals were extracted using Hidden Markov Models (for details, see [1,37,45]). Although convergence was easily achieved with the External SVM Clustering algorithm (see the Methods), convergence to a global optimum was not guaranteed.

In [31], we see that a small value of Kernel-SSE (herein referred to as SSE) is shown to provide us with a reliable cluster validation measure. The Exteranl SVM Clustering (SVM-Relabeler) algorithm does not use an objective function, and the hope is that by running the algorithm in its purest form, the resulting clusters are reliable solutions. However, running this algorithm in this basic fashion does not consistently provide us with a satisfying clustering solution. In fact, the solution space can be divided into three sets: successful, local-optimum, and unsuccessful. Unsuccessful solutions and local optima solutions are undesirable and the objective is to find a method to eliminate their usage by simply re-clustering for objectively improved clustering (via SSE scoring, for example). Since, the solutions in the unsuccessful set are expected to be easily identified in any experiment that calculates the SSE of a randomly labeled data set, they can be simply eliminated by post-processing. In a control experiment we have randomly labeled the dataset 5000 times and calculated the SSE distribution for the experiment. The resulting distribution has a good fit to Johnson's SB distribution and is illustrated in the histogram of Fig. 11.38. Using a fitted distribution one can calculate the p-value of a given SSE. For a SSE threshold of 170.5 (accidentally very unlikely) we can directly eliminate the unsuccessful set.

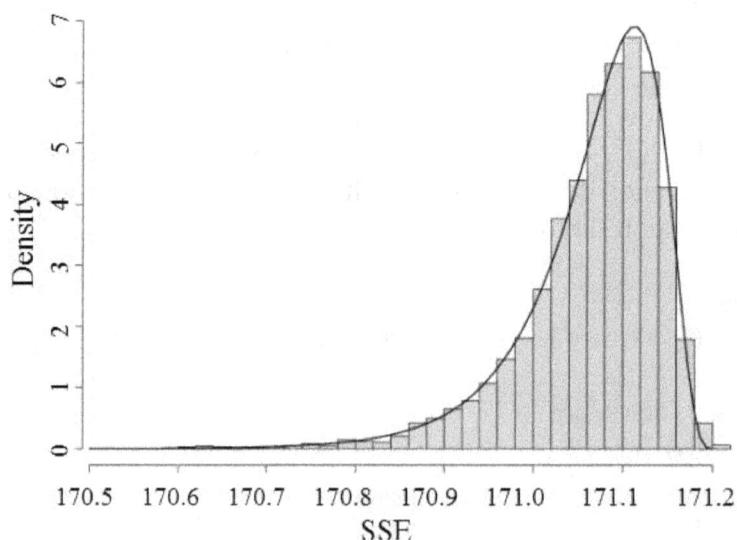

Fig. 11.38. Nanopore feature vector data (in standard 150 component, L1-norm, format) is randomly labeled 5000 times followed by evaluation of SSE values and production of a histogram of those values as shown. The resulting

distribution has a good fit to Johnson's SB distribution with gamma= −5.5405, delta = 1.8197, lambda = 2.7483, epsilon = 168.46.

To substantially reduce the local optimum solutions, however, thresholding does not scale well. One solution is to use a simple hill climbing algorithm which is to run the algorithm for a sufficiently long number of iterations to find the solution with the lowest SSE value. To do this, the clustering algorithm is run repeatedly and randomly initialized every time. A solution is accepted as the best solution if it has a lower SSE than the previously recorded value. This can be a very slow learning process, and is a familiar scenario in statistical learning, and one of the popular solutions in those situations works well here as well – simulated annealing.

It is observed that random perturbation by flipping each label at some probability, p_{pert}, is often sufficient to switch to another subspace where a better solution could be found. (Note that $p_{pert} = 0.50$ has the effect of random reinitialization and $p_{pert} = 1$ flips the entire labels.) The hope is that perturbation with $p_{pert} \leq 0.50$ results in a faster convergence. Reliability can be achieved by searching through the solution space. To do this efficiently, Monte Carlo Methods could be used by taking advantage of perturbation to evaluate the neighboring configuration. The procedure described next uses a modified version of Simulated Annealing to achieve this desired reliability.

As shown in Fig. 11.39 left, top panel, constant perturbation with $p_{pert} = 0.10$ results in a local-optimum solution that could be otherwise avoided by using a perturbation function depending on the number of iterations of unchanged SSE (Fig. 11.39 right, top panel). These results were produced using an exponential cooling function, $T_{k+1} = \beta^k T_k$, with $\beta = 0.96$ and $T_0 = 10$. The initial temperature, T_0 should be large enough to be comparable with the change of SSE, ΔSSE, and therefore increase the randomness by making the Boltzman factor $e^{-\Delta SSE/T} \approx e^0$, while β (< 1) should be large enough to speed up the cooling effect.

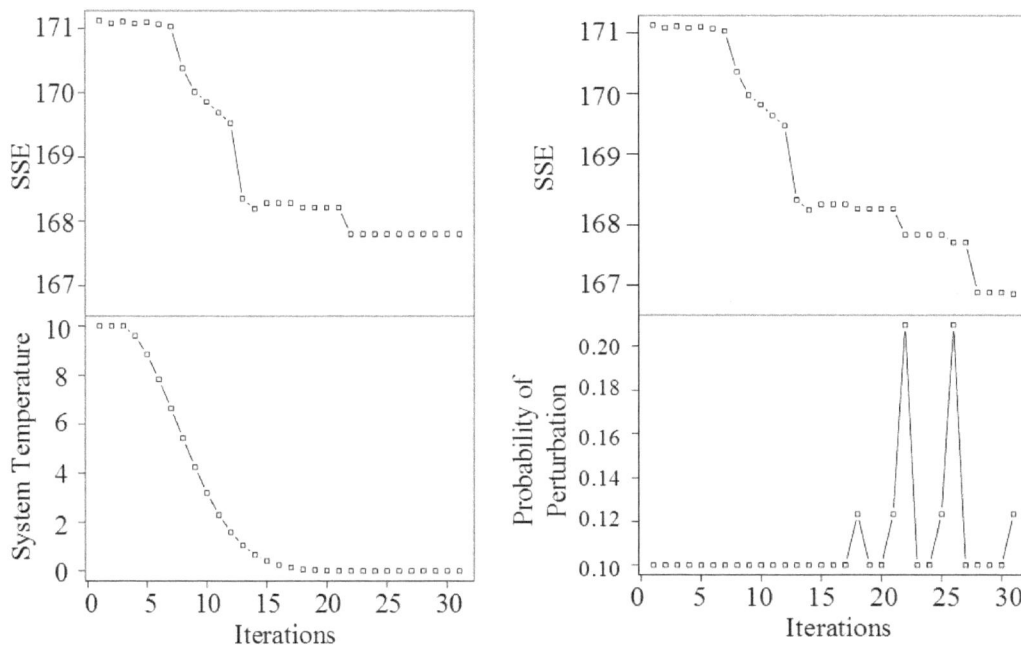

Fig. 11.39. (left) Simulated annealing with constant perturbation, (right) Simulated annealing with variable perturbation. As shown in left, top panel,

simulated annealing with a 10% initial label-flipping results in a local-optimum solution. In the right panel this is avoided by boosting the perturbation function depending on the number of iterations of unchanged SSE (right, top panel). These results were produced using an exponential cooling function, $T_{k+1} = \beta^k T_k$, with $\beta = 0.96$ and $T_0 = 10$.

In the effort shown in Fig.s 11.39 & 11.40, it was found that random perturbation and hybridized methods (with more traditional clustering methods) could help stabilize the clustering method, but often at significant cost to its performance edge over other clustering methods (apparently due to getting stuck in local minima traps to which the other parametric clustering methods are susceptible). The 'pure' SVM-external clustering method appears to offer very strong solutions about half the time – which allows for optimization simply by repeated clustering attempts and looking for the most tightly clustered (smallest SSE) solution. This suggested a simulated annealing approach for greater computational efficiency, as shown in Fig. 11.39 (recent work with Genetic Algorithms, not shown, exhibit even stronger stability). Results of this effort (Fig. 11.39) significantly improve and stabilize the SVM clustering process.

Given the wide variety of dissimilar tuning parameters in the SVM classification process alone, tests on SVM classification with genetic algorithm (GA) based tuning seems optimal. The very robust and rapid auto-tuning with the GA approach on SVM classification in initial tests strongly suggests that this, or any swarm intelligence search/tuning paradigms, offer important refinement to the SVM-classification efforts and critical refinement to the single-convergence initialization SVM-clustering efforts.

11.8.4 Stabilized, multiple-convergence, SVM-External Clustering
Re-examining the same dataset using the Absdiff kernel (gamma = 1.8) and computing SSE, but now iterating with multiple convergences instead of perturbations.

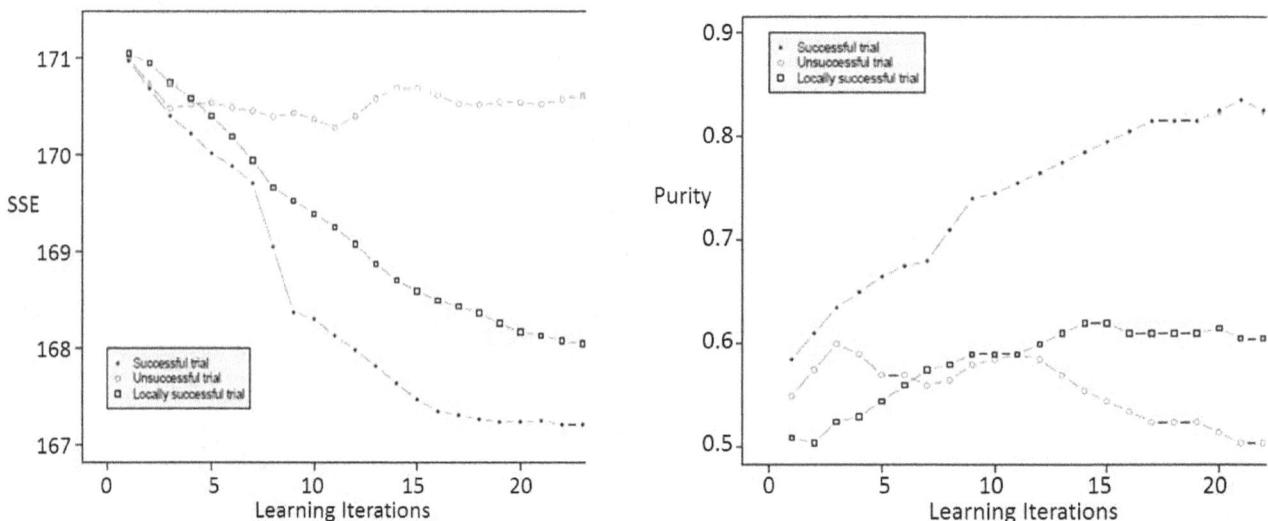

Fig. 11.40. Multiple-convergence, SVM-External Clustering. Three multiple clustering convergences (different trials) of SVM-Relabeler algorithm demonstrating the range of the possible solution space as measured by SSE and purity (a 'successful', an unsuccessful, and a partly-successful trial). Choosing the good SSE external measure (Left Panel) typically provides a generalized clustering that has high purity (Right Panel). The improvments in Purity and SSE with learning iterations are shown. Once Learning slows (SSE unimproved), a

restart for a new convergence clustering is done. Usually in the first two or three attempts a strongly performing converegence is seen as with the example shown here.

Support Vector Machine methods are described for classification, clustering, as well as aiding with signal analysis and pattern recognition on stochastic sequential data. Analysis tools for stochastic sequential data, Markovian (or causal) data for example, have broad-ranging application in that almost any device producing a sequence of measurements can be made more sensitive, or "smarter," by efficient learning of measured signal/pattern characteristics via HMM/SVM methods. The SVM and HMM/SVM application areas described here include cheminformatics, biophysics, and bioinformatics. The cheminformatics application examples pertain to channel current analysis on the alpha-hemolysin nanopore detector.

Markov-based statistical profiles, in a log likelihood discriminator framework, can be used to create a fixed-length feature vector for Support Vector Machine (SVM) based classification [1]. Part of the idea of the method is that whenever a log likelihood discriminator can be constructed for classification on stochastic sequential data, an alternative discriminator can be constructed by 'lifting' the log likelihood components into a feature vector description for classification by SVM. Thus, the feature vector uses the individual log likelihood components obtained in the standard log likelihood classification effort, the individual-observation log odds ratios, and 'vectorizes' them rather than sums them. The individual-observation log odds ratios are themselves constructed from positionally defined Markov Models (pMM's), so what results is a pMM/SVM sensor method. This method may have utility in a number of areas of stochastic sequential analysis, including splice-site recognition and other types of gene-structure identification, file recovery in computer forensics ('file carving'), and speech recognition.

The Multiple-convergence initialized SVM-clustering approach to unsupervised learning provides another non-parametric means to clustering. In preliminary work, it is found that the SVM-based clustering method also offers prospects for inheriting the very strong performance of standard SVMs from the supervised classification setting. This offers a remarkable prospect for knowledge discovery and enhancing the scope of human cognition – the recognition of patterns and clusters without the limitations imposed by assuming a parametric mode and 'fitting' to it, where resolution of the identified clusters can be at an accuracy comparable to the supervised setting (i.e., where cluster identities are already specified).

The new approach is to first obtain *multiple* SVM convergences from separatet initializations (two might suffice, for example, in many situations) and thereby obtain the confidence magnitudes on data points, and their nearest neighbors (if repeatedly have the same neighbors, have high linkage to them). This is used to inform a label-flipping process to arrive at an improved clustering solution on further iterations and analysis. For example, one approach is to establish a high-linkage high-confidence label set (labels retained or flipped accordingly) and a low-linkage, low-confidence, label set (some, according to criteria, may be flipped as well, or dropped). The magnitude comparison in the simplest 'multiple' convergence result would involve two convergences, with the difference in confidence value for a particular training instance producing a line segment, and for all the training instances, their two-convergent point-differences would provide a collection of line-segments. The most stable part of the line-segment 'field', that of the high-linkage high-confidence data instances, can then be used, for example, to provide indication of structure to guide tuning efforts and label-flipping criteria.

SVMs are fast, easily trained, discriminators, for which strong discrimination is possible without over-fitting complications. SVMs are firmly grounded as variational-calculus based optimization methods that are constrained to have structural risk minimization (SRM), unlike neural net classifiers, such that they provide noise tolerant solutions for pattern recognition. An SVM determines a hyperplane that optimally separates one class from another, while the structural risk minimization (SRM) criterion manifests as the hyperplane having a thickness, or "margin," that is made as large as possible in the process of seeking a separating hyperplane. The SVM approach thereby encapsulates model fitting and discriminatory information in the choice of kernel in the SVM, and a number of novel kernels have been shown here. SVMs are good at both classifying data and evaluating a confidence in the classifications given, which leaves an opening for use of metaheuristics to bootstrap into a clustering capability, as explored in a number of algorithmic variations in this paper. SVM use in clustering appears to be a very robust platform and, from initial results shown here, promises to be one of the best clustering approaches. In this paper we have shown a number of SVM classification algorithms and new SVM/metaheuristics bootstrap algorithms for clustering.

11.8.5 SVM-External Clustering – Algorithmic Variants
11.8.5.1 Multiple-convergence initialized (steepest ascent) SVM-clustering
The Multiple-convergence initialized SVM-clustering approach to unsupervised learning provides another non-parametric means to clustering. In preliminary work we have found that the SVM-based clustering method also offers prospects for inheriting the very strong performance of standard SVMs from the supervised classification setting. This offers a remarkable prospect for knowledge discovery and enhancing the scope of human cognition – the recognition of patterns and clusters without the limitations imposed by assuming a parametric mode and 'fitting' to it, where resolution of the identified clusters can be at an accuracy comparable to the supervised setting (i.e., where cluster identities are already specified).

The new approach is to first obtain *multiple* SVM convergences at initialization (two might suffice, for example, in many situations) and thereby obtain the confidence magnitudes on data points, and their nearest neighbors (if repeatedly have the same neighbors, have high linkage to them). This is used to inform a label-flipping process to arrive at an improved clustering solution on further iterations and analysis. For example, one approach is to establish a high-linkage high-confidence label set (labels retained or flipped accordingly) and a low-linkage, low-confidence, label set (some, according to criteria, may be flipped as well, or dropped). The magnitude comparison in the simplest 'multiple' convergence result would involve two convergences, with the difference in confidence value for a particular training instance producing a line segment, and for all the training instances, their two-convergent point-differences would provide a collection of line-segments. The most stable part of the line-segment 'field', that of the high-linkage high-confidence data instances, can then be used, for example, to provide indication of structure to guide tuning efforts and label-flipping criteria.

11.8.5.2 Projection Clustering – clustering in Decision space

SVM methods for clustering are described that are based on the SVM's ability to not only classify, but also to give a confidence parameter on its classifications. Even without modifying the label information (passive clustering), there is often strong clustering information in an SVM training solution. One such instance occurs when one set, the positives, are a known signal species (or collection of species). If you have mixture data with known and unknown signal species, and wish to identify (i.e., cluster) the unknown species, then an SVM training attempt with the mixture taken as negatives leads to a cluster identification method via an SVM "projection-score" histogram. (i.e., cluster partitioning in Decision Space). Real channel blockade data has been examined in this way, biotinylated DNA hairpin blockades comprised the positives, and scored as a sharp peak at around 1.0. The mixture signals seen after introduction of streptavidin cluster with scores around 0.5, corresponding to (unbound) biotinylated DNA hairpin signals, and signals that score < -1.0, corresponding to the streptavidin-bound biotinylated DNA hairpins. SVM projection clustering can be a very powerful clustering tool in and of itself as can be seen in this cheminformatics application.

11.8.5.3 SVM-ABC

New subtleties of classification-separation are possible with support vector machines via their direct handling and direct identification of data instances. Individual data points, in some instances, can be associated with "support vectors" at the boundaries between regions. By operating on labels of support vectors and focusing on training on certain subsets, the SVM-ABC algorithm offers the prospect to delineate highly complex geometries and graph-connectivity:

Split the clustering data into sets A, B and C
- A: Strong negatives
- C: Strong positives
- B: Weak negatives and weak positives
- Train an SVM on Data from A (labeled negative) and B (labeled positive)
- The support vectors: SV_AB
- Similarly train a new SVM on Data from C (labeled positive) and B (labeled negative)
- The support vectors: SV_CB
- Our objective is that the SV_AB and SV_CB sets have their labels flipped to be set A and C
- Regrow set A and C into the weak 'B' region.
- If an element of SV_AB is also in SV_BC, then the intersection of these sets are the elements that should be flipped to class B (if not already listed as class B).
- Stop at the first occurrence of any of these events
- Set B becomes empty
- Set B does not change

The SVM_ABC Algorithm may offer recovery of subtle graph-like connectedness between cluster elements, a weakness of manifold-like separability approaches such as parametric-based clustering methods.

11.8.5.4 SVM-Relabeler

The SVM classification formulation is used as the foundation for clustering a set of feature vectors with no *a priori* knowledge of the feature vector's classification. The non-separable SVM solution guarantees convergence at the cost of allowing misclassification. The extent of slack is controlled through the regularization constant, C, to penalize the slack variable, ξ. If the random mapping $((x_1,y_1),...,(x_m,y_m)) \in X^m \times y$ is not linearly separable when ran through a binary SVM, the misclassified features are more likely to belong to the other cluster. Moreover, by relabeling those heavily misclassified features and by repeating this process we arrive at an optimal separation between the two clusters. The basics of this procedure is presented in Algorithm 1, where $\hat{y}$ is the new cluster assignment for x and θ contains ω, α, y'.

Algorithm 1: SVM-Relabeler

Require: *m*, x
1. $\hat{y} \leftarrow$ Randomly chosen from $\{-1,+1\}$
2. repeat
3. $\theta \leftarrow doSVM(x, \hat{y})$
4. $\hat{y} \leftarrow doRelabel(x, \theta)$
5. until $\hat{y}$ remains constant

The *doSVM*() procedure can be any standard and complete implementation of an SVM classifier with support for nonlinear discriminator function. The idea is that *doSVM*() has to converge regardless of the geometry of the data, in order to provide the *doRelabel*() procedure with the hyperplane and other standard SVM outputs. After this procedure, *doRelabel*() reassigns some (or all) of the misclassified features to the other cluster. If $D(x_i,\theta)$ is the distance between x_i feature and the trained SVM hyperplane, then heavily misclassified feature, $x_{j \in J}$ could be selected by comparing $D(x_j,\theta)$ to $D(x_{j'},\theta)$ for all $j' \in J$. Algorithm 2 clarifies the basic implementation of this procedure.

Algorithm 2: doRelabel() Procedure

Require: Input vector: x
            Cluster labeling: $\hat{y}$
SVM model: θ
Confidence Factor: αIdentify misclassified features:
$x'^+ \leftarrow K$ misclassified features with $\hat{y} = +1$
$x'^- \leftarrow L$ misclassified features with $\hat{y} = -1$
1. for all i^{th} component of x'^+ do
2. if $i/K \sum_{j=1}^{K} D(x'^+_j,\theta) < \alpha D(x'^+_j,\theta)$ then
3. $\hat{y}_i^+ \leftarrow -1$
4. end if
5. end for
6. for all ith component of x'^- do
7. if $1/L \sum_{j=1}^{L} D(x'^-_j,\theta) < \alpha D(x'^-_j,\theta)$ then
8. $\hat{y}_i^- \leftarrow +1$
9. end if
10. end for

11.8.5.5 SV-Dropper

In most applications of clustering, the dataset is composed of *leverage* and *influential* points. *Leverage* points are subsets of the dataset that are highly deviated from the rest of the cluster, and removing them does *not* significantly change the result of the clustering. In contrast, *influential* points are those in the highly deviated subset whose inclusion or removal significantly changes the decision of the clustering algorithm. Effective, identification of these special points is of interest to improve accuracy and correctness of the clustering algorithm. A systematic way to manage these deviants is given by the SV-Dropper algorithm..

As depicted in Algorithm 3, SVM is initially trained on the clustered data; the weakest of the cluster data – those closest to the hyperplane, i.e., the support vectors – are dropped thereafter. This processed is repeated until the desired ratio of accuracy and number of data dropped is achieved.

Algorithm 3: SV-Dropper Algorithm

Require: Input vector: x
         Cluster labeling: $\hat{y}$
1.   let:
         $x^+ \leftarrow K$ features with $y = +1$
$x^- \leftarrow L$ fatures with $\hat{y} = -1$
2.   repeat
3. $\theta \leftarrow doSVM(x, y)$
4.   for all features, x_j,
5.   drop feature, x_j, if $|D(x_j, \theta)| < 1$ end for
6.   until desired ratio of SSE and number of data dropped

11.8.5.6 Rayleigh's criterion clustering algorithm

Rayleigh's criterion, also known as the Rayleigh Limit, is used for the resolution of two light sources. In the case of two laser beam sources falling upon a single slit, the resolution limit is defined by the single-slit interference pattern where one source's maximum falls on the first minimum of the diffraction pattern of the second source. This definition is used for resolving distant stars as singletons or identification of binary star systems, etc. In the case of laser optics, the resolution of two sources can be pushed *beyond* the Rayleigh limit due to tracking the statistics of the individual photons that arrive. The relevance of all of this is that resolving two sources is equivalent to saying that a binary clustering solution exists, i.e., that the data is separable to some degree. If the clustering algorithm tracks the data instances individually, as it does with our SVM-external approach, we have a scenario analogous to the resolution in laser optics beyond the "Rayleigh limit".

11.9 Exercises

(**Ex. 11.1**) Write code that generates two clusters, then write code that scores the SSE of the two clusters.

(**Ex. 11.2**) Implement K-means (using sample Perl code given) and use it to resolve the two clusters generated in (Ex. 11.1).

(**Ex. 11.3**) Implement K-NN (using sample Perl code given) and use it to perform 5-fold cross-validation on a labeled set of test data. Create the labeled test data with one cluster generation getting one label (+), and a separate cluster generation (perhaps partly overlapping) getting a different label (−). From the cross-validation compute average of {TP,TN,FP,FN} and resultant {SN,SP}.

(**Ex. 11.4**) Prove that the perceptron finds a solution (a local minima) in a finite number of learning steps (even though exploring an infinite solution space). Following notation introduced earlier and using the steps outlined in [64]:

Suppose we have solution, a set of weights, w^*, that separates the data. Let's start at $w(0)=0$ and show that $w(t)$ gets more aligned with w^* with every learning update:

    (a) Let $\rho = \min_{1 \leq n \leq N} y_n(w^* \cdot x_n)$, show $\rho > 0$.

    (b) Show that $w(t) \cdot w^* \geq w(t-1) \cdot w^* + \rho$, and conclude that $w(t) \cdot w^* \geq t\rho$ (use induction)

    (c) Show that $\|w(t)\|^2 \leq \|w(t-1)\|^2 + \|x(t-1)\|^2$ (x(t-1) was misclass. by w(t-1)....)

    (d) Show by induction that $\|w(t)\|^2 \leq tR^2$, where $R = \max_{1 \leq n \leq N} \|xn\|$

    (e) Using (b) and (d) show that: $w(t) \cdot w^*/\|w(t)\| \geq \sqrt{t}\frac{\rho}{R}$ and $t \leq R^2 \|w^*\|^2 /\rho^2$

Typically convergence happens much quicker than indicated by $t < R^2 \|w^*\|^2 /\rho^2$, often by a factor of 100, the bad news is you don't know ρ in advance, so don't know the number of iterations until convergence.... This is a big problem because with significant iterations without convergence, you don't know if more iterations are required, or if you are dealing with data that is non-separable......

(**Ex. 11.5**) Re-derive Eq.s (11.2)-(11.5).

(**Ex. 11.6**) Re-derive analysis for Eq.s (11.7)-(11.8).

(**Ex. 11.7**) Re-derive equations in Sec. 11.3.6.

(**Ex. 11.8**) Re-derive equations in Sec. 11.4.1.

(**Ex. 11.9-11-11**)
For the following questions begin by first getting the SVM code (in Perl) provided in Sec. 11.4.5 working. Then do the following:

(Ex. 11.9) Run the code as is by entering at the prompt: ./Binary_Classifier.pl (which uses SVM_Discriminator.pm), you should see the learning process of the code, and eventually a score result is appended to the 'scores' file. Then directly modify and change the kp value from 0.1 in the script to ten other values, generate scores for each, plot the 11 results of your 'brute force' tuning effort. What was your best (SN,SP) score pair?

(Ex. 11.10) Let's automate the brute-force tuning. Run the following:

```
#!/usr/bin/perl
use strict;
my @kernels = ("absdiff0.5","gaussian","sentropic","poly");
my @sigmas = (0.0001, 0.001, 0,005, 0.01, 0.05, 0.1, 0.5, 0.7, 1.0, 2.0);

my $kernel;
my $sigma;
foreach $kernel (@kernels) {
   foreach $sigma (@sigmas) {
      `./Binary_Classifier.pl $kernel $sigma`;
   }
}
```

Note the use of perl's "backtick" operator to execute shell commands (perl can be used as ashell environment called, you guessed it, a "perl shell").

Describe the tuning outcomes. Is there a kernel that always works (where all sigmas result in a convergent training process and thus get scored with a line appended in the 'scores' file)? Is there a kernel that rarely works for choice of sigma?

(Ex. 11.11) Let's demonstrate the 'bag learning' capabilities of the SVM:
(i) in the training data file, change half of the positive label data to have negative label – thereby create a smaller (pure) positive set, and a mixed 'negative' set. Run the SVM with the optimal Kp value identified in (Ex. 11.9) with the first half of the data.
(ii) with the second half of the data as test, and get a histogram on confidence scores.
(iii) identify a cutoff for identifying 'true negatives', thereby select out this true negative set.
(iv) use the true negatives and the pure positive set to train a new SVM (with cleaned data), then use the old (original) test data to see how well it performs.

Chapter 12

Search Metaheuristics

12.1 Trajectory-based Search Metaheuristics

    12.1.1 Optimal-fitness configuration trajectories -- fitness known

    12.1.2 Optimal-fitness trajectories -- fitness *function* not known

    12.1.3 Fitness configuration trajectories with non-optimal updates

12.2 Population-based Search Metaheuristics

    12.2.1 Population with evolution

    12.2.2 Population with large group interaction -- swarm intelligence

    12.2.3 Population with Indirect Interaction via Artifact

Many search methods have been encountered in the context of 'tuning' on the previous acquisition, classification, and clustering methods (especially tuning on the SVM in the last chapter). Tuning is searching for an optimal configuration. Methods and metaheuristics to perform searches are now described in a more general context.

12.1 Trajectory-based Search Metaheuristics

If you have a configuration that you need to optimize, and for any configuration you can evaluate its 'score', or 'fitness', then a variety of metaheuristics have been developed for configuration selection or model tuning, both by Man and by Nature. If the configuration fitness can be determined from a *differentiable* function of its configuration parameters, then classic gradient ascent (or descent) can be used to optimize the configuration by making learning steps that climb (for maximization type optimization, see Fig. 12.1). If the fitness function has a second derivative, then an improved version has been known for over 400 years, Newton's method, which involves calculation of the Hessian to get a higher order correction that avoids overshooting on reaching optima. In practice, local minima 'traps' require repeated attempts with randomly initialized and repeated gradient ascent efforts in order to seek a global optimum -- enter the modern era where use of computers now makes such problems directly addressable, and often fully resolvable.

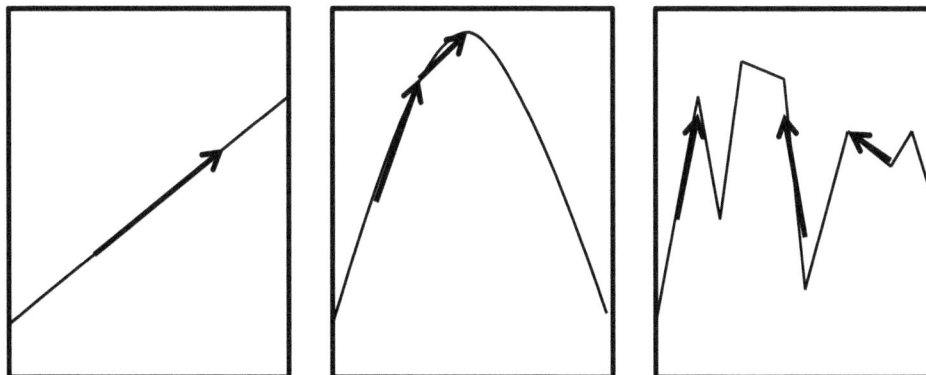

Fig. 12.1 Gradient Ascent, Newton's Ascent, Newton's Ascent with restart.

12.1.1 Optimal-fitness configuration trajectories -- fitness function known and sufficiently regular

Suppose the fitness function, F(x), is known, we can then simply choose to move, from a current configuration 'position' in the direction that fitness is increasing the most.

12.1.1.1 Metaheuristic #1: Euler's Method – 1st-order gradient ascent

If the configuration's fitness can be determined from a differentiable function of its configuration parameters, then gradient ascent (or descent) can be used to optimize the configuration (see Fig. 12.2).

(1) Calculate $x_{i+1} = x_i + \eta_i \nabla F(x)$, where η_i is the 'learning rate', assumed constant for the discussion to follow, but could vary with further iterations such as in some simulated annealing approaches. For small enough learning rate must have $F(x_{i+1}) \geq F(x_i)$. Choosing a learning rate that is large enough to converge quickly, yet not overshoot badly, is balanced against the smaller learning rate that can more precisely optimize. This is a data dependent learning rate selection and often requires simple tuning tests on the choice of learning rate (before initialization).

(2) repeat (1) until no change in x.

Problem: can easily overshoot, and tends to oscillate around local minima without halting simply.

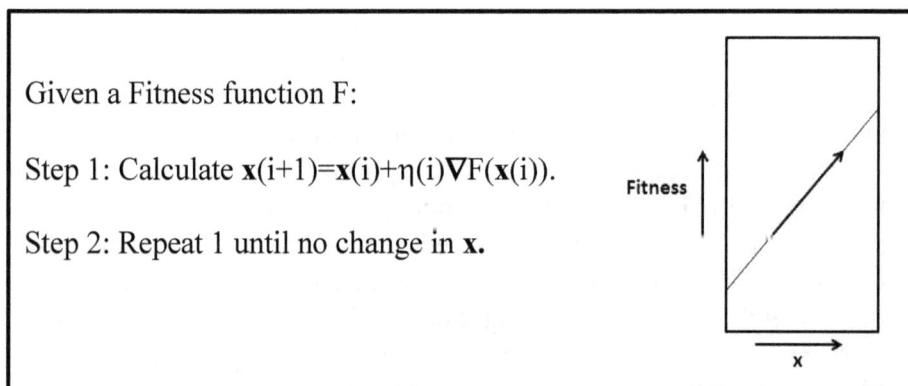

Given a Fitness function F:

Step 1: Calculate $x(i+1)=x(i)+\eta(i)\nabla F(x(i))$.

Step 2: Repeat 1 until no change in **x.**

Fitness

x

Fig. 12.2 Metaheuristic #1: Euler's Method – 1st-order gradient ascent.

12.1.1.2 Metaheuristic #2: Newton's Method – 2nd-order gradient ascent

If the fitness function has a second derivative, then an improved version has been known for over 400 years, Newton's method, which involves calculation of the Hessian to get a higher order correction that avoids overshooting on reaching optima (see Fig. 12.3).

(1) Calculate $x_{i+1} = x_i + \eta_i \nabla F(x)/[H\, F(x)]$, where η_i is the 'learning rate', assumed constant for the discussion to follow, and $H\, F(x)$ is the Hessian of $F(x)$. For small enough learning rate must have $F(x_{i+1}) \geq F(x_i)$. As before, this is a data dependent learning rate situation and often requires simple tuning tests on the choice of learning rate (before initialization).

(2) repeat (1) until no change in x.

Problem: local minima 'traps' require repeated attempts with randomly initialized and repeated gradient ascent efforts in order to seek a global optimum.

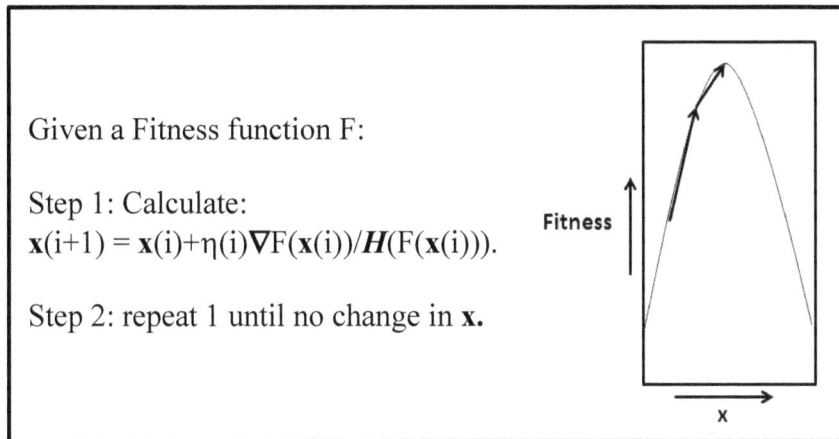

Fig. 12.3 Metaheuristic #2: Newton's Method – 2nd-order gradient ascent.

12.1.1.3 Metaheuristic #3: gradient ascent with (random) restart
The use of computers now makes algorithmic aspects of the solution, such as 'random restart' (according to some specification), accessible in a way that was impossible before the having modern computational tools (see Fig. 12.4):

(1) Calculate $x_{i+1} = x_i + \eta_i \nabla F(x)$, where η_i is the 'learning rate', assumed constant for the discussion to follow, but could vary with further iterations such as in some simulated annealing approaches. For small enough learning rate must have $F(x_{i+1}) \geq F(x_i)$. Choosing a learning rate that is large enough to converge quickly, yet not overshoot badly, is balanced against the smaller learning rate that can more precisely optimize. This is a data dependent learning rate selection and often requires simple tuning tests on the choice of learning rate (before initialization).

(2) repeat (1) until no change in x.

(3) randomly restart, repeat (1)-(2) until overlapping global coverage is achieved.

Problem: local minima in *lower dimensional* settings often can't be overcome with random restart methods (reduces to randomly searching too large a space).

Step 1: Calculate $\mathbf{x}(i+1) = \mathbf{x}(i) + \eta(i) \nabla F(\mathbf{x}(i))/H(F(\mathbf{x}(i)))$.

Step 2: repeat 1 until no change in $\mathbf{x}$.

Step 3: randomly restart, repeat 1 and 2 until new halt, then repeat until no change in $\mathbf{x}$ compared to optimum before restart.

Fitness

x

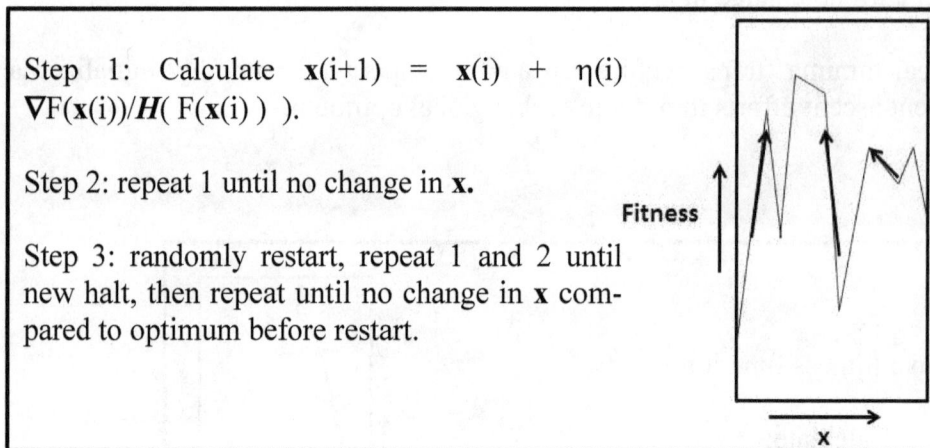

Fig. 12.4 Metaheuristic #2: Newton's Method – 2nd-order gradient ascent.

12.1.2 Optimal-fitness configuration trajectories -- fitness *function* not known

Suppose you have a score (or fitness), but the function is not known. To adopt the terminology of [343], a configuration "tweak" will refer to randomly changed configuration settings by some perturbatively bounded amount. In other words, we always start with some configuration that is 'live', in that it has a perturbatively defined score or fitness at the indicated configuration setting, and we want to evolve the configuration towards one with an improved score or fitness via a series of 'tweaks'. Suppose we tweak the configuration and the new configuration has a better score, we can then take the better configuration as our working optimum and iterate with another tweak, if now the new configuration has worse score, we won't switch to the new configuration, but stay with what we've got, and then iterate again, this is what is known as the "Hill Climbing" optimization algorithm.

The standard Hill Climbing algorithm should more aptly be named 'blind hill climbing' because there's no equivalent of 'looking around', it's akin to gradient ascent in that there is clear choice of up or down hill, but it is not akin to Newton's refinement as there is no ability to "look ahead" (with a second derivative correction in the case of Newton's method). This can be improved by generating multiple tweak configurations on a given parent configuration and selecting the one providing the best score from that test set. This is known as steepest ascent hill climbing, where the sampled steepest ascent approach serves as an approximation to gradient ascent (when a differentiable fitness function is known), and in some cases will also approximate the correction indicated in Newton's method (the steepest ascent sampling and maximal selection precludes the overshooting complication). Of course, the expense of this approximately matching performance between steepest ascent and gradient ascent is that steepest ascent requires multiple tweaks at each step, while gradient ascent, informed as it is by the knowledge of the differentiable fitness function, only requires one tweak at each step. What levels the playing field between the differentiable function and not-known function scenarios, however, is that even with a differentiable function the function may admit numerous local minima, and thus require that its global optima be sought by further refinements, 'random restart' in particular, where we randomly restart the whole algorithm in a different part of the configuration space and hope for a better result. The fact that even the differentiable case will typically require random restart, however, means that the multiple tweak steepest ascent is not so onerous a burden over that of a single-tweak differentiably extrapolatable formulation. This will be especially so, if the "looking around" burden of the multiple tweaks at each steepest ascent step can be handled by metaheuristics in part of a directed (partially) random restart, as will be described.

12.1.2.1 Metaheuristic #4: (Blind) Hill Climbing

Note, the specification of the methods is pure algorithmic... there is no calculus (Fig. 12.5).

(1) Perform Tweak on the current configuration. In other words, generate a new configuration that is a random, locally bounded, perturbation of the current configuration (involving in one or more perturbed parameters).

(2) If tweak configuration scores better then current best case, then make the tweak configuration the new best case, otherwise ignore.

(3) Repeat (1)-(2) until some exit condition met (no improvements for MAX tries, for example).

Problem: has similar weaknesses to Method #1.

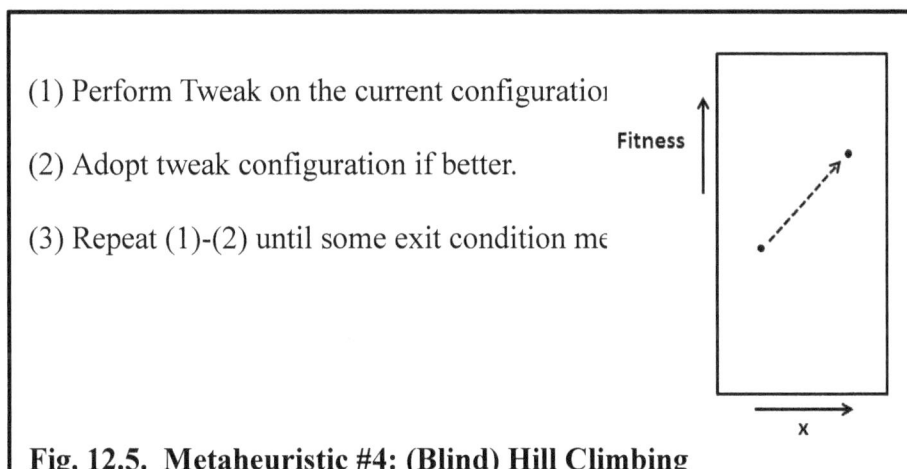

(1) Perform Tweak on the current configuratioɪ

(2) Adopt tweak configuration if better.

(3) Repeat (1)-(2) until some exit condition me

Fitness

x

Fig. 12.5. Metaheuristic #4: (Blind) Hill Climbing

12.1.2.2 Metaheuristic #5: Steepest Ascent Hill Climbing

Note, the specification of the methods is pure algorithmic... there is no calculus (Fig. 12.6).

(1) Generate N Tweak configurations from the current configuration.

(2) If the best tweak configuration score is better then current best case, then make the tweak configuration the new best case, otherwise ignore.

(3) Repeat (1)-(2) until some exit condition met (no improvements for MAX tries, for example).
Problem: has similar weaknesses to Method #2.

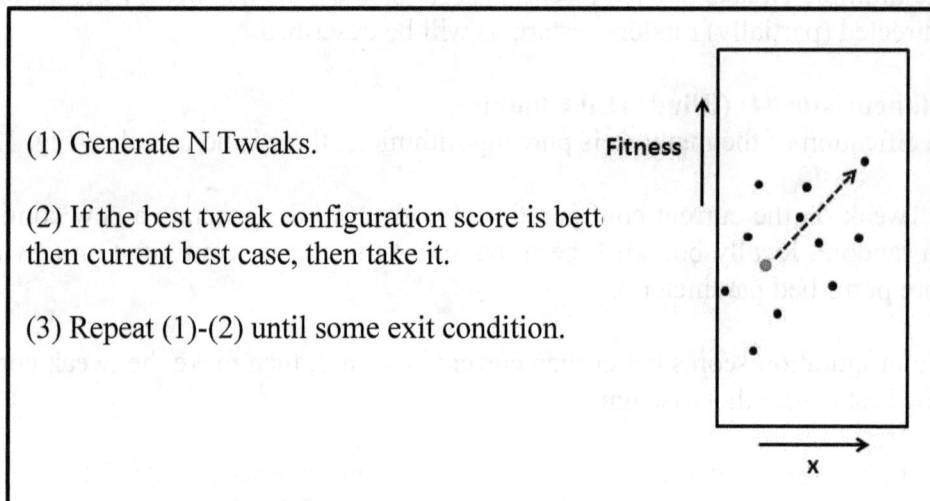

Fig. 12.6. Metaheuristic #5: Steepest Ascent Hill Climbing

12.1.2.3 Metaheuristic #6: Steepest Ascent Hill Climbing with restart

In gradient ascent with random restarts the idea is to find a global optimum by eventually restarting in the region of configuration space covered by the global optimum's footprint. Now we have less information, so can't perform a Newton's method refinement as easily, but we still have the random restart and instead of gradient ascent we have steepest ascent hill climbing. So, what is often the case is that the challenge is not the diffentiability of the fitness function, if it is even known, but in finding a global optimum when local optima are numerous (see Fig. 12.7-12.10).

(1) Generate N Tweak configurations from the current configuration.
(2) If the best tweak configuration score is better then current best case, then make the tweak configuration the new best case, otherwise ignore.
(3) Repeat (1)-(2) until some exit condition met (no improvements for MAX tries, for ex-ample)
(4) randomly restart, repeat (1)-(3) until overlapping global coverage is achieved.
Problem: has similar weaknesses to Method #3.

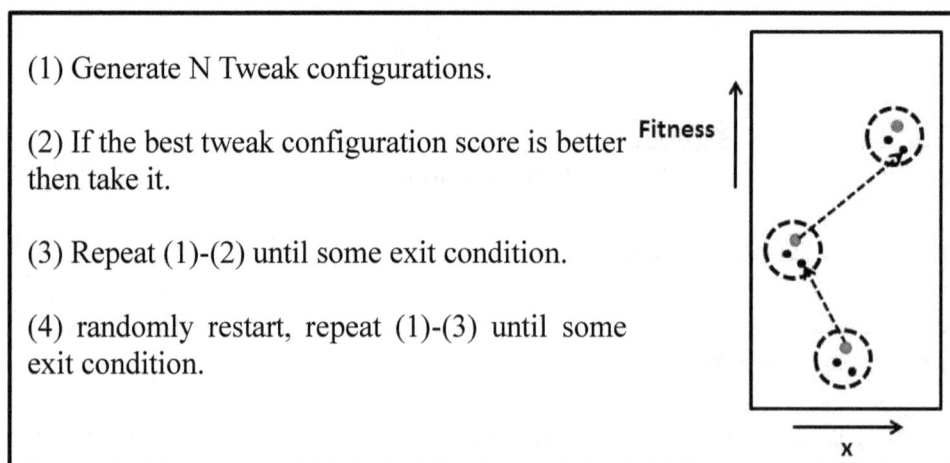

Fig. 12.7. Metaheuristic #6: Steepest Ascent Hill Climbing with restart

366

12.1.3 Fitness configuration trajectories with non-optimal updates
Our ability to assess a score, or assign a fitness, allows for a collection of metaheuristics that basically reduce to 'look around and take the best way forward' via a series of tweaks. This isn't possible for some problems, however, because the 'looking around' part isn't that informative, e.g., the fitness landscape has sections that are at a fixed level (with noise variations about that level, for example). This is the larger problem of the simple globalization algorithm, via random restart: if the fitness landscape or configuration space is too large random restart won't offer a solution, even if it can, in a reasonable amount of time. This is where more clever metaheuristics are involved, to extend to a global optimization algorithm.

Global Optimization
One of the weaknesses of the brute force random restart approach mentioned so far is that the tweak involved is with a *bounded* perturbative change, which may *already* exclude the possibility of reaching the solution sought (given the computational resources and a reasonable amount of time). So one generalization is to allow for tweaks that are unbounded, but in some perturbatively stable way, such as with a Boltzmann factor for regularization, and in doing so we arrive at the Simulated Annealing approach:

12.1.3.1 Metaheuristic #7: Simulated Annealing Hill Climbing
(1) Perform Tweak on the current configuration.

(2) The tweak configuration is taken with probability=$(1/N)\exp[(F(tweak)-F(best))/T]$, where N is a normalization factor, and T is a 'temperature', e.g., a Boltzmann probability factor for occasionally selecting a lower scoring, possibly non-local, configuration.

(3) Repeat (1)-(2) until some exit condition met (no improvements for MAX tries, for example).

Problem: has similar weaknesses to Method #6 and #3.

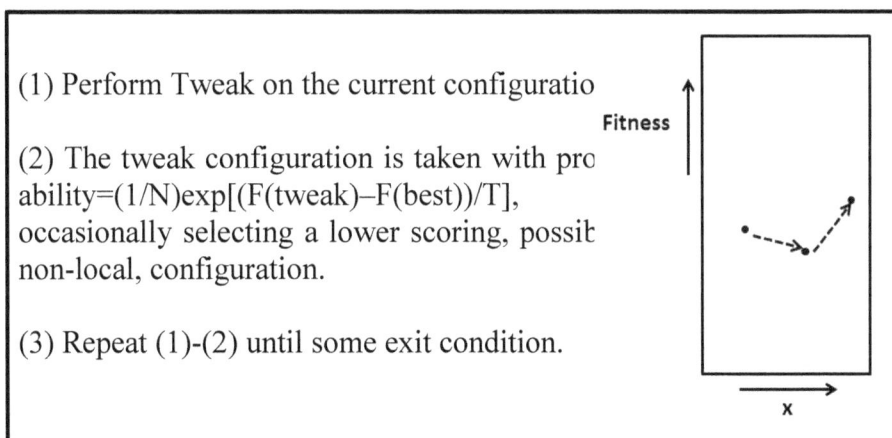

(1) Perform Tweak on the current configuratio

(2) The tweak configuration is taken with pro ability=$(1/N)\exp[(F(tweak)-F(best))/T]$, occasionally selecting a lower scoring, possit non-local, configuration.

(3) Repeat (1)-(2) until some exit condition.

Fig. 12.8. Metaheuristic #7: Simulated Annealing Hill Climbing

12.1.3.2 Metaheuristic #8: Simulated Annealing Hill Climbing with random restart

(1) Perform Tweak on the current configuration.

(2) The tweak configuration is taken with

$$probability = (1/N)exp[(F(tweak) - F(best))/T],$$

where N is a normalization factor, and T is a 'temperature', e.g., a Boltzmann probability factor for occasionally selecting a lower scoring, possibly non-local, configuration.

(3) Repeat (1)-(2) until some exit condition met (no improvements for MAX tries, for example).

(4) randomly restart, repeat (1)-(3) until overlapping global coverage is achieved.

Problem: has similar weaknesses to Method #3.

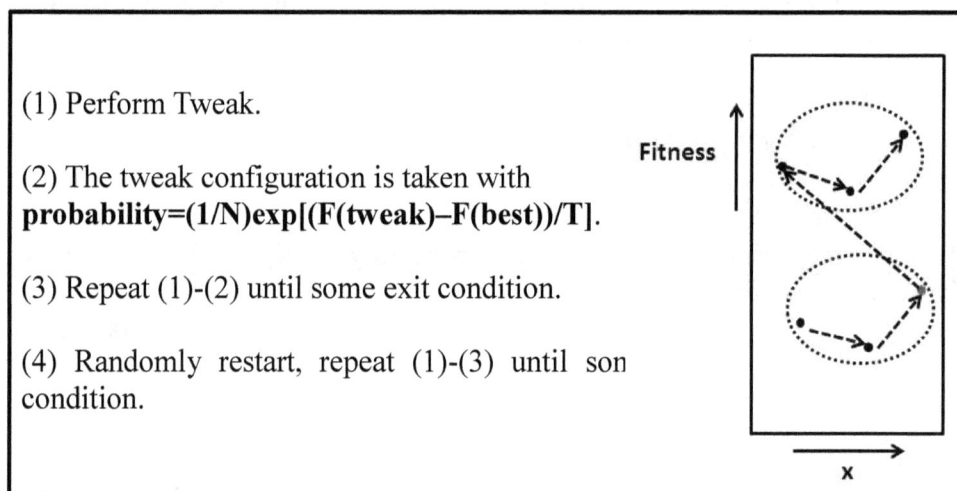

(1) Perform Tweak.

(2) The tweak configuration is taken with **probability=(1/N)exp[(F(tweak)–F(best))/T]**.

(3) Repeat (1)-(2) until some exit condition.

(4) Randomly restart, repeat (1)-(3) until son condition.

Fitness

x

Fig. 12.9. Metaheuristic #8: Simulated Annealing random restart

12.1.3.3 Metaheuristic #9: Taboo Search

Taboo search can be seen as a form of simulated annealing in that lower scores can be selected, here by an exclusion rule where configuration areas visited are 'taboo' from revisiting again 'too soon'. Taboo search can also be extended into a variant that operates on the configuration components, known as component-based taboo search.

Simulated annealing and Taboo search enhancements to the steepest ascent hill climbing algorithm involve use of multiple configuration samples (tweaks), where the steepest ascent sample space is constrained according to choice of learning heuristic. If implemented efficiently what can result is a sampling that is focused on the allowed sample space region (without wasting time generating configurations to reject due to taboo, or reject due to below-threshold probability).

(1) Generate N Tweak configurations from the current configuration.

(2) ***Eliminate configurations seen in recent memory***; perform selection on best of the remainder.

(3) Repeat (1)-(2) until some exit condition met (no improvements for MAX tries, for example).

Problem: has similar weaknesses to Method #3.

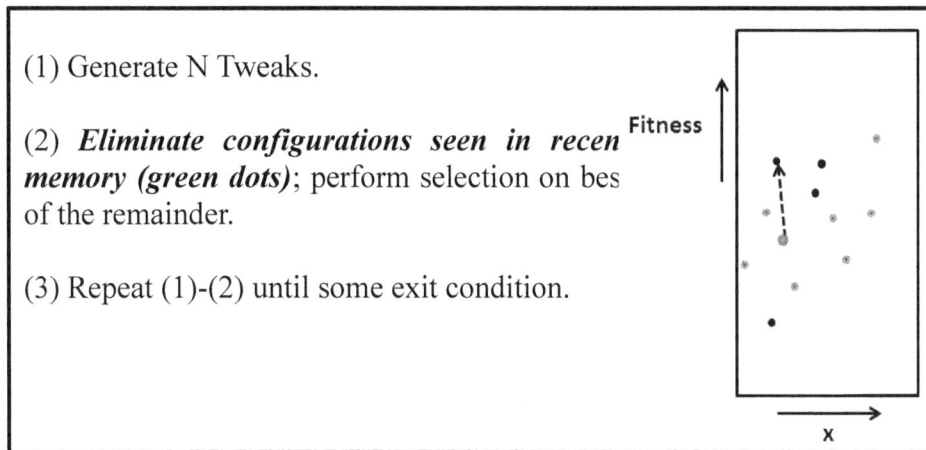

(1) Generate N Tweaks.

(2) ***Eliminate configurations seen in recen*** memory (green dots); perform selection on bes of the remainder.

(3) Repeat (1)-(2) until some exit condition.

Fig. 12.10. Metaheuristic #9: Taboo Search

12.1.3.4 Metaheuristic #10: Tabu Search with restart
Taboo search can be seen as a form of simulated annealing in that lower scores can be selected, here by an exclusion rule where configuration areas visited are 'taboo' from revisiting again 'too soon'.

(1) Generate N Tweak configurations from the current configuration.
(2) Eliminate configurations seen in recent memory; perform selection on best of the remainder.
(3) Repeat (1)-(2) until some exit condition met (no improvements for MAX tries, for example).
(4) randomly restart, repeat (1)-(3) until overlapping global coverage is achieved.
Problem: has similar weaknesses to Method #3.

12.1.3.5 Metaheuristic #11: Component-based Tabu Search
Taboo search can also be extended into a variant that operates on the configuration ***components***, known as component-based taboo search.

(1) Generate N Tweak configurations from the current configuration.
(2) Eliminate configurations involving component usage seen in recent memory; perform selection on best of the remainder.

(3) Repeat (1)-(2) until some exit condition met (no improvements for MAX tries, for example).
Problem: has similar weaknesses to Method #3.

12.1.3.6 Metaheuristic #12: Component-based Tabu Search with restart
Taboo search can also be extended into a variant that operates on the configuration *components*, known as component-based taboo search.

(1) Generate N Tweak configurations from the current configuration.
(2) Eliminate configurations involving component usage seen in recent memory; perform selection on best of the remainder.
(3) Repeat (1)-(2) until some exit condition met (no improvements for MAX tries, for example).
(4) randomly restart, repeat (1)-(3) until overlapping global coverage is achieved.
Problem: has similar weaknesses to Method #3.

12.2 Population-based Search Metaheuristics
In seeking global optimization metaheuristics we are starting to see more sophisticated configuration selection at the component level, on the one hand, and at the population level, on the other hand, especially as we work with the probabilistic simulated annealing approach and the history-based taboo approach, especially with the component-based versions of the latter. This is because the population and history aspects point to a general metaheuristics that operates on populations of configurations (or populations of 'agents' that interact as intermediaries to determining a configuration selection). The notion of 'history' also must address the conveyance of this information or 'artifact'. In the case of ACO, described in what follows, this will be via stygmergy.

12.2.1 Population with evolution
A fixed-size (or size otherwise constrained) population of configurations can have a birth/death cycle or be static. If it has a birth/death cycle, one popular method is the evolutionary computation approach (Darwinian evolution; asexual reproduction) (see Fig. 12.11):

12.2.1.1 Metaheuristic #13: Evolutionary Optimization (Darwinian Evolution; asexual reproduction)

(1) Starting population of parent configurations ("parents") undergoes initial selection according to cut-off (truncation selection) that is chosen.
(2) Those surviving produce offspring, typically via a simple configuration tweak mutation, and those child configurations ("children") are then added to the pool of the current population.
(3) Repeat.

Depending on algorithm, the parents may be selected against generationally also (such as for salmon). The reproduction step can be done by the population all at once (generationally), as described here, or individually, out-of-phase, as commonly done with the GA's given next.

As we work with the probabilistic simulated annealing approach and the history-based taboo approach it becomes apparent that the population and history aspects of these methods point to a general metaheuristics that operates on populations of configurations, or populations of 'agents' that interact as intermediaries to determining a configuration selection. The notion of 'history' also must address the conveyance of this information via 'artifact'. In the case of ACO, described in what follows, this will be via stygmergy.

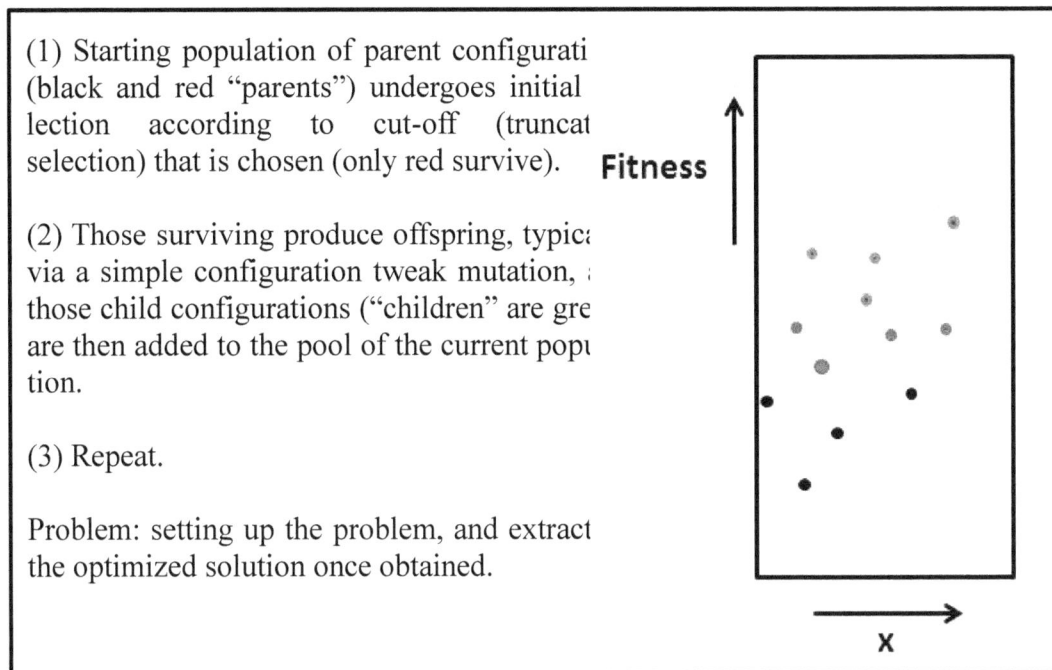

(1) Starting population of parent configurati
(black and red "parents") undergoes initial
lection according to cut-off (truncat
selection) that is chosen (only red survive).

Fitness

(2) Those surviving produce offspring, typica
via a simple configuration tweak mutation,
those child configurations ("children" are gre
are then added to the pool of the current popu
tion.

(3) Repeat.

Problem: setting up the problem, and extract
the optimized solution once obtained.

X

Fig. 12.11. Metaheuristic #13: Evolutionary Optimization (Darwinian Evolution; asexual reproduction). Depending on algorithm, the parents may be selected against generationally also (such as for salmon). The reproduction step can be done by the population all at once (generationally), or individually.

12.2.1.2 Metaheuristic #14: Genetic Algorithm (Darwinian Evolution; sexual reproduction – binary interaction)

(1) Starting population of parent configurations (black and red "parents") undergoes initial selection according to cut-off (truncation selection) that is chosen (only red survive).
(2) Those surviving produce offspring, typically via both simple configuration tweak mutation and non-local configuration component-level swapping, and those child configurations ("children" shown green) are then added to the pool of the current population.
(3) Repeat.
Problem: setting up the problem, and extracting the optimized solution once obtained.

12.2.1.3 Evolutionary Algorithm Parameters
Both of the evolutionary algorithms have tuning parameters in their manner of iteration that shift between less reliance on what has been learned (random search) and strong use of existing information (highly directed gradient ascent). These parameters can be summarized as follows:

Population Size: if population is one, then we are back to simpler hill climbing optimization, with just one configuration tweak under consideration. If the population is unduly large, then we are just looking at everything, e.g., we have random search. If the population is maintained at a more optimal medium size, we arrive at a form of steepest ascent.

Selection pressure: if the selection pressure is high only the very best survive, if only one this reduces to steepest ascent hill climbing. If the selection pressure is low, most survive, and thereby arrive at population that 'walks' from current population via series of configuration 'tweaks', thus have a random walk search.

Generational pressure: if there are many children per parent(s), then we obtain many samples with mutations in the neighborhood of those parents, a form of steepest ascent hill climbing. If there are only a few children have a optimization procedure more akin to simple hill climbing.

Mutation Rate: If the mutation rate is large, we return to a random search since no memory or learning is retained in the decision process. If mutation rate is small, we can fine-tune the optimization on solution. If the mutation is local we may need to use random restart methods to recover global optimization capabilities, even minimally. If the mutation is non-local, such as with simulated annealing, and with sexual reproduction in GA with swapped sections of configuration components allowed, then have improved ability to probe global configuration space.

Populations with interactions (and sub-populations, e.g., speciation)
Once we consider that the configurations in a population may interact with one another, we have a situation where different sub-populations may be given (and now not trivially decouple), i.e., speciation is possible in the evolutionary population. From there whole ecologies of evolutionary complexity can be developed.

12.2.2 Population with group interaction -- swarm intelligence
With population-based interactions have possible direct coordination between agents (sexual reproduction providing cross-over mutation in GA's, as mentioned above, and swarm activity that provides global information to all agents with action defined accordingly to desired local and global swarm behavior, as defined in what follows:

12.2.2.1 Metaheuristic #15: Particle swarm optimization (PSO) (Lamarckian Evolution)
Particle swarm optimization (PSO) also takes its cue from Biology, but not from evolutionary model, but from a swarm model. Here the population is static (the other case than the birth/death cycle case), and there is no selection of any kind. Now the configurations in the population are themselves directly tweaked in response to new information obtained. This is a form of directed mutation and is part of a Lamarckian evolutionary paradigm. The configurations are often viewed as describing particles in a space and the configurations undergo directed mutation, 'motion', in the configuration space, with motion towards the best known configuration, where three levels of knowledge are weighed in the balance: (i) the fittest configuration ascertained by a particular during its history; (ii) the fittest configuration ascertained by the informants of a particular particle (often just a randomly chosen set of particles); and (iii) the fittest configuration discovered by any particle.

12.2.3 Population with Indirect Interaction via Artifact
With population-based interaction also have possible *indirect* interactions between agents. One indirect interaction between agents in a population is stygmergy, such as leaving a mark, as with ants and their pheromone markers. In a broader sense, have interaction of a

population with an artifact in general. This broader category includes the refinement of tools as artifacts and places human evolution in the context of co-evolution with self via artifact (with evolution in the artifact as well, e.g., our improved arrowhead production capability is one of the distinguishing marks of modern human over the Neanderthals). A critical new tool for humans is the computer. We have seen the rapid evolution of the computer's capabilities and sophistication in our lifetimes. Perhaps the original self-replication life-cycle used RNA as an artifact of its operation, giving rise to "RNA World" based life. Perhaps protein began as an artifact of RNA World evolution that co-evolved into a critical part of the organism. Similarly, it not clear where co-evolution with computer as artifact will lead for humans, but it will clearly tap into newfound potential as a new co-evolutionary niche is now open for exploration. The role of artifact is thus, subtle, and can change in the co-evolutionary process. Perhaps someday we will have a "Pinocchio effect" whereby a computer-based artifact becomes self-sufficient (and eventually self-replicating). In this evolutionary history of computer-based life, perhaps Man's role will also be forgotten, but more likely is that we would probably still be there, as a cog in the machine, as with prior co-evolutionary partners displaced by their artifacts , but still extant, typically with a role that is higher up in the information-packaging process chain).

12.2.3.1 Metaheuristic #16: Ant colony optimization (ACO) (swarm intelligence; stygmergy; have co-evolution with artifact)

"no ants"!

(1) Population is based on "ant trails", made by selecting components one-by-one based on their pheromones (can be viewed as a component weight).

(2) Evaporate the pheromones a little (reduce the component weights a little).

(3) Assess fitness of each trail, update weights (pheromone) of components on the trail according to the trails fitness.

12.2.3.2 Other Population-based search metaheuristics

Sometimes even more involved population metaheuristics are needed, with greater handling of constraints, and the methodology blends into the FSA-based modeling with greater complexity, and we must fall back on the standard information measures to help guide, which brings us full circle to involving the FSA-based methods described in Ch. 2., and they, in turn, are more clearly defined in their own internal tuning needs given the advance model search ("tuning") that can be encompassed with the metaheuristics described here.

Population agent algorithms:
Bee
Harmony
Firefly
Bat
Cuckoo
Bacterial Foraging Optimization

Immune algorithms:
Clonal selection algorithm
Negative selection algorithm
Artificial immune recognition system
Immune network algorithm
Dendritic Cell algorithm

<u>Neural Algorithms:</u>
Perceptron
Hopfield Network
Learning Vector Quantization
Self-organizing Map (SOM)

Hybridization of any of the methods shown are found to be even more powerful → **co-evolutionary algorithms** are a specific type of hybridization known to allow the "No free lunch theorem" to be violated, opening the door to a proof of the "feasibility of search" to parallel the breakthrough proof (basis for machine learning) that shows the "feasibility of (statistical) learning".

Chapter 13
Stochastic Sequential Analysis (SSA)

A protocol has been developed for the discovery, characterization, and classification of localizable, approximately-stationary, statistical signal structures in stochastic sequential data, such as the channel current data to be described in Ch. 14.

The stochastic sequential analysis (SSA) methods described in what follows, provide a robust and efficient means to make a device or process 'smart' (e.g., a 'smartening' is possible with a software AI effecting the operational role of a Maxwell Demon on the flow of information, instead of flow of hot/cold matter in a preferential manner), with possible enhancement to device (or process) sensitivity and productivity and efficiency, as well as possibly enabling new capabilities for the device or process (via transduction coupling, for example, as with the nanopore transduction detector (NTD) platform). The SSA Protocol can work with existing device or process information flows, or can work with additional information induced via modulation or introduction via transduction couplings (comprising carrier references [344,345], among other things). Hardware device-smartening may be possible via introduction of modulations or transduction couplings, when used in conjunction with the SSA Protocol implemented to operate on the appropriate timescales to enable real-time experimental or operational control, where real-time adaptive pattern recognition is critical.

13.1 HMM and FSA based methods for signal acquisition and feature extraction
Central to the SSA Protocol method are hidden Markov models (HMMs) [1,39]. To realize the potential of the HMM-based methods, however, there must be a means to directly acquire the signals from the 'raw' form. Eventually an HMM can be trained for the acquisition task as well, but it typically must have previously acquired data to do that initial training. Thus the need for a critical, *ad hoc*, front-end to the signal processing to do signal acquisition even if that acquisition is to eventually be done with an HMM. HMMs and support vector machines (SVMs) [1,39,26,37] are core methods in signal processing and pattern recognition. Both HMMs and SVMs are well-founded in the sense that they are mathematically well-defined and have robust learning properties, and, not surprisingly, they are core methodologies in machine learning based signal processing and pattern recognition.

Even if the signal sought is well understood, and a purely HMM-based approach is possible, this is often needlessly computationally intensive (and slow), especially in areas where there is no signal. To address this there are numerous hybrid FSA/HMM approaches (such as BLAST [82]) that benefit from the O(L) complexity on length L signal with FSA processing, with more targeted processing at $O(LN^2)$ complexity with HMM processing (where there are N states in the HMM model). This is not to say that HMMs can't be used in a signal discovery role in their own right, via use of Viterbi and Baum-Welch algorithms with a 'generic' HMM feature extraction using a statistical modal analysis. HMM approaches on stochastic signals, however, like their periodic signal counterparts (Fourier transform based) from classic electrical engineering signal processing, usually involve pre-processing that assumes linear system properties or assumes observation is frequency band limited and not time limited (via stationarity assumption), etc., and indirectly inherits similar time-frequency uncertainty relations, Gabor limit, and Nyquist sampling relations. FSA methods can be used to recover (or extract) signal features missed by HMM or classical electrical engineering signal processing.

Many signal features of interest are time limited and not band limited in the observational context of interest, such as noise 'clicks', 'spikes', or impulses. To acquire these signal features a time-domain FSA (tFSA) is often most appropriate. Human hearing, for example, is a non-linear system that thereby circumvents the restrictions of the Gabor limit to allow musical geniuses, for example, with 'perfect pitch' whose time-frequency acuity surpasses what should be possible by linear signal processing alone [71], such as with Nyquist sampled linear response recording devices that are bound by the limits imposed by the Fourier uncertainty principle (or Benedick's theorem) [72]. Thus, even when the powerful HMM feature extraction methods are utilized to full advantage, there is often a sector of the signal analysis that is only conveniently accessible to analysis by way of FSA's (without significant oversampling), such that a parallel processing with both HMM and FSA methods is often needed (results demonstrating this in the context of channel current analysis [1] will be briefly discussed). Not all of the methods employed at the FSA processing stage derive from standard signal processing approaches, either, some are purely statistical such as with oversampling [73] (used in radar range oversampling [74,75]) and dithering [76] (used in device stabilization and to reduce quantization error [77,78]).

Hidden Markov models, unlike tFSAs, have a straightforward mathematical and computational foundation at the nexus where Bayesian probability and Markov models meet dynamic programming. To properly define or choose the HMM model in a machine learning context, however, further generalization is usually required. This is because the 'bare-bones' HMM description has critical weaknesses in most applications, which are summarized in what follows, along with their 'fixes'. Fortunately, each of the standard HMM weaknesses can be addressed in computationally efficient ways as shown in Ch. 7. The generalized HMMs allows for a generalized Viterbi Algorithm and generalized Baum-Welch Algorithm. The generalized algorithms retain path probabilities in terms of a sequence of likelihood ratios, which satisfy Martingale statistics under appropriate circumstances [57], thereby having Martingale convergence properties (where convergence is associated with 'learning' in this context). Thus, HMM learning proceeds via convergence to a limit state that provably exists in a similar sense to that shown with the Hoeffding inequality [59], via its proven extension to Martingales [63]. The Hoeffding inequality is a key part of the VC Theorem in Machine Learning, whereby convergence for the Perceptron learning process to a solution is proven to exist in a finite number of learning steps [64].

The generalizations that encompass the hidden semi-Markov models (HMMBD), described in what follows, can't be 'rolled into' an equivalent dynamic Bayesian network (DBN), and while the large-clique generalized meta-HMM can be rolled into a theoretically equivalent

DBN, that DBN still has to express the (fully-connected) large-clique generalization, and adopt the same meta-state constraints as the meta-HMM. When standard HMMs are compared to DBN in character recognition [91], the HMM is found to outperform the DBN in terms of both higher recognition rate and lower complexity. In the large-clique generalization the direct HMM dynamic programming implementation of the meta-states and their transitions, for both the Viterbi and Baum-Welch algorithms, this would lead to an even greater performance gap between the generalized HMM and DBN methods. DBN can offer insights into novel HMM embeddings in the meta-HMM, however, but that falls outside the scope of this work, so DBNs won't be discussed further.

A description of the SSA Protocol and SCW communications will now be given, where stochastic phase modulation (SPM), a simple form of SCW communication, has been used in the engineered nanopore transduction detector experiments in Ch. 14 and [1,17]. A description for a pragmatic distributed HMM generalization and implementation is given in Ch. 7. A discussion of how the HMM with binned duration (HMMBD) and meta-HMM algorithmic methodologies enable practical SCW encoding/decoding then follows, where SCW signal processing can be used in a number of settings in science and nanotechnology.

13.2 The Stochastic Sequential Analysis (SSA) Protocol

The SSA protocol is shown in Fig. 13.1-13.4, where Fig. 13.1 shows a general signal-processing flow topology (see Left Panel), and specialized variants for channel current cheminformatics (Center) and kinetic feature extraction based on blockade-level duration observations (Right). The SSA Protocol allows for the discovery, characterization, and classification of localizable, approximately-stationary, statistical signal structures in channel current data, or genomic data, or sequential data in general. The core signal processing stage in Fig. 13.1 is usually the feature extraction stage, where central to the signal processing protocol is a generalized Hidden Markov model. The SSA Protocol also has a built-in recovery protocol for weak signal handling, outlined next, where the HMM methods are complemented by the strengths of other Machine Learning methods.

The sequence of algorithmic methods used in the SSA Protocol, for the information-processing flow topology shown in Fig. 13.1, comprise a weak signal handling protocol as follows: (i) the weakness in the (fast) Finite State Automaton (FSA) methods will be shown to be their difficulty in non-local structure identification, for which HMM methods (and tuning metaheuristics) are the solution. (ii) for the HMM, in turn, the main weakness is in local sensing 'classification' due to conditional independence assumptions. Once in the setting of a classification problem, however, the problem can be solved via incorporation of generalized SVM methods. If facing only classification task (data already preprocessed), the SVM will also be the method of choice in what follows. (iii) The weakness of the SVM, whether used for classification or clustering, but especially for the latter, is the need to optimize over algorithmic, model (kernel), chunking, and other process parameters during learning. This is solved via use of metaheuristics for optimization such as simulated annealing, genetic algorithm optimization, and particle swarm optimization. (iv) The main weaknesses in the metaheuristic effort is partly resolved via use of the "front-end" methods, like the FSA, and partly resolved by a knowledge discovery process using the SVM clustering methods. The SSA Protocol weak signal acquisition and analysis method thereby establishes a robust signal processing platform.

The HMM methods are the central methodology or stage in the SSA Protocol, particularly in the channel current cheminformatics (CCC) protocol or implementation, in that the other stages can be dropped or merged with the HMM stage in many incarnations. For example, in some CCC analysis situations the time-domain Finite State Automaton (tFSA) methods could be totally eliminated in favor of the more accurate (but time consuming) HMM-based approach to the problem, with signal states defined or explored in much the same setting, but with the optimized Viterbi path solution taken as the basis for the signal acquisition.

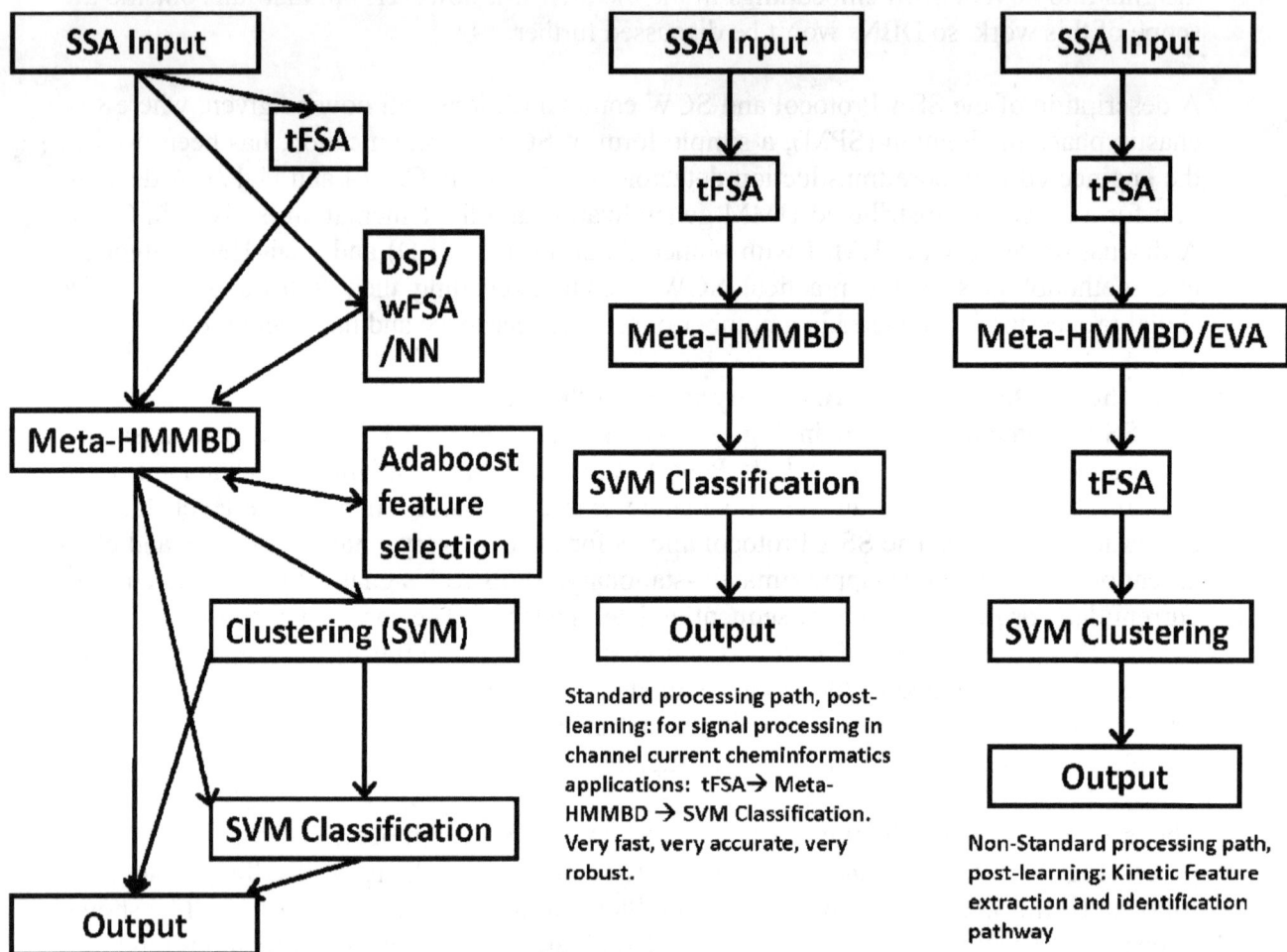

Figure 13.1. Left. The general stochastic sequential analysis flow topology. **Center.** The general signal processing flow in performing channel current analysis is typically Input → tFSA→ Meta-HMMBD → SVM → Output. **Right.** Notable differences occur in channel current cheminformatics during state discovery when EVA-projection (emission variance amplification projection), or a similar method, is used to achieve a quantization on states, then have Input → tFSA → HMMBD/EVA (state discovery) → meta-HMMBD-side → SVM → Output. While, in gene-finding just have: Input → meta-HMMBD-side → Output. In gene-finding, however, the HMM internal 'sensors' are sometimes replaced, locally, with profile-HMMs [1] (equivalent to position-dependent Markov Models, or pMM's, see Methods), or SVM-based profiling [1], so the topology can differ not only in the connections between the boxes shown, but in their ability to embed in other boxes as part of an internal refinement.

The HMM features, and other features (from neural net, wavelet, or spike profiling, etc.) can be fused and selected via use of various data fusion methods, such as a modified Adaboost selection (from [1]). The HMM-based feature extraction provides a well-focused set of 'eyes' on the data, no matter what its nature, according to the underpinnings of its Bayesian statistical representation. The key is that the HMM not be too limiting in its state definition, while there is the typical engineering trade-off on the choice of number of states, N, which impacts the order of computation via a quadratic factor of N in the various dynamic programming calculations (comprising the Viterbi and Baum-Welch algorithms among others).

The HMM 'sensor' capabilities can be significantly improved via switching from profile-MM (pMM) sensors to pMM/SVM-based sensors, as indicated in [1,26], where the superior performance and generalization capability of this approach was demonstrated.

In standard band-limited (and not time-limited) signal analysis with periodic waveforms, sampling is done at the Nyquist rate to have a fully reproducible signal capability. If the sample information is needed elsewhere, it is then compressed (possibly lossy) and transmitted (a 'smart encoder'). The received data is then decompressed and reconstructed (by simply summing wave components, e.g., a 'simple' decoder). If the signal is sparse or compressible, then compressive sensing [145] can be used, where sampling and compression are combined into one efficient step to obtain compressive measurements (the simple encoding in [145] since a set of random projections are employed), which are then transmitted. On the receiving end, the decompression and reconstruction steps are, likewise, combined using an asymmetric 'smart' decoding step. This progression towards asymmetric compressive signal processing can be taken a step further if we consider signal sequences to be equivalent if they have the same stationary statistics. What is obtained is a method similar to compressive sensing, but involving stationary-statistics generative-projection sensing, where the signal processing is non-lossy at the level of stationary statistics equivalence. In the SCW signal analysis the signal source is generative in that it is describable via use of a hidden Markov model, and the HMM's Viterbi-derived generative projections are used to describe the sparse components contributing to the signal source.

In SCW encoding the modulation of stationary statistics can be man-made or natural, with the latter in many experimental situations involving a flow phenomenology that has stationary statistics. If the signal is man-made, usually the underlying stochastic process is still a natural source, where it is the changes in the stationary statistics that is under the control of the man-made encoding scheme. Transmission and reception are then followed by generative projection via Viterbi-HMM template matching or via Viterbi-HMM feature extraction followed by separate classification (using SVM). So in the SCW approach the encoding is even simpler (possibly non-existent, directly passing quantized signal) and is applicable to any noise source with stationary statistics (the case for many experimental observations). The decoding must be even 'smarter', on the other hand, in that generalized Viterbi algorithms are used, and possibly other machine learning methods as well, SVMs in particular. An example of the stationary statistics sensing with a machine learning based decoder is described in application to channel current cheminformatics studies in what follows.

13.2.1 (Stage 1) primitive feature identification
This stage is typically finite-state automaton based, with feature identification comprising identification of signal regions (critically, their beginnings and ends), and, as-needed, identi-

fication of sharply localizable 'spike' behavior in any parameter of the 'complete' (non-lossy, reversibly transformable) classic EE signal representation domains: raw time-domain, Fourier transform domain, wavelet domain, etc. (The methodology for spike detection is shown applied to the time-domain in Ch. 3.) Primitive feature extraction can be operated in two modes: off-line, typically for batch learning and tuning on signal features and acquisition; and on-line, typically for the overall signal acquisition (with acquisition parameters set – e.g., no tuning), and, if needed, 'spike' feature acquisition(s).

The FSA method that is primarily used in the channel current cheminformatics (CCC) signal discovery and acquisition is to identify signal-regions in terms of their having a valid 'start' and a valid 'end', with internal information to the hypothesized signal region consisting, minimally, of the duration of that signal (e.g., the duration between the hypothesized valid 'end and hypothesized valid 'start'). One approach along these lines is a signal 'fishing' protocol " …constraints on valid 'starts' that are weak (with prominent use of 'OR' conjugation) and constraints on valid 'ends' that are strong (with prominent use of 'AND' conjugation)." Another approach to the signal analysis involves identifying anomalously long-duration regions. Identification of anomalously-long duration regions in the more sophisticated Hidden Markov model (HMM) representation would require use of a HMM-with-duration to not lose the information on the anomalous durations, which is one of the application areas for the HMMBD method (as discussed in Ch. 7).

Once identification rules, often threshold-based, are established for the signal start's and signal end's, then those definitions can be explored/used in signal acquisition. As those definitions are tuned over, by exploring the different signal acquisition results obtained with different parameter settings, the signal acquisition counts can undergo radical phase transitions, providing the most rudimentary of the holistic tuning methods on the primitive feature acquisition FSA (Ch. 3 for example). By examining those phase transitions, and the stable regimes in the signal counts (and other attributes in more involved holistic tuning), the recognition of good parameter regimes for accurate acquisition of signal can be obtained. As more internal signal structure is modeled by the FSA, the holistic tuning can involve more sophisticated tuning recognition of emergent grammars on the signal sub-states. The end-result of the tuning is a signal acquisition FSA that can operate in an on-line setting, and very efficiently (computation on the same order as simply reading the sequence) in performing acquisition on the class of signals it has been 'trained' to recognize. On-line learning is possible via periodic updates on the batch learning state/tuning process. For typical SSA (and CCC) applications, the tFSA is used to recognize and acquire 'blockade' events (which have clearly defined start and stop transitions).

13.2.2 (Stage 2) feature identification and feature selection
This stage in the signal processing protocol is typically Hidden Markov model (HMM) based, where identified signal regions are examined using a fixed state HMM feature extractor or a template-HMM (states not fixed during template learning process where they learn to 'fit' to arrive at the best recognition on their train-data, the states then become fixed when the HMM-template is used on test data). The Stage 2 HMM methods are the central methodology/stage in the CCC protocol in that the other stages can be dropped or merged with the Stage 2 HMM in many incarnations. For example, in some data analysis situations the Stage 1 methods could be totally eliminated in favor of the more accurate HMM-based approach to the problem, with signal states defined/explored in much the same setting, but with the optimized Viterbi path solution taken as the basis for the signal acquisition structure

identification. The reason this is not typically done is that the FSA methods sought in Stage 1 are usually only O(T) computational expense, where 'T' is the length of the stochastic sequential data that is to be examined, and 'O(T)' denotes an order of computation that scales as 'T' (linearly in the length of the sequence). The typical HMM Viterbi algorithm, on the other hand, is $O(TN^2)$, where 'N' is the number of states in the HMM. Stage 1 provides a faster, and often more flexible, means to acquire signal, but it is more hands-on. If the core HMM/Viterbi method can be approximated such that it can run at O(TN) or even O(T) in certain data regimes, for example, then the non-HMM methods in stage 1 could be phased out. Such HMM approximation methods present a data-dependent branching in the most efficient implementation of the protocol. If the data is sufficiently regular, direct tuning and regional approximation with HMM's may allow Stage 1 FSA methods to be avoided entirely. For general data, however, some tuning and signal acquisition according to Stage 1 will be needed (possibly off-line) if only to then bootstrap (accelerate) the learning task of the HMM approximation methods.

The HMM emission probabilities, transition probabilities, and Viterbi path sampled features, among other things, provide a rich set of data to draw from for feature extraction (to create 'feature vectors'). The choice of features is optimized according to the classification or clustering method that will make use of that feature information. In typical operation of the protocol, the feature vector information is classified using a Support Vector Machine (SVM). This is described in Stage 3 to follow. Once again, however, the Stage 3 classification could be totally eliminated in favor of the HMM's log likelihood ratio classification capability at Stage 2, for example, when a number of template HMMs are employed (one for each signal class). This classification approach is inherently weaker and slower than the (off-line trained) SVM methodology in many respects, but, depending on the data, there are circumstances where it may provide the best performing implementation of the protocol.

Stochastic carrier wave encoding/decoding
Using HMMBD we have an efficient means to establish a new form of carrier-based communications where the carrier is not periodic but is stochastic, with stationary statistics. The HMMBD algorithmic methodology, [346], enables practical stochastic carrier wave (SCW) encoding/decoding with this method.

Stochastic carrier wave (SCW) signal processing is also encountered at the forefront of a number of efforts in nanotechnology, where it can result from establishing or injecting signal modulations so as to boost device sensitivity. The notion of modulations for effectively larger bandwidth and increased sensitivity is also described in [344,345]. Here we choose modulations that specifically evoke a signal type that can be modeled well with a HMMD but not with a HMM. This is a generally applicable approach where conventional, periodic, signal analysis methods will often fail. Nature at the single-molecule scale may not provide a periodic signal source, or allow for such, but may allow for a signal modulation that is stochastic with stationary statistics, as in the case of the nanopore transduction detector (NTD).

13.2.3 (Stage 3) Classification
This stage is typically Support Vector Machine (SVM) based. SVMs are a robust classification method. If there are more classes to discern than two, the SVM can either be applied in a Decision Tree construction with binary-SVM classifiers at each node, or the SVM can internally represent the multiple classes. Depending on the noise attributes of the data, one or the other approach may be optimal (or even achievable). Both methods are typically ex-

plored in tuning, for example, where a variety of kernels and kernel parameters are also chosen, as well as tuning on internal KKT handling protocols. Simulated annealing and genetic algorithms have been found to be useful in doing the tuning in an orderly, efficient, manner. If the feature vectors produced correspond to complete data information/profiling in some manner, such is explicitly the case in a probability feature vector representation on a complete set of signal event frequencies (where all the feature 'components' are positive and sum to 1), then kernels can be chosen that conform to evaluating a measure of distance between feature vectors in accordance with that notion of completeness (or internal constraint, such as with the probability vectors), e.g., the entropic kernel. Use of entropic kernels with probability feature vectors in proof-of-concept experiments have been found to work well with channel blockade analysis and is thought to convey the benefit of having a better pairing of kernel and feature vector, here the kernels have probability distribution measures (with Kulback-Leibler information divergences), for example, and the feature vectors are (discrete) probability distributions.

13.2.4 (Stage 4) Clustering

This stage is often not performed in the 'real-time' operational signal processing task as it is more for knowledge discovery, structure identification, etc., although there are notable exceptions, one such comprising the jack-knife transition detection via clustering consistency with a causal boundary that is described in what follows. This stage can involve any standard clustering method, in a number of applications, but the best performing in the channel current analysis setting is often found to be an SVM-based external clustering approach (see [1,37]), which is doubly convenient when the learning phase ends because the SVM-based clustering solution can then be fixed as the supervised learning set for a SVM-based classifier (that is then used at the operational level).

A computationally 'expensive' HMM signal acquisition at Stage 1 may be necessary for very weak signals, for example, if the typical Stage 1 methods fail. In this situation the HMM will probably have a very weak signal differential on the different signal classes if it were to attempt direct classification (and eliminate the need for a separate Stage 3). In this setting, the HMM would probably be run in the finest grayscale generic-state mode (see Ch. 7), with a number of passes with different window sample sizes to 'step through' the sequence to be analyzed. Then, there are two ways to proceed: (1) with a supervised learning 'bias', where windows on one side of a 'cut' are one class, and those on the other side the other class, can a the SVM classify at high accuracy on train/test with the labeled data so indicated? If so, a transition is identified. In (2) the idea is to use an unsupervised learning SVM-based clustering method where we look for a strong knife-edge split on clustered populations along the sequence of window samples. When this occurs, there is a strong identification of a transition. Since regions are identified (delineated) by their transition boundaries, we arrive at a minimally-informed means for state and state-transition discovery in stochastic sequential data involving HMM/SVM based channel current signal processing.

13.2.5 (All Stages) Database/Data-Warehouse System specification

The adaptive HMM (AHMM) and modified SVM systems require implementation-specific data schema designs, for both input and output. The signal processing algorithms depend on information, represented structurally in the data, the algorithms are both process driven and data driven - these components impact the implementation of the algorithms.

The data schemas are typically implemented for optimal read time and ease of re-use and deployment, and have system dependencies that can be very significant, such as with client data-services involving distributed data access. The data schemas are typically implemented using flat files, low level operating system specific system calls to map data onto virtual memory, Relational Database Management Systems (RDBMS), and Object Database Management Systems (ODBMS). The database schemas are defined in two system contexts, 1) real time data acquisition, which includes feature recognition (AHMM) and classification (SVM), and, 2) data warehousing for client data-service, and for further analysis that can be computationally intensive and requires substantial data processing.

The real-time data acquisition systems associated with the signal processing can be implemented using flat file systems and operating system specific virtual memory management interfaces. These interfaces are optimized to be scalable and high-bandwidth, to meet the requirements of high speed, real-time, data acquisition and storage. The data schemas allow for real-time signal processing such as feature recognition and classification, as well as local storage for subsequent export to a data warehouse, which can be implemented using industry standard RDBMS and ODBMS systems.

13.2.6 (All Stages) Server-based data analysis System specification
The data warehouse data schemas are optimized for applications-specific analysis of the signal processing tools in a distributed, scalable environment where substantial computing power can extend the analysis beyond what is possible in real-time. The local data acquisition systems produce and identify structure in real-time, storing the data locally, while another process can stream the data transparently to an off-site data warehouse for subsequent analysis. The database uses data modeling tools to identify data schemas that work in tandem with the signal processing algorithms. The structure of the data schemas are typically integral to efficient implementation of the algorithms. Substantial off-line data pre-processing, for example, is used to create data structures based on inherent structure identified in the data. An internet-based user interface allows for access to the stored data and provides a suite of server-based, application-specific analysis and data mining tools.

I. Channel Current Cheminformatics (CCC)Protocol

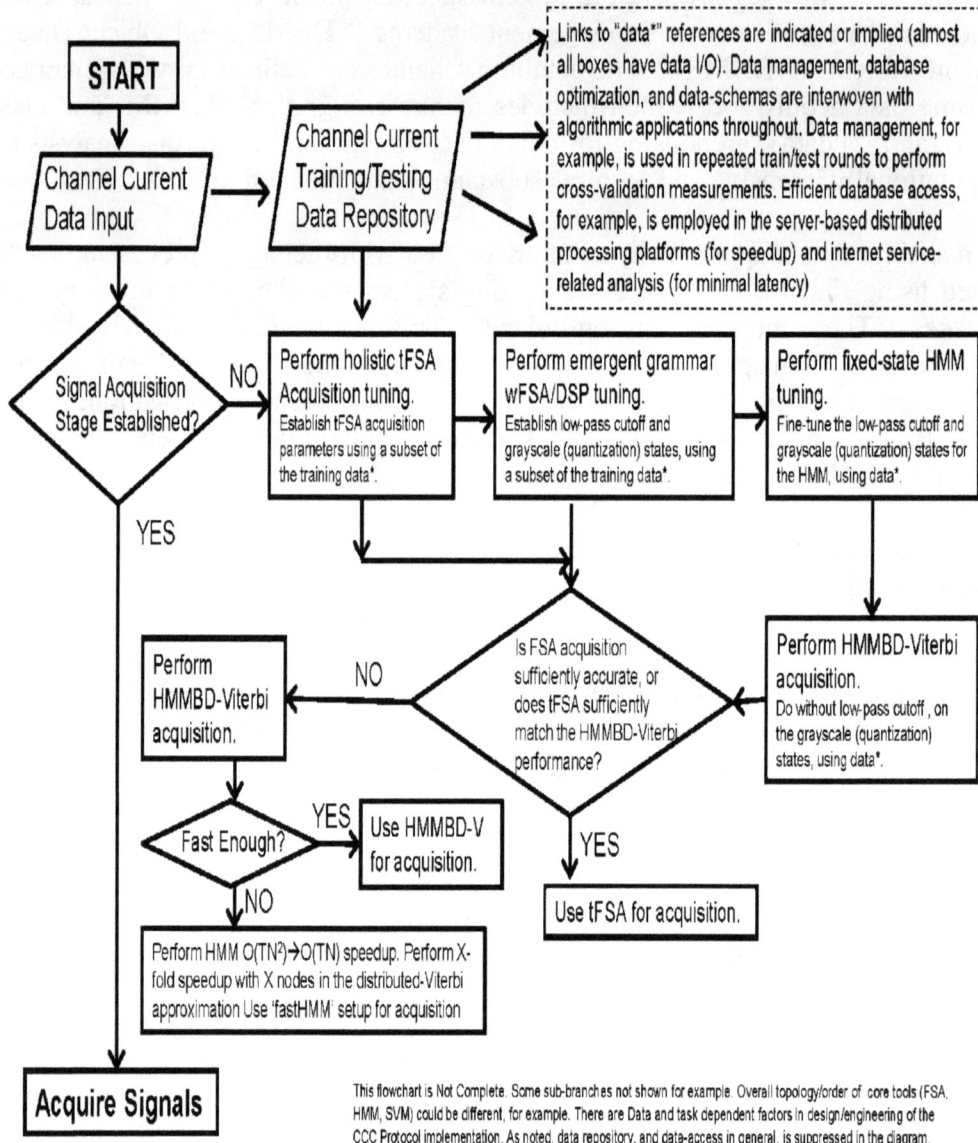

Fig. 13.2. CCC Protocol Flowchart (part 1)

II. Channel Current Cheminformatics (CCC)Protocol

This flowchart is Not Complete. Some sub-branches not shown for example. Overall topology/order of core tools (FSA, HMM, SVM) could be different, for example. There are Data and task dependent factors in design/engineering of the CCC Protocol implementation. As noted, data repository, and data-access in general. is suppressed in the diagram.

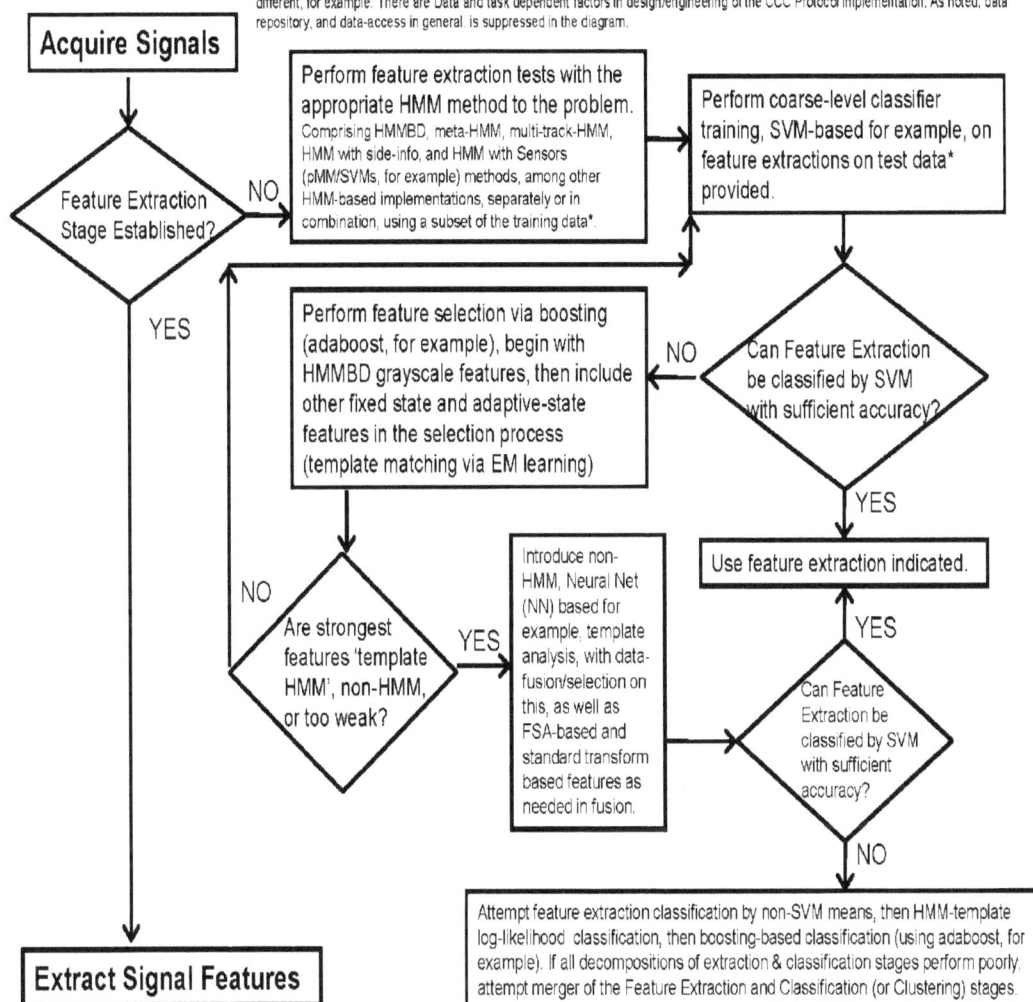

Fig. 13.3. CCC Protocol Flowchart (part 2)

385

III. Channel Current Cheminformatics (CCC)Protocol

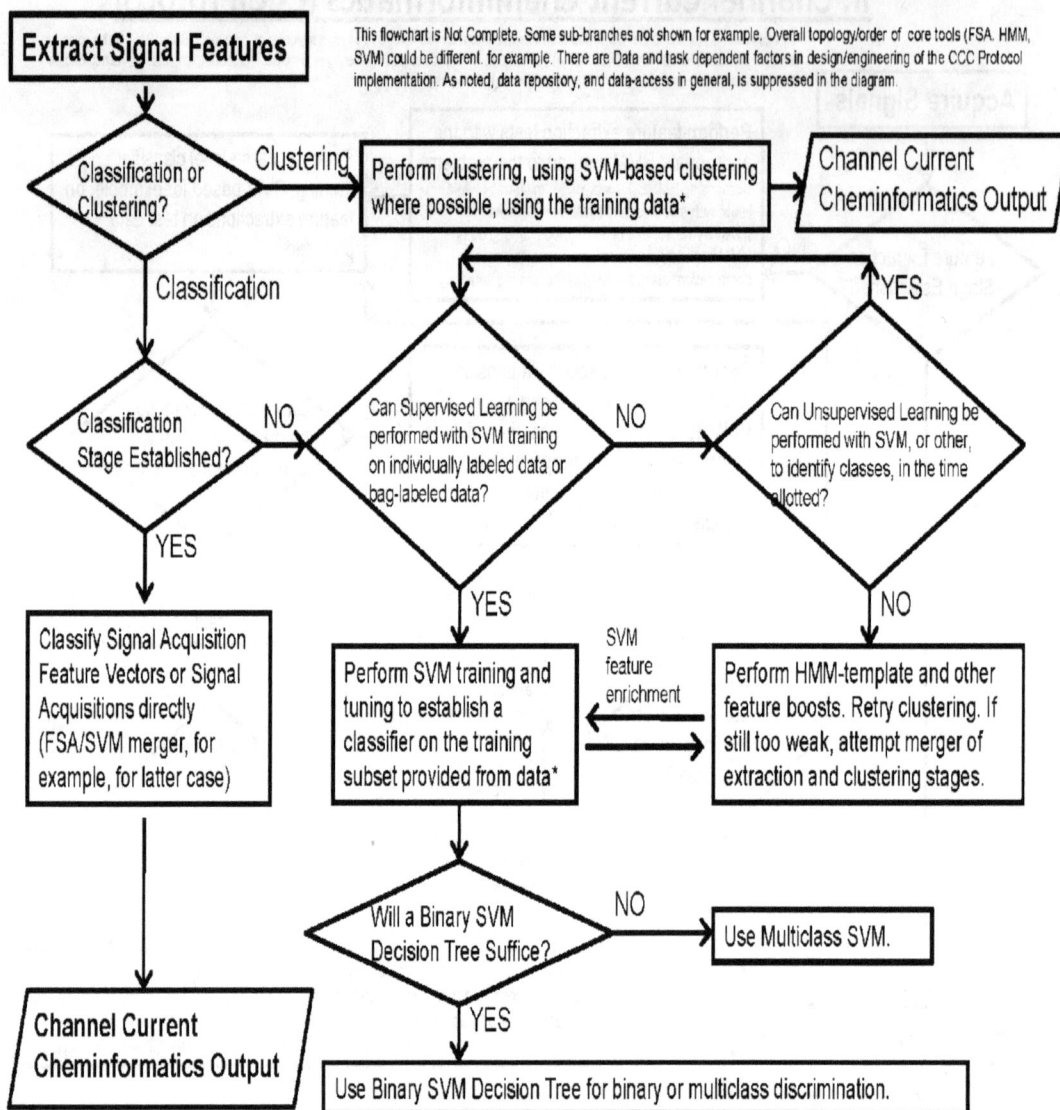

This flowchart is Not Complete. Some sub-branches not shown for example. Overall topology/order of core tools (FSA, HMM, SVM) could be different. for example. There are Data and task dependent factors in design/engineering of the CCC Protocol implementation. As noted, data repository, and data-access in general, is suppressed in the diagram.

Fig. 13.4. CCC Protocol Flowchart (part 3)

13.3 Channel Current Cheminformatics (CCC) implementation of the Stochastic Sequential Analysis (SSA) protocol

NTD, with the channel current cheminformatics (CCC) implementation of the SSA protocol (described in Ch. 14), provides proof-of-concept examples of the SSA methods utilization, and can be used as a platform for finite state communication. From the CCC/NTD starting point it is easier to convey the unique signal boosting capabilities when working with real-time capable HMMBD signal processing [21,346] and other SSA methods. In the larger sense, recognition of stationary statistics transitions allows one to generalize to full-scale encoding/decoding in terms of stationary statistics 'phases', i.e., stochastic phase modulation, a form of stochastic carrier-wave (SCW) communications. Many of the Proof-of-concept experiments described in what follows involve SSA applications, in a CCC implementation or a context for the NTD platform. The SSA Protocol is a general signal processing paradigm for characterizing stochastic sequential data.

In the Nanopore Transduction Detector (NTD) experiments the molecular dynamics of a (single) captured transducer molecule provides a unique stochastic reference signal with stable statistics on the observed, single-molecule blockade, channel current, somewhat analogous to a carrier signal in standard electrical engineering signal analysis. Changes in transient blockade statistics, coupled to SSA signal processing protocols, enables the means for a highly detailed characterization of the interactions of the transducer molecule with binding cognates in the surrounding (extra-channel) environment.
The transducer molecule is specifically engineered to generate distinct signals depending on its interaction with the target molecule. Statistical models are trained for each binding mode, bound and unbound, for example, by exposing the transducer molecule to zero or high (excess) concentrations of the target molecule. The transducer molecule is engineered so that these different binding states generate distinct signals with high resolution. Once the signals are characterized, the information can be used in a real-time setting to determine if trace amounts of the target are present in a sample through a serial, high-frequency sampling process.

Thus, in NTD applications of the SSA Protocol, due to the molecular dynamics of the captured transducer molecule, a unique reference signal with stationary (or approximately stationary) statistics is engineered to be generated during transducer blockade, analogous to a carrier signal in standard electrical engineering signal analysis. The adaptive machine learning algorithms for real-time analysis of the stochastic signal generated by the transducer molecule offer a "lock and key" level of signal discrimination. The heart of the signal processing algorithm is an adaptive Hidden Markov Model (AHMM) based feature extraction method, implemented on a distributed processing platform for real-time operation. For real-time processing, the AHMM is used for feature extraction on channel blockade current data while classification and clustering analysis are implemented using a Support Vector Machine (SVM). In addition, the design of the machine learning based algorithms allow for scaling to large datasets, real-time distributed processing, and are adaptable to analysis on any channel-based dataset, including resolving signals for different nanopore substrates (e.g. solid state configurations) or for systems based on translocation technology. The machine learning software has also been integrated into the nanopore detector for "real-time" pattern-recognition informed (PRI) feedback [1,20]. The methods used to implement the PRI feedback include *distributed* HMM and SVM implementations, which enable the processing speedup that is needed.

A mixture of two DNA hairpin species {9TA, 9GC} is examined in an experimental test of the PRI system. In separate experiments, data is gathered for the 9TA and 9GC blockades in order to have known examples to train the SVM pattern recognition software. A nanopore experiment is then run with a 1:70 mix of 9GC:9TA, with the goal to eject 9TA signals as soon as they are identified, while keeping the 9GC's for a full 5 seconds (when possible, sometimes a channel-dissociation or melting event can occur in less than that time). The results showing the successful operation of the PRI system is shown in Fig. 13.5 as a 4D plot, where the radius of the event 'points' corresponds to the duration of the signal blockade (the

4th dimension). The result in Fig. 13.5 demonstrates an approximately 50-fold speedup on data acquisition of the desired minority species.

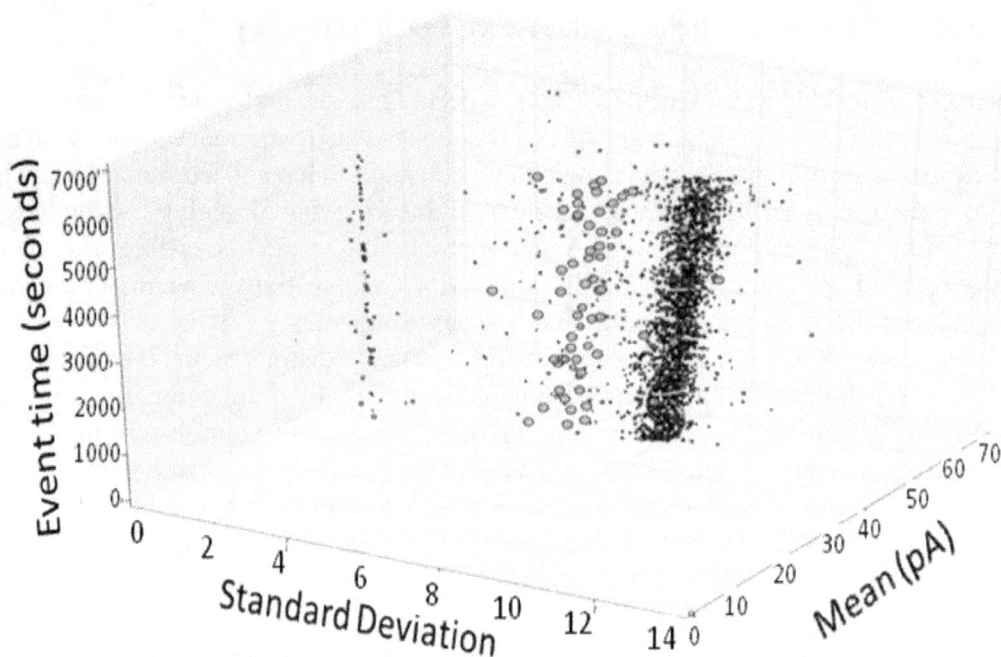

Figure 13.5. PRI Mixture Clustering Test with 4D plot [20]. The vertical axis is the event observation time, and the plotted points correspond to the standard deviation and mean values for the event observed at the indicated event time. The radius of the points correspond to the duration of the corresponding signal blockade (the 4th dimension). Three blockade clusters appear as the three vertical trajectories. The abundant 9TA events appear as the thick band of small-diameter (short duration, ~100ms) blockade events. The 1:70 rarer 9GC events appear as the band of large-diameter (long duration, ~ 5s) blockade events. The third, very small, blockade class corresponds to blockades that partially thread and almost entirely blockade the channel.

To provide enhanced, autonomous reliability, the NTD is self-calibrating: the signals are normalized computationally with respect to physical parameters (e.g. temperature, ph, salt concentration, etc.) eliminating the need for physical feedback systems to stabilize the device. In addition, specially engineered calibration probes have been designed to enable real-time self-calibration by generating a standard "carrier signal." These probes are added to samples being analyzed to provide a run-by-run self-calibration. These redundant, self-calibration capabilities result in a device which may be operated by an entry level lab technician.

Although the nanopore transduction detector can be a self-contained 'device' in a lab, external information can be used, for example, to update and broaden the operational information on control molecules ('carrier references'). For the general 'kit' user (see [1]), carrier reference signals and other systemically-engineered constructs can be used, for example, for a wide range of thin-client arrangements (where they typically have minimal local computational resource and knowledge resource). The paradigm for both device and kit implementations involve system-oriented interactions, where the kit implementation may operate on more of a data service/data repository level and thus need 'real-time' (high bandwidth) system processing of data-service requests or data-analysis requests. Although not as system-dependent on database-server linkages, the more self-contained 'device' implementation will still typically have, for example, local networked (parallelized) data-warehousing, and fast-access, for distributed processing speedup on real-time experimental operations.

13.4 SCW for detector sensitivity boosting

Since an HMM template match can be weighted by its Viterbi path probability, the HMM's generative projection might offer improved efficiency in the compressive sensor method [145] when working with stochastic data with stationary statistics [45]. The HMM's generative capability derives from its ability to be 'run in reverse', e.g., given the learned parameterization of a particular state model, an HMM can produce stochastic data with the same stationary statistics as that which originally was used in the statistical learning process. (The terminology 'emission probability' relates to this generative perspective.) The SCW approach is similar to the compressive sensing approach [145] in that is involves a random (stochastic) projection, but in the SCW approach the stochastic projection is constrained to have stationary statistics and the main area of application is to stochastic sequential analysis. Compressive sensing makes use of a sequence of random projections, while in SCW a sequence of generative projections are done by using template HMMs and compressing stationary statistical parameters according to the generalized Viterbi algorithms. See [1,45,198] for further variations (some using SVMs). Stationary statistical signals that are truly modulatory, e.g., not simply at a fixed level with Gaussian noise fluctuations about that level, will have a sparse data representation in terms of generative feature sets (which is used by SVMs for some classification tasks in [1,45,198]).

New HMM implementations, allow a new form of carrier-based communications where the carrier is not periodic but is stochastic, with stationary statistics. The "stochastic carrier wave" (SCW) approach is not only a means to understand the messages Nature provides (in near-equilibrium flow phenomenologies with stationary statistics), but also provides a hidden carrier method, enabling security and making signal jamming much more difficult. An algorithmic methodology allows for 100-fold, or faster, implementation of a Hidden Markov model with duration (the HMMBD algorithm [19,21,34]), is critical to this encoding/decoding method.SCW communications are found at the forefront of a number of efforts in nanotechnology. This is because nature at the single-molecule scale has a signal modulation that is stochastic, sometimes with stationary statistics. Such is the case with the signal analysis in a nanopore transduction detector (NTD). Thus, further developments with stochastic carrier wave methods would serve both communications efforts and biosensing efforts.

If states have self-transitions with a notably non-geometric distribution on their self-transition 'durations', then a fit to a geometric distribution in this capacity, as will be forced by the standard HMM, will be weak, and HMMD modeling will serve better. In engineered communications protocols, or in engineered, modulated, nanopore transduction detector (NTD) signals, highly non-geometric distributions can be sought. One encoding scheme that is strongly non-geometric in same-state duration distribution is the familiar *long* open-reading-frame (ORF) encoding found in genomic data. This suggests a similar ORF-like encoding scheme to establish a carrier duration peak in the self-transition distribution's tail region, e.g., a second peak in the duration distribution (perhaps one even more skewed from the geometric distribution than the heavy-tail distributions found for ORFs).

The NTD signal analysis demonstrates the simplest stochastic carrier wave utilization, in a biophysics experimental setting. A minor elaboration on the signal analysis, to go from a simple two-state (bound/unbound) signal recognition to a lengthy two-state telegraph signal, then yields the rudimentary implementation for stochastic carrier communications purposes.

13.4.1 NTD with multiple channels (or high noise)

The nanopore transduction detection (NTD) platform involves functionalizing a standard nanopore detector platform in a new way that is cognizant of signal processing and machine learning capabilities and advantages, such that a highly sensitive biosensing capability is achieved. In the NTD functionalization of the standard nanopore detector we design a molecule that can be drawn into the channel (by an applied potential) but be too big to translocate, instead becoming stuck in a bistable 'capture' such that it modulates the ionflow in the *single* nanopore channel established in a distinctive way. An approximately two-state 'telegraph signal' can engineered. If the channel modulator is bifunctional, in that one end is meant to be captured and modulate while the other end is linked to an aptamer or antibody for specific binding, then we have the basis for a remarkably sensitive and specific biosensing capability. The biosensing task is reduced to the channel-based recognition of bound or unbound NTD modulators. Preliminary results demonstrate successful application of this method in a streptavidin (toxin) detection scenario using a biotinylated DNA hairpin. In typical NTD biosensing there is only one (nanometer-scale) channel established in the detector apparatus, however, where other channels bridging the same membrane (bilayer) would do so in parallel with the first (single) channel. In a naïve setting, additional channel noise sources degrade sensitivity and offset gains from having multiple channel 'receptors'. *In the stochastic carrier wave encoding/decoding with HMMD we aim to have multiple channels but avoid signal degradation such that the full benefits of a multiple receptor gain can be realized.*

In the NTD platform, sensitivity increases with observation time in contrast to translocation technologies where the observation window is fixed to the time it takes for a molecule to move through the channel. The key to the sensitivity and versatility of the NTD platform is the unique ability to couple real-time adaptive signal processing algorithms to the complex blockade current signals generated by the captured transducer molecule. The NTD approach can provide exquisite sensitivity and can be deployed in many applications where trace level detection is required.

In the NTD experiments the molecular dynamics of the captured transducer molecule provides a unique stochastic reference signal with (typically or approximately) stable statistics that is generated from the modulating blockade current, analogous to a carrier signal in standard electrical engineering signal analysis. By extension, changes in transient blockade statistics, coupled to sophisticated signal processing protocols, provide the means for a highly detailed characterization of the interactions of the transducer molecule with molecules in the surrounding (extra-channel) environment.

Consider the case where 100 parallel channels are in operation, a scenario that has the potential to increase the sensitivity of the NTD 100-fold, but the signal analysis typically becomes more challenging, and sensitivity gains limited, since there are 100 parallel noise sources.

The HMMD recognition of a transducer signal's stationary statistics, however, is analogous to 'time integration' heterodyning a radio signal with a periodic carrier in classic electrical engineering in that there is improved carrier-signal recognition with longer observation time. In order to introduce a 'time integration' benefit in the recognition of a transducer signal, periodic (or stochastic) modulations may be introduced to the transducer environment. In a high noise background, modulations may allow some of the transducer states to have heavy-tailed, or multimodal, self-transition duration distributions. With these modifications to the signal processing software a single transducer molecule signal is recognizable in the presence of 100's of channels. Increasing the number of channels by 100 and retaining the capability of recognizing a single transducer blockading one of those channels provides a direct gain in sensitivity according to the number of channels (e.g., 100 channels would provide a sensitivity boost of 100). It is important to note that the increase in sensitivity is mostly implemented computationally and does not add complexity or cost to the NTD device itself.

The adaptive machine learning algorithms for real-time analysis of the stochastic signal generated by the NTD transducer molecule are critical to realizing the increased sensitivity of the NTD and offer a "lock and key" level of signal discrimination. The transducer molecule is specifically engineered to generate distinct signals depending on its interaction with the target molecule. Statistical models are trained for each binding mode, bound and unbound, by exposing the transducer molecule to high concentrations of the target molecule. The transducer molecule has been engineered so that these different binding states generate distinct signals with high resolution. In operation, the NTD-biosensing process is analogous to giving a bloodhound a distinct memory of a human target by having it sniff a piece of clothing. Once the signals are characterized, the information is used in a real-time setting to determine if trace amounts of the target are present in a sample through a serial, high frequency sampling process.

The algorithms which describe the stochastic channel current modulations are a pure form of Machine Learning (a branch of Artificial Intelligence) in that there is no assumption of an underlying probability distribution; the statistical representation is directly generated from the data being produced by the molecular dynamics of the transducer molecule. A statistical model that is based on direct observation of the transducer molecule's dynamics eliminates the need for a parameterized statistical model, resulting in a higher resolution of discrimination.

13.4.2 Stochastic Carrier Wave
General methods are proposed for (i) stochastic sequential analysis; (ii) stochastic carrier-wave communications; (iii) holographic HMM extensions; and, (iv) distributed HMM implementations. In method (ii), in particular, we establish a new type of communication process where the carrier wave is a stochastic observation sequence that obeys stationary statistics. In standard periodic carrier wave signal processing convolving with the carrier frequency allows the signal modulations of that carrier to be obtained. Here we have something analogous, but we have a carrier with stationary statistics, not fixed frequency, and can recognize different phases of stationary statistics via HMM methods for class-independent feature extraction, with Support Vector Machines (SVMs) for sparse data classification, or

via HMM methods for class-dependent HMM generative projection (as mentioned in earlier comments).

In standard signal analysis with periodic waveforms, sampling is done at the Nyquist rate and the data compressed and transmitted (a 'smart' encoder). The received data is then de-compressed and reconstructed (by simply summing wave components, e.g., a 'simple' decoder). If the signal is sparse or compressible, then compressive sensing [145] can be used, where sampling and compression are combined into one efficient step to obtain com-pressive measurements (referred to as 'dumb' encoding in [145] since a set of random projections are employed), which are then transmitted. On the receiving end, the decompres-sion and reconstruction steps are, likewise, combined using an asymmetric 'smart' decoding step. This progression towards asymmetric compressive signal processing can be taken a step further if we consider signal sequences to be equivalent if they have the same stationary statistics. What is obtained is a method similar to compressive sensing, but involving sta-tionary-statistics generative-projection sensing, where the signal processing is non-lossy at the level of stationary statistics equivalence. In the SCW signal analysis the signal source is generative in that it is describable via use of a hidden Markov model, and the HMM's Viterbi-derived generative projections are used to describe the sparse components contrib-uting to the signal source. In SCW encoding the modulation of stationary statistics can be man-made or natural, with the latter in many experimental situations that involve flow phe-nomologies that have stationary statistics. If the signal is man-made, usually the underlying stochastic process is still a natural source, where it is the changes in the stationary statistics that is under the control of the man-made encoding scheme. Transmission and reception are then followed by generative projection via Viterbi-HMM template matching or via Viterbi-HMM feature extraction followed by separate classification (using SVM). So in the SCW approach the encoding is even 'dumber' in that it can be any noise source with stationary statistics (the case for many experimental observations), with stationary statistics phase modulation for encoding. The decoding must be even 'smarter', on the other hand, in that generalized Viterbi algorithms are used to perform a generative projection (and possibly other machine learning methods as well, SVMs in particular). An example of the stationary statistics sensing with a machine learning based decoder is described in application to chan-nel current cheminformatics studies in what follows.

In the standard HMM [81,83], when a state 'i' is entered, that state is occupied for a period of time, via self-transitions (with self-transition probability denoted as a_{ii}), until transiting to another state 'j' (with probability a_{ij}). If the same-state interval is given as 'd', the standard HMM description of the probability distribution on state intervals is implicitly given by a geometric distribution (see Ch. 7 for more details). The best-fit geometric distribution, how-ever, is inappropriate in many cases. The standard HMMD replaces the above equation with a $p_i(d)$ that models the real duration distribution of state i. In this way explicit knowledge about the duration of states is incorporated into the HMM.

The original description of an explicit HMMD required computation of order $O(TN^2+TND^2)$ (where T is the sequence length to be examined, N is the number of states in the HMM/HMMD model, and D is the maximum duration length allowed in the HMMD mod-el). The 'D^2' term made the original approach prohibitively computationally expensive in practical, real-time, operations, and introduced a severe maximum-duration constraint on the duration-distribution model. Improvements via hidden semi-Markov models to computations of order $O(TN^2+TND)$ are described in Ch. 7, where the maximum-interval constraint is still employed. In [21] we show that $O(TN^2+TND^*)$ is possible with the HMMBD algorithm, where D^* is the number of binned length states. The HMMBD implementation brings the HMMD modeling within the range of computational viability for many applications. In the HMMBD approach we also eliminate the maximum-duration constraint. We can often reduce to a bin representation with $D^*<10$, such that $D^*<<N$ in many situations, in which case that the HMMBD requires computations of order $O(TN^2)$, the same as for the HMM alone.

One important application of the HMM-with-duration (HMMD) method used in [1,21] includes kinetic feature extraction from EVA projected channel current data (the HMM-with-Duration is shown to offer a critical stabilizing capability in an example in [1] and Ch. 7). The EVA-projected/HMMD processing offers a hands-off (minimal tuning) method for extracting the mean dwell times for various blockade states (the core kinetic information on the blockading molecule's channel interactions).

The HMM-with-Duration implementation, described in [1] and Ch. 7, is being explored in terms of its performance at parsing synthetic blockade signals. In the [1] experiment the synthetic data was designed to have two levels, with lifetime in each level determined by a governing distribution (Poisson and Gaussian distributions with a range of mean values were considered). The results clearly demonstrate the superior performance of the HMMD over the simpler HMM formulation on data with non-geometrically distributed same-state interval durations. With use of the EVA-projection method this affords a robust means to obtain kinetic feature extraction. The HMM with duration is critical for accurate kinetic feature extraction, and the results in [1] suggest that this problem can be elegantly solved with a pairing of the HMM-with-Duration stabilization with EVA-projection.

In Fig. 13.6 we show state-decoding on synthetic data that is representative of a biological-channel two-state ion-current decoding problem, or an encode/decode software radio signal. For this problem 120 data sequences were generated that have two states with channel blockade levels set at 30 and 40 pA (a typical scenario in practice). Every data sequence has 10,000 samples. Each state has emitted values in a range from 0 to 49 pA. The maximum duration of states is set at 500. The mean duration of the 40 pA state is given as 200 samples (typically have one sample every 20 microseconds in actual experiments), while the 30 pA level has mean duration set at 300 samples. The task is to train using 100 of the generated data sequences and attempt state-decoding on the remaining 20 data sequences. Example sequences are shown in Fig. 13.6, along with their decoding when an HMM or an HMMD is employed. The performance difference is stark: the exact and adaptive HMMD decodings are 97.1% correct, while the HMM decoding is only correct 61% of the time (where random guessing would accomplish 50%, on average, in a two-state system). Three parameterized distributions were examined: geometric, Gaussian, and Poisson. Distributions that were segmented and "messy" were also examined. In all cased the HMMD performed robustly, similar to the above, and in all cases the adaptive HMMD optimization performed comparably to the more computationally expensive exact HMMD.

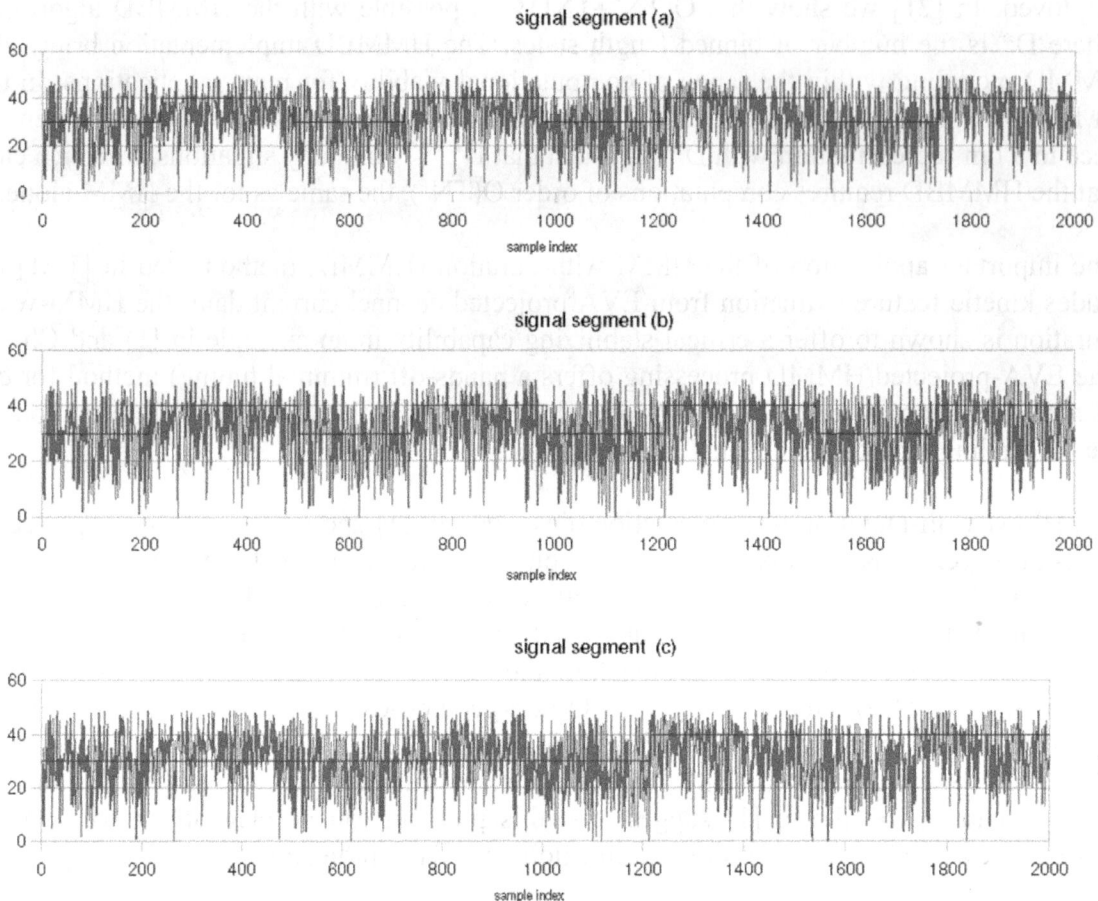

Fig. 13.6. In the figure we show state-decoding results on synthetic data that is representative of a biological-channel two-state ion-current decoding problem. Signal segment (a) (at the top) shows the original two-level signal as the dark line, while the noised version of the signal is shown in red. Signal segment (b) (in the middle) shows the noised signal in red and the two-state denoised signal according to the HMMD decoding process (whether exact or adaptive), which is stable (97.1% accurate) allowing for state-lifetime extraction (with the concomitant chemical kinetics information that is thereby obtained in this channel current analysis setting). Signal segment (c) (at the bottom) shows the standard HMM signal resolution, and its failure to properly resolve the desired level-lifetime information.

Stochastic Carrier Wave (SCW) signal processing occurs in both natural and engineered situations. Whenever Nature is observed with a sequence of observations that have stationary statistics (associated with equilibrium and near-equilibrium flow situations, for example), then the basis for SCW signal processing arises. SCW also parallels all electrical engineering carrier-wave methodologies where periodic wave methods are used in some modulation scheme, thus the number of engineering applications is enormous. AM heterodyning, for example, can be replaced with stochastic carrier wave with pattern recognition informed (PRI) heterodyning. Also have phase modulation equivalence: the standard periodic carrier wave approach has a coherent phase reference, while SCW introduces a stochastic carrier wave with stationary statistics 'phase'. Have similar capabilities as with phased-locked loop (PLL), for example, where the phase tracking is done on SCW encoded information.

Chapter 14

Nanopore Detection

A nanopore detector is based on a membrane that separates two chambers of electrolytic solution with a single nanopore providing a channel across that membrane. The detector is based on ionic current observations when a potential difference is applied across the membrane. Objects drawn into the nanopore cause ionic current blockades that form the basis of the molecular observations (i.e., observations derive from the ionic current imprints, or blockades, due to captured or translocating molecules). With channel current detection, particle analysis can be done on solutions to obtain particle concentrations, solution mixture composition, and even molecular dynamics. Early channel current detectors had millimeter diameters (0.1 mm) and were used to count cell concentrations and mixture compositions [347]. Information obtained about the excluded cell volume was used in classifying blood cells as red or white, for example, the ratio of which provided important data for medical diagnostics. The 100 μm-scale pores of Coulter were devised in the early 1950's.

It wasn't until the early 1970's that nanometer-scale pores were examined [348-350]. Bean made a nanometer-scale channel from crystalline structures (mica) that had defect tracks (from fission events). When etched with HF the normally impervious mica is removed along the defect-track in its crystalline structure. Depending on how this process is controlled, pores have been obtained with diameters ranging down to 6 nm (50 nm diam. pores commercially available). Although this technology has been used for observations on uncharged particles (polystyrene spheres with 90 nm diameter, [349]), it doesn't work as well with charged molecules (like DNA). Another complication is that the etching method for pore construction inevitably leads to long tunnel-like channels, which doesn't provide the best configuration for detector uses. Detection of biomolecules with biologically-based nanometer-scale pores also showed promise at about this time with the work by Hladky and Haydon

[351]. They showed that a biological channel, the bacterial antibiotic gramicidin, could self-assemble in a lipid bilayer to form a functional channel (with currents of order 1 pA). This potentially solved two of the mica-channel problems: the lipid bilayers are very thin, about 5 nm, and the protein-based, biologically functional, nanometer-scale pore seemed better suited to passing charged biomolecules. Gramicidin was too small to detect most biomolecules, however, since it could barely pass molecules the size of the water molecule. It wasn't until 1994 [352] that a sufficiently large pore was studied, α-hemolysin. In the 1994 paper, Bezrukov *et al.* studied the blockades resulting from a charge-neutral polymer: polyethylene glycol (PEG). Later modifications to the gramicidin pore permitted its use as an antibody-modulated (on-off) biosensor, while modifications to the α-hemolysin pore enabled its use as a metal biosensor [353], among other things [354,355]. In 1995 and 1999, α-hemolysin was successfully used for DNA homopolymer translocation studies and classification [356,357]. Nanometer-scale pores then began to be developed in solid-state media [358,359]. Nanopores provide rich opportunities for the future because at nanometer scale a wealth of new prospects arise, from characterizing just about anything that can form a colloidal suspension in electrolytic solutions, to polymers like DNA, to the molecular motions that indicate molecular identity [45,47,48].

One of the key strengths of nanopore detectors is that they analyze populations of single molecules. With signal processing and pattern recognition, this information enables a new type of cheminformatics based on channel current measurements. Single molecule observations are also of interest in biophysics; binding/conformational changes on captured dsDNA end regions, for example, might be tracked and understood using the nanopore blockade signal. DNA regions away from the ends may eventually be studied in a similar manner, using pore-translocation confinement to reveal distinctive conductance/binding properties on those bases threading the pore's limiting aperture constriction. Single molecule classifications permit a number of technical innovations. For sequencing, the single molecule basis of measurement may permit Sanger-type sequencing [360,361] on DNA molecules separated by capillary electrophoresis. If DNA can be translocated slowly enough, through a limiting aperture with dominant contributions to resistance spanning only two or three nucleotides length (about 20 Angstroms for ssDNA, 10 Angstroms for dsDNA), then DNA sequencing of a single molecule may eventually be possible. For single nucleotide polymorphism (SNP) identification, small sample volumes can be used, such that PCR amplification may not be needed. Expression analysis and disease identification (for individualized therapeutics) are just a few of the possibilities. Non-PCR expression analysis may even offer a new level of experimentation on live cells using patch-clamp methods.

14.1 Standard Apparatus

Nanopore detection is based on a nanometer-scale ion channel that can report on the channel-interactions of individual, nanometer-scale, biomolecules. The reporting is via measurements of ion flow through the channel when there is only a single channel, i.e., there is only one conductance path.

Each nanopore experiment described in what follows was conducted using one alpha-hemolysin channel inserted into a diphytanoyl-phosphatidylcholine/hexadecane bilayer, where the bilayer was formed across a 20-micron diameter horizontal Teflon aperture (see Fig. 14.1). The bilayer separates two seventy-microliter chambers containing 1.0 M KCl buffered at pH 8.0 (10 mM HEPES/KOH). A completed bilayer between the chambers was indicated by the lack of ionic current flow when a voltage was applied across the bilayer (using Ag-AgCl electrodes). Once the bilayer was in place, a dilute solution of α–hemolysin (monomer) was added to the *cis* chamber. Self-assembly of the α–hemolysin heptamer and insertion into the bilayer results in a stable, highly reproducible, nanometer-scale channel with a steady current of 120 pA under an applied potential of 120 mV at 23°C (± 0.1°C using a Peltier device). Once one channel formed, further pores were prevented from forming by thoroughly perfusing the *cis* chamber with buffer. Molecular blockade signals were then observed by mixing analytes into the *cis* chamber.

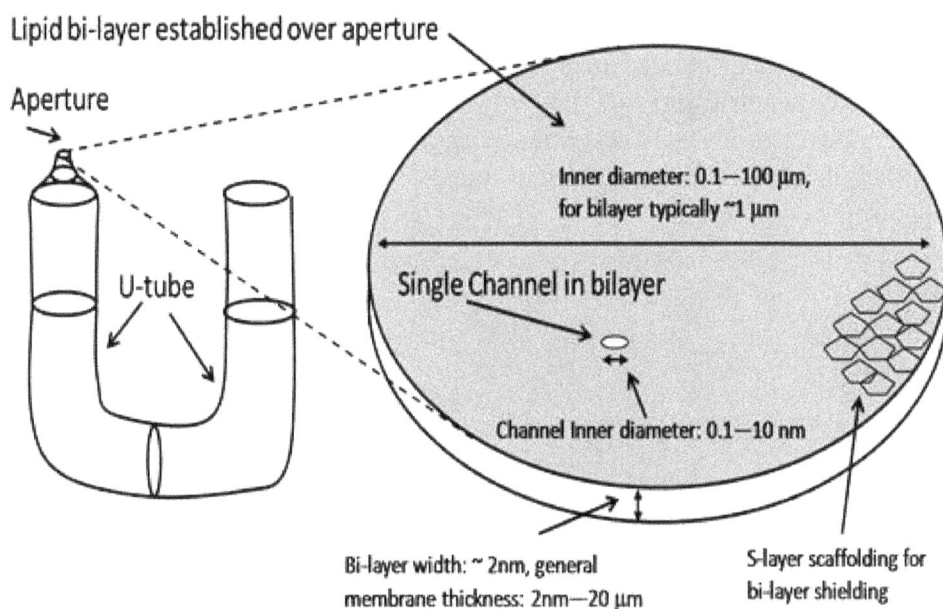

Fig. 14.1. A schematic for the U-tube, aperture, bilayer, and single channel, with possible S-layer modifications to the bi-layer.

14.1.1 Standard operational and physiological buffer conditions
The standard buffer condition for the nanopore detector is 1.0 M KCl with a pH of 8.0. This buffer was found to be most conducive to channel formation and to channels that do not gate. At significantly lower pH the channel is known to gate, if it even forms in the first place, which complicates use of the nanopore detector at physiological conditions (pH 7.0, 100mM NaCl). Since the pH of blood is usually in the range 7.35 to 7.45, and channel formation has been observed at 250 mM KCl, nanopore operation at the high pH and high salt end of the physiological range, relevant for antibody function in the bloodstream, may be possible with minimal alteration to the experimental parameters. Evaluation of antibody/antigen binding efficacy in a physiological buffer environment is particularly important if the nanopore/antibody detector is to be used for clinically relevant screening on the efficacy of antibodies to a given antigen. Biochemically relevant screening on on enzyme activity, for example, requires working with physiological buffer testing.

14.1.2 α-Hemolysin channel stability – introduction of chaotropes
The α-Hemolysin channel is stable up to high salt concentrations (MgCl$_2$ above 2M and KCl up to 4M) and presence of some other additives (urea up to 7M in some experiments, glycerol 5%) at pH around 8.0. Typical pattern of current rise with increase in background

electrolyte, KCl is observed. Specifically, the current versus KCL concentration is obtained in running buffer with composition 1M KCl, 20 mM HEPES (pH 8.0), with HEPES concentration maintained constant as content of KCl is increased.

A limitation in the utility of the nanopore/antibody antigen-binding tester (similarly for a nanopore/aptamer tester) is that once antigen is bound by a channel-captured antibody it is very difficult to effect the release of that antigen. This is a complicating issue in acquiring a large sample of antibody-antigen binding observations. A buffer-based solution to this problem is already known from purifying antibodies through a column containing antigen, where the release of antibodies bound in the column is effected by perfusion with 1.0 M $MgCl_2$. This presents the possibility of weakening the antibody-antigen binding by some choice of buffer in order to obtain large sample sets of binding events. The limitation of this is that the parameters will have likely deviated substantially from the physiological norm. Alternatively, a balanced stoichiometric ratio of antibody to antigen could be rapidly sampled, with lengthy sampling acquisitions only on antibody captures that occur without bound antibody and that then wait to observe antigen binding. Further details on buffer modulation, particularly with chaotropes, is given in [54].

14.2 Controlling Nanopore Noise Sources and Choice of Aperture

The accessible detector bandwidth is limited by noise resulting from 1/f (flicker) noise, Johnson noise, Shot noise, and membrane capacitance noise. In Fig. 14.2, upper left, the current spectral density is shown for the typical bilayer, an open α-hemolysin channel, and a channel with DNA hairpin blockade. For 1.0 M KCl at 23C, the α-hemolysin channel conducts 120 pA under an applied potential of 120 mV. The thermal noise contribution at the 1 GΩ channel resistance has an RMS noise current of 0.4 pA, consistent with Fig. 14.2. Shot noise is the result of current flow based on discrete charge transport. During nanopore operation with 120pA current (with 10KHz bandwidth) there is, similarly, about 0.6 pA noise due to the discreteness of the charge flow. As with Johnson noise, the Shot noise spectrum is white, consistent with Fig. 14.2. The specific capacitance of lipid bilayers is approximately 0.8 $\mu F/cm^2$ (very large due to molecular dimensions), and the specific conductance is approximately 10^{-6} $\Omega^{-1}cm^{-2}$. In order for bilayer conductance to produce less RMS noise current than fundamental noise sources (under the conditions above), the leakage current must be a fraction of a pA. This problem is solved by reducing to less than a 500μm^2 bilayer area, for which less than 0.6 pA leakage current results and for which total bilayer capacitance is at most 4pF. This indicates that a decrease in bilayer area by another magnitude is about as far as this type of noise reduction can go. Preliminary attempts to do this, however, lead to a very unpredictable toxin intercalation rate (possibly due to surface tension factors), among other difficulties.

398

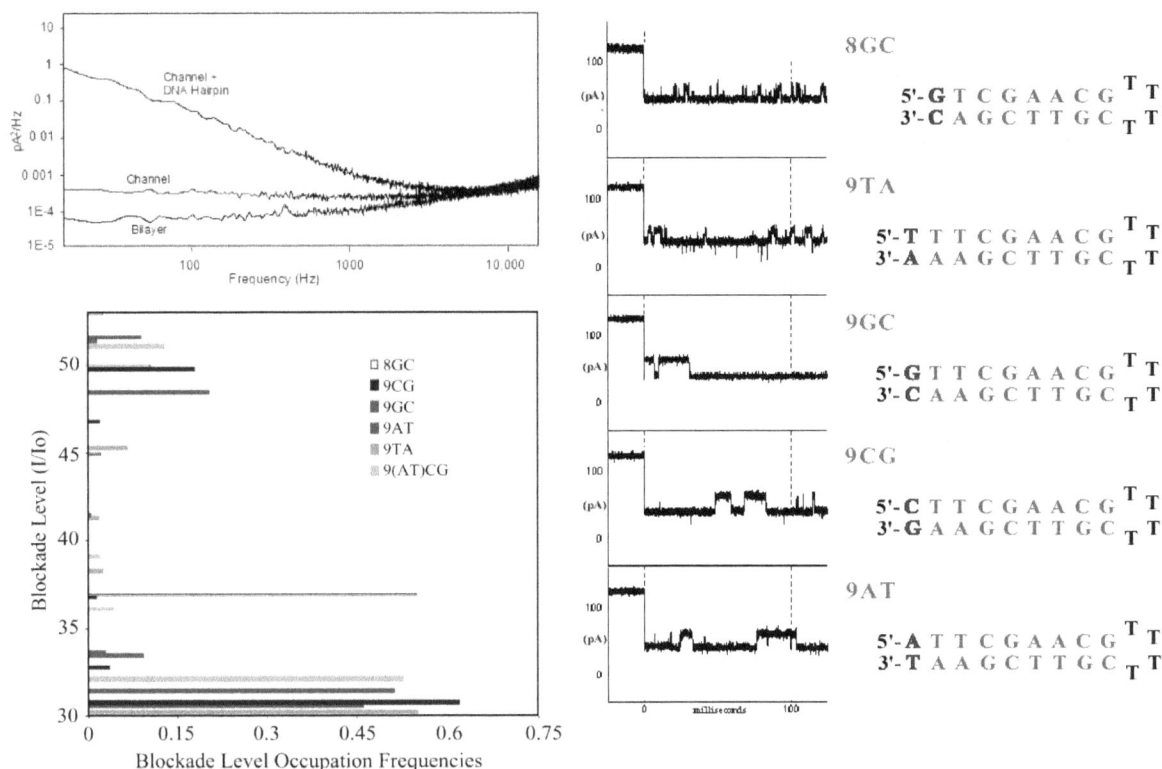

Fig. 14.2. Left. The top panel shows the power spectral density for signals obtained. The bottom panel shows the dominant blockades, and their frequencies, for the different hairpin molecules. **Right. DNA hairpin controls and their diagnostic signals.** The secondary structure of the DNA hairpins is shown on the right, with their highest scoring diagnostic signals shown on the left [45]. Each signal trace starts at approximately120 pA open channel current and all blockades are in a range 40-60 pA upon "capture" of the associated DNA hairpin. Even so, the signal traces have discernibly different blockade structure, which is extracted using an HMM. The signals are aligned at their blockade starts and the demarked time-trace is for 100 ms.

The five DNA hairpins shown in Fig. 14.2 have been studied in [1,45-48,198], where they have been carefully characterized, and are used in other experiments as highly sensitive controls. Use of the controls entails testing a channel, especially an oddly behaving channel, with a known nine base-pair DNA hairpin control. If the familiar, visibly discernible, control blockade signals do not occur, the channels viability is then looked into further. The nine base-pair hairpin molecules examined in the prototype experiment share an eight base-pair hairpin core sequence, with addition of one of the four permutations of Watson-Crick base-pairs that may exist at the blunt end terminus, i.e., 5'-G•C-3', 5'-C•G-3', 5'-T•A-3', and 5'-A•T-3'. Denoted 9GC, 9CG, 9TA, and 9AT, respectively. The full sequence for the 9CG hairpin is 5' CTTCGAACGTTTT CGTTCGAAG 3', where the base-pairing region is underlined. The eight base-pair DNA hairpin is identical to the core nine base-pair subsequence, except the terminal base-pair is 5'-G•C-3'. The prediction that each hairpin would adopt one base-paired structure was tested and confirmed using the DNA mfold server.

14.3 Length resolution of individual DNA hairpins

The α-hemolysin geometry was probed using a series of hairpins, with stem lengths ranging from three to nine base-pairs. The six-base-pair hairpin is described in what follows, while those hairpins longer than six base pairs shared the six-base-pair stem/head at their core. Those hairpins with stems less than six base pairs were constructed by removing base pairs from the six base-pair core sequence. Starting from the three-base-pair hairpin, each base pair addition resulted in a measurable increase in median blockade shoulder lifetime that correlated with the calculated $\Delta\Delta G°$ of hairpin formation (Fig. 14.3).

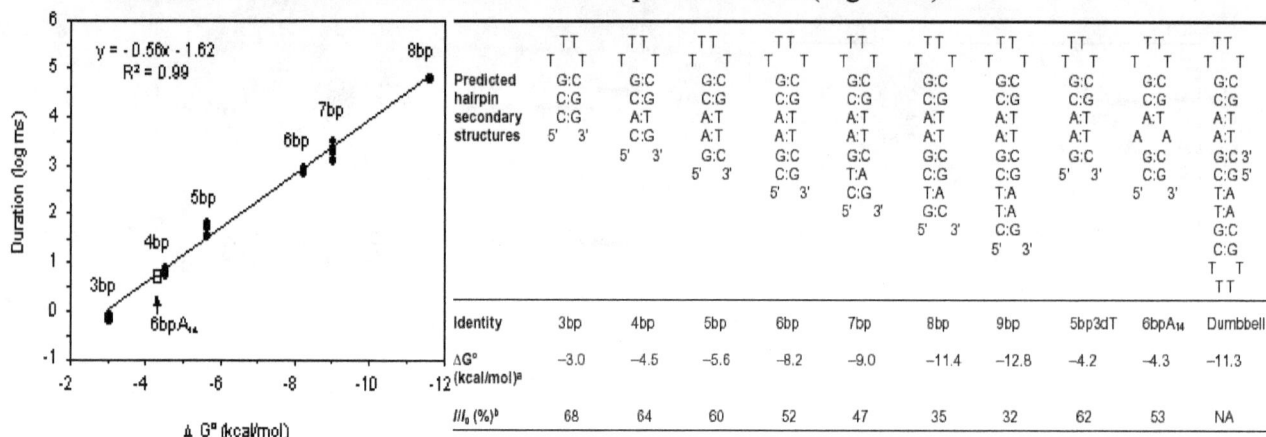

Left graph: $y = -0.56x - 1.62$, $R^2 = 0.99$. X-axis: $\Delta G°$ (kcal/mol). Y-axis: Duration (log ms). Data points labeled 3bp, 4bp, 5bp, 6bp, 7bp, 8bp, 6bpA$_{14}$.

Right table — Predicted hairpin secondary structures:

	3bp	4bp	5bp	6bp	7bp	8bp	9bp	5bp3dT	6bpA$_{14}$	Dumbbell
	T T	T T	T T	T T	T T	T T	T T	T T	T T	T T
	T T	T T	T T	T T	T T	T T	T T	T T	T T	T T
	G:C	G:C	G:C	G:C	G:C	G:C	G:C	G:C	G:C	G:C
	C:G	C:G	C:G	C:G	C:G	C:G	C:G	C:G	C:G	C:G
	C:G	A:T	A:T	A:T	A:T	A:T	A:T	A:T	A:T	A:T
	5' 3'	C:G	A:T	A:T	A:T	A:T	A:T	A:T	A A	G:C 3'
		5' 3'	C:G	G:C	G:C	G:C	G:C	G:C	C:G	C:G 5'
			5' 3'	C:G	T:A	C:G	C:G	5' 3'	5' 3'	T:A
				5' 3'	C:G	T:A	T:A			T:A
					5' 3'	G:C	T:A			G:C
						5' 3'	C:G			C:G
							5' 3'			T T
										T T

Identity	3bp	4bp	5bp	6bp	7bp	8bp	9bp	5bp3dT	6bpA$_{14}$	Dumbbell
$\Delta G°$ (kcal/mol)[a]	−3.0	−4.5	−5.6	−8.2	−9.0	−11.4	−12.8	−4.2	−4.3	−11.3
I/I_0 (%)[b]	68	64	60	52	47	35	32	62	53	NA

Figure 14.3. Left. Standard free energy of hairpin formation vs. shoulder blockade duration. **Right.** DNA Hairpins studied on the prototype nanopore detector.

Standard free energy of hairpin formation was calculated using the mfold DNA server (see Fig. 14.3 Right), and correlated with median duration of hairpin shoulder blockades (solid circles). Each point represents the median blockade duration for a given hairpin length acquired using a separate α-hemolysin pore on a separate day. Median blockade durations and $\Delta G°$ for the equivalent of the 6 bp hairpin with a single mismatch (6bpA$_{14}$, Fig. 14.3 Right) are represented by open squares. All experiments were conducted in 1.0 M KCl at 22 ±1 °C with a 120 mV applied potential. (Increasing stem length also resulted in a 10 μs increase in median duration of the terminal spike, consistent with longer, but still microsecond time-scale, ssDNA translocation on the dissociated hairpin.) A downward trend in shoulder current amplitude was also observed from I/I_0 equal to 68% for a 3 bp stem to I/I_0 equal to 32% for a 9 bp stem (see Fig. 14.3 Right).

The time-domain FSA passed 529 of the six-base-pair hairpin events to the SVM and 3185 of all other events (see Fig. 14.4. Left). Blockade events caused by six-base-pair hairpins were classified against blockades caused by 3,4,5,7 and 8 base-pair hairpins (see Fig. 14.4 Right). Because selectivity was relaxed at the FSA, there were many ambiguous signals with SVM scores near zero. Using an additional set of independent data, the SVM can be trained to exclude these by introducing a rejection region (the region between dashed lines in Fig. 14.4 Right). The events that were rejected were primarily fast blockades similar to those caused by dumbbell hairpin (which can't translocate, see [48] for further details) or acquisition errors caused by the low selectivity threshold of the FSA. When 20% of the events were rejected in this manner, the SVM scores for the six-base-pair hairpin discrimination achieved a sensitivity of 98.8% and a specificity of 98.8%. Sensitivity is defined as true positives/(true positives + false negatives), and specificity is defined as true positives/(true positives + false positives). (A true positive is an event in the test data that comes from the positive class and is assigned a positive value; a false positive occurs when the SVM assigns a positive score to an event in the test data when that event actually comes from the negative class. A false negative is an event that is assigned a negative value, but actually comes from the positive class.) Similar results were obtained for each class of hairpins depicted in Fig. 14.4 Left. Overall the SVM achieved an average sensitivity of 98% and average specificity of 99%. Thus, the stem length of an individual DNA hairpin was determined at single base-pair resolution.

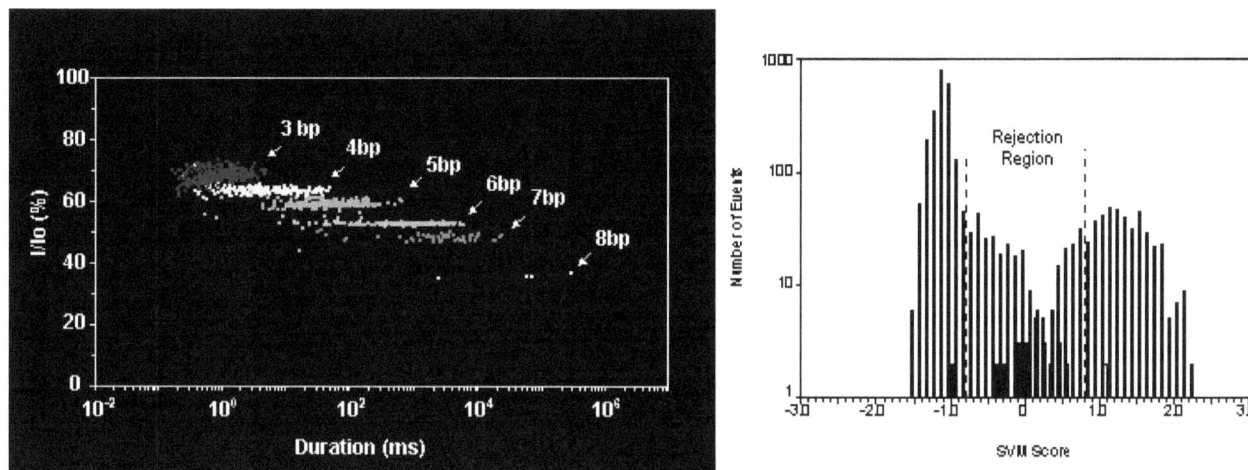

Figure 14.4. Left. Event diagram for DNA hairpins with 3 to 8 base-pair stems. Events were selected for adherence to the shoulder-spike signature. Each point represents the duration and amplitude of a shoulder blockade caused by one DNA hairpin captured in the pore vestibule. The data for each hairpin are from at least two different experiments run on different days. Median I/I_0 values for each type of hairpin varied by at most 2%. The duration of the 9 bp hairpin blockade shoulders were too long for us to record a statistically significant number of events. Control oligonucleotides with the same base compositions as the DNA hairpins, but scrambled, caused blockade events that were on average much shorter than the hairpin events and that did not conform to the shoulder-spike pattern. **Right.** Classification of the 6bp hairpin (solid bars) versus all other hairpins (open bars) by SVM. Note the log scale on the Y axis. The dashed lines mark the limits of the rejection region. The boundaries of the rejection region were determined by independent data, not *post hoc*, on the data shown. The events that were rejected were primarily fast blockades similar to those caused by loops on the dumbbell hairpin (Table 4.1) or acquisition errors caused by the low selectivity threshold of the FSA.

14.4 Detection of single nucleotide differences (large changes in structure)

DNA hairpins with single nucleotide differences were examined in a context where those differences were expected to lead to significant differences in the hairpin molecule's secondary structure. The first hairpin considered involved alterations to the loop of the standard five-base-pair hairpin with a 4-deoxythymidine loop (**5bp4dT** in Fig. 14.3 Right) to one with a 3-deoxythymidine loop (**5bp3dT** in Fig. 14.3 Right). The **5bp3dT** hairpin caused pore blockades in which the shoulder amplitude was increased ~2 pA and the median shoulder duration (21 ms) was reduced 3-fold relative to the same hairpin stem with a 4-deoxythymidine loop (**5bp** in Fig. 14.3 Right). Typical events are illustrated in Fig. 14.5.

401

The FSA acquired 3500 possible five-base-pair hairpin signals from ten minutes of recorded data. The SVM classification for this data set (Fig. 14.5) gave sensitivity and specificity values of 99.9% when 788 events were rejected as the unknown class. The second example involved the hairpin stem. Introduction of a single base-pair mismatch into the stem of a six-base-pair hairpin ($T_{14} \rightarrow A_{14}$, **6bpA$_{14}$** in Fig. 14.3 Right) caused an approximately 100-fold decrease in the median blockade shoulder duration relative to a hairpin with a perfectly matched stem (**6bp** in Fig. 14.3 Right). Typical events are shown in Fig. 14.5. This difference in duration is consistent with the effect of a mismatch on ΔG° of hairpin formation (Fig. 14.3 Left), and it permitted a 90% separation of the two populations using the manually applied shoulder-spike diagnostic. When analysis was automated, the FSA acquired 1031 possible events from ten minutes of recorded data (Fig. 14.5). With the aid of wavelet features that characterized the low frequency noise within the shoulder current, the SVM was able to discriminate the standard six-base-pair hairpin from the mismatched six-base-pair hairpin with sensitivity 97.6% and specificity 99.9% while rejecting only 42 events.

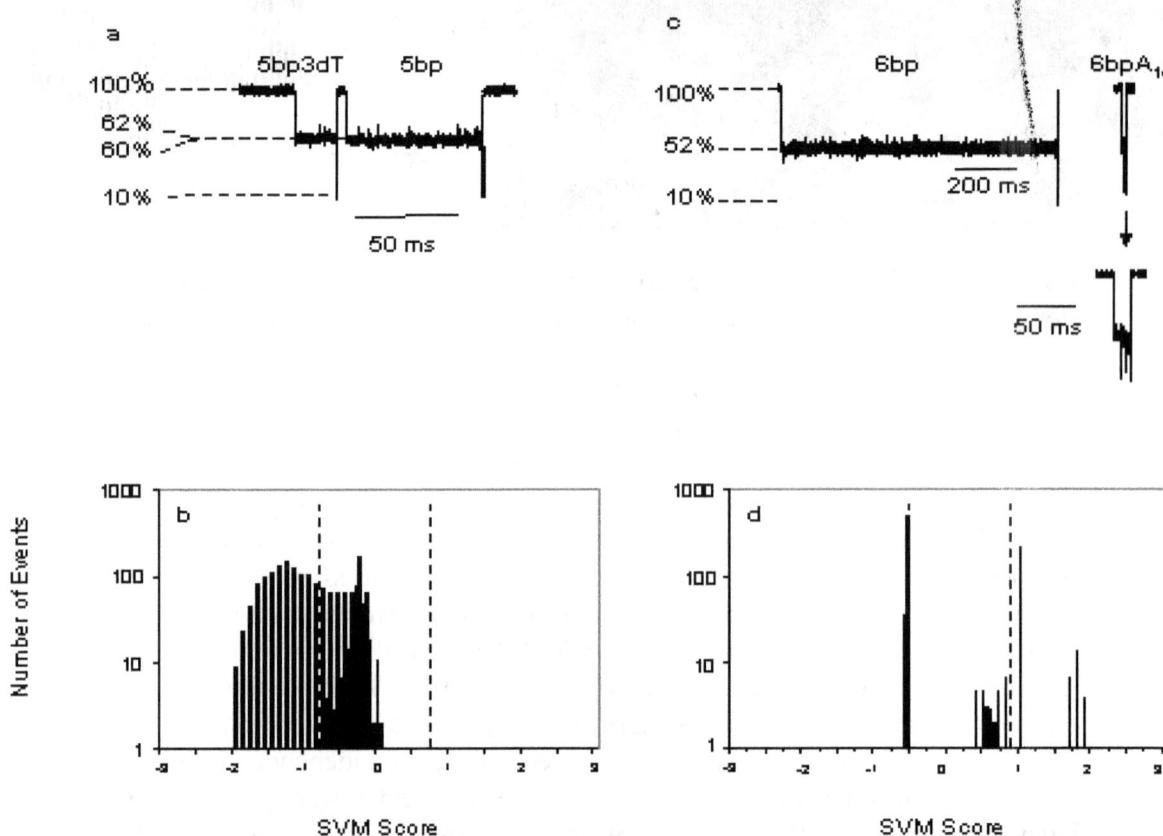

Figure 14.5 Detection of single nucleotide differences between DNA hairpins. **a,** Comparison of typical current blockade signatures for a 5bp hairpin and a 5bp hairpin with a three-dT loop. The standard 5bp hairpin event has a two percent deeper blockade than the 5bp3dT hairpin. **b,** Histogram of SVM scores for 5bp hairpins (filled bars) versus 5bp hairpins with three-dT loops (clear bars). **c,** Comparison of typical current blockade signatures for a standard 6bp hairpin and a 6bp hairpin with a single dA_3-dA_{14} mismatch in the stem. The 6bpA$_{14}$ event is expanded to show the fast downward spikes. These rapid, near-full blockades and the much shorter shoulder durations are the main characteristics identified and used by SVM to distinguish 6bpA$_{14}$

hairpin events from 6bp hairpin events. **d,** Histogram of SVM scores for 6bp hairpins (filled bars) versus 6bpA$_{14}$ hairpins (clear bars).

14.5 Blockade Mechanism for 9bphp

More involved than the classification or sequencing of a molecule is the actual understanding of that molecule's kinetic behavior as revealed by the ionic current blockade information measured by the nanopore detector. In the discussion of blockade mechanism that follows, for the nine-base-pair hairpins, the remarkable sensitivity of the nanopore device becomes apparent. This indicates that the α-hemolysin nanopore detector is likely to be an important tool for single-molecule observation and manipulation.

Ionic flow through the α-hemolysin channel was strongly modulated by the terminal base-pair on DNA hairpins with stem-length nine or more base-pairs. This modulation was most apparent on the nine base-pair hairpins, where the blockade states were discerned with the shortest time-constants (lifetimes). The lower level blockade states for the DNA hairpins are found to have lifetimes that correlate with the energy of dissociation on the terminal bond [47]. An anti-correlation with terminal bond energy is found for the density of lower level blockade spikes.

A working model has been developed to explain the mechanisms underlying the current transitions for the observed 9bp hairpin blockades (Fig. 14.6). The model requires that the 9bp duplex stem is long enough so that the terminal base pair can interact with amino acids in the vestibule wall and that a frayed end can reach the limiting aperture (at lysine-147). This is a reasonable assumption because circular dichroism assays indicate that the 9bp hairpin stem is a B form duplex in bulk phase. The length per base-pair of B form DNA is 3.38 angstroms, therefore the total stem length is approximately 30.4 angstroms. The distance between the narrowest part of the vestibule mouth at threonine-9 and the pore limiting aperture at lysine-147 is 33 angstroms. Therefore, if the hairpin loop is perched at the ring formed by threonine-9, the 9bp stem would reach within 3 angstroms of the limiting aperture. Given the uncertainty about the exact position of the hairpin loop and the 1.9Å precision of the α-hemolysin X-ray crystal structure [362], not to mention effects from waters of hydration and ion fixed-layers, this distance is probably accurate within ±1 bp. Upon capture of a 9bp blunt hairpin, the initial conductance state (I_{IL}/I_o = 35%, where IL stands for intermediate level) is caused by orientation and immobilization (on the millisecond time scale) of the hairpin due to an electrostatic bond formed between the terminal base pair of the hairpin stem and residues in the vestibule wall. The predominant interaction is binding between the nucleotide in the 3' position and the protein. This state initiates virtually all events because it is entropically favored. The dwell time, τ_{IL}, for the intermediate conductance state is largely independent of base pair identity or orientation because the bases are hydrogen bonded to one another and the interaction with the surface is due to the terminal 3' phosphodiester anion. If, however, the 3' nucleotide is unpaired (i.e. a dangling nucleotide) its identity does matter in terms of the duration of τ_{IL}. Preliminary results show that single nucleotide 3' overhangs have dwell times in the IL state with order dA>dC. This suggests that the unpaired bases hydrogen bond or stack against residues in the pore vestibule. The IL state invariably transitions to the upper conductance state, UL. This state (I_{UL}/I_o = 48%) corresponds to desorption of the terminal base pair from the protein wall and orientation of the hairpin stem along the axis of the electric field and the axis of ionic flow. Current is higher in this state because the low resistance path along the major groove leads relatively unimpeded from the pore mouth to the limiting aperture. From the UL conductance state, the hairpin may return to the IL state or it may transition into a third conductance state, LL, where the residual current is equal to 32% of the open channel current. Residence time in this state is dependent upon terminal base pair identity and orientation. In this state, it is hypothesized that the nucleotide at the 5' end of the duplex stem is adsorbed to the pore wall so that the 3' nucleotide is positioned directly over the pore-limiting aperture. Thus, when the duplex end frays, the 3' strand may extend and penetrate the limiting aperture resulting in the transient spikes.

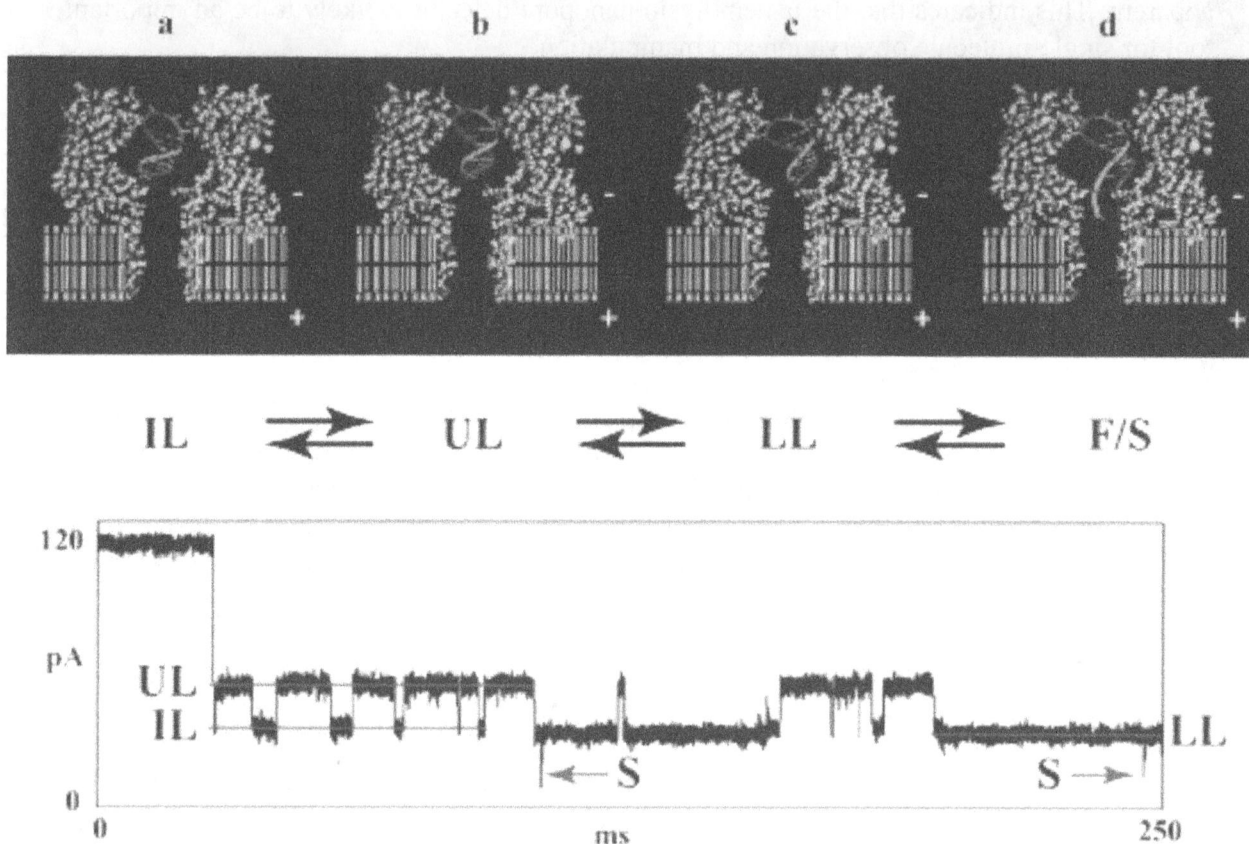

Figure 14.6 Blockade Mechanism. The intermediate level (IL) conductance state initiates most blockades and always transitions to the upper level conductance state (UL). This is explained by binding of the hairpin terminus to the vestibule interior (IL) followed by desorption of the DNA from the protein wall and orientation of the stem along the axis of the electric field (UL). Transitions from the UL state were either back to the IL state or to the lower level conductance state (LL). From the LL state there were brief transitions to nearly full blockade, denoted by F/S for fray/spike conductance state. The LL and F/S states are both thought to involve binding between the hairpin's terminal 5' base and the pore's limiting aperture. The brief F/S state behavior is explained by a terminus-fraying event that is accompanied by extension by the terminal 3' base into the limiting aperture. Part of the evidence for this is a strong spike (fraying) frequency correlation with the different terminus binding energies. Asymmetric base addition or phosphorylation (at the terminal 3' and 5' positions) is part of the evidence for the asymmetric roles for 5' binding (LL and F/S) and 3' fraying/extension (F/S).

Beyond hydrogen bonding and steric considerations, some of the terminus dynamics was influenced by the nearest-neighbor base-pair (i.e. stacking energies), which indicated that the penultimate base-pair might be readable as well. Next-to-nearest-neighbor influence on the terminal base-pair dynamics was thought to be much less, and this was consistent with the minor changes in blockade signatures on hairpins whose ends were the same but that have different base-pairings further up their stems. This drop-off in sensitivity bodes well for terminus classification on *generic* duplex DNA. At the same time, gross changes in stem base-pairs, such as a change from a Watson-Crick base pair to a Hoogsteen (or wobble) base-pair, resulted in distinctly different blockade signatures [47], which bodes well for SNP assaying schemes.

Residual channel current decreases as blockading DNA hairpins increase their stem length from 3 to 8 base-pairs. For DNA hairpins with stems shorter than 8 base-pairs, multiple states were not clearly discernible, presumably because the hairpins were too short to bind to the channel favorably or interact with the current/force constriction near the limiting aperture. For 9 base-pair hairpins, and longer, a clear 1/f noise (flicker noise) is discernible (Fig. 14.2, top) – a preliminary indication of the single-molecule binding kinetics described in Fig. 14.6 (and in detail in [47]). HMM/EM characterization on the five classes of hairpin signatures revealed the existence of two major conductance blockade levels, one minor level intermediate between them, and one to three other statistically relevant levels depending on the hairpin (a pre-processed form, found by HMM/EM level identification, and use of EVA-projection, is shown in Fig. 14.2, bottom). By examining the transition probabilities between the various levels it was found that blockades typically began in the less common intermediate level and from there almost always transitioned to the UL blockade level. The mechanism described in Fig. 14.6 hypothesizes that the upper level (UL) blockade state is unbound. A result that strengthens this hypothesis, is that the UL blockade levels are approximately the same for 8, 9, 10, 11, and 12 base-pair DNA hairpins. This plateau occurs well before that of the other blockade levels – the lower level (LL) blockades, for example, continue to become greater as the hairpin stem length is increased from 8 base-pairs to 10, beyond which it plateaus as well. Beyond 10 base-pairs the hairpin is simply longer than the depth of the channel's *cis*-vestibule, so further base addition causes it to "stick-out further", but cause negligibly greater occlusion of flow than that caused by the fully blockaded *cis*-vestibule. With base-pair addition, however, there arrives greater residual charge, thus greater force drawing the molecule into the vestibule (and slightly deeper channel blockades are seen consistent with this) and dominance of the LL state in the blockade ("toggling") signal. The explanation for the early UL plateau centers on the tight flow geometry between channel and captured hairpin. In such a geometry, much of the ionic flow is confined to be in or near the grooves of the captured DNA molecule. For the unbound molecule, this groove flow can be directed towards the limiting aperture by appropriate orientation of the hairpin molecule. The unbound molecule, thus, appears to cause a gap junction "short circuit" effect, where the contribution to the ionic current is not significantly altered as the hairpin is extended across a 3 base-pair (approx. 1nm) gap separating the hairpin terminus from the vestibule's limiting aperture.

A critical understanding derived from the 9-base-pair DNA hairpin analysis is that if the UL blockade state is unbound at its terminus there is the possibility that conformational kinetics might be observable at the pore-captured polymer end. This motivated examination of a set of dsDNA termini that had already been examined using NMR. Results (in [47]) show agreement with NMR via number of low energy conformational states observed [47].

14.6 Conformational Kinetics on Model Biomolecules

Two conformational kinetic studies have been done, one on DNA hairpins with HIV-like termini, the other on antibodies. The objective of the DNA HIV-hairpin conformational study was to systematically test how DNA dinucleotide flexibility (and reactivity) could be discerned using channel current blockade information (see [35], for a complete description of the results pertaining to this study). The structural and physical properties of DNA depend upon nucleotide sequence, as is manifest in differences in three dimensional structure and anisotropic flexibility. Despite the multitude of crystallographic studies conducted on DNA, however, it is still difficult to translate the sequence-directed curvature information obtained through these tools to actual systems found in solution. Information on the DNA molecules' variation in structure and flexibility is important to understanding the dynamically enhanced DNA complex formations that are found with strong affinities to other, specific, DNA and protein molecules. An important example of this is the HIV attack on cells:one of the most critical stages in HIV's attack is the enzyme mediated insertion of viral into human DNA, which is influenced by the dynamic-coupling induced high flexibility of a CA dinucleotide step positioned precisely two base-pairs from the blunt terminus of the duplex viral DNA. This flexibility appears to be critical to allowing the HIV integrase to perform its DNA modifications. The CA dinucleotide presence is also a universal characteristic of retroviral genomes [363,364]. The behavior of the DNA hairpins containing the CA dinucleotide at different positions relative to their blunt-end termini, is studied in [35] using a nanopore detector. The nanopore detector feature extraction makes use of HMM-based feature extraction and SVM-based classification/clustering of "like" molecular kinetics. We hypothesized that the DNA hairpin with CA dinucleotide, positioned two base-pairs from the blunt terminus, would have "outlier" channel current statistics qualitatively differentiable from the other DNA hairpin variants. This is found to be the case, where the UL state, corresponding to the unbound terminus state, has shortest life for hairpin labeled CA_3 (with the CA dinucleotide step two basepairs from the blunt terminus). Since the UL state is hypothesized to be unbound, the fact that it has the shortest lifetime on average is an indication of the associated molecule's propensity to be bound to the channel (binding site is unknown at this time, although the work in [47] suggests some likely binding sites on the channel). In other words, CA_3 has strongest interaction with channel (and surroundings), as hypothesized, and neighboring variants (CA_2, CA_4), that have GC pairs shifted one base-pair shifted closer and further from the terminus, share this property to a lesser extent. Note: the "CA" notation refers to a dinucleotide step along the backbone of the self-annealed ssDNA strand in the hairpin molecule, while the GC base-pair described is part of that strand annealing, with the 'G' base-paired to the 'C' referred to in the CA-step. The molecules with GC pairs that are more than 1 base-pair distant behave similarly to eachother; the DNA hairpin with no GC pair also separates with its own characteristic curve.

14.7 Channel Current Cheminformatics
14.7.1 Power Spectra and Standard EE Signal Analysis

Typical power spectra for captured nine-base-pair DNA hairpins are shown in Fig. 14.7, along with a spectrum for the open channel. Below 10 kHz, the current fluctuation caused by the captured DNA molecule (i.e. the blockade noise) is greater than all other noise sources. Such blockade noise typically arises from changes in DNA conformation (molecular structure), changes in DNA configuration (molecular orientation, including waters of hydration), and changes in chemical bonds (internally or with surrounding channel). The power spectra for all the signals examined in [45] had approximately Lorentzian profiles, indicative of a predominately two-state switching process (seen as random telegraph noise). Discriminating between the DNA hairpins on the basis of their power spectral (or other Fourier transform properties, or wavelet properties) is possible for small sets of hairpins. For larger sets of hairpins, or for very similar hairpins like here, the HMM-based feature extraction proved critical, due to their strengths at extracting features from aperiodic (stochastic) sequential data. HMMs can be used for classification as well as feature extraction. Here, HMMs are used for feature extraction in conjunction with a fast, highly accurate, pattern recognition method, known as a Support Vector Machine (SVM). The resulting signal processing and pattern recognition architecture enabled real-time single molecule classification on blockade samplings of only 100 milliseconds [45]. With modern computational methods and hardware it is possible to extract the resolving power of the nanopore instrument for real-time classification and handling.

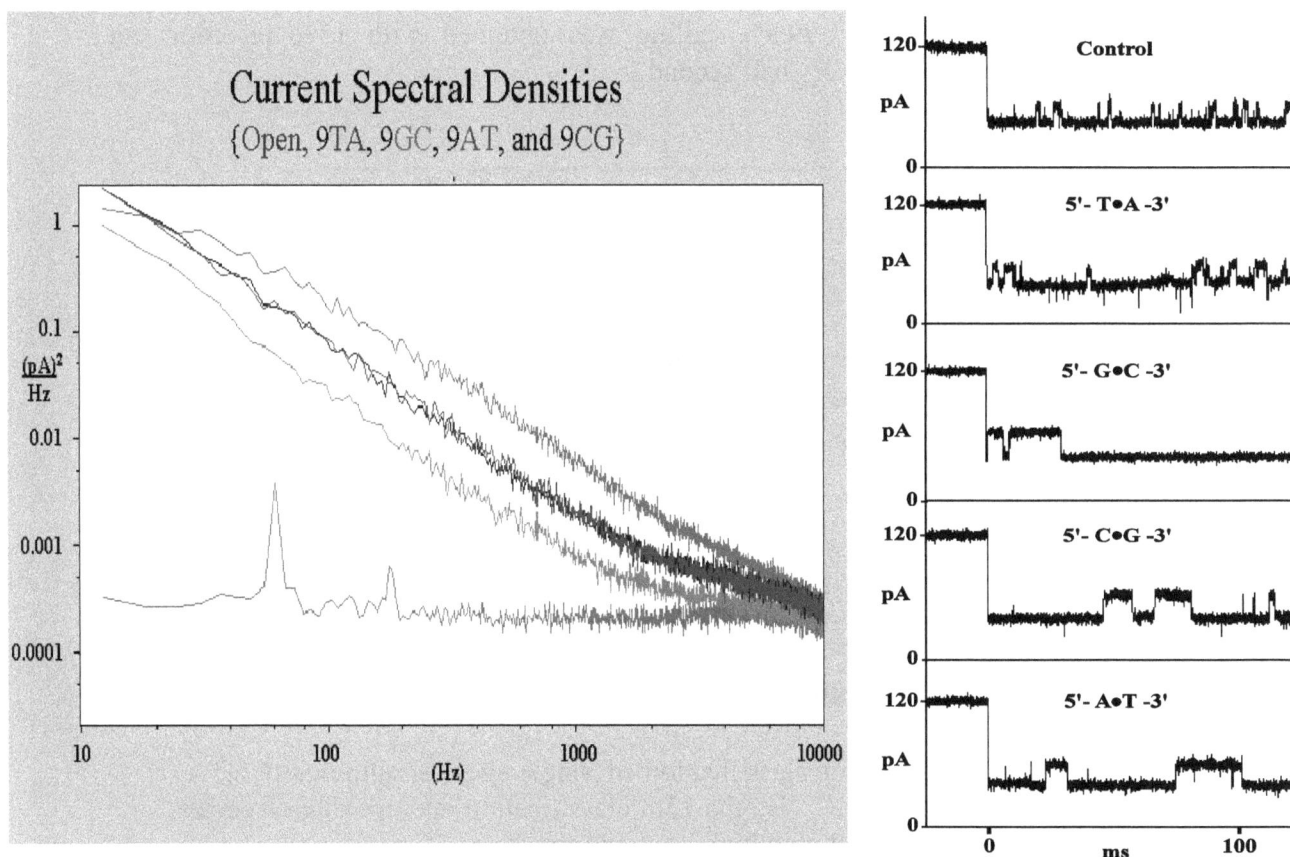

Figure 14.7 Left. Typical power spectra for captured nine-base-pair DNA hairpins and the open channel. **Right.** Typical blockade signatures for each of the five classes of DNA hairpins. The nine base-pair hairpins differ in only their terminal base pairs.

14.7.2 Channel current cheminformatics for single-biomolecule/mixture identifications

Using the testing protocol, we were able to determine which of five species of DNA hairpin had been added to the *cis* chamber of the nanopore device. This was achieved in less than six seconds with 99.6% accuracy. The five species of DNA hairpins consisted of a control hairpin and four hairpins that differed only in their terminal base-pairs (Fig. 14.7). The variants were chosen to include the two possible Watson-Crick base pairs and the two possible orientations of those base pairs at the duplex ends. The core 8bp stem and 4 dT loop were identical with the primary sequence 5'-TTCGAACGTTTTCGTTCGAA-3', where the base-paired compliments are underlined. The eight base-pair hairpin that was used as a control had the primary sequence 5'-GTCGAACGTTTTCGTTCGAC-3'. *These results were for test data drawn from nanopores established on days other than those used to generate the training data (shown on next page).*

Figure 14.8 shows the scoring for multiple observation days, with the number of single molecule sampling/classifications ranging from 1 to 30. At 75% weak signal rejection, approximately 15 classification attempts were needed to classify the type of single-species solution being sampled; final solution classification was obtained in six seconds on average. If training and testing were done on data drawn from the same set of days of nanopore operation, albeit different samples, 99.9% calling was obtained with 15% rejection, and throughput was about one call every half second.

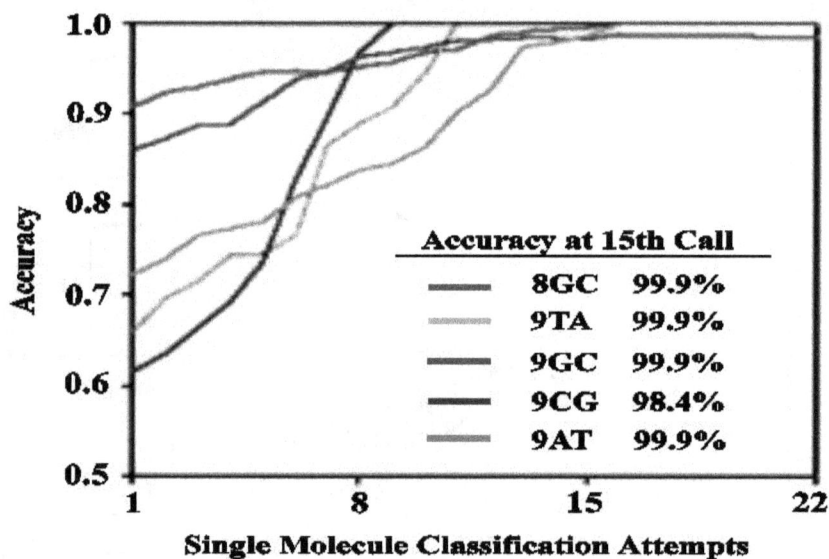

Figure 14.8 Accuracy for classification of single-species solutions of 9TA, 9GC, 9CG, 9AT, and 8GC. By the 15th classification attempt single-species solutions can be identified with high accuracy (inset).

Identification of two hairpins in mixtures was also attempted. Figure 14.9 shows the percentage of 9TA classification in a 3:1 mixture of 9TA to 9GC. (Although the mixture preparations are estimated to be ±10% of their stated mixture ratios, calibration and testing of aliquots from the same mixture compensates for such common error.) The assay on 9TA concentration asymptotes to 75% ± 1%, consistent with the 3:1 ratio, and the assay error drops to 1% after approximately 100 individual molecule classification attempts (completed in 40 seconds).

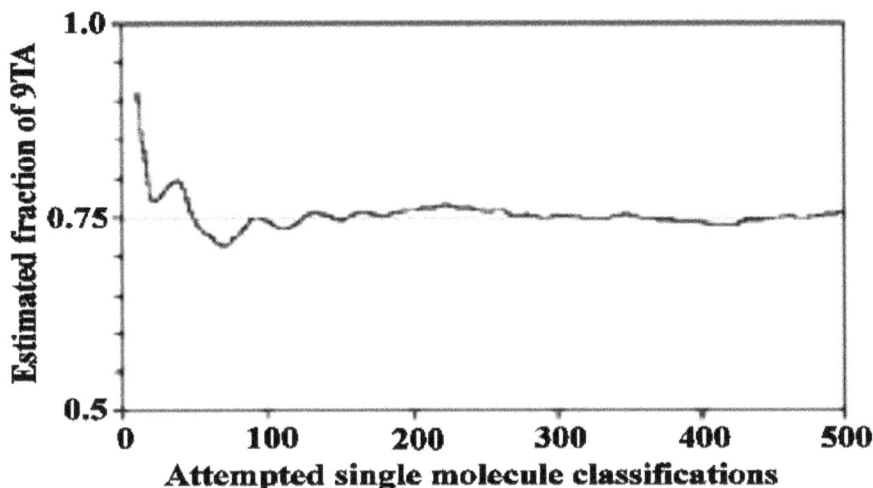

Figure 14.9 Classification on a 3:1 mixture of 9TA and 9GC hairpin molecules as a function of single molecule acquisitions. The 3:1 mole ratio is accurately identified within 1% error after 100 observations (about 40 seconds).

HMM/EM characterization on the five classes of hairpin signatures revealed the existence of two major conductance blockade levels, one minor level intermediate between them, and one to three other statistically relevant levels depending on the hairpin. By examining the transition probabilities between the various levels it was found that blockades typically began in the less common intermediate level and from there almost always transitioned to the greater conductance blockade level. (See Ch. 7 for further details.)

With completion of FSA preprocessing, an HMM is used to remove noise from the acquired signals, and to extract features from them. The HMM configuration used for control probe validation is implemented with fifty states that correspond to current blockades in 1% increments ranging from 20% residual current to 69% residual current [1]. In this HMM application the HMM states, numbered 0 to 49, corresponded to the 50 different current blockade levels in the sequences that are processed. The standard "grayscale" HMM, or 'generic HMM', feature extraction setup is then done: the state emission parameters of the HMM are initially set so that the state j, $0 <= j <= 49$ corresponding to level $L = j+20$, can emit all possible levels, with the probability distribution over emitted levels set to a discretized Gaussian with mean L and unit variance. All transitions between states are possible, and initially are equally likely. Each blockade signature is de-noised by 5 rounds of Expectation- Maximization (EM) training on the parameters of the HMM. After the EM iterations, 150 parameters are extracted from the HMM. The 150 feature vectors obtained from the 50-state HMM-EM/Viterbi implementation are: the 50 dwell percentage in the different blockade levels (from the Viterbi trace-back states), the 50 variances of the emission probability distributions associated with the different states, and the 50 merged transition probabilities from the primary and secondary blockade occupation levels (fits to two-state dominant modulatory blockade signals). Variations on the HMM 50 state implementation are made as necessary to encompass the signal classes under study.

The 150-component feature vector extracted for each blockade signal is then classified using a trained Support Vector Machine (SVM). The SVM training is done off-line using data acquired with only one type of molecule present for the training data (bag learning). Further details on the SVM and overall channel current cheminformatics signal processing are detailed in [1].

14.7.3 Channel Current Cheminformatics: feature extraction by HMM

The HMM-based profiling used for feature extraction provided better discrimination than the wavelet-based profiling used in previous efforts [48]. The improved signal resolution on channel blockades with HMMs is not new [365]. (The wavelet-domain FSA that generates the blockade-level profiling does have the advantage, however, of being hundreds of times faster than the HMM processing in this instance.) The better performance with HMM processing indicated that signal analysis benefited from parsing structural information in the stochastic sequence of blockade-states. Parsing structures in stochastic data is a familiar problem in gene prediction, where Hidden Markov Models (HMMs) have been used to great advantage [366]. Typically with gene prediction, however, HMMs are operated at a high level that parses coding starts and stops, etc., with feature scoring on starts and stops performed at a lower level by neural net or related statistical methods. For channel current analysis, the HMM extracts structural features without identifying them, effectively operating at the lower level, and used with EM [81], accomplishing de-noising on the blockade-state structure [365] prior to extracting those features.

A single HMM/EM process was used to perform the feature extraction in the experiments that follow. If separate HMMs were used to model each species, the HMM/EM processing could also be operated in a discriminative mode. This requires multiple HMM/EM evaluations (one for each species) on each unknown signal as it is observed. Increased computational burden would thus be added at the worst place: the expensive feature extraction stage. Ssemi-scalable, species-specific processing could be considered for the HMM/EM in an indirect manner, by using prior HMM/EM characterization of the species to identify a reduced set of features relevant to each species. The reduced feature set relates to physical characterizations of the captured molecule, such as level states, their time-constants, and allowed level transitions.

Samples using blockade signatures of longer duration (prior to truncation) require fewer rejections to achieve the same signal classification accuracy. A situation that would probably favor longer signal samples than the 100 ms used here was seen in attempts to read more of the DNA hairpin end-sequence than the terminal base pair. Preliminary indications are that the penultimate base pairs can probably also be identified using longer signal samples (17 species with control). Scaling the classification task from 5 to 17 species may also require refinements to the feature extraction, such as the species specific HMM feature extractions mentioned above.

Tests with mixtures of hairpins required an added calibration due to the nanopore's different acceptance rates for different hairpins (i.e., there are different free energy barriers to capture). This finding was consistent with a model for hairpin capture (see below) in which hairpins are captured by an entropically accessible binding site. It is also in agreement with the brief intermediate level state typically observed at the start of the signal blockades.

14.7.4 Bandwidth limitations

Nanopore-based detection is limited by the kinetic time-scale of the molecular blockade states, where the molecular blockade states typically correspond to binding and dissociation (analyte-channel binding, or antibody-antigen binding, for example), or due to internal conformational flexing. It is hypothesized that it is possible to probe higher frequency realms than those directly accessible at the operational bandwidth of the channel current based device, or due to the time-scale of the particular analyte interaction kinetics, by modulated excitations. This can be accomplished by chemically linking the analyte or channel to an "excitable object", such as a magnetic bead, excited by laser pulsations, for example. In one configuration, the excitable object can be chemically linked to the analyte molecule to modulate its blockade current by modulating the molecule during its blockade. In another configuration, the excitable object is chemically linked to the channel, to provide a means to modulate the passage of ions through that channel. Studies involving the first, analyte modulated, configuration, indicate that this approach can be successfully employed to keep the end of a long strand of duplex DNA from permanently residing in a single blockade state (see next Sec.). Similar study of magnetic beads linked to antigen may be used in the nanopore/antibody experiments if similar single blockade level, "stuck", states occur with the captured antibody (at physiological conditions, for example).

Examples of excitable objects include microscopic beads (magnetic and non-magnetic), fluorescent dyes, charged molecules, etc. Bead attachments can couple in excitations passively from background thermal (Brownian) motions, or actively by laser pulsing and laser-tweezer manipulation. Dye attachments can couple excitations via laser or light (UV) excitations to the targeted dye molecule. Large, classical, objects, such as microscopic beads, provide a method to couple periodic modulations into the single-molecule system. The direct coupling of such modulations, at the channel itself, avoids the low Reynolds number limitations of the nanometer-scale flow environment. For rigid coupling on short biopolymers, the overall rigidity of the system also circumvents limitations due to the low Reynolds number flow environment. Similar consideration also come into play for the dye attachments, except now the excitable object is typically small, in the sense that it is usually the size of a single (dye) molecule attachment. Excitable objects such as dyes must contend with quantum statistical effects (at the single-molecule level), so their application may require time averaging or ensemble averaging (where the ensemble case might involve multiple channels observed simultaneously). In both of the experimental configurations, a multi-channel platform may be used to obtain rapid ensemble information. In all cases the modulatory injection of excitations may be in the form of a stochastic source (such as thermal background noise), a directed periodic source (laser pulsing, piezoelectric vibrational modulation, etc.), or a chirp (single laser pulse or sound impulse, etc.). If the modulatory injection coincides with a high frequency resonant state of the system, informative low frequency excitations may result, i.e., excitations that can be monitored in the usable bandwidth of the channel detector. Increasing the effective bandwidth of the nanopore device greatly enhances its utility in almost every application, particularly those, such as DNA sequencing, where the speed with which blockade classifications can be made is directly limited by bandwidth restrictions.

14.8 Channel-based detection mechanisms
14.8.1 Partitioning and translocation-based ND biosensing methods

The standard Nanopore Detector (ND) detection paradigm, that is predominantly translocation (or dwell-time) based, is shown in Fig. 14.10 side-by-side with the Nanopore *transduction* detector paradigm. Fig. 14.11 elaborates on the possible ND detection platform topologies possible with translocation-based approaches, where the difference in translocation times is often the critical information that is used. The difference in dwell times can depend on the off-binding time of the target binding entity (possibly in a high strain environment), where binding failure allows polymer (ssDNA) translocation to complete (and the channel blockade to end). By this mechanism, and its variants, bound probes can be distinguished from unbound. There are specificity limits on the melting-based detection, however, that are not a problem in the NTD approach.

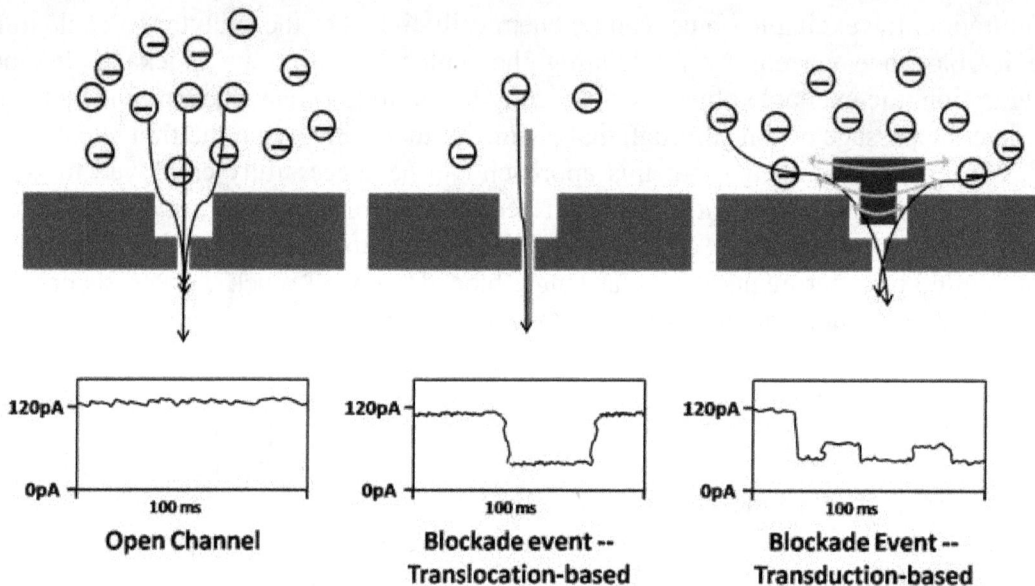

Fig. 14.10. Translocation Information and Transduction Information . Left. Open Channel . **Center.** A channel blockade event with feature extraction that is typically dwell-time based. A Single-molecule coulter counter. **Right.** Single-molecule transduction detection is shown with a transduction molecule modulating current flow (typically switching between a few dominant levels of blockade, dwell time of the overall blockade is not typically a feature -- many blockade durations will not translocate in the time-scale of the experiment, for example, active ejection control is often involved).

14.8.2 Transduction *vs.* Translation

There are two ways to functionalize measurements of the flow (of something) through a 'hole': (1) translocation sensing; and (2) transduction sensing. The translocation methods in the literature are typically a form of a 'Coulter Counter', with a wide range of channel dimensions allowable, that typically measures molecules non-specifically via pulses in the current flow through a channel as each molecule translocates. The transduction biosensing method, on the other hand, requires nanopore sizes that are much more restricted, to the 1-10nm inner diameters that might capture, and not translocate, most biomolecules. Transduction functionalization uses a channel flow modulator that also has a specific binding moiety, the transducer molecule. In transduction, the transducer molecule is used to measure molecular characteristics *indirectly*, by using a transducer/reporter molecule that binds to certain molecules, with subsequent distinctive blockade by the bound, or unbound, molecule complex. One such transducer, among many studied, was a channel-captured dsDNA "gauge" that was covalently bound to an antibody. The transducer was designed to provide a blockade shift upon antigen binding to its exposed antibody binding sites. In turn, the dsDNA-antibody transducer platform then provides a means for directly observing the *single molecule* antigen-binding affinities of any antibody in single-molecule focused assays, in addition to detecting the presence of binding target in biosensing applications.

There are two approaches to utilizing a nanopore for detection purposes: translocation /dwell-time (T/DT) based approaches, which strongly relies on blockade dwell-times, and nanopore transduction detection (NTD) based approaches, which functionalizes the nanopore by utilizing an engineered blockade molecule with blockade features typically not including dwell-time.

Translocation/dwell-time methods introduce different states to the channel via use of the frequency of channel blockades, from a series of individual molecular blockades (often during their translocation). The strongest feature employed in translocation/dwell-time discrimination, and often the only feature, is the blockade dwell-time where the dwell-time is typically engineered to be associated with the lifetime until a specific bond failure occurs. Other feature variations include time *until* a bond-formation occurs, or simply measuring the approximate length of a polymer according to its translocation 'dwell'-time.

14.8.3 Single-molecule *vs.* Ensemble
When the extra-channel states correspond to bound or unbound, there are two protocols for how to set up the Nanopore Transduction Detection (NTD) platform: (1) observe a sampling of bound/unbound states, each sample only held for the length of time necessary for a high accuracy classification. Or, (2), hold and observe *a single* bound/unbound system and track its history of bound/unbound states. The single molecule binding history in (2) has significant utility in its own right, especially for observation of critical conformational change information not observable by any other methods (critical information for understanding antibodies, allosteric proteins, and many enzymes). The ensemble measurement approach in (1), however, is able to benefit from numerous further augmentations, and can be used with general transducer states, not just those that correspond to a bound/unbound extra-channel states.

Fundamentally, the weaknesses of the standard ensemble-based binding analysis methods are directly addressed with the single-molecule approach, even if only to do a more informed type of ensemble analysis. The role of conformational change during binding, in particular, could potentially be directly explored in this setting. This approach also offers advantages over other single-molecule translation-based nanopore detection approaches in that the transduction-based apparatus introduces two strong mechanisms for boosting sensitivity on single-molecule observation: (i) engineered enhancement to the device sensitivity via the transduction molecule itself; and (ii) machine learning based signal stabilization with highly sensitive state resolution. NTD used in conjunction with recently developed pattern recognition informed sampling capabilities [20] greatly extends the usage of the single-channel apparatus. For medicine and biology, NTD and machine learning methods may aid in understanding multi-component interactions (with co-factors), and aid in designing co-factors according to their ability to result in desired binding or modified state.

In ensemble *single-molecule* measurements (via serial detection process), the pattern recognition informed (PRI) sampling on molecular populations provides a means to accelerate the accumulation of kinetic information. PRI sampling over a population of molecules is also the basis for introducing a number of gain factors. In the ensemble detection with PRI approach [20], in particular, one can make use of antibody capture matrix and ELISA-like methods [1], to introduce two-state NTD modulators that have concentration-gain (in an antibody capture matrix) or concentration-with-enzyme-boost-gain (ELISA-like system, with production of NTD modulators by enzyme cleavage instead of activated fluorophore). In the latter systems the NTD modulator can have as 'two-states', cleaved and uncleaved binding moieties. UV- and enzyme-based cleavage methods on immobilized probe-target can be designed to produce a high-electrophoretic-contrast, non-immobilized, NTD modulator, that is strongly drawn to the channel to provide a 'burst' NTD detection signal [1].

14.8.4 Biosensing with high sensitivity in presence of interference

Clinical studies have shown an abundance of protein-based disease markers that accumulate in the blood of patients suffering from chronic kidney disease. In the case of the Bioscience PXRF01marker the stage of kidney disease is linearly correlated (r=.83) indicating that the more severe the disease, the greater the accumulation of the marker in the bloodstream of patients. The NTD biosensing platform provides a tool for quantifying the relationship between PXRF01 and its biosystem interactants with an unparalleled fidelity. With higher quantification of PXRF01 a more accurate characterization of the disease biomarker and kidney disease progression can be established. Greater sensitivity translates directly to earlier diagnosis and improved outcomes. The electrophoretic nature of the biosensing platform also allows for significant advantage in dealing with interference agents, whether in the blood sample itself, say, or due to contaminants, since the reporter molecule can be designed to have a charge that easily separates it from the interference agents. (This is why blood can be scraped off the dirty floor at a crime scene and still accurately report on the identity or identities of those present.)

14.8.5 Nanopore Transduction Detection Methods

Transduction methods introduce different states to the channel via observations of changes in blockade statistics on a single molecular blockade event that is modulatory. This is a specially engineered arrangement involving a partially-captured, single-molecule, channel modulator, typically with a binding moiety for a specific target of interest linked to the modulator's extra-channel portion. The modulator's 'state' changes according to whether its binding moiety is bound or unbound. For further comparative analysis, see Table 14.1 below:

(1) Feature Space. The T/DT approach typically has a single feature, the dwell time. Sometimes a second feature, the fixed blockade level observed, is also considered, but usually not more features sought (or engineered) than that. The NTD approach has multiple features, e.g., blockade HMM parameters, etc., with number and type according to modulator design objectives.

(2) Versatility. T/DT: highly engineered/pre-processed for detection application to a particular target. NTD: requires minimal preparation/augmentation to the transduction platform via use of separately provided binding moieties (antibody or aptamer, for example) for particular target or biomarker (which are then simply linked to modulator)

(3) Speed. T/DT: Slow: entire detection "process" is at the channel, and typically restricted on processing speed to the average time-scale feature (dwell-time) for the longest-lived blockade signal class. NTD: Fast: feature extraction not dependent on dwell-time. Very low probability to get a false positive.

(4) Multichannel. T/DT: Method not amenable to multichannel gain with single-potential platform (can't resolve single-channel blockade signal with multichannel noise). NTD: Have multichannel gain due to rich signal resolution capabilities of an engineered modulator molecule.

(5) Feature Refinement/Engineering. T/DT: No buffer modifications or off-channel detection extensions via introduction of substrates; the weak feature set limited to dwell-time doesn't allow such methods to be utilized. NTD: Have "lock-and-key" level signal resolution. The introduction of off-channel substrates in the buffer solution can increase sensitivity.

(6) Multiplex capabilities. T/DT: Each modified channel is limited to detect a single analyte or single bond-change-event detection, so no multiplexing without brute force production of arrays of T/DT detectors in a semiconductor production setting. NTD: Supports multi-transducer, multi-analyte detection from a single sample. Supports multichannel with a single aperture.

Table 14.1. Comparative analysis of the Translocation/Dwell-Time (T/TD) and Nanopore Transduction Detection (NTD) approaches.

The nanopore transduction detection (NTD) platform involves functionalizing a nanopore detector platform in a new way that is cognizant of signal processing and machine learning capabilities and advantages, such that a highly sensitive biosensing capability is achieved. The core idea in the NTD functionalization of the nanopore detector is to design a molecule that can be drawn into the channel (by an applied potential) but be too big to translocate, instead becoming stuck in a bistable 'capture' such that it modulates the ion-flow in a distinctive way (Fig. 14.2 shows some controls). An approximately two-state 'telegraph signal' has been engineered for a number of NTD modulators. If the channel modulator is bi-functional in that one end is meant to be captured and modulate while the other end is linked to an aptamer or antibody for specific binding, then we have the basis for a remarkably sensitive and specific biosensing capability. The biosensing task is reduced to the channel-based recognition of bound or unbound NTD modulators (or formed/unformed NTD modulators if target is ssDNA).

In order to have a *capture* state in the channel with a *single* molecule, a true nanopore is needed, not a micropore, and to establish a coherent capture-signal exhibiting non-trivial stationary signal statistics, which is the modulating-blockade desired, the nanopore's limiting inner diameter typically needs to be sized at approximately 1.5nm for duplex DNA channel modulators (precisely what is found for the alpha-hemolysin channel). The modulating-blockader is captured at the channel for the time-interval of interest by electrophoretic means, which is established by the applied potential that also establishes the observed current flow through the nanopore.

The NTD molecule providing the channel blockade has a second functionality, typically to specifically bind to some target of interest, with blockade modulation discernibly different according to binding state (DNA annealing examples are shown in what follows). NTD modulators are engineered to be bifunctional: one end is meant to be captured and modulate the channel current, while the other, extra-channel-exposed end, is engineered to have different states according to the event detection. Examples include extra-channel ends linked to binding moieties such as antibodies, antibody fragments, or aptamers. Examples also include 'reporter transducer' molecules with cleaved/uncleaved extra-channel-exposed ends, with cleavage by, for example, UV or enzymatic means. By using signal processing with pattern recognition to manage the streaming channel current blockade modulations, and thereby track the molecular states engineered into the transducer molecules, a biosensor or assayer is enabled.

Nanopore transduction detection (NTD) works at a scale where physics, chemistry, and biomedicine methodologies intersect. In some applications the NTD platform functions like a biosensor, or an artificial nose, at the single-molecule scale, e.g., a transducer molecule rattles around in a single protein channel, making transient bonds to its surroundings, and the binding kinetics of those transient bonds is directly imprinted on a surrounding, electrophoretically driven, flow of ions. The observed channel current blockade patterns are engineered or selected to have distinctive stationary statistics, and changes in the channel blockade stationary statistics are found to occur for a transducer molecule's interaction moiety upon introduction of its interaction target. In other applications the NTD functions like a 'nanoscope', e.g., a device that can observe the states of a single molecule or molecular complex. With the NTD apparatus the observation is not in the optical realm, like with the microscope, but in the molecular-state classification realm. NTD, thus, provides an unprecedented new technology for characterization of transient complexes. The nanopore detection method uses the stochastic carrier wave signal processing methods developed and described in prior work [1], and comprises machine learning methods for pattern recognition that can be implemented on a distributed network of computers for real-time experimental feedback and sampling control [20]. Details on engineering NTD transducers are given in [9] and what follows.

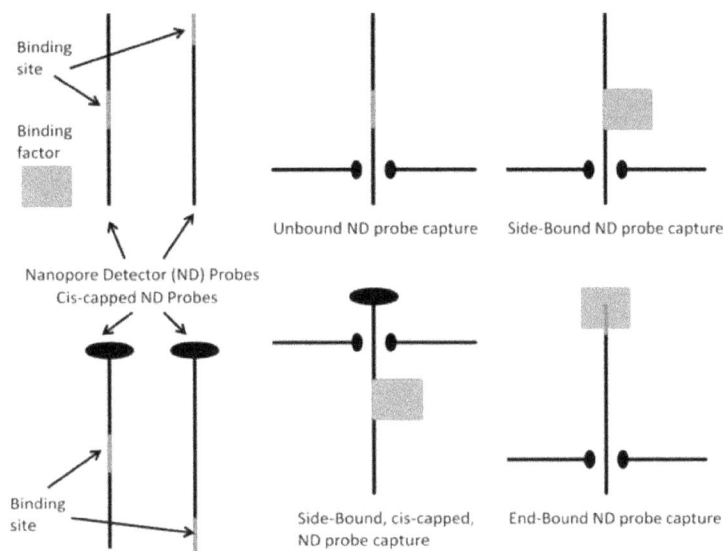

Fig. 14.11. Nanopore Detector detection topologies involving polymer translocation or threading. The detection event is given by polymer (ssDNA in [399,367-385]) translocations that are delayed if bound (side and end configurations shown). If bound entity is on the trans side (with cis-side capped, or vice versa), and bound entity is a processive DNA enzyme, then sequencing may be possible as described in [375,386-389].

Things to 'contact' with the channel: Aptamers

Aptamers are synthetically-derived, single-stranded, RNA or DNA molecules up to ~80 oligonucleotides in length with a high affinity towards bonding to specific targets. In 1990, a new method dubbed SELEX (Systematic Evolution of Ligands by EXponential Enrichment) provided a process of producing aptamers from random DNA or RNA libraries ([390] and [391]). Application of real-time PCR in the production of aptamers has contributed to the growing effectiveness of aptamers in a variety of research areas today [392,393].The main advantages of aptamers over antibodies are that aptamers are more durable (i.e., longer shelf life, do not require in vivo conditions, can sustain high immune response and toxins), are more obtainable (i.e., cost effective, quicker to make, easily modified, uniformity due to synthetic origin), and have greater specificity and sensitivity (i.e., the degree of binding target recognition, lack of cross-species overlap) [392,393]. Aptamers may bind with anything from dyes, drugs, peptides, proteins, metal ions, antibodies, and enzymes. The values of Kd range between ~pML^{-1} to ~nML^{-1}, better than that of antibodies [392,394,395]. Aptamers are now replacing antibodies as detection reagents, in particular, due to having several advantages over antibodies: versatility, the creation of a lab-on-a-chip to process, low detection limits, simpler reactions to perform, diversity and specificity of aptamer-target binding properties [393]. The use of aptamer beacons has been used in flow cytometry [395], in place of antibody-based assays [393,396] and most abundantly in studies of specific proteins [394,397,398].

Things to 'contact' with the channel: Immunoglobulins

The immunoglobulin molecule IgG is often described as a bifunctional molecule: one region for binding to target antigen, the other region for mediating effector function. Effector functions include binding of the antibody to host tissues, to various cells of the immune system, to some phagocytic cells, and to the first component (C1q) of the classical complement system. Activation of the immune system in response to a specific antigen is an amazing example of how a series of protein phosphorylation and dephosphorylation reactions convert a cell surface event to changes in DNA transcription and cell replication.

The structure of the IgG antibody forms three globular regions that are attached to each other in the middle of its grouping. The overall shape of the structure forms a Y configuration. At the base of this structure is the Constant (Fc) region where the effector functions take place and at the tips of the two arms, both referred to as the variable region (Fab), are the antigen binding sites. These variable regions are tethered to the trunk of the Y shaped molecule by a flexible hinge which allows for a high degree of arm movement. The relative size of the antibody is about three times the size of the alpha-hemolysin channel. Its length from base (Fc) to arm tip (Fab) is 25 nm and the width of each globular arm ranges from 6-10nm.

The forces binding antigen to antibody are an important and difficult area of study. Hydrophobic bonds, in particular, are very difficult to characterize by existing crystallographic and other means, and often contribute half of the overall binding strength of the antigen-antibody bond. Hydrophobic groups of the biomolecules exclude water while forming lock and key complementary shapes. The importance of the hydrophobic bonds in protein-protein interactions, and of critically placed waters of hydration, and the complex conformational negotiation whereby they are established, may be accessible to direct study using nanopore detection methods in future developments of this technology.

14.9 The NTD Nanoscope
Nanopore event transduction is done using single-molecule biophysics, engineered information flows, and nanopore cheminformatics. Nanopore transduction detection (NTD) is a unique platform, or 'nanoscope', for detection and analysis of single molecules. Proof-of-Concept experiments shown in what follows indicate a promising approach for single nucleotide polymorphism (SNP) detection, and other biosensing, for clinical diagnostics. This is accomplished via use of the channel-blockade signals produced by engineered event-transducers or by signal-profiled channel modulators in general. The transducer molecule is a bi-functional molecule: one end is captured in the nanopore channel while the other end is outside the channel. This extra-channel end is typically engineered to bond to a specific target: the analyte being measured. When the outside portion is bound to the target, the molecular changes (conformational and charge) and environmental changes (current flow obstruction geometry and electro-osmotic flow) result in a change in the channel-binding kinetics of the portion that is captured in the channel. The change in channel interaction kinetics generates a change in the channel blockade current (which is engineered to have a signal unique to the target molecule). The transducer molecule is, thus, a bi-functional molecule which is engineered to produce a change in its stationary-statistics channel-blockade profile upon binding to cognate. For detection of DNA molecules, the binding can itself lead to NTD modulator *formation*, including formation of the modulator function itself (a duplex DNA molecule annealed to form a Y-branching, for example).

NTD Methods for SNP detection alone offers the tantalizing prospect of medical diagnostics and cancer screening by highly accurate assaying of targeted genomic regions. Common methods for SNP detection are typically PCR-based, thus inherit the PCR error rate (0.1% in some situations). The percentages of minority SNP population might be 0.1%, or less, in instances of clinical interest, thus the PCR error rate is critically limiting in the standard approach. Although standard methods for SNP detection have high sensitivity, they typically lack high specificity and versatility. As will be shown, the Nanopore Transduction Detector is a unique platform with both high sensitivity and high specificity.

An interdisciplinary perspective is important to understanding the experimental approach, so initial background describes nanopore electrochemistry and single-molecule biophysics and how the biophysics information flows can result in stationary statistics observations. Then details are provided on the use of engineered stationary statistics signal processing in device enhancement, and communication, as inferred from the selected nanopore detector (ND) blockade sensing experimental results that are shown.

14.9.1 Nanopore Transduction Detection (NTD)

The nanopore transduction detection (NTD) platform [1,17,27,36] comprises a single nanometer scale channel that allows a single ionic current flow across a membrane and an engineered, or selected, channel blockading molecule. The channel blockading molecule is engineered or selected such that it provides a current modulating blockade in the detector channel when drawn into the channel. The channel is chosen such that it has inner diameter at the scale of that molecule or one of its molecular-complexes. For most biomolecular analysis implementations this leads to a choice of channel that has inner diameter in the range 0.1-10 *nanometers* (see Fig. 1). Given the channel's size it is referred to as a nanopore in what follows.

The nanopore transduction detection (NTD) platform [1,17,27] includes a single nanometer scale channel and an engineered, or selected, channel blockading molecule. The channel blockading molecule is engineered to provide a current modulating blockade in the detector channel when drawn into the channel, and held, by electrophoretic means. The channel has inner diameter at the scale of that molecule. For most biomolecular analysis implementations this leads to a choice of channel that has inner diameter in the range 0.1-10 *nanometers* to encompass small and large biomolecules, where the inner diameter is 1.5 nm in the alpha-hemolysin protein based channel used in the results that follow (see Fig. 14.12). Given the channel's size it is referred to as a nanopore in what follows. In efforts by others 'nanopore' is sometimes used to describe 100-1000 nm range channels, which are here referred to here as micropores.

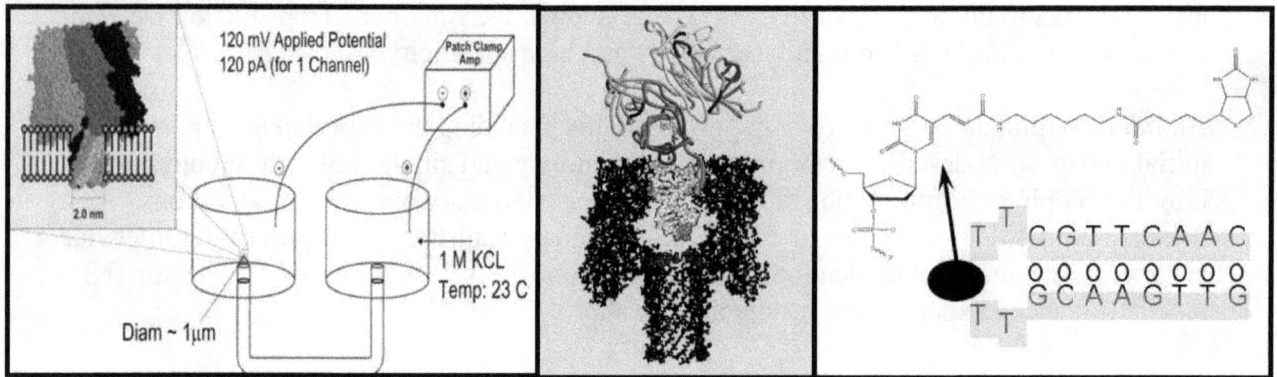

Figure 14.12. Schematic diagram of the Nanopore Transduction Detector
[17]. **Left**: shows the nanopore detector consists of a single pore in a lipid bilayer which is created by the oligomerization of the staphylococcal alpha-hemolysin toxin in the left chamber, and a patch clamp amplifier capable of measuring pico Ampere channel currents located in the upper right-hand corner. **Center**: shows a biotinylated DNA hairpin molecule captured in the channel's cis-vestibule, with streptavidin bound to the biotin linkage that is attached to the loop of the DNA hairpin. **Right**: shows the biotinylated DNA hairpin molecule (Bt-8gc).

In order to have a *capture* state in the channel with a *single* molecule, a nanopore is needed. In order to establish a coherent capture-signal exhibiting non-trivial stationary signal statistics the nanopore's limiting inner diameter typically needs to be sized at approximately 1.5nm for duplex DNA channel modulators (precisely what is found for the alpha-hemolysin channel). The modulating-blockader is captured at the channel for the time-interval of interest by electrophoretic means.

The NTD molecule providing the modulating blockade in what follows has a second functionality, to specifically bind to some target of interest such that its blockade modulation is discernibly different according to binding state (see the DNA annealing examples in [27-29]). Thus, the NTD modulators are engineered to be bifunctional in that one end is meant to modulate the channel current, while the other end is engineered to have different states according to the event detection, or event-reporting, of interest. Examples include extra-channel ends linked to binding moieties such as antibodies or aptamers. Examples also include 'reporter transducer' molecules with cleaved/uncleaved extra-channel-exposed ends, with cleavage by UV or enzymatic means [1]. By using pattern recognition to process the channel current blockade modulations, and thereby track the molecular states, a biosensor is thereby enabled.

With the NTD apparatus the observation is not in the optical realm, like with the microscope, but in the molecular-state classification realm. NTD, thus, provides a technology for characterization of transient complexes. The nanopore detection method uses the stochastic carrier wave signal processing methods developed and described in prior work [1], and comprises machine learning methods for pattern recognition that can be implemented on a distributed network of computers for real-time experimental feedback and sampling control [20].

420

In assaying applications the nanopore detector offers two types of analysis: (1) direct glyco-form assaying according to blockade modulation produced directly by the analyte interacting with the nanopore detector, which works on negatively charged glycosylation and glycation profiling best ; and (2) indirect isomer assaying by means of surface feature measurements using a specifically binding intermediary, such as with the antibody used in HbA1c testing. A mixture of the direct and indirect assaying methods may be necessary for complex problems of interest.

One of the most challenging nanopore assaying applications is for discriminating between isomers, approximately mass equivalent molecular variants, or aptamers [1,11]. Other nanopore-based efforts include DNA sequencing applications, and nanopore device physics studies in general, including with channels other than alpha-hemolysin.

The components comprising the nanopore transduction detection (NTD) platform [6,7] include a single nanometer scale channel that allows a single ionic current flow across a membrane and an engineered, or selected, channel blockading molecule. The channel blockading molecule is engineered or selected such that it provides a current modulating blockade in the detector channel when drawn into the channel, and held, by electrophoretic means. The channel is chosen such that it has inner diameter at the scale of that molecule or one of its molecular-complexes. For most biomolecular analysis implementations this leads to a choice of channel that has inner diameter in the range 0.1-10 *nanometers* to encompass small and large biomolecules and molecular complexes, where the inner diameter of 1.5 nm is utilized in the alpha-hemolysin protein based channel used in the results that follow (see Fig. 14.12).

The NTD molecule providing the modulating blockade has a second functionality, typically to specifically bind to some target of interest such that its blockade modulation is discernibly different according to binding state. Thus, the NTD modulators are engineered to be bifunctional in that one end is meant to be captured, and modulate the channel current, while the other, extra-channel-exposed end, is engineered to have different states according to the event detection, or event-reporting, of interest. By using signal processing to process the channel current blockade modulations, and thereby track the molecular states engineered into the transducer molecules, a biosensor or assayer is thereby enabled. By tracking transduced states of a coupled molecule undergoing conformational changes, such as an antibody, or a protein with a folding-pathway associated with disease, direct examination of co-factor, and other, influences on conformation can also be assayed at the single-molecule level.

The nanopore detection method uses the stochastic carrier wave signal processing methods developed and described in prior work [1,27,27], and comprises machine learning methods for pattern recognition that can be implemented on a distributed network of computers for real-time experimental feedback and sampling control [20]. Pattern recognition informed sampling capabilities greatly extends the usage of the single-channel apparatus, including learning the avoidance of blockades associated with channel failure when contaminants necessitate, and nanomanipulation of a single-molecule under active control in a nanofluidics-controlled environment.

The nanopore transduction detection (NTD) system, deployed as a biosensor platform, possesses highly beneficial characteristics from multiple technologies: (i) the specificity of antibody binding, aptamer binding, or nucleic acid annealing; (ii) the sensitivity of an engineered channel modulator to specific environmental change; and (iii) the robustness of the electrophoresis platform in handling biological samples.

A critical component in the NTD system is the transducer molecule. A NTD transducer is typically a compound molecule that serves to transduce the conformational or binding state of a molecule of interest into different channel current modulations. A NTD transducer can often be constructed by covalently tethering a molecule of interest to a nanopore channel modulator. In previous work, using inexpensive (commoditized) biomolecular components, such as DNA hairpins, as channel-modulators, and antibodies as specific binding moieties (with inexpensive immuno-PCR linkages to DNA), experiments were done to analyze individual antibodies and DNA molecules, their conformations, glycosylations, and their binding properties. It was found that in many applications the DNA-based transducers worked well, but in efforts to extend the methodology to biosensing and glycosylation profiling the DNA modulators often had too short a lifetime until melting. To make matters worse, the DNA-based modulators often had internal conformational freedom of their own that complicated analysis of any linked molecule's conformational changes. Worst of all, sometimes the DNA modulators only modulated when unbound (and the NTD method works best with clearly different modulatory states). Efforts to fix the non-modulatory aspect were partly solved by using a laser-tweezer apparatus to drive distinctive stochastic modulatory blockades in the DNA modulator. This was accomplished by introducing a periodic laser-tweezer 'tugging' on channel-modulator variants that had a biotinylated portion that was bound to a streptavidin-coated magnetic bead (another commoditized component). With modulations 'reawakened', however, the number of types of blockade signal appeared to proliferate significantly, and it wasn't clear if an automated signal analysis could be implemented as had been done previously [1].

Ponderable media flow phenomenology and related information flow phenomenology
The first step in the NTD methodology is to have a stable ion-channel *sized* such that it can be modulated by a single, non-translocating, molecule, where the channel is significantly blockaded, and not at a fixed level. The next step is to *establish a modulated ion-flow* through the ion-channel with an NTD transducer molecule, usually with the molecule electrophoretically drawn into the channel.

A single molecule's blockading interaction upon capture in an ion channel can be 'self-modulating' upon capture (i.e., without a dominant interaction state), and this has been found in a number of experiments [1,27,36,41,198]. Self-modulatory blockaders each have unique blockade signatures that can be resolved to very high confidence over time. Given the engineering freedom to design the self-modulatory molecules, and the generalizations in the standard periodic carrier based signal processing to stationary statistics carrier based signal processing [344,345], we arrive at a means to leverage ponderable media flow phenomena, and interaction kinetics, into a stochastic carrier wave signal processing problem that can be solved by efficient dynamic programming table computational methods [225,346].
At the nanometer-scale of the nanopore experiment the Reynold's number of the flow is incredibly small (10^{-10}). Thus the flow environment is not fluid-like in a familiar sense. The fluid strongly damps transverse vibrations, for example, so no string-like-motion on poly-

mers. The motions are strongly driven by electrostatic forces and steric constraints and have significant thermal energy contributions, such that a stochastic process is effectively obtained in typical measurements.

14.9.2 NTD: a versatile platform for biosensing

The use of a channel modulator introduces significant, engineered, signal analysis complexity, that we resolve using artificial intelligence (machine learning) methods. The benefit of this complication is a significant gain in sensitivity over T/TD, that uses a 'sensing' moiety covalently attached to the channel itself, where they have a T/TD-type blockade 'lifetime' event, with minimal or no internal blockade structure engineered [299]. The NTD approach, on the other hand, has significant improvement in versatility, e.g., we can 'swap out' modulators on a given channel, in a variety of ways, since they are not covalently attached to the channel. The improvements in sensitivity derive from the measurable stationary statistics of the channel blockades (and how this can be used to classify state with very high accuracy). The overall improvement in versatility is because all that needs to be redesigned for a different NTD experiment (or binding assay) is the linkage-interaction moiety portion of the bifunctional molecules involved. There is also the versatility that *mixtures* of different types of transducers can be used, a method that can't be employed in single-channel devices that use covalently bound binding moieties (or that discriminate by dwell-time in the channel).

At the nanopore channel one can observe a sampling of bound/unbound states, each sample only held for the length of time necessary for a high accuracy classification. Or, one could hold and observe a single bound/unbound system and track its history of bound/unbound states or conformational states. The *single* molecule detection, thus, allows measurement of molecular characteristics that are obscured in ensemble-based measurements. Ensemble averages, for example, lose information about the true diversity of behavior of individual molecules. For complex *bio*molecules there is likely to be a tremendous diversity in behavior, and in many cases this diversity may be the basis for their function. There can also be a great deal of diversity via post-translational modifications, as well, such as with heterogeneous mixtures of protein glycoforms that typically occur in living organisms (e.g., for TSH and hemoglobin proteins in blood serum and red blood cells, respectively). The hemoglobin 'A1c' glycoprotein, for example, is a disease diagnostic (diabetes), and for TSH, glycation is critical component in the TSH-based regulation of the endocrine axis. Multi-component regulatory systems and their variations (often sources of disease) could also be studied much more directly using the NTD approach, as could multi-component (or multi-cofactor) enzyme systems. Glycoform assays, characterization of single-molecule conformational variants, and multi-component assays are significant capabilities to be developed further with the NTD approach, further details on NTD assaying will follow in a later section.

In NTD applications we seek DNA modulators with specific, non-linear, topologies, such as Y-shaped DNA duplexes, to obtain molecules whose non-translocating blockades modulate the channel . We include shorter nucleic acids, with channel modulating and simple, DNA-complement, annealing properties, in the collection of DNA-based 'NTD aptamers' described in the NTD biosensor applications that follows. This is because the detection of ssDNA can enable the NTD-transducer's channel-modulatory formation, for direct signal validation, as will be described in what follows.

Nanopore transduction detection provides an inexpensive, quick, accurate, and versatile method for performing medical diagnostics. It is hypothesized that NTD biomarkers can be developed for early stage disease detection with femtomolar to attomolar sensitivity (see Table 14.2) for doing the standard clinical tests of the future. The potentially incredible sensitivity of the NTD targeting on biomarkers also provides a significant new tool for public health and biodefense in general.

In the preliminary results shown in what follows, we first demonstrate a 0.17 µM streptavidin sensitivity in the presence of a 0.5 µM concentration of detection probes with a 100 second detection window. The detection probe is a biotinylated DNA-hairpin transducer molecule (Bt-8gc) [1]. In repeated experiments we see the sensitivity limit ranging inversely to the concentration of detection probes. If taken to its limits, with established PRI sampling capabilities [20], and with stock Bt-8gc at 1mM concentration conveniently available, we believe it is possible to boost probe concentration almost three magnitudes. In doing so, we would boost sensitivity by similar measure, until the minimal observation time needed to reject limits this gain mechanism (see Table 14.2).

METHOD	SN
Low-probe concentration, 100s obs.	100 nM
High probe conc, 100s observation	100 pM
High probe conc, <u>long observation (~1dy)</u>	100 fM *
TARISA (conc. gain), 100s observation	100 fM
TERISA (enzyme gain), 100s obs.	100 aM **
Electrophoretic contrast gain, 100 s	1.0 aM

Table 14.2. Sensitivity limits for detection in the streptavidin-biosensor model system. *We have done 1 -1.5 day long experiments in other contexts, but not longer. Thus, current capabilities, with no modifications to the NTD platform for specialization for biosensing, can achieve close to 100 fM sensitivity by pushing the device limits and the observation window. **Only a slow enzyme turnover of 10 per second is assumed.

Detection in the attomolar regime (see Table 14.2) is critical for early discovery of type I diabetes destructive processes and for early detection of Hepatitis B. Early PSA detection currently has a 500 aM sensitivity. For some toxins, their potency, even at trace amounts, precludes their usage in the typical antibody-generation procedures (for mAb's that target that toxin). In this instance, however, aptamer-based NTD probes can still be obtained.

14.9.3 NTD Platform

The components comprising the NTD platform include an engineered molecule that can be drawn, by electrophoretic means (using an applied potential), into a channel that has inner diameter at the scale of that molecule, or one of its molecular-complexes, a means to establish a current flow through that nanopore (such as an ion flow under an applied potential), a means to establish the molecular capture for the timescale of interest (electrophoresis, for example), and the computational means to perform signal processing and pattern recognition (see Fig. 14.13 & 14.14).

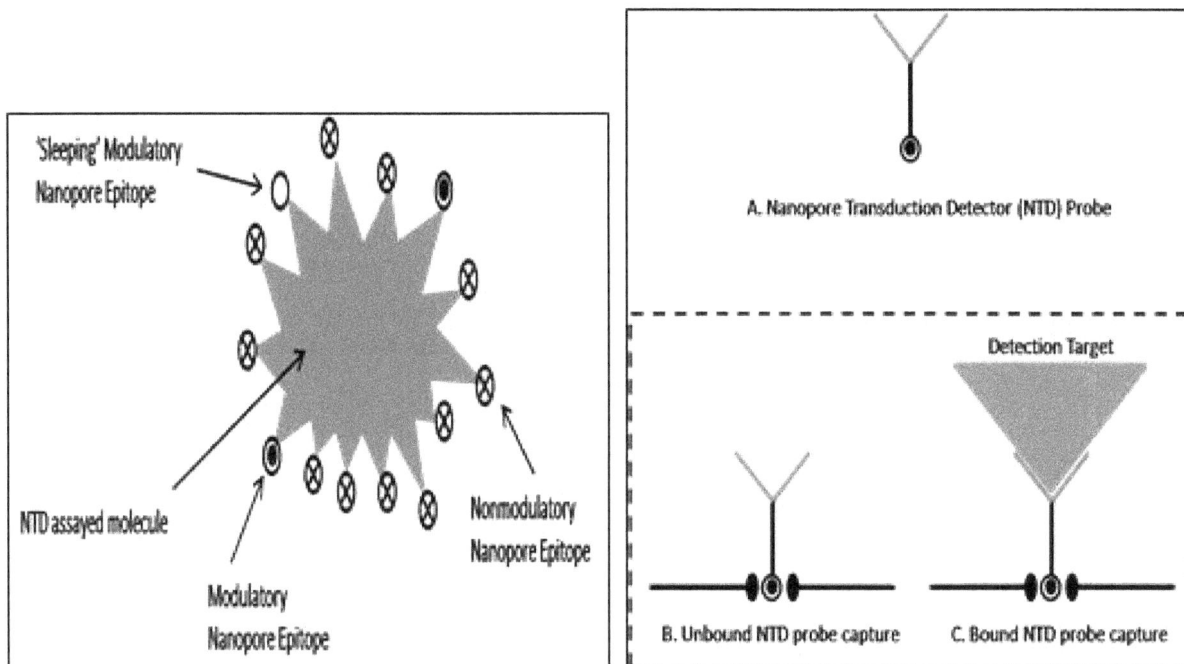

Fig. 14.13. Right. Nanopore Transduction Detector (NTD) Probe – a bifunctional molecule (A), one end channel-modulatory upon channel-capture (and typically long-lived), the other end multi-state according to the event detection of interest, such as the binding moieties (antibody and aptamer, schematically indicated in bound and unbound configurations in (B) and (C)), to enable a biosensing and assaying capability. **Left.** NTD assayed molecule (a protein, or other biomolecule, for example) Antibodies (proteins) are NTD assayed in the Proof-of-Concept Experiments, for example. Nanopore epitopes may arise from glyocprotein modifications and provide a means to measure surface features on heterogeneities mixture of protein glycoforms (such mixtures occur in blood chemistry, commercially available test on HbA1c glycosylation common, for example). A molecule may be examined via NTD sampling assay upon exposure to nanopore detector, (or molecular complex including molecule of interest).

The channel is sized such that a transducer molecule, or transducer-complex, is too big to translocate, instead the transducer molecule is designed to get stuck in a 'capture' configuration that modulates the ion-flow in a distinctive way.

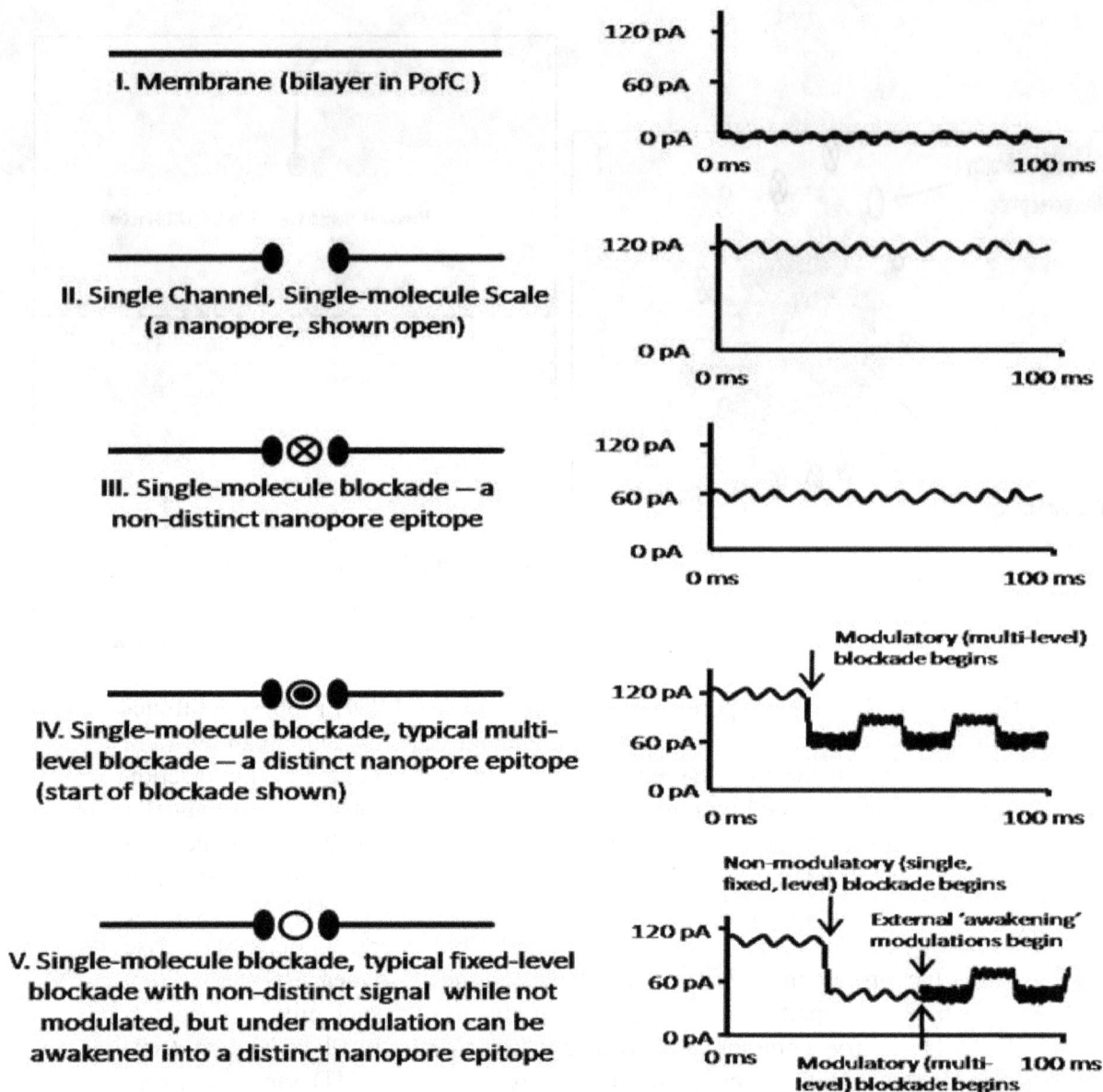

Fig. 14.14. The various modes of channel blockade are shown: I. No channel – e.g., a Membrane (bilayer). II. Single Channel, Single-molecule Scale (a nanopore, shown open). III. Single-molecule blockade, a brief interaction or blockade with fixed-level with non-distinct signal -- a non-modulatory nanopore epitope. IV. Single-molecule blockade, typical multi-level blockade with distinct signal modulations (typically obeying stationary statistics or shifts between phases of such). V. Single-molecule blockade, typical fixed-level blockade with non-distinct signal while not modulated, but under modulation can be awakened into distinct signal, with distinct modulations.

The NTD modulators are engineered to be bifunctional in that one end is meant to be captured, and modulate the channel current, while the other, extra-channel-exposed end, is engineered to have different states according to the event detection, or event-reporting, of interest. Examples include extra-channel ends linked to binding moieties such as antibodies,

426

antibody fragments, or aptamers. Examples also include 'reporter transducer' molecules with cleaved/uncleaved extra-channel-exposed ends, with cleavage by, for example, UV or enzymatic means. By using signal processing to track the molecular states engineered into the transducer molecules, a biosensor or assayer is thereby enabled. By tracking transduced states of a coupled molecule undergoing conformational changes, such as an antibody, or a protein with a folding-pathway associated with disease, direct examination of co-factor, and other, influences on conformation can also be assayed at the single-molecule level. The channel blockade modes in an NTD experiment thus make special use of channel current modulation scenarios (with stationary statistics), see Fig.s 14.13-14.17 for further details.

14.9.4 NTD Operation

When the extra-channel states correspond to bound/unbound, there are two protocols for how to set up the NTD platform: (1) observe a sampling of bound/unbound states, each sample only held for the length of time necessary for a high accuracy classification. Or, (2), hold and observe a single bound/unbound system and track its history of bound/unbound states. The single molecule binding history in (2) has significant utility in its own right, especially for observation of critical conformational change information not observable by any other methods. The ensemble measurement approach in (1), however, is able to benefit from numerous further augmentations, and can be used with general transducer states (see Fig. 14.15), not just those that correspond to a bound/unbound extra-channel states.

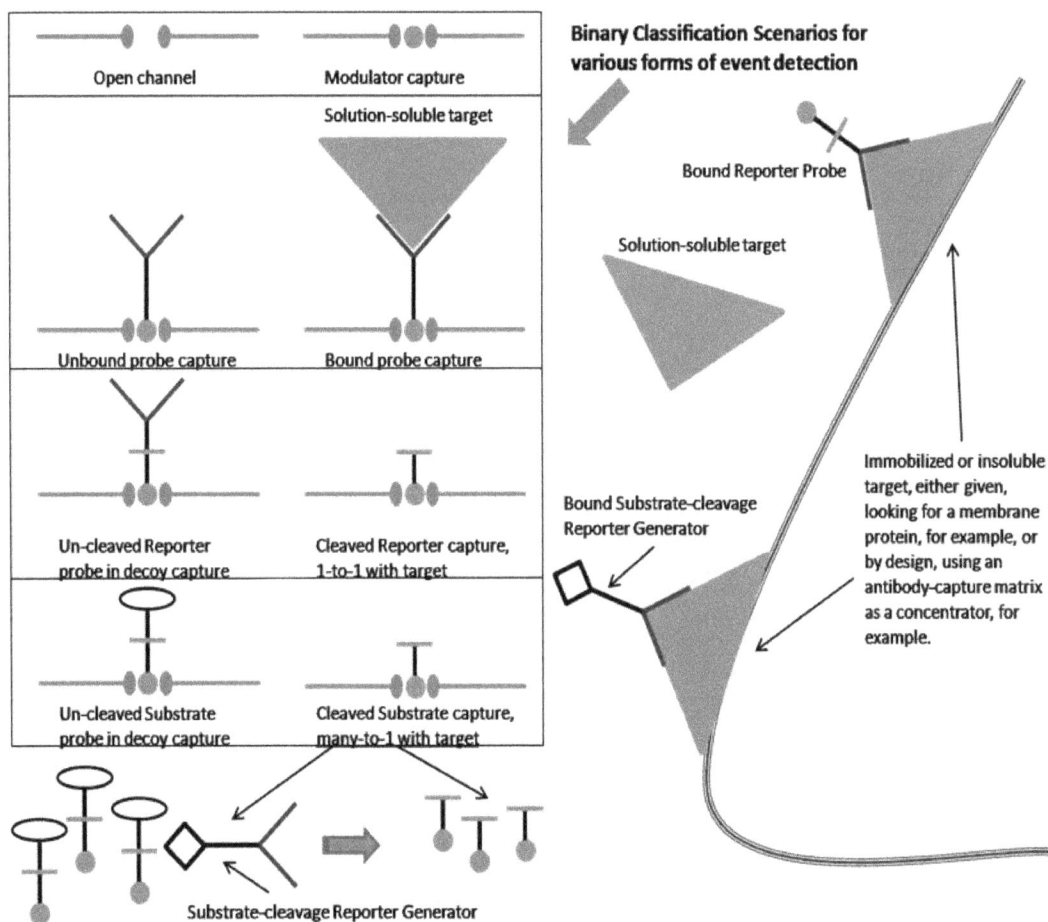

Fig. 14.15. Probes shown: bound/unbound type and uncleaved/cleaved type.

The pattern recognition informed (PRI) sampling 'acceleration', in ensemble-based measurements, for example, provides a means to accelerate the accumulation of kinetic information in most situations [20]. Furthermore, the sampling over a population of molecules is the key to a number of other gain factors that may be realized. In the ensemble detection with PRI approach [20], in particular, one can make use of antibody capture matrix and ELISA-like methods [400], to introduce two-state NTD modulators that have concentration-gain (in an antibody capture matrix) or concentration-with-enzyme-boost-gain (ELISA-like system, with production of NTD modulators by enzyme cleavage instead of activated fluorophore production). (Note that in the latter systems the NTD modulator is simply specified as 'two-state', where here we typically don't have bound/unbound, but cleaved/uncleaved instead.) In the ensemble evaluations, with the aforementioned off-channel-engineered event gain factors, we can introduce a NTD probe substrate that thoroughly probes the sample presented if some element of the probe-target system is immobilized, or significantly reduced in mobilization (see Fig. 14.15). In this circumstance, UV- and enzyme-based cleavage methods on immobilized probe-target can be designed to produce a high concentration, or concentration burst, of NTD modulators, that will be strongly drawn to the channel and provide a UV-event correlated 'burst' concentration detection signal.

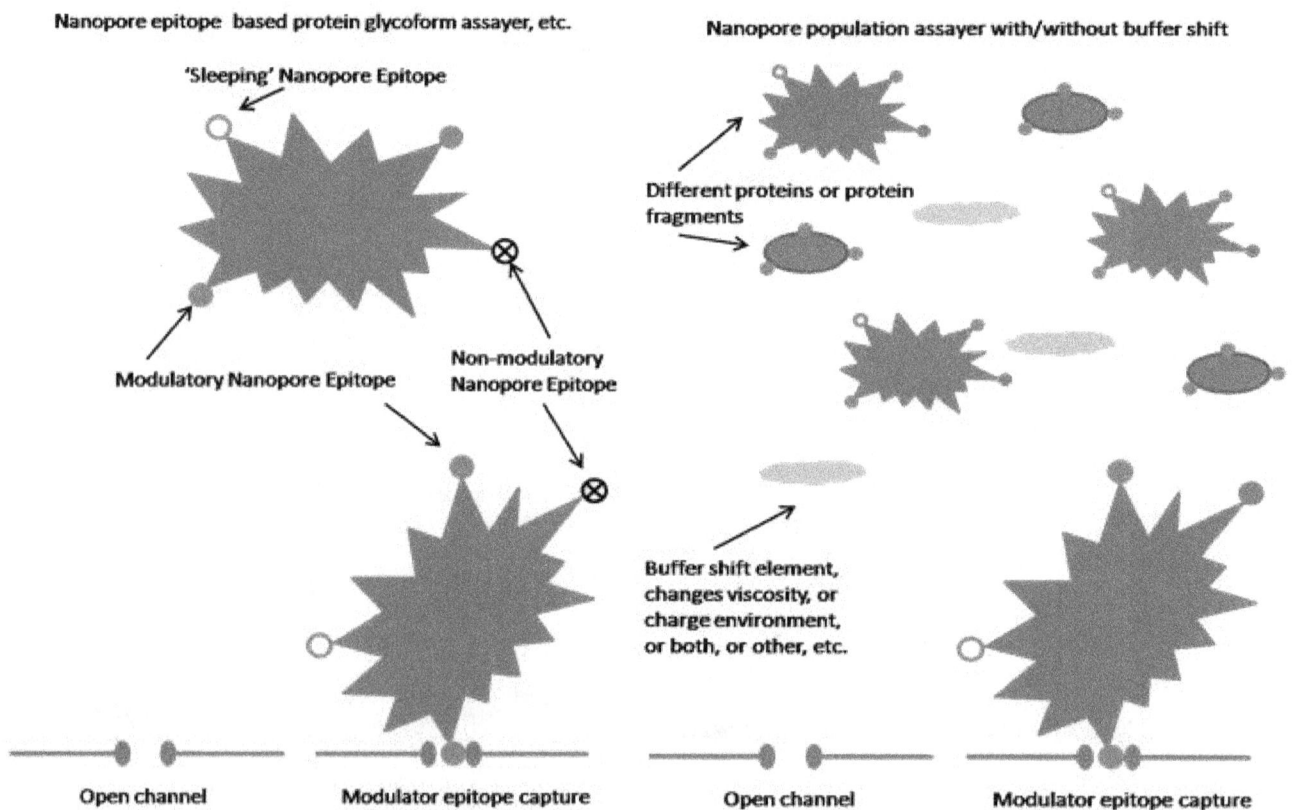

Fig. 14.16 (Left). Nanopore epitope assay (of a protein, or a heterogenous mixture of related glycoprotein, for example, via glycosilation that need not be enzynatically driven, as occurs in blood, for example). **(Right). Gel-shift mechanism.** Electrophoretically draw molecules across a diffusionally resis-

tive buffer, gel, or matrix (PEG-shift experiments). If medium in buffer, gel, or matrix is endowed with a charge gradient, or a fixed charge, or pH gradient, etc., isoelectric focusing effects, for example, might be discernable.

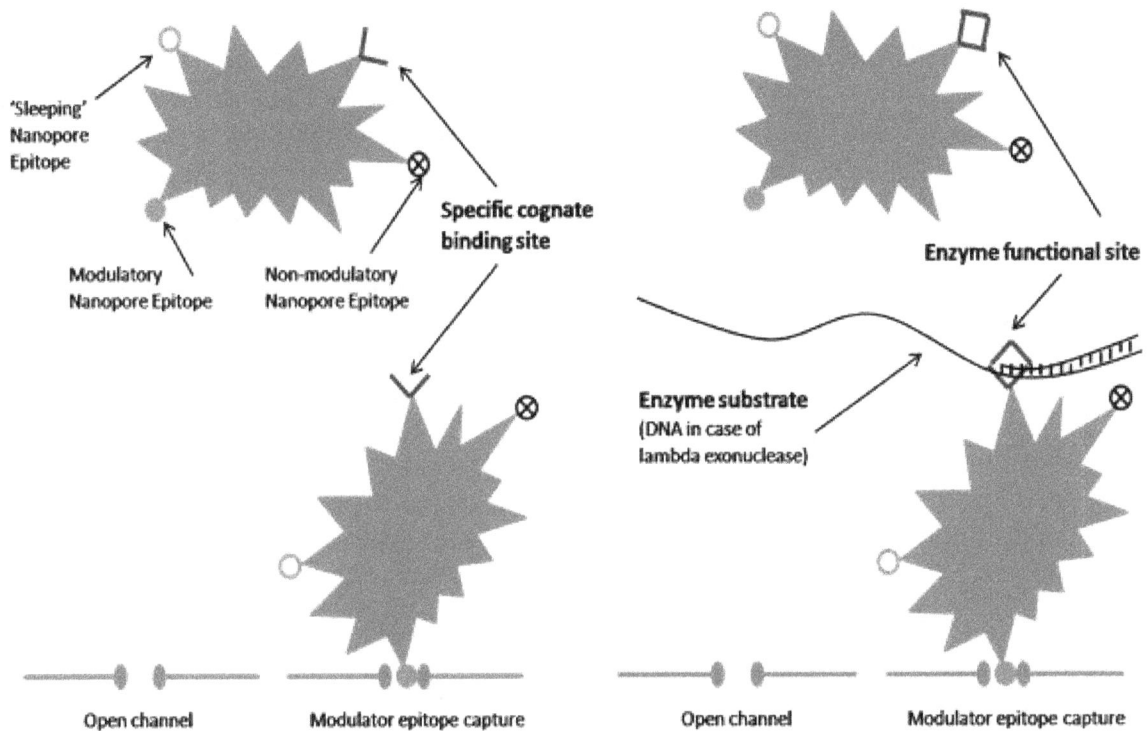

Fig. 14.17 (Left). Oriented modulator capture on protein (or other) with specific binding (an antibody for example). **(Right).** Oriented modulator capture on protein (or other) with enzymatic activity (lambda exonuclease for example).

A multi-channel implementation of the NTD can be utilized if a distinctive-signature NTD-modulator on one of those channels can be discerned (the scenario for trace, or low-concentration, biosensing, see Fig. 14.18). In this situation, other channels bridging the same membrane (bilayer in case of alpha-hemolysin based experiment) are in parallel with the first (single) channel, with overall background noise growing accordingly. In the stochastic carrier wave encoding/decoding with HMMD (Ch. 7 & 8), we retain strong signal-to-noise, such that the benefits of a multiple-receptor gain in the multi-channel NTD platforms can be realized (see Proof-of-Concept Results for further details).

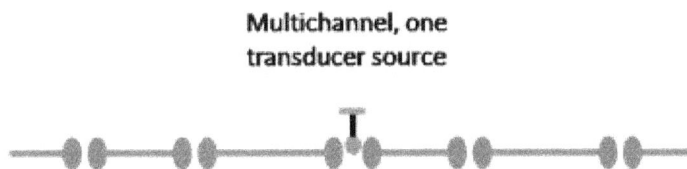

Fig. 14.18. Multichannel scenario, with only one blockade present (at low concentration, for example).

14.9.5 Driven modulations

It is possible to probe higher frequency realms than those directly accessible at the operational bandwidth of the channel current based device (~200 kHz), or due to the time-scale of the particular analyte interaction kinetics, by introducing modulated excitations. This can be accomplished by chemically linking the analyte or channel to an excitable object, such as a magnetic bead, under the influence of laser pulsations. In one configuration, the excitable object can be chemically linked to the analyte molecule to modulate its blockade current by modulating the molecule during its blockade. In another configuration, the excitable object is chemically linked to the channel, to provide a means to modulate the passage of ions through that channel. In a third experimental variant, the membrane is itself modulated (using sound, for example) in order to effect modulation of the channel environment and the ionic current flowing though that channel. Studies involving the first, analyte modulated, configuration (Figs. 14.19 & 14.20), indicate that this approach can be successfully employed to keep the end of a long strand of duplex DNA from permanently residing in a single blockade state. Similar study of magnetic beads linked to antigen may be used in the nanopore/antibody experiments if similar single blockade level, "stuck," states occur with the captured antibody (at physiological conditions, for example). Likewise, this approach can be considered for increasing the antibody-antigen dissociation rate if it does not occur within the time-scale of the experiment. It may be possible, with appropriate laser pulsing, or some other modulation, to drive a captured DNA molecule in an informative way even when not linked to a bead, or other macroscopic entity (Fig. 14.21).

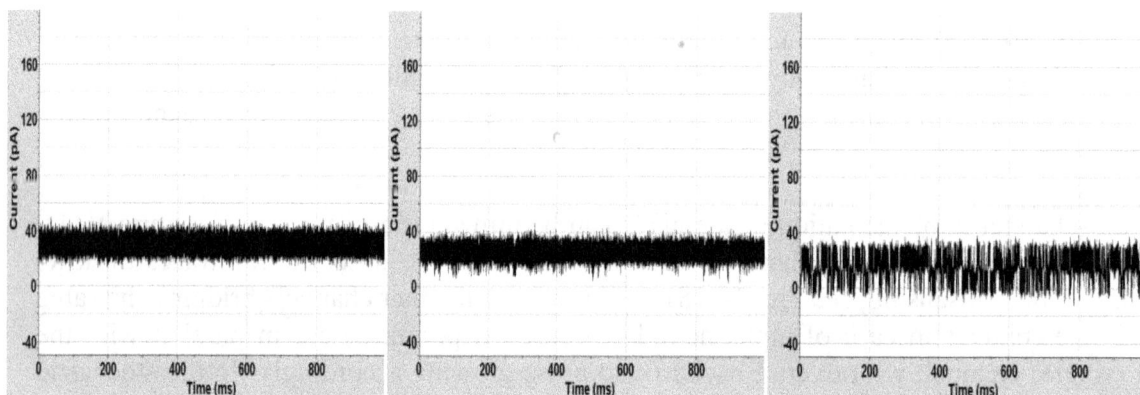

Fig. 14.19. A (Left) Channel current blockade signal where the blockade is produced by 9GC DNA hairpin with 20 bp stem. (Center) Channel current blockade signal where the blockade is produced by 9GC 20 bp stem with magnetic bead attached. (Right) Channel current blockade signal where the blockade is produced by c9GC 20 bp stem with magnetic bead attached and driven by a laser beam chopped at 4 Hz. Each graph shows the level of current in picoamps over time in milliseconds.

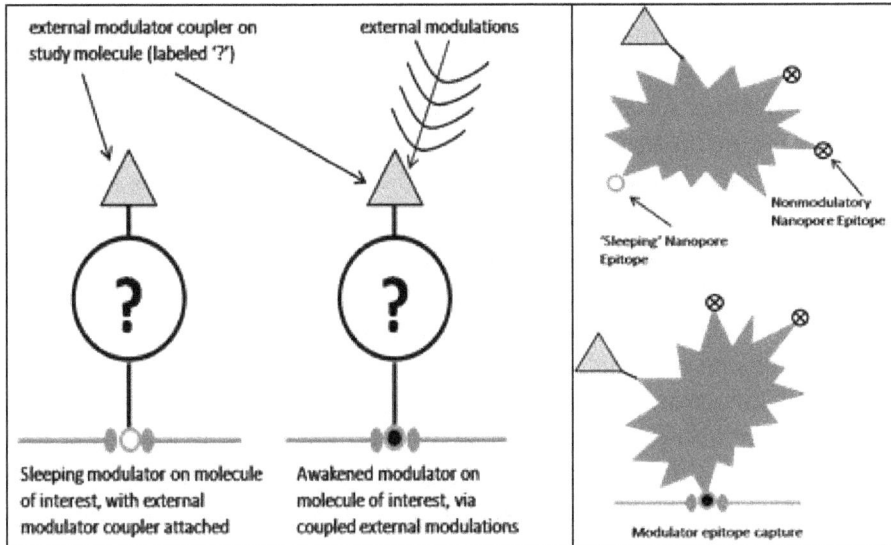

Fig. 14.20 (Left). Study molecule with externally-driven modulator linkage to awaken modulator signal. **(Right).** Study molecule with externally-driven modulator linkage to awaken modulator signal, with epitope-selection to obtain sleeping epitope , then determine its identity, and based on known modulator-activation driving signals, proceed with driving the system to obtain a modulator capture linkage.

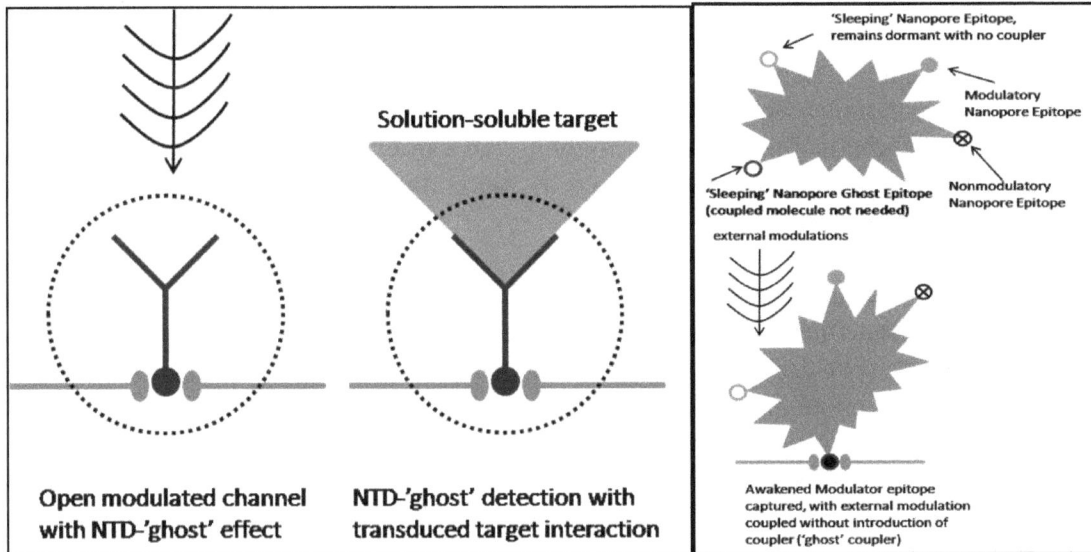

Fig. 14.21 (Left). Same situation as in cases with linked-modulator, but more extensive range of external modulations explored, such that, in some situations, a sleeping nanopore epitope is 'awakened' (modulatory channel blockades produced), and the target molecule does not require a coupler attachment., e.g., using external modulations with no coupler, may be able to obtain 'ghost' transducers in some situations. **(Right).** 'Sleeping' Nanopore Ghost Epitope (coupled molecule not needed).

14.9.6 Driven modulations with multichannel augmentation

The *S. aureus* alpha-hemolysin pore-forming toxin that is used to produce our single-channel nanopore-detector self- oligomerizes to derive the energetics necessary to create a channel through the bi-layer membrane. In the nanopore construction protocol, the process is limited to the creation of a single channel. It is possible to allow the process to continue unabated to create 100 channels or more. The 100 channel scenario has the potential to increase the sensitivity of the NTD, but the signal analysis becomes more challenging since there are 100 parallel noise sources. The recognition of a transducer signal is possible by the introduction of 'time integration' to the signal analysis akin to heterodyning a radio signal with a periodic carrier in classic electrical engineering. In order to introduce a 'time integration' benefit in the transducer signal, periodic (or stationary stochastic) modulations can be introduced to the transducer environment. In a high noise background, modulations can be introduced such that some of the transducer level lifetimes have heavy-tailed distributions. With these modifications to the signal processing software a single transducer molecule signal could be recognizable in the presence of 100 channels or more. Increasing the number of channels by 100 and retaining the capability of recognizing a single transducer blockading one of those channels provides a direct gain in sensitivity according to the number of channels (e.g., 100 channels would provide a sensitivity boost of two orders of magnitude). It is important to note that this type of increase in sensitivity is mostly implemented computationally and does not add complexity or cost to the NTD device.

The single-channel biosensing methods used here can be generalized to where many channels are present, where each channel offers parallel conductance paths for the ionic current, and where each channel is augmented with antibody (or aptamer) to establish a background collection of channel/antibody signals that is modifiable in the presence of antigen. Such 'passive' multi-channel methods offer similar capabilities to surface plasmon resonance approaches for characterizing binding affinity. Multiple antibody (aptamer) species can be present in this multi-channel operation. Anything that can evoke an antibody response (or SELEX selection, for aptamers) can be taken as the antigen or collection of antigens for which the bio-sensing is designed.

Multichannel with modulation is shown in Fig. 14.22, where modulation forces a population inversion, such that state durations are strongly non-geometrically distributed. Even without such modulations, however, there may be a strong enough signal recognitionwith the HMM methods without duration modeling enhancements.

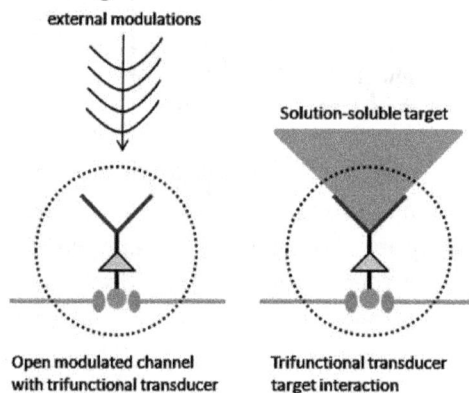

Fig. 14.22. External modulations with transducer with coupler, a trifunctional molecule.

14.10 NTD Biosensing Methods

NTD biosensing methods can involve a DNA modulator with linkages to an aptamer, antibody, or some other binding moiety, including simply a ssDNA overhang. The linkages needed to connect a DNA-based channel-modulator to a DNA-based aptamer involves a trivial join of the underlying ssDNA sequences involved. The linkage needed to connect a DNA-based channel-modulator to an antibody *could* involve use of linker technology, and this has been used in the past with dsDNA hairpins [30], but another, more commoditized route to be discussed, easily accessible with use of the NADIR refined Y-shaped DNA channel modulators [27,28], is that the antibody need merely be 'tagged' with the appropriate ssDNA strand, e.g., where the DNA sequence is complement to part of the 'Y' shaped DNA channel modulator, and antibody tagging with DNA is a standard service for use in immuno-PCR. Proof-of-Concept Biosensing Experiments are described for the streptavidin-biotin and DNA annealing model systems, a pathogen/SNP detection prototype, and for aptamer and antibody based detection.

14.10.1 Model biosensor based on streptavidin and biotin

A biotinylated DNA-hairpin that is engineered to generate two signals depending on whether or not a streptavidin molecule is bound to the biotin (see Figs. 14.23). Results in Fig. 14.23 (Right) suggest that the new signal class on binding is actually a racemic mixture of two hairpin-loop twist states. At T=4000 urea is introduced at 2.0 M and gradually increased to 3.5 M at T=8,100.

The transducer molecule in the NTD "Streptavidin Toxin Biosensor" configuration consists of a bi-functional molecule: one end is captured in the nanopore channel while the other end is outside the channel. This exterior-channel end is engineered to bond to a specific target: the analyte being measured. When the outside portion is bound to the target, the molecular changes (conformational and charge) and environmental changes (current flow obstruction geometry and electro-osmotic flow) result in a change in the channel-binding kinetics of the portion that is captured in the channel. This change of kinetics generates a change in the channel blockade current which represents a signal unique to the target molecule.

Some of the transducer molecule results from [17,27] are shown in Fig. 14.23, for a biotinylated DNA-hairpin that is engineered to generate two unique signals depending on whether or not a streptavidin molecule is bound.

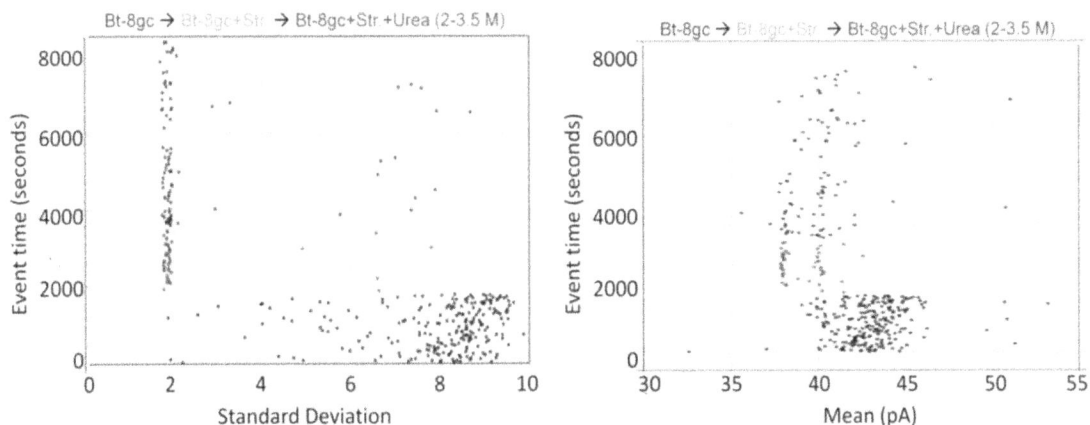

Figure 14.23. Left. Observations of individual blockade events are shown in terms of their blockade standard deviation (x-axis) and labeled by their obser-

vation time (y-axis) [17,27]. The standard deviation provides a good discriminatory parameter in this instance since the transducer molecules are engineered to have a notably higher standard deviation than typical noise or contaminant signals. At T=0 seconds, 1.0 μM Bt-8gc is introduced and event tracking is shown on the horizontal axis via the individual blockade standard deviation values about their means. At T=2000 seconds, 1.0 μM Streptavidin is introduced. Immediately thereafter, there is a shift in blockade signal classes observed to a quiescent blockade signal, as can be visually discerned. The new signal class is hypothesized to be due to (Streptavidin)-(Bt-8gc) bound-complex captures. **Right**. As with the Left Panel on the same data, a marked change in the Bt-8gc blockade observations is shown immediately upon introducing streptavidin at T=2000 seconds, but with the mean feature we clearly see two distinctive and equally frequented (racemic) event categories. Introduction of chaotropic agents degrades first one, then both, of the event categories, as 2.0 M urea is introduced at T=4000 seconds and steadily increased to 3.5 M urea at T=8100 seconds.

In the NTD platform, sensitivity increases with observation time [24] in contrast to translocation technologies where the observation window is fixed to the time it takes for a molecule to move through the channel. Part of the sensitivity and versatility of the NTD platform derives from the ability to couple real-time adaptive signal processing algorithms to the complex blockade current signals generated by the captured transducer molecule. If used with the appropriately designed NTD transducers, NTD can provide excellent sensitivity and specificity and can be deployed in many applications where trace level detection is desired. The monoclonal antibody-based NTD system, deployed as a biosensor platform, possesses highly beneficial characteristics from multiple technologies: the specificity of monoclonal antibody binding, the sensitivity of an engineered channel modulator to specific environmental change, and the robustness of the electrophoresis platform in handling biological samples. In combination, the NTD platform can provide trace level detection for early diagnosis of disease as well as quantify the concentration of a target analyte or the presence and relative concentrations of multiple distinct analytes in a single sample.

In [17,27] a 0.17 μM streptavidin sensitivity is demonstrated in the presence of a 0.5 μM concentration of detection probes, with only a 100 second detection window. The detection probe is the biotinylated DNA-hairpin transducer molecule (Bt-8gc) described in Fig. 1. In repeated experiments, the sensitivity limit ranges inversely to the concentration of detection probes (with PRI sampling) or the duration of detection window. The stock Bt-8gc has 1mM concentration, so a 1.0 mM probe concentration is easily introduced. (Note: The higher concentrations of transducer probes need not be expensive on the nanopore platform because the working volume can be very small: *cis* chamber volume is 70 μL, and could be reduced to 1.0 μL with use of microfluidics.) In [17,27] the selectivity of the detector in the presence of interference agents, such as albumin and sucrose and a variety of antibodies (without specific binding to biotin or the channel) was also examined, and a control transducer molecule with the same six-carbon linker arm from the DNA hairpin, but without the biotin 'fishing lure' binding site, was introduced, where it was shown that no interaction (via change of blockade signal) was observed upon introduction of streptavidin, as expected.

14.10.2 Model system based on DNA annealing
14.10.2.1 Linear DNA annealing test

Proof of Concept experiments for DNA annealing were initially tested for detection of a specific 5-base ssDNA molecule, where we have a linear molecule with a bulge in the center. To one side of the bulge is the blunt-ended stem sequence like that used in one of our DNA hairpin controls, where the bulge is now in the position of the hairpin's loop. To the other side of the bulge is a cap-section of base-pairs followed by an overhang section of length five bases. A similar set of experiments is performed with the "Y-aptamer", a Y-shaped DNA complex with one arm of the Y with an overhang (6Ts), while the other arm is capped with a 4dT loop. The base of the Y is a stem of 10 base-pairs length, prior to the Y-nexus of the molecule. Here the Y-nexus is in the place of the bulge, or the hairpin loop. Nine or ten base-pairs is approximately the length in dsDNA from the mouth of the channel to its limiting aperture. The significance of this length in the modeling is due to its delicate placement of the end of the captured molecule over the high electrophoretic field strength zone near the limiting aperture of the channel, permitting operation in transduction model. The overhang's binding strength can be adjusted by tailoring its length in both of these experiments, and in future work this will also permit a highly precise study of DNA annealing.

The linear duplex DNA molecule, with bulge, and ssDNA overhang, is given below. Examples of the signals that occur when a properly annealed duplex is captured are shown in Fig. 14.24. Fig. 14.24 compares signal traces before/after in terms of their standard 150-component feature set. The linear aptamer with bulge consists of annealing the following two ssDNA strands:

(1) 5'-GAGGCTTGG TTT CAATAGGTA-3'
(2) 5'-ATTG TTT CCAAGCCTC-3'

The complementary 5 nucleotide ssDNA sequence (3):
(3) 5'-TACCT-3'

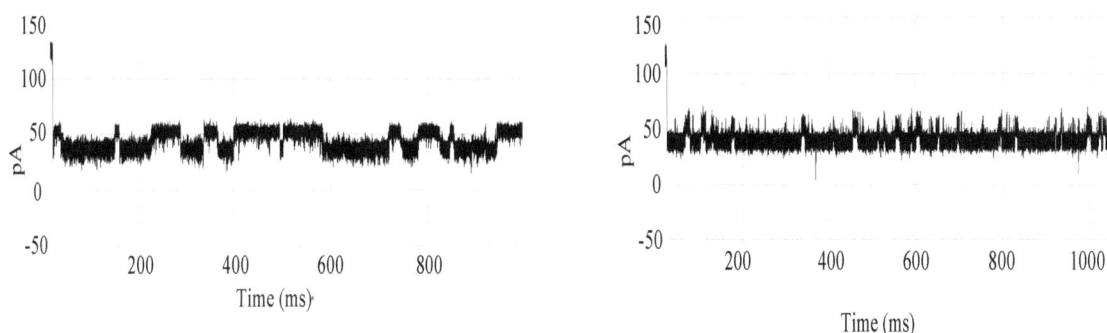

Fig. 14.24 Pseudo-aptamer: DNA overhang binding complement – signal blockades. Left: Before introduction of 5-base ssDNA complement. **Right:** After introduction of complement.

14.10.2.2 'Y' DNA annealing test

The Y-aptamer DNA molecule consists of a three-way DNA junction created by annealing two DNA molecules:
(1) 5'-CTCCGTCGAC GAGTTTATAGAC TTTTTT-3'
(2) 5'-GTCTATAAACTC GCAGTCATGCTTTTGCATGACTGC GTCGACGGAG-3'

For the resulting Y-aptamer, one of the junctions' arms terminate in a 4dT-loop and the other arm has a 6T overhang in place of a 4dT-loop. Preliminary results are shown in Fig. 14.25. The blunt ended arm has to be carefully designed such that when it is captured by the nanopore it produces a toggling blockade. One of the arms of the Y-shaped aptamer (Y-aptamer) has a TATA sequence, and is meant to be a binding target for TBP. In general, any transcription factor binding site could be studied (or verified) in this manner. Similarly, transcription factor could be verified, or the efficacy of a synthetic transcription factor could be examined.

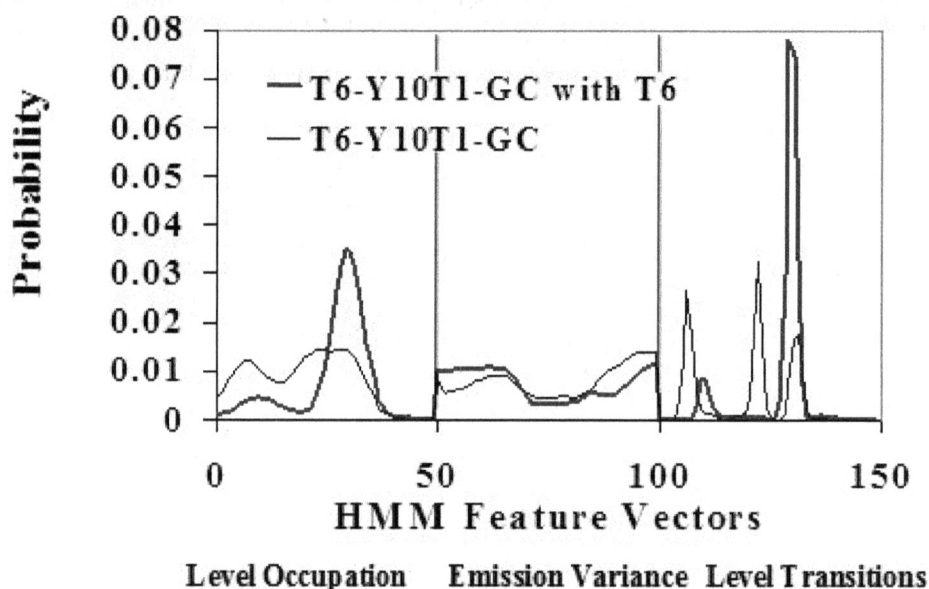

Fig. 14.25. Y-aptamer with DNA overhang that binds complement. Left: signal profiles before and after binding. Right: the dwell-time distributions on the three dominant levels indicated in the *unbound* blockade signal. The profiles aresurprisingly different, the bound case, with annealed complement, appears to be more "stable", with only two dominant blockade levels. This is consistent with it being a molecule with fewer degrees of freedom (with 6T overhang now annealed to 6A complement).

14.10.3 Y-aptamer with use of chaotropes to improve signal resolution

In the nucleic acid annealing studies on the NTD platform described in [17,27] (see Fig. 14.26), the introduction of chaotropes allows for improved nucleic acid annealing identification.

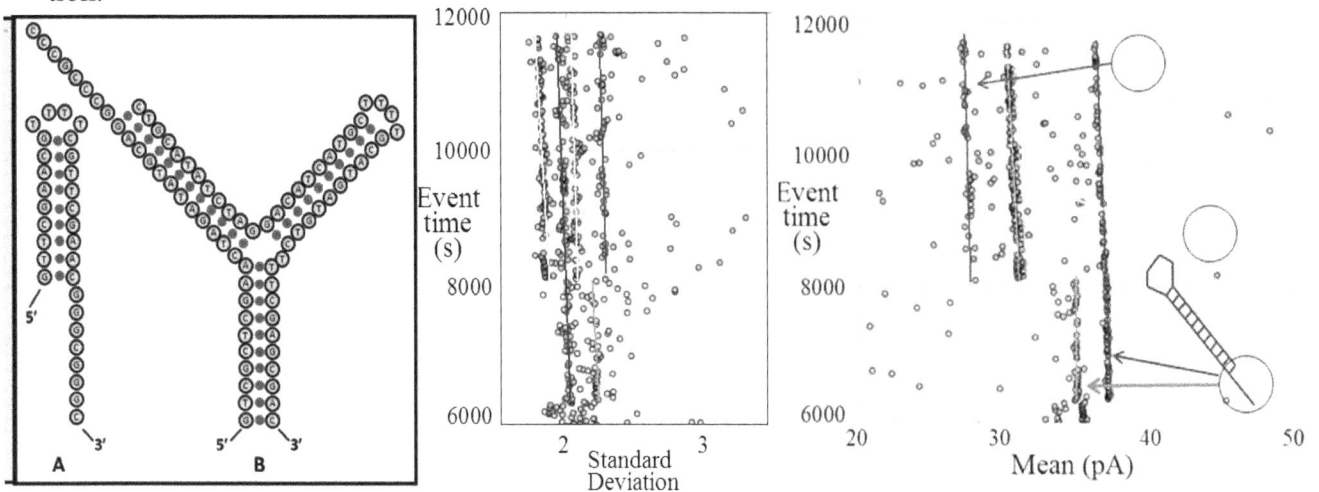

Figure 14.26. Eight-base annealing using a NTD Y-transducer [17]. Left: The DNA hairpin and DNA Y-nexus transducer secondary structures with sequence information shown. **Center and Right: Y-shaped DNA transducer with overhang binding to DNA hairpin with complementary overhang.**

The ability of the of the NTD apparatus to tolerate high chaotrope concentration, up to 5M urea, was demonstrated in [14]. DNA hairpin control molecules have demonstrated a manageable amount of isoform variation even at 5M urea (Sec. 14.12.1.1).

In Fig. 2, only a portion of a repetitive validation experiment is shown, thus time indexing starts at the 6000th second. From time 6000 to 6300 seconds (the first 5 minutes of data shown) only the DNA hairpin (sequence details in [17]) is introduced into the analyte chamber, where each point in the plots corresponds to an individual molecular blockade measurement. At time 6300 seconds urea is introduced into the analyte chamber at a concentration of 2.0 M. The DNA hairpin with overhang is found to have two capture states (clearly identified at 2 M urea). The two hairpin channel-capture states are marked with the green and red lines, in both the plot of signal means and signal standard deviations. After 30 minutes of sampling on the hairpin+urea mixture (from 6300 to 8100 seconds), the Y-shaped DNA molecule is introduced at time 8100. Observations are shown for an hour (8100 to 11700 seconds). A number of changes and new signals now are observed: (i) the DNA hairpin signal class identified with the green line is no longer observed – this class is hypothesized to be no longer free, but annealed to its Y-shaped DNA partner; (ii) the Y-shaped DNA molecule is found to have a bifurcation in its class identified with the yellow lines, a bifurcation clearly discernible in the plots of the signal standard deviations. (iii) the hairpin class with the red line appears to be unable to bind to its Y-shaped DNA partner, an inhibition currently thought to be due to G-quadruplex formation in its G-rich overhang. (iv) The Y-shaped DNA molecule also exhibits a signal class (blue line) associated with capture of the arm of the 'Y' that is meant for annealing, rather than the base of the 'Y' that is designed for channel capture.

14.10.4 Pathogen Detection, miRNA detection, and miRNA haplotyping

In clinical diagnostics, as well as in biodefense testing, patient blood samples can be drawn for the purpose of assaying the DNA content. Obviously there will be a preponderance of human DNA in such a sample, but if there is infection then trace amounts of the associated viral or bacterial DNA will be present as well. The question then arises as to how to detect unique elements of bacterial DNA sequence that are singled-out for detection, with very high sensitivity and specificity. This may be possible in the NTD approach, with annealing-based detection along the lines described earlier and in [17,27,28], where ssDNA sequences are targeted for detection of approximate length 22 base sub-sequences. A 22-mer is shown in Fig. 14.26, 'B'-labeled secondary structure, in the leftmost, linear, ssDNA segment. The Y-shaped secondary structure in Fig. 14.26 ('B') shows the blueprint for a NTD ssDNA probe for any targeted ssDNA segment, upon 'recognition' (annealing-based), a Y-shaped channel modulator is engineered to occur. If not the correct modulator, due to a few mismatches or inserts (particularly at the Y-nexus), then the difference can be discerned with high discrimination. All that is needed is a specific set of enzyme digestion steps on the DNA sample to 'chop' it into shorter segments, and leave targeted regions at the ends of (some) of the resulting ssDNA digests → so as to obtain-dsDNA annealed targets with probe match as in Fig. 14.26 ('B'), where the excess ssDNA length (beyond the 22-mer match template) is left to dangle off of one end, as shown for the eight-base segment shown in Fig. 14.26 ('B'). In ongoing work target-segment annealing with high specificity is being explored in the presence of large polymer extensions to the annealing target.

In clinical diagnostics, as well as in biodefense testing, patient blood samples can be drawn for the purpose of assaying the DNA and glycoprotein contents. In the case of DNA there will be a preponderance of the individual's own genomic DNA in such a sample, but if there is infection then trace amounts of the associated viral or bacterial DNA will be present as well. One of the questions that then arises is how to detect unique elements of bacterial DNA sequence with very high sensitivity and specificity. In [1] annealing-based detection is explored, where Y-shaped NTD transducer results are shown for tests involving an eight base ssDNA target [17,27]. The method can be extended to other lengths of targeted ssDNA, using annealing-based recognition. For longer lengths we can arrive at interesting detection scenarios for pathogens or for miRNA's (some possibly pathogenic). The known pathogen ssDNA targets could be longer, 15-25 bases say, to enable unique identifiers respective to a particular pathogen. For miRNA detection probes could be designed for ssDNA target annealing that is in the 7-15 base range.

MicroRNA detection follows a similar approach to the pathogen detection problem, but now typically working with a much shorter length nucleic acid detection target, a miRNA sequence based annealing target. In this setting often have similar 'informed' analysis to pathogen detection analysis.

The detection of SNPs via annealing is demonstrated with the Y-shaped DNA transduction molecule that is minimally altered, and such that the SNP variant occurs in the Y-nexus region. In preliminary work with Y-transducers [17,27] we demonstrate how *single-base insertions or modifications at the nexus of the Y-shaped molecule can provide clearly discernible changes in channel-blockade signals*. The design of the Y-transducer for SNP detection was similar to the process mentioned in [17,27] for *na*nopore-detector *dir*ected (NADIR) searches for aptamers based on bound-state lifetime measurements. The NTD method provides a viable prospect for SNP variant detection to very high accuracy -- possibly equaling the accuracy with which the NTD can discern DNA control hairpins that only differ in terminal base-pair (greater than 99.999% for sufficiently long observation time).

Y-DNA modulator platforms for biosensing can also provide a simple linker platform for use with antibody binding moieties, where a 'linker' aptamer can be used that is covalently linked to the common base of the antibody (IgG) molecule (using a DNA tagged antibody approach). Aptamer tuning can also be enhanced in the nanopore setting using nanopore directed SELEX (referred to as NADIR in [17,27]), where binding strength can be selected to be not too strong or weak according to the desired tuning on the observed binding lifetimes, as seen in the state durations of the observed state noise.
Linkage of ssDNA to antibody is commonly done in immuno-PCR preparations, so another path with rapid deployment is to make use of a linkage technology that is already commoditized, e.g., a good NTD signal can then be produced with immuno-PCR tagged antibodies that are designed to anneal to another DNA molecule to form an NTD 'Y-transducer'.

The explosive geographic expansion of the Zika virus provides another reminder that rapid diagnostic tools for new viral infections is an ever increasing need. The rapid deployment of a fast diagnostic tool in the example of the Zika virus is all the more pertinent given that the virus has been shown to be the cause of microcephaly in the fetuses of exposed pregnant women, along with results indicating possible brain damage (Guillain-Barre reaction) to a significant fraction of those exposed. A rapid development, deployment, and evaluation of a Zika virus diagnostic would afford the patient the critical time needed to undergo aggressive prophylactic measures. Similarly, certain fungal infections need to be diagnosed as early as possible (cryptococcus neoformans, for example, can disrupt and cross the blood-brain barrier). The treatments for many fungal infections are highly toxic, however, such that they will only be undertaken if infection is highly likely.

Pathogens that are suspected can potentially be probed in a matter of hours using an NTD platform with the methods described here using probes designed according to the pathogen's genomic profile. Unknown pathogens would first need to either have their genomes sequenced (less than a day) if sufficient DNA already available, or a sample directly measured via a test assay template (same procedure as for biomarker discovery) for assay-level fingerprint determination, then testing for that pathogen fingerprint in the patient.

The NTD platform can be enhanced to be a rapid annealing-based detection platform due a recently established ability to operate under high chaotropic conditions (up to 5M urea), which allows measurement of collective binding interactions such as nucleic acid annealing with other simpler binding and related complexes thereby eliminated and effectively filtered from the analysis task. What remains to be done is to establish a general production method for creating a NTD transducer for the sequence of interest, and this is described in Sec. 14.13.

14.10.5 SNP Detection
The proposed test of DNA SNP annealing is with the Y-shaped DNA transduction molecule shown in Fig. 14.26 ('B') that is minimally altered, and such that the SNP variant occurs in the Y-nexus region. For the case where digestion can't conveniently provide extension only to one-side, a Y-shaped annealed dsDNA molecule can still be obtained, but such that the ssDNA extensions outside the annealed region are now free to extend on both arms of the Y-molecule.

SNP variant detection is reduced to resolving the signals of two Y-shaped duplex DNA molecules, one with mismatch at SNP, one with Watson-Crick base-pairing match at SNP. In preliminary studies of Y-shaped DNA molecules, numerous Y-shaped DNA molecules were considered. Three variants that successfully demonstrated the easily discernible, modulatory, channel blockade signals are shown in Figs. 7.27 [17]. In those variants we considered the Y-nexus with and without an extra base (that is not base-paired). And if an extra base is inserted we explore the three positions at the Y (left and middle inserts shown in the left and center Y-molecules shown in Fig. 7.27.

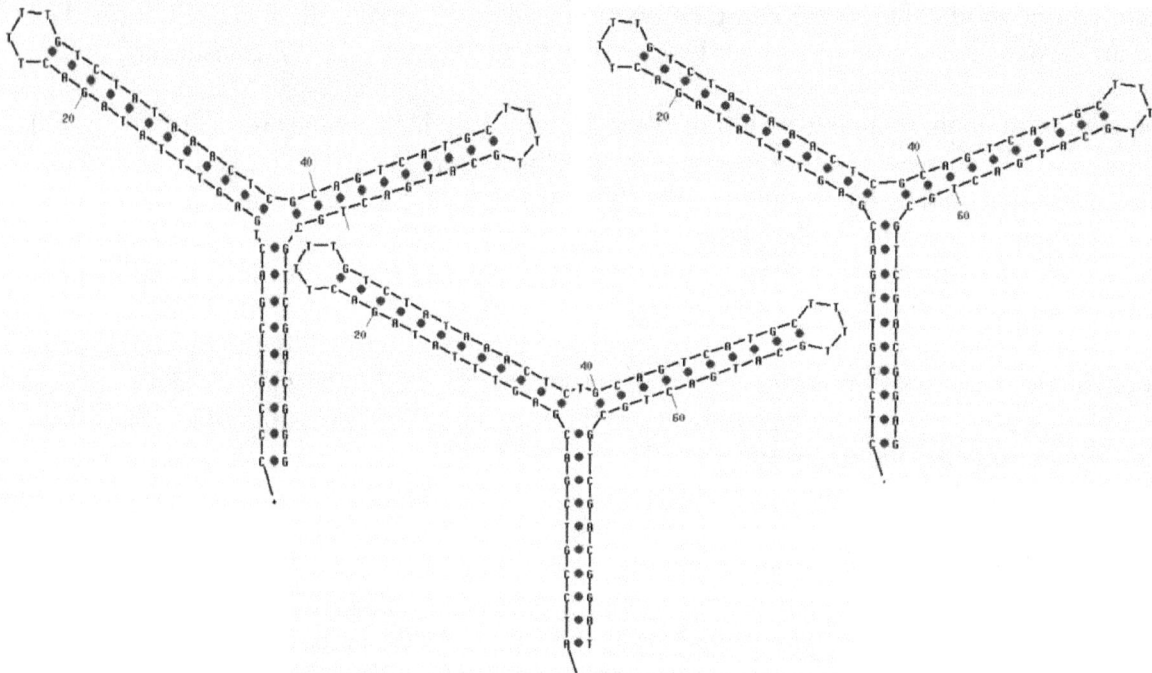

Fig. 7.27. Shown are Y-shaped aptamers that have shown they have capture states with the desired blockaded toggling.

The DNA molecule design we are currently using consists of a three-way DNA junction created: 5'-CTCCGTCGAC GAGTTTATAGAC TTTT GTCTATAAACTC GCAGTCATGC TTTT GCATGACTGC GTCGACGGAG-3'. Two of the junctions' arms terminate in a 4T-loop and the remaining arm, of length 10 base-pairs, is usually designed to be blunt ended (sometimes shorter with an overhang). The blunt ended arm has to be carefully designed such that when it is captured by the nanopore it produces a toggling blockade. One of the arms of the Y-shaped aptamer (Y-aptamer) has a TATA sequence, and is meant to be a binding target for TBP. In general, any transcription factor binding site could be studied (or verified) in this manner. Similarly, transcription factor could be verified by such constructions, or the efficacy of a synthetic transcription factor could be examined. The other Y-aptamer, used in the integrase binding analysis, is shown in Fig. 7.27 (both sequence and secondary structure).

A preliminary test of DNA SNP annealing can be done with the Y-shaped DNA transduction molecule shown in Fig. 7.28, which is minimally altered (e.g., mostly common sequence identity) from the Y-annealing transducer introduced in Fig. 7.27.

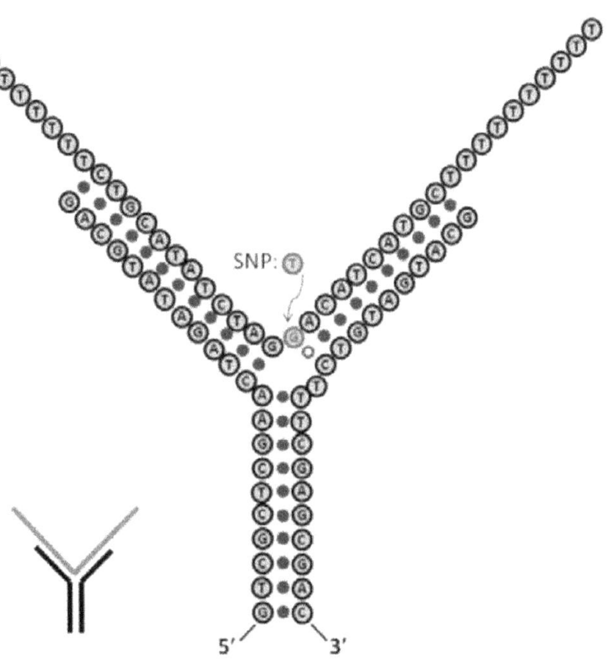

Fig. 7.28. The Y-SNP with test complex is shown at the base-level specification and at the diagrammatic level, where a SNP base is as indicated. If the SNP is its variant form (typically only one other base possibility is common), then a base-pairing will not occur at the nexus of the Y-SNP shown (with the red base becoming a 'T' in the variant as indicated). This allows discrimination between the annealed forms with high accuracy, while also discerning from the signals produced by the non-annealed Y-SNP, where there is no target-bound, or only non-specific molecular interactions imparting much less conformational structure as occurs with the matching (or mostly matching) annealing interaction.

Once the Y-SNP transducer has been tested on a single-species of short overhang length test molecules the next experimental challenge will be to detect SNP variants using the Y-SNP transducer probe in the presence of a heterogeneous length mixture (some with target SNP region of interest), with overhang as shown in Fig. 14.29.

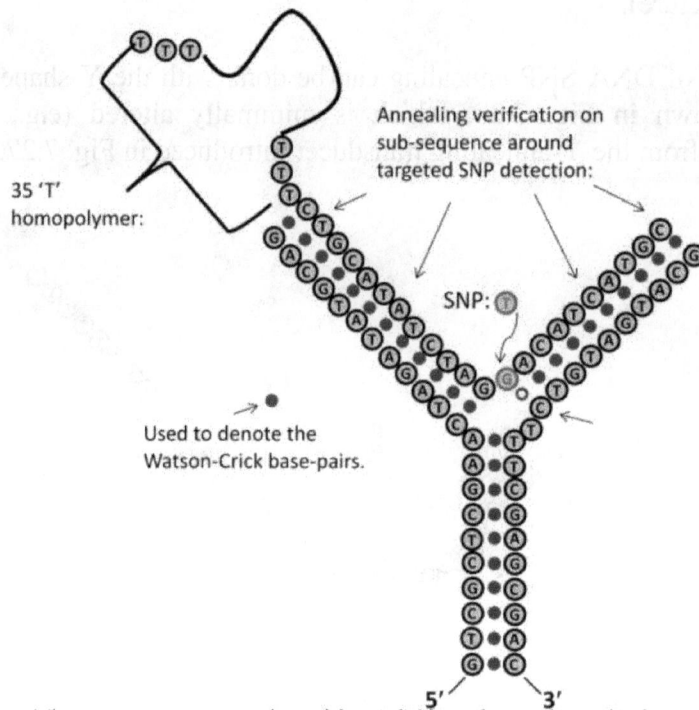

Fig. 14.29. The Y-SNP test complex with 35 dT length overhang is shown at the base-level specification, where a SNP base is as shown. If the SNP is its variant form (typically only one other base possibility is common), then a base-pairing will not occur at the nexus of the Y-SNP shown. This allows discrimination between the annealed forms with high accuracy, while also discerning from the signals produced by the non-annealed Y-SNP, where there is no target-bound, or only non-specific molecular interactions imparting much less conformational structure as occurs with the matching (or mostly matching) annealing interaction.

The value of 35 'T's on the extension is to also match the approximate extension, with same 'Y'-sequence (except for a 4 dT cap) as the previously 'blunt-ended' annealed conformation. SNP variant detection is reduced to resolving the signals of two Y-shaped duplex DNA molecules, one with mismatch at SNP, one with Watson-Crick base-pairing match at SNP. From the above it is clear that the NTD method provides a viable prospect for SNP variant detection to very high accuracy (possibly the accuracy with which the NTD can discern DNA control hairpins that only differ in terminal base-pair, greater than 99.999%). SNP detection via *translocation-based* methods, on the other hand, must discern between two SNP variants according to the different dwell times of the complement-template annealed SNPs, until dissociation from the template allows translocation of the blockading dsDNA annealed conformation.

14.10.6 Aptamer-based Detection

Aptamers are especially appropriate for study by nanopore detection due to the fact they can be designed with an end to be captured and modulate a nanopore (i.e., the captured end is dsDNA) while other parts of the aptamer are intended to bind a specific target. This directly provides a NTD transducer if one or both of the bound/unbound states (captured in the channel at the dsDNA end) provides distinctive channel modulations. The binding statistics derived from the study of aptamers in a nanopore detector can also be used in the design of the aptamer itself, e.g., NADIR selection instead of further SELEX-based selection [17]. In Fig. 14.30 we see the first aptamer test case to be considered, where we seek to detect thrombin [402] in one case, and IgG [401] in another. We use the thrombin aptamer found by Ikebukuro et al [402], it is selected via SELEX and EMA and is a 31-mer, linked by a 4 dT spacer to link to the Y-transducer (see Fig. 14.30).

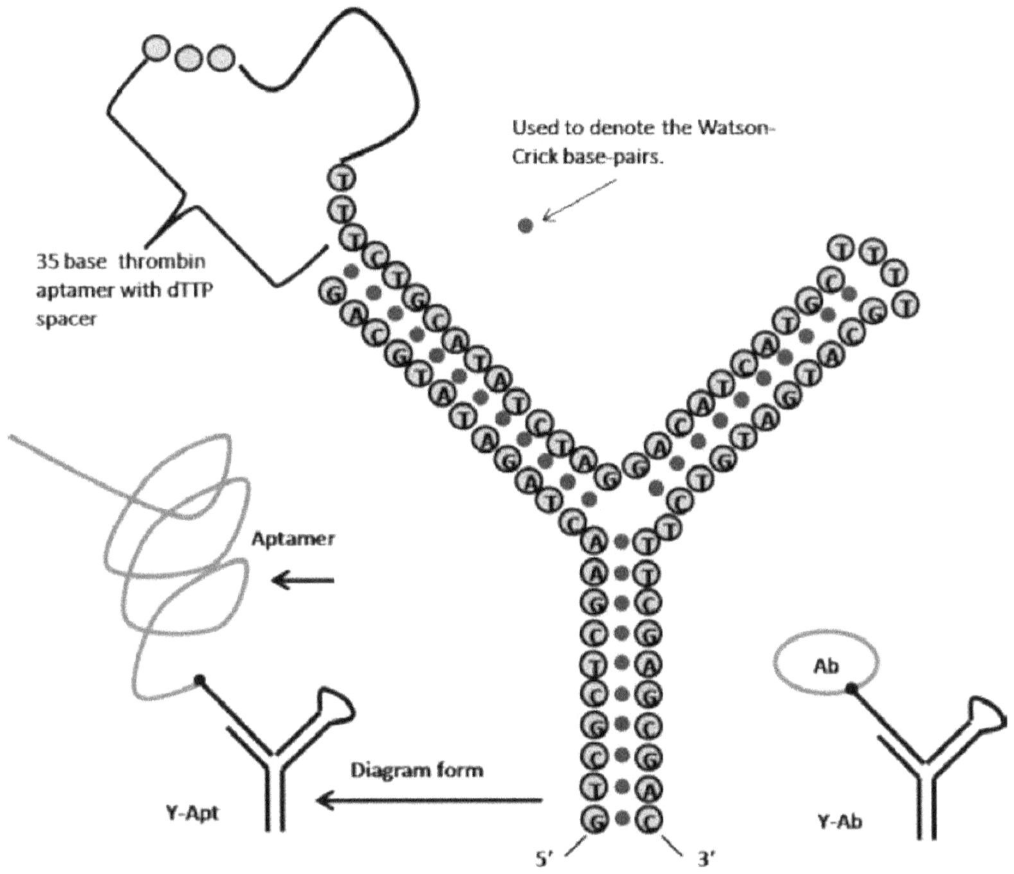

Fig. 14.30 The thrombin aptamer from [402] is 5'-CACTGGTAGGTTGGTGTGGTTGGGGCCAGTG-3'.

NaDir SELEX

In using the NADIR refinement process to arrive at the Y-transducer used in the DNA annealing test [17], we have demonstrated how *single-base insertions or modifications at the nexus of the Y-shaped molecule can have clearly discernible changes in channel-blockade signal*. Y-molecules as DNA probes with single point mutations discernible at the Y-nexus are explored in [17] (see Fig.s 14.27 and 14.31). What is described in [17] is a linkage to a *na*nopore-detector *dir*ected (NADIR) search for aptamers that is based on bound-state lifetime measurements (or some other selection criterion of interest). NADIR complements and augments SELEX in usage.

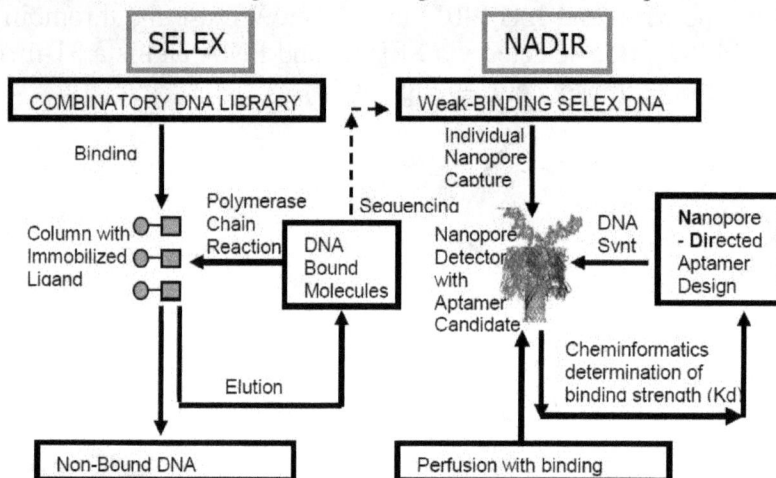

Fig. 14.31. The determination of aptamers can be done (or initiated) via Systematic Evolution of Ligands by Exponential Enrichment (SELEX), as shown schematically on the left. What is proposed here is a linkage to a *na*nopore-detector *dir*ected (NADIR) search for aptamers that is based on bound-state lifetime measurements. NADIR complements and augments SELEX in usage: SELEX can be used to obtain a functional aptamer, and NADIR used for directed modifications (for stronger binding affinity, for example).

14.10.7 Antibody-based Detection

Linkage of ssDNA to antibody is commonly done in immuno-PCR preparations, so another path with rapid deployment is to make use of a linkage technology that is already commoditized, e.g., the molecules required for the antibody-based biosensing with this approach are simple (non-specialty) molecular components. The core issue to be tested here is whether a good NTD signal can be produced with immuno-PCR tagged antibodies that are designed to anneal to another DNA molecule to form an NTD 'Y-transducer' (see Fig. 14.30, lower right). From previous efforts [30], with more complicated EDC linkages between a modified thymine and an antibody (see Fig. 14.34), it is clear that there are strong prospects for success with this method. What is sought is not just further validation of the method, however, but a less expensive, accessible, platform from which to refine and develop NTD-based systems.

Some mAb blockades produce a very clean toggling between two levels (see Fig. 14.38 for antibody description and some typical blockade signals). The mAb interference modulatory signals are easily discerned from a modulatory signal of interest, however, especially with increased observation time as needed. Aside from being an interference agent, antibodies offer a direct means for having a NTD transducer since their modulatory blockade signals are observed to change upon introduction of antigen. The problem with using an antibody directly as a transducer in a biosensor arrangement is that the antibody produces multiple blockade signal types (a dozen or more) just by itself (without binding). This weakness for use directly as a biosensor (they can still be linked indirectly as in [30]) is because the antibody is a glycoprotein that has numerous heterogeneous glycosylations and glycations, with many molecular side-groups that might be captured by the nanopore detector to produce modulatory blockades. If the purpose is to study the post-translational modifications (PTMs) themselves, a glyco-profile of the antibody in other words, then the numerous signal types seen are precisely the information desired. A more complete analysis of antibody blockades on the nanopore detector is beyond the scope of this paper, and will be in a separate paper. Some further details on the Antibody structure and its direct glyco-profiling is still given next, however, since similar PTMs can be analyzed on other proteins of critical biomedical interest.

Managing antibodies as easily identifiable interference or transducer

Antibodies are the secreted form of a B-cell receptor, where the difference between forms is in the C-terminus of the heavy chain region. Fig. 14.32 shows the standard antibody schematic. Standard notation is shown for the constant heavy chain sequence ('CH', 'H', and 'S' parts), variable heavy chain region ('VH' part), the variable light chain region ('VL' part), and constant light chain region ('CL' part). The equine IGHD gene for the constant portion of the heavy chain has exons corresponding with each of the sections CH1,H1,H2,CH2,CH3,CH4(S), and for the membrane-bound form of IGHD, there are two additional exons, M1 and M2 for the transmembrane part, thus, CH1, H1, H2, CH2, CH3, CH4(S), M1, M2 [329]. In Fig. 14.32, the long and short chains are symmetric from left to right, their glycosylations, however, are generally not symmetric. Critical di-sulfide bonds are shown connecting between chains, each of the VH and CH regions typically have an internal disulfide bond as well. The lower portion of the antibody is water soluble and can be crystallized (denoted Fc). The upper portion of the antibody is the antigen binding part (denoted Fab).

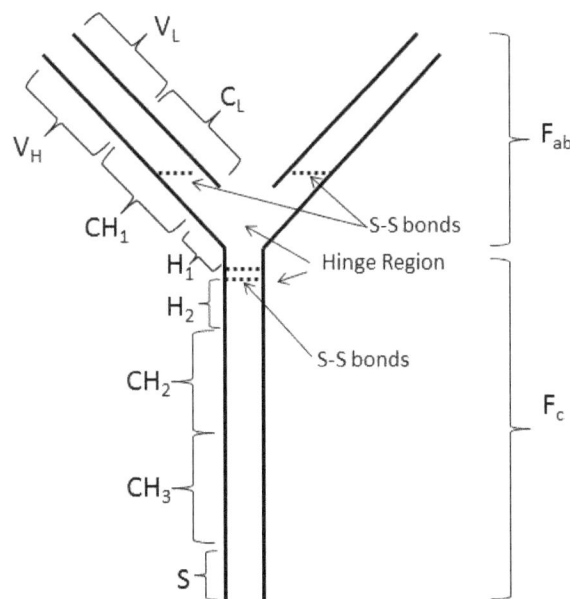

Fig. 14.32. The standard antibody schematic [329]. Standard notation is shown for the constant heavy chain sequence ('CH', 'H', and 'S' parts), vari-

able heavy chain region ('VH' part), the variable light chain region ('VL' part), and constant light chain region ('CL' part). The full heavy chain sequence is derived from recombination of the VH part and {CH,H,S} parts (where the secretory region S is also called CH4). The long and short chains are symmetric from left to right, their glycosylations, however, are generally not symmetric. Critical di-sulfide bonds are shown connecting between chains, each of the VH and CH regions typically have an internal disulfide bond as well. The lower portion of the antibody is water soluble and can be crystallized (denoted Fc). The upper portion of the antibody is the antigen binding part (denoted Fab).

Fig. 14.33 shows a typical antibody N-glycosylation (exact example for equine IGHD [25]). One possible N-glycosylation site is indicated in region CH2, and three possible N-glycosylation sites are indicated in region CH3. N-glycosylation consists of a covalent bond (glycosidic) between a biantennary N-glycan (in humans) and asparagine (amino acid 'N', thus N-glycan). The covalent glycosidic bond is enzymatically established in one of the most complex post translational modifications on protein in the cell's ER and Golgi organelles, and usually only occurs in regions with sequence "NX(S/T) – C-terminus" where X is 'anything but proline' and the sequence is oriented with the C-terminus as shown. Licensed therapeutic antibodies typically display 32 types of biantennary N-glycans 329], consisting of N-acetyl-glucosamine residues (GlcNAc, regions '1'); mannose residues (Man, regions '2'); galactose residues (Gal, regions '3'), and Sialic Acid Residues (NeuAc, regions '4'), as shown in Fig. 14.33. The N-glycans are classified according to their degree of sialylation and number of galactose residues: if disialylated (shown) have A2 class. If asymmetric and monosialylated have A1 class. If not sialylated then neutral (N class). If two galactose residues (shown) then G2 class, if one, then G1 class, if zero, then G0 class. If there is an extra GlcNAc residue bisecting between the two antennae +Bi class (–Bi shown). If a core fucose is present (location near GlcNAc at base), then +F (–F shown). So the class shown is G2-A2. The breakdown on the 32 types is as follows: 4 G2-A2; 8 G2-A1; 4 G1-A1; 4 G2-A0; 7 G1-A0; 4 G0-A0 [329]. The N-glycans with significant acidity (A2 and A1) are 16 of the 32, so roughly half of the N-glycans enhance acidity. The other main glycosylation, involving O-glycans, occurs at serine or threonine (S/T). The main non-enzymatic glycations occur spontaneously at lysines ('K') in proteins in the blood stream upon exposure to glucose via the reversible Maillard reaction to form a Schiff Base (cross-linking and further reactions, however, are irreversible and associated with the aging process).

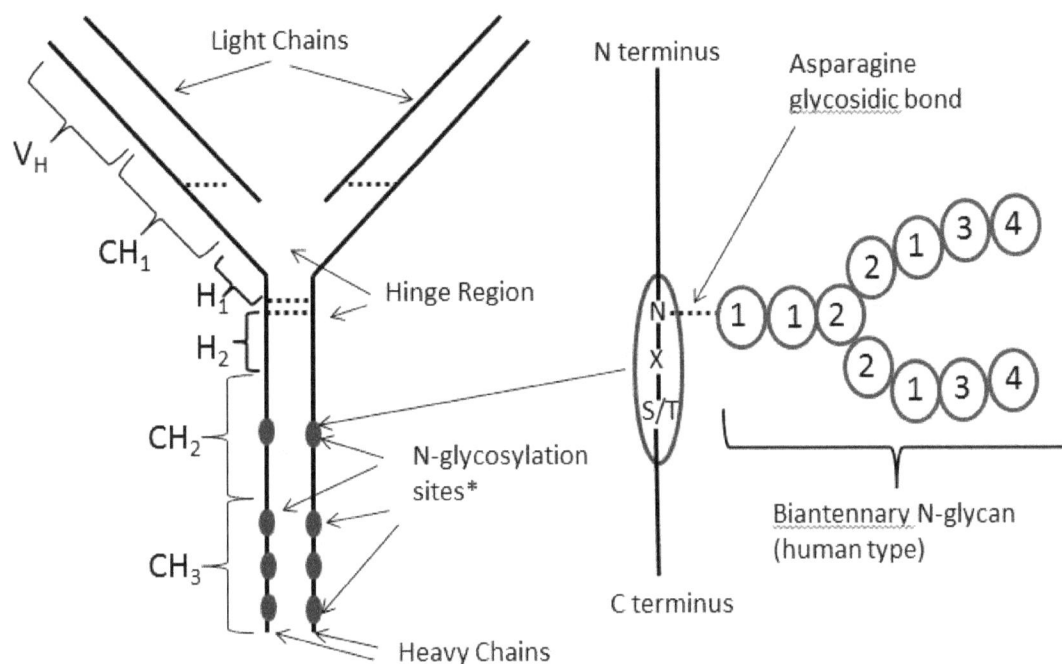

Fig. 14.33. Typical antibody N-glycosylation [329]. A schematic for typical antibody N-glycosylation is shown (drawn from results on the equine IGHD gene [329,330]), where one possible N-glycosylation site is indicated in region CH2, and three possible N-glycosylation sites are indicated in region CH3. N-glycosylation consists of a covalent bond (glycosidic) between a biantennary N-glycan (in humans) and asparagine (amino acid 'N', thus N-glycan). The covalent glycosidic bond is enzymatically established in one of the most complex post translational modifications on protein in the cell's ER and Golgi organelles, and usually only occurs in regions with sequence "NX(S/T) – C-terminus" where X is anything but proline and the sequence is oriented with the C-terminus as shown. Licensed therapeutic antibodies typically display 32 types of biantennary N-glycans, consisting of N-acetyl-glucosamine residues (GlcNAc, regions '1'); mannose residues (Man, regions '2'); galactose residues (Gal, regions '3'), and Sialic Acid Residues (NeuAc, regions '4'). The N-glycans are classified according to their degree of sialylation and number of galactose residues: if disialylated (shown) have A2 class. If asymmetric and monosialylated have A1 class. If not sialylated then neutral (N class). If two galactose residues (shown) then G2 class, if one, then G1 class, if zero, then G0 class. If there is an extra GlcNAc residue bisecting between the two antennae +Bi class (–Bi shown). If a core fucose is present (location near GlcNAc at base), then +F (–F shown). So the class shown is G2-A2. The breakdown on the 32 types is as follows: 4 G2-A2; 8 G2-A1; 4 G1-A1; 4 G2-A0; 7 G1-A0; 4 G0-A0. The N-glycans with significant acidity (A2 and A1) are 16 of the 32, so roughly half of the N-glycans enhance acidity. The other main glycosylation, involving O-glycans, occurs at serine or threonine (S/T). The main non-enzymatic glycations occur spontaneously at lysines ('K') in proteins in the blood stream upon exposure to glucose via the reversible Maillard reaction to form a Schiff Base (cross-linking and further reactions can be irreversible).

The base of the antibody plays the key role in modulating immune cell activity. The base is called the Fc region for 'fragment, crystallizable', which is the case, and to differentiate it from the Fab region for 'fragment, antigen-binding' that is found in each of the arms of the

Y-shaped antibody molecule (see Fig. 14.32). The Fc region triggers an appropriate immune response for a given antigen (bound by the Fab region). The Fab region gives the antibody its antigen specificity; the Fc region gives the antibody its class effect. IgG and IgA Fc regions can bind to receptors on neutrophils and macrophages to connect antigen with phagocyte, known as opsonization (opsonins attach antigens to phagocytes). This key detail may explain the modulatory antibody interaction with the nanopore channel. IgG, IgA, and IgM can also activate complement pathways whereby C3b and C4b can act as the desired opsonins. The C-termini and Fc glycosylations of an antibody's heavy chain, especially for IgG, is thus a highly selected construct that appears to be what is recognized by immune receptors, and is evidently what is recognized as distinct channel modulator signals in the case of the NTD. Using NTD we can co-opt the opsonization receptor-binding role of the Fc glycosylations (and mAB glycations and glycosylations in general), and C-terminus region, to be a channel modulating role. This may also permit a new manner of study of the critical opsonization role of certain classes of antibodies (and possibly differentiate the classes in more refined ways) by use of the nanopore detector platform. The channel may provide a means to directly measure and characterize antibody Fc glycosylations, a critical quality control needed in antibody therapeutics to have correct human-type glycosylation profiles in order to not (prematurely) evoke an immunogenic response.

14.10.7.1 Small target Antibody-based detection (linked modulator)

IgG antibodies may vary in net charge but are nowhere near as negatively charged as the DNA hairpin molecules examined in [27,30]. Differences in channel interaction are often attributed to its net charge and its electrophoretic mobility. To improve the antibody's affinity for the channel and to aid in signal classification, a complex of antibody and DNA hairpin is sometimes used. The result is the increase in channel affinity and a significant reduction in capture class configurations (see Fig. 14.34 for further details), while still retaining binding detection sensitivity. The *small*-antigen biosensing results (described here) complements those for *large*-antigen biosensing (presented in the next section). The large antigen study done here is also notable in that it involves direct use of the antibody as a bifunctional reporter molecule. This leads to complications with capture, and uniqueness in the orientation of that capture, but may offer a more sensitive detection approach since there is not a linkage separating the bound/unbound complex from the channel flow environment.

A DNA hairpin with EDC linkage to an antibody is shown in Fig. 14.34, and examined in [30]. When the DNA portion of this linked complex inserts itself into the alpha hemolysin channel it creates a definable toggle signal that serves as reliable "carrier signal" for monitoring any changes of molecular state (such as binding). In our first study of DNA-hairpin linked antibody complexes [30], we used an anti-biotin-antibody (Stressgen) as our binding element linked to our DNA hairpin. (Note, as one of many control tests, we see that the blockade toggle signal is relatively unchanged after addition of excess biotin.)

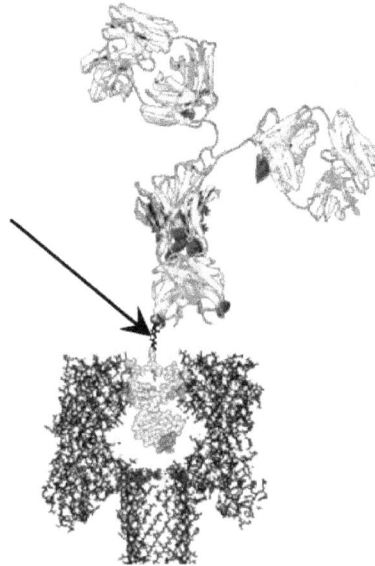

Fig. 14.34A. DNA hairpin bound to Antibody via an EDC-linker. Approximately shown to scale. Arrow points to the Internal Amino Thymine Modification with Primary Amine on a six carbon spacer arm. Primary amine can be crosslinked using 1-Ethyl-3-(3-dimethylaminopropyl) carbodiimide hydrochloride (EDC) to the peptide carboxyl terminus of the antibody heavy chain. This crosslinkage results in a covalent bond between the primary amine and the carboxyl.

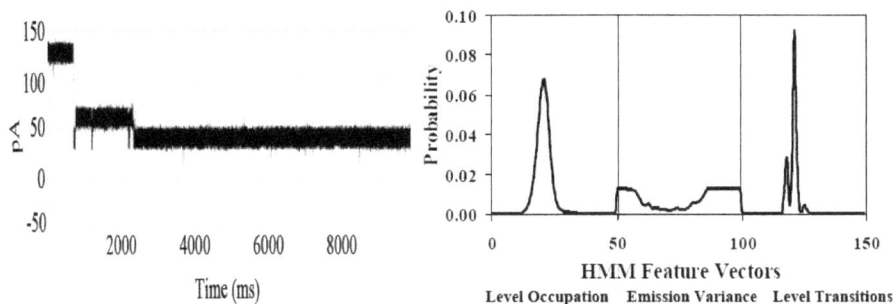

Fig. 14.34B. Antibody linked to DNA-Hairpin Blockade signal and HMM Profile. (See [30] for description of HMM profile.)

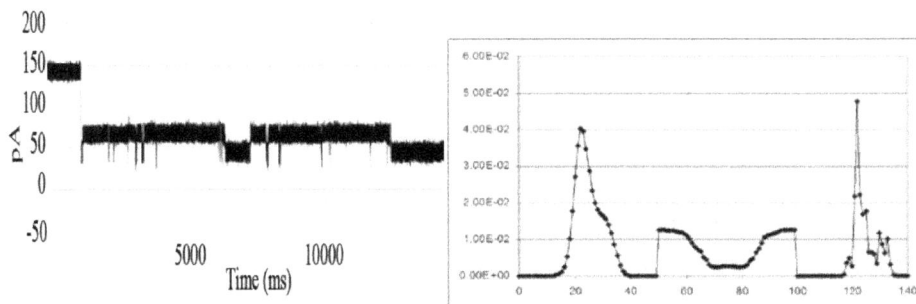

Fig. 14.34C. Antibody linked to DNA-Hairpin, now bound to its target antigen (biotin) – new blockade signal, and associated HMM profile. Antigen binding to an EDC-linked Antibody/DNA-Hairpin, where stem of the

449

hairpin is captured in the Nanopore Detector. (See [30] for description of HMM profile.)

The clarity of the current blockade signal for Ab-antigen binding and Ab-pore interaction was examined by varying the composition of working buffer in presence of urea and $MgCl_2$. In one series of experiments, mentioned above, we used free antibody molecule interacting with the nanopore detector, where the antibody (anti-biotin) molecule is introduced to our nanopore device to produce the characteristic two-state telegraph signal (Fig. 14.34). The blockade signal for the antigen is practically unaltered by excess antigen: even 100 fold excess of biotin does not change the blockade signal considerably (Fig. 14.35). The signal changes greatly in presence of urea, however, in a relatively small concentration. Here the duration of any event to occupy upper state level becomes shorter and the total probability value of upper level decreases with urea concentration rise.

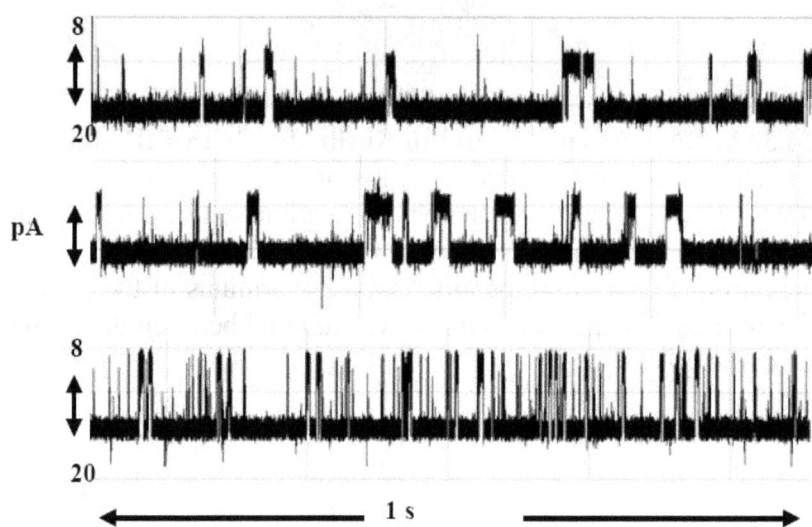

Fig. 14.35. DNA-hairpin signals. Top, No biotin concentration. Middle, low-to-high biotin concentration (1000-fold excess). Bottom. low urea concentration.

14.10.7.2 Large target Antibody-based detection

For large-antigen antigen-binding studies, different versions of copolymer (Y,E)-A—K ('large' targets) were originally prepared to allow study of the effect of antigenic mass and valency of binding upon the observations in [30]. In this and other studies involving direct antibody interactions with the channel, however, we found that antibodies themselves typically produce a variety of 'long-lived' blockades at the channel themselves, sometimes modulatory, even possibly producing clear 'toggle' signals as shown in the study cases in Fig. 14.36.

It is found that the antibody blockade signal alters shortly after introduction of antigen, as Fig. 14.37 shows upon addition of a moderately high concentration (100 μg/ml) of 200kD multivalent synthetic polypeptide (Y,E)-A—K. Presumably, these changes are the result of antibody binding to antigen. The time before the blockade signal is altered is also interesting; it ranges from seconds to minutes (not shown). This presumably is a reflection of antibody affinity.

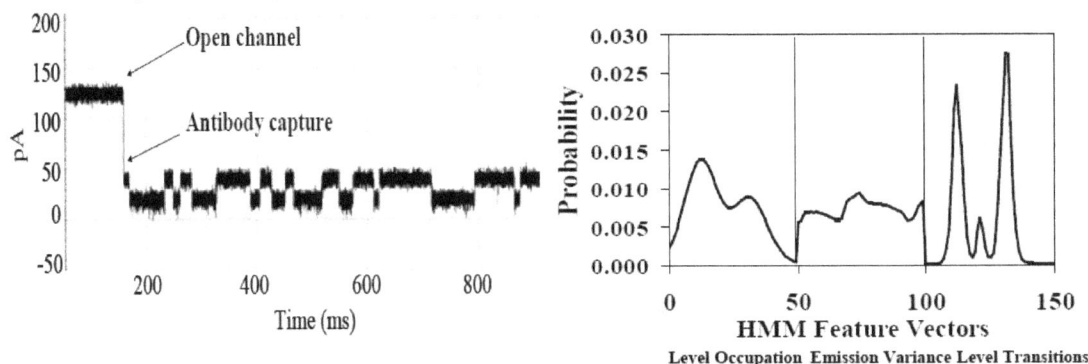

Fig. 14.36. Example that provides a very clear, stable, blockade direct by an Ab. Left: A toggle signal is generated as a channel-captured region of the molecule (IgG) wiggles above the limiting aperture of the alpha-hemolysin channel varying the ionic current between two transient states. **Right:** Antibody Toggle HMM Signal Profile. The 150 feature vectors obtained from the 50-state HMM-EM/Viterbi implementation in [1,30] are: the 50 dwell percentage in the different blockade levels (from the Viterbi trace-back states), the 50 variances of the emission probability distributions associated with the different states, and the 50 merged transition probabilities from the primary and secondary blockade occupation levels (fits to two-state dominant modulatory blockade signals).

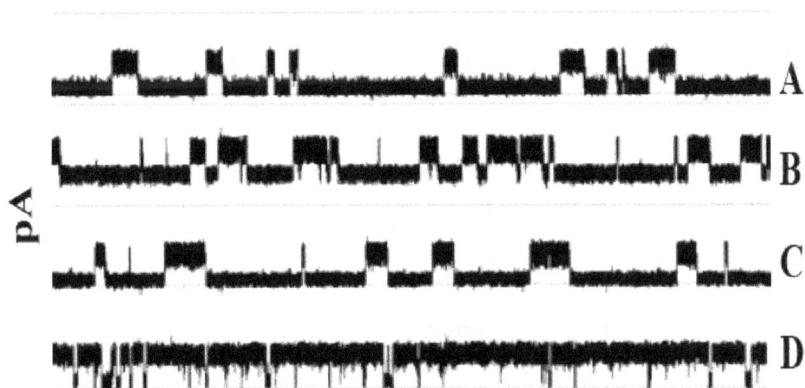

Fig. 14.37. Antibody-Antigen binding – clear example from specific capture orientation. Each trace shows the first 750 ms of a three minute recording, beginning with the blockade signal by an antibody molecule that has inserted (some portion) into the Alpha-hemolysin channel to produce a toggle signal (A). Antigen is introduced at the beginning of frame (A). Changes to the toggle signal are discernible in frame D, indicating the binding event between the antibody and antigen has taken place.

Direct antibody nanopore blockades are examined further in Fig. 14.38, Left, where the different capture signals provided by a single antibody species provide a 'nanopore epitope' mapping or assay of the antibody's surface features, including glycations and nitrosilations, as described in the following section. Typical captures seen after introduction of antigen are shown for the same system in Fig. 14.38, Right. Fig 14.39 shows a possible indication of a multivalent binding signal (the Ab being bivalent).

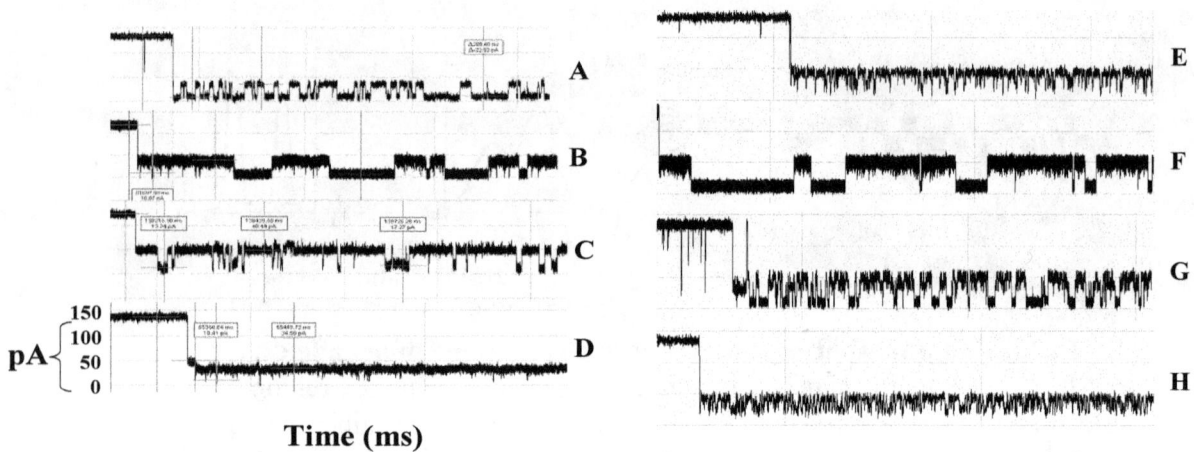

Fig. 14.38. Antibody Signal Classes and Ab-Antigen Signal Classes. A-D: various IgG region captures and their associated toggle signals (1 second traces). E-F: various IgG+Antigen region captures and their associated toggle signals (1 second traces). Each blockade signal was identified visually and represents a commonly observed signal class. Note the changes in dwell times for the upper and lower current levels in each signal class. We find a higher current level bias in the level occupancy as a result of binding with the antigen molecule.

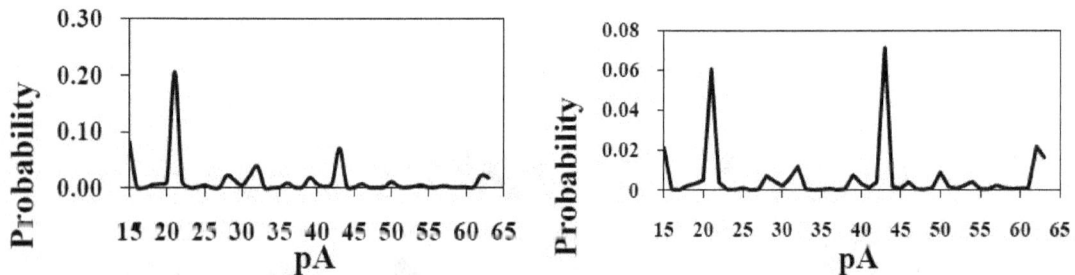

Fig. 14.39. Multivalent antigen binding. Left Panel: First Antibody Antigen Binding – 1st 50 feature components extracted from the HMM. **Right Panel:** Shifts in the values of these 1st 50 HMM feature components indicate a possible second Antibody Antigen Binding (same molecular capture). The first 50 components of the 150 feature vectors obtained from the 50-state HMM-EM/Viterbi implementation are the dwell percentages in the different blockade levels from the Viterbi trace-back states (approximately the Histogram in that range).

14.11 NTD Assaying Methods

A single bound/unbound system can be held, observed, and its history of bound/unbound states can be tracked. The *single* molecule state-tracking with lengthy time averages allows measurement of molecular characteristics that are obscured in ensemble-based measurements. The ensemble averages, that underlie most approaches, lose information about the true diversity of behavior of individual molecules. For complex biomolecules there is likely to be a tremendous diversity in behavior, and in many cases this diversity may be the basis for their function.

Molecular (protein) diversity via post-translational modifications can be examined as well, such as with heterogeneous mixtures of protein glycoforms that typically occur in living organisms (e.g., for TSH and hemoglobin proteins in blood serum and red blood cells, respectively). The hemoglobin 'A1c' glycoprotein is a disease diagnostic (diabetes) [1,13], and for TSH, glycation is critical component in the TSH-based regulation of the endocrine axis. Multi-component regulatory systems and their variations (often sources of disease) could also be studied much more directly using the NTD approach, as could multi-component (or multi-cofactor) enzyme systems. In what follows, NTD assaying applications will be described for enzyme studies and for nanopore-epitope sampling on complex proteins.

The NTD approach may provide an excellent method for examining enzymes, and other complex biomolecules, particularly their activity in the presence of different co-factors. There are two ways that these studies can be performed: (i) the enzyme is linked to the channel transducer, such that the enzyme's binding and conformational change activity may be directly observed and tracked or, (ii) the enzyme's substrate may be linked to the channel transducer and observation of enzyme activity on that substrate may then be examined. Case (i) provides a means to perform DNA sequencing if the enzyme is a nuclease, such as lambda exonuclease. Case (ii) provides a means to do screening, for example, against HIV integrase activity (for drug discovery on HIV integrase inhibitors).

An example of a transient interaction that has been examined involves interaction of HIV integrase with its consensus DNA binding terminus [27]. One use of the nanoscope is as drug-discovery assayer in settings where measurements are made of transient interactions, such as HIV transcriptase interactions with DNA in the presence of interference agents or competitive inhibition molecules (decoy aptamers, for example).

HIV integrase binding to viral-DNA appears to favor the high flexibility of a CA/TG dinucleotide positioned precisely two base-pairs from the blunt terminus of the duplex viral DNA (and experimentally verified with the nanoscope in the conformational analysis shown in [28]). The CA/TG dinucleotide presence is a universal characteristic of retroviral genomes. Deletion of these base pairs impedes the integration process and it is believed that the unusual flexibility imparted by this base-pair on the terminus geometry is necessary for the binding to integrase. Once bound to integrase the viral DNA molecule is modified by removal of the two residues at the 3'-end together with subsequent insertion into the host genome.

14.11.1 DNA enzyme analysis: Integrase
DNA termini are of critical importance for certain retroviral integrases and other biological processes – being able to study them, even comparatively, offers new avenues for understanding and drug selection (HIV integrase blockers). Information on the DNA molecules' variation in structure and flexibility is important to understanding the dynamically enhanced (naturally selected) DNA complex formations that are found with strong affinities to other, specific, DNA and protein molecules. An important example of this is the HIV attack on cells. The DNA terminus properties of retroviral DNA molecules are found to exhibit greater flexibility than similar sequences, often marked by an increase in the number of blockade states, such as in the upper-level fine structure for the molecule terminating with GACG-3' [35].

One of the most critical stages in HIV's attack is the binding between viral and human DNA. The DNA molecule studied in this instance consists of the HIV consensus terminus at the end of the Y-aptamer arm in Fig. 14.40 – where it is exposed for binding to integrase. Since this molecule presents another blunt-ended dsDNA for capture, it is no surprise that such events occur. The signal analysis must separate between two classes of signal associated with these two dominant forms of capture -- associated with capture of the two blunt-ended DNA regions (at the base of the Y and at the end of the integrase-binding arm). With appropriate capture of the molecule at the base of the Y, this permits direct examination of protein binding to the terminal DNA region.

The NTD approach may provide the best means for examining other enzymes, and other complex biomolecules, particularly their activity in the presence of different co-factors. There are two ways that these studies can be performed: (i) the enzyme is linked to the channel transducer, such that the enzyme's binding and conformational change activity may be directly observed and tracked or, (ii) the enzyme's substrate may be linked to the channel transducer and observation of enzyme activity on that substrate may then be examined. Case (i) provides a means to perform DNA sequencing if the enzyme is a nuclease, such as lambda exonuclease. Case (ii) provides a means to do screening, for example, against HIV integrase activity (for drug discovery on HIV integrase inhibitors).

A variation of the Y-aptamer used previously is used to observe interaction events between that terminus and HIV DNA integrase. Preliminary binding observations are shown in Fig. 14.40. More detailed signal profiles are shown in Fig. 14.41 (Left), where the three most common signal classes are shown for the HIV Y-aptamer (left side), with right side images zoomed in to a time-scale more than 100 times shorter. Similarly, a more detailed figure is shown in Fig. 14.41 (Right), where the a signal class is shown that is not seen when HIV Y-aptamer is introduced without addition of integrase. In that figure, a possible binding event might be shown at the change in signal pattern from fixed level that ends in the yellow box, (with actual end transition shown in the pink box).

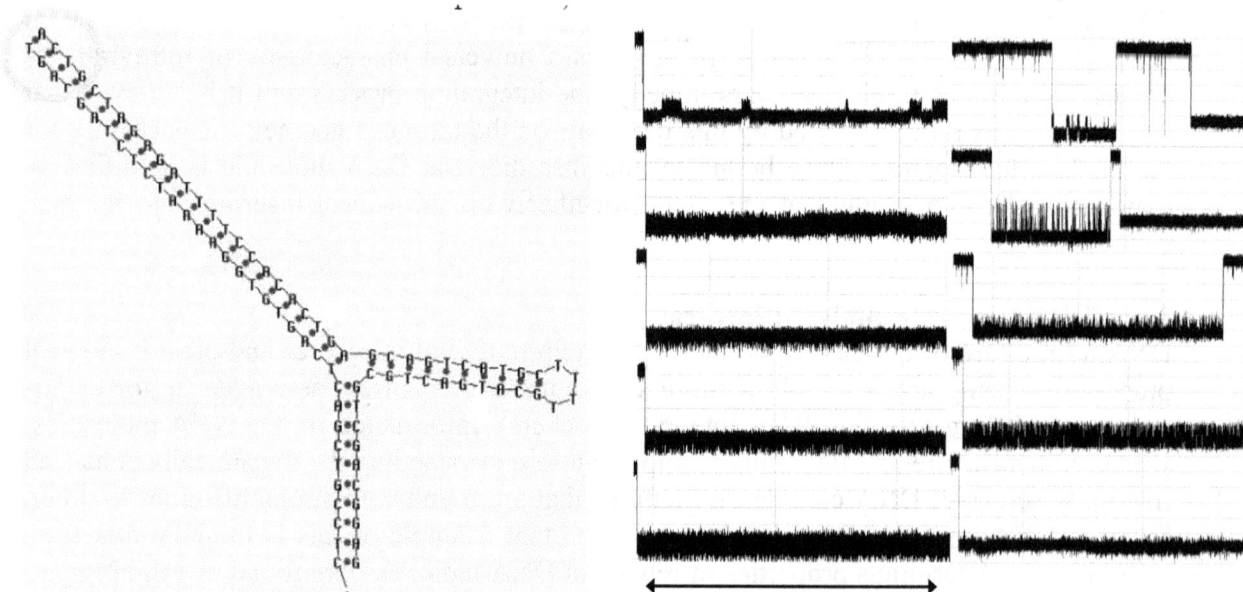

Fig. 14.40. Left: the mfold secondary structure map of the Y-aptamer used in the integrase binding study. Integrase will bind to the blunt-ended arm shown

454

in the yellow circle, where the HIV DNA Terminus consensus sequence has been place. **Right:** Blockade signals produced before (left) and after (right) introduction and possible binding of HIV Integrase to the HIV-corresponding terminus of one arm of a channel-captured y-shaped aptamer. The time elapsed during each frame is approximately three seconds.

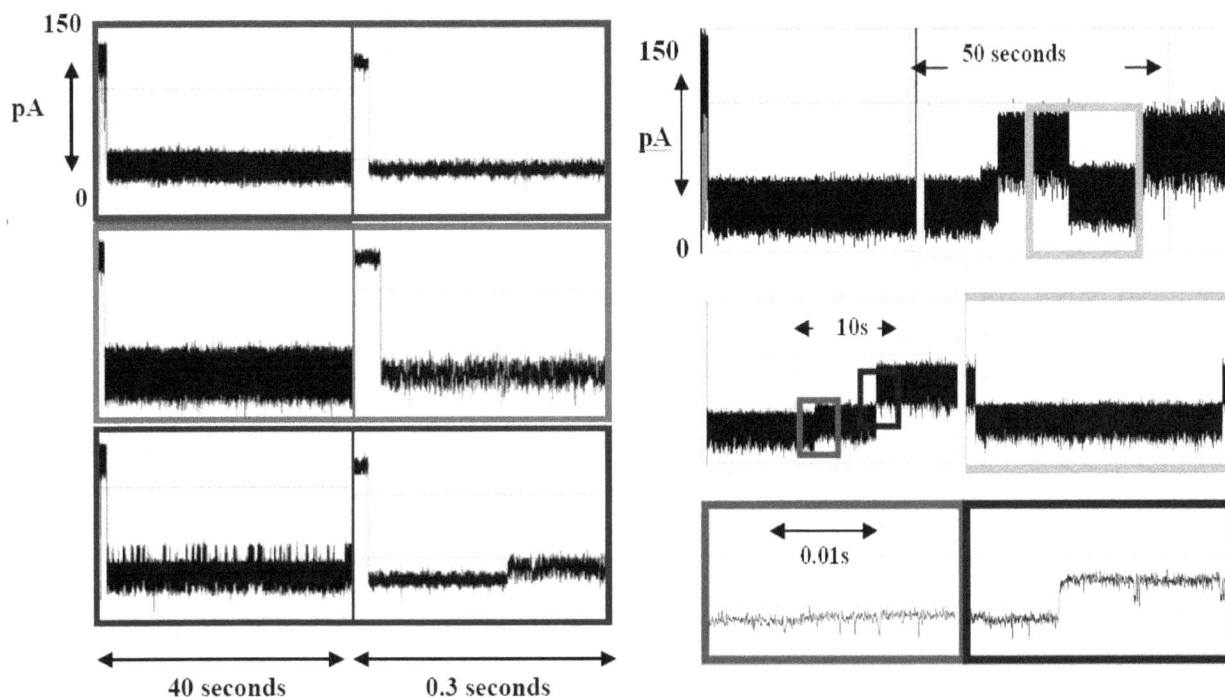

Fig. 14.41 (Left). Three most common signal classes for HIV Y-aptamer. Right and left boxes are identical signals shown at two different time scales. **(Right).** New type of HIV Y-aptamer Blockade Signal only seen after introduction of HIV Integrase to detector (with the Y-aptamer already present). Possible binding event observed at the change in signal pattern from fixed level that ends in the yellow box, (with actual end transition shown in the pink box).

14.11.2. Single-molecule serial assaying
14.11.2.1 DNA-Protein complex Assaying: Aptamer-TBP

Upon addition of the alpha-hemolysin monomers to the *cis*-well, according to the standard nanopore protocol, the toxin oligomerizes to form a water-filled transmembrane channel in the phospholipid bilayer. Next, the TY10T1-GC aptamer was applied through refluxing to this environment and began to engage the alpha-hemolysin channel. Upon capture of a single TY10T1-GC aptamer at the channel there is an immediate and overall current reduction. Thereafter, the steady flow of ions through the channel was alternately blockaded at levels corresponding to approximately 40% and 60% of baseline, hypothesized to correspond with the binding/unbinding of the aptamer's blunt-ended terminus to the surrounding vestibule walls. These fluctuations in ionic current were measured and recorded as a blockade pattern. The two-level dominant blockade signal is shown in Fig. 14.42 for T-Y10T1-GC.

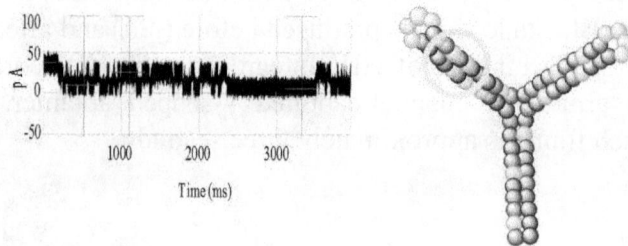

Fig. 14.42. The TY10T1-GC NTD-aptamer, with signal sample.

In an attempt to demonstrate the nanopore detector's capacity for describing the transcription factor/transcription factor binding site interaction, we examined the TBP/TATA box complex following the nanopore protocol. TBP, a subunit of transcription factor TFIID, was selected for its broad commercial availability and nominal price. TFIID is the first protein to bind to DNA during the formation of the pre-initiation transcription complex of RNA polymerase II (RNA Pol II). The TATA box, located in the promoter region of most eukaryotic genes, assists in directing RNA Pol II to the transcription initiation site downstream on DNA. For our transduction molecular system, the TATA box is located on a 4dT-loop terminating arm of our Y-aptamer, which was prepared in the lab by annealing to two DNA hairpin molecules. The base stem of our bifunctional Y-aptamer is designed to target and bind the area around the limiting aperture of the alpha-hemolysin channel, while the arm containing the TATA box binds the TBP.

We find that some of the blockade signals are only seen after introduction of TBP, which is hypothesized to be the sought after indication of TBP/TATA Box complex formation. The automated signal analysis profiles for T-Y10T1-GC w/wo TBP are shown in Fig. 14.43. The experiment is also repeated (not shown), with the receptor arm elongated several base pairs for more distal receptor placement from the channel environment, in order to ensure accommodation for the TATA binding protein (TBP), with similar indication of binding in our experiments.

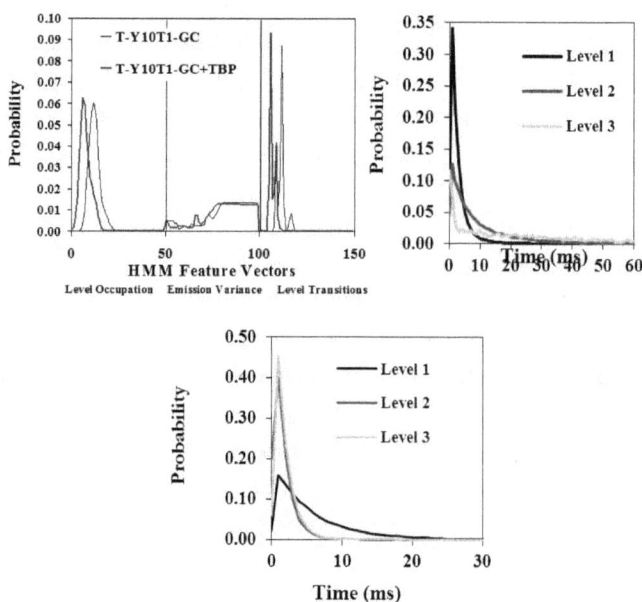

Fig. 14.43. Left. Standard 150-component HMM-based feature extraction for collections of T-Y10T1-GC blockade signals, w/wo TBP. After the EM itera-

456

tions, 150 parameters are extracted from the HMM. The 150 feature vectors obtained from the 50-state HMM-EM/Viterbi implementation in [29] are: the 50 dwell percentage in the different blockade levels (from the Viterbi trace-back states), the 50 variances of the emission probability distributions associated with the different states, and the 50 merged transition probabilities from the primary and secondary blockade occupation levels (fits to two-state dominant modulatory blockade signals). **Right.** Dwell Time at Each Level for T-Y10T1-GC (see Fig. 14.43 to visually identify the three levels – with two dominating). **Bottom Center.** Dwell Time at Each Level for T-Y10T1-GC + TBP (sample signal blockade not shown).

When TBP binds to the TATA box, it creates a nearly ninety degree bend in the DNA. This strong conformational change allows for strand separation. This is possible since the binding region of DNA is rich with the weaker two-hydrogen bond interactions of adenine and thymine. Once the strand separation occurs, RNA Pol II gains entry and begins transcription of the gene. The conformational deformity precipitated by the binding of TBP to DNA may be largely responsible for the alteration of the blockade signal originating after the introduction of TBP. Further results are sought in this area to explore the ability to observe conformational changes.

14.11.2.2   Glycoprotein assayer

NTD can operate as an HbA1c glycoform assayer (see next section for initial observations involving antibodies) to improve the knowledge of hemoglobin biochemistry (and that of heterogeneous, transient, glycoproteins in general). This could have significant medical relevance as a gap exists between what is known about hemoglobin biochemistry and how HbA1c information is used in the management of diabetic patients. The definition of 'HbA1c' is complex as HbA1c is a heterogeneous mixture of non-enzymatically modified hemoglobin molecules (whose concentration in blood is in part genetically determined). In clinical applications, HbA1c is used as if it were single complex with glucose whose concentration is solely influenced by glucose concentration. It may be possible, using an NTD platform, to improve diabetes management by introducing a new assaying capability to directly close the gap between the basic and clinical knowledge of HbA1c. It may be possible, perhaps optimal, to apply NTD in direct nanopore detector-to-target assays in combination with indirect NTD-to-target assays, for purposes of characterizing post-translational protein modifications (glycations, glycosylations, nitrosilations, etc.), see Fig. 14.44.

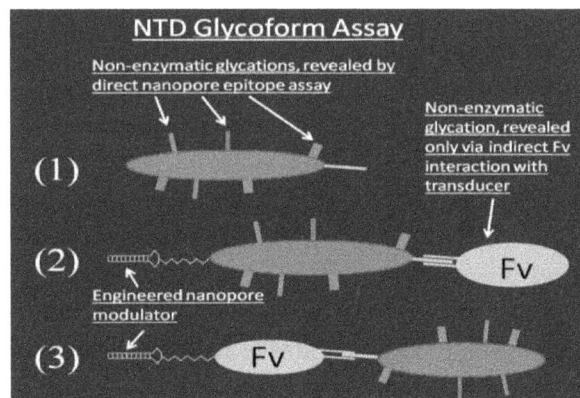

Fig. 14.44. NTD-based glycoform assays. Three NTD Glycoform assays are shown. Assay method (1) shows a protein with its post-translational modifica-

tions in orange (e.g., non-enzymatics glycations, glycosylizations, advanced glycation end products, and other modifications). Assay method (2) shows a protein of interest linked to a channel modulator. Direct channel interactions (blockades) with the protein modifications are still possible in this instance, but are expected to be dominated by the preferential capture of the more greatly charged modulator capture. Changes in that modulator signal upon antibody Fv interactions with targeted surface features provide an indirect measure of those surface feature. Assay method (3) shows an antibody Fv that is linked to modulator, where, again, a binding event is engineered to be transduced into a change of modulator signal.

The endocrine axis, thyroid stimulating hormone (TSH) in particular, is regulated via a heterogenous mixture of TSH molecules with different amounts of glycation (and other modifications). The extent of TSH glycation is a critical regulatory feedback mechanism. Tracking the heterogenous populations of critical proteins is critical to furthering our understanding and diagnostic capabilities for a vast number of diseases. Hemoglobin molecules provide a specific, on-the-market, example -- here extensive glycation is more often associated with disease, where the A1c hemoglobin glycation test is typically what is performed in many over-the-counter blood monitors. The NTD testing of surface features of the protein can be done before or after digestion or other modification of the test molecule as a means to further improve signal contrast on the identity and number of possible protein modifications, as well as other surface features.

Part of the complexity of glycoforms, and other modifications, of proteins such as hemoglobin and TSH, is that these glycoforms are present as a heterogeneous mixture, and it is the relative populations of the different glycoforms that may relate to clinical diagnosis or identification of disease (such as prion exposure [403]). To this end, a protein's heterogeneous mixture of glycations and other modified forms can be directly observed with a NT-detector, and this constitutes the clinically relevant data of interest, not simply the concentration of some particular glycoform. Furthermore, it is the transient, dynamic, changes of the glycoform profile that is often the data of interest, such that a 'real-time' profile of glycoform populations may be of clinical relevance, and obtaining such real-time profiling of modified forms (glycoforms, etc.) would be another area of natural advantage for the NTD approach.

The protein modification assays have indirect relevance for public health and biodefense. This is because the degree of glycation of a patients hemoglobin is an early indication of their disease state (if any, or simply 'glycation' age otherwise). This is because the *hemoglobin that is actively used in transporting oxygen throughout the body is analogous to a 'canary- in-the-coalmine' in that it provides an early warning about insipient complications or past chemical or nerve agent exposures.* Red blood cells (that carry hemoglobin) typically live for 120 days – providing a 120-day window into past exposures and a 120-day average on the regulatory load induced by those exposures. In the future, if a mysterious gulf-war syndrome is encountered, and there is concern about a low-level exposure to a nerve agent, examining the hemoglobin glycation profiles, and similar profiles on other blood serum constituents, would provide a rapid (30 min.) assessment of biodefense status.

NTD detection and assaying provides a new technology for characterization of transient complexes, with a critical dependence on 'real-time' cyberinfrastrucure that is integrated into the nanopore detection method using machine learning methods for pattern recognition and their implementation on a distributed network of computers for real-time experimental feedback and sampling control.

Thyroid stimulating hormone (TSH) is present as a heterogeneous mixture of TSH molecules with different amounts of glycation (and other modifications). The extent of TSH glycation is a critical regulatory feedback mechanism. Tracking the heterogeneous populations of regulatory proteins is required to further our understanding and diagnostic capabilities for a vast number of diseases. Hemoglobin molecules are an example where specific, on-the-market, glycation diagnostics are in use -- here extensive glycation is often associated with disease, where the A1c hemoglobin glycation test is typically what is performed in many over-the-counter blood monitors.

A nanopore-based glycoform assay could be performed on modified forms of the proteins of interest, i.e., not just native, but deglycosylated, active-site 'capped', and other forms of the protein of interest, to enable a careful functional mapping of all surface modifications. Pursuant to this, the methodology could also be re-applied with digests of the protein of interest, to further isolate the locations of post-translational modifications when used in conjunction with other biochemistry methods.

Part of the complexity of glycoforms, and other modifications, of proteins such as hemoglobin and TSH, is that these glycoforms are present as a heterogeneous mixture, and it is the relative populations of the different glycoforms that may relate to clinical diagnosis or identification of disease. To this end, a protein's heterogeneous mixture of glycations and other modified forms could be directly observed with the NTD Nanoscope setup, allowing direct access to the clinically relevant data of interest, not simply the concentration of one glycoform. Furthermore, it is the *transient*, dynamic, changes of the glycoform profile that is often the data of interest, such that a 'real-time' profile of TSH glycoform populations are of clinical relevance, and obtaining such real-time profiling of modified forms (glycoforms, etc.) in physiological buffer conditions is an area of natural advantage for the NTD approach.

In conjunction with protein digests and HPLC, nanopore detection of glycation may provide a powerful new means to assay the post-translational modifications present for a given protein (in whole or via its digests), including their changing molecular complexations. This has profound significance for the understanding and treatment of a variety of diseases, including diabetes, where post-translational modifications to hemoglobin are an important biomarker for disease diagnosis and treatment.

14.11.2.3 Antibody Assayer: A new window into understanding antibody function
Upon binding to antigen, a series of events are initiated by the interaction of the antibody carboxy-terminal region with serum proteins and cellular receptors. Biological effects resulting from the carboxy-terminal interactions include activation of the complement cascade, binding of immune complexes by carboxy-terminal receptors on various cells, and the induction of inflammation. Nanopore Detection provides a new way to study the binding/conformational histories of individual antibodies. Many critical questions regarding antibody function are still unresolved, questions that can be approached in a new way with the nanopore detector. The different antibody binding strengths to target antigen, for example, can be ranked according to the observed lifetimes of their bound states. Questions of great interest include: are allosteric changes transmitted through the molecule upon antigen

binding? Can effector function activation be observed and used to accelerate drug discovery efforts?

Thus, real-time analysis of antibody IgG binding affinity might be possible using a nanopore detector to better understand antibody-antigen binding affinities and the conformational changes that initiate signal pathways. Although some surface features clearly elicit blockade signals that are modulatory, not all surface features of interest will exhibit blockade signals when drawn to the channel and in these instances antibody or aptamer based targeting of those features could be used, where the antibody or aptamer is linked to a channel modulator that then reports on the presence of the targeted surface feature indirectly, e.g., the NT-biosensing setup.

A nanopore-based glycoform assay could be performed on modified forms of the proteins of interest, i.e., not just native, but deglycosylated, active-site 'capped', and other forms of the protein of interest, to enable a careful functional mapping of all surface modifications. Pursuant to this, the methodology could also be re-applied with digests of the protein of interest, to further isolate the locations of post-translational modifications when used in conjunction with other biochemistry methods.

14.12 NTD Signal Stabilization and Interference Handling

Operation of an alpha-hemolysin nanopore transduction detector is found to be surprisingly robust over a critical range of pH (6-9), including physiological pH=7.4 and PCR pH=8.4, and extreme chaotrope concentration, including 5M urea. The engineered transducer molecule that is captured in the standard alpha-hemolysin nanopore detector, to transform it into a transduction detector, appears to play a central role in this stabilization process by stabilizing the channel against gating during its capture. This enables the nanopore transduction detector to operate as a single molecule 'nanoscope' in a wide range of conditions, where tracking on molecular state is possible in a variety of different environmental conditions. In the case of streptavidin biosensing, results are shown for detector operation when in the presence of extreme (5M) urea concentration. Complications involving degenerate states are encountered at higher chaotrope concentrations, but since the degeneracy is only of order two, this is easily absorbed into the classification task as in prior work. This allows useful detector operation over a wide range of conditions relevant to biochemistry, biomedical engineering, and biotechnology.

Results are shown for nanopore transduction detection based on biotin-streptavidin interactions (very strong), and antibody-antigen interactions. Extensive results are shown to validate the NTD Nanoscope results using standard methods from isoelectric focusing (IEF) gels and capillary electrophoresis (CE). Further results for the Streptavidin-Biotin biosensor are shown confirming the NTD Nanoscope binding of Bt-8gc to streptavidin in urea with concentrations up to 5M, where IEF Gel and CE validation results are found to be in agreement. Results on antibody binding are also provided, along with validation results, building off preliminary work. The validation results show antibody binding with biotin as antigen in urea concentrations up to 2M, with validation by IEF Gels.

14.12.1. Biotin-Streptavidin Binding Experiments
14.12.1.1. The BT-8gc transducer viability in urea up to 5M concentrations
In some instances, chaotropes (such as urea) are used to weaken the binding affinity, or DNA-DNA annealing affinity, of molecules studied with the nanoscope, such that binding

tests can be performed with numerous on/off transitions in the lifetime of the experiment. In the case of DNA-DNA annealing, the collective binding that occurs can remain sufficiently strong in the presence of chaotrope such that it provides a clear contrast with non-collective binding interactions and can greatly improve signal quality. For this reason, and others, understanding the response of the channel and transducers in the presence of chaotropes is useful. The NTD approach will benefit most where the transducers provide little change, or have just a few states, when in channel blockade with change in chaotrope concentration. From high voltage capture strain prior studies it was found that the Bt-8gc blockades exhibit two different capture blockade signals. This is hypothesized to be due to two states of the transducer itself, probably due to two accessible loop 'twists' conformations, one not normally accessible without capture-strain. Two transducer states that are degenerate (being simply due to hypothesized racemization on molecules with different loop conformations) is a manageable complication with the automated pattern recognition, but clearly reveals how at the single DNA-hairpin level of resolution we can see changes in molecular conformation (and terminus regions, as shown previously). Thus, a racemization over capture states with two loop "twists" was hypothesized to occur upon introduction of chaotropic agents (urea 2.0 M – 5.0 M), and this result is confirmed in Fig. 14.45. (A crude schematic for the twists is envisaged, from a top-down view of the hairpin loop, to look like the yin-yang symbol boundary that bows in to the left at the top, then to the right at the bottom, and the reverse for the other twist conformation.)

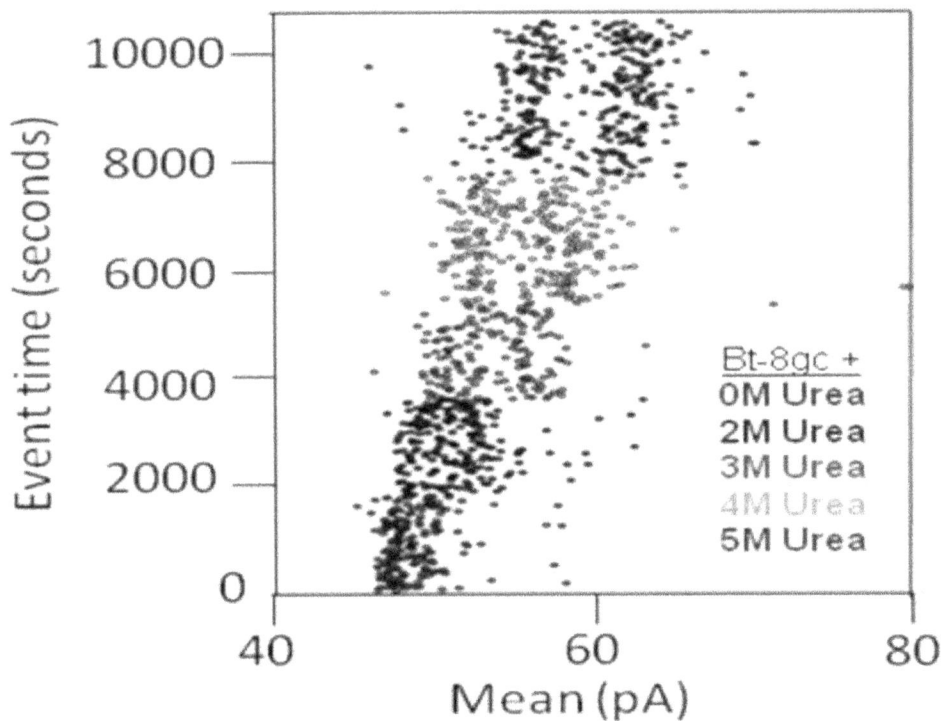

Figure 14.45. Sufficiently strong Urea concentration (5M) results in racemization of the two loop capture-variants, while weaker urea (<2M) does not. The results show Bt-8gc measurements at 30 minute intervals (1800 s on vertical axis) with urea concentration 0, 2, and 3M, 45 minutes at 4M, and 60 minutes at 5 M, with signal blockade mean on the x-axis, with results consistent with the two-state loop hypothesis, and consistent with the observation of such not due to zero or weak urea content but due to high strain due to mass and charge effects upon binding to the large streptavidin molecule.

The α-hemolysin channel demonstrates a high tolerance to high salt concentration and the presence of chaotropic agents, which is important to establish a platform for the study of binding between other molecules under such conditions. By varying the composition of running buffer it is possible to control the interaction of analyzed molecules with the nanopore or with each other. In what follows, tests are shown of the impact on binding affinity between streptavidin, or mAb, and biotin upon introduction of chaotropic agents. This demonstrates new capabilites in nanopore detector applications.

14.12.1.2. Observations of Biotin-Streptavidin Binding on the NTD Nanoscope

Preliminary results on streptavidin biosensing were shown for urea concentration up to 3.5M. The resolution of the bound/unbound Bt-8gc is greater than 99.99% accurate in less than 100 ms, with greater accuracy if longer observation time is used. The analysis uses the signal processing pipeline described in Sec. X on channel current cheminformatics where a 150-component feature extraction is done on each blockade signal. Using just two 'human-friendly' features based on each signal's maximum and minimum blockade values in that 100 ms observation window, a surprisingly clear separation of the molecular classes is easily discerned, as well as the role of urea in weakening interactions where bound states are reduced in observation frequency and unbound states increased. Initially, at 0M urea, two clusters are easily discerned by eye. One corresponds to the Bt-8gc blockades, the other corresponds to the (Streptavidin) – (Bt-8gc) complex. Upon introduction of urea, signals for Bt-8gc unbound start to shift the Bt-8gc cluster, where direct quantification of the cluster results is directly accessible from the cheminformatics analysis.

14.12.1.3. Bt-8gc -- Streptavidin Binding validation using IEF Gels w/wo chaotropes

Complex formation between the biotinylated DNA hairpin (Bt-8gc) and streptavidin is shown on the NTD Nanoscope -- this result is validated via electrophoretic mobility shift analysis with isoelectric focusing in Fig. 14.46. The standard gel analysis can't resolve presence of different isoforms in a single 'band' of gel, but Nanopore augmentation of gel electrophoretic methods, may offer a means to resolve components within the bands.

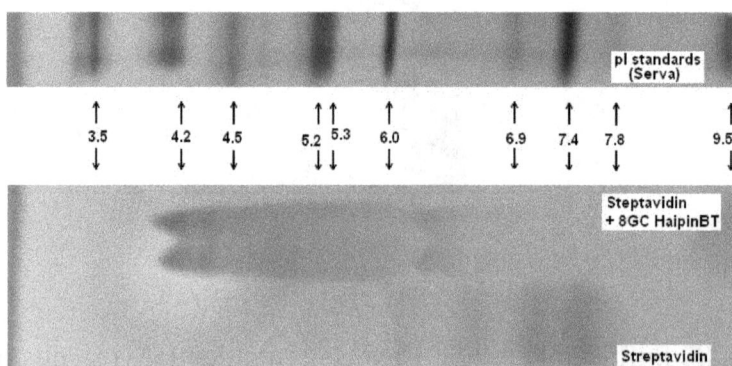

Figure 14.46. Biotinylated DNA hairpin (Bt-8gc) and streptavidin complex verification.

Electrophoretic methods provide a means to study the process of complex formation. Depending on the affinity (thermodynamic constant value) and the kinetics of the reaction, different electrophoretic techniques can be used. For highly stable complexes, the isoelectric focusing technique can be applied [14]. This electrophoresis technique has the advantage of extremely high resolution that allows maximally complete detection of existing heterogeneity in complex population, due to both multi-valent interaction and initial heterogeneity of interacting species.

In Fig. 14.47 we show the gel IEF results describing the interaction of streptavidin and biotinylated hairpins. Due to very strong interaction between the streptavidin and biotin the complex is extremely stable: it does not break apart for hours and IEF detects practically no presence of free streptavidin. In Fig. 14.47 the IEF spectra of streptavidin and streptavidin incubated with an excess of the biotinylated hairpins Bt-8gc and Bt-9gc, are shown. For the streptavidin, the two major components are visible (with their pIs at 7.1 and 7.5, approximately). After targeting with hairpin those streptavidin isoforms convert to two new bands (pI 4.2 and pI 4.35). We hypothesize that there exists a one to one correspondence between the two above pairs of major components (before and after the complexation takes place). According to our theoretical calculation such a high pI shift can be achieved when all four binding sites of the streptavidin molecule are targeted. Here we used the technique allowing for predicting the electric charge vs. pH relationship for a protein molecule based on the amino acid composition, or more generally, any biopolymer with known content of so-called ionogenic groups. The approach has limitations connected with the dissociation scheme selected for the model and the exact values of the dissociation, but typically serves as a reasonably good approximation for isoelectric point calculation or protein titration curve behavior. The latter are often used as tool for optimizing various electrophoretic of chromatographic separations of intact or labelled proteins (with covalent or non-covalent interaction). With an excess of hapten, heterogeneity does not become more pronounced (although, by shorter incubation time or deficit or hairpin, some reaction products are detectable in the middle acidic range – pH 5-6.5).

One should expect that during the electrophoretic experiment, the reacting mixture becomes quickly divided to single components, so the complex is subjected to decay. The decay above, still, occurs rather slowly, as it may be seen from the Fig 14.47. When the interaction is not as strong, the IEF method may not detect the complex formation. In particular, we did not detect any product that may correspond to a complex for anti-GFP Mab and its binding partner, GFP (data not shown).

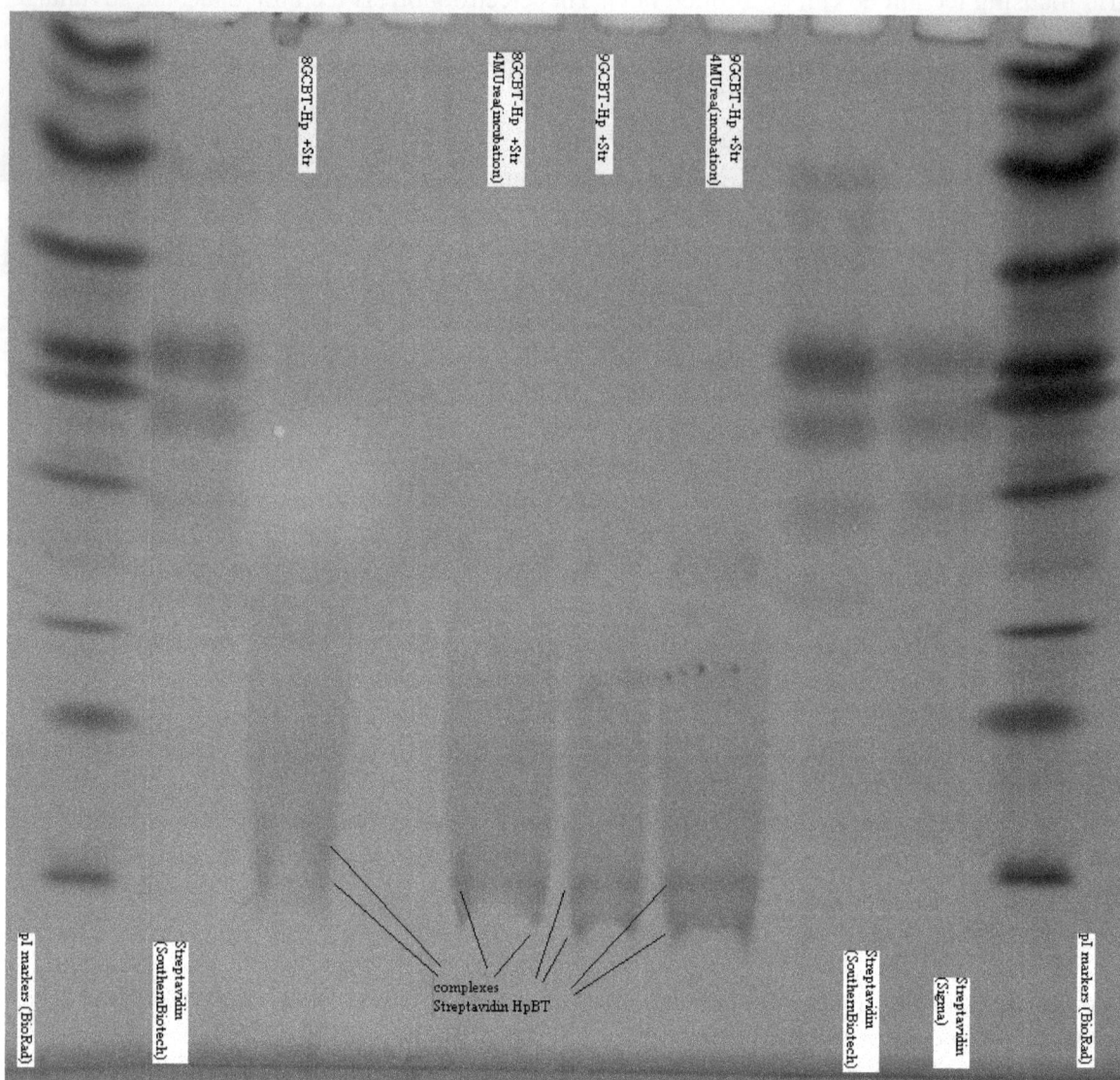

Figure 14.47. Complexes examined for streptavidin and biotinylated hairpins (Bt-8gc and Bt-9gc). Isoelectric focusing 3-10 pH range is implemented using a vertical system. Incubation time was 40min. Urea concentration in the sample buffer was 4M (with no urea in the gel). Outer lanes: pI markers (BioRad). Inner lanes from left: (1) Streptavidin (Southern biotech); (2) Biotinylated 8GC hairpin + Streptavidin; (3) Biotinylated 8GC hairpin + Streptavidin + 4M urea incubation; (4) Biotinylated 9GC hairpin + Streptavidin; (5) Biotinylated 9GC hairpin + Streptavidin + 4M urea incubation; (6) Streptavidin (Southern biotech); (7) Streptavidin (Sigma). The notation at the bottom of inner lanes (2)-(5) marks the complexes of streptavidin and the biotinylated DNA hairpins. (The well pronounced pI –shift of the protein-hairpin complex is due to the presence of strong acidic moiety of DNA.)

14.12.1.4. Bt-8gc -- Streptavidin Binding using CE w/wo chaotropes

We also used capillary electrophoresis (CE), as an alternative to IEF gel electrophoresis, since the CE processing time is much shorter, on the order of minutes. CE may be employed for analysis of fast chemical reactions (fast decay, etc.). Similar to chromatographic separation, capillary electrophoresis provides an opportunity to determine reaction kinetics although the accuracy of these calculations is not very high. The CE technique also has certain advantages due to its suitability for study of complex formation at different pH and in presence of additives modulating the interaction (salt ions and other charged compounds). Results of CE experiments on (streptavidin)--(biotinylated hairpin) complexation have been obtained. The experiments aim to confirm complex formation, and its relative concentration decrease, under chaotropic conditions. Complex formation (streptavidin-Bt-8gc) is clearly exhibited as new peak appearance on electropherogram when the mixture of streptavidin and DNA is analyzed. It becomes possible to separate the same components, previously detected by gel IEF.

The standard sample introduction scheme for two interactions substances is performed as a test: Streptavidin plug is introduced first (hydrodynamically), followed by the DNA plug. The two substances moving in the opposite directions interact very briefly, but sufficient to see side effects of complex formation. The complex has lower mobility and it is eluted second, after unbound DNA. The part of streptavidin which did not react with biotinylated DNA continues its moving towards anode and thus does not pass though the detector. In capillary electrophoresis of streptavidin/biotinylated hairpin (Bt-8gc) complex using sequential injection (Fig. 14.48), a streptavidin sample plug is pressure introduced first, following by the second one of DNA. The DNA plug passes though the protein (streptavidin) and the interaction time is 2sec. By reducing the sample load and varying the DNA/protein ratio it was possible to separate two streptavidin-DNA complexes. (The more acidic complex pI=4.3approx. is eluted first). The existence of two major isoforms for complex is in accordance with our previous results on gel IEF. (Injection time/pressure from the bottom to the top: 5s/0.5psi(prot)-0.5psa(DNA); 5s/0.5psi(prot)-0.3psa(DNA); 5s/0.2psi(prot)-0.1psa(DNA). Run at 250Kv/cm.

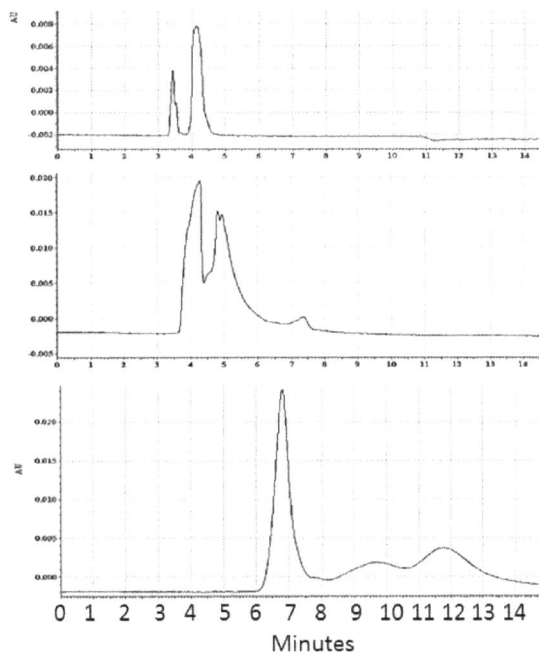

Figure 14.48. Capillary electrophoresis of equilibrium mixture, streptavidin/biotinylated hairpin (Bt-8gc) in presence of urea. Urea concentration increase suppresses the complex formation. Upper panel: 2.5M urea running

465

buffer. Sample – equilibrium mixture, no urea. Middle panel: 2.5M urea running buffer. Sample – equilibrium mixture, 4M urea. Left and right peaks on the two upper panels represent DNA and streptavidin-DNA complex, accordingly. The concentration of complex decreases with chaotrope concentration. In the case of 8M urea concentration (lower panel) no complex formation is observed. The markings on the x-axes are in minutes.

By adding urea in the running buffer, even in the absence of urea in the sample buffer, one changes the electropherograms, beginning with indications of population shift, i.e., different proportion between the complex and unbound hairpin. Further increase in urea concentration decreases the ratio between the complex and free Bt-8gc (here the concentration of urea in running buffer does not have a significant impact). Finally, very high urea concentration results in essential changes: the streptavidin is apparently mostly in its denatured form, although some capability of binding biotin still remains. Urea concentration increase influences the elution time. Several different effects act simultaneously, in particular, dielectric constant and viscosity change. In addition, there is a possibility of electroosmotic flow modulation. The most pronounced effect, apparently, is the conformation changes induced by urea; this explains considerable reduction in migration times both for denatured protein and DNA.

14.13 Nanopore Transducer Engineering and Design
14.13.1 Transduction channel-modulator capability via laser modulation
Biomolecules are in size-ranges that are well-sized for interaction with the alpha-hemolysin based nanopore detector. Duplex DNA can't translocate the channel, for example, being captured at one end instead, but ssDNA can translocate. It is discussed in [45] that the end of the DNA molecule can be read for nine base-pair DNA molecules with very high accuracy based on the telegraph-like modulatory signals directly elicited during their channel interactions. DNA hairpins with lengths greater than roughly twelve base-pairs no longer elicit channel modulations, residing at a fixed-level blockade. If the high accuracy of the DNA terminus read can be extended to DNA hairpins at longer lengths, then highly efficient Sanger-style DNA sequencing might be possible on the Nanopore platform. In [1,36], a 20 base-pair hairpin with a magnetic bead attachment was studied with this in mind. The 20 base-pair hairpin (bphp) with magnetic bead produced a fixed level blockade that was similar to the blockade of the 20 bphp with no bead attachment (see Fig. 14.49 – another version of Fig. 14.19 information placed here for convenience). In the presence of appropriate laser modulations with a chopped beam, channel blockade modulations resulted (Fig. 14.49 Right Panel). It was found that the modulatory signals were distinctive in this 're-awakened' configuration. Regarded in a different sense, the captured 20 bphp provides a terminus-dependent transform on the injected laser modulation that allows the terminus to be identified as in the 9bphp analysis, presumably with similar high accuracy given sufficient observation time. Thus Sanger sequencing on the NTD platform appears possible with use of laser modulations (but without dyes). Perhaps what's more interesting, however, is simply that a molecule producing a fixed level blockade upon capture was successfully induced into a unique telegraph-like blockade signal by use of laser modulations.

Biomolecules in general, such as DNA, RNA, protein, and glycoprotein, typically provide channel blockades at a fixed level. If their blockades can be induced into telegraph-like signals via introduction of laser modulations, then the critical modulatory signal aspect of the transducer can be made ubiquitous, allowing close inspection of any molecule, via its states, when interacting with the nanopore.

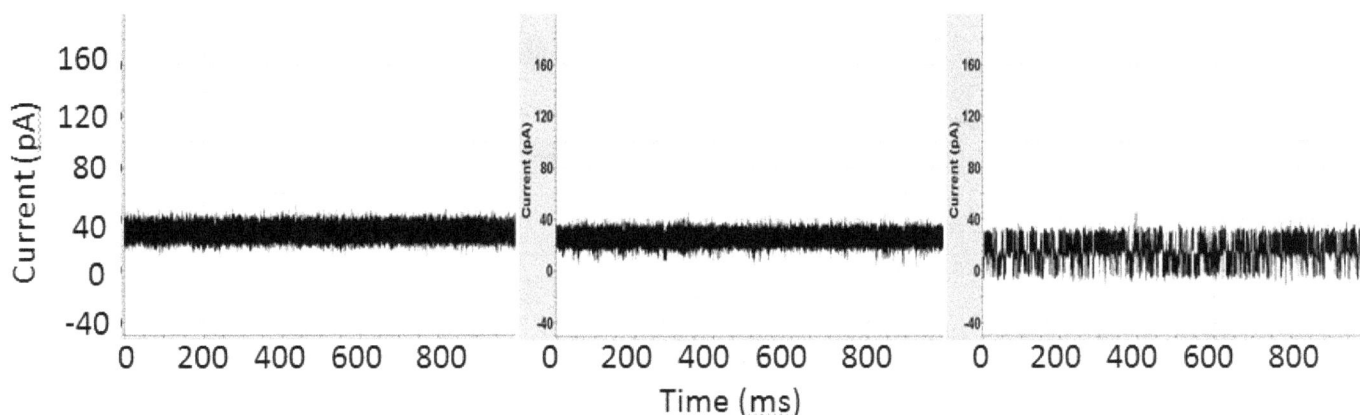

Figure 14.49. A (Left) Channel current blockade signal where the blockade is produced by 9GC DNA hairpin with 20 bp stem [36]. (Center) Channel current blockade signal where the blockade is produced by 9GC 20 bp stem with magnetic bead attached. (Right) Channel current blockade signal where the blockade is produced by c9GC 20 bp stem with magnetic bead attached and driven by a laser beam chopped at 4 Hz. Each graph shows the level of current in picoamps over time in milliseconds.

14.13.2 NTD Transducer Design

The *bound* state of the transducer/reporter molecule is sometimes found to not transduce to a different toggling ionic current flow blockade, but to a fixed-level blockade (i.e., the transducer provides distinctive channel modulation when unbound, but not so distinctive fixed-level channel blockades when bound). It is important for *both* the bound and unbound transducers to have distinctive channel modulations in order to have automated high-precision state identification and tracking (and allow for multiplex assaying). In this instance, the switch to a fixed-level blockade was thought to be an effect of the large electrophoretically held complex forcing the channel-captured end to reside in one blockade state. This was previously explored in experiments where a streptavidin-coated magnetic bead was attached to biotinylated DNA hairpins known to be good modulators or poor channel modulators. Once a streptavidin coated magnetic bead was attached to the biotinylated hairpins, it was found that gently pulsing the nanopore channel environment with a chopped laser beam (a laser-tweezer tugging) allowed a distinctive channel modulation to result (see Fig. 14.49). It was found more recently that the induced blockade modulations occur in two types (described in detail in [14] for chaotrope induced; and in [36], for early laser-tweezer induced results. Further laser tweezer results showing the different, overlapping, modes will be given in Sec. X, where the experiments are performed with a DNA-hairpin transducer as in previous studies. In terms of the convenient Y-transducer, however, the same could be done by simply making use of the unused arm, as shown in Fig. 14.50 (further discussion in [9]).

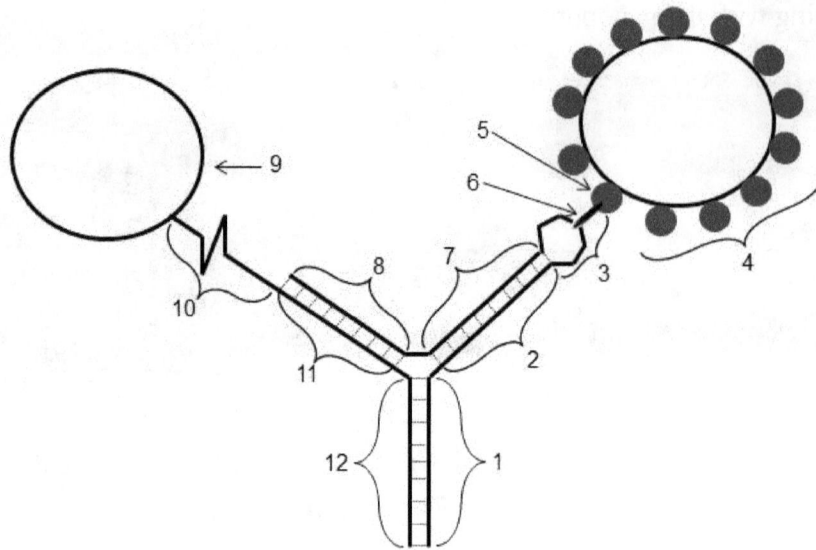

Figure 14.50. Y-laser transducer for high-specificity binding detection or individual protein binding & conformational change study [9]. The Y-transducer is meant to have a study molecule, region 9, attached by a single stranded nucleic acid linker, region 10, that is possibly abasic (non-base-pairing), that is linked to a single stranded nucleic acid region, region 11 & 12, that is meant to anneal to a second nucleic acid to create the Y-shaped nucleic acid construct shown.

In Fig. 14.50 the annealed Y-transducer is comprised of two, possibly LNA/RNA/DNA chimeric, nucleic acids, where the first single stranded nucleic acid is indicated by regions 1-3 and 7-8 and the second nucleic acid is indicated by regions 10-12. The paired regions {1,12}, {2,7}, and {8,11} are meant to be complements of one another (with standard Watson-Crick base-pairing), and designed such that the annealed Y-transducer molecule is meant to be dominated by one folding conformation (as shown). Region 3 is a biotin-modified thymidine loop, typically 4-5 dT in size (here 5dT shown with 2 dT, a biotinylated dT, then another 2 dTs), that is designed to be too large for entry and capture in the alpha-hemolysin channel, such that the annealed Y-transducer only has one orientation of capture in the nanopore detector (without bead, region 4, attached). Region 4 is a streptavidin coated magnetic bead (that is susceptible to laser-tweezer impulses). The base region, comprising regions {1,9}, is designed to form a duplex nucleic acid that produces a toggling blockade when captured in a nanopore detector. The typical length of the base-paired regions is usually 8, 9 or 10 base-pairs. The study molecule (region 9), an antibody for example, has linkage to single stranded nucleic acid via a commoditized process due to the immuno-PCR industry so is an inexpensive well-established manufacturing approach for the molecular construction. The Y-transducer on the left will not form if the 'immuno-PCR tagged' antibody is not present, which provides an additional level of event detection validation. If region 9 is a DNA enzyme that is processively acting on a DNA substrate this may provide a new means for nucleic acid sequencing.

NTD transducers are typically constructed by covalently linking a binding moiety of interest to a nanopore current modulator, where the modulator is designed to be electrophoretically drawn to the channel and partly captured, with its captured end distinctively modulating the flow of ions through the channel. Using inexpensive (commoditized) biomolecular components, such as DNA hairpins, this allows for a very versatile platform for biosensing, and given the high specificity high affinity binding possible, this also allows a very versatile platform for assaying at the single molecule level, even down to the single isoform level, e.g., molecular substructure profiling, such as glycosylation profiling. (Glycosylation profiling can also be done directly for some molecules that directly produce toggling blockades, antibodies in particular. Glycosylation profiling is of critical importance in the development of the most effective antibody treatments.) Two complications with the transducer design, however, are (1) the convenient DNA-based modulators are often short-lived; and (2) the overall transducer's bound state often doesn't modulate. The first is shown to be solved using locked nucleic acid (LNA) nucleosides, the second is solved by introducing a third functionality for receiving laser-tweezer impulses by means of a covalently attached magnetic bead (another commoditized component). A description of the detector's robust performance in the presence of numerous interference agents with very low analyte concentration was also needed, and this is now much more clearly affirmed. LNA Y-transducers with magnetic bead attachment and laser pulsing gives rise to a generic modulator arrangement (see Fig. 14.50), that modulates even when bound, to allow NTD probing over long timescales on biological system components. An inexpensive commoditized pathway for constructing nanopore transducers is thereby obtained.

Two problems with the NTD approach are, thus, revealed in the Bt-8gc transducer study: (1) the aforementioned fixed-level blockade by the *bound* transducer; and (2) isomer splitting on the transducer itself under high strain conditions (such as high chaotrope). In the next section we show how to eliminate both of these problems using transducer designs.

Transducer instability: short lifetime and isomer splitting under strain
Two twist conformations, due to different configurations in the hairpin loop and stem duplex conformation (such as B, B*, or A/B conformation duplex DNA), have been suspected from results on the DNA hairpins under other strain conditions, such as high voltage settings [1]. Thus, it is consistent that two types of DNA hairpin channel blockade modes appear in the laser-tweezer experiments. The two modes are thought to be rigid-body configuration changing, or 'toggling', and internal DNA hairpin configuration changing, or 'twisting'. Although the resulting toggle/twist mode signal analysis is more complicated when working with channel modulators, especially if induced by laser-tweezer, this is actually a highly favorable result since additional modulatory modes beyond the physically associated toggling and twisting are not seen. A bound transducer can now generically provide a modulatory state by use of a bead attachment with laser excitation, with high-strain modal proliferation apparently limited to two types, which is a very manageable situation given sufficient observation time. Thus, the stochastic carrier wave analysis [1] can proceed as before, only with more training data needed to 'learn' the more complicated background 'carrier wave' signal's characteristics. The transducer problem, thus, remains tractable with laser-tweezer generalized (ubiquitous) transducer design. Furthermore, there is the ability to turn the twist mode type of internal signaling to our advantage in specialized transducer designs.

The problem with the DNA transducers with short lifetimes (in the electrophoretically-driven capture strain environment), and the internal mode transmission (excessive twist mode) transducers, is they have too much internal freedom. If it was possible to 'lock-up' some of the internal twist motion, then a stronger hairpin might result, and one less likely to have twist modulations on top of toggle modulations. Such nucleic acid variants exist and are known as locked nucleic acid nucleosides (LNAs). They are a nucleic acid analogue where the ribose ring is locked into a highly favorable configuration for Watson-Crick base-pairing. The locking is accomplished by forming a methylene bridge from the 2'-O atom to the 4'-C atom of the ribose ring. LNA oligonucleotides can be synthesized using standard phosphoamidite chemistry (e.g., is compatible with standard enzymatic processes) and can be incorporated into chimeras with RNA and DNA. The high affinity of LNA for complementary DNA or RNA provides improved specificity and stability, and is resistant to exo- and endonucleases for use in both *in vivo* and *in vitro* settings. The increased affinity leads to much more stable LNA hairpin and other LNA duplex configurations. This has special significance in the NTD setting where specially designed DNA hairpin and Y-transducer molecules have already been identified for use as event transduction molecules, and minor alterations on these transducers for the LNA form (see Methods) are obtainable that retain the transduction properties, but now with the long-lived and improved specificity and affinity attributes of LNAs [9]. LNA versions of the biotinylated hairpins explored in [9], where streptavidin binding occurs where one twist appears to dominate (so only toggle modes are non-trivial), and the lifetimes of the LNA/DNA chimeric transducer molecules in the high-strain capture environment of the nanopore is now on the order of hours instead of minutes.

The generic Y-transducer for annealing-based detection (no laser-tweezer needed) could have a form like in Fig. 14.51, where the regions with high LNA content are shown in dashed boxes, protecting the molecule in those regions from terminus fraying, loop opening, or nexus opening.

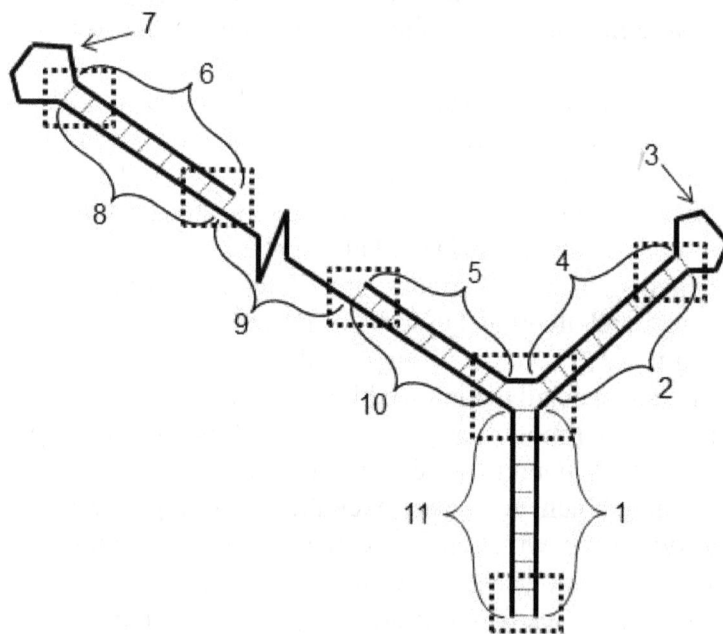

Figure 14.51. Y-transducer for annealing-detection for presence of specified viral digests [9]. The boxed regions indicate favorable areas for LNA substitution to protect the molecule in those regions from base-pair fraying at the terminus, loop-opening, or nexus-branchings.

Appendix A

Perl System Programming in Linux

A.1 Getting Linux and Perl in a Flash (drive)

A.2 Linux and the command shell

A.3 Perl programming: I/O, primitives, string handling, regex

A.1 Getting Linux and Perl in a Flash (drive)

The operating system (OS) environment is part of the programming environment in what follows since *systems* level programming techniques for using the Perl code will be used, including using Perl as a 'shell' scripting language (all of this terminology will be reviewed in what follows).

If you have a Mac (OS X) then you are already running a type of Linux behind the scenes. There are many pitfalls for a beginner programmer with using Macs, however, including use of many of the text editors. So using the Mac environment requires care with the choice of editors, such as using Sublime Text.

If you are running an older Windows machine (not Windows 10) then I suggest a bootable USB drive that has some type of Linux (mine has Mint on 128G and cost $30). The procedure for preparing a bootable USB drive will be outlined below. If you have Win 10 then, like with the Mac, you can run a version of Linux on the machine while Win 10 is running – you just need to learn how to access it. If you have a chromebook, you have a version of Linux running behind the scenes (like the Mac's) – here, however, saving work on the computer can be tricky when accessing Linux, so an inexpensive USB drive is still needed as a simple/safe memory.

If you have Win7, most Win8, or anything earlier than Win7, then you can get Linux via a bootable USB drive. This approach requires that you change the boot order in the BIOS of your computer so that it tries to boot from USB drive first. Plugged into the USB drive will be a bootable USB drive prepared according to the steps below.

If you don't have a computer, and want both Windows and Linux capabilities cheaply, then you might consider getting a bootable USB drive (with Linux) and a Windows laptop. You will want to get, at a minimum, a used Win7 laptop, with at least 4G RAM (where BIOS access isn't difficult, a Dell, for example), cost approx. $150, and also get a 32G or greater flash drive, cost approx. $20.

Set up a Linux OS USB drive, aka flash-drive (also called a pendrive, or thumb-drive), by going to www.pendrivelinux.com . This approach changes the boot order in the BIOS to try to boot from USB first.

Any system where you can access the BIOS, you can take over the system via flash drive.....
Which reminds me:

Be Good.
...no running around with a (usb) ax

Free software for simulating a Linux environment, called 'VirtualBox', can also be set up to run on any OS, and this provides an alternative means to have a Linux OS. A minicomputer option for Linux is also possible, known as the Raspberry Pi ($35) that plugs into your TV or monitor via HDMI. To get VirtualBox → Go to www.virtualbox.org, and follow instructions from there.

A.2 Linux and the command shell

The Linux (Unix) OS:
- provides an extensive set of computational utilities and maintenance utilities (several hundred) – an ideal software development environment
- takes full advantage of available hardware (can run efficiently on a micro-, mini-, or super-computer)
- 95% of the OS is written in C, a portable, machine-independent, language (only the drivers are machine-dependent, as they should be)
- multitasking was part of the original design, not an afterthought
- effective data sharing/privacy also part of the original design

Device Driver Level
- a separate program exists for interacting with each device
- the drivers execute on behalf of the kernel only (no user access)
- all devices appear as files to Unix programs, this permits a standardized device interface and enhances inter-process communication (piping, etc.)

The Kernel
- performs process management and interprocess communication (IPC)
- performs file management
- performs main memory management (RAM optimization with AI)
- performs disk management (cache optimization with AI)
- performs peripherals management

The System Call Interface
- Unix access at its lowest level, consists of function calls known as system calls
- system calls allow the user to manipulate processes, files, and other system resources.

- system calls are the most reliable function calls on the system (having stood the test of time and heavy usage) and are more secure than other function calls for the same reason.

The Language Libraries: prewritten/pretested functions exist for most programming languages. The relevant libraries and system calls define the application programmer's interface (API).

The UNIX Shell: starts at logon, interprets commands entered.

Applications: Programs that run via a combination of library calls and system calls. Since library calls are themselves composed of system calls, use of library calls can often be slower.

Directory and File Manipulations:
'ls' tells you the contents of your "working directory"
'ls –la' lists all content including hidden files

Your working directory when you first log in is your "home directory" (with name tied to your username). To change directories to a different working directory use the 'cd' command to change to one of the directories shown when you enter 'ls –la'..

'cd ..' changes to parent directory for your "working directory"
'cd child_directory' changes to the subdirectory indicated
'mv file_a file_b' renames file_a as file_b
'mv file_a dir_x' moves file_a to dir_x
'cp file_a file_b' copies file_a to file_b
'cp file_a dir_x' copies file_a to dir_x
'less file_a' opens file_a in readonly mode (q to quit)
'vi file_a' opens file_a in vi edit mode (some cmds are like less)
Ubuntu and other Linux typically have a simple gui editor 'gedit'

Some UNIX commands: cut, bg and fg, nice, nohup, set and setenv, umask, less.
Some UNIX utilities: cat, chmod, chown, df, finger, ftp, grep, head, more, ping, rsh and ssh, sty, telnet, top, which.

A.3 Perl programming: I/O, primitives, string handling, regex

Let's get started, try the following:

1. Login to Linux a Linux system.
2. Open a file named program1.pl in your favorite editor (use gedit as default) and type three lines:

```
#!/usr/bin/perl –w
# your basic "Hello World" program.
print "Hello World!\n";
```

3. Save the edited file.

4. Enter on the command line: "chmod u+x program1.pl".
5. Execute the program by typing ./program1.pl at the command prompt and hitting enter.

Something like that should work……. and print "Hello World" to standard out (STDOUT), which is the terminal screen, and we've thereby demonstrated we have perl and print capability. In the next section redirection will be briefly covered to describe redirection of what would have gone to screen (STDOUT) to some other file (STDOUT is seen by the linux OS as a file).

Let's learn more Perl syntax and then write some more programs:

Most computer languages have a sequence of lines of commands, each line ending in ';' (Python is the main exception, with no ';' end-of-line syntax).

$x = "Hello ";
$y = "World\n";
$sentence = $x . $y;

In the above example you see the introduction of scalar variables $x and $y, that are set to the string values indicated in quotes, and each command is terminated with a semicolon. The scalar variable $sentence is then set to the value of $x concatenated with the value of $y. The concatenation is indicated by the period operator '.'.
The command

print "$sentence";

will print "Hello world" to the terminal screen as before. Notice how this print statement involves a (scalar) variable, $sentence, inside the quotes. Perl performs what's known as variable interpolation in this instance. Simply put, it substitutes "Hello World\n" for what should be printed as in the previous example.
Suppose your scalar variable holds a number (integer) instead:

$x = 8;

We can increase the value held in the variable $x by 7 by the command

$x = $x + 7;

The new value held in $x will now be 15. Notice that the line of code is not an algebraic statement! If it were it would be a false statement as we would be saying x = x+7, and if we cancel the x's we get 0=7, which is false. So in programming instructions in general (not just Perl syntax examples), it must be remembered that the code is for an operational instruction.

Often there is a close correspondence between an algebraic expression and its code implementation, but there is a fundamental difference just the same. The variable on the left side of the equals sign is known as an 'lvalue' for this reason in programming languages jargon, where 'lvalue' stands for 'left value'. What's occurring operationally is the computer performs the algebraic manipulations indicated on the right hand side of the equals sign, and the result is placed in the memory location of the variable indicated on the left hand side of the equals sign.

It turns out that the above example is very common in programming, where a variable is often modified, and then the new value placed back into that same variable. Many languages have a shorthand syntax to emphasize precisely this type of operation:

$x += 7; is equivalent to the above line of code: $x=$x+7;

In Perl, if you have a string that you want to concatenate strings to, you could have something like:

$x = "c";
$sentence = "ab";
$sentence .= $x;
Where the last instruction can be 'unpacked' to mean:
$sentence = $sentence . $x;
Which would yield an updated value for $sentence of "abc".

Consider the list, or array, of values: (first, second, third). In Perl this is simply coded with the following syntax:

@vars = ("first", "second", "third");

Let's now try to accees the information and print it to the screen:

print "$vars[1] is after $vars[0] and before $vars[2]\n";

The individual variables in the array are simply accessed by using the array name followed by square brackets with a number inside the brackets that indicates which individual variable is being accessed.

Notice two important details. First, the indexing into the array starts at an index value '0' not '1'! So $vars[0] is accessing the string "first" that is listed first in the array. Second, since the indexed variable is single valued, it is a scalar, thus must be referenced as '$vars[0]' with a '$' symbol at the start, not '@'! The result of the print statement would thus read:

"second is after first and before third" (where the quotes are not shown in the actual printout).
Array indexing that starts at 0 is an annoying artefact that results from how the array variable information is represented in memory, and it is a shared convention for all computer languages that the indexing in arrays always starts at 0.

The reason for this is actually quite straightforward. Think of variables as actually being containers that hold the values they are 'set equal to' in their container (memory) space. In the case of an array, the different values in the array are held in a contiguous sequence of memory locations, where the memory location of the first element of the array is simply that indicated when referencing the array. The second element of the array is one position over from the start of that contiguous memory block for the array, so is indexed with value '1', similarly for the indexing into the other array positions.

Perl is very friendly with array data. Perl allows two arrays to be concatenated:
@combined = (@first_array, @second_array);

Perl allows elements to be added to the front or back of an array with similar syntax:
@new_array_front = ($new_element, @old_array);
@new_array_back = (@old_array, $new_element);

Perl allows arrays to be created that range over values in an obvious numerical or alphabetical sequence, where:

@alpha = ('a' .. 'z');

results in the array holding the letters of the alphabet (all lower case). Perl allows sections, or a 'slice', of an existing array to be taken by indexing the individual positions, or a range of positions, such as with

@slice = @alpha[4, 10 .. 15];

Which results in an array ('e','k','l','m','n','o','p'). You've seen what print does when presented with a scalar variable, what about when presented with an array variable? Very similar, but with an array you have multiple elements to print, and the question arises as to whether there is any delimiter between the printing of the individual values. Perl has a special variable, '$,', that allows you to specify that delimiter. The default for $, is a space, but you may want to specify it directly to be sure by simply including the command:

$, = " ";

If we now do the print:

print @slice;

we get as output to the terminal screen:

"e k l m n o p"

Perl also allows the elements of an array to be 'joined' to form a string, where a delimiter can be specified in the join command:

join '+', ('apple','orange','banana');

evaluates to: "apple+orange+banana"

The reverse of this can be done as well, where a string can be split into is constituent parts according to a specified delimiter. If no delimiter is given, the splitting occurs at the individual character level:

$seq = "acgtag";
@arrayseq = split //, $seq;

The delimiter for the splitting is given between the '/' symbols, and as nothing is given in this example, the splitting defaults to individual character level, with the result that the array @arrayseq is now ('a','c','g','t','a','g').

When dealing with an associative array, or hash variable, the process is much the same. We might declare a hash variable with the name "hash" with the code:

%hash;

We might then set up an associative memory between the strings 'key' and 'value' by:

$hash{"key"}="value";

Notice again that when setting an individual lvalue or accessing an individual hash entry, the special character in the hash variable changes from '%' to '$' similar to what occurred with the array variable entries. Consider the following print statement:

print "Each key is associated with a $hash{"key"}.\n";

which results in the output:

"Each key is associated with a value."

Most languages do not have a hash data *primitive*. Convenient hash variable primitives make Perl very effective in informatics applications where associative memory is often a fundamental aspect of the problem.

Now that we've seen the different variable types, the next thing to consider is operations between them. There are operators that involve one variable (unary), two variables (binary), and three variables (trinary). The most common unary operators are negation (use of the negative sign) and increment. There are two forms of the increment operator:
++$a;
and
$a++;

When given simply as shown these are both the same as '$a+=1;' which is the same as '$a=$a+1;', e.g., incrementing by one. The increment operators can be used in compound commands, however, and that's when they act differently:

$b=++$a; → increment $a first, then $b assigned that value
$b=$a++; → $b assigned $a value, then $a incremented.

If either of the above operations is done a significant amount in your programming, then either is good programming style. If there isn't a lot of increment/assign operations then the combined compound expressions are bad style, and the a good, readable, style convention is to simple use $a++ always for increment, and avoid compound increment forms entirely.

Binary operations are the most prevalent, including standard mathematical operations such as addition, multiplication, etc., as well comparison evaluation, equality evaluation, bitwise operations, and assignment operations:

Comparison Operators: <, >, <=, >=, <=>, lt, gt, le, ge, cmp
Equality Operators: ==, !=, eq, ne
Logical Operators: (||,or), (&&,and), (!,not), xor
Bitwise Operators: <<, >>, &, |, ^, ~
Assignment Operators: =, +=, -=, *=, /=, %=, **=, .=, x=, and more, where
op1 operator= op2; → op1=op1 operator op2; such as $a += 1; → $a=$a+1;

Variables, and operations involving them, are accessed in programs according to control structures (if-then conditionals) and (repeated) loop structures. The group of commands, or code 'blocks', that are run conditionally or in some loop, then form the core of the imperative programming design. Sometimes variables only 'exist', or are only made use of, while in a particular code block. Where a variable 'lives' and can be accessed is referred to as the variable's 'scope'. A variable introduced in a particular block of code, usually only can be accessed inside that block. Before the advent of object oriented coding, the careful management of code blocks and variable scopes within those blocks, was a key aspect of software engineering to have 'safe' code with minimal errors and maximal, safe, reusability in other programs.

Examples of the syntax for conditionals and loops:

Basic Conditional construct:
if (EXPR1) BLOCK_1
[elsif (EXPR2) BLOCK_2] …
[else BLOCK_N]

Basic Loop constructs:
"while (cond-expr) BLOCK" , which is open ended on a conditional, like a file read operation.
"for ([init-expr]; [cond-expr]; [loop-expr]) BLOCK", which exits after a max number of iterations, if not sooner.
"foreach [[my] $loop_var] (list) BLOCK", which loops in association with the items of a list (when possible, 'foreach' preferred over 'for').

As with human languages, many aspects of programming languages can best be learned by example, so rather than continue with further syntax rules, the discussion will now turn to actual code examples in Ch. 2-4, and show syntax and software engineering issues in actual implementations. ***The Ch. 2-4 examples will be doubly informative as well as they will also serve as a means to review basic probability and statistics definitions and methods.***

Appendix B

Physics

The Calculus of Variations

As Scientists we seek explanations (hypotheses) and subject them to tests and refinements. Elaborate explanations are more easily refuted, such that refinement typically leads to pared-down, simple explanations. The most efficient way to proceed given this well-known interplay between hypothesis complexity and robust modeling is to seek *simple* physical explanations before more complicated ones. The latter, pragmatic, notion is often referred to as "Occam's Razor," for the William of Occam phrase "causes shall not be multiplied beyond necessity." (From "nunquam ponenda est pluralitas sine necesitate" [311].) From the success of the scientific method with Occam's Razor it appears that nature effects an "economy of means" [312]. The hypotheses that underpin most of physical theory, in fact, can be described in concise, elegant, terms via extremal hypotheses. The study of extremal properties advanced greatly with the theological, philosophical and mathematical explorations of Gottfried Leibniz, who postulated that our world is organized such that it is "the best of all possible worlds." To pursue the study of extremal properties, Leibniz and Newton, separately, invented calculus to have the mathematical framework they needed. Leibniz, in particular, described how variation in an "action" would be extremal in describing a motion. An exact definition of action was not given by him, however, or by Maupertuis who followed (who popularized only the minimum action version of the principle). The exact definition of the action only came with the rigorous explorations by Euler and Lagrange roughly thirty years later. Our legacy from these early explorers is a remarkably succinct description of physical properties using the calculus of variations.

Physics unifications and applications
The calculus of variations is sometimes referred to as the mathematics of "optimal forms." This is misleading if optimal forms are taken to be solely of a geometrical nature, because physical observation also reveals optimal forms that are distributional (among other things – e.g., there are sequential and other optimals, such as Martingales, etc.). In conventional physical descriptions geometric and distributional variational components are treated separately, often with one set of parameters held constant, such as an unchanging geometry. Recent research into unifying quantum mechanical and general relativistic descriptions of nature, however, reveal that at such unification the independence between geometric degrees of freedom and distributional degrees of freedom might be precisely what is lost. In those studies it was found that global variations in the geometric description of the idealized physical systems analyzed (black holes for example) can be analytically related to (global) variations of a distributional description for that system [313-317] In effect, this would unify not only quantum mechanical and general relativistic descriptions of nature, but also the remaining statistical mechanical (thermodynamic) description of nature. From the thermodynamics perspective, there is one critical variational principle, the Second Law of thermodynamics: an isolated body in equilibrium has the maximum entropy that physical circumstances will allow [189,190]. A number of physicists have noted that the property that entropy always increases may relate to the "arrow of time," and unifications such as the above appear to support such a notion. The Laws of Thermodynamics have many equivalent

formulations, other than the classical description the most significant description is that stemming solely from the extremal principle of maximum entropy, known as the Jaynesian approach to thermodynamics [173].

The classic variational calculus application to physics describes moving bodies using the Lagrangian or Hamiltonian formalisms (which are related by a Legendre transformation). The Lagrangian variational formulation is based on "configuration space" where elements are described in terms of positions x_i and their corresponding velocities v_i. Variation of a function, the "Lagrangian," then yields the equations of motion when the variation is extremized. The Lagrangian, L, is often written in terms of kinetic energy contributions, T, and potential energy contributions, U: $L(x_i, v_i, t) = T(x_i, v_i, t) - U(x_i)$. The classic case is where the kinetic energy is $mv^2/2$, for which variation leads to $F = ma$, Newton's Second Law. In general, the kinetic aspect of the motion is defined to be solely a description of the motion itself, devoid of explanation or causation. There is still substantial information in the kinetic representation, however, as this is where one's geometric assumptions enter the problem [318] (here a Galilean frame of reference on time). The m term then encodes the inertial concept and serves double duty as the dimensionful parameter linking acceleration to force. The dynamics, then, is whatever makes the description work (balances the equations). Different objects may share similar geometric "backgrounds," i.e., the kinetic energy part, but their dynamical description may differ in any way conceivable – encoded as force (or potential energy when working from the Lagrangian). Not all descriptions of motion need be fundamentally empirical in the dynamical parts of their descriptions, however, as Einstein's theory of gravitation attests. When expressed in a Lagrangian variational context, as first done by Hilbert, Einstein's theory can be shown to give a full description of both the kinematical and dynamical components of the motion entirely within a geometric construction (where geometry itself is dynamical). What is particularly satisfying about this presentation of Einstein's theory is that it depends on a minimum amount of structure (Occam's Razor): if a covariant tensorial theory is presumed to exist (the unstated kinematic structure), and if one disallows spontaneous creation of energy, disallows rotational instabilities (change in rotation with no torque applied), assumes three space and one time dimension (locally Lorentzian manifold exhibited by Maxwell's electromagnetic equations), and assumes the algebraic topology notion that the boundary of a boundary is zero (for example the boundary of a flat disk is taken to be the circle at its perimeter, and the boundary of that circle, a line with no ends, is zero), then one obtains, *uniquely*, Einstein's theory of gravitation [319].

Physics & Statistics

To really get an understanding of physics and its relation to statistics it is necessary to put it into the context of the four fundamental "theories," or epistemological divisions of modern physics. Those theories are general relativity, quantum mechanics, the theory of elementary particles, and statistical mechanics.

General relativity is concerned with the structure of spacetime. Such a simple statement of what the theory is concerned with is not possible for the other three theories. General relativity has its flaws, however, most notable being its incompatibility with an even more successful theory, quantum mechanics. The incompatibility between general relativity and quantum mechanics is not a problem most of the time, however, since they are typically applied at greatly different scales: general relativistic effects are barely noticeable with anything smaller than the largest planetary objects, while quantum mechanical effects are barely noticeable with anything larger than the tiniest motes of dust.

On a fundamental level, quantum mechanics is not on as firm a footing as general relativity, even though its successful applications number far greater and have been confirmed to much greater precision. The first problem is concerned with the very interpretations of the theory. Reminiscent of the Bayesian vs. Frequentist split in statistical inference; in quantum mechanics there is not agreement over interpretations of the quantum mechanical wavefunction itself, and even where there is agreement on ontological aspects, there is still opportunity for disagreement when it comes to taking measurements (associated with a reduction of state or wavefunction collapse). This is because the description of measurement processes is separate from the description of evolution processes. For measurements described in terms of a reduction of state, the process of that reduction is a fundamental unknown. Some reduction models fundamentally depend on the observer, these are known as *subjective* reduction models (and are prone to metaphysical arguments on consciousness causing reduction), while other models are based on *objective* reduction. Some of the more interesting objective reduction schemes have as their basis an entropic argument. Related to the measurement problem is why large groupings of atomic particles should lose their quantum mechanical properties and behave "classically". In other words, why does the quantum mechanical wavefunction decohere in such a way that we perceive the familiar reality of distinct objects? To answer this question Murray Gell-Mann (Nobel prize for quarks) and others have looked into the entropic properties of the very algorithms used in describing physics theory. This work on "algorithmic entropy" ties directly to the work of Chaitan and Zurek [320-323]. In the machine learning context, algorithmic entropy was first introduced in terms of the minimum description length (MDL) method for controlling complex fitting models [324]. The structural risk minimization (SRM) approach behind Vapnik's Support Vector Machine discrimination method also attempts to encapsulate, in the variational foundations of the formalism, the notion of minimal, necessary, structure (Occam's Razor again).

In the theory of elementary particles one contends with the old reductionist question concerning the underlying building blocks of the universe (and with the advent of the force concept, what are the underlying forces between these objects). Why there should even be a reductionist aspect to reality is partly what the aforementioned work of Gell-Mann and others attempts to find out. Due to its more phenomenological basis in scattering observations, this branch of physics is much more of a gray area than the previous two discussed.

The first three theories describe matter and its interactions. At this point it might appear that there is no further room for another "fundamental" theory. But there still remains the connection between the small, isolated, system approximation typically employed in the non-statistical models and the large, non-isolated, "real world" of our experience. The theories of thermodynamics and statistical mechanics provide such a link between the microscopic description of the non-statistical theories and macroscopic (non-isolated) reality. At first it might seem that the theories of thermodynamics and statistical mechanics should relate to trivial representations of statistical relationships. But the statistical relationships themselves come into question as to their fundamental nature. The problem is tautological in that the various "laws" of statistics, such as the law of large numbers, are themselves mathematical formulations based on phenomenologically observed "truths." Ergodicity on a specified region of phase space, for example, has been shown to be a generalization of the law of large numbers [251]. The notion of equilibrium from thermodynamics is another analogue of this law of large numbers. Once we begin to identify the core metaphysical assumptions underlying many of the notions in statistics, we begin to reassemble the set of concepts, in the physical setting, that are familiar from the discipline of thermodynamics. What becomes evident in such explorations is that thermodynamics is unavoidably a fourth fundamental theory of physics, contrary to the expectations of many early researchers in statistical mechanics, who sought to eliminate thermodynamic-like principles as independent laws. Concepts such as equilibrium, temperature, and entropy, are now considered elements of the statistical description of nature that is as fundamental as the kinematical and dynamical descriptions [251,325,326]. Of the four fundamental theories of physics, thermodynamics is the oldest and least understood. This suggests that further progress in our fundamental understanding of reality will require advances in representing statistical phenomenology, so as to better understand thermodynamics, possibly in a unifying context with the other theories.

Information Optimization: Inference via maximum entropy
The Principle of Maximum Entropy, first stated by Jaynes as a general rule of inference in statistical mechanics, offers arguments in favor of Shannon's choice for entropy, particularly the recovery of the classical distributions of physics under appropriate constraints [327].

The Maximum Entropy Principle: Let X, an element of R^n, denote a random variable whose probability distribution $p(\mathbf{X})$ is unknown. Assume, however, that the distribution is subject to mathematical constraints. The principle states that, of all the distributions that satisfy the constraints, we should choose the distribution that provides the greatest Shannon entropy for $\mathbf{X}$. A generalization of this principle applies when a distribution $q(\mathbf{X})$, which estimates $p(\mathbf{X})$, is known (in addition to the constraints). The generalized principle is the minimum relative-entropy principle: of the various distributions $p(\mathbf{X})$ which satisfy the constraints: choose the distribution with minimal relative entropy $D(p\|q)$. The generalized principle is particularly relevant when working with stationary states ("stationary states play a role in the thermodynamics of irreversible processes similar to that played by states of equilibrium in classical thermodynamics" --- [191]), in which case its known as the principle of minimum production of entropy [195-197].

Information optimization: The distributions of nature via maximum entropy
Using the Shannon entropy measure it is possible to derive the classic probability distributions of statistical physics by maximizing the Shannon measure subject to appropriate linear momentum constraints. Constrained variational optimizations involving the Shannon entropy measure can, thus, provide a unified framework with which to describe all, or most, of statistical mechanics. This follows because the classic distributions can themselves be taken to form the basis of most statistical mechanical descriptions. This is known because of a research program begun by Maxwell, who argued that the Gaussian distribution might be taken to be fundamental. What developed after Maxwell was the proliferation of "fundamental" distributions, taken to be on a par with the fundamental laws of physics by many statistical physicists at the turn of the century. The distributions included the Maxwell-Boltzmann, Bose-Einstein, Fermi-Dirac, and Intermediate distributions, all of which are shown to be derivable within the maximum entropy formalism. The maximum entropy method for defining statistical mechanical systems has been extensively studied in [173].

Both statistical estimation and maximum entropy estimation are concerned with drawing inferences from partial information. The maximum entropy approach estimates a probability density function when only a few moments are known (where there are an infinite number of higher moments). The statistical approach estimates the density function when only one random sample is available out of an infinity of possible samples. The maximum entropy estimation may be significantly more robust (against over-fitting, for example) in that it has an Occam's Razor argument that "cuts both ways" – use *all* of the information given and avoid using any information not given. This means that out of all of the probability distributions consistent with the set of constraints, choose the one that has maximum uncertainty, i.e., maximum entropy [168].

At the same time that Jaynes was doing his work, essentially an optimization principle based on Shannon entropy, Soloman Kullback was exploring optimizations involving a notion of probabilistic distance known as the Kullback-Leibler distance, referred to above as the relative entropy [174]. The resulting minimum relative entropy (MRE) formalism reduces to the maximum entropy formalism of Jaynes when the reference distribution is uniform. The information distance that Kullback and Leibler defined was an oriented measure of "distance" between two probability distributions. The MRE formalism can be understood to be an extension of Laplace's *Principle of Insufficient Reason* (e.g., if nothing known assume the uniform distribution) in a manner like that employed by Khinchine in his uniqueness proof, but now incorporating constraints.

In *Entropy Optimization Principles with Applications* [168], Kapur and Kesavan argue for a generalized entropy optimization approach to the description of distributions. They believe every probability distribution, theoretical or observed, is an entropy optimization distribution, i.e., it can be obtained by maximizing an appropriate entropy measure, or by minimizing a relative entropy measure with respect to an appropriate *a priori* distribution. The primary objective in such a modeling procedure is to represent the problem as a simple combination of probabilistic entities that have a simple set of moment constraints. Generalized measures of distributional distance can also be explored along the lines of generalized measures of geometric distance. In physics, not every geometric distance is of interest, however, since the special theory of relativity tells us that spacetime is locally flat (Lorentzian, which is Euclidean on spatial slices), with metric generalization the Riemannian metrics. Likewise, perhaps not all distributional distance measures are created equal either. What the formalism of Information Geometry [23-25] reveals, among other things, is that relative entropy is uniquely structureless (like flat geometry) and is perturbatively stable, i.e., has a well-defined Taylor expansion at short divergence range, just like the locally Euclidean metrics at short distance range.

Appendix C

Math

C.1 Martingales and convergence

C.2 Hoeffding Inequality

C.1 Martingales
Martingale Definition
A stochastic process $\{X_n; n=0,1, \ldots\}$ is martingale if, for $n=0,1, \ldots$,

1. $E[|X_n|] < \infty$
2. $E[X_{n+1}|X_0, \ldots, X_n] = X_n$

Def.: Let $\{X_n; n=0,1, \ldots\}$ and $\{Y_n; n=0,1, \ldots\}$ be stochastic processes. We say $\{X_n\}$ is martingale with respect to (w.r.t) $\{Y_n\}$ if, for $n=0,1, \ldots$:

1. $E[|X_n|] < \infty$
2. $E[X_{n+1}|Y_0, \ldots, Y_n] = X_n$

Examples of Martingales:

(a) Suns of independent random variables: $X_n = Y_1 + \ldots + Y_n$.

(b) Variance of a Sum $X_n = (\sum_{k=1}^n Y_k)^2 - n\sigma^2$

(c) Have induced Martingales with Markov Chains! ….

(d) For HMM learning, sequences of likelihood ratios are martingale….

The asymptotic equipartition theorem (AEP) and Hoeffding Inequalities (critical in Ch. 11) have both been generalized to Martingales.

Induced Martingales with Markov Chains
Let $\{Y_n; n=0,1, \ldots\}$ be a Markov Chain (MC) process with transition probability matrix $P=\|P_{ij}\|$. Let f be a bounded right regular sequence for P:

$f(i)$ is non-negative and $f(i)=\sum_{k=1}^n P_{ij}f(j)$. Let $X_n=f(Y_n)$ → $E[|X_n|]< \infty$ (since f is bounded).

Now have:
$E[X_{n+1}|Y_0, \ldots, Y_n]$
$= E[f(Y_{n+1})|Y_0, \ldots, Y_n]$
$= E[f(Y_{n+1})|Y_n]$ (due to MC)
$= \sum_{k=1}^n P_{Y_n, j}f(j)$ (def . of P_{ij} and f)
$= f(Y_n)$
$= X_n$

In HMM learning have sequences of likelihood ratios, which is a martingale, proof:
Induced Martingales with Sequences of Likelihood Ratios
Let $Y_0, Y_1, \ldots$ be iid rv.s and let f_0 and f_1 be probability density functions. A stochastic process of fundamental importance in the theory of testing statistical hypotheses is the sequence of likelihood ratios:

$$X_n = \frac{f_1(Y_0)f_1(Y_1)\ldots f_1(Yn)}{f_0(Y_0)f_0(Y_1)\ldots f_0(Yn)}, n = 0, 1, \ldots$$

Assume $f_0(y) > 0$ for all y:

$$E[X_{n+1} \mid Y_0, \ldots, Y_n] = E[X_n \left(\frac{f_1(Y_{n+1})}{f_0(Y_{n+1})}\right) \mid Y_0, \ldots, Y_n] = X_n E[\frac{f_1(Y_{n+1})}{f_0(Y_{n+1})}]$$

When the common distribution of the Y_k's (used in the 'E' function) has f_0 as its probability density, have:

$$E[\frac{f_1(Y_{n+1})}{f_0(Y_{n+1})}] = 1$$

So, $E[X_{n+1} \mid Y_0, \ldots, Y_n] = X_n$
So likelihood ratios are martingale when the common distribution is f_0.

Supermartingales and Submartingales
Let $\{X_n; n=0,1, \ldots\}$ and $\{Y_n; n=0,1, \ldots\}$ be stochastic processes. Then $\{X_n\}$ is called a ***supermartingale*** with respect to $\{Y_n\}$ if, for all n:

    (i) $E[X_n^-] > -\infty$, where $x^- = \min\{x,0\}$

    (ii) $E[X_{n+1}|Y_0, \ldots, Y_n] \leq X_n$

    (iii) X_n is a function of $(Y_0, \ldots, Y_n)$ (explicit due to inequality in (ii))

The stochastic process $\{X_n; n=0,1, \ldots\}$ is called a ***submartingale*** w.r.t $\{Y_n\}$ if, for all n:

    (i) $E[X_n^+] > -\infty$, where $x^+ = \max\{x,0\}$

    (ii) $E[X_{n+1}|Y_0, \ldots, Y_n] \geq X_n$

    (iii) X_n is a function of $(Y_0, \ldots, Y_n)$

With Jensen's inequality for convex function φ and conditional expectations have:
$$E[\varphi(X)|Y_0, \ldots, Y_n] \geq \varphi(E[X|Y_0, \ldots, Y_n])$$
So, have means to construct submartingales from martingales (with supermartingales the same aside from a sign flip).

Martingale Convergence Theorems
Under very general conditions, a martingale X_n will converge to a limit random variable X as n increases.

Theorem

(a) Let $\{X_n\}$ be a submartingale satisfying

$$\sup_{n \geq 0} E[|X_n|] < \infty$$

Then there exists a r.v. X_∞ to which $\{X_n\}$ converges with probability one:

$$Prob\left(\lim_{n \to \infty} X_n = X_\infty\right) = 1$$

(b) If $\{X_n\}$ is a martingale and is uniformly integrable, then, in addition to the above, $\{X_n\}$, converges in the mean:

$$\lim_{n \to \infty} E[|X_n - X_\infty|] = 0$$

And $E[X_\infty] = E[X_n]$, for all n.

A sequence is uniformly integral if:

$$\lim_{c \to \infty} \sup_{n \geq 0} E[|X_n|I\{|X_n| > c\}] = 0$$

Where I is the indicator function: 1 if $|X_n|>c$, and 0 otherwise.

'Maximal' Inequalities for Martingales

Chebyshev's inequality applied to a sequence can be 'tightened' to a finer inequality known as the Kolmogorov inequality in terms of the maximum of the sequence. This carries over to Martingales:

Let $\{X_n; n=0,1, \ldots\}$ be iid rvs with $E[X_i]=0 \ \forall \ i$ and $E[(X_i)^2]=\sigma^2 < \infty$. Define $S_0 = 0$, $S_n = X_1+\ldots+X_n$, for $n \geq 1$. From Chebyshev's Inequality:

$$\varepsilon^2 Prob(|S_n| > \varepsilon) \leq n\sigma^2, \ \varepsilon > 0$$

A finer inequality is possible:

$$\varepsilon^2 Prob\left(\max_{0 \leq k \leq n} |S_n| > \varepsilon\right) \leq n\sigma^2, \ \varepsilon > 0$$

Known as the Kolmogorov inequality, it can be generalized to provide a maximal inequality on submartingales:

Lemma 1: Let $\{X_n\}$ be a submartingale for which $X_n \geq 0$ for all n. Then for any positive λ:

$$\lambda \, Prob\left(\max_{0 \leq k \leq n} |X_k| > l\right) \leq E[X_n]$$

Lemma 2: Let $\{X_n\}$ be a non-negative supermartingale then for any positive λ:

$$\lambda \, Prob\left(\max_{0 \leq k \leq n} |X_k| > l\right) \leq E[X_0]$$

Mean-Square Convergence Theorem for Martingales

Let $\{X_n\}$ be a submartingale w.r.t $\{Y_n\}$ satisfying, for some constant k, $E[(X_n)^2] \leq k < \infty$, for all n. Then $\{X_n\}$ converges as $n \to \infty$ to a limit r.v. X_∞ both with probability one and in mean square:

$$Prob(\lim_{n \to \infty} X_n = X_\infty) = 1, \quad \text{and} \quad \lim_{n \to \infty} E[|Xn - X_\infty|^2] = 0,$$

Where $E[X_\infty] = E[X_n] = E[X_0]$, for all n.

Martingales w.r.t σ-field formalism

Review of axiomatic probability theory, have three basic elements:

(1) The sample space, a set Ω whose elements ω correspond to the possible outcomes of an experiment;

(2) The family of elements, a collection F of subsets A of Ω (the sigma fields). We say that the event A occurs if the outcome ω of the experiment is an element of A;

(3) The probability measure, a function P defined on F and satisfying:

(i) $0 = P[\varnothing] \leq P[A] \leq P[\Omega] = 1$ for $A \in F$

(ii) $P[A_1 \cup A_2] = P[A_1] + P[A_2] - P[A_1 \cap A_2]$ for $A_i \in F$

(iii) $P[\cup_{n=1}^{\infty} A_n] = \sum_{n=1}^{\infty} P[An]$ if $A_i \in F$ are mutually disjoint.

Then, the triple (Ω, F, P) is called a probability space.

Backwards Martingale Definition (w.r.t sigma sub-fields)

Let $\{Z_n\}$ be rv's on a probability space (Ω, F, P) and let $\{G_n; n=0,1, \ldots\}$ be a decreasing sequence of sub sigma-fields of F, viz.,

$$F \supset F_n \supset F_{n+1}, \text{ for all n.}$$

Then $\{Z_n\}$ is called a backward martingale w.r.t. $\{G_n\}$ if for $n=0,1, \ldots$:

(i) Z_n is G_n-measurable

(ii) $E[|Z_n|] < \infty$, and

(iii) $E[Z_n | G_{n+1}] < Z_{n+1}$

$\{Z_n\}$ is a backwards martingale, iff $X_n = Z_{-n}$, $n=0,-1,-2,\ldots$ forms a martingale w.r.t $F_n = G_{-n}$, $n=0,-1,-2,\ldots$

Backwards Martingale Convergence Theorem

Let $\{Z_n\}$ be a backwards martingale w.r.t a decreasing sequence of sub sigma-fields $\{G_n\}$. Then:

$$Prob(\lim_{n \to \infty} Z_n = Z) = 1, \quad \text{and} \quad \lim_{n \to \infty} E[|Z - Z_n|] = 0,$$

and $E[Z_n] = E[Z]$, for all n.

Strong Law of Large Numbers Proof

Let $\{X_n; n=1,2, \ldots\}$ be iid rvs with $E[|X_1|] < \infty$. Let $\mu = E[X_1]$, $S_0 = 0$, and $S_n = X_1 + \ldots + X_n$, for $n \geq 1$. Let G_n be the sigma field generated by $\{S_n, S_{n+1}, \ldots\}$. We can derive the strong law of large numbers from the observation that $Z_n = S_n/n$ ($Z_0 = \mu$), forms a backward martingale w.r.t G_n. Have $E[|Z_n|] < \infty$ and Z_n is G_n-measurable by construction, so just need relation (iii):

$$S_n \equiv E[S_n|S_n] = E[S_n|S_n, S_{n+1}, \ldots] = E[S_n|G_n] = \sum_{k=1}^{n} E[X_k|G_n] = nE[X_k|G_n],$$

with the last equality for $1 \le k \le n$, thus:

$$Z_n = S_n/n = E[X_k|G_n]$$

So, $E[Z_{n-1}|G_n] = (n-1)^{-1} E[S_{n-1}|G_n] = (n-1)^{-1} \sum_{k=1}^{n-1} E[X_k|G_n] = Z_n$!!!

Now use backward martingale convergence theorem to show the strong law:

$$Prob\left(\lim_{n\to\infty} \frac{S_n}{n} = \mu\right) = 1$$

Stationary Processes

A **stationary** process is a stochastic process $\{X(t), t \in T\}$ with the property that for any positive integer 'k', and any points $t_1, \ldots, t_k$, and h in T, the joint distribution of $\{X(t_1), \ldots X(t_k)\}$ is the same as the joint distribution of $\{X(t_1+h), \ldots X(t_k+h)\}$.

An ergodic theorem gives conditions under which an average over time

$$\overline{x_n} = \frac{1}{n}(x_1 + \cdots + xn)$$

of a stochastic process will converge as the number n of observed periods becomes large. The strong law of large numbers is one such ergodic theorem.
Stationary processes provide a natural setting for generalization of the law of large numbers since for such processes the mean value is a constant m=E[X_n], independent of time. Just as there are strong and weak laws of large numbers, there are a variety of ergodic theorems.....

Strong Ergodic Theorem

Let $\{X_n; n=0,1, \ldots\}$ be a strictly stationary process having finite mean m=E[X_n]. Let

$$\overline{X_n} = \frac{1}{n}(X_0 + \cdots + X_{n-1})$$

be the sample time average. Then, with probability one, the sequence $\{\overline{X_n}\}$ converges to some limit rv denoted $\bar{X}$:

$$Prob(\lim_{n\to\infty} \overline{X_n} = \bar{X}) = 1, \quad \text{and} \quad \lim_{n\to\infty} E[|\bar{X} - \overline{X_n}|] = 0,$$

and E[$\overline{X_n}$] = E[$\bar{X}$] = m.

Asymptotic Equipartition Property (AEP)

$$\lim_{n\to\infty}\left[-\frac{1}{n}\log p(X_0, \ldots, X_{n-1})\right] = H(\{X_n\})$$

With probability one, provided $\{X_n\}$ is ergodic.

Proof: For $\{X_n\}$ a stationary ergodic finite Markov chain use relation that:

$H(\{X_n\}) = \lim_{k\to\infty} H(Xk|X_1, \ldots, X_{k-1})$ Or $H(\{X_n\}) = \lim_{l\to\infty} \frac{1}{l} H(X_1, \ldots, X_l)$

$H(X_n|X_0, \ldots, X_{n-1}) = -\sum_{i,j} \pi(i) P_{ij} \log P_{ij}$, where $\pi(i)$ is the prior on X_i and P_{ij} is the transition probability to go from X_i to X_j. Thus

$H(\{X_n\}) = -\sum_{i,j} \pi(i) P_{ij} \log P_{ij}$, while,

$-\frac{1}{n} \log p(X_0, \ldots, X_{n-1}) = \frac{1}{n} \sum_{i=0}^{n-2} W_i - \frac{1}{n} \log \pi(X_0)$, where $W_i = -\log P_{i,i+1}$

The ergodic theorem applies:

$$\lim_{n\to\infty} \left[-\frac{1}{n} \log p(X_0, \ldots, X_{n-1}) \right] = E[W_0] = -\sum_{i,j} \pi(i) P_{ij} \log P_{ij} = H(\{X_n\})$$

The general AEP proof uses the backwards martingale convergence theorem instead of the ergodic theorem.

De Finetti's Theorem

Let $\{X_n; n=0,1, \ldots\}$ be an infinite sequence of rv's. They are said to be exchangeable if for any finite cardinal number n and any two finite sequences $i_1, \ldots, i_n$ and $j_1, \ldots, j_n$ (with each of the i's distinct and each of the j's distinct), the two sequences

$$X_{i_1}, \ldots, X_{i_n} \text{ and } X_{j_1}, \ldots, X_{j_n}$$

both have the same joint probability distribution.
iid → exchangeable, but not the reverse.

C.2 Hoeffding Inequality

Hoeffding's inequality provides an upper bound on the probability that the sum of random variables deviates from its expected value (Wassily Hoeffding, 1963 [59]). It's generalized to martingale differences by Azuma [63] and to functions of rvs $\{X_n\}$ with bounded differences by McDiarmid [232] (where function is empirical mean of the sequence of variables: $\bar{X} = \frac{1}{n}(X_1 + \ldots + X_n)$ recovers the special case of Hoeffding).
Recall:
Let $X_1, \ldots, X_n$ be independent random variables. Assume that the X_i are almost surely bounded: $P(X_i \in [a_i, b_i]) = 1$. Define the empirical mean of the sequence of variables as:

$$\bar{X} = \frac{1}{n}(X_1 + \ldots + X_n)$$

Hoeffding (1963) proves the following:

$$P(\bar{X} - E[\bar{X}] \geq k) \leq \exp\left(-\frac{2n^2 k^2}{\sum_{i=1}^{n}(b_i - ai)^2}\right)$$

$$P(|\bar{X} - E[\bar{X}]| \geq k) \leq 2 \exp\left(-\frac{2n^2 k^2}{\sum_{i=1}^{n}(b_i - ai)^2}\right)$$

For each X almost surely bounded have another relation if $E(X) = 0$ known as the Hoeffding Lemma:

$$E[e^{\lambda X}] \leq \exp\left(\frac{\lambda^2 (b-a)^2}{8}\right)$$

The proof begins with showing the Lemma as the hard part.......

Hoeffding Lemma Proof

Since $e^{\lambda X}$ is a convex function, we have

$$e^{\lambda X} \leq \frac{b-X}{b-a} e^{\lambda a} + \frac{X-a}{b-a} e^{\lambda b} , \quad \forall \, a \leq x \leq b$$

So,

$$E[e^{\lambda X}] \leq E\left[\frac{b-X}{b-a} e^{\lambda a} + \frac{X-a}{b-a} e^{\lambda b}\right] = \frac{b}{b-a} e^{\lambda a} + \frac{-a}{b-a} e^{\lambda b} \quad \text{(last is since E[X]=0)}$$

The convexity method involves a line interpolation, let's shift to those parameters with p = -a/(b-a), and introduce hp = -aλ (so have h = λ(b-a)):

$$\frac{b}{b-a} e^{\lambda a} + \frac{-a}{b-a} e^{\lambda b} = e^{\lambda a}[1\text{-}p + p \, e^{\lambda(b-a)}] = e^{-hp}[1\text{-}p + p \, e^{h}]$$

$E[e^{\lambda X}] \leq e^{L(h)}$, where L(h) = -hp + ln(1-p+pe^{h}) $\rightarrow$ L(0) = 0.
L'(h) = -p + pe^{h}/(1-p+pe^{h}) $\rightarrow$ L'(0) = 0.
L''(h) = p(1-p)e^{h} $\rightarrow$ L''(0) = p(1-p).
L$^{(n)}$(h) = p(1-p)e^{h} > 0

Using Taylor series for L(h):

L(h) = L(0) + hL'(0) + $\frac{1}{2}$h^{2}L''(0) + (more positive terms at higher order in h)

L(h) $\leq \frac{1}{2}$h^{2} p(1-p)

Since we have E[X]=0, have p=-a/(b-a) is $\in$ [0,1], so classic logistic function, where the maximum value of p(1-p) on range [0,1] is ¼ (when p=1/2), so:

L(h) $\leq \frac{1}{8}$h^{2} and $E[e^{\lambda X}] \leq e^{\frac{1}{8}\lambda^2(b-a)^2}$

Hoeffding Inequality Proof (for further details, see [233])

Consider Sum on iid X_i , where $S_m = m\bar{X}$ where $\bar{X}$ has m terms in its empirical average:

$$P(S_m\text{-}E[S_m] \geq k) \leq e^{-tk} \, E[e^{t(S_m - E[S_m])}] \quad \text{(Chernoff Bounding Technique)}$$

$$= \prod_{i=1}^{m} e^{-tk} \, E[e^{t(X_i - E[X_i])}] \quad (\{X_n\} \text{ are iid})$$

$$\leq \prod_{i=1}^{m} e^{-tk} e^{\frac{1}{8}t^2(\text{bi-ai})^2} \quad \text{(Hoeffding Lemma)}$$

$$= e^{-tk} e^{\frac{1}{8}t^2 \sum_{i=1}^{m}(\text{bi-ai})^2}$$

Have f(t) = -tk+$\frac{1}{8}$t^{2} $\sum_{i=1}^{m}(\text{bi} - \text{ai})^2$; Choose t=4k/$\sum_{i=1}^{m}(\text{bi} - \text{ai})^2$ to minimize the upper bound to get:

$$\mathbf{P(S_m\text{-}E[S_m] \geq k) \leq e^{-2k^2/\sum_{i=1}^{m}(\text{bi-ai})^2}}$$

$$\mathbf{P(\bar{X}\text{-}E[\bar{X}] \geq k) \leq e^{-2m^2k^2/\sum_{i=1}^{m}(\text{bi-ai})^2}}$$

Chernoff Bounding Technique:
$$P[X \geq k] = P[e^{tX} \geq e^{tk}] \leq e^{-tk} \, E[e^{tX}] \quad \text{(Chernoff uses Markov Inequality on last)}$$

492

References

1. Winters-Hilt, S. "Machine-Learning based sequence analysis, bioinformatics & nanopore transduction detection." ISBN: 978-1-257-64525-1. (2011).

2. Winters-Hilt, S. Unified propagator theory and a non-experimental derivation for the fine-structure constant. Advanced Studies in Theoretical Physics, Vol. 12, 2018, no. 5, 243-255. https://doi.org/10.12988/astp.2018.8626.

3. Winters-Hilt, S. The 22 letters of reality: chiral bisedenion properties for maximal information propagation. Advanced Studies in Theoretical Physics, Vol. 12, 2018, no. 7, 301-318. https://doi.org/10.12988/astp.2018.8832.

4. Winters-Hilt, S. RNA-dependent RNA polymerase encoding artifacts in eukaryotic transcriptomes. Int. J. Mol. Genet Gene Ther 2(1), 2017: doi http://dx.doi.org/10.16966/2471-4968.108.

5. Winters-Hilt S, Evanilla J (2017) Characterization of Fish Stock Diversity via EST Based miRNA Trans-Regulation Profiling. Int J Mol Genet Gene Ther 3(1): doi http://dx.doi.org/10.16966/2471-4968.110.

6. Winters-Hilt, S. Distributed SVM Learning and Support Vector Reduction. International Journal of Computing and Optimization, Vol. 4, 2017, no. 1, 91 – 114.

7. Winters-Hilt, S. Clustering via Support Vector Machine boosting with simulated annealing. International Journal of Computing and Optimization, Vol. 4, 2017, no. 1, 53 – 89.

8. Winters-Hilt, S. Finite State Automaton based signal acquisition with Bootstrap Learning. International Journal of Computing and Optimization, Vol. 4, 2017, no. 1, 159 – 186.

9. Winters-Hilt, S. Nanopore Transducer Engineering and Design. Int J MolBiol Med 2(1): doi http://dx.doi.org/10.16966/ijmbm.108 (2017).

10. Winters-Hilt, S. Biological System Analysis Using a Nanopore Transduction Detector: from miRNA Validation, to Viral Monitoring, to Gene Circuit Feedback Studies. Advanced Studies in Medical Sciences, 5(1), 13 – 53. doi.org/10.12988/asms.2017.722 (2017).

11. Winters-Hilt, S. Isomer-Specific Trace-Level Biosensing Using a Nanopore Transduction Detector. Clinical and Experimental Medical Sciences, 5(1), 35-66. doi.org/10.12988 cems.2017.722 (2017).

12. Winters-Hilt, S. and A. Lewis. Alt-Splice Gene Predictor Using Multitrack-Clique Analysis: Verification of Statistical Support for Modelling in Genomes of Multicellular Eukaryotes. Informatics 2017, 4, 3; doi:10.3390/informatics4010003 (2017).

13. Winters-Hilt, S. Exploring protein conformation-binding relationships and antibody glyco-profiles using a nanopore transduction detector. Molecules & Medicinal Chemistry 2016; 2: e1378. doi: 10.14800/mmc.1378 (2016).

14. Winters-Hilt, S. and A. Stoyanov. Nanopore Event-Transduction Signal Stabilization for Wide pH Range under Extreme Chaotrope Conditions. Molecules 2016, 21(3), 346 (2016).

15. Winters-Hilt, S. Feynman-Cayley Path Integrals select Chiral Bi-Sedenions with 10-dimensional space-time propagation, Advanced Studies in Theoretical Physics, Vol. 9, 2015, no. 14, 667-683 (2015).

16. Winters-Hilt, S. Channel current cheminformatics and stochastic carrier-wave signal processing. International Journal of Computing and Optimization, Vol. 4, 2017, no. 1, 115 – 157.

17. Winters-Hilt, S., E. Horton-Chao, and E. Morales. The NTD Nanoscope: potential applications and implementations. BMC Bioinformatics; 12 (Suppl 10): S21 (2011).

18. Winters-Hilt, S. and C. Baribault. A Meta-state HMM with application to gene structure identification in eukaryotes. EURASIP Journal of Advances in Signal Processing, Special Issue on Genomic Signal Processing (2010).

19. Winters-Hilt, S., Jiang, Z., and C. Baribault. Hidden Markov model with duration side-information for novel HMMD derivation, with application to eukaryotic gene finding EURASIP Journal of Advances in Signal Processing, Special Issue on Genomic Signal Processing, 2010.

20. Eren AM, Amin I, Alba A, Morales E, Stoyanov A, and Winters-Hilt S. Pattern Recognition Informed Feedback for Nanopore Detector Cheminformatics. Accepted paper in book "Advances in Computational Biology", to be published by Springer in Advances in Experimental Medicine and Biology, AEMB 2010 book series.

21. Winters-Hilt S and Jiang Z. A hidden Markov model with binned duration algorithm. IEEE Trans. on Sig. Proc., Vol. 58 (2), Feb. 2010.

22. Winters-Hilt S. Nanopore Cheminformatics based Studies of Individual Molecular Interactions. Ch. 19 in Yanqing Zhang and Jagath C. Rajapakse, editors, Machine Learning in Bioinformatics, John Wiley & Sons, 2009.

23. Alexander Churbanov, Stephen Winters-Hilt, Eugene V Koonin and Igor B Rogozin. Accumulation of GC donor splice signals in mammals. Biology Direct 2008, 3:30.

24. Churbanov, Alexander and S. Winters-Hilt. Implementing EM and Viterbi algorithms for Hidden Markov Model in linear memory. BMC Bioinformatics 2008, 9:228.

25. Churbanov A and Winters-Hilt S. Clustering ionic flow blockade toggles with a Mixture of HMMs. BMC Bioinf. 9 S9, S13 (2008).

26. Roux B and Winters-Hilt S. Hybrid SVM/MM Structural Sensors for Stochastic Sequential Data. BMC Bioinf. 9 S9, S12 (2008).

27. Winters-Hilt S. The alpha-Hemolysin Nanopore Transduction Detector -- single-molecule binding studies and immunological screening of antibodies and aptamers. BMC Bioinf. 8 S7, S12 (2007).

28. Thomson K, Amin I, Morales E, and Winters-Hilt S. Preliminary Nanopore Cheminformatics Analysis of Aptamer-Target Binding Strength. BMC Bioinf. 8 S7, S14 (2007).

29. Winters-Hilt S., Davis, A, Amin, I, and Morales E. The Nanopore Cheminformatics of Individual Transcription Factor Binding Site Interactions. BMC Bioinf. 8 S7, S10 (2007).

30. Winters-Hilt S, Morales E, Amin, I., and Stoyanov, A. Nanopore Cheminformatics Analysis of Single Antibody-Channel Interactions and Antibody-Antigen Binding. BMC Bioinf. 8 S7, S20 (2007).

31. Winters-Hilt S and Merat S. SVM Clustering. BMC Bioinf. 8 S7, S18 (2007).

32. Churbanov A, Baribault C, Winters-Hilt S. Duration learning for nanopore ionic flow blockade analysis. BMC Bioinf. 8 S7, S14 (2007).

33. Landry M, Winters-Hilt S. Analysis of nanopore detector measurements using machine learning methods, with application to single-molecule kinetic analysis. BMC Bioinf. 8 S7, S12 (2007).

34. Winters-Hilt, S and C Baribault. A novel, fast, HMM-with-Duration implementation – for application with a new, pattern recognition informed, nanopore detector. BMC Bioinf. 8 S7, S19 (2007).

35. Winters-Hilt, S., Landry M, Akeson M, Tanase M, Amin I, Coombs A, Morales E, Millet J, Baribault C, and Sendamangalam S. Cheminformatics Methods for Novel Nanopore analysis of HIV DNA termini. BMC Bioinformatics 2006, Sept. 26, 7 S2: S22.

36. Winters-Hilt, S: Nanopore Detector based analysis of single-molecule conformational kinetics and binding interactions. BMC Bioinformatics 2006, Sept. 26, 7 S2: S21.

37. Winters-Hilt S, Yelundur A, McChesney C, Landry M: Support Vector Machine Implementations for Classification & Clustering. BMC Bioinformatics 2006, Sept. 26, 7 S2: S4.

38. Iqbal R, Landry M, Winters-Hilt S: DNA Molecule Classification Using Feature Primitives. BMC Bioinformatics 2006, Sept. 26, 7 S2: S15.

39. Winters-Hilt S: Hidden Markov Model Variants and their Application. BMC Bioinformatics 2006, 7 S2: S14.

40. Deamer, David W. and S. Winters-Hilt, "Nanopore analysis of DNA." Encyclopedia of Nanoscience and Nanotechnology, Ed. H. S. Nalwa. 2005. Vol. 7, pgs 229-235.

41. Winters-Hilt, S., "Single-molecule Biochemical Analysis Using Channel Current Cheminformatics," *Fourth International Conference on Unsolved Problems of Noise and Fluctuations, June 6–10, 2005.*

42. Winters-Hilt, S. and M. Akeson, "Nanopore cheminformatics," *DNA and Cell Biology, Vol. 23 (10), Oct. 2004.*

43. Winters-Hilt, S., "Nanopore detection using channel current cheminformatics," *SPIE Second International Symposium on Fluctuations and Noise, 25-28 May, 2004.*

44. Winters-Hilt S, "Highly Accurate Real-Time Classification of Channel-Captured DNA Termini," *Third International Conference on Unsolved Problems of Noise and Fluctuations,* 2003.

45. Winters-Hilt, S., W. Vercoutere, V. S. DeGuzman, D. Deamer, M. Akeson, and D. Haussler, "Highly Accurate Classification of Watson-Crick Base-Pairs on Termini of Single DNA Molecules," *Biophys. J.* Vol. 84, pg 967, 2003.

46. DeGuzman V, Winters-Hilt S, Solbrig A, Sughrue W, Deamer D, Haussler D, Akeson M. Sequence-dependent fraying of single DNA molecules measured in real time at 5 angstrom resolution using an ion channel. *Biophys J.* 2003 84(2):490A-490A Part 2 Suppl.

47. W. Vercoutere, S. Winters-Hilt, V. S. DeGuzman, D. Deamer, S. Ridino, J. T. Rogers, H. E. Olsen, A. Marziali, and M. Akeson, "Discrimination Among Individual Watson-Crick Base-Pairs at the Termini of Single DNA Hairpin Molecules," *Nucl. Acids Res. Vol.31, 1311-1318,* 2003.

48. W. Vercoutere, S. Winters-Hilt, H. Olsen, D. Deamer, D. Haussler, and M. Akeson, "Rapid Discrimination Among Individual DNA Molecules at Single Nucleotide Resolution Using an Ion Channel," *Nature Biotechnology,* Vol. 19, pg 248, 2001.

49. Winters-Hilt S, I. H. Redmount, and L. Parker, "Physical distinction among alternative vacuum states in flat spacetime geometries," *Phys. Rev. D* 60, 124017 (1999).

50. Friedman J. L., J. Louko, and S. Winters-Hilt, "Reduced Phase space formalism for spherically symmetric geometry with a massive dust shell," *Phys. Rev. D* 56, 7674-7691 (1997).

51. Louko J, J. Z. Simon, and S. Winters-Hilt, "Hamiltonian thermodynamics of a Lovelock black hole," *Phys. Rev. D* 55, 3525-3535 (1997).

52. Louko J and S. Winters-Hilt, "Hamiltonian thermodynamics of the Reissner-Nordstrom-anti de Sitter black hole," *Phys. Rev. D* 54, 2647-2663 (1996).

53. Winters-Hilt, S. "Informatics and Machine Learning, from Martingales to Metaheuristics." (2019)

54. Winters-Hilt, S. "The Nanoscope." (2019)

55. Winters-Hilt, S. "Lagrangian Physics and Unified Propagator Theory." (2020)

56. Cox, R. T. 1946. Probability, Frequency and Reasonable Expectation. Am. J. Physics 14, 1.

57. Karlin, S. and Taylor, H. M. A First Course in Stochastic Processes. Acad. Press, 2nd Ed. 1975.

58. Andrey Andreyevich Markov. Theory of Algorithms. Academy of Sciences of the USSR, 1954.

59. Hoeffding, W. Probability Inequalities for sums of bounded variables. Journal of the American Statistical Association 58 (301) 13-30.

60. Kullback S: *Information Theory and Statistics.* Dover; 1968.

61. Shannon, C.E. 1948. A mathematical theory of communication. Bell Sys. Tech. Journal, 27: 379-423, 623-656.

62. Khinchine, A. I. 1957. Mathematical foundations of information theory. Dover.

63. Azuma, K. Weighted sums of certain dependent random variables. Tohoku Math. J. Vol. 19, No. 3, 1967.

64. Abu-Mostafa, Y.S., Magdon-Ismail, M., and Lin, H.-T. Learning from Data. AMLBook, 2012.

65. Freund, Y. and Schapire, R. E. A decision-theoretic generalization of on-line learning and an application to boosting. Journal of Computer and System Sciences 55. 1997.

66. Kapur JN and Kesavan HK. *Entropy optimization principles with applications.* Academic Press; 1992.

67. Jaynes E. 1997. *Paradoxes of Probability Theory*. Internet accessible book preprint: http://omega.albany.edu:8008/JaynesBook.html.

68. Amari S; Dualistic Geometry of the Manifold of Higher-Order Neurons. Neural Networks, Vol. 4(4), 1991:443-451.

69. Amari S: Information Geometry of the EM and em Algorithms for Neural Networks. Neural Networks, Vol. 8(9), 1995:1379-1408.

70. Amari S and Nagaoka H: *Methods of Information Geometry.* 2000. Translations of Mathematical Monographs Vol. 191.

71. Oppenheim, J.N., and Magnasco, M.O. (2012), Human Time-Frequency Acuity Beats the Fourier Uncertainty Principle. Phys Rev Lett. 110(4).

72. Benedicks, M. (1985), On Fourier transforms of functions supported on sets of finite Lebesgue measure, J. Math. Anal. Appl. 106 (1): 180–183.

73. Silicon Laboratories Inc. Improving ADC Resolution by Oversampling and Averaging. Retrieved 17 January 2015.

74. Torres, S.M. and Zrnic, D.S. Whitening in Range to Improve Weather Radar Spectral Moment Estimates. Part I: Formulation and Simulation. J. Atmospheric and Oceanic Tech. 20 (Nov. 2003).

75. Torres, S.M. and Zrnic, D.S. Whitening of Signals in Range to Improve Estimates of Polarimetric Variables. J. Atmospheric and Oceanic Tech. 20 (Dec. 2003).

76. Pohlmann, K.C. (2005). Principles of Digital Audio. McGraw-Hill Professional. ISBN 0-07-144156-5.

77. Schuchman, L. Dither Signals and Their Effect on Quantization Noise. IEEE Trans. Communications 12 (4): 162–165. (Dec. 1964).

78. Analog Devices: A Technical Tutorial on Digital Signal Synthesis. 1999. http://www.analog.com/static/imported-files/tutorials/450968421DDS_Tutorial_rev12-2-99.pdf

79. Cormen, T. H., C. E. Leiserson, and R. L. Rivest. 1989. Introduction to Algorithms. MIT-Press, Cambridge, USA.

80. Majoros, W.H., M. Pertea and S. L. Salzberg . TigrScan and GlimmerHMM: two open source *ab initio* eukaryotic gene-finders. Bioinformatics, 2004 Nov 1(16):2878-9.

81. Durbin, R., S. Eddy, A. Krogh, and G. Mitchison. 1998. Biological sequence analysis: probalistic models of proteins and nucleic acids. Cambridge, UK New York: Cambridge University Press.

82. Altschul, S., Gish, W., Miller, W., Myers, E., Lipman, D., Basic local alignment search tool. Journal of Molecular Biology **215** (3): 403–410, (1990).

83. Rabiner, L.R. A tutorial on hidden markov models and selected application in speech recognition. Proceedings of the IEEE, 77:257-286, 1989.

84. Moises Burset and Roderic Guigo. Evaluation of gene structure prediction programs. Genomics, 34:353-367, 1996.

85. Mathé C., M.-F. Sagot, T. Schiex and P. Rouzé. Current methods of gene prediction, their strengths and weaknesses. Nucleic Acids Research, 2002, Vol. 30, No. 19 4103-4117

86. Stanke, M., R. Steinkamp, S. Waack, and B. Morgenstern. AUGUSTUS: a web server for gene finding in eukaryotes. Nucleic Acids Research, 2004, Vol. 32, W309-W312.

87. Stanke, M. and Waack, S. Gene prediction with a hidden Markov model and new intron submodel. (2003) Bioinformatics, 19(Suppl. 2) ii215-ii225.

88. Guigo, R., Agarwal, P., Abril, J., Burset, M. and Fickett, J.W. An assessment of gene prediction accuracy in large DNA sequences. (2000) Genome Res., 10, 1631-1642.

89. Mian, S., A. Krogh and D. Haussler. A hidden markov model that finds genes in e. coli dna. Nucleic Acids Research, 22:68-78, 1994.

90. Lu, D. Motif Finding. UNO MS thesis 2009, Advisor – S. Winters-Hilt.

91. Alkhateeb, J. H., Pauplin, O., Ren, J, Jiang, J. Performance of hidden Markov model and dynamic Bayesian classifiers on handwritten Arabic word recognition. Knowledge-based Systems, Vol. 24, Issue 5, July 2011, pp. 680-688.

92. Venkataramaanan L., Sigworth, F. J., Applying hidden Markov models to the analysis of single ion channel activity. Biophys J. 2002 Apr;82(4):1930-42.

93. Ferguson, J.D. Variable duration models for speech. Proceedings of Symposium on the Application of Hidden Markov models to Text and Speech, pages 143-179, 1980.

94. Ramesh, P., and J.G. Wilpon. Modeling state durations in hidden markov models for automatic speech recognition. Proceedings of IEEE International Conference on Acoustics, Speech and Signal Processing, 1:381-384, 1992.

95. Yu, SZ. and H. Kobayashi. An efficient forward-backward algorithm for an explicit-duration hidden markov model. IEEE Signal Processing Letters, 10:11-14, 2003.

96. Johnson, M.T. Capacity and complexity of hmm duration modeling techniques. IEEE Signal Processing Letters, 12:407-410, 2005.

97. Ghahramani, Z. and M. Jordan. Factorial hidden markov models. Machine Learning, 29:245-273.

98. Singer, Y., S. Fine and N. Tishby. The hierarchical hidden markov model: Analysis and applications. Machine Learning, 32:41, 1998.

99. Murphy, K. and M. Paskin. Linear time inference in hierarchical hmms. Proceedings of Neural Information Processing Systems, 2001.

100. Miklos I, Meyer I: A linear memory algorithm for Baum-Welch training. BMC Bioinf. 2005, 6(231).

101. Perry A. Stoll and Jun Ohya. Applications of hmm modeling to recognizing human gestures in image sequences for a man-machine interface. IEEE International Workshop on Robot and Human Communication, pages 129-134, 1995.

102. Jorg Appenrodt Mahmoud Elmezain, Ayoub Al-Hamadi and Bernd Michaelis. A hidden markov model-based continuous gesture recognition system for hand motion trajectory. IEEE Conference Proceeding, 2008.

103. J. Appenrodt M. Elmezain, A. Al-Hamadi and B. Michaelis. A hidden markov model-based isolated and meaningful hand gesture recognition. International Journal of Electrical, Computer, and Systems Engineering, 3:156-163, 2009.

104. E. Augustin S. Knerr and D. Price. Hidden markov model based word recognition and its application to legal amount reading on french checks. Computer Vision and Image Understanding, page 404, 1998.

105. M. Schenkel and M. Jabri. Low resolution, degraded document recognition using neural networks and hidden markov models. Pattern Recognition Letters, 3:365{371, 1998.

106. J. Vlontzos and S. Kung. Hidden markov models for character recognition. IEEE Transactions on Image Processing, 1992.

107. A. Najmi J. Li and R.M. Gray. Image classification by a two-dimensional hidden Markov model. IEEE Transactions on Signal Processing, 48, 2000.

108. R. A. Olshen J. Li, R. M. Gray. Multiresolution image classification by hierarchical modeling with two-dimensional hidden Markov models. IEEE Transactions on Information Theory, 2000.

109. M.S. Wu C.L. Huang and S.H. Jeng. Gesture recognition using the multi-pdm method and hidden markov model. Image and Vision Computing, 18:865, 2000.

110. J. Garcia-Frias and P. M. Crespo. Hidden markov models for burst error characterization in indoor radio channels. IEEE Transactions on Vehicular Technology, 1997.

111. J.P. Hughes E. Bellone and P. Guttorp. A hidden markov model for downscaling synoptic atmospheric patterns to precipitation amounts. Climate Research, 2000.

112. C. Raphael. Automatic segmentation of acoustic musical signals using hidden markov models. IEEE Transactions on Pattern Analysis and Machine Intelligence, 21:1998, 360.

113. Joseph A. Kogan and Daniel Margoliash. Automated recognition of bird song elements from continuous recordings using dynamic time warping and hidden markov models: A comparative study. Journal of the Acoustical Society of America, 1998.

114. Cortes C, and Vapnik VN, "Support Vector Networks", Machine Learning, 20:273-297. 1995.

115. V.N.Vapnik. The Nature of Statistical Learning Theory. New York: Springer- Verlag, 1995.

116. V.N.Vapnik. Statistical Learning Theory. New York: Wiley, 1998.

117. Burgess CJC. A tutorial on support vector machines for pattern recognition. Knowledge Discovery and Data Mining, 2(2):121–167, 1998.

118. J. Platt, *Sequential Minimal Optimization: A Fast Algorith for Training Support Vector Machines*, Microsoft Research Tech. Rep. MSR-TR-98-14, 1998.

119. Platt JC. Fast Training of Support Vector Machines using Sequential Minimal Optimization. In *Advances in Kernel Methods -- Support Vector Learning.* Edited by Scholkopf B, Burges CJC, and Smola AJ. MIT Press, Cambridge, USA; Ch. 12. 1998.

120. Vapnik, V. N. 1999. The Nature of Statistical Learning Theory (2nd Ed.). Springer-Verlag, New York.

121. Graf HP, Cosatto E, Bottou L, Durdanovic I, and Vapnik VN. Parallel Support Vector Machines: The Cascade SVM, in proceedings NIPS, 2004.

122. Armond, Kenneth C. Jr. Distributed Support Vector Machine Learning. (2008). University of New Orleans Master's Thesis in CS, Advisor Stephen Winters-Hilt.

123. McChesney, C. SVM-based Clustering. (2006). University of New Orleans Master's Thesis in CS, Advisor Stephen Winters-Hilt.

124. Merat, S. Clustering via supervised support vector machines. (2008). University of New Orleans Master's Thesis in CS, Advisor Stephen Winters-Hilt.

125. Zhang, H. Distributed Support Vector Machines with Graphical Processing Units. (2009). University of New Orleans Master's Thesis in CS, Advisor Stephen Winters-Hilt.

126. Girosi F and Poggio T. Regularization algorithms for learning that there are equivalent to multilayer networks. Science, 247:978–982, 1990.

127. Scholkopf B, Williamson RC, Smola AJ. Regularization algorithms for learning that there are equivalent to multilayer networks. Science, 247:978–982, 1990.

128. Doursat R, Geman S, and Bienstock E. Neural network and bias/variance dilemma. Neural Computation, 4(2):1–58, 1992.

129. Kleinberg J. An impossibility theorem for clustering. Proc. of the 16th conference on Neural Information Processing Systems, (12), 2002.

130. Bishop CM. Neural Networks for Pattern Recognition. Oxford University Press, 1995.

131. Schapire RE and Freund Y. A decision-theoretic generalization of on-line learning and an application to boosting. J. Comput. Syst. Sci., 55(1):119–139, 1997.

132. Crammer K and Singer Y: On the Algorithmic Implementation of Multiclass Kernel-based Vector Machines. Journal of Machine Learning Research 2 (2001) 265-292

133. G.Ratsch K. Tsuda K. Muller, S. Mika and B. Schölkopf, *An introduction to kernel-based learning algorithms*, IEEE Trans. Neural Netw. 12, 2001, no. 2, 181–201.

134. Osuna E; Freund R, and Girosi. F: An improved training algorithm for support vector machines. In *Neural Networks for Signal Processing VII*. Edited by Principe J, Gile L, Morgan N, and Wilson E. editors. IEEE, New York; 1997: 276-85.

135. Joachims T: Making large-scale SVM learning practical. In *Advances in Kernel Methods -- Support Vector Learning*. Edited by Scholkopf B, Burges CJC, and Smola AJ. MIT Press, Cambridge, USA;. 1998: Ch. 11.

136. Crammer K and Singer Y: On the Algorithmic Implementation of Multiclass Kernel-based Vector Machines. Journal of Machine Learning Research 2 (2001) 265-292

137. Hsu CW and Lin CJ: A Comparison of Methods for Multi-class Support Vector Machines. IEEE Transactions on Neural Networks, 13; 2002:415-425

138. Lee Y, Lin Y and Wahba G: Multicategory Support Vector Machines. Technical Report 1043, Department of Statistics, University of Wisconsin, Madison, WI, 2001. http://citeseer.ist.psu.edu/lee01multicategory.html

139. Duda RO, Hart PE and Stork DG, *Pattern classification*, Second Edition, John Wiley and Sons, New York, 2001.

140. Keerthi SS, Shevade SK, Bhattacharyya C and Murthy KRK: Improvements to Platt's SMO algorithm for SVM classifier design. *Neural Computation,* Vol. 13, 2001:637-649

141. Ben-Hur A, Horn D, Siegelmann HT, Vapnik V: Support Vector Clustering. Journal of Machine Learning Research 2; 2001:125-137.

142. Scholkopf B, Platt JC, Shawe-Taylor, J Smola AJ, Williamson RC: Estimating the Support of a High-Dimensional Distribution. Neural Computation, 13, 1999:1443—1472.

143. Yang J, Estivill-Castro V, Chalup SK: *Support Vector Clustering Through Proximity Graph Modeling. In Proceedings, 9th International Conference on Neural Information Processing (ICONIP'02)*, 2002:898-903.

144. Fisher RA. The use of multiple measurements in taxonomic problems. Annals of Eugenics, 7:179–188, 1936.

145. Donoho, D. Compressed sensing. IEEE Trans. On Information Theory, 52(4), pp. 1289 - 1306, April 2006.

146. DeFelice, L. J. 1981. Introduction to membrane noise. Plenum Press, New York.

147. Ziemer, R. E. and W. H. Tranter. 1985. Principles of Communications; Systems, Modulation, and Noise (2nd Ed.). Houghton Mifflin Company, Boston.

148. Seven-Year Wilson Microwave Anisotropy Probe (WMAP) Observations: Sky Maps, Systematic Errors, and Basic Results" (PDF). nasa.gov. http://lambda.gsfc.nasa.gov/product/map/dr4/pub_papers/sevenyear/basic_results/wmap_7yr _basic_results.pdf.

149. Lunine, J.I. 1999. Earth:evolution of a habitable world, Cambridge University Press, United Kingdom, ISBN 0521644232.

150. "'Life Chemical' detected in comet". BBC News, August 18, 2009.

151. Lepot, Kevin, Karim, Benzerara, Gordon E. Brown, Pascal Phillipot (2008). Microbially influenced formation of 2.7 billion-year-old stromatolites", Nature Geoscience 1: 118-21. Doi10.1038/ngeo107.

152. Forterre P. The two ages of the RNA World, and the transition to the DNA World: a story of viruses and cells. Biochemie 2005, 87(9-10):793-803.

153. Forterre P. The origin of viruses and theor possible roles in major evolutionary transirions. Virus Res 2006. 117(1):5-16.

154. Warmflash, David, and Benjamin Weiss. "Did life come from another world?" Scientific American: 64-71, http://www.sciam.com/article.cfm?articleID=00073A97-5745-1359-94FF83414B7F0000&pageNumber=1&catID=2.

155. Witt AN, Vijh UP, Gordon KD (2003). "Discovery of Blue Fluorescence by Polycyclic Aromatic Hydrocarbon Molecules in the Red Rectangle". *Bulletin of the American Astronomical Society* **35**: 1381. Archived from the original on 2003-12-19. http://web.archive.org/web/20031219175322/http://www.aas.org/publications/baas/v35n5/aas203/189.htm.

156. Battersby, S. (2004). Space molecules point to organic origins. Retrieved January 11, 2004 from http://www.newscientist.com/article/dn4552-space-molecules-point-to-organic-origins.html

157. Koonin, E.V., and Dolja, V.V. 2006. Evolution of complexity in the viral world: the dawn of a new vision. Virus Res. 117:1-4.

158. Dobzhansky, Theodosius. Genetics of the evolutionary process. Columbia University Press (1970), ISBN 0231083068.

159. Darwin, Charles (1859). *On The Origin of Species*. pp. 503. ISBN 0801413192. http://en.wikisource.org/wiki/On_the_Origin_of_Species_(1859)/Chapter_XIV.

160. Dawkins, Richard (1996) [1986]. *The Blind Watchmaker*. New York: W. W. Norton & Company, Inc. pp. 148–161. ISBN 0-393-31570-3

161. Joan Y. Chiao and Katherine D. Blizinsky. Culture–gene coevolution of individualism–collectivism and the serotonin transporter gene. Proc Biol Sci. 2010 February 22; 277(1681): 529–537.

162. Susantha Goonatilake: The Evolution of Information: Lineages in Gene, Culture, and Artefact. Pinter Publishers 1991.

163. Bell, Philip John Livingstone (Sep 2001), "Viral eukaryogenesis: was the ancestor of the nucleus a complex DNA virus?", *Journal of molecular evolution* **53** (3): 251–256

164. D'Herelle F: The Bacteriophage; Its role in immunity. Baltimore, Williams and Wilkins, 1922.

165. Haldane JB S. The Origin of Life. Rationalist Annual 1928, 148:3-10.

166.McClintock, B. (1950). The origin and behavior of mutable loci in maize. Proc. Natl;. Acad Sci U.S.A. 36 (6):344-55.

167. Arnaud, F., et. al. A paradigm for virus-host coevolution: sequential counter-adaptions between endogenous and exogenous retroviruses. PloS Pathog 3(11): e170. Nov. 2007. doi10.1371/journal.ppat.0030170.

168. M. Worobey, A. Bjork, J .O. Wertheim. Point, Counterpoint: The evolution of pathogenic viruses and their human hosts. Annu. Rev. Ecol. Evol. Syst. 2007. 38:515-40.

169. Lobo, F.P., et al. Virus-Host co-evolution: common patterns of nucleotide motif usage in *Flaviviridae* and their Hosts. PLoS ONE 4(7): e6282. Doi:10.1371/journal.pone.0006282.

170. Smith, S.E.P., J. Li, K. Garbett, K. Mirnics, and P. H. Patterson. Maternal immune activation alters fetal brain development through interleukin-6. J. Neurosci., Oct. 3 2007, 27(40):10695-10702.

171. Brown, A.S., Prenatal infection as a risk factor for schizophrenia. Schizophr Bull 32:200-202.

172. Brown, A.S., Susser E.S. Inutero infection and adult schizophrenia. Ment Retard Dev. Disabil Res Rev 8:51-57.

173. Brown, A.S., Begg, M.D., Gravenstein, S., Schaefer, C.A., Wyatt, R.J. Bresnahan, M., Babulas, V.P. and Susser, E.S. Serologic evidence of prenatal influenza in the etiology of schizophrenia. Arch Gen Psychiatry 61:774-780.

174. Reddy, P.S., et al. Seneca Valley Virus, a systematically deliverable oncolytic picornavirus, and the treatment of neuroendacrine cancers. J. Natl. Cancer Inst. 99, 1623-1633.

175. Bandea, C.I. The origin and evolution of Viruses as molecular Organisms. Nature Proceedings: hdl:10101/npre.2009.3886.1.

176. Zgao, H, Gao, X., and Zhu, L. A virus co-evolution genetic algorithm based on niche technology. Icla pp. 894-899, 2006 IEEE International Conference on Information Acquisition, 2006.

177. Tamura, K., Mutoh, A., S. Kato, and H. Itoh. Genetic Algorithm adopting selective virus infection. Proc. (365) Articial and computation Intelligence, 2002.

178. Fire, A, Xu S, Montgomery MK, Kostas SA, Driver SE, Mello CC. 1998. Potent and specific genetic interference by double-stranded RNA in *Caenorhabditis elegans. Nature* 391:806-11.

179. Bernstein E, Caudy AA, Hammond SM, Hannon GJ. 2001. Role for a bidentate nuclease in the initiation step of RNA interference. Nature 409:363-66.

180. Siolas, D., Lerner C., Burchard, J., et al. Synthetic shRNAs as potent RNAi triggers. Nat Biotechnol 2005; 23(2): 227-231.

181. Kanzaki, L.I.B., S.S. Ornelas, and E. R. Arganaraz. RNA interference and HIV-1 infection. Rev. Med. Virol. 2008; 18: 5-18.

182. Weinberg, M.S. and K.V. Morris. Are Viral-Encoded microRNAs mediating latent HIV-1 infection? DNA Cell Biol. 2006 April; 25(4): 223-231. Doi:10.1089/dna.2006.25.223.

183. Yeung, M.L., et al. Changes in microRNA expression profiles in HIV-1 transfected human cells. Retrovirology 2005, 2:81. Doi:10.1186/1742-4690-2-81.

184. Valeri, N., et al. Epigenetics, miRNAs, and human cancer: a new chapter in human gene regulation. Mamm Genome (2009) 20:573-580.

185. Gabuzda, DH, Lawrence K, Langhoff E, Terwilliger E, Dorfman T, et al. 1992. Role of Vif in replication of human immuinodeficiency virus type 1 in CD4+ T lymphocytes. J. Virol. 66:6489-95.

186. Sheehy AM, Gaddis, NC, Choi, JD, Malim, MH. 2002. Isolation of human gene that inhibits HIV-1 infection and is suppressed by viral Vif protein. Nature 418:646-50.

187. Mangeat, B, Turelli, P., Liao, S., Trono D. 2004. A single amino acid determinant governs the species-specific sensitivity of APOBEC3G to Vif action. J. Biol. Chem. 279:14481-83.

188. Zhang, H, Yang, B, Pomerantz, RJ, Zhang, C, Arunachalam, SC, Gao, L. 2003. The cytadine deaminase CEM15 unduces hypermutation in newly synthesized HIV-1 DNA. Nature 424:94-98.

189. Conticello, SG, Thomas, CJ, Petersen-Mahrt SK, Neuberger MS. 2005. Evolution of the AID/APOBEC family of polynucleotide (deoxy)ctyidine deaminases. Mol. Biol. Evol. 22:367-77.

190. Evidence of s sedimentary origin of clay materials in the Mawrth Vallis region, Mars. J.R. Michalski and Eldar Z. Noe Dobroe. NASA.

191. NASA mission News 2008-227. NASA Orbiter finds Martian rock record with 10 beats to the bar.

192. Cheng S, Fockler C, Barnes WM, Higuchi R (1994). "Effective amplification of long targets from cloned inserts and human genomic DNA". *Proc Natl Acad Sci.* **91** (12): 5695–5699

193. Wolpert, D.H. and W.G. Macready. No Free Lunch Theorems for Optimization. IEEE (1997) Transactions on Evolutionary Computation1, 67.

194. Wolpert, D.H. and W.G. Macready. Coevolutionary free lunches. IEEE (2005) Transactions on Evolutionary Computation, 9(6): 721-735.

195 Raspe, R.E. Baron Munchhausen's Narrative of his Marvellous Travels and Campaigns in Russia. London 1785.

196. IEEE Standard 100 Authoritative Dictionary of IEEE Standards Terms, Seventh Edition, IEEE Press, 2000 ISBN 0-7381-2601-2 page 123.

197. Winters-Hilt, S. Method and System for Stochastic Carrier Wave Communications, Radio-Noise Embedded Steganography, and Robust Self-Tuning Signal Discovery and Data-Mining. Pat. Pend. June, 2015; 62/186827.

198. Winters-Hilt, S. Machine Learning Methods for Channel Current Cheminformatics, Biophysical analysis, and Bioinformatics. (2003). PhD Dissertation, UCSC.

199. Oppenheim, A. V., A. S. Willsky, and I. T. Young. 1983. Signals and Systems. Prentice-Hall, New Jersey.

200. Pearce, B.K.D., Tupper, A.S., Pudritz, R.E., and P.G. Higgs. Constraining the Time Interval for the Origin of Life on Earth. Astrobiology, Vol. 18, No. 3. (2018). https://doi.org/10.1089/ast.2017.1674.

201. Dyson, F. J. Origins of Life. Second edition. (1999).

202. Margulis, L. Origin of Eukaryotic Cells. (1970).

203. Margulis, L. Symbiosis in Cell Evolution. (1981).

204. Margulis, L. and D. Sagan. What is Life? (1995).

205. Amils, R.et al. From Río Tinto to Mars: The Terrestrial and Extraterrestrial Ecology of Acidophiles. https://doi.org/10.1016/B978-0-12-387044-5.00002-9.

206. Wei, R., T.G. Martin, U. Rant, H. Dietz. DNA Origami Gatekeepers for solid-state nanopores. Angewandte Chemie Vol 51 (20) 4864-4867. (2012).

207. Sanger, F., *et al.* 1977. DNA sequencing with chain-terminating inhibitors. *Proc. Natl. Acad. Sci. U.S.A.* 74, 5463 – 5467.

208. Sanger F. and Coulson AR (May 1975). A rapid method determing sequences in DNA by primed synthesis with DNA polymerase. J. Mol. Biol. 94 (3):441-8.

209. Smith LM, Sanders JZ, Kaiser RJ, *et al* (1986). Fluorescence detection in automated DNA sequence analysis. *Nature* **321** (6071): 674–9.

210. Smith LM, Fung S, Hunkapiller MW, Hunkapiller TJ, Hood LE (April 1985). The synthesis of oligonucleotides containing an aliphatic amino group at the 5' terminus: synthesis of fluorescent DNA primers for use in DNA sequence analysis. *Nucleic Acids Res.* 13 (7): 2399–412.

211. Murphy, K.; Berg, K.; Eshleman, J. (2005). Sequencing of genomic DNA by combined amplification and cycle sequencing reaction. *Clinical chemistry* **51** (1): 35–39.

212. Sengupta, D.; Cookson, B. (2010). SeqSharp: A general approach for improving cycle-sequencing that facilitates a robust one-step combined amplification and sequencing method. *The Journal of molecular diagnostics : JMD* **12** (3): 272–277.

213. Meinkoth J, Wahl G: Hybridization of nucleic acids immobilized on solid supports. *Anal Biochem* 1984, 138:267-284.

214. Maskos U, Southern EM: Parallel analysis of oligodeoxynucleotide (oligonucleotide) interactions. I. Analysis of factors influencing oligonucleotide duplex formation. *Nucleic Acids Res* 1992, 20:1675-1678.

215. Augenlicht L H; Kobrin D Cloning and screening of sequences expressed in a mouse colon tumor. Cancer research 1982;42(3):1088-93. 1982

216. Liu, S., L. Lin, P. jiang, D. Wang and Y. Xing. A comparison of RNA-seq and high-density exon array for detecting differential gene expression between closely related species. Nucleic Acids Research, 2010, Sept. 1-11.

217. Fakhrai-Rad, H., J. Zheng, and T.D. Willis et al. SNP discovery in pooled samples with mismatch repair detection. Genome Res. 2004 14: 1404-1412.

218. http://genomics.xprize.org/archon-x-prize-for-genomics/prize-overview

219. Braslavsky, I., B. Hebert, E. Kartalov, and S.R. Quake. Sequence information can be obtained from single DNA molecules. PNAS 2003 Vol. 100, No. 7, 3960-3964.

220. Bao, Y.P., M. Huber, T-F. Wei, S.S. Maria, J.J. Storhoff. SNP identification in unamplified human genomic DNA with gold nanoparticle probes. Nucleic Acids Res., 2005, Vol. 33, No. 2, e15.

221. Krane, D.E., and M.L. Raymer. Fundamental Concepts of Bioinformatics. (2003).

222. Henikoff S, Henikoff JG. Automated assembly of protein blocks for database searching. *Nucleic Acids Res.* **19**(23):6565–6572. (1991).

223. Henikoff, S. and Henikoff, J.G. Amino Acid Substitution Matrices from Protein Blocks. PNAS 89, 10915-10919. (1992).

224. Winters-Hilt, S.N. and Robert L. Adelman. Methods and systems for sequential analysis and nanopore detector signal analysis using stochastic sequential analysis (SSA) methods such as hidden Markov models (HMMs). PCT patent filing Feb. 2011.

225. Winters-Hilt, S., Hidden Markov model based structure identification using (i) HMM-with-Duration with positionally dependent emissions and incorporation of side-information into an HMMD via the ratio of cumulants method; and/or (ii) meta-HMMs and higher-order HMMs with gap and sequence-specific (hash) interpolated Markov models and Support Vector Machine signal boosting; and/or (iii) topological structure identification; and/or (iv) multi-track, parallel, or holographic HMMs; and/or (v) distributed HMM methods via Viterbi-path based reconstruction and verification; and/or (vi) adaptive null-state binning for O(TN) computation. Patented, February 2010.

226. Bousso, Raphael. "The Holographic Principle". http://arxiv.org/pdf/hep-th/0203101.Rev. Mod. Phys. 74, 825–874 (2002).

227. Winters-Hilt, S. and R. Adelman. Method and System for Characterizing or Identifying Molecules and Molecular Mixtures. USPTO Filing. Meta Logos Inc. 2010.

228. Stephen N. Winters-Hilt & Robert L. Adelman. Methods and systems for structure identification, pattern recognition, signal analysis, bioinformatics, and nanopore detector cheminformatics. Patent Pending, January 2011.

229. Stephen N. Winters-Hilt and Robert L. Adelman. Methods and systems for nanopore biosensing. PCT patent filing Feb. 2011.

230. Stephen N. Winters-Hilt and Robert L. Adelman. . Methods and systems for classification, clustering, pattern recognition, and nanopore detector cheminformatics, using Support Vector Machines (SVMs). Patent Pending, February 2011.

231. Jiang, Z. Binned HMM with duration: variations and applications. (2010). University of New Orleans PhD Dissertation in CS, Advisor Stephen Winters-Hilt.

232. McDiarmid, Colin (1989). "On the Method of Bounded Differences". *Surveys in Combinatorics*. 141: 148–188.

233. Mohri, M., et al. Foundations of Machine Learning. (2012).

234. Fire, A., Xu, S., Montgomery, M., Kostas, S., Driver, S., Mello, C. Potent and specific genetic interference by double-stranded RNA in Caenorhabditis elegans. Nature, 1998, 391 (6669): 806–811.

235. Bernstein E., Caudy AA, Hammond SM, Hannon GJ (Jan 2001). Role for a bidentate ribonuclease in the initiation step of RNA interference. Nature. 409 (6818): 363–6.

236. Valeri, N., et al. Epigenetics, miRNAs, and human cancer: a new chapter in human gene regulation. Mamm Genome (2009) 20:573-580.

237. Iyer, L.M., Koonin, E.V., and Aravind L. Evolutionary connection between the catalytic subunits of DNA-dependent RNA polymerases and eukaryotic RNA-dependent RNA polymerases and the origin of RNA polymerases. BMC Struct Biol. 2003 Jan 28;3:1.

238. Forterre, P. Displacement of cellular proteins by functional analogues from plasmids or viruses could explain puzzling phylogenies of many DNA informational proteins. Mol Microbiol. 1999 Aug;33(3):457-65.

239. Legendrea, M., et al. In-depth study of Mollivirus sibericum, a new 30,000-yr old giant virus infecting Acanthamoeba. PNAS, September 8, 2015, E5327–E5335.

240. Iyer, L.M., Balaji, S., Koonin, E.V., and L. Aravind. Evolutionary genomics of nucleocytoplasmic large DNA viruses. Virus Research 117 (2006) 156–184.

241. Oliveira, G.P., et al. Promoter Motifs in NCLDVs: An Evolutionary Perspective. Viruses 2017, 9, 16.

242. Kobiler, O., Drayman, N., Butin-Israeli, V. and A. Oppenheim. Virus strategies for passing the nuclear envelope barrier. Nucleus 3:6, 2012; 526–539.

243. Fay, N. and N. Panté. Nuclear entry of DNA viruses. Frontiers in Microbiology 6(467), 2015.

244. Cohen, S., Au, S., and N. Panté. How viruses access the nucleus. Biochimica et Biophysica Acta 1813 (2011) 1634–1645.

245. Wang, G., Shimada, E., Zhang, J., Hong, J.S., Smith, G.M., Teitell, M.A, and C. M. Koehler. Correcting human mitochondrial mutations with targeted RNA import. PNAS 109(13), 2012, 4840–4845.

246. Shaheen, H.H. and A. K. Hopper. Retrograde movement of tRNAs from the cytoplasm to the nucleus in Saccharomyces cerevisiae. PNAS 102(32), 2005, 11290–11295.

247. O'Neill, R.E. Jaskunas. R., Blobeli, G., Palese, G.P., and J. Moroianu. Nuclear Import of Influenza Virus RNA Can Be Mediated by Viral Nucleoprotein and Transport Factors Required for Protein Import.The Journal of Biological Chemistry 270(39), 1995, 22701-22704.

248. Marfori, M., et al. Molecular basis for specificity of nuclear import and prediction of nuclear localization. Biochimica et Biophysica Acta 1813 (2011) 1562–1577.

249. Bryant, H.E., Wadd, S.E., Lamond, A.I., Silverstein, S.J., and J.B. Clements. Herpes Simplex Virus IE63 (ICP27) Protein Interacts with Spliceosome-Associated Protein 145 and Inhibits Splicing prior to the First Catalytic Step. J. of Virology 75(9), 2001, 4376-4385.

250. Dubois J, Terrier O, Rosa-Calatrava M. Influenza viruses and mRNA splicing: doing more with less. mBio 5(3):e00070-14. 2014. doi:10.1128/mBio.00070-14.

251. De Maio FA, Risso G, Iglesias NG, Shah P, Pozzi B, Gebhard LG, et al. The Dengue Virus NS5 Protein Intrudes in the Cellular Spliceosome and Modulates Splicing. PLoS Pathog 12(8): e1005841. 2016. doi:10.1371/journal.ppat.1005841

252. Rogozin, I.B., Carmel, L., Csuros, M. and E.V. Koonin. Origin and evolution of spliceosomal introns. Biology Direct 2012, 7:11.

253. Forterre, P. Genomics and early cellular evolution. The origin of the DNA world. C R Acad Sci III. 2001; 324(12):1067-76.

254. Forterre, P. Three RNA cells for ribosomal lineages and three DNA viruses to replicate their genomes: A hypothesis for the origin of cellular domain. PNAS, 2006, 103(10), 3669-3674.

255. Zong, J., Yao, X., Yin, J., Zhang, D., and H. Mac. Evolution of the RNA-dependent RNA polymerase (RdRP) genes: Duplications and possible losses before and after the divergence of major eukaryotic groups. Gene 447(1), 2009, 29-39.

256. Sigova, A., Rhind, N., and P.D. Zamore. A single Argonaute protein mediates both transcriptional and posttranscriptional silencing in Schizosaccharomyces pombe. Genes & Dev. 2004. 18: 2359-2367.

257. Takemura, M. Poxviruses and the origin of the eukaryotic nucleus. J Mol Evol. 2001 May; 52(5): 419-25.

258. Bell P.J. Viral eukaryogenesis: was the ancestor of the nucleus a complex DNA virus? J Mol Evol. 2001 Sep, 53(3):251-6.

259. Vellai T., Takacs K., and Vida G. A new aspect to the origin and evolution of eukaryotes. J Mol Evol. 1998 May;46(5):499-507.

260. Gaudin, M., et al. Extracellular membrane vesicles harbouring viral genomes. Environ Microbiol. 2014 Apr;16(4):1167-75.

261. Forterre, P. and M. Gaia. Giant viruses and the origin of modern eukaryotes. Curr Opin Microbiol. 2016 Jun; 31:44-9.

262. Hale, C.R., Zhao, P., Olson, S., Duff, M.O., Graveley, B.R., Wells, L., Terns, R.M., and M.P. Terns. RNA-Guided RNA Cleavage by a CRISPR RNA-Cas Protein Complex. Cell, 2009 Nov, 139, 945–956.

263. Makarova, Kira S, et al. Unification of Cas Protein families and a simple scenario for the origin of CRISPR/cas Systems. Biology Direct 2011:6.

264. Kostyrka G. What roles for viruses in origin of life scenarios? Stud Hist Philos Biol Biomed Sci. 2016, Oct;59:135-44.

265. Tessera, M. Origin of Evolution versus Origin of Life: A Shift of Paradigm. Int. J. Mol. Sci. 2011, 12, 3445-3458.

266. Boyer M, et al., 2009. Giant Marseillevirus highlights the role of amoebae as a melting pot in emergence of chimeric microorganisms. Proc Natl Acad Sci U S A. 2009 Dec 22; 106(51):21848-53.

267. Boyer, M., Madoui, M. A., Gimenez, G., La Scola, B., & D. Raoult. 2010. Phylogenetic and phyletic studies of informational genes in genomes highlight existence of a 4 domain of life including giant viruses. PLoS One. 2010 Dec 2;5(12):e15530.

268. Nasir, A., Kim, K. M., & G. Caetano-Anolles. 2012. Giant viruses coexisted with the cellular ancestors and represent a distinct supergroup along with superkingdoms Archaea, Bacteria and Eukarya. BMC Evol. Biol. 12:156.

269. Yutin, N., Wolf, Y. I., Raoult, D., & E. V. Koonin. 2009. Eukaryotic large nucleo-cytoplasmic DNA viruses: clusters of orthologous genes and reconstruction of viral genome evolution. Virol. J. 6:223.

270. Bell, P. J. 2001. Viral eukaryogenesis: was the ancestor of the nucleus a complex DNA virus? J. Mol. Evol. 53(3): 251-256.

271. Iyer, L. M., Aravind, L., & E. V. Koonin. 2001. Common origin of four diverse families of large eukaryotic DNA viruses J. Virol. 75(23):11720-34.

272. Saini, H. K., & D. Fischer. 2007. Structural and functional insights into Mimivirus ORFans BMC Genomics. 8: 115.

273. Jagus, R., Bachvaroff, T. R., Joshi, B., & A. R. Place. 2012. Diversity of Eukaryotic Translational Initiation Factor eIF4E in Protists. Comp. Funct. Genomics. 2012:134839.

274. Bell, P. Meiosis: Its Origin According to the Viral Eukaryogenesis Theory. http://dx.doi.org/10.5772/56876.

275. Stanke M. and B. Morgenstern. AUGUSTUS: a web server for gene prediction in eukaryotes that allows user-defined constraints. Nucleic Acids Research, 2005, Vol. 33, W465–W467

276. Rajapakse, J. C. and L. S. Ho. Markov Encoding for Detecting Signals in Genomic Sequences. IEEE/ACM Transactions on Computational Biology and Bioinformatics, Vol. 2, No. 2,, pgs. 131-142.

277. Cheng S, Fockler C, Barnes WM, Higuchi R (1994). "Effective amplification of long targets from cloned inserts and human genomic DNA". *Proc Natl Acad Sci.* **91** (12): 5695–5699

278. Taher, L., O. Rinner, S. Garg, A. Sczyrba, M. Brudno, S. Batzoglou and B. Morgenstern. AGenDA: homology-based gene prediction. Bioinformatics Vol. 19 no. 12 2003, pages 1575–1577.

279. Sonnenburg S., A. Zien, and G. Ratsch . ARTS: accurate recognition of transcription starts in human. Bioinformatics Vol. 22 no. 14 2006, pages e472–e480.

280. Do J.H. and D-K. Choi. Computational Approaches to Gene Prediction . The Journal of Microbiology, April 2006, Vol. 44, No. 2. p.137-144

281. Korf I. Gene finding in novel genomes. BMC Bioinformatics 2004, 5:59.

282. Mathe C., M.-F. Sagot, T. Schiex and P. Rouze . Current methods of gene prediction, their strengths and weaknesses. Nucleic Acids Research, 2002, Vol. 30 No. 19, 4103-4117.

283. Allen, J. E., W. H. Majoros, M. Pertea and S. L. Salzberg. JIGSAW, GeneZilla, and GlimmerHMM: puzzling out the features of human genes in the ENCODE regions. Genome Biology 2006, 7(Suppl 1):S9

284. Noguchi, H., Park, J., Takagi, T.: MetaGene: prokaryotic gene finding from environmental genome shotgun sequences. Nucleic Acids Res. 2006 , 34 (19) :5623-30

285. Taher L., O. Rinner, S. Garg, A. Sczyrba, M. Brudno, S. Batzoglou, and B. Morgenstern. Agenda: homology-based gene prediction. *Bioinformatics*, 19(12):1575-1577, Aug 2003.

286. van Baren MJ, Koebbe BC, Brent MR. Using N-SCAN or TWINSCAN to predict gene structures in genomic DNA sequences. Curr Protoc Bioinformatics. 2007 Dec;Chapter 4:Unit 4.8.

287. Sanja Rogic, Alan K Mackworth, and B.F. Francis Ouellette, "Evaluation of Gene-Finding Programs on Mammalian Sequences," Genome Res. 2001. 11: 817-832, pp. 817-832, 2001.

288. Dunham I., Shimizu N., Roe B.A. & Chissoe S. (1999) The DNA sequence of human chromosome 22. Nature 402, 489-95.

289. Moises Burset and Roderic Guigo, "Evaluation of Gene Structure Prediction Programs," Genomics, vol. 34, pp. 353-367, 1996.

290. Liu H. , H. Han, J. Li and L. Wong. DNAFSMiner: A Web-Based Software Toolbox to Recognize Two Types of Functional Sites in DNA Sequences. http://sdmc.i2r.a-star.edu.sg/DNAFSMiner/.

291. Sonnenburg S., G. Schweikert, P. Philips, J. Behr and G. Rätsch . Accurate splice site prediction using support vector machines. BMC Bioinformatics 2007, 8(Suppl 10):S7

292. Degroeve, S., Y. Saeys, B. De Baets, P. Rouzé and Y. Van de Peer. SpliceMachine: predicting splice sites from high-dimensional local context representations. Bioinformatics, Vol. 21 no. 8 2005, pages 1332–1338

293. Muro, E.M., R. Herrington, S. Janmohamed, C. Frelin, M. A. Andrade-Navarro and N. N. Iscove. Identification of gene 3' ends by automated EST cluster analysis. PNAS, December 23, 2008, vol. 105, no. 51, pgs. 20286–20290.

294. Bellora N., D. Farre and M. Mar Alba. PEAKS: identification of regulatory motifs by their position in DNA sequences. Bioinformatics, Vol. 23 no. 2 2007, pages 243–244.

295. X. He, X. Ling, and S. Sinha. Alignment and Prediction of cis-Regulatory Modules Based on a Probabilistic Model of Evolution. PLoS Computational Biology 2009,Volume 5, Issue 3, Pgs 1-14.

296. Lu, D. Motif Finding. UNO MS thesis in CS, 2009, Advisor – Prof. S. Winters-Hilt.

297. Shinozaki D., T. Akutsu and O. Maruyama. Finding optimal degenerate patterns in DNA sequences. Bioinformatics Vol. 19 Suppl. 2 2003, pages ii206–ii214

298. Frickey T. and G. Weiller. Mclip: motif detection based on cliques of gapped local profile-to-profile alignments. Bioinformatics, Vol. 23 no. 4 2007, pages 502–503

299. de Hoon, M.J.L., S. Imoto, J. Nolan and S. Miyano . Open source clustering software. Bioinformatics, Vol. 20 no. 9 2004, pages 1453–1454

300. Wang G., T. Yu and W. Zhang. WordSpy: identifying transcription factor binding motifs by building a dictionary and learning a grammar. Nucleic Acids Research, 2005, Vol. 33, W412–W416

301. The *C. elegans* Sequencing Consortium. "Genome sequence of the nematode *C. elegans*: a platform for investigating biology". Science 282 (5396): 2012–2018,

302. Fickett J.W. and C.-S. Tung, "Assessment of protein coding measures.," Nucleic Acids Res. 20:6441–6450, pp. 6441-6450, 1992.

303. Snyder E.E.and Stormo G.D., "Identification of protein coding regions in genomic DNA.," J. Mol. Biol. 248:1-18, pp. 1-18, 1995.

304. Fickett J.W., "The gene identification problem: An overview for developers," Computers Chem. Vol 20, No. 1, pp. 103-118, 1996. [Online]. http://www.nslij-genetics.org/gene/1996.html

305. Du Preez J.A. and D.M. Weber, "High-order hidden Markov modelling," in Communications and Signal Processing, 1998. COMSIG '98. Proceedings of the 1998 South African Symposium on, University of Cape Town, Rondebosch, 7-8 Sept. 1998, pp. 197-202.

306. Reese M.G., Frank H. Eeckman, David Kulp, and David Haussler, "Improved splice site detection in Genie," RECOMB '97: Proceedings of the first annual international conference on Computational molecular biology, pp. 232-240, January, 1997.

307. Xie, Z., Fan, B., Chen, C., and Z. Chen. An important role of an inducible RNA-dependent RNA polymerase in plant antiviral defense. PNAS May 22, 2001 98(11).

308. Siegel, R.W., Bellon, L., Beigelman, L., and C.C. Kao. Use of DNA, RNA, and Chimeric Templates by a Viral RNA Dependent RNA Polymerase: Evolutionary Implications for the Transition from the RNA to the DNA World. J. Virol. 1999, 73(8):6424-6429.

309.Pandey, S.P., Gaquerel, E., Gase, K., and I. T. Baldwin. RNA-Directed RNA Polymerase3 from Nicotiana attenuata Is Required for Competitive Growth in Natural Environments. Plant Physiology, 2008, 147:1212–1224.

310. Di Serio, F., de Alba, A-E. M., Navarro, B., Gisel, A., and R. Flores. RNA-Dependent RNA Polymerase 6 Delays Accumulation and Precludes Meristem Invasion of a Viroid That Replicates in the Nucleus. J. Virol. 2010, 84(5):2477-2489.

311. Horie, M., et al. An RNA-dependent RNA polymerase gene in bat genomes derived from an ancient negative strand RNA virus. Sci Rep 2016 May 13;6:25873.

312. Crombach, A. and P. Hogeweg. Is RNA-dependent RNA polymerase essential for transposon control? BMC Systems Biology 2011, 5:104.

313. Pelczar, H., Woisard, A., Lemaıtre, J.M., Chachou, M., and Y. Andeol. Evidence for an RNA Polymerization Activity in Axolotl and Xenopus Egg Extracts. PLoS ONE, 2010 Dec, 5(12).

314. Nolan, T. , G. Cecere , C. Mancone , T. Alonzi , M. Tripodi, C. Catalanotto and C. Cogoni. The RNA-dependent RNA polymerase essential for post-transcriptional gene silencing in Neurospora crassa interacts with replication protein A. Nucl. Acids Research 36(2), 2008, 532-538.

315. Forrest, E.C., C. Cogoni , and G. Macino. The RNA-dependent RNA polymerase, QDE-1, is a rate-limiting factor in post-transcriptional gene silencing in Neurospora crassa. Nucl. Acids Research 32(7), 2004, 2123-2128.

316. Lipardi, C. and B. M. Paterson. Identification of an RNA dependent RNA polymerase in Drosophila establishes a common theme in RNA silencing, Fly, 4:1, 30-35, 2010.

317. Fraenkel-Conrat, H. RNA-dependent RNA polymerases of plants. Proc. Natl. Acad. Sci. USA, 1983, 80, 422–424.

318. Wang Y., Qu J., Ji S., Wallace A.J., Wu J., Li Y., Gopalan V., and Ding B. A Land Plant-specific Transcription Factor Directly Enhances Transcription of a Pathogenic Noncoding RNA Template by DNA-dependent RNA Polymerase II. Plant Cell 28:1094-1107.

319. O'Sullivan, J.M., Tan-Wong, S.M., Morillon, A., Lee, B., Coles, J., Mellor, J., and N. J. Proudfoot. Gene loops juxtapose promoters and terminators in yeast. Nature Genetics 36(9), 2004.

320. Mikoshiba, K., Tsukada, Y., Haruna, I. and Watanabe, I. RNA-dependent RNA synthesis in rat brain. Nature, 1974, 249, 445–447.

321. Downey, K. M., Byrnes, J. J., Jurmark, J. S. and So, A. G. Reticulocyte RNA-dependent RNA polymerase. Proc. Natl. Acad. Sci. USA, 1973, 70, 3400–3404.

322. Volloch, V., Schweitzer, B. and Rits, S. Uncoupling of the synthesis of edited and unedited COIII RNA in Trypanosoma brucei. Nature, 1990, 343, 482–484.

323. Volloch, V., Schweitzer, B., Zhang, X. and Rits, S. Identification of negative-strand complements to cytochrome oxidase subunit III RNA in Trypanosoma brucei. Proc. Natl. Acad. Sci. USA, 1991, 88, 10671–10675.

324. Middlebrook R.D. (1989). "Null Double Injection and the Extra Element Theorem". *IEEE Transactions on Education*. 32 (3): 167–180. doi:10.1109/13.34149.

325. Feynman, R.P. There's plenty of room at thebottom: An invitation to enter a new field of physics. Engrg Sci 23:22 (1960).

326. D.B. Craig, E. Arriaga, J.C.Y. Wong, H. Lu, and N.J. Dovichi. The life and death of a single enzyme molecule. *Analytical Chemistry* 70, 39A-43A (1998).

327. D.B. Craig, E. Arriaga, J.C.Y. Wong, H. Lu, and N.J. Dovichi. Studies on single alkaline phosphatase molecules: reaction rate and activation energy of a reaction catalyzed by a single molecule and the effect of thermal denaturation-The death of an enzyme. *Journal of the American Chemical Society* 118, 5245-5253 (1996).

328. D.Y. Chen and N.J. Dovichi. Single-molecule detection in capillary electrophoresis: molecular shot noise as a fundamental limit to chemical analysis. *Analytical Chemistry* 68, 690-696 (1996).

329. Bettina Wagner, Donald C. Miller, Teri L. Lear,and Douglas F. Antczak. The Complete Map of the Ig Heavy Chain Constant Gene Region Reveals Evidence for Seven IgG Isotypes and for IgD in the Horse. J Immunol 2004; 173:3230-3242.

330. Daryl Fernandes. Demonstrating Comparability of Antibody Glycosylation during Biomanufacturing. European Biopharmaceutical Review. Summer 2005. pp 106 -110.

331. In-Geol Choi and Sung-Hou Kim. "Evolution of protein structural classes and protein sequence families". PNAS 103.38 (2006), pp. 14056-61. DOI: 10.1073/pnas.0606239103. PMID: 16959887.

332. Arstila, TP; Casrouge, A; Baron, V; Even, J; Kanellopoulos, J; Kourilsky, P. "A direct estimate of the human alphabeta T cell receptor diversity". Science. 286 (5441): 958-61. (1999).

333. Winters-Hilt, S. "Immune Repertoire Profiling Using Nanopore Transduction," Patent Pending 2019.

334. Sakmann B, Neher E. Patch clamp techniques for studying ionic channels in excitable membranes. Annu Rev Physiol. 1984;46:455-72.

335. "The Nobel Prize in Physiology or Medicine 1991". nobelprize.org. Nobel Media AB.

336. Zhang, H. Reversal of HIV-1 Latency with Anti-microRNA Inhibitors. Int J Biochem Cell Biol. 2009 Mar; 41(3): 451–454.

337. Liang, Ruqiang, David J Bates, and Eugenia Wang. Epigenetic Control of MicroRNA Expression and Aging. Curr Genomics. 2009 May; 10(3): 184–193.

338. Bantounas, I., L A Phylactou1 and J B Uney. RNA interference and the use of small interfering RNA to study gene function in mammalian systems. J Mol Endocrinol. 2004 Dec;33(3):545-57.

339. Agarwal, Vikram, George W Bell, Jin-Wu Nam, David P Bartel. Predicting effective microRNA target sites in mammalian mRNAs. eLife 2015;4:e05005.

340. Yang W, Chendrimada TP, Wang Q, Higuchi M, Seeburg PH, Shiekhattar R, Nishikura K. Modulation of microRNA processing and expression through RNA editing by ADAR deaminases. Nat Struct Mol Biol (2006) 13: 13-21.

341. Zanghirati G and Zanni L, "A parallel solver for large quadratic programs in training support vector machines", Parallel Computing, Vol. 29, pp.535-551, 2003.

342. Eppstein D and Bern M. Approximation algorithms for geometric problems, pages 296–345. Approximation algorithms for NP-hard problems. PWS Publishing Co, 1996.

343. Luke, Sean. 2009. Essentials of Metaheuristics, Lulu.

344. Winters-Hilt, S., and Pincus, S. Nanopore-based biosensing. PATENT, UNO filing, 2004.

345. Winters-Hilt, S. , and Pincus, S. Channel current cheminformatics and bioengineering methods for immunological screening, single-molecule analysis, and single molecular-interaction analysis. PATENT, UNO filing, 2005.

346. Winters-Hilt, S.; U.S. Provisional Patent Application No. 61/233,732. Title: A Hidden Markov Model With Binned Duration Algorithm (HMMBD). August 13, 2009. Re-filing: Winters-Hilt, S.; U.S. Provisional Patent Application No. 61/234,885. Title: An Efficient Self-Tuning Explicit and Adaptive HMM with Duration Algorithm. August 18, 2009

347. Coulter, W. H. 1953. U.S. Patent No. 2.656.508, issued 20 Oct. 1953.

348. DeBlois, R.W. and Bean, C.P. 1970. Counting and sizing of submicron particles by the resistive pulse technique. Rev. Sci. Instr. 41: 909-916.

349. Bean, C.P. 1972. The physics of porous membranes – neutral pores. *In:* Membranes. G. Eisenman, ed. pp. 1-54. Marcel Dekker, New York.

350. DeBlois, R.W., Bean, C.P. and Wesley, R.K.A. 1977. Electrokinetic measurements with submicron particles and pores by the resistive pulse technique. J. Coll. Interface Sci. 61: 323-335.

351. Hladky, S.B. and D.A. Haydon. 1972. Ion transfer across lipid membranes in the presence of gramicidin A. Biochim. Biophys. Acta 274: 294-312.

352. Bezrukov, S.M., I. Vodyanoy, V.A. Parsegian. 1994. Counting polymers moving through a single ion channel. Nature 370 (6457), pgs 279-281.

353. Braha, O., B. Walker, S. Cheley, J. Kasianowicz, L. Song, J.E. Gouaux, and H. Bayley. 1997. Designed protein pores as components for biosensors. In: Chemistry & Biology (London). 4: 497-505.

354. Bayley, H. 2000. Pore planning: Functional membrane proteins by design. J. Gen. Physiol. 116. 1a.

355. Bayley, H., Braha, O. & Gu, L.Q. 2000. Stochastic sensing with protein pores. *Advan Mater* 12, 139-142.

356. Kasianowicz, J.J., E. Brandin, D. Branton, and D.W. Deamer. 1996. Characterization of Individual Polynucleotide Molecules Using a Membrane Channel. Proc. Natl. Acad. Sci. USA 93(24), 13770-73.

357. Akeson M, D. Branton, J.J. Kasianowicz, E. Brandin, D.W. Deamer. 1999. Microsecond Time-Scale Discrimination Among Polycytidylic Acid, Polyadenylic Acid, and Polyuridylic Acid as Homopolymers or as Segments Within Single RNA Molecules. Biophys. J. 77(6):3227-3233.

358. Li, J., C., D. McMullan, D. Stein, D. Branton, and J. Golovchenko. 2001. Solid state nanopores for single molecule detection. Biophys. J. 80. 339a.

359. Li, J., D. Stein, C. McMullan, D. Branton, M. J. Aziz, and J. A. Golovchenko, 2001. Ion Beam Sculpting on the Nanoscale. *Nature* .

360. Sanger, F., *et al.* 1977. DNA sequencing with chain-terminating inhibitors. *Proc. Natl. Acad. Sci. U.S.A.* 74, 5463 – 5467.

361. Maxam, A . M. and W. Gilbert. 1977. A new method for sequencing DNA . *PNAS* 74, 560-564.

362. Song L., M.R. Hobaugh, C. Shustak, S. Cheley, H. Bayley, and J.E. Gouaux, 1996. Structure of Staphylococcal Alpha-Hemolysin, a Heptameric Transmembrane Pore. Science 274 (5294):1859-1866.

363. Chow SA, Vincent KA, Ellison V, Brown PO. Reversal of integration and DNA splicing mediated by integrase of human immunodeficiency virus. *Science.* 1992;**255**:723–726.

364. Scottoline BP, Chow S, Ellison V, Brown PO. Disruption of the terminal base pairs of retroviral DNA during integration. *Genes Dev.* 1997;**11**:371–382.

365. Chung, S-H., and P. W . Gage. 1998. Signal processing techniques for channel current analysis based on hidden Markov models. *In* Methods in Enzymology; Ion channels. Part B. 420-437.

366. Krogh, A., I. S. Mian, and D. Haussler. 1994. A hidden Markov model that finds genes in E.coli DNA. Nucl. Acids Res. 22. 4768-4778.

367. Ma, L. and S.L. Cockroft. Biological Nanopores for single-Molecule Biophysics. ChemBioChem 2010, 11, 25-34.

368. J. Nakane, M. Wiggin, A. Marziali. A nanosensor for transmembrane capture and identification of single nucleic acid molecules. *Biophys. J.* 2004, 87, 3618.

369. D. Stoddart, A. J. Heron, E. Mikhailova, G. Maglia, H. Bayley. Single-nucleotide discrimination in immobilized DNA oligonucleotides with a biological nanopore. *Proc. Natl. Acad. Sci. USA* 2009, 106, 7702–7707.

370. J. Sánchez-Quesada, A. Saghatelian, S. Cheley, H. Bayley, M. R. Ghadiri. Single DNA rotaxanes of a transmembrane pore protein. *Angew. Chem.* 2004, 116, 3125–3129.

371. J. Sánchez-Quesada, A. Saghatelian, S. Cheley, H. Bayley, M. R. Ghadiri. Single DNA rotaxanes of a transmembrane pore protein. *Angew. Chem. Int. Ed.* 2004, 43, 3063–3067.

372. D. B. Amabilino, J. F. Stoddart. Interlocked and Intertwined Structures and Superstructures. *Chem. Rev.* 1995, 95, 2725–2829.

373. E. R. Kay, D. A. Leigh, F. Zerbetto. Synthetic molecular motars and mechanical machines. *Angew. Chem.* 2007, **119**, 72–196;

374. E. R. Kay, D. A. Leigh, F. Zerbetto. Synthetic molecular motars and mechanical machines. *Angew. Chem. Int. Ed.* 2007, **46**, 72–191.

375. S. L. Cockroft, J. Chu, M. Amorin, M. R. Ghadiri. A single-molecules nanopore device detects DNA polymerase activity with single-nucleotide resolution. *J. Am. Chem. Soc.* 2008, **130**, 818–820.

376. N. Mitchell, S. Howorka. Chemical tags facilitate the sensing of individual DNA strands with nanopores. *Angew. Chem. Int. Ed.* 2008, **47**, 5476–5479.

377. S. Howorka, L. Movileanu, O. Braha, H. Bayley. Kinetics of duplex formation for individual DNA strands within a single protein nanopore. *Proc. Natl. Acad. Sci. USA* 2001, **98**, 12996–13001.

378. L.-Q. Gu, O. Braha, S. Conlan, S. Cheley, H. Bayley. Stochastic sensing of organic analytes by a pore-forming protein containing a molecular adapter. *Nature* 1999, 398, 686–690.

379. Y. Astier, O. Braha, H. Bayley. Toward single molecule DNA sequencing: direct identification of ribonucleoside and deoxyribonucleoside 5-monophosphates by using an engineered protein nanopore equipped with a molecular adapter. *J. Am. Chem. Soc.* 2006, 128, 1705–1710.

380. J. Clarke, H.-C. Wu, L. Jayasinghe, A. Patel, S. Reid, H. Bayley. Continuous base identification for single-molecule nanopore DNA sequencing. *Nat. Nanotechnol.* 2009, 4, 265–270.

381. M. M. Mohammad, S. Prakash, A. Matouschek, L. Movileanu. Controlling a single protein in a nanopore through electrostatic traps. *J. Am. Chem. Soc.* 2008, 130, 4081–4088.

382. L. Movileanu, S. Howorka, O. Braha, H. Bayley. Detecting protein analytes that modulate transmembrane movement of a polymer chain within a single protein pore. *Nat. Biotechnol.* 2000, 18, 1091–1095.

383. H. Xie, O. Braha, L.-Q. Gu, S. Cheley, H. Bayley. Single-molecule observation of the catalytic subunit of cAMP-dependent protein kinase binding to an inhibitor peptide. *Chem. Biol.* 2005, 12, 109–120.

384. S. Cheley, H. Xie, H. Bayley. A genetically-encoded pore for the stochastic detection of a protein kinase. *ChemBioChem* 2006, 7, 1923–1927.

385. B. Hornblower, A. Coombs, R. D. Whitaker, A. Kolomeisky, S. J. Picone, A. Meller, M. Akeson. Single-molecule analysis of DNA-protein complexes using nanopores. *Nat. Methods* 2007, 4, 315–317.

386. Y. Astier, D. E. Kainov, H. Bayley, R. Tuma, S. Howorka. Stochastic detection of motor protein-RNA complexes by single-channel current recording. *ChemPhysChem* 2007, 8, 2189–2194.

387. S. Benner, R. J. A. Chen, N. A. Wilson, R. Abu-Shumays, N. Hurt, K. R. Lieberman, D. W. Deamer, W. B. Dunbar, M. Akeson. Sequence-specific detection of individual DNA polymerase complexes in real time using a nanopore. *Nat. Nanotechnol.* 2007, 2, 718–724.

388. N. Hurt, H. Wang, M. Akeson, K. R. Lieberman, *J. Am. Chem. Soc.* 2009, 131, 3772–3778.

389 N. A. Wilson, R. Abu-Shumays, B. Gyarfas, H. Wang, K. R. Lieberman, M. Akeson, W. B. Dunbar. Electronic control of DNA polymerase binding and unbdining to single DNA molecules. *ACS Nano* 2009, 3, 995–1003.

390. Ellington AD, Szostak J: In vitro selection of RNA molecules that bind specific ligands. *Nature* 1990 , 346:818-22.

391. Tuerk C, Gold L: Systematic evolution of ligands by exponential enrichment: RNA ligands to bacteriophage T4 DNA polymerase. *Science* 1990 , 249:505-10.

392. Jayasena SD: Aptamers: an emerging class of molecules that rival antibodies in diagnostics. *Clin Chem* 1999 , 45:1628-1650.

393. Proske D, Blank M, Buhmann R, Resch A. Aptamers – basic research, drug development, and clinical applications. *Appl Microbiol Biotechnol* 2005 , 69:367-374.

394. Hamaguchi N, Ellington A, Stanton M. Aptamer beacons for the direct detection of proteins. *Anal Biochem* 2001 , 294:126-131.

395. Ulrich H, Martins AH, Pesquero JB. RNA and DNA aptamers in cytomics analysis. *Cytometry Part A* 2004 , 59A:220-231.

396. Brody EN, Gold L. Aptamers as therapeutic and diagnostic reagents. *J Biotechnol* 2000 , 74:5-13.

397. Yamamoto R, Baba T, Kumar PK. Molecular beacon aptamer fluoresces in the presence of Tat protein of HIV-1. *Genes Cells* 2000 , 5:389-396.

398. Yamamoto R, Katahira M, Nishikawa S, Baba T, Taira K, Kumar PK. A novel RNA motif that binds efficiently and specifically to the Tat protein of HIV and inhibits the transactivation by Tat of transcription in vitro and in vivo. *Genes Cells* 2000 , 5(5):371-388.

399. Howorka, S., S. Cheley, and H. Bayley, "Sequence-specific detection of individual DNA strands using engineered nanopores," Nat. Biotechnol., vol. 19, no. 7, pp. 636–639, July 2001.

400. Winters-Hilt, S. Biosensing processes with substrates, both immobilized (Immuno-absorbant matrices) and free (enzyme substrate): Transducer Enzyme-Release with Immuno-absorbent Assay (TERISA); Transducer Accumulation and Release with Immuno-absorbent Assay (TARISA); Electrophoretic contrast substrate. Patent, UNO Filing 2009.

401. Ding, S., C. Gao, Li-Qun Gu. Capturing single molecules of immunoglobulin and Ricin with an aptamer-encoded glass nanopore. Ana. Chem 2009 ac9006705.

402. Ikebukuro, K., Y. Okumura, K. Sumikura, I. Karube. A novel method of screening thrombin-inhibiting DNA aptamers using an evolution-mimicking algorithm. Nucl. Acids Res. 2005, Vol. 33 (12).

403. Race, R.E., A. Raines, T.G. M. Baron, M.W. Miller, A. Jenny, and E.S.Williams. Comparison of Abnormal Prion Protein Glycoforms Paterns from Transmissable Spongiform Encepphalography Agent-Infected Deer, Elk, Sheep, and Cattle. Journal of Virology, Dec. 2002, p. 12365-12368.

404. Tornay, S.C. 1938. Ockham: Studies and Selections. Open Court Publishers.

405. Hildebrandt, S. and A. Tromba. 1996. The Parsimonious Universe. Springer-Verlag.

406. Feynman, R.P. and A.R. Hibbs. 1965. Quantum Mechanics and Integrals. McGraw-Hill.

407. Birrell, N.D. and P.C.W. Davies. 1982. Quantum fields in curved space. Cambridge University Press.

408. Louko, J. and B.F. Whiting. 1995. Phys. Rev. D 51.

409. Goodstein, D.L. 1975. States of Matter. Prentice-Hall, New Jersey.

410. Morse, P.M. 1969. Thermal physics (2nd Ed.). Benjamin/Cummings, Reading, MA.

411. Lindsay, R.B. and H. Margenau. 1981. Foundations of Physics. Ox Bow Press.

412. Thorne, K.S., C.W. Misner, and J.A. Wheeler. 1973. Gravitation. W. H. Freeman.

413. Chaitan, G.J. 1987. Algorithmic Information Theory. Cambridge University Press.

414. Zurek, W.H. 1989. Algorithmic randomness and physical entropy. Phys. Rev. A 40, 4731-4751.

415. Zurek, W.H. 1989. Thermodynamic cost of computation, algorithmic complexity and the information metric. Nature 341, 119-124.

416. Zurek, W.H. 1990. Complexity, entropy and the physics of information. Proceedings of the 1988 Workshop on the Complexity, entropy and physics of Information.

417. Rissanen, J. 1983. A universal prior for integers and estimation by minimum description length. Annals of Statistics, 11, 416-431.

418. Sklar, L. 1993. Physics and Chance. Cambridge Univerisity Press.

419. Frieden, B. R. 1998. Physics from Fisher Information. Cambridge.

420. Guttmann, Y.M. 1999. The concept of probability in statistical physics, Cambridge.

421. Jumarie, G. 1990. Relative Information: theories and applications. Springer-Verlag. (Springer series in synergetics, v. 47).

422. Katchalsky, A. and P. F. Curran. 1965. Nonequilibrium Thermodynamics in Biophysics. Harvard University Press, Cambridge, MA.

423. Prigogine, I. 1973. A United Foundation of Dynamics and Thermodynamics. Chemica Scripta 4: 5-32.

424. Prigogine, I. 1984. Order out of Chaos. Bantam Books, New York.

425. Landau, L.D. and E.M. Lifshitz. 1987. Fluid Mechanics (2nd Ed.). Pergamon Press, New York.

biomedical	445,460		bootable	471
biomedicine	416		Boxcar	59,75,76
biomolecular	13,95,187,192,237,246,249,266,419,421,422,469		boxcar	73,75,76
			BSV	330,338,339,340,348
			BSVs	338,339,340
biomolecule	96,100,256,408,425		buffer	258,266,268,269,397
Biomolecules	395,406,466		buffers	266
biomolecules	13,53,90,104,265,395,396,412,418,419,421,423,452,453,454		Cache	319,320,323
			cache	472
			caching	297
bionanotech-nology	256		Calculus	28,479
			calculus	2,3,39,77,272,354,365,479,480
biophysical	9			
biophysics	9,13,255,353,390,396,418,419		calibration	388,408,410
			cannabinoids	269
biopolymer	90,95,463		cannabis	260
biopolymers	411		cannamimetic	265
Biosensor	433		CAP	196
biosensor	266,269,396,416,420		cap	105,157,195,435,442
biosphere	258		capacitance	398
Biosystem	265		capacitive	73
biosystem	265,267,414		capacity	104,389,456
biotech	464		Capillary	465
Biotechnology	87,106		capillary	109,259,396,460,464
biotechnology	92,96,99,259,460		capsid	101,188
Biotin	460,462		carbodiimide	449
biotin	420,433,434,448,449		catalyst	258
Biotinylated	462,464		catalysts	94,258
biotinylated	355,390,420,422,424		cDNA	108,110
BLAST	5,88,125,126,140,165,199,243,247,375		cDNAs	93
			CDS	202,203
blast	111		CE	460,464,465
BLAT	125		chaotrope	437,460,461,466,467
blood	13,263,395,397,414,400		chaotropes	268,269,397,398,437
blossum	125		chimeras	470
BLOSUM	120,125		chimeric	257,468,470
Blosum	121,122,126		chiral	261,262
Blot	106,107		chiralities	261
blot	106		chromato-graphic	463,465
Blots	106			
bond	100,109,111,256,262		Chromatog-raphy	108
boost	79,80,131,141,145,288,310,344,381,391,414,424,428,432			
			chromatog-raphy	107
boosted	8		chromebook	471
boosting	108,146,150,211,296		chromosomal	98
boosts	61,67,142,143,145		CHROMOSOME	204
boot	471			

Chromosome	46,118,204,227	crosscorrela-tion	78
chromosome	118,199,202,227	crosslinkage	449
Chromosomes	189,202,204,217	crosslinked	449
chromosomes	118,185,189,196,198	crossvalidation	213
circoviridae	188	crystalline	257,395
circuit	5,94,255,265,267,268,405	crystallizable	447
		crystallization	258
Circuits	255,265	crystallized	257,261,445,446
circuits	255,265,266,267	crystallographic	406,418
Classifier	271,273,287,298,304	crystallography	257,260,261,269
classifier	82,131,141,144,145,100	crystals	257
Classifiers	271,333	CstF	198,241,252,253
classifiers	65,145,272,273,291,200	cytadine	104
Cluster	356,357	cytochrome	248
cluster	7,120,250,274,276,270	cytokines	103
clusters	120,273,276,277,278	cytometry	417
clutter	41	cytoplasm	195
cm	398,465	cytosine	101,120
cmds	473	cytosol	87,97,100,103,105,188,191,192,194,195,250,257
coevolution	250		
coevolutionary	87,232,373,374		
cofactor	13,423,453	Database	382,383
cofactors	413	database	10,120,125,126,199,200
Comets	88,89	databases	115,188
comets	89	datawarehous-ing	389
commensalism	249		
compartment	95,96,256	DBN	376,377
Compartmen-talization	185	DBNs	377
		DdDp	101,188,265
compartmen-talization	87,89,94,95,113	ddNTP	109
		ddNTPs	109
compartmen-talizations	185,190,257	DdRp	92,101,105,188,193,100
		deaminase	104
compart-mentalizing	19	deaminases	268
		decode	393
compartments	95,97	decoder	12,379,392
Compression	140	Decoding	133
compression	12,78,145,146,147,379,392	deglycosylated	459,460
		Deinococcus	54,58,186
Compressive	389	Deletion	453
copolymer	450	deletion	118
Coulter	395,412	deletions	118,202,203
coulter	412	delimit	80
covalent	446,447,449,463	delimiter	50,51,52,476,477
covalently	13,412,422,423,439,400	delimiters	52,80
CRISPR	187,191,193,237	denoised	394
CRISPRi	98,185,190		

deoxynucleo-tides	109	dNTP	109
deoxythymi-dine	401	DROSHA	112
		Drosha	191
dephosphoryla-tion	418	Drosophila	226
		dsDNA	188,189,195,196,222
detergent	260	dsRNA	96,97,103,104,188,190,191
detergents	257		
diabetes	13,268,423,424,453,400	Earth	32,88,89,90,91,92,111,112,113,118
diabetic	457		
diagnosed	439	earth	88,91
diagnosis	414,434,458,459	ecologies	372
diagnostic	13,110,145,146,399,400	econometric	2
diagnostics	109,110,395,418,423	econometrics	1
Dicer	103,104,112,190,191	ecotype	241,253
dichroism	403	EDC	444,448,449
dideoxynucleo-tide	109	EET	255
		electrochemis-try	12,107,419
diffraction	257,357		
diffuse	253	electrodes	397
diffusion	108	electrolyte	398
digest	106	electrolytic	395,396
digests	438,459,460,470	electromagnet-ic	480
Dimension	289,293		
dimension	108,285,289,290,293	electronics	267
dimensional	129,261,274,284,285	electrons	267
dimensionality	43,296,325	electroosmotic	466
dimensionful	480	electrophero-gram	465
dimensions	261,272,274,285,326		
Dimer	206	electrophero-grams	466
dimer	148,150,151,168,205		
dimerization	267	Electrophoresis	107,108
dimers	201,205,206,207,229	electrophoresis	107,109,396,422,424
dimethyla-minopropyl	449	Electrophoretic	424,462
		electrophoretic	68,107,414,416,419,400
dinucleotide	23,24,45,46,99,209,212,406,453	Electrophoreti-cally	428
		electrophoreti-cally	13,107,265,416,422,400
dinucleotides	23,24		
dinucleoties	23	electrostatic	260,403,423
diphtheria	57	Emergence	185
diphytanoyl	396	emergence	89,90,91,185,190
diploid	26,118,119	Emergent	17,30,67
disialylated	446,447	emergent	1,27,30,31,32,67,88,250,261,266,380
dithering	3,376		
divalent	107	emerges	95
DNAtranspos-ons	98	emerging	193,252
		encapsulate	481
		encapsulated	90,91,294

encapsulates	272,354	ESTs	243,251,252
encapsulating	168	Euclidean	40,43,57,168,297,325,3 26,330,483
Encapsulation	90		
encapsulation	27,41,90,101,111,249,2 50	euclidean	43
		Eukaryogenesis	191,194
encephaly	257	eukaryogenesis	54,96,97,105,106,112,1 85,191,192,193,194,195 ,196,246,247,248,249
enclosing	81,250,286,287,347,300		
enclosure	195		
encode	101,187,239,262,393	eutectic	89,90,91,95
encoded	26,59,76,88,98,101,192, 194,199,203,205,241,24 2,244,246,286,394,480	EVA	7,8,11,14,130,134,140,1 42,143,168,378,393
		eva	142,181,182
		exogenous	102,249,260
encoder	12,379,392	Exonuclease	101
encodes	54,97,256,480	exonuclease	429,453,454
endocanna- binoid	260	Expectation	27,28,34,134,136,143,1 49,166,409
endocanna- binoids	260	expectation	27,30,34,59,138
		extremophiles	111
endocrine	13,423,453,458	extremum	39
endocytosis	195	extrinsic	8,127,131,199,200,200
endogenous	102,112,249,260	Fab	263,418,445,446,447
endonuclease	106,119	FASTA	21,22
endonucleases	94,99,106,470	fasta	42,44,46,47
endoplasmic	100	femtomolar	424
endosymbio- genesis	96	fingerprint	195,439
		fingerprinting	53
endosymbiont	191,192,194	fingerprints	143
endosymbionts	105,192,193	Fitness	361,362,363,367
Endosymbiosis	249	fitness	96,97,104,287,330,332, 333,361,362,364,366,36 7,373
endosymbiosis	105,193,194,195,246		
endosymbiotic	97,249		
Epigenetic	191		
epigenetic	104	Fixation	119
epigentics	104	fixation	119
epistemological	480	Flanking	117
Epitope	431	flanking	119
epitope	110,426,428,431,451	fluorescence	268
epitopes	425	fluorescent	257,411
equilibrium	32,389,394,465,466,400	fluorescently	109
equine	263,445,446,447	fluorophore	106,414,428
Equipartition	489	fold	111,117,202,203,204
equipartition	169,485	folded	108
Ergodic	489	Folding	256
ergodic	78,489,490	folding	129,421,427,468
Ergodicity	481	folds	202,217,219,269
ergodicity	39	fray	68,404
ERVs	102,103	frayed	403

fraying	69,78,404,470
frays	69,404
Frequentist	26,481
frequentist	26
ftp	473
FTs	77
fucose	446,447
GEL	107
Gel	107,108,428,460
gel	107,108,109,429,462
Gematria	87,99,112
gematria	93,97,255,262
geminiviruses	188
GenBank	202
Genbank	117,202,203,221,239
genbank	33,34,35,57,111,183,239,240,243
geneFinder	61,62,63,64,79,80
genefinder	61,64,80
Genefinders	115
genefinding	199
GeneID	201,209,210,212
generative	12,39,379,389,392
GENIE	211
Genie	210
GENSCAN	211
Genscan	210
geographic	240,439
geologic	103
geological	88,90
geologically	91
Geology	32
geology	32
Geometric	30,31,218
geometric	8,30,31,32,34,40,121,128,139,143,154,156,158,162,183,208,218,243,244,278,297,298,306,324,325,329,330,389,390,392,393,479,480,483
geometrical	479
geometrically	143,393,432
geometries	295,355
Geometry	40,483
geometry	38,40,330,356,400,405,418,433,453,479,480,483
Geophysical	87,88
geophysical	87
GFF	214
gff	214
GFP	463
ghIMM	56
ghIMMs	142
GHMM	138
gHMM	14,133
GHMMs	127,141,148,156,165
gIMM	52,56,117,139,142,149,150,220
gIMMs	52,142
globular	256,262,418
glu	99,263
glucosamine	446
glucose	263,446,447,457
gly	99,263
glycan	446,447
glycans	446,447
glycation	13,110,259,263,421,400
glycations	256,263,264,445,446
glycerol	397
glycine	89
glyco	445
Glycoform	13,423,457
glycoform	107,421,457,458,459
glycoforms	13,423,425,453,458,400
glycol	396
Glycoprotein	457
glycoprotein	13,261,423,428,438,400
Glycoproteins	255,263
glycoproteins	107,110,457
glycosidic	446,447
glycosilation	428
Glycosylation	469
glycosylation	100,115,255,258,263
glycosylations	100,264,422,445,446
glycosylizations	458
glyocprotein	425
Golgi	269,446,447
GPCR	259
GPCRs	260
GPU	129,141,166,273,288
Gramicidin	396
gramicidin	396
grammar	67,97

grammars	380	holonomic	301
grayscale	141,382,409	Homologous	118
groove	403,405	homologous	104
grooves	405	homology	126,127,157,199,201
GTF	226,227,228	homopolymer	100,396
gtf	226	Hood	109
guanine	92,101,120,268	Hoogsteen	92,405
haploid	26	hormone	13,260,458,459
haplotyping	438	hormones	260
Heaviside	289	horse	5,195
heavytailed	391	HPLC	108,459
helix	92,100,256	HSMM	8,128,156,157,159,160
Hemoglobin	458,459	hybrid	5,140,344,345,346,370
hemoglobin	13,261,423,453,457,400	Hybridization	374
Hemolysin	395,397	hybridization	100,109,110,256,374
hemolysin	9,259,353,396,397,390	hydrophilic	95,100,256,260
Hepatitis	424	Hydrophobic	418
HEPES	397,398	hydrophobic	95,100,108,120,126,200
heptamer	397	hydrophobicity	90,93,95,97,107,112,255,262
HERV	112		
Hessian	361,362	hydrothermal	89
heterodyning	140,391,394,432	hypermutates	104
heterotrimeric	241,260	hypermutation	104
heuristic	52,53,61,68,79,80,306,310,324,325,330,368	hypermuta-tional	104
heuristics	167,295,298	Hyperplane	275,299
hexadecane	396	hyperplane	272,273,275,284,285
hexamer	25,26,57,79,200,203	hyperplanes	272,274,284,285,294
hexamers	25,26,37,79	hypershere	326
hexaploidal	118	hypershperical	326
HF	395	hypersphere	274,326
HGT	97,98	hyperspherical	287,326
HHMM	156	hyperspherical-ly	326
hIMM	56,132,149,150,220		
hIMMs	142	hypersurface	284,298
histocompati-bility	202	IEF	108,460,462,463,464
		IgG	264,417,418,439,443
Histogram	143,402,403,452	IGHD	263,445,446,447
histogram	50,58,81,112,350,355,359	IgM	448
		immobilites	108
Histograms	54	immobilization	109,403
histograms	54,58,81,244	immobilized	106,107,108,109,414
Hoeffding	6,169,290,291,292,370	IMMs	142
Holistic	67	immunofluo-rescent	257
holistic	52,60,67,70,267,380		
Holographic	129	immunogenic	264,448
holographic	129,391	immunoglobu-	417

linux	474	Martingale	6,34,116,127,149,168,3 76,485,486,488
Lipid	90,190	martingale	32,33,131,149,159,160, 168,169,485,486,487,48 8,489,490
lipid	91,95,111,266,396,398, 420	Martingales	6,30,149,168,169,376,4 79,485,486,487
Lipids	95	martingales	32,486
lipids	256,260	megaviridae	111,192
Liposomal	95	megavirus	104
LLN	30,31	megaviruses	105,193
LLR	131,141,155	meiosis	195
LNA	468,469,470	meiotic	195
LNAs	470	melanogaster	226,248
lncRNA	113	Mellin	78
localizable	10,67,68,129,375,377,3 80	Messenger	259
localized	5,211	messenger	110,185,259,260,267
Lorentz	326	Messengers	255,259
Lorentzian	78,330,407,480,483	messengers	260,267,269
lowpass	75	metabalome	91
lysine	403	Metabolic	112
lysines	263,446,447	metabolic	87,88,91,108,112,190,1 94,265,266
lysogenic	195	metabolism	90,91,96
Mab	463	metabolites	266
mAB	264,448	Metagenomic	110
mAb	264,424,444,462	metagenomic	110
Machiavelli	58	Metaheuristic	287,332,362,363,364
macrophages	448	metaheuristic	11,103,106,377
magnetic	88,91,411,422,430,466, 467,468,469	Metaheuristics	271,324,361,370
magnetosphere	91	metaheuristics	2,4,10,11,103,272,287,3 31,332,333,354,361,365 ,367,370,373,377
magnets	40,41	metaHMMBD	130,220,378
maltoporin	259	metal	107,396,417
mammalian	35,97,185,198,220,233, 235	metals	258,260
mammals	34,103,117,185,220,200	metaphysical	481
mannose	446,447	metastate	220
MAP	29	metastates	200,221
Map	374	meteor	91
map	58,274,285,287,326,300	meteoric	91,118
mapped	196,278,296,347	meteorite	89,90,111
mapping	99,117,119,141,262,200	meter	58
maps	80,189,194,269	methanogen	113
Margin	272,273	methylated	101,105,106
margin	209,212,272,274,275	Methylation	101
Markovian	127,166,167,353	methylation	196
Mars	89,90,91,92,111,112,11 3,118		
Marseillesvirus	105,193		

palindromic	106	phenomeno-logical	39,481
panspermia	89	phenomeno-logically	481
parametric	273,332,341,352,353	phenomenolo-gies	389
parasitic	96,98,248,249	phenomenolo-gy	12,379,422,482
parsimoniae	292	phenomenon	32,289
parsimony	292	phenomologies	392
Parsing	410	phenotype	241,242,250
parsing	126,199,200,223,393	phenotypes	241,250,253
partition	39,227,340	pheromone	372,373
Partitioning	411	pheromones	373
partitioning	204,227,355	phosphate	89,92,93,106
Pathogen	438	phosphatidyl-choline	396
pathogen	259,433,438,439	phosphoam-idite	470
pathogenic	438	phosphodiester	92,100,109,262,403
Pathogens	439	phospholipid	455
pathogens	259,438,439	phosphoryla-tion	108,404,418
pathological	166	photorefractive	257
pathologies	297	photosynthesis	89
pathology	308,309	phylogenetic	57,105,193
paths	91,132,164,165,166,100	phylogenetical-ly	34
pathway	33,88,100,190,193,266,421,427,469	Pi	145,472
pathways	91,269,448,460	pI	108,463,464,465
PEG	396,429	pi	82,83,92,156,157,158,392
Peltier	397	piezoelectric	411
Peptide	100	piggybacking	156,159
peptide	87,95,99,100,102,107,111,256,258,259,260,262,269,449	Pinsker	329
peptides	256,259,269,417	plasma	259
peptidyl	94,99	plasmid	98,106,189
Perceptron	6,271,283,284,374,370	plasmids	98
perceptron	283,284,293,358	plasmon	432
perceptrons	272	Polarization	313,315
PERL	319	polarization	297,308,309,313,314
Perl	2,4,17,18,20,22,23,50,61,82,214,271,319,321,358,471,473,474,475,476,477	polarized	315
perl	2,18,22,33,34,41,46,57,62,63,64,83,85,86,279,281,319,321,359,473,474	poleflipping	91
		polyA	105,252,253
		polyadenylated	241
Phage	110	polyadenyla-tion	192,197,198,199,241
phage	97,106,110	polycistronic	105,185,187,237,238
phagocyte	448		
phagocytes	448		
phagocytic	418		

recursive	6,122,123,124,134,130		79,381,387,389,392,394
recursively	6,122,123,134,135,130	secreted	263,445
recusively	6	secretory	100,269,446
Repertoire	255	sedenions	261
repertoire	111,241,265	sedimentary	113
replicase	188	Sedimentation	88
replicative	90,188	sedimentation	87,89,91
Replicator	90,95	sediments	90
replicator	90,91,92,95	selenocysteine	99,263
replicators	94	SELEX	92,96,108,417,432,439, 443,444
reporter	12,266,268,412,414,400	selfassemble	396
resonance	432	selfsplicing	93,192
resonant	411	Separability	272,299
Retrogenes	118	separability	245,272,274,296,299
retrogenes	118	Separable	275
retrotranspos-on	93,191	separable	14,143,272,274,275,200
Retrotranspos-ons	118	serine	446,447
retrotranspos-ons	98	serotonin	106
retroviral	249,406,453	serum	13,423,453,458,459
retrovirus	103,112,119	Shannon	17,18,19,23,24,27,33,34 ,37,38,39,40,41,43,57,2 53,329,482,483
retroviruses	98,102,249	shannon	18,19,20,23,24,25,33,41 ,42,57
Reynold	422	Sialic	446,447
Reynolds	411	sialylated	446,447
Rho	93	sialylation	446,447
rho	214	siRNA	187,191,194,237,248
ribose	92,470	siRNAs	102,103,104,190,248
ribosomal	99	SNP	109,110,197,241,242
Ribosome	99	SNPs	106,110,197,241,438
ribosome	53,94,95,99,101,111,18 8,196,249,258,260	Southern	106,109,464
Ribosomes	100,105	spliceosomal	96,185,192,194,195,100
ribosomes	99,100,260	spliceosomally	234
riboswitches	92,268	spliceosome	93,94,95,96,97,187,188, 192,193,195,197,220,23 1,233,234,235,237,238, 247,248,249
ribozyme	92,93,94,99,111,250	spliceosomes	96,111
Ribozymes	92	splices	200,224,232
ribozymes	92,94,95,99,111	splicesome	187,195,237
rRNA	92,94,99	SPM	377
scaffolding	200,210	SRM	144,271,272,284,286
Scalable	269	SSA	9,10,11,14,127,129,131, 140,141,142,143,146,16 5,273,375,377,378,380, 386,387
scalable	112,140,165,241,242		
Scan	81		
scan	3,4,50,53,59,60,68,72,7 4,76,140,216		
SCW	9,12,140,141,375,377,3		

Transcriptomes	237
transcriptomes	7,61,185,190,192,194,195,244,246,247,248,250
Translation	105,412
translation	37,96,97,100,101,187,188,195,196,200,237,256,262,413
translational	13,53,100,115,255,258,268,423,445,446,447,453,457,459,460
transliterated	43
transliteration	43
translocate	13,390,400,412,415,400
translocated	396
translocates	412
translocating	14,395,422,423
Translocation	412,413,415
translocation	387,390,396,400,411
translocations	417
transmem-brane	103,445,455
transporter	106,259
transporters	259
transporting	458
Transposable	102
transposable	98
Transposase	98
transposase	98,102,249
transpose	98
Transposition	102
transposition	98
transposon	94,98,102,104,111,112,118,190,191,248,249,257
Transposons	98,102,118,119
transposons	93,97,98,102,104,112,118,257
triginta-duonions	261
tRNA	92,99,202
TSH	13,423,453,458,459
TSS	189,190
underflow	116,138,180,306,330
Urea	461,464,465,466
urea	269,397,433,434,437
UTR	117,189,192,196,198
UTRs	242,243,247,268
UV	241,253,411,414,416

vesicle	95,193
vesicles	91,95
vestibule	401,403,404,405,420
viscosity	466